# Fün *and educ* F... go With Kids

## in Southern California

A comprehensive guide through Los Angeles, Orange, Riverside, San Bernardino, San Diego, and Ventura Counties, plus Big Bear and Palm Springs!

# By Susan Peterson

Fun Places Publishing, California
www.funplaces.com

Copyright © 1998 by Susan Peterson

Published by Fun Places Publishing
P.O. Box 376
Lakewood, California 90714-0376
(562) 867-5223
sales@funplaces.com
www.funplaces.com

ISBN 0-9646737-3-8

Printed in the United States of America.

Fourth Edition - October, 1998
Third Edition - May, 1997
Second Edition - May, 1996
First Edition - May, 1995

# ACKNOWLEDGMENTS

A book is _never_ put together alone! I especially want to thank:

**My husband**, Lance, who is also my best friend and partner. His computer skills have turned my ideas and typing into a readable format; his love, prayers, and encouragement have kept me going. Thank you, honey - you are God's greatest gift to me;

**My three boys** (who are the only kids I know that sometimes ask, "Can we please stay home?"):
Kellan (age 11), whose brilliant mind conceived the title;
Bryce (age 8), whose artistic ability is displayed on the cover; and
Terrell (age 6), who is the last jewel in my crown;

**My parents**, Jan and Joe Gallagher. From my mother, I inherited a love of travel and adventure, and the desire to do things well. From my father, I inherited organizational skills and the ability to get up early in the morning to get something accomplished;

**My in-laws**, Joyce, Pete, and Lerri Peterson, who have blessed us with consistent support, encouragement, and love;

**My sister** and one of my best friends, Beth Davidson, who helped me develop this idea, listened to my whining (I catch it from my kids), and just loves me;

**My sister**, Sandy Krupinsky, who has been excited for me about all the good things;

**My best friend,** Renee McKenzie, my "earth mother" who kept me focused, prayed for me, gave me support, and often watched my little darlings so I could do some serious writing about fun places;

**My wonderful editors**, without whom this book would be rife with ~~eros! erors!~~ oops, errors! How humbling it is to hand something you've poured your heart and time into writing to someone else to read. How much more humbling to get back those precious writings with lots of red marks! Some of my favorite comments include, "I have no idea what you mean" and "Did you make this word up?" Thank you all for taking time out of your busy schedules to read, edit, and gently (and sometimes sarcastically) redirect my writing efforts: Pauline Hirabayashi, Mary Kettles, Cathy Martinez, Pat Raymer, Eileen Verosko, and Kathleen Yanelli. A special thanks goes to a treasured friend, mentor, and editor - my 96-year-old grandmother (who still runs circles around me) - Dora (Dee-Dee) Demme; and

**All of the people** associated with places mentioned in this book that were so willing to talk with me, send me information, and enable my family to come and visit.

Thank you, THANK YOU, **THANK YOU**!!

# TABLE OF CONTENTS

# INTRODUCTION and LEGEND EXPLANATION

In this world there are specifically fun places to go with kids, and there are places we go and bring our kids, anyhow. I think going shopping is great, but while I'm looking at clothes, my boys think it's fun to climb in the clothing racks and maybe even pull off a ticket or two to bring home as "prizes." This is not a fun family outing. I've tried to do the weeding for you so that anywhere you choose to go in this guidebook, whether it's an all-day outing or just for an hour, would be an enjoyable time for you and your child. Some places are obvious choices; some places you might have simply forgotten about; some are hidden treasures; and some are new attractions.

The book is set up by category. Under each category, counties are listed alphabetically; under each county, attractions are listed alphabetically. Note: Names of places in all capital letters, used in a description (e.g. DISNEYLAND), are separately listed attractions in the book. Note: The word "ages" stands for recommended ages. It is meant to be an aid to help you decide if an attraction is appropriate and/or meaningful for your child. Some of the age restrictions, however, are designated by the place you are visiting. Tips: Look for discount coupons for main attractions in hotel lobbies and visitors centers. Also, if you belong to AAA, ask if admission to the attraction you're visiting is discounted for members.

Next to most of the places described are symbols, meant to be at-a-glance guidelines. The **sun** indicates the average amount of time needed to see this attraction. You might decide you need more or less time - this is just a guideline. The **dollar signs and exclamation mark** are price guidelines. They incorporate *the entrance cost for one adult, a 10-year-old child, and the parking fee* (if there is one). If you have more than one child, or one who gets in for free, your cost will vary. The **birthday cake** symbol represents an attraction that is a good place to 1) have a birthday party (the place may or may not have a separate party room), or 2) incorporate with a birthday party.

| | | | | |
|---|---|---|---|---|
| ☀ | = | 15 minutes to 1 hour | ! | = FREE! |
| ◑ | = | 1½ hours to half a day | !/$ | = FREE, but bring spending money. |
| ☼ | = | all day | $ | = 1¢ - $5 |
| | | | $$ | = $5.01 - $10 |
| ♨ | = | good place for a birthday party | $$$ | = $10.01 - $20 |
| | | | $$$$ | = $20.01 - $40 |
| | | | $$$$$ | = over $40 |

# NEVER LEAVE HOME WITHOUT THESE ESSENTIALS

1) **SNACKS**: Always carry snacks and a water bottle with you and/or in the car. Listening to a child whine because he is hungry or thirsty can drive any sane parent over the edge. (And kids will not stop this endearing behavior until they actually get their food or drink!)

2) **MAP**: I would be lost without it! Invest in a street-finder map such as *The Thomas Guide* or *Rand McNally Streetfinder*.

3) **TISSUES AND/OR WIPES**: For obvious reasons.

4) **QUARTERS**: A few quarters tucked away in a container in the car can come in handy for phone calls, those snacks I told you to pack but you forgot, metered parking, or arcade games.

5) **TOYS/BOOKS/GAMES**: Keeping little fingers busy helps keep little hands out of trouble. (Check out "Educational Toys, Books, and Games" under the IDEAS/RESOURCES section.)

6) **TAPES**: Audio tapes can get kids singing instead of fussing. (And if kids cry really loud, just turn up the volume of the tape even louder!) We've found story tapes to be a real blessing, too. (See "Audio Tapes" under the IDEAS/RESOURCES section.)

7) **FIRST AID KIT**: Fill it with the essentials including band aids, ointment, adhesive tape, scissors, an ice pack, Benedryl®, disposable gloves, and Tylenol™ (both children's and adults').

8) **ROADSIDE EMERGENCY KIT**: This kit should contain jumper cables (know how to use them!), flares, a flashlight, batteries, extra drinking water, tools, matches, etc.

9) **JACKET**: Pack a light jacket or sweater for the unexpected change in weather or change of plans. Throw in a change of clothes, too, for little ones who don't always make it to the bathroom in time. (This last tip could save your outing from being cut short.)

10) **BLANKET**: We use ours mainly for picnics, but it doubles as an "I'm cold" helper, and is handy for other emergencies.

11) **FANNY PACK**: Even if your kids are still in the diaper/stroller stage, a fanny pack is great for keeping your hands free to either help your children or grab them before they dart away.

12) **SUNSCREEN**: With our weather, we almost always need it.

13) **CAMERA AND FILM**: Capture those precious moments in a snap!

14) **A SENSE OF HUMOR!**

# MISCELLANEOUS TIDBITS

1. **MATCHING OUTFITS** - Dress your kids in the same shirt (no, I don't mean one big shirt), or at least shirts of the same color (orange, yellow, and red are bright choices) when you go on an outing. I thought this would look silly, but while we do get stares and comments, I can find my kids at just a glance. If kids balk at wearing the same-colored shirt, invest in solid color baseball caps. Not only can you spot your children quickly, but hats help shade their faces from the sun.

2. **TAPE RECORDER** - A movie camera is a great idea, but sometimes I find it too bulky. Carry a hand-size audio tape recorder and press "record" at any time. This is a great way to document trips and get genuine reactions, as well as impromptu stories, songs, arguments, etc.

3. **EXPECTATIONS** -
   A.  Be Aware - Simply because you have a fun outing planned, whether it's going to the "happiest place on earth" or just an hour of play, please don't expect your child to necessarily enjoy every moment of it. Know and expect that your child will probably fuss about something, or seemingly nothing. Beware of the fun-stealers - tiredness and hunger. Visit places before or after nap time, and always bring food, even if you just ate.
   B.  Be Prepared - Call ahead and make sure the place you want to visit is open, especially if there is something that you particularly want to see; check off your list of essentials; set realistic expectations for all participants; be flexible; and go for it!
   C.  Family Mottos - We no longer promise our kids that we'll take them on an outing. A promise, as any parent knows, cannot be broken; it is an absolute. A plan, however, can be altered depending on weather, circumstance, and/or attitude! One of our family mottos is, "It's a plan, not a promise." Another one is, "Oh well." Feel free to use either or both as the situation warrants.

# SOME IDEAS TO EXTEND THE
# MAGIC OF YOUR OUTING

1. **PHOTO ALBUMS** - Buy your child an inexpensive 35mm camera (even a disposable one) and let him document the fun you have together. Keep ticket stubs and brochures. Have your older child keep a journal of his travels; where he went, when, and what he liked best. Give younger children duplicate pictures (or ones that aren't going in the family album) so each child can put together his/her own album. Use craft scissors with patterned blades for creative cutting. Have kids use acid-free construction paper and stickers for decorations. Coming up with captions can be lots of fun - and funny! Spending this time together is a great way to extend a trip and continue making special memories. Note: Photo albums with magnetic pages will discolor your pictures eventually, but ones that use acid-free paper will not. See Photo Albums under the IDEAS/RESOURCES section in back of the book.

2. **COLLECTIONS** - Collect key chains, pencils, or other inexpensive souvenirs from each place you go, and keep them on display. This is a fun reminder of the places you've gone to. I collect three patches from every place we visit, and sew them onto blankets. Each child has his own blanket. (To make the blankets, I folded over twin-size flannel sheets, with thin batting in between, and sewed the edges together. Then I sewed a few semi-straight lines, both vertically and horizontally to "quilt" it.) I hand sew the patches on as we get them. My kids love their "travel blankets."

3. **EDUCATION** - Spend some time doing a little (or a lot) of research about a particular place (or time period) before you visit. It will make your outing more meaningful and make a lasting impression upon your child. Think of your field trip as curriculum supplement! Call the attraction to get a brochure on it or use an encyclopedia to look up pertinent information, or do some on-line research on the web. Other educational aids to enhance your outing include:
   A) Stories - If you're going apple picking, for instance, read stories that have something to do with apples, such as Johnny Appleseed, William Tell, Snow White, Adam and Eve, Sir Isaac Newton, and specifically, *The Giving Tree* by Shel Silverstein or *Ten Apples on Top* by Theo LeSieg.
   B) Theme books - There are thematic study books for almost every subject written. (Teacher Created Materials, Inc., P.O. Box 1040, Huntington Beach, CA 92647, has over fifty thematic unit study books available.) Each book includes lessons and projects that incorporate math, arts and crafts, history, science, language arts, and cooking, into a study about one particular subject. (i.e. weather, birds, the human body, holidays, etc.)

C) Spelling words - Give your child a spelling list pertaining to the attraction you are visiting.

D) Maps - Have older children use a map to track your way to and from your outing - this is an invaluable skill, especially if they learn to do it correctly!

E) Flash cards - Take pictures of the places you go. Put the picture on a piece of construction paper and write the facts about the attraction on the back. "Laminate" it with contact paper. Use the cards as flash cards. Tip: If you're not a picture taker, buy postcards instead.

F) Bingo - Get duplicate pictures made of the places you go. Make bingo boards and cards. If the kids get a match, however, they have to tell you at least one fact about the place before they can put their chip on the board.

4. **LISTEN TO AUDIO TAPE** - Nothing refreshes you memory about a trip like playing back on-the-road commentary. (See Miscellaneous Tidbits.)

These are just a few ideas - I'm sure you'll come up with many of your own!

5. **YOUR IDEAS -**

# ROAD GAMES

"Are we almost there yet?" and "I'm bored!" (along with "I have to go to the bathroom!") are common cries from children (and adults) who are traveling. Tapes, books, toys, and snacks all help to keep kids entertained, as do car games. Here are just a few of our favorites with brief explanations on how to play:

FOR THE YOUNGER SET:
**MISSING LETTER ABC SONG** - Sing the ABC song, leaving out a letter. See if your child can figure out what letter is missing. Now let your child sing (or say) the alphabet, leaving out a letter. Suggest correct (and incorrect) letters and see if your child agrees with you on what letter is missing. (Tip: Know your alphabet!)

**MISSING NUMBER GAME** - Count up to a certain number and stop. See if your child can figure out what number comes next. Now let your child do the counting. See if he/she agrees with what you say the next number should be.

**COLOR CAR GAME** - Look out the window for just red cars (or just blue or just green, etc.). Each time your child sees a red car, he/she can shout "red!" (or "blue!" or "green!", etc.) Count together the number of cars of a particular color you see on your trip. Your child can eagerly share at night, "Daddy, we had a fifteen-red-car day!" A variation of this game is to count a particular type of car; VW Bugs is the popular choice for our family.

**ABC WORD GAME** - A is for apple; B is for bear; etc. Encourage your child to figure out words that start with each letter of the alphabet.

FOR OLDER CHILDREN:
**ALPHABET SIGN GAME** - Each person, or team, looks for a word outside the car (i.e. billboards, freeway signs, bumper stickers, etc.) that begins with each letter of the alphabet. When the words are found, the person, or team, shouts it out. The words must be found in alphabetical order, starting with the letter A. Since words beginning with a Q, X, or Z are hard to find (unless you're near a Quality Inn, X-Ray machine, or a Zoo), players may find these particular letters used in any word. A word on a sign, billboard, etc., can only be used once, by one player or team member. Other players must find their word in another sign, billboard, etc. The first one to get through the alphabet wins! Warning #1: Try to verify that the word has been seen by more than just the player who shouted it out, or learn to trust each other. Warning #2: From personal experience: If the driver is competitive and wants to play, make sure he/she keeps his/her eyes on the road!

**ALPHABET WORD GAME** - This is a variation on the above game. Instead of finding words that begin with each letter of the alphabet, each player must look outside the car and describe his surroundings using letters of the alphabet, in sequential order. This game can be played fast and gets creative, depending on the quick-thinking skills of the people playing. Example: Someone who is on the letter D might look at the land and see dirt; a person looking for an S might say soil; someone else who is on the letter G might say ground. All are correct. Players may use the same point of reference as long as the exact same word is not used. Whoever gets through the alphabet first wins.

**GHOST** - (Or whatever title you choose.) The object of this game is to add one letter per turn and be in the process of spelling a word, without actually spelling out a word. Players take turns adding letters until someone either spells a word, or can't think of another letter to add without spelling a word. A player may try to bluff and add a letter that doesn't seem like it spells a word. If he gets challenged by someone asking what he is spelling, he must come up with a legitimate word. If he doesn't, he loses the round. (If he does have a word, however, than the challenger loses that round.) Whoever spells a word or can't think of a letter to add, gets a G. The second time he loses a round, he gets an H, etc. Whoever earns G-H-O-S-T (i.e. loses 5 rounds) is eliminated from the game. Example: Player 1 says the letter "B." Player 2 adds the letter "E." (Words must be at least 3 letters long to count as a word.) Player 3 says "T." Player 3 gets a G, or whatever letter-round he is on. He loses the round even if his intent was to spell the word "better" because "bet" is a word.

**WORD SCRAMBLE** - Make sure players have a piece of paper and a writing implement. Using a word on a sign or billboard, or using the name of the place you are visiting, see how many other words players can make. To spice up the game, and add stress, set a time limit. Whoever has the most words wins. A variation is that letters are worth points: 2 letter words are worth 2 points, 3 letter words are worth 5 points, 4 letter words are worth 8 points, etc. The player with the most points wins. (Although a player may have fewer words, he/she could win the game by being long-worded.) Note: This game can be played for only a brief period of time by players who are prone to motion sickness.

FOR ALL AGES:
**BINGO** - This is the only game that you have to prepare for ahead of time. Make up bingo-type cards for each child. Cards for younger children can have pictures of things kids would typically see on their drive (although this depends on where you are traveling, of course): a blue car, McDonalds, a cow, a pine tree, etc. Cards for older children can have pictures, signs, license plates, and/or words that they would typically see on their drive: exit, stop, a traffic light, curvy road ahead, etc. Use magazines, newspapers, etc., and glue the pictures and words onto posterboard, one card per child. Tip: Have your kids help you prepare the cards as it's a fun project. Use raisins (or M&Ms) as markers and when your child has bingo (or has seen a certain number of objects on his card), he can eat his reward. For those parents who intend to use the bingo boards more than once, "laminate" them with contact paper. Put small pieces of velcro on a part of each picture or sign on the card and make (non-edible) markers that have the other part of velcro on them. (This will keep markers from sliding off the cards during sudden turns!) Keep the cards and markers together in a plastic baggy in the car.

**20 QUESTIONS** - This time-honored game has many variations. (Our version is usually called 40 Questions.) The basic rules are for one player to think of a well-known person, or at least someone well-known to your children, and for other players to ask questions about the person to try to find out his/her identity. Only yes or no answers can be given. Whoever figures out the mystery person, in 20 questions or less, wins. Tip: Encourage players to ask general questions first to narrow down the field. (Inevitably, my youngest one's first question is, "Is it George Washington?") Teach them to ask, for instance: "Is it a man?"; "Is he alive?"; "Is he real?"; "Is he a cartoon?"; "Is he on T.V.?"; "Is he an historical figure?"; "Is it someone I know personally?" You get the picture. For a variation of the game, think of an object instead of a person. (Tip: Tell the others players first, though, about the switch in subject matter.)

**3 THINGS IN COMMON** - This is a great thinking game that is easily adaptable for kids of all ages. One person names 3 words (or things) that have something in common. Everyone else takes turns guessing what that something is. Examples for younger children: #1) sky, ocean, grandpa's eyes (or whomever). Answer: Things that are blue. #2) stop sign, fire truck, Santa's suit. Answer: Things that are red. Examples for older kids and adults: #1) house, butter, horse. Answer: Things that have the word fly at the end of them. #2) chain, missing, sausage. Answer: Things that can end with the word link. #3) tiger, nurse, sand. Answer: Kinds of sharks. My favorite example is the one my middle child came up with: #4) lion, Jesus, Budweiser. Answer: They are all kings! (Who says kids aren't affected by commercials?)

**I'M GOING ON A PICNIC. . .** - This game tests a player's abilities to remember things and remember them in order. Player 1 starts with the words, "I'm going on a picnic" and then adds a one word item that he will bring. The next player starts with the same phrase, repeats player 1's item, and then adds another item, and so on. Play continues until one of the players can't remember the list of things, in order, to bring on a picnic. Example: Player 1 says, "I'm going on a picnic and I am going to bring a ball." Player 2 says, "I'm going on a picnic and I'm going to bring a ball and a kite." Variations of the game include adding items in alphabetical order or adding items beginning with the same letter.

xviii

PLEASE be aware that although the facts recorded in this book are accurate and current as of October, 1998:

• HOURS CHANGE!
• EXHIBITS ROTATE!
• ADMISSION COSTS ARE RAISED WITHOUT FANFARE!
• PLACES CLOSE, EITHER TEMPORARILY OR PERMANENTLY!

To avoid any unexpected (and unpleasant) surprises:

## Always, ALWAYS, *ALWAYS*
CALL BEFORE YOU GO TO AN ATTRACTION!!!

## AMUSEMENT PARKS

Webster's definition of amusement is: "To cause to laugh or smile; entertainment; a pleasant diversion." So, from roller coasters to water slides - have fun!

Tip: If you *really* enjoy a particular amusement park, look into getting season passes. Also, many parks offer discounts on admission after 3pm or 4pm.

KENAN

## PACIFIC PARK

(310) 260-8744 / www.pacpark.com    *$$*

*Foot of Colorado Boulevard, on Santa Monica Pier, Santa Monica*

(Exit Santa Monica Fwy [10] N. on 4th St., L. on Colorado Blvd. It dead ends at the pier.)

The major kid-attraction on the Santa Monica pier is Pacific Park. It has eleven family rides, including six kiddie rides. The rides include a fifty-five-foot Ferris wheel, an historic carousel (with horses, camels, and lions), bumper boats, and a ship that swings back and forth, like a pendulum. A three-minute, motion simulator ride features either of two action films. Each simulated ride costs $4. The Backyard Circus is a free event where kids are invited to be a part of the circus by dressing up and then using their imaginations to be tightrope walkers, clowns, etc. See SANTA MONICA PIER, under the Piers and Seaports section, for details about the pier.

> **Hours:** Open in the summer Sun. - Thurs., 10am - 10pm; Fri. - Sat., 10am - midnight. Open the rest of the year Mon. - Thurs., 11am - 6pm; Fri., 11am - midnight; Sat., 10am - midnight; Sun., 10am - 10pm. Note: Not all the rides are open Mon. - Thurs. during the school year.
> **Admission:** Rides cost between $1 - $3 each.
> **Ages:** 2 years and up.

## RAGING WATERS

(909) 592-6453 / www.raging-waters.com    *$$$$$*

*111 Raging Waters Drive, San Dimas*

(Exit San Bernardino Fwy [10] N. on the 210 Fwy, or follow the Orange Fwy [57] where it turns into the 210 Fwy; exit at Raging Waters Dr.)

What a cool place to be on a hot day! Raging Waters is out*rage*ous with its fifty acres of chutes, white-water rapids, slides, drops, enclosed tubes (which make these slides dark and scary), a wave pool, lagoon areas, and sandy beaches. The rides run the gamut from a peaceful river raft ride in only three feet of water, to the ultimate in daredevil, such as plunging headfirst on High Extreme, a 600-foot ride off a 100-foot tower, or riding the blistering El Nino.

The younger set reigns at Kids Kingdom. They enjoy splashing around in this water area designed just for them. It has a big water play structure to climb on that shoots out water, plus tyke-size water slides and a tire swing. Elementary-school-aged kids have their own, separate, fantastic, activity pool with slides, a ropes course, and Splash Island. The Island is a five-story treehouse with slides, water cannons, and a huge bucket on top that spills over gallons of water.

Life vests are available at no extra charge. Inner tubes are available at no charge for some of the rides, but you must wait in long lines to get them. On busy days, I recommend renting a tube ($5). A picnic area is available just outside the main entrance gate. Outside food is not allowed inside, but there are many food outlets throughout the park. Hot tip: Wear water shoes, or sandals, because the walkways get very hot.

**Hours:** Open mid-April through May, and Labor Day through October, on weekends only from 10:30am - 6pm. Open Memorial Day through June, Mon. - Fri., 10:30am - 6pm; Sat. - Sun., 10am - 7pm. Open July through August, Mon. - Fri., 10am - 9pm; Sat. - Sun., 9:30am - 9pm.

**Admission:** $21.99 for 48" and taller; $14.99 for seniors and kids under 48"; children 2 years and under are free. After 4pm, prices are $14.99 for 48" and taller; $10.99 for seniors and kids under 48". Purchase season passes by May and save $! Parking is $6.

**Ages:** 1½ years and up.

## SIX FLAGS HURRICANE HARBOR                    ☼

(818) 367-5965 or (805) 255-4111 / www.sixflags.com                    $$$$$

*Magic Mountain Parkway, Valencia*

(Exit Golden State Fwy [5] W. on Magic Mountain Pky. It's right next to Magic Mountain.)

Pirates and lost tropical islands are the themes creatively integrated throughout every attraction in this twenty-two-acre water park. Older kids enjoy the swashbuckling thrill of the vertical drops, enclosed tube rides, and a combination of the two in the tallest enclosed speed slide this side of the Mississippi. The wave pool is a hit for those practicing surfing techniques. The five-person raft ride is fun without being too scary, and the lazy, looping river ride in only three feet of water is great for everyone in the family.

Relax in lounge chairs while your younger children play in a shallow pool with mini-slides, cement aquatic creatures, and a wonderful water play structure. The next harbor over is ideal for elementary-school-aged mateys to get wet and play on board the "floating" pirate ship. An adult activity pool is great for swimming, plus it has a net for water volleyball and, of course, it also has a few slides. Sand volleyball is available, too.

Tube rentals run between $6 and $8, although tubes are included in some of the rides. Food is available to purchase inside the Harbor as outside food is not allowed in. Hot tip: Wear water shoes, or sandals, as the walkways get very hot. Note: The Harbor shares the same parking lot as Magic Mountain.

**Hours:** Open May and September on weekends only from 10am - 6pm. Open June through Labor Day daily from 10am - 7pm.

**Admission:** $19 for adults and kids 48" and taller; $12 for seniors and kids under 48"; children 2 years and under are free. Parking is $7. Combo tickets for Hurricane Harbor and Magic Mountain are $46 for adults and kids 48" and taller; $30 for kids under 48"; children 2 years and under are free.

**Ages:** 1½ years and up.

## SIX FLAGS MAGIC MOUNTAIN                    ☼

(818) 367-5965 or (805) 255-4111 / www.sixflags.com                    $$$$$

*Magic Mountain Parkway, Valencia*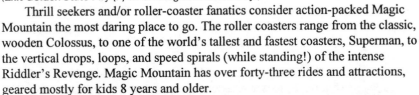
(Exit Golden State Fwy [5] W. on Magic Mountain Pky.)

Thrill seekers and/or roller-coaster fanatics consider action-packed Magic Mountain the most daring place to go. The roller coasters range from the classic, wooden Colossus, to one of the world's tallest and fastest coasters, Superman, to the vertical drops, loops, and speed spirals (while standing!) of the intense Riddler's Revenge. Magic Mountain has over forty-three rides and attractions, geared mostly for kids 8 years and older.

Besides riding the coaster, some of our other highlights here include Yosemite Sam Sierra Falls, which is a raft ride through tubes ending in water, the Log Ride, Jet Stream, bumper cars, and a visit to Pirate's Cove. The Sky Tower is a "must-do" for all ages because it affords a 360-degree view of the park and the surrounding area. Bugs Bunny World is ideal for the younger and shorter crowd (under 54"). The ten rides here include race cars, mini-prop planes, a roller coaster (of course) and, my children's favorite, the Tweety Bird Cage ride, which is a ride in an oversized bird cage.

Magic Mountain has entertainment such as live music, stunt shows, water shows, and interactive shows for younger kids such as Bugs Bunny in Rabbit Hood. Cyclone Bay is toward the back of the park, where specialty shops are the specialty. Bayshore Candy is an especially sweet stop as kids can watch fudge, caramel apples, and all sorts of mouth-watering delights being made before their very eyes.

If it's real food that you're hankering for, try Mooseburger Lodge. The waiters and waitresses sing, a moose talks, and the dessert, chocolate "moose," is served in an edible chocolate shell.

Wear walking shoes because although there are lots of grassy, shady areas to rest, Magic Mountain is spacious and hilly. Be on the lookout for Looney Tunes characters throughout the park. (If you want wet, summertime fun check out SIX FLAGS HURRICANE HARBOR, right next door to Magic Mountain.)

**Hours:** Open April through October daily from 10am - 6pm. Call for extended summer hours. Open the rest of the year weekends and holidays only from 10am - 6pm.

**Admission:** $36 for adults and kids 48" and taller; $20 for seniors; $18 for kids under 48"; children 2 years and under are free. Parking is $7. Combo tickets for Magic Mountain and Hurricane Harbor are $46 for adults and kids 48" and taller; $30 for kids under 48"; children 2 years and under are free.

**Ages:** 1½ years and up.

# UNIVERSAL STUDIOS HOLLYWOOD                    ☼

(818) 508-9600 / www.mca.com/unicity                    *$$$$$*

*Universal Center Drive, Universal City*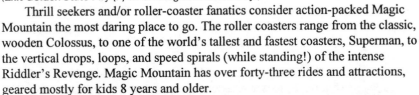

(Heading NW on Hollywood Fwy [101], exit NE on Universal Center Dr. Heading SE on 101, exit R. on Lankershim. At the end of the off ramp, turn L. on Cahuenga Blvd., L. on Universal Center Dr.)

This huge, unique, Hollywood-themed amusement park is really one of the world's biggest and busiest motion picture and television studios. Personal advice is to go on the forty-five-minute, guided tram tour first, as lines get long later on. The tour takes you behind the scenes, through several of Hollywood's original and most famous backlots. Along the way, some of the elaborate special effects that you'll encounter are: a confrontation with King Kong; the shark from *Jaws*; Earthquake - The Big One, where buildings collapse and a run-away big-rig crashes within inches of you, followed by fire and a flood coming toward you; and more disasters, such as the Collapsing Bridge and the Flash Flood. Some of it can get a bit overwhelming for younger kids.

Want to go Back to the Future? Be prepared for an intense, jolting, simulated experience through the Ice Ages, into the mouth of a Tyrannosaurus Rex, and to the year 2015.

Down on the lower lot, kids can fly on a bike with E.T. and visit his planet. Although a little darker in tone, this ride is best described as Disneyland's "it's a small world" meets a world of E.T.'s. If you are at least 46" tall, enter through the gates of Jurassic Park as you river raft through the primordial forest. It starts off as a peaceful ride, but it ends up as a very wet, terrifying, face-to-face encounter with bellowing dinosaurs! Follow this ride with Backdraft, where you literally feel the heat of the hottest attraction here. (You'll dry off from the Jurassic waters.) This sound stage becomes a fiery furnace, ablaze with ruptured fuel lines and melting metal. In the sound stage show of Cinemagic, you can watch or take part in some of the special effects created for big and small screens. Lovers of Lucy can visit the heart-shaped facility and "walk through" her career, with the aid of photos, videos, costumes, and other memorabilia.

As Universal Studios is synonymous with quality productions, the live shows here are entertaining and highlighted with special effects. Some of the current shows include Animal Actors Show, Beetlejuice Review, and the Wild, Wild, Wild West Stunt Show, which is a funny western farce employing great stunts. (Get there early to watch the Charlie Chaplin character interact with the crowd.) Waterworld is the "coolest" production here with explosive stunts and special effects that blow you out of the water. The interactive Totally Nickelodeon show is totally fun. Based on Nickelodeon shows, a few audience members are invited to compete on teams doing some very silly games and activities. The ultimate prize? Getting slimed! Some of Universal's shows are seasonal, and/or performed on weekends and holidays only.

There are many unique shops at Universal, too. Universal Ranch is tops on our list because kids can dig through a bin of rocks and fill up a small pouch for only $3.50.

Dine at the restaurants inside the Studios, or try two that are just outside the studio gates: MARVEL MANIA, a comic book restaurant, and COUNTRY STAR, an eating establishment with good ol' country cookin'. Look under the Edible Adventures section for more details on both restaurants.

Get an early start for your adventure at Universal Studios, and don't forget to bring your camera for some wonderful photo opportunities.

If you're interested in "edutainment," ask about the Universal Studios

Hollywood Course of Study Program. Fourth through twelfth grade students are introduced to a variety of subjects on a field trip here, including dinosaurs, sound effects, and careers in advertising and entertainment. Other programs include assemblies at Universal, for seventh through twelfth graders, where speakers and live performances address important issues facing today's youth. Kids can then spend the remainder of the day at Universal Studios. Call (800) 959-9688 for more information on these programs.

Check out the adjacent UNIVERSAL CITYWALK, listed under the Potpourri section, for unusual shopping and dining experiences.

**Hours:** Open the majority of the year daily 9am - 7pm. During the peak summer season, it's open daily 8am - 10pm. Call to find out the hours for the day of your visit. Tours in Spanish are available Sat. and Sun. Closed Thanksgiving and Christmas.

**Admission:** $38 for adults; $33 for seniors; $28 for ages 3 - 11; children 2 years and under are free. (Certain discounts available through AAA.) Parking is $7. Season passes are a good deal at $69 for adults; $59 for seniors; $54 for kids. Passes allow you priority tram boarding and complimentary parking.

**Ages:** 3 years and up.

# ADVENTURE CITY

(714) 827-7469  / www.imenu.com/adventurecity
*10120 S. Beach Boulevard, Anaheim*
(Exit Artesia Fwy [91] S. on Beach Blvd. It's 2 miles S. of Knott's Berry Farm on the left hand side in the Hobby City complex on the Anaheim/Stanton border.)

My family travels a lot and one of our favorite cities to visit is Adventure City. This clean, two-acre little theme park, located in the HOBBY CITY complex (look under the Potpourri section), is perfect for younger children. The colorful city scene facades throughout resemble storybook illustrations. The ten rides, designed to accommodate parents, too, include a wonderful train ride around the "city," a roller coaster, an airplane ride, and a bus with wheels that goes 'round and 'round. Kids can have a really hot time dressing up in full fireman apparel before (or after) they "drive" around on the 9-1-1 vehicle ride.

Adventure City also offers do-it-yourself face painting, a few video and arcade games, plus terrific interactive, educational puppet shows at the theater. After the show, the puppeteers come out and allow kids to try their hand at puppeteering. Classes in puppeteering are also available. Thomas the Tank play area has a huge wooden train set that encourages toddlers' imaginations to go full steam ahead. A small petting zoo has goats, sheep, chickens, bunnies, and a llama. Mount Adventure is a rock climbing wall just the right size for kids (and adults) to scale. It's twenty-five feet high and cost $3 per person to climb.

The food is good and reasonably priced. Note: You may not bring your own food inside, but there is a small picnic area just outside the gates. Come and spend a delightful day in this city!

**Hours:** Open in the summer Mon. - Thurs., 10am - 5pm; Fri., 10am - 8pm; Sat., 11am - 9pm; Sun., 11am - 8pm. Open the rest of the year Fri., 10am - 5pm; Sat. - Sun., 11am - 7pm. Call for holiday hours.

**Admission:** $4.95, which includes admission, puppet shows, face painting, Thomas the Tank area, and entrance to the petting farm, for age 1 year and up; $10.95 includes all of the above, plus unlimited rides. Children under 12 months are free. Individual rides are $1.25 per ride for all ages.

**Ages:** 1 - 10 years.

## DISNEYLAND ☼

(714) 781-4565 / www.disneyland.com                                   $$$$

*1313 Harbor Boulevard, Anaheim*

(Exit Santa Ana Fwy [5] S. on Harbor Blvd. Or, exit Garden Grove Fwy [22] N. on Harbor Blvd.)

The world-famous "happiest place on earth" amusement park has so many things to do, see, and ride on, that entire books are written about it. The following description is just a brief overview.

The park is "divided" into different sections and each section favors a particular theme. The following attractions are just *some* of the highlights in these various areas. •**Fantasyland** is located mostly inside the castle "walls." Rides include Mr. Toad's Wild Ride, Alice in Wonderland (where the ride vehicle is shaped liked a caterpillar), a carousel, etc. This area is definitely geared for the younger set, although some of the images on the rides may be scary for them. Storybook Land is a boat ride through canals lined with miniature buildings that are from Disney's classic tales. Fantasyland also features Matterhorn Bobsled (a roller coaster), and "it's a small world," where a slow moving boat takes you past animated children from all over the world dressed in their culture's attire and singing the theme song in their native language. (If you didn't know the song at the beginning of the ride, you will never forget it afterward.) •**Mickey's Toontown** is put together at crazy, cartoonish angles. Meet Mickey and Minnie in "person" at each of their houses and get your picture taken with him/her. Kids enjoy Goofy's Bounce House, the scaled down roller coaster ride, sitting in cars that look like they are straight out of a cartoon, as well as just running all around this toddler-friendly "town." Roger Rabbit is the most popular ride here as riders sit in a car that they can actually spin around. •**Frontierland** features Big Thunder Mountain Railroad (a roller coaster), Mark Twain River boat (which looks authentic), and Tom Sawyer's Island. On the island, kids can climb on (fake) rocks, go through secret passages in the rocks, and play at the frontier fort. •**New Orleans Square** boasts of Pirates of the Caribbean. Yo ho, yo ho, with its catchy music and cannons "blasting" under a nighttime setting, it's a pirate's life for me. The Haunted Mansion is a ride through, well, a haunted mansion, that showcases various ghosts. •**Critter Country** has an un*bear*ably funny show starring singing country bears. Splash

Mountain, a wet roller coaster ride, is also here. •**Adventureland** has the thrilling (and jolting) Indiana Jones Adventure roller coaster ride. You'll encounter snakes, skeletons, a huge boulder rolling toward your jeep, and other dangers. Height restrictions apply as younger children will most likely be frightened of the content. Climb the Swiss Family Robinson Treehouse and imagine living like that. •**Tomorrowland,** with its sixty-four-foot mobile of gold, spinning planets, ushers in a new era. Zoom through the darkness of outer space in Space Mountain, one of the fastest roller coaster rides at Disneyland. Bump along through Star Tours, a motion simulator ride. *Honey, I Shrunk the Audience* is an exciting 3D movie experience. Warning: If you do not like mice, keep your feet off the floor. Be entertained by film tributes to past and future technology while waiting in line for Rocket Rods, a ride in a speeding, futuristic car. We could have stayed inside the Innoventions building all day. This showcase that rotates (remember G.E. Carousel of Progress?) features educational and entertaining computer and video games on the first floor. I can only liken the second level to a terrific, hands-on, science "museum" that features technology and games of the future. Play virtual reality games, listen to the rhythm of human heart beats, and use a ultrasound machine on a model pregnant woman to see how the baby is forming inside her.

The themed parades and shows are truly memorable. They are usually based on Disney's latest animated films. *Fantasmic* is usually shown daily in the summer, and on the weekends only, the rest of the year. This twenty-five-minute show is produced by Tom Sawyer's Island. The central storyline is that Mickey Mouse's imagination battles evil forces. Fountains of water create a misty "screen" for film images from *The Sorcerer's Apprentice*, *Dumbo*, *Little Mermaid*, and others. Boats with lights cruise by with characters on board that re-enact scenes from movies, like the scene in *Peter Pan* where Peter fights Captain Hook. Fire flashes on the water, fireworks explode, and the finale is played with a thunderous symphony of music. Summer nights, actually May through Labor Day, bring a magic of their own to the Magic Kingdom as a spectacular fireworks display is shot off nightly at 9:30pm. Call for a complete list of show information and times.

Main Street, U.S.A. is perfect for all your mini (and Mickey) shopping needs. Your child's favorite Disney characters are strolling all around the park, so keep your eyes open and your camera ready. Tip: Quite a few of the characters are gathered at Town Square when Disneyland opens in the morning. Come spend at least a day at the "Magic Kingdom." Epcot West, a completely new addition for Disneyland, is under construction. Current plans call for it to open around the year 2000.

**Hours:**   Open daily in the summer from 8am - 1am. Open the rest of the year Mon. - Thurs., 9:30am - 6pm; Fri. - Sat., 9am - midnight; Sun., 10am - 10pm. Hours do fluctuate, so call before you visit.

**Admission:**   $38 for adults; $36 for seniors; $28 for ages 3 - 11; children 2 years and under are free. Parking costs $7. Ask about 2 or 3 day passes. Several times throughout the year Southern California residents are offered a substantial discount on admission.

**Ages:**   All

# KNOTT'S BERRY FARM

(714) 220-5200 / www.knotts.com
*8039 Beach Boulevard, Buena Park*
(Exit Artesia Fwy [91] S. on Beach Blvd.)

$$$$$

The atmosphere of the Old West is re-created throughout most of California's original theme park. The Old West Ghost Town has a humorous Wild West Stunt Show, an old-fashioned Stagecoach ride, train rides, a huge wooden-trestle roller coaster (opening '99) named Ghost Rider, lots of stores with a Western motif, and usually some cowboys hanging around. Indian Trails has tepees to go in, Indian crafts to see, and terrific shows featuring Native American dancers.

Fiesta Village's rides and shops have a Mexican theme. Enter Jaguar, a 2,700-foot long roller coaster, through a Mayan-styled pyramid temple and experience ancient wonders (and a fun ride!). Check out Windjammer, a dual track racing roller coaster at the Boardwalk area. Zap and get zapped with laser tag, a fast-moving action game which costs $5 per person to play. One of the most popular rides at Knott's is Kingdom of the Dinosaurs (guess why?), though it's a bit dark and scary for younger kids. Beware - the Roaring Rapids ride **will** get you wet. There are roller coasters, bumper cars, and many other amusement park rides and attractions at Knott's.

Kids 2 to 7 years old can spend almost the whole day in Camp Snoopy. This "camp" has kiddie rides, ball pits, a petting zoo, pony rides, and a large Snoopy bounce.

There are also "hidden" parts to Knott's Berry Farm. For instance, in front of Roaring Rapids is a small, but terrific, Ranger Station. Inside, kids can see and hold a variety of insects and arachnids such as a giant millipede and a hissing cockroach. They can also pet a snake and touch animal pelts. The Edison Room in Camp Snoopy is a great first exposure to the science of how things work, utilizing magnets, generators, etc. A lot can be learned about the Old West and Native American life styles by talking to some of the costumed employees, visiting the old-fashioned schoolroom, and using some of the stores as mini-museums. There are many terrific educational tours available through Knott's education department. Learn about our early American heritage, pan for gold, explore Indian Trails with an Indian guide, learn about energy in motion, go on a natural history adventure, and much more! Call (714) 220-5244 for information on field trips.

In addition to Knott's Berry Farm's rides and attractions, there are twenty-six shops; delicious restaurants, including the famous Mrs. Knott's Chicken Dinner Restaurant; the Good Time Theater, where major entertainers, including

Snoopy, perform; and a full-size reproduction of INDEPENDENCE HALL.
(Look under the Potpourri section for a description of the hall.)

**Hours:** Open in the summer, Sun. - Thurs., 9am - 11pm; Fri. - Sat., 9am - midnight. Open the rest of the year Mon. - Fri., 10am - 6pm; Sat., 10am - 10pm; Sun., 10am - 7pm. Hours may vary. Closed Christmas.

**Admission:** $36 for adults; $26 for seniors and ages 3 - 11; children 2 years and under are free. (Certain discounts available through AAA.) Parking is $7. Knott's offers numerous special admission deals throughout the year, including some for California residents and some for admissions after 4pm.

**Ages:** All

# WILD RIVERS WATERPARK
(949) 768-WILD (9453) / www.go-wildrivers.com
*8770 Irvine Center Drive, Irvine*
(Exit San Diego Fwy [405] S. on Irvine Center Dr.)

☼
$$$$$

This park's all wet with twenty acres of over forty water rides and attractions! The mild to wild rides include a relaxing river raft ride, wave pools (one has "real-size" waves), completely enclosed slides (i.e. dark and scary), and vertical drops. My boys also enjoyed shooting the rapids, and the opportunity to go belly-sliding down Surf Hill.

Younger kids have their own terrific water play area at Pygmy Pond. It has a climbing structure that shoots out water, a gorilla swing, just-their-size slides, and kiddie tube rides. Tunnel Town offers both wet and dry fun with twisting and turning tunnels to crawl through.

Two pools just for swimming are also here. One pool is three-and-a-half-feet deep, while the other is a bit deeper and has a water basketball area. All of this, and plenty of sun-bathing opportunities, makes Wild Rivers a fantastic beach alternative.

Picnic areas are available outside the park, as no outside food may be brought in. Locker rentals are $4. Additional tube rentals are available. Hot tip: Wear water shoes, or sandals, as the cement walkways get very hot.

**Hours:** Open May through mid-June and mid-September through the beginning of October on weekends only from 11am - 5pm. Open mid-June through mid-September daily from 10am - 8pm.

**Admission:** $21.95 for adults; $9.95 for seniors; $14.95 for spectators; $17.95 for ages 3 - 9; children 2 years and under are free. Parking is $4. After 4pm, admission is only $9.95 for ages 3 years and up. Ask about Monday Carloads, when admission is $40 for up to eight people after 4pm.

**Ages:** 1½ years and up.

# CASTLE AMUSEMENT PARK
(909) 785-4140

◑
$$$

*3500 Polk Street, Riverside*                                          🎂

(Exit Riverside Fwy [91] N. on La Sierra Ave., R. on Diana St., L. on Polk St. It's between
the Galleria at Tyler and La Sierra Ave., and visible from the freeway.)

Castle Amusement Park has a lot of action packed into only twenty-five
acres. The compactness of the park makes it easy to walk all around. It has four
scenic and challenging eighteen-hole miniature golf courses; a three-level arcade
with over 400 video games and games of skill, plus a redemption center; and
over thirty rides and attractions! The rides include the log ride (which will get
you wet), a huge carousel, roller coasters, a Ferris wheel, a few train rides, pony
rides, Nascar go-karts, etc. There are plenty of "big kids" rides, as well as
delightful kiddie rides. The atmosphere here reminds me of Coney Island in that
the flashy rides are interspersed with carnival-type games.

The park's Petting Zoo features thirty-five to forty animals at any given
time, although the selection of animals changes frequently. You might see
camels, kangaroos, goats, sheep, cows, horses, potbellied pigs, rabbits, ostriches,
pheasants, and/or a bison!

The massive BIG TOP FOOD 'N' FUN RESTAURANT (look under the
Edible Adventures section) looks like a circus Big Top, complete with a large
circus elephant statue outside. Pizza tops the list of food, but chicken nuggets,
burgers, hot dogs, and salads are available, too. There are more arcade games in
here, and shows are occasionally performed on stage to keep kids entertained
while eating.

Special events and package deals are on going at Castle Park, so call for a
schedule and more information.

**Hours:**   Miniature golf and the arcade area are open Sun. - Thurs.,10am -
10pm; Fri. - Sat., 10am - 11pm. The ride park is open Fri., 6pm -
10pm; Sat., noon - 10pm; Sun., noon - 8pm. During summer
hours and holidays the entire park is open extended hours. The
petting zoo is open on weekends only from noon - 9pm. Big Top
Restaurant is open daily from 11am - 10pm.

**Admission:**   There is no general admission fee. Miniature golf is $5.50 for
adults; $3.75 for seniors and children 11 years and under. Rides
require between two to five tickets, depending on the age of the
rider. (Children 10 years and under need fewer tickets.) Ride
tickets are 50¢ each; $10 for 22; $18 for 50. Passes, which
include all the rides except go karts and pony rides, are $16 for
adults; $14 for children 11 years and under. Pass prices are
subject to change. Pony rides are $1 each. Nascar go karts are $4
per ride. The petting zoo costs $1; children under 12 months old
are free. Parking is free before noon; $3 after noon.

**Ages:**   All

# LAKE DOLORES                                                  ☼

(760) 257-1233                                                      *$$$$*

*72 Hacienda Road, Newberry Springs*                               🎂

(Exit Mojave Fwy [15], S. on Harvard St. [20 minutes E. of Barstow], L. on Hacienda Rd.)
Shooby do wop wop over to Lake Dolores, a Route 66-themed water park. Listen to oldies songs playing over the sound system, check out the cool retro cars and old-time gas pumps throughout the park, and look over the vintage Harley Davidson mounted on a rotating display at the front entrance. This high desert oasis brings refreshment to a parched community with its twelve water slides that range from enclosed, spiraling body slides with full 360 degree turns, to a six-person river raft ride (a ride for the family), to open-topped slides. For a change of pace, float around on the circular Lazy River - a slow moving river raft ride. Children can splash around in the two water play areas designed just for them. One has small waterfalls and kiddie-size slides. The other features a big umbrella with water pouring over its sides, a few slides, and a large water play structure with handles to pull to squirt out water. Life jackets and most inner tubes are included with your admission price. Tube rentals are available (and advisable on a really crowded day). There are grassy areas, picnic tables, and plenty of food booths. No outside food is allowed in. Tip: Instead of your blue suede shoes, wear water shoes as the cement pathways can get hot. The lakeside area can be rented by a group. The rental fee includes swimming in the large lake and the opportunity to rent paddle boats. Ask about the on-site RV campground.

**Hours:** Open mid-May through Labor Day daily from 11am - 9pm. Open weekends through September from 11am - 9pm. Hours are subject to change.

**Admission:** $17.95 for adults; $10.95 for seniors; $12.95 for ages 3 - 9; children 2 years and under are free. Parking is $3.

**Ages:** All

# PHARAOH'S LOST KINGDOM

(909) 335- PARK (7275) / www.pharaohslostkingdom.com
*California Street, Redlands*
(Exit San Bernardino Fwy [10] N. on California St. It's the first pyramid off the Fwy.)
Mummies (and daddies) looking for a place to keep kids royally entertained have found their answer at Pharaoh's Lost Kingdom. Enter through the giant Sphinx. Inside is a massive number of arcade, video, and virtual reality games. On the upper level, take your best shot in Laser Tag. With over 5,000 square feet of darkness, mazes, obstacle courses, and opponents just waiting to zap you, the twelve-minute game is action-packed. All this is only the tip of the pyramid!
Outside, the Race Car Complex offers three different tracks - kiddie, Grand Prix, and a banked Indy speed track; some height restrictions apply. Bumper boats are another great family attraction. Travel to ancient and exotic lands via the four, nine-hole miniature golf courses. The holes don't have a lot of challenging obstacles, but they are intriguingly embellished. For an adrenaline rush, dare to try Sky Coaster, a harnessed "ride" that lets you fly and swing from over 100-feet high for $20; height and age restrictions apply. The fifteen amusement rides, geared for young kids and older kids (i.e. adults), include a Ferris wheel, carousel, Tilt-A-Whirl, bumper cars, mini motorboats, etc. A large

children's soft play area with ball pits, slides, tubes, and obstacle courses is also in this area.

We found a lot of fun at Pharaoh's Lost Kingdom water park. Climb up the central tower to go down the six slides that range from enclosed body slides with a sheer drop, to open tube rides that hurtle riders down. Enjoy a blissful raft ride in three feet of water on the Endless River, a large circular river encompassing the water park. Body or board surf with the wave machine at Riptide. Younger children have their own wading pool with a big water play structure and slides. Another activity pool, for elementary-school-aged kids, has a few short slides, a water volleyball area, and a challenging ropes course over hard foam mummies and tiles. A beach and a sand volleyball court are also here. King Tut never had it so good! Note that there are two full-service snack bars here and that no outside food is allowed in.

**Hours:**  Open Sun. - Thurs., 10am - 10pm; Fri. - Sat., 10am - midnight. The amusement rides usually open in the early afternoon. The water park is open daily 10am - 8pm, April through October. Call for its "off season" hours.

**Admission:**  Laser tag, bumper cars, race car rides, and miniature golf, cost $4.95 each. Amusement park rides cost between $1 to $3 each. Children under two years are not permitted on the rides. Admission to the water park is $14.95 for ages 11 and up; $10.95 for ages 3 - 10; children 2 years and under are free. A silver passport, which includes unlimited amusement rides and 5 attractions, is $14.95 for ages 11 and up; $10.95 for ages 3 - 10. A gold passport, which is unlimited amusement rides, attractions, and entrance to the water park, is $29.95 for ages 11 years and up; $19.95 for ages 3 - 10. Parking is $3.

**Ages:**  2 years and up.

# BIG RIVER COUNTRY WATER PARK

(760) 742-1921

*Rt. 76 and Segnme Oaks Road, on the La Jolla Indian Reservation, Pauma Valley*

(Exit Escondido Fwy [15] E. on Route 76, up about 25 windy mountain miles, R. on Segnme Oaks Rd.)

The woods along Route 76 hold a refreshing summer treat - a small water park! The park has five slipping, zipping, dipping slides, some that gently twist and some that drop straight down! Younger children have their own large shallow pool area with slides, water play structures, and floating foam animals. The setting is attractive with shade trees and picnic areas - you can even bring your own food inside. Volleyball courts, a general store, a full-service snack bar, showers, and lockers are also here. Look up an adjacent attraction, LA JOLLA INDIAN RESERVATION CAMPGROUND / TUBING ON SAN LUIS REY RIVER, under the Great Outdoors section.

**Hours:**    Open on weekends from mid-May to mid-June, and the month of
September, 10am - 6pm. Open mid-June, July, and August, Wed.
- Sun. from 10am - 6pm.

**Admission:**  $11.95 for 48" and over; $7.95 for kids under 48"; seniors and
children 2 years and under are free.

**Ages:**     2 years and up.

## LEGOLAND CALIFORNIA ☼

(760) 438-LEGO (5346) / www.lego.com/legoland/california          $$$$$

*1 Lego Drive, Carlsbad*

(Exit San Diego Fwy [5] E. on Palomar Airport Rd. It's next to the flower fields.)

  Lego mania will reach an all-time high when the 128-acre Legoland
California opens in 1999 featuring family rides, shows, interactive attractions,
areas to build and play with Legos™, and restaurants. (There are two other
Legolands, one in Denmark and one in England.) Over thirty *million* Legos
create the models used in and around this unique amusement park (and you will
get tired of reading the word "Lego" by the end of this entry). The following are
some highlights of the six main attraction areas:
  •**Village Green** is an imagination garden, comprised mostly of Duplo bricks.
Take a boat ride through an enchanted forest, past animated fairy tales settings.
Ride in a Lego jeep through a jungle that has ninety animals made of Legos. The
Waterworks area lets visitors turn a handle and aim water spray at objects and
pretend animals to bring them to "life." Playtown has a maze to crawl through, a
train ride, an ambulance and police motorcycle to "drive", and lots more. A
magic show and puppet theater round out this area. •**The Ridge** is situated in the
center of the park and helps orient guests. Sit in outward facing seats and pull
yourselves up a thirty-five foot tower, then free fall down. At the base of a tower
is a walk-through maze. For another perspective, pedal around an elevated,
circular track. •**Fun Town** offers age appropriate driving schools, in Lego-
looking cars, complete with a traffic jam and drivers licenses issued at the end of
a spin around the track. Other attractions here include piloting a kid-size
helicopter up and down via a joystick; maneuvering a bumper boat around buoys
(and other boats); seeing inhabitants of the rain forest, ancient Egypt, and the
Arctic (Legos and their builders really are amazing); watching a stage show;
touring a small-scale Lego factory to see how the bricks are made and packaged;
and eating an ice cream at the Cool Cafe where a Lego Robot Band performs.
•The medieval-themed **Castle Hill** has a roller coaster that takes riders through a
castle and into a cave past a fire-breathing dragon. Kids can also mount a
"horse" and take part in a simulated joust; have adventures at a playground that
has rope climbs, cargo nets, and slides; pan for "gold" and "gems" to be
exchanged for a Lego medallion; and take a nature walk, past model of native
animals, of course. •**Miniland** re-creates five areas of the U.S. constructed in
1:20 scale. Each area has fourteen to thirty-three animations and some
interactivity: New England Harbor has farmlands, a traditional harbor and a
shipyard, and underwater divers exploring a sunken ship; Washington, D.C. is

impressive with its Lincoln Memorial, Washington Monument, White House, a presidential motorcade, baseball games, etc; New York City showcases the Manhattan and Brooklyn bridges, Central Park (i.e. joggers, the zoo, etc.), Times Square complete with police cars with lights and siren, and the Statue of Liberty; California Coast combines beaches and mansions in Beverly Hills with cable cars and Ghiradelli Square; and New Orleans offers paddle steamers on the river front, plantation houses, Mardi Gras, and the sound of jazz. •The mostly hands-on **Imagination Zone** offers both free-play opportunities and structured workshops and contests for all ages. Inspiration is all around, such as a twelve-foot submarine, a Technic T-Rex, and a fifteen-foot Einstein. A learning center here also features computers with Lego software. The Imagination Zone theater shows a ten-minute movie in which you help choose the outcome via control devices - very cool.

A picturesque part of the Legoland landscaping is a large lake, where families can take a "cruise" and see more - what else - Lego animals and characters!!

**Hours:** To be announced.

**Admission:** At press date, the admission price was scheduled for $32 for adults; $25 for seniors and ages 3 - 16; children 2 years and under are free. Parking is $5.

**Ages:** Geared for ages 2 - 12, but are you ever too old to play with Legos?

## THE WAVE

(760) 940-WAVE (9283) / www.ci.vista.ca.us/wave

*161 Recreation Drive, Vista*

(Exit 78 Fwy N. on Vista Village Dr., R. on Broadway, L. on Recreation Dr.)

Catch a wave at The Wave on the Flow Rider wave machine. Swoosh on down the four water slides here - two are enclosed, and two are convertible-style (no tops). Some height restrictions apply. Slip 'n slide down the fifth slide, which is short, slopes gently, and ends into Crazy River, a large ring of water that encircles the slide and lounge area. For those 48" and under, there is also a small, children's water play area with climbing apparatus that has water spouting out and a few slides. The large rectangular pool, usually used for lessons and the swim team, is open to the public during Wave hours. There are a limited number of picnic tables here, as well as a few grassy areas for picnicking or sunbathing. You may bring in your own lounge chairs. Lockers, double inner tubes, life vests, and shade pavilions are all available for a small fee. Use of single inner tubes and body boards are included in your admission price. Outside food is not allowed in, but there is a full-service snack bar here that sells food at very reasonable prices. Have big time fun at this small water park!

**Hours:** Open the end of May through the beginning of June, and the month of September, on weekends and holidays from 11am - 5pm. Open the beginning of June through Labor Day daily from 10:30am - 5:30pm.

**Admission:**   $9.25 for ages 7 to 59 years; $6.25 for seniors and ages 3 - 6;
children 2 years and under are free. Spectators pay the full
admission price, but if their wristbands are dry when they leave,
they receive a $7 refund.

**Ages:**   1½ years and up.

## WHITE WATER CANYON

(619) 661-7373 / www.whitewatercanyon.com                              *$$$$$*

*2052 Otay Valley Road, Chula Vista*

(From San Diego Fwy [5], exit E. on Main St., turns into Otay Valley Rd. From Jacob
Dekema Fwy [805], exit E. on Otay Valley Rd., about 2 miles. It's near the Coors
amphitheater.)

The wild, wild West was never so wild, wild and wet! San Diego's liquid
gold - White Water Canyon water park - is set in a re-created, western gold
mining town, circa 1890. The park is spread over thirty-two acres with a large,
centrally located grassy area. The kids come here in hordes to plunge down the
sixteen water slides lined up side by side: six inner-tube slides, six body slides,
and four speed slides.

Rip the curl in the wave pool, where waves can reach up to three-and-a-half-
feet high. This huge pool can hold hundreds of swimmers and surfer "wannabes"
at one time. Fort White Water is a four-story, interactive family water play
structure with water cannons to shoot, cargo nets to crawl and climb on, and a
floating lily-pad bridge across the pool. Going across on the "lily pads" is more
challenging than it looks. A large toddler play area has mini slides and a
climbing structure in shallow waters. Still Water River is a restful inner tube ride
where you float along a continuous river that encircles a good portion of the
park.

White Water Canyon also features a softball field, sand volleyball courts, a
game arcade area, lockers, and showers. If you get hungry, choose from three,
full-service eateries, or snack from one of the "stands" scattered throughout the
park. No outside food is allowed inside the park. Suit up, saddle up, and mosey
on over to this western-themed water park, where your expectations for a fun
time will surely pan out. Hot tip: Wear water shoes, or sandals, as the cement
pathways can get hot.

**Hours:**   Open May through mid-June, September, and October, on
weekends only from 10am - 6pm. Open mid-June through Labor
Day daily from 10am - 6pm.

**Admission:**   $21.99 for 48" and taller; $14.99 for seniors; $15.99 for kids
under 48"; children 2 years and under are free. Parking is $4.

**Ages:**   2 years and up.

## ARTS AND CRAFTS

Children have creative urges and need a place to express themselves. Since art classes are offered in a dizzying array of fluctuating times and prices, most of the places listed here are paint-it-yourself ceramic stores, along with a variety of other places, that assist your young artists in developing their talents - move over Monet! Note: Museums are also great resources for arts and crafts workshops.

## COLOR ME MINE

Beverly Hills - (310) 247-1226; Costa Mesa - (949) 515-8612; Encino -            *$$$$*
(818) 784-0400; Huntington Beach - (714) 960-3834; Laguna Hills -
(949) 380-8510; Laguna Niguel - (949) 240-6884; Long Beach - (562)
433-4177; Los Angeles - (323) 465-1680; Santa Monica - (310) 393-
0069; Studio City - (818) 762-4434; Torrance - (310) 325-9968; Tustin -
(714) 505-3975; Valencia - (805) 284-2927; Venice - (310) 581-0525 /
www.colormemine.com
    Do your kids have an artistic flair? Or think they do? Color Me Mine is a
delightful, cozy, paint-your-own ceramic store. Kids can express themselves by
first choosing their own ceramic piece, and then their own palette. White
dinosaurs, dolphins, mugs, plates, and more will be transformed into vibrant
works of art that will be treasured forever, or at least a while. My boys were so
intent on their artistry that the hours just flew by. Warning: This recreational
activity can become quite addicting! Pieces are glazed and fired, then ready to be
picked up in a day or two.
       **Hours:**     Open Sun. - Thurs., 11am - 10pm; Fri. - Sat., 11am - 11pm.
  **Admission:**   Prices for mugs and vases start at $6. There is a $7 an hour fee
                   charged, per painter, plus a fee (usually $3) for glazing.
        **Ages:**    4 years and up.

## KID'S ART

(818) 248-2483 - the main number for all the centers.                           *$$$$$*
*Kid's Art is located in the cities of Clairmont, Glendora, La Canada,*
*Northridge, Pasadena, Tarzana, and Valencia.*
    This small, wonderful classroom is a great setting for teaching kids realistic
fine art skills using mediums such as drawing, painting, charcoal, pastel, and
water color. Subject matter covered includes still life, landscape, animals,
cartooning, and more. Each class has one instructor per eight students, so there is
plenty of individualized instruction. The room has an intimate feel with kid-size
easels, and kid-level shelves all around that hold stuffed animals, vases with
flowers, and other objects to inspire your young artist. Week-long summer
workshops are also offered in clay, animation, etc.
       **Hours:**     Classes are given after school Tues. - Fri., and on Sat.
  **Admission:**   Classes vary in cost. A one-hour class, once a week for four
                   weeks, costs $56. There is also a $15 first-time registration fee,
                   plus a drawing course material fee of $10.
        **Ages:**    5 years and up.

## BARNSDALL ART PARK / JUNIOR ART CENTER

(213) 485-4474                                                                  *!/$$$*
*4814 Hollywood Boulevard, Los Angeles*
(Exit Hollywood Fwy [101] E. on Hollywood Blvd, up a driveway to the park and center.)
    This art park/center is comprised of four facilities: 1) The Jr. Art Center with
on-going classes for ages 3 to 17 that range from film making and animation to

drawing and pottery; 2) Barnsdall Art Center which offers classes for adults; 3) L.A. Municipal Art Gallery, (213) 485-4581, that has year round exhibitions for adults; and 4) two small children's galleries that feature rotating exhibits, such as art work produced by kids, or by illustrators of children's books.

Another key element is Sunday Open Sunday (yes, this is the real name of it), which is offered thirty-five Sundays a year at various art sites and locations throughout the Los Angeles area. These free, two-hour workshops produce an eclectic array of collages, paintings, cardboard houses, jewelry, masks, etc.

The art park also has the famed Hollyhock House designed by Frank Lloyd Wright. Unlike most house tours, the emphasis is almost entirely on the architecture, not on the few furnishings inside the house.

**Hours:** Call for class and event information.
**Admission:** Free to the small galleries and Sunday Open Sunday. Class fees range from $18 - $36.
**Ages:** 3 years and up.

## CAROUSEL CERAMICS                                              ☼
(818) 879-8292                                                   $$$$
*31149 Via Colinas, Suite 604, Westlake Village*
(Exit Ventura Fwy [101] N. on Lindero, L. on Via Colinas. It's in an industrial park, on a corner curve, next to Grason's art supply store.)

This workshop studio stocks the largest quantity of bisque, greenware, and plaster pieces I've ever seen. Two rooms are fully stocked with statues, figurines, picture frames, bowls, mugs, vases, dinner sets, etc. Long tables are completely set up for you to design and paint your piece. There are many finished samples at the studio that lend inspiration. Carousel, however, is not your typical paint-a-piece-in-one-session place. It is primarily a teaching studio where instructors give formal classes for groups or individuals. Just a few of the several classes offered throughout the year include acrylic painting on glass, painting wisteria or dogwood flowers on greenware, etc. One-on-one tutoring is available for brush strokes, handmade flowers, airbrushing, drybrushing, glazing, and more. With such a variety of items to choose from, and all of this assistance being offered, even I could produce a work of art here! Come create a special gift, or make coming here a hobby and start your own heirloom collection.

**Hours:** Open Mon, Fri., and Sat., 10am - 6pm; Tues. and Thurs., 10am - 9pm. (Closed Wed. and Sun.)
**Admission:** The cost of your piece, plus the brushes, paints, and other supplies you purchase. The owner will work out a price for those who want to use the store's supplies.
**Ages:** 5 years and up.

## JUPITER - FUN FROM A DIFFERENT PLANET                         ☼
(818) 707-9797                                                   $$$$
*30875 Thousand Oaks Boulevard, Westlake Village*
(Exit Ventura Fwy [101] N. on Thousand Oaks Blvd. It's in a small shopping center on the corner of Thousand Oaks Blvd. and Lindero Canyon Rd.)

This paint-it-yourself ceramic store is well supplied with an array of pieces to paint, as well as the paints, sponges, stencils, brushes, etc., for decorating them. As an added benefit, there is a small, children's corner (for the quick-finishing artists in the family) equipped with a table, books, crayons, and a few toys. What a fun outing - and you come home with something better than a Happy Meal toy!

**Hours:** Open Tues. and Thurs., 11am - 5pm; Wed. and Fri., 11am - 8pm; Sat., noon - 8pm; Sun., noon - 6pm.

**Admission:** Items begin at $3.50. The studio fee, which includes paints and all the other tools of the trade, depends on the price of your item. For instance, for a piece costing $7.50 or less, the studio fee is $6; for a piece costing $10.50 to $15 the studio fee is $10.

**Ages:** 4 years and up.

## KAR-LAN'S KRAFTS

(805) 251-7924

*17743 Sierra Highway, Canyon Country*

(Exit Golden State Fwy [5] N. on Antelope Valley Fwy [14], N. on Via Princessa, R. on Sierra Hwy.)

Kids kan kultivate their kreativity at Kar-Lan's Krafts. Both plastercraft and ceramics are available to paint and glaze at this roomy and well-lit krafts store. Please note that plastercraft items are more fragile than ceramic pieces, but they are also less expensive. This is a wonderful way to spend an hour or so together!

**Hours:** Open Tues. - Fri., 10:30am - 6pm (open Wed. and Thurs. until 9pm); Sat., 11am - 5pm.

**Admission:** Prices start at $2 for a piece of unfinished art, plus $5 a day for paint and brushes. Firing costs extra, depending on the size of the piece.

**Ages:** 4 years and up.

## KID'S PAINT PLACE

(909) 699-4941

*27540 Inez Road, Temecula*

(Exit Temecula Valley Fwy [15] on Rancho California Rd., L. on Inez, R. Town Center. It's in the Target shopping center.)

As the title suggests, this place is for kids. Parents may paint if they promise to behave themselves. Most of the store contains plaster items to paint, and there are specific shelves designated for younger children. Use of the paints and brushes are included in the price of the item.

**Hours:** Open Mon. - Sat.,10:30 - 6pm; Sun., noon - 5pm. Closed holidays.

**Admission:** Magnets start at $3.25. An average price for an item, which includes paint and time, is $7.

**Ages:** 4 years and up.

## THE MAGIC PAINT BRUSH

(818) 505-6477                                        *$$$$*

*11309-A Ventura Boulevard, Studio City*

(Exit Ventura Fwy [101] S. on Laurel Canyon Blvd., L. on Ventura Blvd.)

Look at all the different things you can decorate here with a paint brush! Paint your own ceramic or plaster piece and take home a beautiful vase, mug, figurine, coaster, and more. The Magic Paint Brush also offers classes on drawing, making clay models, and candle making - turn a ceramic item you've painted into a candle! Ask about the Kids' After School Club classes, too. Prices include all the implements and accessories that you'll need for each project such as paints, brushes, smocks, glaze, paraffin wax, etc. One of my favorite features about this store is that there isn't an hourly fee charged - just a flat fee for painting. In fact, a shelf here is nicknamed "works in progress." Tip: This is a great place for a birthday party or any kind of party.

**Hours:**   Open Mon. - Sat., 11am - 9pm; Sun., noon - 6pm.
**Admission:**   The cost of your item, plus $8 painting fee per piece for adults; $5 for children 5 years and under. Classes vary in price.
**Ages:**   4 years and up.

## MUDD BEACH (Manhattan Beach)

(310) 318-2242                                        *$$$$*

*1113 Manhattan Avenue, Manhattan Beach*

(Going S. on San Diego Fwy [405], exit S. on Inglewood Ave., R. on Manhattan Blvd. Or, going N. on 405, exit N. on Hawthorne Blvd., L. on Manhattan Blvd. Once on Manhattan Blvd., take it almost to the end and turn L. on Manhattan Ave.)

Help mold your children's artistic talents by signing them up for a class that could include working with clay. Or, get your children fired-up about art by encouraging them to paint some of the wonderful ceramic pieces here. Choose from a wide variety of animal figures, picture frames, children's tea sets, etc. With over fifty colors of paint, and a bright cheerful atmosphere, your kids will have a great time at Mudd Beach.

A small gallery of retail art is also here to lend inspiration. Some of the unique pieces for sale include mosaic mirrors and tables, candles, hand blown glass, etc.

**Hours:**   Open Sun. - Mon., 11am - 8pm; Tues. - Thurs., 11am - 9pm; Fri. - Sat., 10am - 9pm.
**Admission:**   Small ceramic pieces start at $3. Other costs include $5.50 an hour per painter, and a $2 firing fee per piece.
**Ages:**   4 years and up.

## MUDD BEACH (Pasadena)

(626) 449-4050                                        *$$$$*

*148 West Colorado Boulevard, Pasadena*

(Going E. on the Ventura Fwy [134], exit E. on Colorado Bvld. From Foothill Fwy [210], exit S. on Fair Oaks Ave., R. on Colorado Blvd. It's between De Lacey and Pasadena Ave. Validated parking is free for the first two hours before 6pm; after 6pm it's $1.50 an hour.)

See MUDD BEACH (Manhattan Beach) for details.

**Hours:** Open Mon., noon - 7pm; Tues. - Thurs., 11am - 9pm; Fri., 11am - 11pm; Sat., 10am - 11pm, Sun., 11am - 7pm.

**Ages:** 4 years and up.

## PAINT & FUN

(818) 708-2152

*19458 Ventura Boulevard, Tarzana*

(Exit Ventura Fwy [101] S. on Reseda Blvd., R. on Ventura Blvd. It's on the corner of Shirley and Ventura.)

With a paintbrush in one hand and a plaster or ceramic ornament, statue, or part of a place setting in the other, plus paints in all the colors of the rainbow to choose from, your child is in his/her own little art heaven. The set-up is smartly arranged, as items are on shelves on one wall, while tables with paint are against the opposite wall - less opportunity for broken pieces! For more ambitious artists, T-shirt painting is also available. Paint & Fun is great place to make special gifts, or to have a birthday party.

**Hours:** Open daily from 10am - 6pm.

**Admission:** The cost for a plaster work of art starts at $3; ceramic starts at about $12; T-shirt painting begins at $12. There is no per hour fee charge, and paints, etc., are included in the price of your piece.

**Ages:** 4 years and up.

## PAINT PALACE

(818) 541-1875

*3600 Ocean View Boulevard, #4, Glendale*

(From Foothill Fwy [210], exit S. on Ocean View Blvd. Going N. on Glendale Fwy [2], exit W. on Verdugo Blvd, L. on Ocean View Blvd. Paint Palace is on the corner of Ocean View Blvd. and Broadview, on the bottom floor of a two-story mini mall.)

This paint-your-own studio offers plaster figurines, refrigerator magnets, ornaments, frames, holiday decorations, sports items, etc., for your child's painting enjoyment. Smocks, paints, brushes, and inspiration are all provided. Note: The pieces generally do not last as long as glazed ceramic items, but they cost less, kids enjoy coming here just for the fun of creating, and you can take home your object d'art the same day.

**Hours:** Open in the summer Sun. - Fri., 11am - 6pm; Sat., 10am - 6pm. Open the rest of the year, Wed. - Mon. from 11am - 6pm.

**Admission:** Prices range from $3 - $20, with the average piece costing $7. Paints and studio time are included in the price of the item.

**Ages:** 4 years and up.

## PLANET PAINT

(310) 442-8118                                                          $$$$

*11677 San Vicente Boulevard, #206, Los Angeles*

(Exit San Diego Fwy [405] W. on Wilshire Blvd., R. on Barrington, R. on San Vincente. It's in Brentwood Gardens mall, on the 2nd floor.)

Planet Paint specializes in birthday parties and encouraging kids to have fun while painting their own ceramic piece to take home. Choose from a wide variety of statues, cups, plates, and frames. A birthday party includes two hours of painting, glazing and firing, party favors, decorations, supervision, and a special plate for the guest of honor.

**Hours:**  Open Tues. - Sat., 11am - 9pm; Sun., noon - 7pm.

**Admission:**  Cost of the item, ranging from $3 to $50 (average $12), plus $6 per hour per person. Birthday parties, for 8 - 10 people, are $100, plus the price of each party goer's ceramic item. You can bring in your own food.

**Ages:**  4 years and up.

## A PERSONAL TOUCH

(714) 693-8777                                                          $$$$

*5655 East La Palma Avenue, Suite 125, Anaheim*

(Exit Riverside Fwy [91], N. on Imperial Hwy, L. on La Palma Ave.)

Come to this inviting store to make a keepsake designed with a personal touch. There are several ceramic pieces to choose from such as animal figurines, plates, trinket boxes, sports balls (e.g. baseballs, footballs, etc.), mugs, and oven tiles for hand or footprints. Paints, brushes, and studio time are all included in the hourly fee. Having trouble deciding on how to paint your item? Look around at the finished products for ideas. Kids love expressing themselves in the creative fashion that A Personal Touch encourages, and it is so much better than watching TV!

**Hours:**  Open Mon., noon - 9pm; Tues. - Sat., 11am - 9pm; Sun., noon - 5pm.

**Admission:**  The price of your ceramic item, plus a flat fee of $6 for adults; $4 for children 12 years and under. Glazing and firing cost between $2 to $5, depending on the size of the piece.

**Ages:**  4 years and up.

## ARTMAKER

(562) 596-8896                                                          $$

*12371 Seal Beach Boulevard, Seal Beach*

(Exit San Diego Fwy [405] N. on Seal Beach Blvd. It's in Rossmoor Shopping Center.)

Are your kids crafty? I mean that question in the artistic sense. Whether your answer is "yes" or "no," they will thoroughly enjoy their visit to the Artmaker. Each arts and crafts session features a special project or two, with only general instructions given so that imaginations have free reign. Recycled and everyday materials such as newspaper, egg cartons, glitter, glue, ribbons, buttons, paints, and milk jugs, become party hats, bird feeders, banners, etc. A snack is provided for your starving artists, and a bubble machine is turned on to entertain those who are done early. (Did you know that if you wet your hands, you can catch and hold a bubble?)

The Artmaker is decorated with children's creations, lending inspiration to your artists. Parents, you can assist your younger kids, or just relax as staff is on hand to help out. As an added bonus, when your child is done crafting, you can just leave without having to clean up the inevitable mess! The Artmaker has become a favorite place for my kids to come and create. Tip: This is a great place for a birthday party!

**Hours:** Classes are offered at varying times throughout the week, including mornings for Mommy/Daddy and Me, after school for older children, and every Sat. from 1pm - 2pm. Call for a schedule, and for adult class information, too.

**Admission:** One-hour classes are $8 per artist. Other classes start at $10 per artist.

**Ages:** 2 years and up, depending on the class.

## CERAMIC CREATIONS

$$$$

(949) 458-7067
*24000 Alicia Parkway, Mission Viejo*
(Exit San Diego Fwy [5] N.E. on Alicia Pkwy.)

Come visit Ceramic Creations and let your creative juices flow! Choose from vases, mugs, Disney figurines, bowls, etc., and paint it with your special flare. My kids sometimes choose very interesting color combinations, but that is part of what makes their pieces so special. Tip: Designing your keepsake can take time, so be prepared to spend a few hours here. Your item will be glazed and fired and ready to be picked up in a day or two.

**Hours:** Open Mon. - Tues., 11am - 6pm; Wed. - Fri., 10am - 9pm; Sat. - Sun., 10am - 6pm.

**Admission:** The price of your item, plus $4 per hour per painter for studio time, which includes paint, brushes, glazing, and firing.

**Ages:** 4 years and up.

## IRVINE FINE ART CENTER

!/$$

(949) 724-6880
*14321 Yale Avenue, Irvine*
(Exit Santa Ana Fwy [5] S. on Culver, L. on Walnut, L. on Yale. It's in HERITAGE PARK.)

Irvine Fine Art Center is host to various monthly exhibits of art work and photography by students, and/or by local artists. The Center also offers special programs and holds numerous art classes such as watercolor, drawing, calligraphy, cartooning, etc. Two of the on-going classes are listed below:

The **Children's Open Studio** is an after-school, drop-in program for elementary-aged kids. This semi-structured class provides a great opportunity for kids to be creative using a variety of materials such as clay, papier-mache, paints, etc. It is also a wonderful environment for making new friends. Supervision, materials, and fun are all provided.

The **Teen Open Studio** is an open-ended ceramics class for high schoolers. An instructor is available for assistance. All materials are provided. (Also look up HERITAGE PARK [Irvine], under the Great Outdoors section, for an adjacent attraction.)

**Hours:** Tour the Center, Mon. - Thurs., 9am - 9pm; Fri., 9am - 5pm; Sat., 9am - 3pm; Sun., 1pm - 5pm. Children's Studio is offered Mon. - Fri. from 3pm - 5:30pm. Teen Studio is offered Tues. and Thurs. from 4pm - 6pm. (Days are subject to change.)

**Admission:** The Center is free. Children's Studio is $9 per child, per visit, or purchase a multiple-day pass and save money. Teen Studio is $5 per visit.

**Ages:** 6 - 11 years for Children's Open Studio; 13 - 18 years for Teen Open Studio.

## IT'S YOU                                                                     ☼

(949) 673-5969                                                                  $$$$

*2919 East Coast Highway, Corona Del Mar*                                       ♨

(Take the San Diego Fwy [405] or the Costa Mesa Fwy [55] to the Corona Del Mar Fwy [73], turns into MacArthur Blvd. Exit MacArthur Blvd. S. on East Coast Hwy.)

Bowls, mugs, figurines, jewelry boxes, frames, etc., are just a few of the ceramic pieces available to you at It's You. Pick out an item, and with paints and stencils galore to use, let your creative side take over, or at least have fun making something you can take home. This is a great indoor activity for kids (and adults) who will treasure what they've made.

**Hours:** Open Mon. - Sat., 11am - 9pm; Sun., 11am - 6pm.

**Admission:** Items cost between $2 - $40, plu $6 per hour per painter - the clock doesn't start ticking until you actually start painting. Glazing and firing cost between $1 - $5, depending on the size of your item.

**Ages:** 5 years and up.

## PLAY IN THE MUD TO GO                                                        ☼

(714) 680-4367                                                                  $$$$

*at the location of your choosing!*                                            ♨

Pam, the owner of Play in the Mud, is a talented artist and teacher who brings ceramic painting to you. She supplies the figurines, mugs, plates, vases, frames, tiles, etc., as well as the paints, brushes, stencils, and glaze. You supply the place and a minimum of eight painters. What a great idea for birthday parties, girl/boy scouts gatherings, bridal showers (I know this is a kid's book, but adults are reading, too!), or any kind of get together.

**Hours:** Call to make a reservation.

**Admission:** The price of the piece, plus $6 per person. Ask about special scout programs.

**Ages:**   4 years and up.

# ARTOPIA
(619) 283-1653
*3191 Thorn Street, San Diego*
(Exit 805 Fwy at Northpark/University, L. on University, L. on 32$^{nd}$ St. It's on the corner
of Thorn and 32$^{nd}$.)
    Do your kids have that glazed look in their eyes? Then bring them to
Artopia where they can pick out any piece of unfinished ceramic to paint, glaze,
and fire. Choose from a wide assortment of pieces, such as dinnerware, vases,
figurines, etc. Creative kids (and adults) can literally sit for hours, designing and
painting their masterpieces freehand. I, on the other hand, rely on others' ideas,
and on using stencils. Either way, it's a great activity and the finished product is
always a special keepsake. Note: On a beautiful day, and San Diego has so many
of them, you can paint outside in the courtyard.
    **Hours:**   Open Thurs. - Fri., noon - 8pm; Sat. - Sun., noon - 6pm. Call for
                an appointment for other times and days.
**Admission:**   The price of your piece, usually between $4 - $40, includes
                paints, glazing, and firing.
    **Ages:**   4 years and up.

# CERAMICAFE
(619) 231-7991
*860 5$^{th}$ Avenue in the Gaslamp Quarter, San Diego*
(Going S. on San Diego Fwy [5], exit W. on Ash St., L. on 6$^{th}$ Ave., R. on Market, L. on 5$^{th}$
Ave. Going N. on 5, exit S. on 6$^{th}$ Ave., R. on Market, L. on 5$^{th}$ Ave. It's one block away
from Horton Plaza.)
    "You've got a style all your own" can be taken several different ways. At
the Ceramicafe, your children can develop a style all their own by choosing a
mug, plate, figurine, picture frame, etc., to design and paint any way they want.
What fun! This classy, paint-your-own ceramic studio is located in the historic
and romantic Gaslamp Quarter, so explore some of the unique stores before or
after your time painting here.
    **Hours:**   Open during the summer Mon. - Thurs., 11am - 10pm; Fri. - Sat.,
                11am - midnight. Open the rest of the year Mon. - Thurs., 2pm -
                10pm; Fri. - Sat., noon - midnight; Sun., noon - 8pm.
**Admission:**   The cost of your item, which ranges between $5 - $45, includes
                paints, glazing, and firing.
    **Ages:**   5 years and up.

# PAINT, GLAZE, AND FIRE!
(760) 633-2254
*937 1$^{st}$ Street, Suite 109, Encinitas*
(Exit San Diego Fwy [5] W. on Encinitas Blvd., L. on 1$^{st}$ St. By the lumberyard next to the
sheriff's station.)
    Ready, set, go, to Paint, Glaze, and Fire! This fun, paint-your-own ceramic

store offers lots of items to choose from such as plates, bowls, flower pots, goblets, salt and pepper shakers, animal figurines, and more. Kids will have a field day picking out colors and thinking of ways to design their chosen piece. Warning: This recreational activity can become habit forming! Finished masterpieces may be picked up in a day or two, after they've been glazed and fired.

**Hours:** Open Mon. - Sat., 10am - 8pm; Sun., 10am - 6pm.
**Admission:** $2 - $24 per piece, plus $6 a day for adults; $4 a day for children 12 years and under.
**Ages:** 4 years and up.

## PAINT PALS CLUBHOUSE

(805) 581-4676
*1716 Erringer Road, #106, Simi Valley*
(Exit Simi Valley - San Fernando Valley Fwy [118] S. on Erringer Rd. It's on the N.E. corner of Heywood St. and Erringer.)

Clubhouses weren't this much fun when I was a kid! The colorfully decorated Paint Pals Clubhouse offers paint-your-own bisque, and a whole lot more. One section has shelves of items to paint, plus long tables and all the paint, brushes, smocks, etc., needed. Popular items include sunflowers, pigs, jars with ceramic lids, magnets, and picture frames. Creating a masterpiece is a terrific activity. But, while moms (this one, anyway) sometimes take longer to do a project than kids do, there are plenty of other things here to keep the younger set busy. Karaoke is a popular option, and whether or not children can actually sing on key seems to be irrelevant. Next to the stage are costumes for dressing up. Toward the back of the store, and through a short tunnel of mirrors, is a small black light maze that my boys enjoyed going through. Kids can also play with soft foam blocks, make "pictures" in a shadow room, try to solve metal shape puzzles, blow giant bubbles, and visit the live reptiles on exhibit - snakes, turtles, lizards, and frogs.

**Hours:** Open during the school year Tues. - Thurs. and Sun.,10am - 6pm; Fri. - Sat., 10am - 8pm. Closed Mon. Open in the summer on Mon. from 10am - 6pm, in addition to its other days and hours.
**Admission:** $1 per child (toddlers, too) entrance fee; free to adults. Items cost from $2.50 on up, which includes use of the paints and other supplies. Karaoke is 50¢ for one song; $1 for 3 songs.
**Ages:** 3 years and up.

# BEACHES

Beaches are a "shore" bet for a day of fun in the sun. Along with sand and water play, in-line skating, and/or biking, some beaches have playgrounds, picnic tables, and waveless waters that make them particularly younger-kid friendly. This section includes just a few suggestions of where to go beaching.

Tip: If you and your family are Orange County beach bunnies, consider purchasing a parking pass for $50. The pass price is $30 for seniors. For an additional $25, you will also receive a pass for the Orange County Regional Parks. For more information, call (949) 661-7013.

## CABRILLO BEACH

(310) 548-2645

*3720 Stephen M White Drive, San Pedro*

(Take Harbor Fwy [110] to the end, L. on Gaffey St., L. on 9<sup>th</sup> St., R. on Pacific Ave., almost to the end, L. on 36<sup>th</sup> St., turns into Stephen M White Dr.)

The beach has a gated entrance, wonderful sandy stretches, a playground, and rock jetties to climb out on. See CABRILLO MARINE AQUARIUM, under the Zoos and Animals section, as this terrific museum is adjacent to the beach (and it's free!).

**Hours:** Open daily sunrise to 10:30pm

**Admission:** $6.50 per vehicle.

**Ages:** All

## LEO CARRILLO STATE BEACH

(805) 986-8591 - state beach; (818) 880-0350 - camping info; (800) 444-7275 - camping reservations.

*36000 Pacific Coast Highway, Malibu*

(Exit Ventura Fwy [101] S. on Westlake Blvd. [Hwy 23], turns into Mulholland Hwy., turns into Decker Rd. Go to the end, and turn R. on Pacific Coast Hwy.)

Leo Carrillo combines the best of everything that's enjoyable about the beach - a beautiful, sandy beach; good swimming and surfing; sea caves to carefully explore; tidepools; a playground; lifeguards; and nature trails. Camping near the beach (campsites are a five minute walk from the beach) makes this one of our favorite campgrounds. Each campsite has a fire pit and picnic table. Pack a sweater!

**Hours:** Open daily 7am - dusk.

**Admission:** $6 per vehicle. Camping starts at $17 a night, Sun. - Thurs.; $18, Fri. - Sat. Each campsite can have up to 8 people and 2 vehicles.

**Ages:** All

## MARINA BEACH or "MOTHERS' BEACH"

(562) 570-3100

*5839 Appian Way, Long Beach*

(Take San Gabriel River Fwy [605] to Garden Grove Fwy [22] W., exit on Studebaker and eventually head S., R. on Westminster, R. on Appian Way, which is just over a bridge. It's across from the Long Beach Marina.)

This beach is aptly nicknamed because it is a mother/child hang out. There are waveless waters in this lagoon-type setting, lifeguards, a nice grassy playground, and barbecues. Single and double kayak rentals are available daily during the summer, and weekends only the rest of the year.

**Hours:** Open daily sunrise to 10:30pm.

**Admission:** Bring either lots of quarters for parking - 25¢ for each half hour - or get here early to park on the street for free. Kayak rentals are $5 an hour for a single; $15 an hour for a double.

**Ages:** All

## SEASIDE LAGOON

(310) 318-0681

*200 Portofino Way, Redondo Beach.*

(Exit San Diego Fwy [405] S. on Western, R. on 190th St., which turns into Anita St., which then turns into Herondo St., L. on Harbor Dr. It's on the S.W. Corner of Harbor Dr. and Portofino Way.)

Have a swimmingly good time at the Seaside Lagoon. This large, saltwater lagoon is heated by a nearby steam generating plant, so the average water temperature is seventy-five degrees. Warm waveless waters, plus a lifeguard, make it an ideal swimming spot for little ones. There is also a beach, playground, snack bar (sponsored by Ruby's), barbecues, picnic tables, and volleyball courts.

**Hours:** Open daily Memorial Day through Labor Day from 10am - 5:45pm. Open in September on weekends only from 10am - 5:45pm.

**Admission:** $3.50 for adults; $2.50 for ages 2 - 17; children under 2 years are free.

**Ages:** All

## VENICE BEACH

(310) 392-4687                                                                     *!*

*Ocean Front Walk, between Washington Boulevard and Rose Avenue, Venice*

(Exit San Diego Fwy [405] W. on Venice Blvd. Park at the end of Venice or Washington Blvds., or in lots along Speedway.)

I think Southern California's reputation of being offbeat, quirky, etc., comes directly from Venice Beach. This area actually has a stretch of beach, but visitors come here mainly to stare at and mingle with the eclectic Venice population of jugglers, street musicians, performers of all types, artists, vendors, skaters, etc. Two hot spots here are Muscle Beach, where weight lifters of all levels pump iron, and the International Chess Park. This park, south of Santa Monica pier and north of Venice pier, has rows of picnic tables where players run the gamut of older, scruffy-looking men to teens in street clothing. Watch and learn strategies as players compete in traditional play or speed chess. Venice Beach also has a bike path, playground, basketball courts, shops, boardwalk, and restaurants.

**Hours:** Open daily sunrise to sunset.

**Admission:** Free, although parking may cost.

**Ages:** All

## ALISO BEACH

(949) 661-7013                                                                     *$*

*31131 Pacific Coast Highway, Laguna Beach*

(Exit San Diego Fwy [5] S. on Laguna Fwy, which turns into Laguna Cyn., L. on Pacific Coast Highway. Or, exit San Diego Fwy [5], S. on Crown Valley Pky., R. on P.C.H.)

This beautiful, cove-like beach has a small playground, plus barbecues, picnic tables, and a short pier.

**Hours:** Open daily 7am - 10pm.

**Admission:**   Metered parking is 75¢ an hour (or a parking pass).
**Ages:**   All

# BOLSA CHICA STATE BEACH

(714) 846-3460
*Pacific Coast Highway, Huntington Beach*
(Exit Garden Grove Fwy [22] S. on Bolsa Chica Rd., R. on Warner Ave., L. on Pacific Coast Highway. Or, going N. on San Diego Fwy [405], exit E. on Warner Ave., L. on P.C.H.)

There are six miles of beach here that are ideal for families because of the picnic areas (campfires are allowed), outdoor showers, five snack bars, and beach rentals. Year round camping in self-contained vehicles is allowed, but there are no hook ups. No tent camping is permitted.
**Hours:**   Open daily 6am - 9pm.
**Admission:**   $6 per vehicle. Camping Sun. - Thurs. is $23; Fri. - Sat., $24.
**Ages:**   All

# CORONA DEL MAR STATE BEACH and TIDEPOOL TOURS

(949) 644-3044
*On Poppy Avenue and Ocean Avenue, Corona Del Mar*
(Take the San Diego Fwy [405] or the Costa Mesa Fwy [55] to the Corona Del Mar Fwy [73] which turns into MacArthur Blvd., S. on East Coast Highway, R. on Poppy Ave.)

Come for a few hours of tidepool exploration, then spend the rest of the day playing at the adjacent beach. Tidepools are a rich natural resource and a fascinating way for kids to learn about marine life. You are welcome to investigate the tidepools on your own, or sign up for a guided tour. After giving a short lecture, tour guides are helpful in pointing out interesting animal and plant life.

Just a short drive away, off Ocean Boulevard, is the big beach of Corona Del Mar. Besides sand and water, Big Corona provides fire rings, picnic tables, volleyball courts, and a snack bar.
**Hours:**   Open daily sunrise to sunset. Tidepool tours are given by reservations only.
**Admission:**   $6 per vehicle for regular day use. Tours are $25 per group, up to thirty people, which includes parking fees.
**Ages:**   3 years and up.

# CRYSTAL COVE STATE PARK BEACH

(949) 494-3539
*East Coast Highway, between Laguna Beach and Newport Beach, Laguna Beach*
See CRYSTAL COVE STATE PARK, under the Great Outdoors section, for details.

## DANA COVE PARK or "BABY BEACH"

*Dana Point Harbor Drive, Dana Point*
(Exit San Diego Fwy [5] N. on Pacific Coast Highway, L. on St. of the Green Lantern,
L. on Cove Rd. It's at the bottom of Cove Rd.)

"Baby Beach" offers picnic tables, barbecues, free parking, and showers. Lifeguards oversee the waveless waters.

**Hours:**  Open daily sunrise to sunset.

**Admission:**  Free

**Ages:**  All

## DOHENY STATE BEACH PARK

(949) 496-6172

*25300 Dana Point Harbor Drive, Dana Point*
(Exit San Diego Fwy [5] N. on Pacific Coast Highway, L. on Doheny State Beach Pky.)

Doheny State Beach Park is big and absolutely gorgeous. The park is divided into three parts. The northern area, also accessible by metered parking off Puerto Place, is for day use. It is five acres of grassy, landscaped picnic area, with barbecue grills and fire rings along the beach. The rocky area is ideal for tidepool exploration during low tide. Since Dana Point Harbor is right next door, this is also a perfect spot to watch the boats sail in and out.

The central section, south of the San Juan Creek, is a campground with 121 sites. Farther south is another day use area with fire rings, beach volleyball, and showers. Throughout the entire stretch of the park there are sandy beaches and beckoning ocean waves!

A small Interpretative Center is to your left as you go through the entrance gates. It contains a simulated tidepool (not a touch tank), with sea stars and leopard sharks. The mural-covered wall has wood shells that pose questions such as, "Do all sharks kill?" Lift the shell tab for the answer. There are also a few tanks of fish, plus taxidermied animals, fossils, and skeletons of a fox, raptor, and whale.

**Hours:**  The park is open daily from 6am - 6pm. Summer hours are daily from 6am - 10pm. The Interpretative Center is usually open Fri. - Mon., but call for hours first.

**Admission:**  $5 per vehicle for day use. Admission to the Interpretative Center, when it is open, is free. Mon. - Fri. camping prices range from $17 a night for an inland site to $22 a night for a beachfront site; weekends are $1 more per site.

**Ages:**  All

## MAIN BEACH / HEISLER PARK

(949) 497-0716

*Cliff Drive & Myrtle Street, Laguna Beach*
(From San Diego Fwy [5], take Laguna Fwy S., which turns into Laguna Canyon Rd. [133]. Before the end, take Cliff Dr. to the R. and follow it to the beach. Exit Laguna Canyon Rd. [133] S. on Pacific Coast Highway [1] for Main Beach.)

I mention this park and beach together because they are on either side of

Highway 133. Both are incredibly popular (i.e. crowded) and noted for their
unparalleled views of the ocean. The water is clear, and the horizon seems to go
on forever.

Some activities available at Heisler Park are lawn bowling, shuffleboard,
and biking or skating on the paved paths. Main Beach offers a grass play area
along with basketball courts, volleyball courts, and a small playground. This is a
terrific place for beaching it and for swimming. Good luck finding a parking
spot, though!

**Hours:** Both are open daily sunrise to sunset.
**Admission:** Free. Most parking is metered.
**Ages:** All

# NEWPORT DUNES RESORT MARINA
(949) 729-3863
*1131 Backbay Drive, Newport Beach*
(Take Newport Fwy [55] S.W. to end, which turns into Newport Blvd., L. on W. Coast
Hwy., L. on Jamboree Rd., L. on Backbay Dr. Or, from Corona Del Mar Fwy [73], exit
S.W. on Jamboree Rd., R. on Backbay Dr. before E. Coast Hwy.)

Toddlers to teens will enjoy the enclosed acres of clean beach here, along
with a waveless lagoon and a myriad of boating activities. There is a large
fiberglass, stationary whale, nicknamed Moe B. Dunes, in the water for kids to
swim out to, and one on the beach. The playground equipment includes a pirate
ship to climb aboard - ahoy mateys!

Remember the joys of collecting seashells? Newport Dunes is one of the rare
beaches around that still has shells. Note: Shellmaker Island and UPPER
NEWPORT BAY ECOLOGICAL RESERVE (look under the Great Outdoors
section) are adjacent to the resort marina.

If you forget to bring food, have no fear of a growling tummy as a grocery
store and cafe are inside the gates, just around the corner from the beach. Two
outdoor showers are also available. RESORT WATER SPORTS (see the
Transportation section) rentals is located in the park for your kayaking,
pedalboat, windsurfing, etc., needs.

Overnight camping is available here and there are plenty of RV hook-ups.
Free-standing (i.e. no stakes) tent camping is allowed, too. The surroundings are
pretty; activities for campers such as crafts, ice cream socials, and special movie
showings are offered; and the Dunes has a swimming pool, indoor showers, and
laundry facilities. What more could you want out of life? This local resort is my
kind of "roughing it" vacation!

**Hours:** Open daily from 8am - 10pm.
**Admission:** $6 per vehicle. Camping prices range from $27 - $45 a night,
depending on location and camping equipment.
**Ages:** All

## SEAL BEACH                                                      ☼
*Main Street, Seal Beach*                                          !/$
(Exit San Diego Fwy [405] S. on Seal Beach Blvd., R. on Pacific Coast Highway, L. on 🎂
Main St.)

   This beach has lifeguards, a pier, great swimming, and a playground. My
kids love to gather the crabs crawling along the pier wall and put them in
buckets. (We let them go before we go home.) Take a walk on the pier as the
coastline view is terrific. There is also a RUBY'S diner (see the Edible
Adventures section) at the end of the pier. Directly across the street from the
beach is Main Street, which is lined with unique shops and restaurants.
   **Hours:**   Open daily sunrise to sunset.
   **Admission:**   Park along the street or in a nearby lot for free for a few hours, or
                    pay a $5 entrance fee for the day at the parking lot at the beach.
   **Ages:**    All

## CHILDREN'S POOL BEACH                                          ☿
*At the foot of Jenner Street, La Jolla*                           !
(Exit San Diego Fwy [5] W. on La Jolla Village Dr., L. on Torrey Pines Rd., R. on   🎂
Prospect Pl., which turns into Prospect St. Leave the car at the S. end of Prospect
St., or park anywhere you can.)

   One of the most popular family beaches around is Children's Pool Beach,
aptly named because the ocean water is partially enclosed by a seawall in a pool-
type swimming hole. Everything is here to ensure a great day at the beach - sand,
water, a cave to explore, tidepools, lifeguards, and rocks to climb on. The rocks
along the breakwater have a sturdy guard rail. Just past the northeast green lawns
is the La Jolla Underwater Park, which is a haven for divers and snorkelers.
   **Hours:**   Open daily.
   **Admission:**   Free
   **Ages:**    All

## LA JOLLA COVE                                                  ☿
*Coast Boulevard, La Jolla*                                        !
(Exit San Diego Fwy [5] W. on La Jolla Village Dr., L. on Torrey Pines Rd., R. on Prospect
Pl., R. on Coast Blvd.)

   In this beautiful seaside city is a wonderful cove, which is a favorite spot for
exploring tidepools, and watching or participating in some great surfing,
snorkeling, scuba diving, and swimming. The cove is located near the SEAL
ROCK MARINE MAMMAL RESERVE, listed under the Zoos and Animals
section.
   **Hours:**   Open daily.
   **Admission:**   Free
   **Ages:**    All

## LA JOLLA SHORES BEACH                                          ☼
*La Vereda, La Jolla*                                              $
(Exit San Diego Fwy [5] W. on La Jolla Village Dr., L. on Torrey Pines Rd., R. on Calle   🎂
De La Plata, L. on Avenida De La Playa, R. on La Vereda.)

This beach comes fully loaded for a full day of fun! The nearly two-mile stretch of beach offers year-round lifeguard service, rest rooms, showers (a parent's essential), and a few playgrounds for the kids, complete with swing sets and climbing apparatus. Enjoy your time at the beach, and maybe even incorporate a drive around picturesque La Jolla with a visit here.

**Hours:** Open daily
**Admission:** Free - good luck with parking!
**Ages:** All

## SILVER STRAND STATE BEACH / CORONADO BEACH                                              ☼

*Coronado*                                                                              !/$

(Exit San Diego Fwy [5] W. on 75 and cross over the Coronado Bridge, L. on Orange Ave. For Coronado Beach, turn R. at R H Dana Pl., which turns into Ocean Blvd. For Silver Strand State Beach, stay on Orange as it turns into Silver Strand Blvd. The toll is $1 to Coronado and the return trip is free. If you are car pooling, cross the bridge using the right lane, at no charge.)

Silver Strand State Beach is one of the longest strips (seven miles) of beautiful white sandy beach. Part of the beach is Coronado Beach, situated in front of the famous HOTEL DEL CORONADO (look under the Tours section). A terrific bike path also begins near the hotel. The waters are warm and the surf isn't too intense, which is good for younger children. There are picnic areas and lots of room to throw footballs and Frisbees.

**Hours:** Open daily
**Admission:** Free
**Ages:** All

## EDIBLE ADVENTURES

To market, or a restaurant,
  or maybe high tea,
We'll go together,
  my child and me;
Or maybe we'll stop
  for an ice-cream cone,
Or go apple picking,
  and then head for home.

## BENIHANA OF TOKYO

$$$$

Anaheim - (714) 774-4940; Beverly Hills - (323) 655-7311; City of
Industry - (626) 912-8784; Encino - (818) 788-7121; Marina Del Rey -
(310) 821-0888; Newport Beach - (949) 955-0822; San Diego - (619)
298-4666; Torrance - (310) 316-7777

Enjoy the "show" and the food at Benihana. These restaurants feature
hibachi-style cooking, so the food is prepared on a grill right in front of you.
Knives flash as your food is chopped up seemingly in mid-air, as well as on the
frying table, with lightning speed - this is the show part. (Don't try this at home.)
Although my kids are not normally prone to trying new foods, they readily taste
new entrees here because the food is fixed in such an intriguing way!

The atmosphere is unique and the food, which ranges from chicken to
seafood to steak, is delicious. Adult lunch prices range from $7.50 to $11;
dinners, from $15 to $22. Kids' meals range from $6 to $6.95 for a choice of
chicken, steak, or shrimp. Their meals also come with soup or salad, shrimp
appetizer, and ice cream. Several Benihanas have a koi pond and a traditional
Japanese arched bridge as part of their outside decor.

**Hours:**    Open daily for lunch, 11:30am - 2pm; for dinner, 5pm - 10pm.
**Ages:**    5 years and up.

## BULLWINKLE'S RESTAURANT

$$$

El Cajon - (619) 593-1155; Fountain Valley (ironically, though, there are
no fountain shows at this location) - (714) 841-6469; Upland - (909)
946-9555; Vista - (760) 945-9474
*El Cajon - 1155 Graves Avenue; Fountain Valley - 16922 Magnolia
Avenue; Upland - 1560 W. 7th Street; Vista - 1525 W. Vista Way*

Fa*moose* Bullwinkle's Restaurants are adjacent to FAMILY FUN
CENTERS (see the Family Pay and Play section) in the city's listed above.
Eating here is always a highlight for my kids. The woodsy-themed, family-
oriented restaurants serve great food at delicious prices. Menu selections include
pizza ($10.95 for a medium-sized), ribs ($7.45, and it comes with a biscuit), a
sixteen-piece chicken meal ($19.95, and it comes with eight biscuits), salads, and
more. Kids' meals average $2.79 for a choice of chicken nuggets, a hot dog,
ribs(!), or a hamburger. Each meal comes with fries, a drink, and ice cream. Most
of the restaurants feature Rocky and Bullwinkle cartoons on the T.V. monitors
and/or they have a small stage where the electronic figures of Rocky and
Bullwinkle come out and tell jokes. Children enjoy the water show, too, where
fountain waters "dance" to music and change colors via spotlights. Come here to
eat, and then play at the Family Fun Centers, because your kids won't let you go
home without doing so. Food and fun - what more could you want?!

**Hours:**    Open Sun. - Thurs., 11am - 10pm; Fri., 11am - 11pm; Sat., 10am
- 11pm.
**Ages:**    All

## CHUCK E. CHEESE

Check your yellow pages for a local listing. / www.chuckecheese.com   $$$
    These popular indoor eateries and play lands for young kids offer kiddie
rides and video and arcade games, as well as the all-important prize redemption
centers. Many facilities also have play areas with tubes, slides, and ball pits.
Chuck E. Cheese, the costumed rat mascot, is usually walking around giving
hugs and high fives. An electronic version of Chuck E. performs several stage
shows throughout the day.
    Every child's favorite food is served here - pizza! A salad bar is available,
too. Note: This place is often noisy at peak lunch and dinner times, especially on
weekends when crowds descend.

**Hours:** Usually open during the week from 10am - 9pm; on the
weekends from 10am - 11pm. Call for a particular location's
hours.

**Admission:** Free admission, but count on spending money on pizza and
tokens.

**Ages:** 2 - 11 years.

## FARMER'S MARKETS

Many cities host a weekly farmer's market. These markets usually consist of
open-air (outside) booths set up for customers to purchase fresh produce, bakery
goods, meats, and more - taste the difference! Freshly-cut flowers are often
available, too. Indulge yourself and let your kids pick out a "new" food to try.
We think the food and ambiance of a market is much more enticing than a
grocery store. Please call your local city hall or chamber of commerce to see if
there is a farmer's market near you. Here are just a few of the cities that I know
of that host a market: Calabasas, Coronado, Costa Mesa, Julian, Long Beach,
Mission Valley, Oceanside (with llama rides!), Ojai, Pacific Beach, Palm
Springs, Riverside, Tustin, and Woodland Hills.

## HARD ROCK CAFE

La Jolla - (619) 454-5101; Los Angeles - (310) 276-7605; Newport   $$$
Beach - (949) 640-8844; San Diego - (619) 456-7225; Universal City -
(818) 622-7625 / www.hardrock.com
*La Jolla - 909 Prospect Street; Los Angeles - 8600 Beverly Boulevard;*
*Newport Beach - 451 Newport Center Drive, near Fashion Island; San*
*Diego - 801 4ᵗʰ Avenue, near Horton Plaza; Universal City - 1000 Universal*
*Center Drive, at Universal CityWalk*
    This has become the "in" place to eat and hang out if you are a rock 'n roll
fan. Each Cafe has its own unique memorabilia displayed in glass cases on the
walls, but the essence of all the cafes - paying tribute to music industry legends
and the hot artists of today, and promoting an environmentally aware motto,
"Save the Planet" - is the same. Hard Rock Cafe is part restaurant and part
museum, so before or after your meal, take a walk around to see your favorite
musician's guitar, record album, or stage costume on exhibit. And, oh yes, rock

music is constantly played. Souvenir T-shirts and glasses bearing the Cafe's logo and location (as they are restaurants throughout the world) have become collectible items among Hard Rock Cafe enthusiasts.

The Cafe at UNIVERSAL CITYWALK (look under the Potpourri section) has a gigantic electric guitar out front. Inside are numerous guitars (one is covered with snake skin), a few saxophones, a cool-looking car spinning on a pedestal, a gleaming motorcycle, gold records, autographed items, and an outfit worn by Elton John.

Menu items include Chinese chicken salad ($7.99), burgers (average $7), barbeque ribs ($12.99), fajitas ($10.99), T-bone steaks ($15.99), and sandwiches (average $7.50). Personal dessert favorites include chocolate chip cookie pie ($3.99) and Heath Bar rain forest nut crunch sundae ($4.99). Kids' meals are $5.99 each and come with applesauce, fries, and a beverage in a souvenir cup. Meal choices include macaroni and cheese, a burger, a hotdog, chicken tenders, or a grilled cheese sandwich.

**Hours:** Open daily for lunch and dinner.

**Ages:** 5 years and up.

## THE OLD SPAGHETTI FACTORY

*$$$*

Factories are in the following cities: Duarte - (626) 358-2115; Fullerton - (714) 526-6801; Hollywood - (323) 469-7149; Newport Beach - (949) 675-8654; Rancho Cucamonga - (909) 980-3585; Riverside - (909) 784-4417; and San Diego - (619) 233-4323

These elegant "factories" have posh, velvet seats in a variety of colors. The overhead fabric lamps are from a more genteel era. The old world antiques and the dark, rich furniture exudes a quiet, classy atmosphere. Yet, the restaurants are also very kid friendly. Old Spaghetti Factories usually have a train or trolley car to eat in - this is a highlight. The franchised restaurants differ only in regional decor. For instance, the one in Riverside, being in a citrus city, has orange crate labels on the walls.

The food is fine fare, such as spaghetti (what a surprise!), with a wonderful variety of sauces to choose from, and pastas such as lasagna, tortellini, and ravioli. Prices range from $3.50 to $7.50. Kids' meals cost between $3.25 to $3.95 for a choice of pasta and a choice of sauces (with or without meat), plus a salad, beverage, and dessert.

**Hours:** Open Mon. - Thurs., 11:30am - 3pm and 5pm - 10pm; Fri., 11:30am - 3pm and 5pm - 10:30pm; Sat. - Sun., 11:30am - 10pm.

**Ages:** 4 years and up.

## OLIVIA'S DOLL HOUSE and TEA ROOM

*$$$$$*

Newhall - (805) 222-7331; Thousand Oaks - (805) 381-1553; West Hollywood - (310) 273-663

*Newhall - 22700 Lyons Avenue; Thousand Oaks - 1321 E. Thousand Oaks Boulevard, #110; West Hollywood - 8804 Rosewood Avenue*

These small, Victorian-style house-like buildings are beautifully decorated with flowers and lace - a little girl's dream come true. Young ladies can dress up in gowns and jewelry; have their hair, make-up, and nails done; and enjoy hors d'oeuvres, finger sandwiches, and dessert. (Forget about little girls - this sounds like a mom's dream come true!) Parties are given by reservation only.

**Hours:** Open for parties by reservation.
**Admission:** Parties start at $225 and include cake and party favors.
**Ages:** 4 years and up.

## PLANET HOLLYWOOD

Beverly Hills - (310) 275-7828; San Diego - (619) 702-7827; Santa Ana $$$
- (714) 434-7827 / www.planethollywood.com
*Beverly Hills - 9560 Wilshire Boulevard; San Diego - 197 Horton Plaza; Santa Ana - 1641 W. Sunflower Boulevard, across from South Coast Plaza.*

There are several Planet Hollywoods throughout Southern California, and the rest of the world. These very Hollywood restaurants literally have the handprints of co-owners Demi Moore, Arnold Schwarzenegger, Bruce Willis, and Sly Stallone all over them. Film and television memorabilia abound such as costumes, parts of sets, and photographs. Just a few of the featured items at the Beverly Hills location, for instance, are the original *Batman* costume, an astronaut costume from *Apollo 13*, and the carousel horse ridden in *Mary Poppins*. Memorabilia is definitely a main attraction at Planet Hollywood. The food is California cuisine, which actually encompasses everything - pizza, pasta, burgers, ribs, chicken, salads, etc. Prices range from $6.95 to $16. The kids' menu offers pizza, cheeseburgers, chicken fingers, spaghetti, hot dogs, or cheese quesadilla for $5.95. Their meals include fries and a beverage.

**Hours:** Open daily 11am - 11:30pm.
**Ages:** 4 years and up.

## RUBY'S

(800) HEY RUBY (439-7829) / www.rubys.com $$$
*Call for the one nearest you.*

These 1940's-style diners offer good food and have a terrific atmosphere for kids. They've readily become one of our favorite places to eat. Old-fashioned-looking jukeboxes that play your favorite oldies; red vinyl booths and bar stools; and the kind of attentive service that all but disappeared years ago, are some of Ruby's trademarks. Since the restaurants are franchised, each one is slightly different in decor (some have trains going around on tracks overhead), and in their choice of menu items. Most breakfast choices include omelettes ($4.89), waffles ($3.79), etc. Lunch and dinner foods include a wide selection of burgers (beef, turkey, veggie, or chicken), for an average cost of $5. Salads, sandwiches, and soups are available, too. The delicious concoctions from the soda fountain, including flavored sodas and old-fashioned ice cream desserts, keep us coming back for more. Kids' meals range from $2.99 to $3.79 for a choice of a grilled cheese sandwich, corn dog, hamburger, chicken fingers, etc. Their meals come with fries, a small drink, and a kid-size ice cream cone. Note: You'll find Ruby's at the end of several Southern California piers, kind of like a pot of gold.

**Hours:**  Open daily for breakfast, lunch, and dinner.

**Ages:**  All

## BEN BOLLINGER'S CANDLELIGHT PAVILION

(909) 626-1254  / www.candlelightpavilion.com

*455 W. Foothill Boulevard, Claremont*

See BEN BOLLINGER'S CANDLELIGHT PAVILION, under the Shows and Theaters section, for details.

## CARTOONSVILLE EATERIE AND FUNHOUSE

(310) 207-6070

*12121 Wilshire Boulevard, Suite 207, Los Angeles*

(Exit Santa Diego Fwy [405] W. on Wilshire Blvd. It's on the N.E. corner Wilshire and Bundy Dr. Garage parking is available on nearby Amherst Ave. Parking is free, with validation, for the first 2 hours. It's $1.35 for each additional 20 minutes; $9.50 maximum.)

Enter this upscale eaterie and funhouse through its third component, a retail store that sells T-shirts, hats, Barbie dolls, etc. Cartoonsville appeals to parents because of its fine cuisine served in a relaxing atmosphere. The kids like it because of the fun food, the colorful and friendly environment, and the adjacent playroom. The restaurant has wooden chairs with smiley faces carved in them, carpeting printed with cartoonish words like "zowie!", fanciful lamps, and several glass-encased displays containing toys such as robots, trucks, jack-in-the-boxes, dolls, etc. One display showcases eighteen Barbies. A wall display features a large lunch box collection. A few video monitors show cartoons, of course, although you can't hear the dialogue over the piped-in music. Note: An outside covered patio eating area, with nice, redwood furniture, is also available for your dining pleasure.

Menu choices include Caesar salad ($8.95), chicken tostada ($8.95), hamburger ($7.95), New York steak ($16.95), baby back ribs ($14.95), and a selection of pastas and pizzas. Cheesecake and sundaes ($4.99 each) are some of the dessert choices. Kids can choose from a burger, chicken fingers, pasta, or a hot dog ($4.95 each), or kid-size ribs or pizza ($5.25 each). All childrens' entrees include fries, fruit, and a beverage in a souvenir cup.

Adults can sit in the restaurant while keeping an eye and ear out for their kids, who can play in the small, adjoining funhouse room at no extra charge. Families are also welcome to just come play in the funhouse room, at no charge. The room, geared for ages 10 and under, has a multi-level play structure with enclosed tubes and twisty slides, a few kiddie rides, video games, and some token-taking games such as skee ball. Note: The ticket redemption center requires a minimum of twenty-five tickets in exchange for a relatively inexpensive prize.

**Hours:**  Open Tues. - Thurs., 11:30am - 9pm; Fri., 11:30am - 10pm; Sat., 11am - 10pm; Sun., 11am - 9pm.

**Admission:** Free for the funhouse. Meal prices are listed above.
**Ages:** 1 - 10 years.

## COUNTRY STAR

(818) 762-3939 / www.countrystarrestaurants.com                    $$$$
*1000 Universal Center Drive, Universal CityWalk, Universal City*
(Heading NW on the Hollywood Fwy [101], exit NE at Universal Center Dr. Heading SE on the Hollywood Fwy, exit R. on Lankershim Blvd. off ramp, L. on Cahuenga Blvd., L. on Universal Center Dr. It's next to entrance of Universal Studios Hollywood and CityWalk.)

The entrance to this restaurant is in the shape of a huge, old-time jukebox, but there is nothing dated about County Star. Its investors include Reba McEntire, Vince Gill, and Wynonna. Y'all look down as you enter through the cave-like hallway and you'll see videos of the latest country stars at your feet. Then again, there are video screens everywhere, showcasing your favorite singers from waaay back to the hottest, current stars. The showy decor includes walls lined with guitars, boots, glitzy costumes, and photos, plus a motorcycle spinning on a pedestal in the center of the main room.

Good-old American food is served here, like fried chicken ($12.95), big, beef ribs ($13.95), steaks ($17.95 for filet mignon), and burgers ($7.95), plus sandwiches, like club and barbecue beef ($8.95). Kids, ages 9 and under, have their choice of a hot dog, burger, grilled cheese sandwich, or spaghetti for $4.95. Their meals come with fries, a drink, and a hot fudge sundae. Boy howdy - delightful food and "down-home" singing make Country Star an entertaining dining experience.

**Hours:** Open Mon. - Fri., 11am - 10pm; Sat. - Sun., 11am - 11pm.
**Ages:** 4 years and up.

## DALE'S DINER

(562) 425-7285 / e-mail:dalesdiner@earthlink.net                    $$$
*4229 E. Carson Street, Long Beach*

(Exit Riverside Fwy [91] S. on Lakewood Blvd., L. on Carson St. It's on the corner of Carson and Norse Way)

Hey daddy-o! This 50's diner is a really happening' place. It's decorated with black and white checkered tile floor, turquoise vinyl seats, and a few special booths that look like they were made from the back section of cars from this era. Each table has its own small jukebox. At 25¢ for two songs, your kids can now be introduced to such classics as *Chantilly Lace* and *Purple People Eater*. For breakfast, try a five-egg omelette stuffed with bacon and cheese and served with hash browns or fruit, and toast or a cinnamon roll, for $5.95. Blueberry flapjacks ($3.85) or cinnamon raisin french toast ($3.65) make tasty morning choices, too. Kids' meals, for ages 9 and younger, include two oreo pancakes (about $3), or one egg and one pancake and a piece of bacon (about $3). The lunch and dinner menu offers a Cobb salad ($6.85), pork chops ($7.25), sirloin tip steak kabob ($7.95), deli sandwiches (average $6), hamburgers (average $5), etc. Top off your meal with a chocolate, vanilla, or cherry soda. Kids can choose a burger

and fries, grilled cheese with fries, chili, or a pepperoni pizza for about $3.25.
Beverages are extra. Come in just for dessert sometime and try a piece of fresh-
baked pie ($2.25), or a scrumptious Brownie Saturday, which is alternating
layers of brownies with vanilla ice cream, topped with hot fudge and whipped
cream ($3.95).

**Hours:**   Open Mon. - Fri., 6am - 10pm; Sat. - Sun., 7am - 10pm.
**Ages:**   All

## DC3 RESTAURANT

(310) 399-2323
*2800 Donald Douglas Loop North, Santa Monica*
(Exit Santa Monica Fwy [10] S. on Bundy Dr., R. on Ocean Park Blvd., L. on 28th St. It's
just N. of the Santa Monica airport; adjacent to the MUSEUM OF FLYING.)

Come to DC3 Restaurant for an uplifting dining experience. This art-deco
restaurant is stylish, and has a great view of the planes from Santa Monica
airport landing and taking off. It is most dear to my heart, though, because of the
Jr. Jet kids' program. Kids eat pizza or spaghetti, plus a salad and ice cream, for
free! Then a licensed child care professional - one adult for every four children -
will care for them as they go play in the MUSEUM OF FLYING, which is an
elevator ride down from the restaurant. (Look under the Museums section to
know all the wonderful things this museum has for children to do.) Do you
realize what this means? You can enjoy uninterrupted, adult conversation while
your little darlings are having a great time! Adult meals range from $18.95 to
$26 for your choice of steak, ribs, seafood, etc.

**Hours:**   Hours for the Jr. Jet program vary, although it is usually offered
Tues. - Fri. from 6pm - 9pm. Reservations are needed at least by
2pm of the day you are dining. The restaurant is open for lunch
Mon. - Fri., 11:30am - 2:30pm. It's open for dinner Tues. -
Thurs., 6pm - 9pm; Fri. - Sat., 6pm - 10pm.
**Ages:**   The Jr. Jet program is for ages 3 - 11 years.

## DIVE!

(310) 788-DIVE (3483)
*10250 Santa Monica Boulevard, in the Century City Shopping Center,
Century City.*
(Exit San Diego Fwy [405] N.E. on Santa Monica Blvd. Parking is free for the first three
hours in the underground parking structure of the shopping center.)

Dive! is not just a place to eat, it's an underwater experience. You'll hear
the kids say, "how cool!" as soon as they enter through the hatch door of the
submarine-shaped restaurant. Inside the entrance, to your left, is a periscope that
pokes through the roof so kids can actually see what's going on outside. Note:
The tantalizing buttons in this area are safe to push. The rest of the interior also
replicates a submarine, albeit a more colorful one than is normally found on the
seas. Port hole windows have bubbles in them. Adding to the submerged feeling,
video screens on the walls show actual underwater footage of stingrays, sharks,
and other fish, plus a few shots of backyard pools and Jacuzzis. Music helps set

the mood, too with tunes like *Yellow Submarine*, etc.

The elevator resembles a submarine locker room. Upstairs, a mini-submarine goes around on a track overhead. Even the bathrooms are nautically themed. (Come on - you've got kids - you know they check these things out!)

The food is great. Sub-Starter menu choices include special fries ($2.95), with a choice of seven dips. Sub-stantial salads go from $4.95 for a house salad to $11.95 for a grilled lemon basil chicken breast salad. Dive! also serves pasta, burgers, ribs, and fish. There is a delicious variety of submarine sandwiches at an average cost of $7.95. The desserts taste incredible and are generous in portion so, as their motto "Never DIVE! alone" suggests, share one with a friend. The kids' menu will bait your youngsters' appetites. Choices, all of which include fries, are chicken fingers, pasta, pizza, turkey breast, hot dog, or hamburger for $4.95 to $5.95. For $8.95, the meal also comes with a beverage in a souvenir cup plus an ice-cream dessert. Note: Take advantage of the fact that you are in the Century City Shopping Center, a wonderful outdoor mall with many unique shops and boutiques.

**Hours:**   Open Sun. - Thurs., 11:30am - 10pm; Fri. - Sat., 11:30am - 11pm.

**Ages:**   4 years and up.

## ENCOUNTER RESTAURANT                            ☼

(310) 215-5151                                               *$$$$*

*209 World Way, Los Angeles*

(Exit Imperial Fwy [105] N. on Sepulveda Blvd., follow the signs that say "arrivals." It's at L.A.X. [airport])

Seemingly from a galaxy far, far away comes (a close) Encounter Restaurant that looks like a space station. It is located at the hub of the Los Angeles airport. Earthlings need to take the elevator, with its mood lighting and other-worldly music, up to the restaurant, which overlooks the immediate L.A. area. Note: The nighttime ambiance is almost surreal as hundreds of twinkling lights fill the skyline.

I can't decide if the interior decor, designed by Walt Disney Engineering, is futuristic or from the 60's. The carpet's predominant colors are lime green, dark red, and blue. The booths are white and oblong. The ceiling has blue and purple lights shining through oval and odd-shaped holes. My boys and I sat around the bar and were entertained by the lava lamps. (We are easily amused!) The servers, who are dressed in space uniforms (think *Star Trek*), used hand held drink dispensers shaped like laser guns. The main attractions in this circular restaurant, however, are the windows. They are slanted outward, from the floor to the ceiling. Although looking down out the window made me dizzy, my boys thought it was cool (and a little scary).

The food (and prices) are out of this world. The lunch menu includes grilled salmon with vegetable spaghetti and field greens and a balsamic vinaigrette ($12), mushroom ravioli with vegetables and champagne cream ($12), and sirloin burgers ($10). The dinner selection includes Caesar salad ($10); duck, with mustard-infused raspberry sauce, and saute of wild rice ($27); seared ahi tuna with garlic-scented spinach ($26); and veal chops with chili sauce ($29); plus lamb, sea bass, and more. Sophisticated children's entrees allow kids 12 years and under to indulge in fettuccine ($8), filet of beef ($10), chicken breast ($10), or penne pasta with shrimp ($10). Dessert choices include lemon honey sesame crisps with creme brulee with berries ($6), pecan sweet potato torte and ice cream ($8), and cheesecake ($5).

Make sure to take the separate "observation deck" elevator to go above the restaurant to the open air observation deck. Free telescope viewing is available up here through the partial glass barriers.

**Hours:**   The restaurant is open daily for lunch from 11am - 4pm for lunch; 4pm - 5pm for cocktails and a light dinner. It is open for dinner Sun. - Thurs., 5pm - 10pm and Fri. - Sat., 5pm - 11pm. The observation deck is open daily.

**Admission:**   Prices are mentioned above. The observation deck is free.

**Ages:**   All

## FARMERS MARKET

(323) 933-9211 / www.farmersmarketla.com                      !/$$
*6333 W. 3rd Street, Los Angeles*
(Exit Santa Monica Fwy [10] N. on Fairfax Ave. to 3rd St. It's on the "corner.")

This unique outdoor market, originally founded in 1934, is an eclectic mixture of more than sixty fresh food and produce vendors, and over twenty kitchens that make and sell all sorts of homemade domestic and international favorites. The market can be crowded, but it is a fun place to shop or enjoy lunch. Patrons can order their favorite ethnic food and eat at an outdoor table. Kids love stopping by Littlejohn's English Toffee House stall to watch (and sample) mouth-watering candy being made. At Magee's House of Nuts, they can also see peanuts steadily pouring into a large machine behind glass, being churned around to make very fresh-tasting peanut butter. Across the way from the main marketplace, more than sixty-five retail stores offer unique clothing items and specialty gifts.

**Hours:**   Open in the summer Mon. - Sat., 9am - 7pm; Sun., 10am - 6pm. The rest of the year the market is open Mon. - Sat., 9am - 6:30pm; Sun., 10am - 5pm. Closed major holidays.

**Admission:**   Free, but bring spending money.

**Ages:**   2½ years and up.

## FRILLS

(626) 303-3201                                                $$$$
*504 South Myrtle Avenue, Monrovia*
(Exit San Gabriel River Fwy [605] N. on Myrtle Ave.)

Entering through the doors of Frills is like taking a step back in time. The front Victorian boutique sells vintage clothing and a variety of hats, plus gift items like cards and unusual buttons.

The back part of Frills is a tea room. If you feel inappropriately attired, choose a feather boa and/or a glamorous hat from the dress-up trunk. What fun! The room is charmingly decorated with lacy tablecloths, old-fashioned clothing and hats, and tea sets that are for sale. There are over forty types of tea to choose from, with cinnamon vanilla and cherry being the two most popular with the younger set. Order a meal fit for a king with King's Tea, which includes a hearty meat pie or sausage roll, a variety of tea sandwiches, fresh fruit, cheese, dessert, and of course, tea - $12.50. Other teas (meals) fit for a queen, princess, or peasant are available. All meals are served with fresh-baked bread and a delicious dessert. Children's Tea, a peanut butter sandwich, shortbread, fresh fruit, and tea, costs $8.50. Ask about Frills' special children's programs.

**Hours:** Open Tues. - Sat., 11am - 4pm; Fri., 11am - 7:30pm.
**Admission:** Prices range from $8.50 - $12.50.
**Ages:** 4 years and up.

## GRAND CENTRAL MARKET

(213) 624-2378 $$
*317 S. Broadway Street, Los Angeles*
(Exit Ventura Fwy [101] S. on Spring St., R. on 3rd St., then a quick L. on Hill. The parking structure is between 3rd St. and Hill St.)

This is a fun, aromatic, cultural experience for kids who are used to shopping at grocery stores. There are over forty stalls inside this covered structure that sell everything from exotic fruits and vegetables to octopus and pigs' heads. There are also meat stalls, restaurants, and a bakery. Stop here to shop and/or eat on your way to visit other fun and educational places listed in this book!

**Hours:** Open Mon. - Sat., 9am - 6pm; Sun., 10am - 5:30pm.
**Admission:** Parking is $1 for every fifteen minutes; $8 maximum. Parking is free for ninety minutes, if you purchase merchandise worth $15 or more.
**Ages:** 3 years and up.

## HOLOWORLD

(626) 578-0009 $$$
*620 N. Lake Avenue, Pasadena*

See HOLOWORLD, under the Family Pay and Play section, for details.

## JOHNNY REB'S SOUTHERN SMOKEHOUSE

(562) 866-6455 $$$
*16639 Bellflower Boulevard, Bellflower*
(Exit Artesia Fwy [91] N. on Bellflower Blvd.)

This roadhouse restaurant serves up southern hospitality, as well as good ol' southern cookin'. Walk past the bales of hay and cow bells into the main room with its wood beam ceilings, wooden tables and benches, and rustic ambiance. Large U.S. (and a few other) flags hang from the ceiling. The walls and counter tops are decorated with straw hats, old wash basins, musical instruments, license plates, old-fashioned kitchen gadgets and tools, and pictures of farms framed by shutters. Bluegrass music plays in the background.

The immediate attraction for kids (and adults) is the bowl of peanuts on each table because peanut shells are to be thrown on the floor! (My floor looks like this too, sometimes. The only difference is that kids are allowed to do it here.) I have to mention that even the bathrooms fit into the Ma and Pa Kettle theme because they look like (nice) outhouses, and barnyard noises are piped in.

Our waiter, who wore a long johns shirt, served our beverages in canning jars. Breakfast items include grits ($1.69), omelettes (average $6.50), pancakes (average $4.25), and country ham ($7.99). Meals come with all the fixins'. The children's menu offers an egg and toast, french toast, pancakes, or bacon and egg biscuit, for $1.95 each. The lunch menu is the same as the following dinner menu, only the portions are smaller, so prices are lower. Going along with the southern attitude toward food - anything tastes better when fried - choices include fried green tomatoes, okra, fried sweet potatoes, hushpuppies (i.e. fried cornbread), catfish, and chicken fried steak. Y'all may also select ribs, hamburger, blackened T-bone steak, stuffed Cajun sausage sandwich, chicken salad, and more. Dinner prices range from $7 to $15. The homemade desserts are delicious, especially the peach cobbler. Personal advice - don't even think about dieting, at least for the meal you eat here. The kids' menu offers chicken, catfish, or beef ribs from $3.50 to $4.75. Beverages are extra. Tip: For each paying adult, a child 12 years and under may eat for free on selected Wednesday evenings. "Put some south in your mouth" and grab some grub at Johnny Reb's! Note: Another, smaller, Johnny Reb's is located at 4663 Long Beach Boulevard in Long Beach, (562) 423-7327.

**Hours:**   Open Sun. - Thurs., 7am - 9pm; Fri. - Sat., 7am - 10pm.
**Ages:**    2 years and up.

## MALIBU SPEEDZONE

(626) 913-9663                                                    $$$

*17871 Castleton Street, City of Industry*

See MALIBU SPEEDZONE, under the Family Pay and Play section, for details.

## MARVEL MANIA

(818) 762-7835  / www.marvel.com/mania                           $$$

*1000 Universal Center Drive, Universal CityWalk, Universal City*

(Going S.E. on Ventura Fwy [101], exit R. on Lankershim Blvd., L. on Cahuenga, L. on Universal Center Dr. Going N.W. on the 101, exit N. on Universal Center Dr. The restaurant is located on CityWalk, just outside the Universal Studios Hollywood entrance.)

Here's a pop quiz: Which Spider-Man villain does not trigger the hero's early warning spider-sense? A) Green Goblin B) The Mailman C) Vermin D) Venom. If you answered Venom, you're right. This information won't change your life, but those who grew up with Marvel comics will appreciate knowing that this type of trivia, plus good food and fun, can be enjoyed at Marvel Mania. The Incredible Hulk and other comic book stars are depicted in epic proportions on the outside of the building. The lobby, with its eye-catching flame carpeting, has a full bar along one wall. More importantly, however, it has cylindrical cases that display a rotating statue of Iron Man and other cool memorabilia such as Spider-Man's web-shooter, Silver Surfer's surfboard, and Dr. Strange's cape and amulet.

The restaurant carpeting is a conglomeration of Marvel's most popular figures. Some walls are decorated with larger-than-life comic cut outs and panels featuring Captain America, the Thing, Thor, etc. Parts of the ceiling and other walls jut out at angles giving them a futuristic look, like the inside of a space ship. The front area of the restaurant has a sort of captain's bridge (think *Star Trek*), complete with lighted control panels. A major attraction is a twenty-foot monitor showing cartoons and profiles of Marvel's heroes and villains. Several smaller screens are placed throughout the restaurant, too. Note: The Hulk and Hulkess bathrooms are also themed. Be sure to look in the mirror at "your" reflection.

The delicious menu choices include generous portions of Southwest pizza ($10.95); pastas (averaging $10.50); "Stanwiches," such as ham and cheese, steak, or tasty vegetable combo (about $10); grilled jumbo shrimp ($13.95); and grilled pork with tangy barbecue sauce ($11.50). Save room for dessert. The incredible Butterfinger Bread Pudding, topped with hot caramel and chocolate sauce and ice cream, for $5.95 is to-die-for, well almost. Or, try the equally scrumptious fudge brownie and white chocolate ice cream explosion of Chocolate Volcano for $6.50. For $5.95, children can choose chicken strips, X-Men pasta and sauce, a pizza, a burger, or a hot dog. Their meal comes with french fries, chocolate chip cookies (and chocolate sauce for dipping), and a beverage in a Spider-Man souvenir cup. A retail store completes your adventure in entertainment dining. Visit Universal Studios Hollywood, or stroll around the always-fascinating City Walk for a totally "Marvel"ous outing!

**Hours:**   Open Sun. - Thurs., 11am - 10pm; Fri. - Sat., 11am - 11pm
**Ages:**   All

## PETER PIPER PIZZA

Los Angeles - (323) 773-5502; Pacoima - (818) 899-4848; Sylmar - (818) 837-5996; Whittier - (562) 692-5563 / www.peterpiperpizza.com
*Los Angeles - 6207 Atlantic; Pacoima - 13200 Osborne Street; Sylmar - 12902 Foothill Blvd.; Whittier - 11885 Whittier Blvd. New locations are opening soon in Covina and National City.*

This huge, fun-filled pizza place is very similar to Chuck E. Cheese. Obviously the main food offered here is pizza, but chicken wings and a salad bar are also available. For entertainment, there are ball pits, arcade games, lots of skee ball lanes, and a merry-go-round that is free (yea!). The mascot, a green-spotted purple dinosaur, comes on stage a few times throughout the day/night to

put on a show. The kids love coming here - just cover your ears to block out the din.

**Hours:** Open Sun. - Thurs., 10am - 10pm; Fri. - Sat., 10am - 11pm.
**Admission:** Free, but bring money for food.
**Ages:** 1½ years and up.

## SHOGUN
(626) 351-8945 *$$$$*
*470 N. Halstead Street, Pasadena*
(Exit Foothill Fwy [210] N. on Rosemead Blvd. It's on the corner of Rosemead Blvd. and Halstead St.)

This Japanese-style restaurant has built-in tabletop grills where chefs prepare the food with rapid slicing and dicing movements (and "cool" tricks) in front of your eyes. (See BENIHANA, under this section, as it is a similar type of restaurant.) The "entertainment" is great and the food is delicious. Kids get a real kick out of the presentation, and are more likely to try "new" foods now that they've seen the unique way it has been prepared. Chicken, seafood, and steak are some of the menu selections. Lunch ranges from $8 to $10; dinners from $11 to $26. Kids' meals usually run between $6.95 to $8.95. (Kids are served the same meals as adults, just smaller portions.)

**Hours:** Open Mon. - Fri., 11:30am - 2pm and 5pm - 10pm; Sat., 5pm - 10:30pm; Sun., 4:30pm - 9:30pm.
**Ages:** 4 years and up.

## VINTAGE TEA LEAF
(562) 435-5589 / www.vintagetealeaf.com *$$$$*
*969 East Broadway, Long Beach*
(Exit the Long Beach Fwy [710] E. on Broadway.)

Classical music, bone china, lacy tablecloths, and a homey atmosphere make an afternoon tea at Vintage Tea Leaf a real treat. Offerings here include eighteen different kinds of tea "meals." The staples include soup, fresh-baked scones, cakes, and more than ten varieties of dainty sandwiches. Only at tea places do you find such sandwich combinations as salmon, cream cheese, and lemon capers; mayonnaise and mixed berry jam on cranberry bread; etc. I need to be more adventurous while making sandwiches at home! Ask about specific teas for young children, such as the Teddy Bear Tea, with its chocolate chip scones, chocolate tea (de-caf), bear-shaped sandwiches, and biscuits, served with honey, of course. The Leaf also features almost 100 kinds of tea to drink, each brewed just right.

**Hours:** Open Thurs. - Mon., 11:30am - 6pm.
**Admission:** Prices range, depending on the tea, between $10 - $20 per person.
**Ages:** 3 years and up.

## ALICE'S BREAKFAST IN THE PARK

(714) 848-0690                                                                *$$$*
*6622 Lakeview Drive, Huntington Beach*

(Exit the San Diego Fwy [405] E. on Warner Ave., R. on Edwards St., L. on Central Park
Dr. It's the red building at the end of the parking lot in HUNTINGTON CENTRAL PARK.)

Since breakfast is the most important meal of the day, why not start your day
at Alice's Breakfast in the Park?! The red, barn-like building has a small dining
room packed with antiques and Alice's varied collections, giving it a homey
atmosphere. We also enjoy eating outside at the patio tables by the lake's edge.
This is a delightful treat, especially for kids who don't always like to sit down
throughout a meal. Watch out for the ducks, geese, and other birds that are
usually waddling around, hoping for a handout.

Mmmmm - fresh baked bread or buns are served at all of Alice's breakfasts
and lunches. Try an "outrageously delicious" cinnamon roll; at $2, it's (almost)
big enough for a meal. Breakfast averages $4.95 for two eggs, home fries, and
fruit. The menu offers a wonderful variety of other breakfast favorites, too, as
well as fresh-squeezed orange juice. The lunch menu includes large sandwiches
(average $4.50), salads, burgers, chili, etc. Kids' meals range from $1.95 to
$3.95. Fries and a drink cost an additional $1.25.

The restaurant is located in Huntington Central Park, so after your meal - go
play! See HUNTINGTON CENTRAL PARK / SHIPLEY'S NATURE CENTER
under the Great Outdoors section.

**Hours:**  Open daily 7am - 1:30pm.
**Ages:**  All

## BEST OF FRIENDS TEA ROOM

(714) 633-4710                                                              *$$$$*
*1051 North Meads, Ridgeline Country Club, Orange*

(Exit Costa Mesa Fwy [55] E. on Katella, turns into Villa Park, then Santiago Canyon Rd.,
R. on Orange Park Blvd., L. on Meads.)

It's time to play dress-up, and share a cup of tea with a special child in your
life. The price can include tea, scones, soup, sandwiches, fruit, and dessert, all
served in Victorian surroundings. Reservations are required. Call to inquire
about children's teas, such as Teddy Bear Tea, Alice in Wonderland Tea, and
special holiday teas.

**Hours:**  Tea is served Fri. - Mon., at 10am for breakfast and 1pm for high
tea.
**Admission:**  $15 for adults; $12 for children 7 years and under.
**Ages:**  5 years and up.

## BREAKFAST WITH MINNIE

(714) 956-6755 / www.disneyland.com                                        *$$$$*
*1717 S. West Street at the Pacific Hotel, Anaheim*

(Exit Santa Ana Fwy [5] W. on Katella Ave., R. on West St.)

This breakfast is described as "character dining." I'm still not sure if the "character" reference refers to Disney characters or to my children! The colorful, art-deco-styled restaurant offers a breakfast buffet with an array of delicious foods: omelets made any way you like 'em (my boys considered watching the cook make omelets part of the entertainment), cereal, yogurt, fresh fruit, hash browns, Danish (hungry yet?), mouse-shaped waffles, and smoked salmon. You may also order a la carte from the menu.

Intermittently, Belle and Gaston walk among the tables, making sure to greet and chat with each member of the family. Bring your camera! They also sing songs from *Beauty and the Beast*. Minnie Mouse periodically makes an appearance, dispensing hugs to all the kids and putting on interactive magic shows with the help of Merlin and eager young diners. What fun! Each person also receives a Disney pin as a souvenir.

Take some time, before or after your meal, to ride the glass elevator in the lobby to the top of the hotel. It's not much of a view, but the ride was a thrill for my kids. Sometimes, it's the simple things in life that are the most pleasurable. Visit the adjacent DISNEYLAND HOTEL (look under the Potpourri section) for more fun things to do and see.

    **Hours:**    Open daily from 6:30am - 11am.

  **Admission:**    The buffet costs $14.50 for adults; $8.95 for ages 4 - 12; $3 for children 3 years and under. A la carte menu prices range from $4 to about $11. Parking is free for first three hours, with validation.

      **Ages:**   All

## ELIZABETH HOWARD'S CURTAIN CALL DINNER    ☼ THEATER

(714) 838-1540                                                         $$$$$
*690 El Camino Real, Tustin*                                                 🎂

    See ELIZABETH HOWARD'S CURTAIN CALL DINNER THEATER, under the Shows and Theaters section, for details.

## GOOFY'S KITCHEN                              ☼

(714) 956-6755 / www.disneyland.com                         $$$$
*1150 W. Cerritos Avenue, at the Disneyland Hotel, Anaheim*
(Going S. on Santa Ana Fwy [5], exit W. on Ball Rd., L. on West St., R. on Cerritos. Going N. on 5, exit W. on Katella, R. on West St., L. on Cerritos. It's on the W. side of Disneyland, across the street.)

    For a special, Disney-style meal, come to Goofy's Kitchen for an all-you-can-eat breakfast, lunch, or dinner buffet. Not only are the walls decorated with Disney cartoons, but your children's favorite characters come by the tables for a hug. We were visited by Pluto, Minnie Mouse, Chip (or was it Dale?), John Smith, Miko and, of course, Goofy. Kids even eat a bite or two in between hopping up to touch the costumed characters. Remember to bring your camera!

    We stuffed ourselves at the dinner buffet with prime rib, ham, chicken, seafood, fruit, salad, and scrumptious desserts. (The way my family suffers just to be able to share with you!) The kids have their own food bar that offers familiar favorites like macaroni and cheese, mini-hotdogs, spaghetti, and chicken strips. The lunch buffet consists of salads, fruit, vegetables, pastas, chicken, and more. The kids' lunch buffet is similar to their dinner selection. The breakfast buffet has equally delicious offerings of Mickey-shaped waffles, pancakes, cereal, oatmeal, fruit, omelets, etc.

Goofy's Kitchen offers good food in a fun, family atmosphere. Make your outing even more of a treat by coming early, or staying after mealtime, to walk around and enjoy the hotel grounds. (See DISNEYLAND HOTEL, under the Potpourri section, for details.)

**Hours:** Open daily for breakfast 7am - 11:30am. Open daily for dinner 5pm - 9pm. Open daily for lunch during the summer, during the holidays, and on weekends only the rest of the year from 11:45am - 2:30pm.

**Admission:** Breakfast or lunch buffets are $14.50 for adults; $8.95 for ages 4 - 12; $3 for children 3 years and under. Dinner is $19.95 for adults; $8.95 for ages 4 - 12; $3 for children 3 years and under. Parking is free for the first three hours, with validation.

**Ages:** 1½ years and up.

## MCDONALD'S (with a train theme)
(714) 521-2303
*7861 Beach Boulevard, Buena Park*
(Exit Artesia Fwy [91] S. on Beach Blvd. It's just N. of Knott's Berry Farm.)

We've nicknamed this "Train McDonald's" because the center of the eating area has a large model train exhibit with seating available all around it. Kids (and adults) are enthralled as the train goes around the mountains, through the tunnels, and past villages. Tracks and a train also run overhead.

This McDonald's also offers McThriller, a simulated jolting ride that allows you to experience white water rafting, downhill skiing at breakneck speed, and four other simulations. The cost is $2.50 for adults; $1.50 for kids. Children must be at least 42" tall. The lobby has video games, too.

**Hours:** Open daily. The drive-through is open 24 hours.

**Ages:** All

## MEDIEVAL TIMES
(714) 521-4740 / www.medievaltimes.com                    $$$$$
*7662 Beach Boulevard, Buena Park*

See MEDIEVAL TIMES, under the Shows and Theaters section, for details.

## PLAZA GARIBALDI DINNER THEATER
(714) 758-9014                    $$$$
*1490 S. Anaheim Boulevard, Anaheim*

See PLAZA GARIBALDI DINNER THEATER, under the Shows and Theaters section, for details.

## POFOLKS

(714) 521-8955 / www.pofolks.com

*7701 Beach Boulevard, Buena Park*

(Exit Artesia Fwy [91] S. on Beach Blvd.)

$$$

   PoFolks is a great place to come for home-style cooking and a nice, family atmosphere. The walls are decorated with pictures, toll-paintings, and other things that make it look homey. A model train is running on tracks overhead and there are a few table games to keep kids entertained. Menu choices include soup ($2.49), salads ($5.29 for a chef's), country ham steak ($7.99), home-style dinners like pot roast ($7.99), plus chicken, ribs, and fish. Kids' meal choices include chicken, fish, a burger, a corn dog, or a grilled cheese sandwich for $2.99. Beverages are extra. Tip: McDonald's, just a bit south down the street, has a free magazine called "Welcome" that usually contains discount coupons for PoFolks.

   **Hours:**   Open Sun. - Thurs., 7am - 9:30pm; Fri. - Sat., 7am - 10:30pm.

   **Ages:**   All

## PRACTICALLY PERFECT TEA WITH MARY POPPINS

(714) 956-6755 / www.disneyland.com

*1717 S. West Street, at the Pacific Hotel, Anaheim*

(Exit Santa Ana Fwy [5] W. on Katella Ave., R. on West St.)

$$$$

   Get the kids dressed up and enjoy a spot of tea in this supercalifragilisticexpialidocious tea room. Half of the cozy room is done like a Victorian parlor, with couches and ornate chairs in rose pink hues, while the other half looks like a garden room, with white wicker furniture, climbing green vines, and bird cages. I don't know if it was the somewhat subdued atmosphere, soft music, bone china, or the presentation of dainty finger foods, but when we entered the tea room, my boy's demeanor changed (thankfully) from rambunctious to a bit more proper and gentlemanly-like.

   When Mary Poppins appears, her presence lights up the room. Everyone's favorite nanny makes sure she chats with each person, addressing them entirely in character. She is witty, states that "hugs are most definitely allowed," and periodically entertains with stories and songs. Children especially like the rendition of *Chim-Chiminey* because she powders her nose with soot as she sings. A highlight is dressing up in feather boas and hats (top hats for males) and having your picture taken with Mary Poppins. Tip: Bring your camera!

   The Tea - this is not a full luncheon meal - consists of fresh scones, a tasty assortment of finger sandwiches (the mango and turkey combination, and the sun-dried tomato and cream cheese sandwiches were surprisingly good), sweets to nibble on, and a selection of teas, taken with just a spoonful of sugar. Other beverages are available. Etiquette tips for children: 1) Just one lump of sugar, not five; and 2) Don't sip tea with your spoon still in the cup. Note: The Tea is an hour and a half long and my boys and the young girl with us did get a little antsy.

   Take the time, before or after your tea, to ride the glass elevator in the lobby of the hotel. It's not much of a view, but the ride was a thrill for my kids.

(Sometimes it's the simple things in life that are the most pleasurable.) Visit the adjacent DISNEYLAND HOTEL (look under the Potpourri section) for more fun things to do and see.

**Hours:** Tea is served Wed. at 12:30pm; Sat. at 10am, 12:30pm, and 3pm; Sun. at 12:30pm and 3pm. Additional teas are served in the summer Mon. and Fri. at 12:30pm. Call for special holiday hours. Reservations are required.

**Admission:** $18.95 for adults; $12.95 for children 12 years and under. Parking is free for the first three hours, with validation.

**Ages:** 3 years and up.

## RAINFOREST CAFE (Costa Mesa)

(714) 424-9200 / www.rainforestcafe.com                    $$$

*3333 Bristol Street, South Coast Plaza, Costa Mesa*

(Exit San Diego Fwy [405] N. on Bristol Street. The mall is on the left. Rainforest Cafe is on the bottom level, near Sears.)

Deep in the heart of the Rainforest Cafe, realistic-looking animatronic beasts come to life - gorillas beat their chests, elephants trumpet, and parrots squawk. Periodic thunder and lightening "storms" explode through the restaurant. This is not a quiet place to eat. Cascading waterfalls, fake dense foliage, and "rock" walls add to the atmosphere, as do the jaguars and cheetahs that are partially hidden in the banyan trees. Rain drizzles down from the ceiling around the perimeter of the cafe, ending in troughs of misty waters. You'll enter the cafe under a 6,000 gallon fish tank archway that holds a colorful array of saltwater fish. Two more aquariums are inside the Cafe and one contains beautiful, but poisonous, lionfish. There is always something to grab your attention here!

Savor your meal at a table, or on a bar stool that looks like a giraffe, zebra, frog, or another animal. The delectable menu offers everything from salmon, flatbread pizza, Oriental chicken salad, and Jamaica Me Crazy! porkchops to hamburgers, meatloaf, and lasagna. Prices start at $7.95 and portions are huge. Children's meals average $4.99 for a choice of a grilled cheese sandwich, hot dog, hamburger, pasta linguine, or pizza, and include a drink with a souvenir cup. Desserts are deliciously unique. My favorite was Monkey Business - coconut bread pudding with bits of apricots, topped with shaved chocolate and whipped cream.

The adjacent Rainforest Cafe Retail Village (i.e. store) is themed with equal attention to detail. In the front of the store a (pretend) life-size crocodile resides in a small swamp. He moves around and roars every few minutes. Live macaws and cockatoos are on perches just above the crocodile. A knowledgeable animal care specialist will tell your inquisitive little ones all about the birds. Catch jungle fever and experience the Rainforest Cafe! Note: There is another Rainforest Cafe in Ontario. (Look under this section for the address.)

**Hours:** Open Mon. - Thurs., 11am - 10pm; Fri., 11am - 11pm; Sat., 10:30am - 11pm; Sun., 10:30am - 9pm.

**Ages:** All

## RITZ-CARLTON HOTEL TEA

(949) 240-2000 / www.ritzcarlton.com      $$$$$

*1 Ritz-Carlton Drive, Dana Point*

(Exit San Diego Fwy [5] W. on Camino Los Ramblas, turns into Pacific Coast Hwy [1], L. at Ritz-Carlton Dr.)

The Ritz-Carlton is an incredibly classy hotel. Celebrate your child with a special afternoon of tea in an elegant room that overlooks the ocean. Choose from either Light Tea, with a delectable variety of pastries and tea ($19 per person); Pacific Tea or Traditional Tea, with pastries and scrumptious finger sandwiches, or pastries and a fruit platter ($25 per person); or the Royal Tea, with champagne or a non-alcoholic cocktail, tea, finger sandwiches, pastries, and strawberries and cream ($32 per person). Come early or stay a bit afterwards to explore the gracious hotel and beautiful grounds. Teddy Bear Teas, for families, are offered on selected days in December and include a marionette show. Call for times and details.

    **Hours:**   Seatings for tea are Mon. - Fri. every half hour between 2pm - 4pm; Sat. - Sun. at 2pm and 4:30pm. Call to make reservations.

    **Ages:**   5 years and up.

## SAM'S SEAFOOD "POLYNESIAN SPECTACULAR"

(562) 592-1321 / www.letseatoc.com/info/samsseafood.htm   $$$$

*16278 Pacific Coast Highway, Huntington Beach*

(Exit San Diego Fwy [405] S. on Seal Beach Blvd., L. on Pacific Coast Highway.)

Aloha! Imagine a balmy evening where Hawaiian music plays softly in the background while you're savoring delicious seafood. Welcome to . . . not Hawaii, but Sam's! This tropically themed restaurant offers all this, plus beautiful South Seas murals, a waterfall decorated with flowers and real volcanic rocks, carved wood totem poles, and (padded) bamboo furniture. Dining here is a treat for the senses and palate. Lunch choices include fried clam strips ($4.95), fried jumbo shrimp ($6.50), broiled salmon ($6.50), swordfish steak ($6.50), steak sandwich or hamburger ($4.95 each). Dinner selections include calamari ($13.95), steamed clams ($8.50), prime rib ($14.95), lobster tail ($21.95), or teriyaki steak or barbeque ribs ($13.95 each). The childrens' menu is the same for both lunch and dinner, although the prices are not. It includes fish 'n chips, fried chicken, a grilled cheese sandwich, or a burger, plus fries, for $3.50 for lunch, $4.25 for dinner. Beverages are extra.

If you want to spend more time vacationing at the Pacific islands (via Sam's), come to the three-hour Polynesian Spectacular offered in a "hidden" room just off the main dining area. Seating begins at 7pm, with each party being seated at individual tables. Live music accompanies your meal - feel free to sway along. Although the traditional music is good, two hours of this pre-show fare, including songs sung in native languages, can make a younger child antsy. Dinner selections include prime rib, Mahi Mahi, baby back BBQ ribs, Snow Crab legs, teriyaki shrimp, or Hawaiian-style chicken, accompanied by salad, rice, and dessert. Beverages are served with little paper parasols.

The featured one-hour-and-fifteen-minute show starts at 9pm on a stage that has a waterfall surrounded by rocks and flowers. The singers, dancers, and musicians have Polynesian roots. The variety of performers' costumes include colorful print shirts and dresses, grass skirts, bandeau tops, feather headdresses, etc. The costumes authentically reflect the islands represented throughout the show - Hawaii, Tahiti, Samoa, and New Zealand. Highlights include the Samoan body slap dance (ouch!), graceful hula dances, belly dances (how do they move like that?), and fierce-looking Maori warriors, complete with face paint and spears, who stomp around and stick out their tongues.

Tip: If you're celebrating a birthday, anniversary, or other special event, tell your waiter upon arrival so that the emcee can include it during her announcements. Also, hang loose and go native by wearing a tropical outfit!

**Hours:** Sam's is open daily for lunch from 11:30am - 4pm. Dinner is served Sun. - Thurs., 4pm - 9:30pm; Fri. - Sat., 4pm - 10pm. The Polynesian Spectacular is offered Fri. nights from April through November from 7pm - 10:15pm.

**Admission:** Meal prices are listed above. The Polynesian Spectacular is $29.95 for adults; $23.95 for ages 4 - 11; children 3 years and under are free.

**Ages:** 5 years and up.

## SPAGHETTI STATION

(714) 956-3250 / www.spaghetti-station.com                         *$$$*
*999 W. Ball Road, Anaheim*

(Going S. on Santa Ana Fwy [5], exit Ball Rd. It's on the corner of the off ramp and Ball Rd. Going N. on 5, exit N. on Harbor Blvd., L. on Ball Rd.)

For a taste of the Old West, come eat at Spaghetti Station. The lobby area has a stuffed mountain lion and deer, Butch Cassidy's saddle (yes, it really belonged to him), wooden Indians, and cowboy statues. Either before or after your meal take a "tour" through the rustic restaurant. Lots of terrific Western memorabilia is displayed in glass cases in the rooms, such as lanterns, cowboy boots, woman's lace-up shoes, saddles, musical instruments, guns, arrowheads, tomahawks, and arrows, plus statues of bulls, cowboys, and stagecoaches. Upstairs is a small game room with a billiard table.

Each room has a stone fireplace in a house-like setting. The menu has fun facts about the gold rush and other important Western dates and happenings. Food choices include spaghetti, fixed with a wide variety of sauces, plus ribs, chicken, pizza, salad, etc. Prices range from $5.95 to $13.95. The kids' menu offers pizza, spaghetti, cheese ravioli, or chicken tenders for $4.95 to $5.95. Beverages are $1.50. Although there is a bar toward the front, the rest of the restaurant is great for your little cowhands.

**Hours:** Open Mon. - Fri., 11am - 10pm; Sat., noon - 11pm; Sun., noon - 10pm.

**Ages:** 2 years and up.

## SPEEDWAY INTERNATIONAL RACING BISTRO AND  BAR

(949) 675-5900 / www.thespeedway.com                    *$$$*

*353 E. Coast Highway, Newport Beach*

(Exit Costa Mesa Fwy [55] E. on Coast Hwy [1]. It's past Dover Dr., and over the bay. Free valet parking is available.)

Looking for a restaurant to keep your pit crew happy? Then put it in gear and race over to this Speedway Bistro, where race car enthusiasts enjoy the ambiance and the food. The outside of the building looks like an old drive-in, though it sports a car on its rooftop. The lobby has numerous video screens showing car races, of course. Some Formula race cars, including the fully-injected Formula 5000 car that won first place in a Long Beach Grand Prix, and a few motorcycles are part of the restaurant's decor. Car parts, trophies, autographed racing overalls, signed helmets, and other memorabilia are displayed on the walls. There are several more video monitors throughout the restaurant and the bar area has a large-screen model. So, yes, it does get noisy in here. Note: Seating is also available on the outside patio. For more entertainment, go full throttle at any one of the eight virtual reality race car simulators.

Menu choices include "Pedal to the Metal" cheeseburgers ($6.50), pasta dishes (average $10), roasted chicken ($12.95), seafood (such as sweet Hawaiian prawns at $16.95), and ribs or steak ($16.95), as well as a full array of delicious desserts. Little racers get revved with entree choices ranging from burgers to grilled cheese sandwiches to pizza to fish 'n chips that come in a take-home cardboard car. The $4.95 meal price includes a beverage. Sunday brunches of pancakes ($7.95), omelets (average $8.95), or steak and eggs ($12.95) are served with a glass of champagne, fresh fruit, and a cinnamon roll.

**Hours:** Open Mon. - Thurs., 11:30am - 10pm; Fri., 11:30am - 11pm; Sat., 11:30am - midnight; Sun. - opening times vary, either 4am or 10:30am, depending if there is a race that day. Closing time on Sun. is usually 11pm.

**Ages:** All

## TIBBIE'S MUSIC HALL

(949) 252-0834 / www.tibbiesmusichall.com                    *$$$$$*

*4647 MacArthur Boulevard, Newport Beach*

(Exit San Diego Fwy [405] S. on MacArthur, just S. of the John Wayne Airport.)

See TIBBIE'S MUSIC HALL, under the Shows and Theaters section, for details.

## TINSELTOWN STUDIOS

(714) 937-9090                    *$$$$$*

*Katella Avenue, Anaheim*

See TINSELTOWN STUDIOS, under the Shows and Theaters section, for details.

## VILLA PARK PHARMACY

(714) 998-3030                                                                    !/$

*17821 Santiago Boulevard, Villa Park*

(Going S. on Costa Mesa Fwy [55], exit E. on Lincoln, R. on Santiago (right after the Fwy). Going N. on 55, exit E. on Nohl Ranch Rd., R. on Santiago.)

Chocolate phosphates, sorbet, dot candy - if these things bring back fond memories, or just make you hungry, head to the Villa Park Pharmacy, where old-fashioned fun is not out of date. The soda fountain is right out of the 1800's, with an old marble counter-top and brass bar stools, plus ornate ceiling tiles and ceiling fans. There are a few booths here, too. Sip a Green River, or another specialty juice, or just have an ice-cream cone.

The candy "store" has big glass display cases, just like in an old-time general store, filled with a delicious assortment of candy. Sometimes creamy fudge or caramel apples are being made on the nearby counter-top.

The rest of the store is a wonderful blend of antique fixtures and modern products. For instance, a 1938 ticket agent's booth is now used to sell lotto tickets, while an old-fashioned Post Office in the back is still used as a real Post Office. The store also carries a full line of cards, books, videos, cosmetics, and gifts. And yes, there is a pharmacy here, too.

**Hours:**   Open Mon. - Sat., 9am - 7pm; Sun., 11am - 5pm.

**Ages:**   2 years and up.

## WATSON DRUGS and SODA FOUNTAIN

(714) 633-1050 - restaurant; (714) 532-6315 - pharmacy                    $$$

*116 E. Chapman Avenue, Orange*

(Exit Costa Mesa Fwy [55] W. on Chapman Ave. It's just E. of the shopping center circle.)

Watson Drugs and Soda Fountain, built in 1899, has the distinction of being the oldest drugstore in Orange County. Located in the wonderful shopping center of Old Town, it is a great place to stop for a meal, or just a treat. Part of Watson Drugs is a pharmacy/gift shop. Look up at the eclectic, old-fashioned items on the overhead shelves.

The other half is a retro 40's diner, with a big jukebox, red vinyl seats, and lots of memorabilia, including old license plates that decorate the walls. Breakfast, such as omelets, pancakes, or french toast, costs about $4.25. Lunch, like chicken salad, roast beef, burgers, or tuna melts, costs about $4.75. Dinner, such as steak, fish, or chicken, costs, on the average, $7.75. The kids' menu includes a choice of a hot dog, tuna fish sandwich, or a grilled cheese sandwich for $2.95. Fries are included in the kids' meals, but drinks are extra. Let's not forget the most important food item - dessert! Ice cream floats, sundaes, shakes, etc., are yours for the asking (and the paying). Eat inside and enjoy the ambiance, or choose one of the tables outside, and watch the world go by.

**Hours:**   Open daily from 6:30am - 9pm.

**Ages:**   2 years and up.

# BIG TOP FOOD 'N' FUN RESTAURANT

☼

*$$$*

(909) 785-4141

*3500 Polk Street, Riverside*

(Exit Riverside Fwy |91| N. on La Sierra Ave., R. on Magnolia Ave., R. on Polk St. It's adjacent to CASTLE AMUSEMENT PARK.)

For big time fun, come eat at Big Top Restaurant! The good-sized restaurant resembles a circus big top, complete with a lifelike statue of a circus elephant outside. The inside feels like a circus, too. (Then again, meal times at our house always feel like a circus what with balancing plates of food, kids acting clownish, etc.) Red and white are the predominant colors. Overhead are stuffed animals in acrobatic poses.

The food is good, with pizza being the featured item - $11.75 for a medium, two topping pizza. A salad bar, burgers, hot dogs, sandwiches, soup, and chicken are also available. Kids love to be entertained at meal time (any time!), so the Big Top bear mascot occasionally appears on stage for a short show. There are a few kiddie rides, and a small arcade room with "G-rated" games, plus a redemption center.

Big Top also offers educational tours. For example, a half-hour Pizza Tour is given where kids learn how pizza fits into the four basic food groups, see how pizza is made, and make their own. Then, they get to eat it! $2.50 per person includes the tour, a slice of pizza, a soft drink, and five tokens. For an additional $1.50 each, children can also play a round of miniature golf. A minimum of ten kids are needed for this tour. See CASTLE AMUSEMENT PARK, under the Amusement Parks section, for a description of the adjacent park.

    **Hours:**    Open daily 11am - 10pm.

    **Ages:**    2 years and up.

# TOM'S FARMS

☼

*!/$*

(909) 277- 9992 - general info; (909) 277-4012 - Tom's Hamburgers

*Temescal Canyon Road, Corona*

(Exit Riverside Fwy |91| S. on the 15 Fwy, R. on Temescal Canyon Rd., past the fast food restaurants at the corner.)

Tom's Farms consists of five separate buildings, each one selling different products. The front building has farm fresh produce, dried fruit, nuts, and candies. This is a delicious stop. The adjacent Bird's Nest is unusual with its various live birds and related bird items for sale. The small restaurant, Tom's Hamburgers, offers large portions. Tasty hamburgers start at $2.95. Kids have their choice of a corn dog, grilled cheese sandwich, or a burger, plus fries and a drink for $2.25. An outside eating area is set up around a small pond that has black swans. Beyond the pond are a few penned farm animals to pet. A wine and cheese store also offers baked goods. On weekends only, although not during the month of January, a few craft booths are set up here, too. Grab a snack or eat a meal at this "farm" with a folksy ambiance.

    **Hours:**    Open in the summer daily from 8am - 8pm. Open the rest of the year daily from 8am - 6pm.

**Admission:**   Free
**Ages:**   All

# OAK GLEN / APPLE PICKING & TOURS
(909) 797-6833
*Oak Glen Road, Oak Glen*

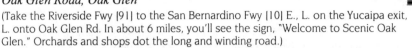

(Take the Riverside Fwy [91] to the San Bernardino Fwy [10] E., L. on the Yucaipa exit, L. onto Oak Glen Rd. In about 6 miles, you'll see the sign, "Welcome to Scenic Oak Glen." Orchards and shops dot the long and winding road.)

Your *delicious* journey into Oak Glen takes you through a town that is ripe with fun things to do. Several orchards offer U-Pic, which means you pick your own apples, raspberries, blackberries, pears, and pumpkins, in season, of course. Most orchards also have wonderful country stores with all sorts of apple concoctions and apple-related items for sale.

Here are a few of our favorites stops:

**Parrish Pioneer Ranch,** 38561 Oak Glen Boulevard, (909) 797-1753: The Ranch has a picnic area, apples (already picked), a few gift shops, and a restaurant. Llamas, goats, and emus are in pens by the parking lot. Weekend entertainment includes Johnny Appleseed, Yodeling Merle (who sings cowboy songs), and Stunt Masters of the Old West shows. These half hour shows take place at the outside theater at 1pm, 2:30pm, and 4pm on weekends, weather permitting. Performances always first include a talk on firearm safety, followed by stunts, a melodrama, or a farce on life in the 1800's. Admission is $2 for adults, $1 for ages 7 to 15, children 6 years and under are free. The shops are open daily from 10am to 6pm.

**Los Rios Rancho,** 39610 Oak Glen Boulevard, (909) 797-1005: This Rancho has a store, a delicious bakery, an orchard with U-Pic fruit, walking trails, and two picnic areas. One area is the large, grassy front lawn that has picnic tables. The other is a pretty, wooded area, with picnic tables, located behind the store. Pony rides - $2 around the track, and a twenty-five-minute, horse-drawn hay ride - $4 for adults, $3 for children, are usually available only on weekends during the harvest season. The hay ride is available for groups with reservations at other times.

Los Rios also offers a crop of year-round educational programs. A forty-five-minute tour of the packing house/cider mill explores the relationship between farming and the environment, and seasonally includes grading apples, pressing cider, taste testing, eating fresh-dipped caramel apples (for an additional fee), etc. A pioneer tour, in which kids relive a day in the life of a pioneer, includes butter making and other chores. Nature programs can include hiking, collecting and studying samples from a pond, and/or studying Native American lifestyles. Take your choice of one to three hour tours by combining any of the above tours. Each tour needs a minimum of ten people, generally costs $3.75 per person, is offered Monday through Friday, and is available by reservation only. On weekends, during certain seasons, the public is welcome to participate in some of the tour activities, with no minimum number required. The packing house/cider mill tour is $1.50; making apple cider costs $6 a gallon; etc. The

Rancho is open January through August, Wednesday through Friday from 10am to 5pm, and Saturday and Sunday from 9am to 5pm. It's open September through December daily from 9am to 5pm.

**Riley's Log Cabin Farm and Orchard,** 12201 S. Oak Glen Boulevard, (909) 797-4061: This orchard has not only U-Pic apples, but also seasonal U-Pic berries and pumpkins. Weekend entertainment includes "Johnny Appleseed" playing his fiddle. A bountiful harvest of year-round tours offered for groups can include a colonial or farm Bible study; participating in frontier skills such as chopping wood and making candles, soap, or rope; building a log cabin; learning old-fashioned dances such as the minuet and/or square dancing; grinding corn and baking Johnny cakes; and making and drinking apple cider. Tour options range from two to six hours, cost between $5 and $10 per person, and require a minimum of twenty students during the week and thirty on the weekend. Parents are encouraged to come along. Bring a sack lunch to enjoy by the pond picnic area. Riley's also hosts outstanding Civil War Re-enactments a few times a year, as well as musical and living history events, hoedowns, and much more. Riley's is closed mid-November through March. Open April to mid-June for tours only. Closed mid-June through August, except for weekends in August when berry picking is available. (Call first.) Open Labor Day through mid-November Tues. - Fri., 10am - 2pm for tours only; open Sat. - Sun., 10am - 4pm for tours and the general public.

**Riley's Farm and Orchard,** 12253 S. Oak Glen Boulevard, (909) 790-2364: Neighboring in-laws own this Riley's farm that also has a U-Pic, a general store, and tours for groups of twenty-five to forty participants. Each tour includes a tractor-drawn hayride, making cider (a fascinating process), drinking cider, eating hot-dipped caramel apples (a personal favorite), and your choice of buttermaking, candlemaking, doing farm chores, or access to the petting farm. $5.50 per person for the two-hour tour is a great deal! Call to make reservations. Riley's is closed mid-December through March. Open April through July for tours only - call for hours. Open August through December daily from 10am - 5pm for tours and to the general public.

**Oak Tree Village,** (909) 797-4020: Located in the center of Oak Glen is the Village, a wonderful place to shop, play, and eat. Kids enjoy walking on the hilly trail through the good-sized animal park. Penned deer, sheep, a llama, goats, and birds are in here, plus a lot of squirrels that are running around freely. Admission is 50¢ for adults, 25¢ for children. On the weekends only, the Village offers pony rides ($3); scale model train rides ($2); panning for (and keeping) real gold ($5); and fishing at the small Trout Pond ($3 per person with poles and bait provided, plus $4.95 per pound for each fish). Up the walkway is Mountain Town, a store with a small cave-like museum that displays taxidermied wildlife. Entrance is 25¢. Along the perimeter of the museum are mini-stores that display merchandise tempting to young shoppers.

Although weekends (especially in October) can be crowded, some orchards will only let you pick apples then, so get an early start on your day's adventure! Call the orchards to find out when your favorite type of apple will be ripe. Tip:

Buy an apple-recipe book, as kids get a little carried away with the joy of picking apples! Note: Oak Glen is beautiful in the spring, when the apple trees are in bloom.

**Hours:** Apple-picking season goes from September through November, with most U-Pics open on the weekends only. Stores, tours, and many other activities are usually open year round.

**Admission:** Pay for U-Pic fruit by the pound. See Los Rios and both Rileys Farms for tour prices.

**Ages:** All ages for most activities; 5 years and up for the educational tours.

## RAINFOREST CAFE (Ontario)

(909) 941-7979 / www.rainforestcafe.com

*One Mills Circle, in Ontario Mills Mall, Ontario*

(Exit San Bernardino Fwy [10] N. on Milliken Ave., R. on Mall Rd. Or, exit Ontario Fwy [15] W. on 4th St. It's on the S.E. corner, near entrance 6.)

See RAINFOREST CAFE (Costa Mesa), under this section, for details.

## BATES NUT FARM

(760) 749-3333

*15954 Woods Valley Road, Valley Center*

(From Escondido Fwy [15] exit E. on Old Castle Rd. which turns into Lilac Rd., R. on Valley Center Rd., E. on Woods Valley Rd.)

Is your family a little nutty? Then join nuts from all over the world at the Bates Nut Farm. This eight-acre farm features a store with rows and rows of nuts (almonds, cashews, walnuts, etc.), dried fruits, and candies. Kids enjoy watching (and smelling) fresh peanut butter being made in machines that are at eye level. The adjacent Farmer's Daughter gift boutique sells books, dolls, collectibles, country crafts, and more.

Outside, kids enjoy the small, animal farm with ducks, geese, sheep, and goats to feed and pet. There are picnic tables and shade trees on the grounds, too. Free fifteen-minute tours of the Bates Nut Farm are given January through August. The tours show and tell a more in depth look at the growing and processing of nuts by going through the roasting room, cold storage room, and packaging room. Call to make a reservation. Call, also, about the many seasonal events held here, such as the pumpkin patch, hayrides, choose n' cut Christmas trees, and arts and crafts fairs. You've got *nut*in' to lose by coming here for a visit!

**Hours:** Open daily 8am - 5pm.

**Admission:** Free, unless you purchase something.

**Ages:** All

## CORVETTE DINER

(619) 542-1001 / e-mail:vetdinrmrg@aol.com

*3946 5th Avenue, Hillcrest, San Diego*

(Exit Cabrillo Fwy [63] E. on Washington St., L. on 5$^{th}$ Ave., L. on University St., L. on 5$^{th}$ Ave. (One way streets). Or, exit Cabrillo Fwy [163] W. on University St., R. on 5$^{th}$ Ave., which is a one-way street. Valet park or circle around the block for self parking.)

This 50's style diner is a really bebopping place to eat! The music played from the deejay's booth; the license plates, neon signs, and hub cabs that decorate the walls; the old gas pumps; the Bazooka bubble gum displays; and the red Corvette (parked inside) all add to the atmosphere of the restaurant. The rest of the decor incorporates black and white checked tiles with blue marbleized vinyl booths. Waiting for a table here can be more fun than usual as you sit on a bench made from the back seat and the fins of an old Cadillac. On Tuesday and Wednesday evenings, from 6:30pm to 9:30pm, be entertained by "Magic Mike," who plies his tricks of the trade and jokes at your table. (Ask him to show your children how to magically stretch their arms.)

The food here is great! A Hawaii 5-O burger (burger with pineapple) or a Philly steak sandwich is $5.95. Other food choices include fish tacos, grilled Reubens, ribs, meatloaf, blackened chicken pasta, salads, etc. Desserts are delectable. They range from Green Rivers to peppermint smoothies to Snickers Pie to Death by Chocolate Cake. Kids' meals are $4.25 for their choice of spaghetti, burger, corn dog, grilled cheese sandwich, or chicken fingers, plus fries, a soft drink, and an ice cream bar. Was life really this good in the fifties?!

**Hours:**   Open Sun. - Thurs., 11am - 11pm; Fri. - Sat., 11am - midnight.
**Ages:**    All

## EDEN CREEK ORCHARD

(760) 765-2102                                                                    $

*1052 Julian Orchards Drive, Julian*

(From San Diego Fwy [5] or Escondido Fwy [15], take 78 Fwy E. to Julian. 78 is Washington St. in Julian. From the 8 Fwy, take 79 N. to Julian, at 78 Jct. turn L. on Main St. Take Main St. N. out of town; it turns into Farmer, turn R. at Wynola Rd., turns into Julian Orchards Dr. It is 2 miles N. of town.)

This bed and breakfast is open year round, although its biggest kid-draw is the U-Pic apple orchards. Apple picking season runs from September through November, depending on the crop. At Eden Creek Orchard, children can pick Golden Delicious, Macintosh, Red Delicious, and/or Jonathons. There is a picnic area on the premises, so bring a lunch.

**Hours:**     Apple picking is available on weekends from 10am - 6pm,
               September through November. Groups may make appointments
               to come during the week.
**Admission:** Current price of apples.
**Ages:**      All

## HORTON GRAND HOTEL / IDA BAILEY'S RESTAURANT

(619) 544-1886                                                                    $$$

*311 Island Avenue, San Diego*

(Going S. on San Diego Fwy [5], exit W. on Imperial Ave., R. on 12th Ave., L. on Island Ave. Going N. on 5, exit at "J" St., continue straight off the off ramp and turn L. at Island.)

Put on the lace gloves, extend your pinky, and enjoy a delicious afternoon tea at this Victorian-style hotel. Afternoon Tea consist of petit fours, finger sandwiches, scrumptious scones, cake, and an assortment of teas. High Tea is a bit more formal and also includes sherry, a sausage roll, and truffle. As this hotel is in the heart of the historic Gaslamp District, take a stroll around before or after your tea to soak in the district's ambiance. There are many unique stores, so both window shoppers and "real" shoppers will be appeased.

**Hours:** Teas are served Tues., Fri., and Sat. from 2:30pm - 5pm.
**Admission:** $9.95 per person for Afternoon Tea; $13.95 for High Tea.
**Ages:** 5 years and up.

## HOTEL DEL CORONADO - TEA TIME

(619) 435-6611 / www.hoteldel.com
*1500 Orange Avenue, Coronado*

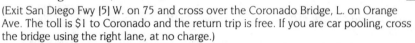

(Exit San Diego Fwy [5] W. on 75 and cross over the Coronado Bridge, L. on Orange Ave. The toll is $1 to Coronado and the return trip is free. If you are car pooling, cross the bridge using the right lane, at no charge.)

This hotel is the creme-de-la-creme of hotels (personal opinion), and tea time here is a true taste of elegance. (Note: You must make some time before or after your tea to explore this incredible hotel and its grounds!) Teas consist of bay shrimp and celery salad on puff pastry; triple-layered cucumber, cream cheese, and watercress sandwiches; New York sirloin carpaccio on ciabatta toast; brie with apple and grape slices decorated with walnuts; smoked salmon with dill on rye bread (it's amazing what kids will try in an etiquettely-correct atmosphere); an assortment of delectable pastries; and a variety of teas, of course. (Also see HOTEL DEL CORONADO under the Tours section.)

**Hours:** Tea is served Sun. at noon, 12:30pm, 2pm, 2:30pm, and 3:30pm.
**Admission:** $14.95 includes the food described above. $21.95 also includes champagne, Belgium truffles, and a chocolate dipped strawberry. Parking in the hotel lot costs $2.50 per hour; street parking, which is limited, is free.
**Ages:** 5 years and up.

## KOOKY'S DINER

(619) 294-2926
*1425 Frazee Road, Mission Valley*

(Exit Cabrillo Fwy [163] E. on Friars Rd., L. on Frazee. It's on the corner, in the shopping center.)

This 50's art deco diner features black and white checked tiles, red vinyl booths, a huge mural of an old-fashioned drive-in, an "antique" jukebox, and lots of photographs of famous stars from this era (e.g. James Dean, Elvis Presley, etc.). The main feature, though, is waitresses on skates, or "skatetresses." My youngest child was slightly disappointed, however, that the busboys didn't wear skates, too! My kids watched our skatetress carefully as the meal was served, to see if she would fall. She didn't.

The menu is extensive, from "Egg-Sullivan" Show breakfast foods to the "Platters" dinner fare. $8.95 buys you a full dinner meal of meat, mashed potatoes or fries, vegetable soup or salad, and bread. Hamburgers, taco salads, sandwiches, roast beef, chicken, etc., cost around $5.95 each. A "Sundae, Sundae, So Good to Me" costs $1.85. The Little Boppers menu offers hamburgers, hot dogs, spaghetti, chicken fingers, etc. Prices range from $1.95 - $3.25. The fourth Saturday of every month is Cruise Night at Kooky's. Vintage cars cruise by, a deejay plays 50's music, and there are contests and giveaways.

    **Hours:**    Open 24 hours.

    **Admission:**    Family Nights are Mon. - Thurs., where one child eats for free with the purchase of an adult entree.

    **Ages:**    All

## SEAU'S, THE RESTAURANT

(619) 291-SEAUS (7328) / www.seau.com    *$$$*

*1640 Camino Del Rio North, #1376, in the Mission Valley Shopping Center, San Diego*

(Going E. on Mission Valley Fwy [8], exit N. on Mission Center Rd., R. on Camino Del Rio Rd. Going W. on 8, exit at Camino Del Rio Rd., turn R. It's next to Robinsons-May.)

San Diego Charger's All-Pro linebacker, Junior Seau, has a two-story restaurant for the good sports in your family to enjoy. Notice how the outside of the restaurant resembles a coliseum. The inside decor is equally eye-catching with a huge mural of Junior Seau, model sports figures in action poses, and signed sports paraphernalia all around such as surfboards, football helmets, baseballs, bats, jerseys, hockey sticks, etc. Suspended T.V. monitors show sporting events, and the huge main screen shows the sports channel. (What a surprise!) Music instead of commentary, however, is heard.

The black table tops have football plays drawn on them. Don't try to erase them, however, because even though it looks like they were done in chalk - they weren't. (We saw others try to do this, too!) Our kids enjoyed watching the pizza maker toss pizzas, and then cook them in the wood-burning stove. The simplest entertainment is sometimes the best kind.

The food goes the whole nine yards - everything we ate was scrumptious. Menu choices run the gamut from burgers ($6.95) and pizza ($9.95) to rib-eyed steak ($13.95) and lobster ravioli ($11.95). The generously-portioned kids' meals range from $3.55 (choice of hot dog, pizza, or burger) to $6.55 (jr. shrimp). They come with fries, fresh homemade ice cream, and a beverage in a small take home sports bottle. Ah, to be 12 years old (or younger) again!

    **Hours:**    Open Sun. - Thurs., 11am - 10pm; Fri. - Sat., 11am - midnight.

    **Ages:**    All

## U.S. GRANT HOTEL

(619) 232-3121    *$$$$*

*326 Broadway, San Diego*                                                  ♨

(Going S. on San Diego Fwy [5], exit W. on Ash St., L. on 4th, R. on Broadway. Going N. on 5, exit S. on 6th Ave., R. on Broadway.)

Old-time elegance permeates tea time in the Grant Hotel lobby. Amid crystal chandeliers, polished mahogany furniture, and beautiful floral arrangements, little girls and boys transform into young ladies and gentlemen, respectively. Savor an assortment of finger sandwiches, scones with fresh cream and preserves, crumpets and pastries, and a fine selection of teas. What a delightful treat! Note: If your children don't care for tea, just request hot chocolate, or juice, for them.

**Hours:** Tea is served Tues. - Sat. from 3pm - 6pm.
**Admission:** $12 per person
**Ages:** 5 years and up

## WELK RESORT THEATER                                                     ☼

(888) 802-7469 / www.welkresort.com                                        *$$$$$*
*8860 Lawrence Welk Drive, Escondido*                                      ♨

See WELK RESORT THEATRE, in the Shows and Theaters section, for details.

## WESTGATE HOTEL                                                          ☼

(619) 557-3650                                                             *$$$$*
*1055 2nd Avenue, San Diego*                                             ♨

(Going S. on San Diego Fwy [5], exit W. on Ash St., L. on 4th Ave., R. on Broadway, R. on 2nd Ave. Going N. on 5, exit S. on 6th Ave., R. on Broadway, R. on 2nd Ave.)

Fashioned after an anteroom at Versailles, children will feel like royalty as they sip their tea and nibble on fancy finger sandwiches, truffles, petit fours, strawberries and cream, and scones topped with preserves, honey, seasonal berries, or Grand Marnier cream. Reservations are requested. (I wanted to write that the food is lip-smacking good, but the refined atmosphere here dictates a more decorous choice of words.) The luxurious surroundings include a Steinway piano, rich tapestries, gilded mirrors, and crystal chandeliers.

**Hours:** Tea is served Mon. - Sat. from 2:30pm - 5pm. Piano music starts at 3pm.
**Admission:** $12.95 for adults; $8 for ages 3 - 8 years from the above set menu. You may also order a la cart.
**Ages:** 5 years and up.

## TIERRA REJADA FAMILY FARMS                                              ☼

(805) 523-8552 / www.underwoodfarmmarket.com                               *$*
*3370 Moorpark Road, Moorpark*                                             ♨

(Exit Ventura Fwy [101] N. on the 23 Fwy, L. on Tierra Rejada Rd., L. on Moorpark Rd.)

There are two ways to enjoy this farm: 1) Stop by the adjacent roadside market to purchase fresh produce (tasty, but boring), or 2) Let the kids pick their own fruits and vegetables. (Ya-hoo - we've got a winner!) This huge working farm has rows and rows (and rows and rows) of seasonal crops including artichokes, strawberries, blackberries, peaches, squash, potatoes, green beans, apricots, apples, onions, garlic, tomatoes, eggplant, peppers, cabbages, pumpkins, melons, corn, and herbs. My boys were excited to eat strawberries they picked from the vines, carrots they pulled from the ground, beans they harvested from the stalks, and other good-for-you foods they won't normally eat, proving that kids really enjoy the fruits (and vegetables) of their labor.

Heavy-duty pull wagons are available to transport your prize pickings (or tired little ones) at no extra charge. A grassy picnic area, with tables, is located at the front of the farm, near the restroom facilities.

The farm offers numerous guided tours of the fields for groups of twenty or more. The tours entail learning about a designated crop (or crops) - care, growth cycle, etc., - as well as picking some to take home. What a great combination of fun and education! Crops do grow seasonally, so call to see what is currently ripe. Tierra Rejada also offers a thirty-minute tractor drawn hayride all around the farm for groups. Tips: Wear sunscreen and walking shoes, prepare to get a little muddy if you visit here after a rain, and bring a cooler to store your fresh produce. Look up PARTY ANIMALS, under the Zoos and Animals section, as it is adjacent to the Farm.

**Hours:** Open daily 9am to about 6pm. Usually closed in December and January. Call first!

**Admission:** Technically free. Crop prices are charged per pound and change per season/availability. The hayride is $1.50 per person for a group of at least twenty people. Tours average about $4 per person, depending on the activity and length of the tour.

**Ages:** All for a visit; 5 years and up for the tours.

# FAMILY PAY AND PLAY

The family that plays together, stays together! Indoor play areas, outdoor miniature golf courses, rock climbing centers, laser tag arenas, etc., are great places to go to spend some special bonding time.

## DISCOVERY ZONE

Check your yellow pages for a local listing.

This giant, wonderfully safe, fun, inside play environment is made for children to run around 'til their hearts are content! It reminds me of three or four McDonald's Play Places™ put together under one roof. There are colorful, plastic, inter-connecting tubes to go through (think kid-size gerbil runs) that create maze-like tunnels. Other fun features include foam-padded obstacle courses, ball pits, air bounces, and slides. Each Discovery Zone differs slightly in the additional activities offered, such as a bungee cord room or a small trampoline. There is a separate play area for toddlers that has the same activities, just scaled down in size. There are also token-taking games and a full-service snack bar. Note: Socks are required to play at Discovery Zone.

With usually just one entrance in and out of the play area, it's possible to just sit, *zone* out, and watch your child. Or, bring knee pads and join in the fun.

**Hours:** Most Discovery Zones are usually open Mon. - Thurs., 10am - 8pm; Fri. - Sat., 10am - 9pm; Sun., 11am - 7pm.

**Admission:** $5.99 for ages 3 - 12; $3.99 for children 2 years and under. Adults play for free with a paid child's admission. (Certain discounts are available through AAA.)

**Ages:** 1½ - 12 years.

## ARROYO MINIATURE GOLF

(323) 255-1506

*1055 Lohman Lane, South Pasadena*

(Going S. on Golden State Fwy [5], exit S. on Orange Grove, R. on Mission. Go straight past Arroyo onto Stoney Dr. Going N. on Pasadena Fwy [110], exit N. on Marmion Way, R. on Pasadena, L. on Arroyo, L. on Stoney Dr. From Mission St., Stoney Dr. winds around to the (big) Arroyo golf course.)

This miniature golf course, adjacent to a real golf course, is very simple (i.e. no fancy castles, difficult obstacles, etc.). It does, however, offer itself as a good little course for practicing your short stroke game at an inexpensive price. So, for the price, practice, and fun of it, why not bring the kids and come play a couple of rounds?!

**Hours:** Open daily from 7am - 10pm.

**Admission:** $1.50 per person per round.

**Ages:** 3 years and up.

## BRIGHT CHILD

(310) 393-4844 / e-mail:brightchild@msn.com

*1415 4<sup>th</sup> Street, Santa Monica*

(Exit Santa Monica Fwy [10] N. on Lincoln, L. on Wilshire, L. on 4<sup>th</sup>. It's next door to Toys R Us. Parking is available in structure #5 and #3, on 4<sup>th</sup> St.)

This large indoor play land offers big time fun for your little ones. It has six slides, four zip lines, a wind tunnel, a mini putting green, a basketball court (with an adjustable rim height), an arts and crafts room, a music room with a karaoke stage, and a toddler room. Whew! Your kids will not want to leave. Classes, geared for particular age groups, are available throughout the week. Instructors encourage learning and agility through activities, games, and using equipment. Outside food is not allowed in, but the cafe here serves good food, such as fresh sandwiches that range between $3.50 to $6.50, and kids' meals that include a sandwich and a drink. Socks must be worn by everyone, including adults. I hope a visit here *bright*ens your day!

**Hours:** Open Thurs. - Tues., 10am - 6pm. Closed Wed.

**Admission:** $8 per child for up to two hours of play; each additional hour is $4. One adult is free with one paid child's admission; additional adults are $4 each. Parking is free for the first two hours in structure #5 or #3.

**Ages:** 6 months to 7 years.

## CLOSE ENCOUNTERS PAINT BALL

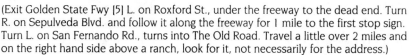

(323) 656-9179 - office; (805) 255-5332 - field /                $$$$$
www.paintballusa.net/clzenc.htm
*22400 The Old Road, Newhall*
(Exit Golden State Fwy [5] L. on Roxford St., under the freeway to the dead end. Turn R. on Sepulveda Blvd. and follow it along the freeway for 1 mile to the first stop sign. Turn L. on San Fernando Rd., turns into The Old Road. Travel a little over 2 miles and on the right hand side above a ranch, look for it, not necessarily for the address.)

Play this version of Capture the Flag while armed with markers (i.e. guns) filled with paint. This makes the game a bit more colorful! You'll be placed on one of two teams. The object of the game is to get the flag from your opponent's base, while dodging paintballs by hiding behind bunkers and trees. The three-a-half-acres of mountainside is a perfect setting to play this rugged game. A referee is on the playing field to insure fair play and help out. Each game lasts about twenty minutes. After you're rested, go for another round. Food is available to purchase, or bring your own, as there is a shaded grove of trees with picnic tables. Tip: Wear pants and other clothing you don't care about, and shoes with good traction. Getting hit stings, so wear a padded shirt or multiply layers to help absorb the hits.

**Hours:** Open to the public Sat. - Sun., 8am - 4:30pm. Groups of thirty or more can reserve play time during the week.

**Admission:** $25 for all-day play, which includes a pistol, goggles, and face mask. There are two types of upgraded guns to rent - constant-air pump rifles at $20 a day, or a semi-automatic, constant-air machine gun at $25, which includes free $CO_2$ for they day. Paintballs cost $10 for 100, or $35 for 500. Call to inquire about discount packages for junior players, ages 10 to 15, such as a Ninja Special. This special includes all-day play, an air rifle, and 100 paintballs for $30. Kids under 18 years old must have a parental consent form in order to play.

**Ages:** 10 years and up.

## CLUB DISNEY (West Covina)

(888) CLUB DIS (258-2347) or (626) 938-1480 / www.clubdisney.com    *$$$*
*2851 Eastland Center Drive, West Covina*

(Exit San Bernardino Fwy [10] N. on Eastland Drive. It's in Eastland Mall and you can see Mickey's wizard hat from the freeway.)

This large indoor play area, designed with Disney's special flair, was created for parents and children to have fun interacting with each other. The attraction called Now Playing is a changing exhibit with hands-on fun that showcases Disney's newest movie release. The *Flubber* exhibit, for instance, featured a tank filled with gooey, green "flubber" that you could play with, as well as some flubber-related paraphernalia. Little ones will enjoy Winnie the Pooh Corner where they can crawl through a log, pound on honey pot drums, and play with large alphabet blocks in a room inside a tree. Four different shows, starring your kids, are put on daily at Applaudeville Theater, including a fashion show and a Mouse House Dance Party. Under the Sea play area offers "shellular" phones for kids to call and converse with each other. The Mousepad has sixteen computers and monitors where visitors can choose from numerous educational games. The main, multi-level play structure has plastic tubes, a thirty-foot slide with twists and turns, and a few areas just to jump around. Socks are required. My favorite room is the Character Creations Art Studio which offers half-hour classes on painting, sculpting, or other artistic endeavors. Each take-home creation centers around a Disney character or theme. The in-house cafe offers a fairly extensive menu and really tasty food. Menu items include chicken Caesar salad ($5.25), Mickey pizzas ($3.50), turkey sandwiches, yogurt, applesauce, hot pretzels, and Cheesecake Factory desserts. Note: The five party rooms are each decorated with a different Disney theme and a wall that has a birthday cake done in fiber optics. Oh, to be five or six years old again! (There is another CLUB DISNEY in Thousand Oaks.)

**Hours:**    Open Tues. - Wed. and Sun., 10am - 7pm; Thurs. - Sat., 10am - 8pm. Open during the summer one hour later. It's usually open on holiday Mondays.

**Admission:**    $8 per person; $7 for seniors; children under 1 year play for free.

**Ages:**    1 - 14 years.

## DISCOVERY ZONE (Lakewood)

(562) 634-1666    *$$*
*4645 Silva, Lakewood*

(Exit Riverside Fwy [91] S. on Lakewood Blvd., L. on Del Amo. D.Z. is in the Lakewood Mall, near JC Penneys.)

This particular Discovery Zone is more modernized than the other Discovery Zones. The inside play area, which reminds me of two McDonald's Play Places™ put together under one roof, has colorful, plastic, inter-connecting tubes to go through that create maze-like tunnels. Other fun features include foam-padded obstacle courses, ball pits, an air bounce, and slides. A separate area for toddlers has similar activities, just scaled down in size. The small arts and crafts area provides drawing supplies and other artistic materials. A form of laser tag is played in the Men in Black room, where there are neon-colored alien targets to shoot. Kid-friendly videos play in the back, adjacent to the food court, and next to a small stage that offers karaoke. Tip: Enjoy a walk around the Lakewood Mall, which is just next door.

**Hours:**   Open Mon. - Thurs., 11am - 8pm; Fri. - Sat., 10am - 9pm; Sun., 11am - 7pm.

**Admission:**   $7.99 for kids 38" tall to 17 years; $4.99 for children under 38"; parents are free with a paid child's admission.

**Ages:**   2 years and up.

## FIGHTER TOWN ENTERTAINMENT (Pasadena)

(626) 577-9896 / www.fightertown.net                                    *$$/$$$$$*

*One Colorado, 35 Hugus Alley, Suite 200, Old Pasadena*

(Take Pasadena Fwy [110] N. to the end, turns into Arroyo Pky., L. on Colorado. Going W. on Foothill Fwy [210], exit S. on Fair Oaks. Going E. on Ventura Fwy [134], exit E. on Colorado. One Colorado is between Colorado, Fair Oaks, Union, and De Lacey Sts. Fighter Town is above the AMC Theaters.)

See FIGHTER TOWN ENTERTAINMENT (Lake Forest) for details. This location offers seven flight simulators, ranging from a single seat cockpit with an internal screen, to a projection screen cockpit, to a double seat cockpit with full motion. After suiting up in flight gear, you'll be briefed for a half hour on the basics of flying and tactical maneuvers. Your simulation, which feels like the real thing, lasts a half hour. Note that a child 5 years or older may join his parent (at no additional charge) in the single control, dual seat cockpit of an EA-6A.

Fighter Town in Old Pasadena also has eight pods (or partially-enclosed booths) for the virtual reality games of Battletech and Red Planet. Choose Battletech, with its slogan of "no guts, no glory," or Red Planet, where you race your vehicle through the canals of Mars. After a briefing on how to navigate a game, you'll be interacting with others on your intense fifteen-minute journey to other worlds - expect the unexpected. Fighter Town covers the gamut in stimulating simulations.

**Hours:**   Open Sun. - Thurs., 11am - 11pm; Fri., 11am - midnight; Sat., 9am - 1am.

**Admission:**   $8.99 for each virtual reality game; $29.99 - $49.99 for airplane simulations, depending on the type of cockpit you choose.

**Ages:**   8 years and up for the virtual reality games; 54" and taller to fly solo in the flight simulator.

## FUNLAND U.S.A.

(805) 273-1407 / www.funlandusa.com                                    *$$$*

*525 W. Avenue P-4, Palmdale*

(Exit Antelope Valley Fwy [14] N. on Ave. P., then a quick L. on Ave. P, L. on 10th St. W., L. on Marketplace.)

This land of fun offers three, themed, ten-hole **miniature golf courses -**

$3.75 per course for adults; children 5 years and under play for free. **Go-karts** are $4.50 for a five-minute ride. Drivers must be 58" or taller and passengers, who may ride for free, need to be at least 3 years old. **Bumper boats** are $4.50 per ride and drivers must be 44". Other attractions here include **batting cages**, a large game aracade area, and a snack bar.

**Hours:**  Open Sun. - Thurs., 10am - 10pm; Fri. - Sat., 10am - 11pm. Open in the summer one hour later.

**Admission:**  Individual attractions are listed above, or purchase a park pass - one round of golf, two rides, twelve tokens, and a soda for $13 per person.

**Ages:**  4 years and up.

## GO KART WORLD

(310) 834-3800
*21830 Recreation Road, Carson*
(Exit San Diego Fwy |405| E. on Carson, take an immediate R. on Recreation Rd.)

Kids 58" and taller, with a parent present, can drive the Turbo slick track cars. If kids are by themselves, they must be at least 18 years old to drive. Rides are $3.50 for four minutes. A mini-Indy track is available for kids 45" and taller at $3.50 a ride. The electric oval kiddie track is $2 for a three-minute ride for children between 3 to 6 years. If you have a group of ten or more, you may rent the track for a birthday party, or whatever.

**Hours:**  Open daily from 11:30am - 11pm.

**Admission:**  Individually priced above.

**Ages:**  3 years and up.

## GOLFLAND ARCADE

(626) 444-5163
*1181 N. Durfee Avenue, South El Monte*
(Exit Pomona Fwy |60| S. at Peck Ave., R. on Durfee.)

What course of action will you take? Choose from four, well-kept miniature golf courses with lots of fun holes. The arcade area is clean and has games, such as air hockey, as well as video games. Tip: McDonald's is only a few buildings away.

**Hours:**  Open Sun. - Thurs., 10am - 11pm; Fri. - Sat., 10am - 1am.

**Admission:**  Miniature golf is $5 for adults; $3 for ages 7 - 12; $2 for children 6 years and under.

**Ages:**  4 years and up.

## GOLF 'N STUFF - FAMILY FUN CENTER (Norwalk)

(562) 863-8338
*10555 E. Firestone Boulevard, Norwalk*
(Exit San Gabriel River Fwy |605| E. on Firestone.)

This big family fun center offers several different ways to have fun, with three themed **miniature golf courses** - $6 for adults, children 5 years and under

are free; plus **Li'l Indy, bumper boats,** and **bumper car** rides - $4 per ride.
Yes, there are also lots of arcade games to be played. This can keep you and the
kids busy for hours - just bring quarters!

**Hours:** Open Sun. - Thurs., 10am - 11pm; Fri. - Sat., 10am - midnight.
Open in the summer an hour later at night.

**Admission:** Attractions are individually priced above, or buy an all-park pass
for $13.50 per person that entitles you to a round of miniature
golf, 4 rides, and 4 tokens.

**Ages:** 4 years and up.

## HOLOWORLD

(626) 578-0009
*620 N. Lake Avenue, Pasadena*
(Exit Foothill Fwy [210] N. on Lake Ave.)

This huge, two-story, alien-themed restaurant and games play area pulsates
with activity and objects that glow with fluorescent colors under black lighting.
The downstairs billiards room, decorated with murals of pool sharks and floating
billiard balls, has several pool tables outlined with fluorescent lights. Practice
your golf swing in this room, too, while interfacing with a large screen virtual
golf course. Choose from over two hundred courses. You're welcome to bring
your own club(s). This room also contains two smaller party rooms and an ice
cream bar offering fresh, homemade ice cream.

The restaurant has four, small, themed sections, each one self contained in
its decor, tables, and fantastic wall murals. Aliens prevail in all of the themes.
The small western-saloon section has a soda bar, painted wood-paneled floors,
real antlers hanging on the wall, and murals of bottles, glasses, and an alien
piano player. The adjoining Native American section has a mock tepee in the
corner, a fake cactus, and a steer's skull, along with murals of the desert and
chairs made out of cowhide. The next area is jungle-themed. It contains a fake
banyan tree, simulated lush green foliage that covers the ceiling, a waterfall, and
a gorilla and a rhino head bursting through walls. Wall paintings in here include
colorful plants and lifelike animals. A large UFO is stationed in the middle of the
space room and an alien has crash-landed upside down in the corner. The walls
show galactic mountains and other-world cities along with planets, comets, etc.
Aluminum tables match the metallic-colored vinyl chairs.

The food is good, the portions are generous, and the prices are decent. Menu
selections include appetizers of popcorn shrimp ($7.99) and fried zucchini rings
($3.99). Choose a main course of burgers and sandwiches (average $7.50),
chicken Caesar salad ($7.99), teriyaki chicken breast ($7.99), tempura fried
shrimp platter ($14.99), or barbecued tri-tip platter ($12.99). Kids can choose a
burger, grilled cheese sandwich, chicken tenders, or fish and chips for $4.99
each. Meals include a drink, fries, and an alien critter souvenir.

The upstairs, with its psychedelic-colored carpeting and video and virtual
reality games, create sensory overload for me. My boys love it, of course. The
short, nine-hole miniature golf course has basic holes with a few twists. Each

hole is outlined with neon lighting. Experience flight in a jet or spaceship in the two-person motion simulator. Our favorite activity here, however, is laser tag. This action-packed game is played wearing vests, while shooting laser guns with visible lasers, and running around in a huge room filled with obstacles to hide behind and surprise your opponents. Each exciting game lasts about twenty minutes.

Note: There are other Holoworlds scheduled to open throughout the Southland within the next year. They are reputed to be more sophisticated, to have larger restaurant areas, and even have some sort of show. Call the above number for information.

**Hours:** Open Mon. - Thurs., 11am - 9pm; Fri., - Sat., 11am - 10pm.

**Admission:** Menu prices are listed above. Laser tag is $7 Mon. - Thurs., $8 Fri. - Sun. Cosmic Golf is $4 Mon. - Thurs., $5 Fri. - Sun. Virtual Golf is $20 per hour Mon. - Thurs., $25 Fri. - Sun. The Motion Simulator is $4 a ride Mon. - Thurs., $5 Fri. - Sun. Pool is $1 per game. Ask about special deals offered throughout the week.

**Ages:** All for the restaurant; 5 years and up for the games

## JUNGLE ISLAND

(818) 882-0800 / e-mail:ourjungle@aol.com
*8919 Reseda Boulevard, Northridge*
(Exit Ventura Fwy [101] N. on Reseda Blvd. (1 block S. of Nordhoff), L. on Rayen for parking behind Jungle Island.)

Your little monkeys will go bananas at this jungle-themed indoor play area. The large room is covered with beautiful wall murals that feature jungle and endangered animals. The main wooden play structure has ladders, a thatched roof, a rope bridge, a few tunnels, and some slides. Little Tykes™ toys such as slides, playhouses, etc., are scattered throughout the room. Youngsters will also enjoy a just-their-size basketball hoop, air hockey game, and a realistic-looking cave room (used for parties). You are welcome to bring your own food into a nice little eating area, or order pizza to be delivered. Jungle Island has two goals - fun, and saving the rainforest. A portion of the proceeds go toward. Ask about special programs and events, and know that this is a great place for a birthday party. Note: Socks are required.

**Hours:** Open Tues. - Fri., 10am - 7pm. The Jungle is reserved on weekends for private parties.

**Admission:** $5 for ages 1 - 8 years; siblings and children 9 - 12 months are $3.50; babies under 9 months and adults are free. Tues. - Fri. from 5:30pm - 7pm admission is $4 for ages 1 - 8 years; siblings and children 9 - 12 months are $2; babies under 9 months and adults are free.

**Ages:** Babies to 8 years.

## LASER STORM (Torrance)

(310) 373-8470     $$

*22535 Hawthorne Boulevard, Torrance*

(Going S. on San Diego Fwy [405], exit S. on Hawthorne Blvd. Going N. on 405, exit W. on Sepulveda Blvd., L. on Hawthorne Blvd.)

    Laser tag is taking kids (and adults) by storm! Power up your laser gun as two teams compete against each other and "shoot" it out in a darkened room. Take cover behind neon-colored partitions, decorated with gak splats, as an opponent aims at you. Or, use the partitions as cover to stealthily sneak up on someone. The ten-minute games are action-packed, and all the running around can literally take your breath away!

  **Hours:**    Open during the school year Mon. - Wed., 3pm - 9pm; Thurs., 3pm - 10pm; Fri., 3pm - 11pm; Sat., 10am - 11pm; Sun., 10am - 8pm. Open in the summer Sun. - Thurs., 10am - 10pm; Fri. - Sat., 10am - 11pm.

**Admission:**    $3.50 per game, Mon. - Fri.; $4.50, Sat. - Sun.

  **Ages:**    5 years and up.

## LASERTREK

(310) 325-7710     $$

*2755 Pacific Coast Highway, #D, Torrance*

(Exit Harbor Fwy [110] R. on Pacific Coast Highway. It's just past Crenshaw Blvd., in a shopping center.)

    Unlike most laser tag lobbies, which are usually dark and filled with loud video games, LaserTrek's lobby is brightly lit and has just a few games. It also has two birthday party rooms. A space theme is prevalent throughout the actual playing arena. Astronauts, rocket ships, other-world cities, etc., painted with glow-in-the-dark paint, decorate the walls, angled partitions, and ramps. Even so, it's dark in here. Fog swirls around the up to twenty-five players as they run after (and from) opposing team members who are likewise trying to "shoot" them with laser guns. Each "hit" registers on that person's vest and he/she is out of the game for a few seconds. Then the action, enhanced by mood music, picks back up again. Each pulse-pounding game lasts ten minutes.

  **Hours:**    Open Mon. - Thurs., 11am - 10pm; Fri., 11am - midnight; Sat., 10am - midnight; Sun., 10am, - 10pm.

**Admission:**    $5 for one game; $9 for two.

  **Ages:**    5 years and up.

## LAZER CRAZE

(818) 889-6633     $$$

*30135 Agoura Road, Suite A, Agoura Hills*

(Exit Ventura Fwy [101] S. on Reyes Adobe, L. on Agoura Rd. It's on the corner.)

    Kids are crazy about Lazer Craze. The darkened lobby is packed with video and arcade games, including skee ball and air hockey. The walls are decorated with old, junky car parts and road signs. A small upstairs room has more video games, and a party room with a balcony that overlooks the laser arena. The snack bar sells soft pretzels, sodas, churros, and the other important foods.

The barely-lit arena looks like a junk yard for cars. It contains a few old cars, oil drums, a robot (!), and other themed stuff. The obstacles scattered all around are splattered with black and neon paint and graffiti-style markings. Depending on the number of players here, the fast-paced, twelve-minute games can be played with two teams of up to twenty-four people, or every man for himself. This unique atmosphere, coupled with the thrill of laser tag, makes Lazer Craze an exciting pit stop.

**Hours:**   Open during the school year Mon. - Thurs., 3pm - 9pm; Fri., 3pm - 11pm; Sat., 10am - 11pm; Sun., 11am - 8pm. Summer and holiday hours are Mon. - Thurs., 11am - 10pm; Fri., 11am - midnight; Sat., 10am - midnight; Sun., 11am - 10pm.

**Admission:**   $6 per player for one game; $11 for two games.

**Ages:**   5 years and up.

## LAZER POWER

(805) 250-4993

*20655 Soledad Canyon Road, #20, Canyon Country*

(Exit Golden State Fwy [5] E. on Valencia Blvd. which turns into Soledad Canyon Rd., turn L. on Reuther Ave., R. into the first driveway.)

Enter into another dimension with the radical game of laser tag. The Lazer Power lobby looks like nighttime, even during the day because the lobby uses black lights. It contains video and arcade games, and a snack bar. The large playing arena has a balcony, and obstacles decorated with flourescent planets and aliens, plus music playing in the background. Up to forty people can play on two opposing teams, both armed with laser guns and vests that light up. "Shoot" it out in a fifteen-minute games of non-stop action.

**Hours:**   Open in the summer Mon. - Thurs., 10am - 10pm; Fri. - Sat., 10am - 11pm; Sun., 11am - 10pm. Open the rest of the year Mon. - Thurs., 3pm - 10pm; Fri., 3pm - 11pm; Sat., 10am - 11pm; Sun., 11am - 10pm.

**Admission:**   $7 per game. $20 includes five hours of play, two slices of pizza, and a soda.

**Ages:**   5 years and up.

## LAZERSTAR (Glendora)

(626) 963-9444 / www.lazerstar.com

*1365 S. Grand Avenue, Glendora*

(Exit Foothill Fwy [210] S. on Grand Ave. It's in a mall.)

See LAZERSTAR (Oxnard), in this section, for details.

## MALIBU CASTLE (Hollywood)

(818) 765-4000

*12400 Vanowen Street, Hollywood*

$$$

(Going N. on Hollywood Fwy [170], exit W. on Victory, R. on Whitsett, R. on Vanowen. Going S. on 170, exit W. on Sherman Way, L. on Whitsett, L. on Vanowen.)

This big castle (is there such a thing as a small castle?) offers your family choices of entertainment, with two **miniature golf** courses complete with scaled down buildings and challenging obstacles to putt around or through - $5.75 for adults, $4.75 for kids under 13 years; **go kart** racing - $4 for a four-minute ride (drivers must be at least 54" tall); **batting cages**; and a slew of video and arcade games.

**Hours:**  Open Mon. - Thurs., 11am - 10pm; Fri., 11am - midnight; Sat., 10am - midnight; Sun., 10am - 11pm.
**Admission:**  Attractions are individually priced above.
**Ages:**  4 years and up.

## MALIBU CASTLE (Redondo Beach)

(310) 643-5167                                                             $$$
*2410 Marine Avenue, Redondo Beach*
(Exit San Diego Fwy [405] N. on Hawthorne, L. on Marine. Or, exit 405 E. on Rosecrans, R. on Inglewood, R. on Marine.)

Hold court at Malibu castle as your little subjects play either one of the two wonderful **miniature golf** courses here. There are video and arcade games inside the castle walls, a ticket redemption area, a full-service snack bar, party rooms, and **batting cages** just outside.

**Hours:**  Open Mon. - Thurs., 11am- 10pm; Fri., 11am - midnight; Sat., 10am - midnight; Sun., 10am - 10pm.
**Admission:**  Miniature golf is $6.95 a round for adults; $3 for seniors; $5.95 for children 12 years and under.
**Ages:**  4 years and up.

## MALIBU SPEEDZONE

(626) 913-9663                                                             $$$
*17871 Castleton Street, City of Industry*
(Exit Pomona Fwy [60] S. on Fullerton Rd., R. on Colima, R. on Stoner Creek. It's on the corner of Stoner Creek and Castleton.)

Ahhhh, the smell of gasoline and the sound of engines being revved! Although SpeedZone is advertised as a racing park for adults, kids can go full throttle here, too. The huge mural and formula race cars on the outside of the massive black and white checkered building reinforce the park's intentions of being dedicated to speed, racing, and competition. Drivers must be at least five feet tall and have a valid driver's license. If you do not have a license, but are at least fifty-eight inches tall, you may drive a two-seater sidewinder racer on the Turbo Track during daytime hours. The four tracks consist of Top Eliminator Dragsters, with cars powered by 300 hp; Grand Prix, with custom-scale-designed Formula One Racers; Turbo Track, which allows wheel-to-wheel racing with up to nineteen other drivers; and Slick Trax, for a spin around the concrete track. SpeedZone is the closest thing to professional racing available to the public.

Two, eighteen-hole miniature golf courses are done in the racing theme motif and include paraphernalia such as gas pumps, tires, and guard rails, plus waterways and bridges. Inside, SpeedZone decor consists of racing flags, murals, photos, a few cars (on the floor and suspended from the ceiling), and signed memorabilia such as helmets and jumpsuits. Even the restaurant table tops are designed to look like race tracks!

The Terrace Bar and outdoor grill offer open seating, or enjoy full-service dining in the Cafe. For $5.95 each, your menu choices include burgers, turkey or cheddar melt sandwiches, hoagies, Cobb salads, and individual pizzas. A chicken or steak meal is available for a few more dollars. Jr. Dragster meals consist of either chicken fingers, a hot dog, or a hamburger, along with fries and a beverage, for $3.50 to $3.95. Your pit crew will also enjoy the dessert selections that include chocolate thunder cheesecake ($3.75) or a scoop of ice cream ($1.50).

Keep the adrenaline pumping with over 100 video, virtual reality, and arcade games in the Electric Alley, plus a prize redemption area. Play basketball or skee ball, or try virtual jetskiing, motocross, or downhill skiing. At the Daytona simulators, up to eight drivers can race against each other on the same track. A day at SpeedZone is not just another day at the races!

**Hours:** Open Sun. - Thurs., 11am - midnight; Fri. - Sat., 11am - 2am. All visitors at SpeedZone after 9pm must be 18 years old or older.

**Admission:** Free entrance. Top Eliminator - $15 for 3 runs; Grand Prix - $2.50 a lap with a 2 lap minimum; Turbo Track and Slick Trax are $5 for 5 minutes. Speedway miniature golf is $6 a round for adults; free for children 5 years and under.

**Ages:** 4 years and up for the restaurant and miniature golf; see above restrictions for driving cars.

## MOUNTASIA                                                    ☼
(805) 253-4FUN (4386)                                          $$$
*21516 Golden Triangle Road, Santa Clarita*                    ⊞
(Exit Golden State Fwy [5] E. on Valencia Blvd. which turns into Soledad Canyon Rd., R. on Golden Oak Rd., L. on Golden Triangle Rd.)

Mountasia offers a mountain of fun for your family! Play either one of two **miniature golf** courses that feature a cascading waterfall. (Note: The zebra course has a hole that goes under the waterfall, inside a cave.) Prices are $5.95 for ages 4 and up; $4.95 for seniors; children 3 years and under are free. Zip around the race track in **go karts** - $4 for a single car; $4.50 for a double car. Height and age restrictions apply. Try to avoid getting wet (or go for it) in the **bumper boats** - $4.50 a ride; a passenger can ride for free. Height and age restrictions apply. Kids at least 48" tall and 6 years old can improve their batting average at the **batting cages**.

Inside Mountasia, skate around the **RollArena** with its constant light and music shows. Ask about their roller hockey games. Day skating sessions go from opening to 4pm and are $4 per skater; night sessions go from 6pm to closing and are $5. Friday and Saturday night sessions are $6. Skate rentals are $2. Stroller

skating, held on Thursday mornings from 8:30am to 10am, is a great sport for
moms to skate around the rink with their kids in strollers - $7 a session, which
includes skate rentals. Experience the speed of car racing or the thrill of riding
roller coasters via Mountasia's motion simulators - $3.50 a ride. A dual-seat
simulator, that actually flips over 360 degrees, is $4.50 a ride. Family-oriented
video and arcade games, a redemption center, and an Express McDonald's are
located inside, too.

| | |
|---|---|
| **Hours:** | Open Sun. - Fri., 10am - 10pm; Sat., 10am - midnight. Call for fall/winter hours, when the park might open later. |
| **Admission:** | Attractions are individually priced above, or purchase a $10 pass that includes one round of miniature golf, one ride on the go-karts, and one ride on the bumper cars. |
| **Ages:** | 4 years and up. |

## MULLIGAN FAMILY FUN CENTER (Torrance)    ☼

(310) 325-3950                                                                *$$$*
*1351 Sepulveda Boulevard, Torrance*
(Exit Harbor Fwy [110] W. on Sepulveda past Normandie. It's on the R. Look for the
sign, as it is easy to miss.)

This center features **batting cages** - $1 for twenty pitches (you can also buy
time, by reservation only); two wonderful **miniature golf** courses - $5.50 for
adults, $4 for seniors and kids ages 4 to 10; children 3 years and under play for
free; **Slic Track** racing - $3.50 for five minutes (height restrictions apply); a
Jungle Gym **play area** with tubes, slides, and ball pits just for children under 60"
- $4 for unlimited time; and the ever-present arcade games.

| | |
|---|---|
| **Hours:** | Open in the summer Mon. - Fri., 10am - 10pm; Sat. - Sun., 10am - 11pm. Open the rest of the year, Mon.- Fri., noon - 10pm; Sat. - Sun., 10am - 10pm. |
| **Admission:** | Attractions are individually priced above. |
| **Ages:** | 2 years through 60" for the play area; 4 years and up for miniature golf. |

## PEPE'S KARTLAND    ☼

(818) 892-9309                                                                *$$*
*8300 Hayvenhurst Place, North Hills*
(Exit San Diego Fwy [405] W. on Roscoe Blvd., R. on Hayvenhurst Ave., L. on
Hayvenhurst Pl.)

Kids at least 4'2" and 7 years old can race around the curvy, asphalt track for
an exhilarating, six-minute ride.

| | |
|---|---|
| **Hours:** | Open Mon. - Thurs., 3pm - 10pm; Fri., 3pm - 11pm; Sat., noon - 11pm; Sun., noon - 11pm. |
| **Admission:** | $4 a ride or purchase a family pass of 16 rides for $40. |
| **Ages:** | 7 years and up. |

## Q-ZAR (Valencia)

(805) 260-3307                  *$$$*

*23460 Cinema Drive #C, Valencia*

(Exit Golden State Fwy [5] E. on Valencia Blvd., R. on Cinema Dr.)

     See Q-ZAR (Chino) for details.

## RACE CITY

(310) 523-4630                  *$$*

*777 West 190th Street, Gardena*

(Take Artesia Fwy [91] W. to end, L. on Vermont, L. on 190th. Or, exit San Diego Fwy [405] at Vermont / 190th, L. on 190th.)

     Go kart drivers on this seven-turn, slick-track (meaning the car can spin out) must be at least 4'6" tall. A kiddie track, which is a small oval track for ages 6 to 10, is also available.

          **Hours:**    Open daily from 11:30am - 11pm.

  **Admission:**    A four-minute ride costs $3.50

           **Ages:**    6 years and up.

## THE ROCK GYM

(562) 983-5500 / home.earthlink.net/~therock      *$$$$*

*600 Long Beach Boulevard, Long Beach*

(Exit San Diego Fwy [405] S. on Long Beach Blvd. It is located on the 2nd floor of the Y.M.C.A. on the corner.)

     Go rock climbing at the beach, Long Beach, that is. The Rock Gym is one of Southern California's largest indoor rock climbing facilities. The huge lead climbing roof, unique bouldering tunnel, and walls jutting out at various angles prove a fitting challenge for your young athletes, and for those who are not so athletically inclined. Both seasoned climbers and those new to the sport will experience a sense of accomplishment as they conquer the rocky obstacles and terrain. Staff is on hand to harness, belay, and encourage climbers. Classes are offered where you can learn to belay you kids and other people. Belay means to stand on the ground, as an anchor, attached to the climber. The multi-colored rocks, embedded in the realistic-looking granite walls, are marked so they can be used as trail guides, though the routes are changed every few months to stimulate your mind and body. Ask about the variety of classes and programs offered. So, if you're feeling caught between a rock and a hard place, come to the Rock Gym for safe, fun exercise for the whole family!

          **Hours:**    The gym is open Mon. and Fri., 11am - 10pm; Tues. - Thurs., 11am - 11pm; Sat. - Sun., 10am - 8pm. Kids' climbs are held on Sat. and Sun. from 1pm - 3pm, and include equipment, instruction, and a belayer.

**Admission:** Kids' climbs are $20 a child. An two-hour introduction class for belaying for kids 12 years and up (this includes adults) is $35, which also includes a week pass to the gym. An all-day pass for adults is $25 if you need a belayer; $15 if you don't. Equipment rental is $6 per day.

**Ages:** 5 years and up.

## ROCKREATION (Los Angeles)

(310) 207-7199 / www.rockreation.com                    *$$$$*

*11866 La Grange Avenue, Los Angeles*

(Exit San Diego Fwy [405] W. on Olympic Ave., N. on Bundy, R. on La Grange.)

See ROCKREATION (Costa Mesa) for details.

**Hours:** The gym is open Mon. and Wed., noon - 11pm; Tues. and Thurs., 6am - 11pm; Fri., noon - 10pm; Sat. - Sun., 10am - 8pm. Kids' Climb, for ages 5 - 15, is offered Mon., Wed., and Sun., 4pm - 6pm; Sat., 3pm - 5pm.

**Admission:** Kids Climb is $20 per participant. Reservations are needed. Kids may climb at any time, if they bring a belayer, for $10 for the day. Rental equipment - shoes, harness, and chalk - is an additional $5. An adult day pass is $15. Belaying classes are offered.

**Ages:** 5 years and up.

## SHERMAN OAKS CASTLE PARK

(818) 756-9459                                           *$$*

*4989 Sepulveda Blvd., Sherman Oaks*

(Exit Ventura Fwy [101] N. on Sepulveda.)

This Castle Park offers royal fun for the whole family. There are three majestic **miniature golf** courses to putt around on, nine **batting cages** (kids must be 8 years old, or at least 4'6", to play in the batting cages), over 100 arcade games, a redemption center, and a full-service snack bar.

**Hours:** Open Sun. - Thurs., 10am - 11pm; Fri. - Sat., 10am - midnight.

**Admission:** Miniature golf is $5.50 for the first round for adults; $4.50 for children 12 years and under. Pay only $1 a round for early bird specials on Sat. and Sun. morning from 10am - 11am.

**Ages:** 4 years and up.

## TREEHOUSE CLUB

(818) 597-8733                                           *$$*

*28716 Roadside Drive, Agoura*

(Exit Ventura Fwy [101] S. on Kanan Blvd., L. on Roadside Dr. It's in a shopping center.)

Feel like you're up a tree about how to entertain your young child? Join the club, the Treehouse Club, that is. This warm and inviting, large indoor playroom features a big wooden treehouse with a ball pit and a twisty slide, a bounce, Little Tykes™ cars, foam play shapes, single-standing Little Tykes™ slides and playhouses, big balls to roll or pounce on, and some run-around space. Other activities throughout the day might include storytelling, circle games, special children's performances (i.e. puppet shows, etc.), and costumed character visits. A small, enclosed infant area has a swing, a crib, and a few toys. Tree murals and kids' music complete the fun atmosphere.

Parents can sit down and enjoy adult conversation while watching the kids play. This way everyone has the opportunity to make new friends! Ask about special events, such as Mommy and Me classes, the twice-a-month family dinners, art classes, parenting seminars, and kids' concerts. Note: During public hours, you may bring in your own food to consume at the eating area, or purchase a snack from the club.

**Hours:** Open play hours are Mon. - Fri., 10am - 4pm. Classes are held at various times. Weekends are reserved for private parties.

**Admission:** Open play is $7 for the first child; $3.50 for each additional sibling; parents play for free. Ask about class and special event prices.

**Ages:** 6 months - 6 years.

## ULTRAZONE (Alhambra)

(626) 282-6178 / www.playultrazone.com
*231 East Main Street, Alhambra*
(Exit San Bernardino Fwy [10] N. on Garfield Ave., R. on Main St.)

See ULTRAZONE (San Diego) for details.

**Hours:** Open most of the year Mon. - Thurs., 4pm - 9pm; Fri., 4pm - midnight; Sat., 11am - midnight; Sun., 11am - 10pm. Summer hours are Sun. - Thurs., noon - 10pm; Fri., noon - midnight; Sat., 11am - midnight; Sun., 11am - 10pm.

**Admission:** $7 a game.

**Ages:** 5 years and up.

## ULTRAZONE (Sherman Oaks)

(818) 789-6620 / www.playultrazone.com
*14622 Ventura Boulevard, Suite 208, Sherman Oaks*
(Exit Ventura Fwy [101] S. on Van Nuys Blvd., R. on Ventura Blvd. It's on the S. side of the street, upstairs. Two hours of parking free with validation.)

It's almost pitch black. You're going through mazes and tunnels trying to find your way to the enemy's base before your enemy finds you. Suddenly, ZAP - you get hit! You realize you've lost your power and now you have to recharge. Where *is* the recharging site? After getting lost several times you find it, and now your infrared sighting helps spy one of "them"! You fire, hit, and score one for your team!

Ultrazone, with over 5,000 square feet of excitement, is the ultimate in laser tag. You carry your own equipment - a vest and laser gun - and play with up to thirty people, or three teams. After a ten-minute briefing, you'll play for fifteen intense minutes. The first game will wear you out, but it's just practice. Now that you've got a handle on how the game is played, go for a second round. Or, just play some video games and grab a bite to eat from the full-service snack bar. Three party rooms are available. Laser tag - there is fun to be had with a game this rad!

**Hours:** Open Mon. - Fri., 2pm - 11pm; Sat., 10am - midnight; Sun., 10am - 11pm.

**Admission:** Games are $7 each. Volume discounts, role playing, and advanced access membership are also available.

**Ages:** 5 years and up, or not afraid of the dark.

## UNDER THE SEA
(818) 343-1533
*18928 Ventura Boulevard, Tarzana*
(Exit Ventura Fwy [101] S. on Tampa, L. on Ventura Blvd., R. on Topeka to park behind the building.)

Murals of mermaids and octopuses submerge your children in a world of play under the sea. This indoor play area has a bounce house, a ball pit, soft play mats, Little Tykes™ cars, a playhouse, and free standing slides. Socks are required in the play area. Ask about classes, including modern dance and Mommy & Me. You are welcome to bring your own food in and enjoy a meal at the picnic tables toward the entrance.

**Hours:** Open Mon. - Fri., 10am - 5pm. Open Sat. and Sun. for private parties.

**Admission:** $7 per child; $3.50 for siblings; adults are free.

**Ages:** 6 months to 7 years.

## BALBOA FUN ZONE
(949) 673-0408
*Main Street, Balboa*
(Take Costa Mesa Fwy [55] to the end, which turns into Newport Blvd., which turns into Balboa Blvd., L. on Main St.)

This strip called the Fun Zone is across the road from the pier. (See BALBOA PIER under the Piers and Seaports section.) The carousel, Ferris wheel, bumper cars, and Scary Dark Ride (that's its real name) are the main attractions here. Rides require one to two tickets, and tickets are $1 each. Arcade games, a clown bounce for younger children ($1 for a few minutes of bouncy fun), and Laser Zone (laser tag) are also here. May the force be with you as you try to zap your opponents in this game of laser tag. The darkened room has bright, florescent markings giving it an other-world, funky feel. Ten minutes of action-packed play costs $5. Call (949) 723-6453 for hours of operation. Craft activities in the Zone include making spin art pictures, filling stretch-neck bottles with multi-colored sand, etc.

Kids also enjoy walking around, shopping, or eating a famous Balboa Bar, an ice-cream bar with toppings. If you're looking for physical activity, bike rentals are available at Oceanfront Wheelworks, located at 105 Main Street.

Rentals are $5 for the first hour for children's bikes, and $12 for tandems. They also have in-line skates and more. Parasailing, (949) 673-3372, is $55 for ten minutes of air time and an hour boat trip. Call for hours of operation. See the Transportation section for harbor cruises launched from this immediate area.

Take the historic Balboa ferry which runs daily from 6:30am to midnight (longer on the weekends) to Balboa Island. At only 35¢ for ages 12 and up, 15¢ for ages 5 to 11, free for children 4 years and under, or $1 for car and driver - the ferry is a fun, affordable way to get to the island. Kids love this mini-adventure. Once on the man-made island, there is not a lot for kids to do. Enjoy a walk on the paved pathway along the beach or perhaps head east toward the main shopping street. Note: The Island can also be reached by exiting Pacific Coast Highway [1] S. on Jamboree Road, where it turns into Marine Ave.

**Hours:** Stores and attractions along the Balboa Fun Zone are usually open Mon. - Thurs., noon - 8pm; Fri., noon - 10pm; Sat., 11am - 10pm; Sun., 11am - 8pm. Summer hours are Mon. - Thurs., 11am - 10pm; Fri., 11am - 11pm; Sat., 10am - 11pm; Sun., 10am - 10pm. Most parking along the street is metered.

**Admission:** Attractions are individually priced above.

**Ages:** All

## CAMELOT

(714) 630-3340
*3200 Carpenter Avenue, Anaheim*
(Exit Riverside Fwy [91] N. on Kraemer/Glassell, R. on La Palma, R. on Shepard, L. on Carpenter. It's next door to FAMILY FUN CENTER (Anaheim).)

This huge castle has dragons, knights in shining armor, and anything else your prince or princess might consider fun decor. Choose from five exciting **miniature golf** courses - $6 for adults, $5 for ages 5 to 11, children 4 years and under are free with a paid adult; Putt's the Dragon **Playground**, which has balls, slides, ziplines, etc., for kids 2½ years through 58" - $3 per hour, $1 for each additional hour; four **waterslides** (usually open from May to September) - $4 for ten rides, $6 for twenty rides, and $8 for an all-day rides pass; over 300 video and arcade games; and the mandatory snack bar, serving pizza and Dryer's ice cream!

**Hours:** Most of Camelot is open in the summer Sun. - Thurs., 10am - midnight; Fri. - Sat., 10am - 1am. The rest of the year it's open Sun. - Thurs., 10am - 11pm; Fri - Sat., 10am - midnight. The water slide is open seasonally, daily from 11am - 6pm. The playground is open weekends only from 11am - 6pm.

**Admission:** Attractions are individually priced above.

**Ages:** 2½ years and up.

## CLIMBX

(714) 843-9919
*18411 Gothard Street, Unit 1, Huntington Beach*

(Exit San Diego Fwy [405] W. on Talbert Ave., L. on Gothard. It's in an industrial section.)

This indoor rock climbing facility is not as large as others we've found, but it has all the essential ingredients - several contoured wall structures built at angles that look and climb like real rock; colorful hand and foot holds that mark a variety of "trails"; a small bouldering cave; twenty-six top ropes; and enough challenges for seasoned climbers, along with lots of encouragement and easier routes for beginners. It's encouraging to know that athletic prowess is not necessary when learning how to climb. This is a sport that teaches balance and thinking while instilling a sense of confidence. Climbers are in a safety harness which is attached to a belayer, so even if one should misjudge a hand or foot hold (which my kids sometimes did on purpose), the climber will not fall, but merely swing in the air. ClimbX marks the spot for indoor fun! Note: This facility has a separate party room.

**Hours:** Open Mon., Sat., and Sun., 11am - 5pm; Tues. - Thurs., 11am - 10pm; Fri., 11am - 8pm.

**Admission:** An all day pass is $12 for adults; $10 for students. Shoe or harness rentals are $3 each, per person, or $5 for both. Introductory classes are $35 for three hours, which includes a week of free climbing.

**Ages:** 5 years and up.

# FAMILY FUN CENTER (Anaheim)

(714) 630-7212

*1041 N. Shepard, Anaheim*

(Exit Artesia Fwy [91] N. on Kraemer/Glassell, R. on La Palma, R. on Shepard. It's next door to CAMELOT, miniature golf.)

This is a fun center, but bring your money because fun costs. The many attractions are include **bumper boats** - $3.50 for kids over 44", $1.50 for kids under 44"; **batting cages**; **go-karts** - $4.25 for a five-minute ride and children must be at least 57" to drive; **Nascars** - $4.50 a drive (height restrictions apply); **battle boats,** which is like riding in a surfaced submarine while shooting balls at your "enemy" in the next boat - $4; and an **outdoor roller-skating rink** - $3 before 5pm, and $4 after 5pm. Skate rentals are $1 extra. The giant **maze craze** is amazing. Walk around the six-feet high partitions and try to find your way out. To actually play the challenging maze game, purchase a card, punch the time clock, and try to find the eight numbers hidden throughout the maze - they could even be up at any of the four towers! The game costs $4 per player. Tip: Keep younger children with you. **Big Top Fun Zone** has ten carnival rides, including a Ferris wheel, a yo-yo swing, and five kiddie rides. Each ride requires two to five tickets, and tickets are 50¢ each. Arcade games and a snack bar are available, too.

**Hours:** Big Top Fun Zone is open during the school year, Fri., noon - 10pm; Sat. - Sun., 11am - 11pm. It is open daily during the summer. The rest of the attractions are open Sun. - Thurs., 11am - 10pm; Fri. - Sat., 11am - midnight. Family Fun is open extended hours during the summer.

**Admission:** Attractions are individually priced above.

**Ages:** 2 years and up.

# FAMILY FUN CENTER (Fountain Valley)

(714) 842-1011
*16800 Magnolia Street, Fountain Valley*
(Exit San Diego Fwy [405] S. on Magnolia.)

$$$

Family Fun Center is fun for the whole family. The attractions here include **miniature golf** - $5.75 for adults, $3.75 for kids 13 years and under; **bumper boats** - $3.75 for a six-minute ride, and kids must be at least 44" to ride by themselves (children under 44" can ride with an adult); **batting cages** - eighteen pitches for $1; and **go karts** - $4.25 for a five-minute ride, and kids must be at least 57" to drive by themselves, $1.75 for additional passengers. The **Kiddie Big Top** has six carnival rides, such as a Ferris wheel and spinning cups, geared for ages 7 and under. Each ride takes three to five tickets and tickets are 50¢ each, or purchase twenty-four tickets for $6; forty-four tickets for $10.

BULLWINKLE'S RESTAURANT (look under the Edible Adventures section) is adjacent to this Family Fun Center.

**Hours:** Miniature golf is open Sun. - Thurs., 9am - 10pm; Fri. - Sat., 9am - midnight. Batting cages are open Mon. - Thurs., noon - 9pm; Fri. - Sun., 9am - 11pm. Go karts are open daily from 2pm - 10pm. The Kiddie Big Top is open Mon. - Fri., noon - 10pm; Sat. - Sun., 9am - 10pm. Family Fun attractions are open extended hours during the summer.

**Admission:** Attractions are individually priced above, or purchase a "pick four," where you pay $12.50 for any four attractions.

**Ages:** 2 years and up.

# FIGHTER TOWN ENTERTAINMENT (Lake Forest)

(949) 855-8802 / www.fightertown.net
*20521 Teresita Way, Lake Forest*
(Exit Santa Ana Fwy [5] N.E. on Lake Forest, go 4 miles, turn R. on Regency., L. on Teresita Way. The next L. is the parking lot.)

$$$$

For older kids aiming to be Top Guns, these seven flight simulators are the next best thing to actually being airborne. Offering different flying perceptions, some cockpits have twenty-seven inch monitors while others have fifteen-foot wall projections. The cockpits are realistic with fully functional avionic control panels, heads-up displays, and hands-on stick and throttle controls. Choose from single seat, dual seat, full-motion, or non-motion simulators. Note that a child 5 years or older may join his parent (at no additional charge) in the dual control cockpits of the side-by-side F-111 or back-to-back F-14.

After suiting up in flight gear, you'll watch a fifteen-minute briefing video on the basics of flying, followed by a briefing on the particulars of your cockpit. Enjoy your half-hour flight as you compete in dog fights against computer-generated opponents or against a buddy in the next plane. You can also participate in a multi-craft air strike mission. You'll be in constant contact with the control tower.

For those who remain grounded, an Officer's Club is available with snacks and drinks to purchase. Monitors in here show what the pilots are experiencing, or take a look from the observation deck, which oversees the darkened pilot's room.

Reservations for a weekend flight should be made two weeks in advance; reservations for a weekday flight, one week. Ask about squadron and wing training, and about aviation youth camps. Another Fighter Town is located in Pasadena.

> **Hours:** Open Mon. - Thurs., 11am - 9pm; Fri., 11am - 11pm; Sat., 9am - 11pm; Sun., 9am - 7pm.
>
> **Admission:** Prices range from $29.99 to $59.99, depending on the type of cockpit you choose.
>
> **Ages:** 54" and taller to fly solo.

## GOLF 'N STUFF - FAMILY FUN CENTER (Anaheim)

(714) 778-4100 $$$

*1656 S. Harbor Boulevard, Anaheim*

(Exit Santa Ana Fwy [5] S. on Harbor. Or, exit Garden Grove Fwy [22] N. on Harbor. It's across the way from Disneyland.)

Come, *par*take in some family fun, and play either one of the deluxe miniature golf courses here that are designed with whimsical buildings and challenging obstacles - $6 a round for adults; children 5 years and under play for free. There are plenty of arcade games available here, too.

> **Hours:** Open Sun. - Thurs., 9am - 10pm; Fri. - Sat., 9am - midnight.
>
> **Admission:** Priced above.
>
> **Ages:** 4 years and up.

## LASER QUEST

(714) 449-0555 $$$

*229 East Orangethorpe Avenue, Fullerton*

(Exit Riverside Fwy [91] N. on Harbor Blvd., R. on Orangethorpe Ave.)

This large arena, with gothic decor, sets the stage for an exciting game of laser tag. Armed with laser guns, and vests with target lights, enter the multi-level maze. Amid the strobe lights, partitions, and loud music, race against the clock to "tag" the opposing team members with laser shots, and score. The fifteen-minute games are fast-paced, and leave you either tired or fired up to play another round! The lounge has video games.

**Hours:** Open Mon. - Thurs., 6pm - 10pm; Fri., 4pm - midnight; Sat., noon - midnight; Sun., noon - 10pm. Open extended hours in the summer.

**Admission:** $7 per game

**Ages:** 5 years and up.

## PALACE PARK

(949) 559-8336

*3405 Michelson Drive, Irvine*

(Exit San Diego Fwy [405] S. on Culver Dr., R. on Michelson. Or, exit San Diego Fwy [405] S. on Jamboree, L. on Michelson.)

This pink palace, which can be seen from the freeway, is definitely a kids' kingdom. There is an almost overwhelming amount of video and arcade games, or, to quote my boys, "Wow!" There is also a ticket redemption center and an Express McDonald's Restaurant. The **simulator** ride offers different adventures for $4 each. Riders must be at least 42" tall. Also inside the castle walls are activities for the younger set, such as kiddie arcade games; **Palace Playland**, which is a two-tiered, soft play area with soft-play mazes, ball pits, tunnels, and slides - $3.50 for all-day play for kids 12 years and under; and **Palace Bouncer**, a castle bounce - $1 for kids under 60".

Outside, are three, terrific, themed **miniature golf** courses with windmills, castles, houses, and other buildings - $6 a round for adults, children 4 years and under are free. Splash Island **bumper boats** are $3.50 a ride, $1 for additional riders and riders must be over 44" tall. I allowed my 11-year old to steer the boat and he did so gleefully - right under the fountain's waters. Oh, the joy of spending time together! The **Slick car race track** is $5 a ride, $1 for additional riders. Drivers must be 60" or taller and riders must be over 44" tall. **Go-carts,** where drivers can be minimum 44" tall, are $3.75 per ride, $1 for additional riders. **Bumper cars** are $2 a bump, I mean ride. **Batting cages** are here, too. In **Laser Storm**, you and your at least 5-year-old child (personal recommendation) enter a darkened, maze-like room with walls that are three-feet high and lit by fluorescent markings. For ten minutes you'll engage in laser tag, which entails alternately safeguarding your base while shooting at the players on the opposing team. It's a blast. The cost is $5 per game.

If the urge strikes, next door is the Irvine Recreation Center with plenty of bowling lanes.

**Hours:** Open Sun. - Thurs., 10am - 11pm; Fri. - Sat., 10am - 1am. Hours may fluctuate.

**Admission:** Attractions are individually priced above or purchase a pass for three attractions and eight tokens for $12, or four attractions and sixteen tokens for $15.

**Ages:** 2 years and up.

## PLANET KIDS (Fountain Valley)

(714) 378-8733 / www.planet-kids.com

*18081 Magnolia St., Fountain Valley*                                    ▦
(Going S. on San Diego Fwy [405], exit S. on Magnolia St. Going N. on 405, exit N. on
Euclid St., L. on Talbert Ave., L. on Magnolia. It's on the corner of Magnolia and
Talbert.)
    See PLANET KIDS (Laguna Hills) for details.

## PLANET KIDS (Laguna Hills)                                         ☼
(949) 831-3500 / www.planet-kids.com                                   $$
*26538 Moulton Parkway, Laguna Hills*                                   ▦
(Exit San Diego Fwy [5] S.W. on La Paz Rd., R. on Moulton Pky. It's in a shopping
center.)

    Bring your earthling offspring to Planet Kids for indoor fun that is out of
this world! Adventure Crater is the main play structure, where kids will run
orbits around you. It has a wooden walkway all around, padded slides, tube
slides, and a ball pit. Go through the tunnel under crater rock and peek out the
windows into a desert diorama.

    The Globe Theater has costumes and karaoke for your budding star. It also
shows (mostly Disney) movies. Nintendo games are featured in the Galactic
Games room - no tokens needed. Mission Control is a space-like shuttle room,
with most of the few computers programmed with educational games that
intrigue ages 5 - 95 years old. Take "pictures" in the Eclipse room against a
photo-sensitive wall as the strobe-like light flashes.

    You'll hear the "music" (i.e. loud noises) before you actually enter the
Lunar Tunes room. For band member "wannabes," or for kids who like to play
with drums and other instruments, this is the place to be. A floor piano has keys
that light up when stepped (or jumped) on (as in the movie *Big*). Another cosmic
component in here is the individual rooms; one contains electric drums, another
has a synthesizer, and a third has karaoke equipment.

    The Tot Spot, designed for kids five years and under, has a complete little
beach area and a climbing play structure with a ball pit and soft foam animals. It
also has a mini-schoolhouse room with toys, books, and a computer.

    The snack bar has food ranging from pizza and soft pretzels to chef salad
and baked potatoes. If you have places to go and things to do (and want to do it
ten times faster without your kids), check into the Blast-Off program. It enables
parents to enroll their children, ages 5 - 13, to stay here for up to four hours of
supervised play. Note: Socks are required in all play areas.

    **Hours:**    Open Wed. - Thurs., 11am - 7pm; Fri., 11am - 9pm; Sat., 10am -
                9pm; Sun., 10am - 7pm. Closed Mon. and Tues.
**Admission:**    $5.95 for ages 1 - 3; $8.95 for ages 4 - 17. Adults play for free
                with a paid child's admission.
      **Ages:**    1½ - 13 years.

## PLANET KIDS (Orange)                                               ☼
(714) 288-4090 / www.planet-kids.com                                   $$
*1536 E. Katella Avenue, Orange*                                       ▦
(Exit Costa Mesa Fwy [55] W. on Katella Ave.)

See PLANET KIDS (Laguna Hills) for details. This location shows signs of being well loved.

## ROCKREATION (Costa Mesa)

(714) 556-ROCK (7625) / www.rockreation.com
*1300 Logan Avenue, Costa Mesa*
(Exit San Diego Fwy |405| S. on Fairview Rd., R. on Baker St., L. on McClintock Wy., R. on Logan Ave.)

$$$$

Get the kids geared up - it's time to *rock* and roll at Rockreation! This huge indoor warehouse/rock climbing gym is a great place for beginners to learn climbing techniques in a safe and controlled environment. It also provides enough rocky terrain for serious climbers to train. The multi-colored rocks of various shapes and sizes jut out from the twenty-seven-foot geometrical walls for handholds and footholds, offering over 150 different climbing routes. Some of the walls are straight up and down, others have slight inclines, while still others have very challenging angles and overhangs. Belayers, those who hold the rope so if you slip you don't fall, are provided at the kids' climbs and for adults who need a climbing buddy. Even if you were to hit rock bottom (which you won't), it's "carpeted" with black foam padding. Kids warm up using a short practice wall. Although my boys were a bit intimidated at first, by the end of our time here, they were really climbing the walls - all the way to the top. Enroll your child in a summer camp or one of the year-round classes offered for various levels and ages. Hang out with your kids here, or better yet, tell them to go climb a rock! Also see ROCKREATION (Los Angeles).

**Hours:**    The gym is open Mon. - Thurs., noon - 10pm; Fri., noon - 9pm; Sat. - Sun., 10am - 7pm. Kids Climb, for ages 6 - 12, is offered Tues. and Thurs., 6pm - 8pm; Sat. - Sun., 3pm - 5pm.

**Admission:**    $15 for the Kids Climb. Reservations are required. Kids may climb here on other days for $10, as long as they bring a belayer. Equipment rental - shoes, harness, and chalk - is an additional $5. An adult day pass is $15.

**Ages:**    Depending on your child's agility - 5 years and up.

## SOUTHLAND HILLS GOLFLAND AND PIZZA

(714) 895-4550
*12611 Beach Boulevard, Stanton*
(Exit Santa Ana Fwy |5| S. on Beach. Or, exit Garden Grove Fwy |22| N. on Beach.)

$$$

*Fore*tunately for miniature golf lovers, Southland Hills has two great courses enhanced by a scaled down windmill, pagoda, fort, etc. - $6 for adults; $4 for seniors; $5 for ages 11 and under. There are also video arcades, a redemption center, and a snack bar that serves pizza and other food. Monday night, after 5pm, is family night, when everyone can play miniature golf for only $4 a round.

**Hours:**    Sun. - Thurs., 10am - 11pm; Fri. - Sat., 10am - midnight.

**Admission:**    Prices are listed above.

**Ages:**    4 years and up.

## VIDEO RACING LEAGUES OF AMERICA

(949) 362-1300

*27792 Aliso Creek Road, Unit B-120, Aliso Viejo*

(Exit San Diego Fwy [5] W. on Aliso Parkway, R. on Aliso Creek Rd. The cross street is Liberty. It's in the corner mall of Windrose Plaza.)

Gentlemen (and ladies), start your engines! This storefront play area, done in racing car decor, offers a lot of vroom for your money. The main attraction is the eight virtual reality race car stations where you'll enjoy the thrill of racing, without the danger. Choosing from six different tracks, climb into the driver's seat, grip the steering wheel, and, while using either automatic or gear shift, put the pedal to the metal. Watch out for the curves! Players can either race against each other, so teams are encouraged to complete in Daytona tournaments, or race against the computer's virtual drivers. Other games can be played on VRLA's two computers and Sony Playstation at no extra charge. There are also a few wireless cars to race around and a few books and puzzles. This place is just as popular with adults as it is with kids. Ask about their party packages and special events.

**Hours:**   Open daily 11am - 9pm, although it might be closed for special bookings.

**Admission:**   Prices vary greatly depending on the date, time, and specials offered. The average race costs between 50¢ to $1.

**Ages:**   5 years and up.

## ADAMS KART TRACK

(909) 686-3826                                                           *$$$$*

*5292 Bell Avenue, Riverside*

(Exit Pomona Fwy [60] N. on Market. It's on the corner of 24th St. and Market.)

The main track, which is six-tenths of a mile of turns, twists, and straight track, is a great introduction to real racing. This race track school offers classes for kart racing, available for kids 5 years and up. Call for a class schedule.

**Hours:**   The track is open Mon. - Wed., 10am - 5pm; Thurs. - Fri., 10am - 9pm; Sat. - Sun., noon - 5pm.

**Admission:**   Bring your own kart for the main track - $25 a day for non-members; $20 for members; $20 for an extra passenger; $8 for spectators. Classes start at $125 for four hours of instruction and racing.

**Ages:**   5 years and up.

## FIREWORKS FAMILY FUN

(909) 222-4777                                                          *$$$*

*12125 Day Street, Moreno Valley*

(Exit Moreno Valley Fwy [60] N. on Day St. It's in the Canyon Swings Plaza.)

Make sparks fly at Fireworks Family Fun! The two, *tee*rific, nine-hole **miniature golf** courses are $3.25 for adults, $2.75 for ages 6 to 11, children 5 years and under are free. (Note that additional games are only $1). **Go karts** are

$3.50 for a five-minute ride with a 57" height requirement to drive; $1 for an additional passenger. **Bumper boats** are $3 a ride with a 47" height requirement for drivers; $1 for an additional passenger. Enter the dark and foggy room to play **Laser Tag.** $5 will buy you eight minutes of adrenaline pumping fun of shooting laser guns at your opponents while trying to avoid getting hit! What fun center could call itself complete without a myriad of arcade games to entice your kids?! Fireworks has 10,000 square feet of such games (i.e. a lot!).

| | |
|---|---|
| **Hours:** | Open Sun. - Thurs., noon - 10pm; Fri. - Sat., noon - midnight. Call first as hours may vary. |
| **Admission:** | Attractions are individually priced above. Ask if their Monday night family special is still on - $25 for a family of 5 to play one of each attraction. |
| **Ages:** | 4 years and up. |

## S.C. VILLAGE PAINTBALL GAMES

(949) 489-9000 / www.scvillage.com

*Hellman, Corona*

(Exit Riverside Fwy [91] N. on Lincoln Blvd., L. on River Rd. It's on the "corner" of Hellman and River Rd.)

Rambos, Terminators, Xenas, and people from all other walks of life are invited to play paintball on this massive, sixty-acre playing field with eleven different settings. Battle it out in desert terrain, jungle tracts, or even in the city of Beirut. Each field has special props which may include a downed helicopter, ambulance, tents, tanks, radar towers, huts, bridges, tunnels, swamp, camouflage netting, and acres of woods or brush. In this updated version of Capture the Flag, paintball guns and non-toxic gelatin capsules (i.e. paintballs) are used. Two teams compete against each other using the props to run around and hide behind. The object of the game is to somehow capture your opponents' flag and return it to your team's flag station. However, if you are hit with a paintball (which can sting), you are out of the game. Games last between twenty to thirty minutes. All games have referees to insure safe and fair play. There are two levels of play - beginner and advanced. Come by yourself or with a group of friends. All amenities, including a food concession, equipment, and supplies are on-site.

| | |
|---|---|
| **Hours:** | Open to the public Sat. - Sun., 7:30am - 4pm. Weekday games are by appointment only. |
| **Admission:** | General admission is $20 per person for half day; $25 for all day. Rental equipment varies in price according to what you want. Goggles/face masks (mandatory) are $5; jumpsuits are $7; guns range from $10 - $15; paintballs start at $6 for 100 rounds; etc. Package deals are available. For instance, a $42 starter package includes half day admission, full mask, pump rifle, 100 rounds of paintball, four $CO_2$ cartridges, and ten paint holders. |
| **Ages:** | At least 10 years old. Kids 10 - 17 years old need parental consent. |

## FAMILY FUN CENTER (Upland)

(909) 985-1313

*1500 West 7ʰ Street, Upland*

(Exit the San Bernardino Fwy [10] N. at either Central or Mountain. You can see it from the freeway.)

Upland Family Fun Center offers fun for everyone in your family! This giant fun center has four, themed **miniature golf** courses. Two of them are indoor, so rainy days won't put a damper on your swing. Prices are $5.75 a round for adults, $3.75 for children 12 years and under. Take a spin on a **go kart** at $4.25 a ride (no sandals allowed) - drivers must be over 57". An additional passenger under this height is $1.50. **Bumperboats** are always fun - $3.50 for kids over 44", $1.50 for riders under this height. There are eight **kiddie rides** here, including a Ferris wheel, roller coaster, mini-airplanes, moonbounce, and soft play area. Each ride or attraction costs three to five tickets. Tickets cost $6 for a book of twenty-four; $10 for a book of forty-four; and $20 for a book of 104. Kids can also practice for the big league at the **batting cages,** or play at the over 100 video and arcade games.

If you've worked up an appetite, BULLWINKLE'S FAMILY RESTAURANT (see the Edible Adventures section for more info on this restaurant), (909) 946-9555, is right next door. Your choice of hamburgers, pizza, chicken, or ribs is served in a fun atmosphere, where there are more arcade games to play. (There is no escape from them.)

**Hours:**    Miniature golf and the arcades are open Mon. - Fri. from 10am - 11pm. The other attractions are open Mon. - Fri., noon - 9pm. All attractions are open Sat. - Sun. from 10am - 11pm. Family Fun is open extended hours during the summer.

**Admission:**    Attractions are individually priced above, or purchase an all-day pass which includes unlimited use of everything, except the arcade games; $17.50 for 58" and taller; $13.50 for 57" and under. The pass is only offered on Fri. after 5pm and all day Sat., Sun., and on holidays. Ask about its daily availability during the summer.

**Ages:**    3 years and up.

## FIESTA VILLAGE

(909) 824-1111

*1405 E. Washington Street, Colton*

(Exit Moreno Valley Fwy [215] E. on Washington.)

Come party at Fiesta Village! There are two, Western-motif **miniature golf** courses - $5 for adults, $4.50 for children 12 years and under; **go karts**, where drivers must be at least 53" tall - $4.50 for a five-minute ride; **batting cages**; **laser tag** - $4.50 for seven minutes of action-packed fun; **bumper cars** - $3.50; and three **waterslides** with a lounging area for spectators - $6 for an all-day pass for ages 4 years and up; $2 for a spectator. Note: There isn't any pool here, just slides. Video arcades and a snack bar are in the lobby.

The Great Gatsby restaurant is adjacent to Fiesta Village, offering pizza, salads, sandwiches, and ice-cream. If you're in the mood to play, there are video and arcade games, air hockey, and a pool table in here.

**Hours:** The dry land activities are open Sun. - Thurs., 10am - 10pm; Fri. - Sat., 10am - 11pm. The waterslides are open weekends only in May and September from 11am - 5pm, and daily in the summer from noon - 6pm.

**Admission:** Attractions priced above.

**Ages:** 4 years and up.

## MULLIGAN FAMILY FUN CENTER (Murrieta)          ☼

(909) 696-9696                                                              $$$
*24950 Madison Avenue, Murrieta*                                            ⛟
(Exit Temecula Valley Fwy [15] W. on Murrieta Hot Springs Rd., R. on Madison Ave.)

Calling all ranch hands: Git along to Mulligan Family Fun Center for some family fun! This western-themed miniature golf center has two impressive **miniature golf** courses. (Note: You can see the red rock boulders, small western buildings, and stagecoaches from the freeway, when you're heading southbound on the I-15.) A round of golf costs $5.50 for ages 11 and up; $4 for 10 years and under. Other attractions include **batting cages**; **bumper boats** - $3.50 for the driver, $1.50 for passengers; **go-karts** - $4 for drivers, $1.50 for passengers; and **kiddie go-karts** - $2.50 for those 40" to 54". Complete your day (or night) on the town by coming in the spacious "town hall," which is done up right fine. First, though, take a look at all the fun props outside, like cowboy mannequins literally hanging around. Inside, the old west motif continues with a jail and kids' saloon (cafe). The cafe serves salads, pizza, hot dogs, chicken strips, and other food essentials. There are also plenty of modern-day shoot out games (i.e. arcade and video games).

**Hours:** Open Mon. - Thurs., 11:30am - 10pm; Fri., 11:30am - 11pm; Sat., 10am - 11pm; Sun., 10am - 10pm. Closed Thanksgiving and Christmas.

**Admission:** Attractions are individually priced above. Unlimited all-day passes are available Mon. - Thurs. for $18 for 56" and taller; $13 for kids under 56". Fri. - Sun. passes are $21 for 56" and taller; $16 for kids under 56".

**Ages:** 3 years and up.

## Q-ZAR (Chino)          ☼

(909) 364-1055                                                              $$$
*5479 Philadelphia Street, Chino*                                           ⛟
(Exit Pomona Fwy [60] N. on S. Central Ave., R. on Philadelphia St.)

The noise level from the action at the video games is the first thing I noticed about Q-Zar. Next, we were briefed on how to play Q-Zar laser tag. Tip: Listen carefully! Although there is the usual set up of two teams playing against each other, and points scored by "shooting" the lights on your opponents vests, gun, or home base, there are also some intricacies of this particular game. For instance, you are given so many shots (and lives) before you must re-energize your gun; after you've been hit your gun tells you it is deactivated, and you cannot hit your opponents for a few seconds; and when your gun is recharging, you can be hit, but temporarily can't retaliate. It gets a bit confusing, but in the heat of the battle, you just run around like crazy anyhow! Q-Zar is definitely ultra high-tech and wildly fun. Games are fifteen minutes long, yet in this massive (4,500 square feet) fluorescent-lit arena, it seems a whole lot longer. Run, duck, hide, point, and shoot - it's time for laser tag!

**Hours:** Open Sun. - Thurs., 10am - midnight; Fri. - Sat., 10am - 1am.

**Admission:** $7 a game. Ask about their "fun packs." One fun pack offers three hours of play and twelve tokens for $19.99.

**Ages:** 5 years and up.

## SCANDIA AMUSEMENT PARK

(909) 390-3092

*1155 S. Wanamaker Avenue, Ontario*

(Exit Ontario Fwy [15] W. on Jurupa, R. on Rockefeller, R. on Wanamaker.)

Vikings might have come to this country just to play at this amusement park! Well, maybe not, but it is a lot of fun and very well kept up. Attractions include two **miniature golf** courses at $5.95 for adults, children 5 years and under play for free; **batting cages;** seventeen **amusement rides** - some for big kids such as a roller coaster, bumper boats, and scrambler, and some for little kids such as a small semi-truck ride around a track, a carousel, and a slide. Tickets cost $1 each or $10.95 for fifteen tickets. Children's rides require one to three tickets; big kids' (or adult) rides require three to six tickets. Arcade games and a snack bar are here, too.

**Hours:** Open in the summer Sun. - Thurs., 10am - midnight; Fri. - Sat. 10am - 1am. Open the rest of the year, Sun. - Thurs., 10am - 10pm; Fri. - Sat., 10am - midnight.

**Admission:** Attractions are individually priced above, or purchase an unlimited pass (excluding arcade games) - $17.95 for 54" and taller; $13.95 for 53" to 37"; $9.95 for kids 36" and under. Inquire about weekday specials.

**Ages:** 3 years and up.

## SCANDIA FAMILY FUN CENTER

(760) 241-4007

*12627 Mariposa Road, Victorville*

(Exit Mojave Fwy [15] E. on Bear Valley Rd.)

Enjoy some high-desert fun at Scandia Family Fun Center. There are two Scandinavian-themed, **miniature golf** courses, with castles, bridges, and other small buildings that add interest - $4.95 for adults, children 5 years and under play for free; **go-karts** and **bumper boats** - $3.95 per ride (height restrictions apply); and **batting cages**. A full-service snack bar, arcade and video games, and

prize redemption center are also here for your enjoyment.
> **Hours:** Open Sun. - Thurs., 10am - 11pm; Fri. - Sat., 10am - midnight.
> **Admission:** Attractions are individually priced above, or buy a pass for $10.95 per person that allows you to play on each attraction once, as well as receive 5 tokens. An unlimited pass is $15.95 per person.
> **Ages:** 4 years and up.

# BELMONT PARK ☼ $$$

(619) 491-2988 - general information; (619) 488-1549 - amusement rides; (619) 488-3110 - The Plunge / e-mail:giant-dipper@worldnet.att.net
*West Mission Bay Drive and West Mission Boulevard, San Diego*
(Exit San Diego Fwy [5] W. on Sea World Dr. and follow the signs to W. Mission Bay Dr.)

Shops and restaurants encircle the ten or so amusement rides at Belmont Park. In the center, is the Giant Dipper Roller Coaster which doesn't have any loops, but has plenty of ups and downs! A replica of the Looff Liberty wooden carousel has horses as well as an ostrich, giraffe, and tiger to ride on. Other amusement rides include bumper cars (drivers must be at least 52"), a Tilt-A-Whirl, and five kiddie rides such as Baja Buggies, Thunder Boats, Submarines, and the Sea Serpent. Rides require between two to five tickets, with tickets costing 75¢ each, or $23.50 for thirty-five tickets. Jumpstart your heart with Trampoline Thing, where you can safely do flips because you're harnessed in - $4 per jumping session. Steer remote-controlled boats around a nifty little harbor, complete with mini docks and houses. Kid-friendly attractions around the perimeter of the rides include virtual reality at Cyber Station, movies at the Venturer Theater, arcade and video games at either Family Arcade or Prime Time, and PIRATE'S COVE, and indoor play area for younger children. (Look under this section for information on the cove.)

While at Belmont Park, take a plunge at The Plunge. This large indoor swimming pool, located on the other side of the movie theater, boasts a beautiful underwater/whale mural, painted by renown marine artist, Wyland. The enclosed pool, kept at 83 degrees, is surrounded by huge windows looking out on palm trees, suggesting a tropical atmosphere. Swim sessions are $2.50 for adults; $2.25 for seniors and children 6 months to 17 years.

Too nice a day to go swimming inside? Go for a dip outside, as the ocean is just a few steps away. The surf and sand, and bike trail on the beach are "shore" to help make your day at the park a good one!
> **Hours:** The stores and restaurants are open daily, usually from 10am - 7pm. In the summer, the rides are open Sun. - Thurs., 11am - 10pm; Fri. - Sat., 11am - 11pm. The rest of the year the rides are open Mon. - Thurs., 11am - 7pm; Fri. - Sun., 11am - 8pm. Call first as hours fluctuate. The Plunge is open daily to the public with swim sessions held at various times.

**Admission:**   Attractions are priced above. Ask about a special deal offered during the week for unlimited kiddie rides plus entrance to Pirate's Cove.

**Ages:**   All

## BOARDWALK

(619) 449-7800
*1286 Fletcher Parkway, El Cajon*
(Going E. on 8 Fwy, exit N. on Johnson Ave., L. on Fletcher Pky. Going W. on 8, go N. on San Vicente Fwy [67] and then immediately exit W. on Broadway, which turns into Fletcher Pky. Going S. on 67, exit W. on Fletcher Pky.)

$$ ☀ \quad SS$$

This Boardwalk is not made of boards, nor is it by the seaside; it is, however, a large indoor amusement center for kids. It's clean with brightly colored games and rides that elicited several, "this is FUN!" comments from my kids. The main attractions are the **carousel** (three tokens), **castle bounce** (three tokens), **bumper cars** (six tokens), **barrel of fun**, which is similar to the teacups ride (three tokens), and **soft play gym** (eight tokens). This two-story soft play area, for kids 60" and under, has balls pits, a mini zip line, slides, and obstacle courses, plus tubes to crawl through. Each token costs 25¢. There are numerous arcade and video games here, as well as fifty, free and 5¢ games. The full-service snack bar offers salads, pizza, pasta, etc., and weekly family deals. Kids meals are $2.25 for a choice of corn dog, chicken nuggets, or pizza, plus fries and a drink. If you feel like scoring more fun, strike out to Parkway Bowl, the connecting bowling alley.

**Hours:**   Open Sun. - Thurs., 11am - 10:30pm; Fri. - Sat., 11am - midnight.

**Admission:**   Attractions are individually priced above. An unlimited play pass is $4.45 Mon. - Thurs., and $5.45 Fri. - Sun. and holidays.

**Ages:**   1½ years - 12.

## FAMILY FUN CENTER (El Cajon)

(619) 593-1155
*1155 Graves Avenue, El Cajon*
(From 8 Fwy, go N. on San Vicente Fwy [67] and then immediately exit at Broadway. At the end of off ramp, turn L. on Graves Ave.)

$$ ☀ \quad SSS$$

Come to this Family Fun Center to play for just an hour, or have fun all day. Green fees pay for two rounds at any of the three nine-hole, themed **miniature golf** courses. Choose Memory Lane (fairy tale motif), Iron Horse (western), and/or Lost Crusade (Egyptian) - $5.75 for adults; $4.50 for seniors and kids 12 years and under. Other attractions include **bumper boats** - $3.50 for adults, $1.50 for passengers (height restrictions apply); **go-karts** - $4.25 for adults, $1.50 for passengers (height restrictions apply); **batting cages**; and the **Kids' County Fair**. The latter is comprised of six rides such as a roller coaster, train ride, Ferris wheel, mini-planes, etc. Each ride costs $1.50, or purchase a book of twenty-four tickets for $6, or forty-four tickets for $10. **Kidopolis** is a multi-level, soft play area with ball pits, slides, and climbing ladders. It's for kids 60"

and under and cost $3.50 for three hours of play. Socks are required. The two-story arcade and video game building is attractively set up. Try virtual reality rides such as skiing the slopes with the Alpine Racer, or jet skiing on Wave Runner. A nickel arcade area is upstairs.

Bullwinkle's Restaurant is also at this fun center and eating here is always a highlight. (See BULLWINKLE'S RESTAURANT under the Edible Adventures section for more tasty details.) Food and fun - what more could you want?!

**Hours:**     Kids' County Fair is open Mon. - Fri., 4pm - 8pm; Sat. - Sun., 10am - 8pm. Other attractions are open Mon. - Thurs., 11am - 10pm; Fri., 11am - 10pm; Sat. - Sun., 11am - 10pm. Hours fluctuate, so please call before you come.

**Admission:** Attractions are individually priced above, or purchase a "pick four," where you may choose any four attractions or rides for $12.50.

**Ages:**      2½ years and up.

## FAMILY FUN CENTER (Escondido)          ☼

(760) 741-1326                                     $$$

*830 Dan Way, Escondido*

(Exit Escondido Fwy [15] E. on Hwy 78, S. on Centre City Pky., R. on Mission Ave., R. on Dan Way.)

This Family Fun Center, just one in a chain of several, is packed with fun activities. The three **miniature golf** courses offer interesting embellishments such as a double-headed dragon, a castle, a windmill, fountains, and miniature housing structures - $5.75 a round for adults; $3.75 for seniors and kids 12 years and under. The **Giant Maze** is an amazing (and confusing) game to play. Purchase a game card, punch the time clock, and then walk/run through the maze, which has numerous partitions and four towers. The object is to find all eight numbers and four letters on your card that are hidden throughout the maze. A game card costs $3.25 per person and average game time is half an hour. The seven rides in **Kiddieland** include a moon bounce, kiddie swing, rocket ship, Ferris wheel, and mini airplanes. Each ride takes four to six tickets costing $6 for twenty-four tickets, $10 for forty-four. Other attractions here are the **batting cages**; **go-karts** - $4.25 per driver (height restrictions apply), $1.50 for passengers under 44"; **bumper boats** - $3.50 (height restrictions apply), $1.50 for passengers under 44"; and video and arcade games. A full-service snack bar is available to take care of the inevitable hunger pangs that kids get when they know food is nearby. If you haven't had enough of kids running around, Chuck E. Cheese is right next door!

**Hours:**     In the summer, Kiddieland is open daily 10am - 8pm. The rest of the attractions are open Sun. - Thurs., 10am - 11pm; Fri. - Sat., 10am - midnight. The rest of the year, Kiddieland is open daily 11am - 6pm. The rest of the attractions are open Sun. - Thurs., 11am - 10pm; Fri. - Sat., 11am - 11pm.

**Admission:**   Attractions are individually priced above. All day/all play passes (not including batting cages and video and arcade games) are $17.50 for 57" and taller; $13.50 for kids under 57". During the school year, the passes can be purchased Fri. after 4pm, or all day Sat., Sun., and on major holidays. They can be purchased daily during the summer.

**Ages:**   2 years and up for Kiddieland; 4 years and up for most of the other attractions.

## FAMILY FUN CENTER (San Diego)

(619) 560-7342

*6999 Clairemont Mesa Boulevard, San Diego*

(Exit Jacob Dekema Fwy [805] E. on Clairemont Mesa Blvd.)

So much fun can be had at just one place! Choose from two, themed **miniature golf** courses: Storybook Land with a castle, Cinderella's pumpkin, the shoe from the old woman who lived in one, etc., or Western Town with a bank, jail, storefront facades, a livery stable, and wagons - $5.75 a round for adults, $3.75 for seniors and children 12 years and under. Other attractions include **go karts** - $4.25 for a five-minute ride, $1.50 for a passenger (height restrictions apply); **Naskarts** - $4.75 per ride (height restrictions apply); **bumper boats** - $3.75 per driver, $1.50 per passenger; **batting cages**; and **Lazer Runner**. This last game is laser tag played inside an inflated, spaceship-looking big bounce. With six to eight players, it's every kid (or adult) for himself/herself. Although this game is played with the usual laser tag equipment of a vest with flashing lights and a laser gun, running around inside a bounce (with obstacles, even!), adds a whole new element of fun. Five minutes of sweaty fun costs $3.75 per person, and players must be at least 5 years old. The **Fun Zone** has seven rides, including teacups, a Ferris wheel, a train ride, a swing, and a fire engine that goes in the air and around and around. Rides cost $2.50 each, or take between four to seven tickets at a cost of $7 for 28 tickets, or $10 for 44. Of course there is a video and arcade game area and a prize redemption center. There is also a separate section for less violent kiddie video games. For those making every nickel count, a special video arcade area has games to play for only 5¢. Fa*moose* Bullwinkle's food is on hand, although it is purchased at a snack bar, not at the usual sit-down restaurant. Ask about group rates and how good grades can translate into free tokens.

**Hours:**   The Fun Zone is open daily in the summer from 10am - 9pm. The rest of the attractions are open daily 10am - midnight. The rest of the year, the Fun Zone is open Fri., 4pm - 9pm; Sat. - Sun., 10am - 10pm. The rest of the attractions are Mon. - Fri., 11am - 11pm; Sat. - Sun., 10am - midnight.

**Admission:**   Attractions are individually priced above. An unlimited pass (except for video and arcade games) costs $21.50 for 57" and over; $17.50 for kids under 57". A "pick four" pass allows you to choose four attractions for $12.50.

**Ages:**   2 years and up.

## FAMILY FUN CENTER (Vista)   ☼

(760) 945-9474   *$$$*

*1525 West Vista Way, Vista*

(Exit 78 Fwy N. on Emerald Ave., R. on W. Vista Way.)

This Family Fun Center really has it all! If you're in a mutinous mood, play the **miniature golf** course with a pirate ship and fountains. If you're feeling rather noble, play King Arthur's course with its huge (relatively speaking) castles and dungeons, and a bridge over water. Golf prices are $5.75 for adults; $3.75 for seniors and kids 12 years and under. **Laser Runner** is an every man/woman/child for himself laser tag game played inside an inflatable battleship bounce. There are soft obstacles to hide behind (or jump on) and even small rooms to run around in. The game is action-packed, sweaty, and fun. The cost is $3.75 for a five-minute game, and children must be 5 years old to play. **Kidopolis** is a huge, four-story soft-play area with slides, obstacle courses, ball pits, tubes and tunnels. This major gerbil run was a major hit with my boys. The cost is $4.95 for kids, who must be 60" or under; two adults can play for free with each paid child's admission. Other attractions here include **batting cages**; **go karts** - $4.25 for drivers, (height restrictions apply), $1.50 for passengers; and **bumper boats** - $3.50 a ride, (height restrictions apply), $1.50 for passengers.

The noisy, but attractive, main two-story building houses numerous video and arcade games. A nickel arcade section is upstairs. Bullwinkle's Restaurant is also here serving up its tasty family fare, along with a fun atmosphere. Rocky and Bullwinkle cartoons play on the television monitors and a spotlight flashes colored lights on a fountain in front of the stage while the water "dances" to the music. (See BULLWINKLE'S RESTAURANT under the Edible Adventures section for more details.)

**Hours:**   Kidopolis is open Mon. - Fri., noon - 8pm; Sat. - Sun., 10am - 8pm. The other attractions are open Mon. - Fri., 11am - 10pm; Sat. - Sun., 10am - 11pm.

**Admission:**   Attractions are individually priced above, or purchase a "pick four" pass which entitles the participant to choose any four attractions for $12.50.

**Ages:**   2 years and up.

## FUN-4-ALL   ☼

(619) 427-1473   *$$$*

*950 Industrial Boulevard, Chula Vista*

(Exit San Diego Fwy [5] E. on "L" St., S. on Industrial Blvd.)

This small, family amusement park has an older, well-used, **miniature golf** course with a nautical theme - $5 a round for adults, $4 for kids 12 years and under; a fun **bumper boat** ride around a few islands - $3.75 per person; **go-karts** - $3.75 (height restrictions apply); and **batting cages**. There are also several video and arcade games inside the main building, and a full-service snack bar.

**Hours:** Open in the summer daily from 9am - midnight. Open the rest of the year daily 10am - 10pm.

**Admission:** Attractions are individually priced above, or play one of every attraction, plus receive a soda, for $12 per person.

**Ages:** 4 years and up.

## HIDDEN VALLEY PAINTBALL
(760) 737-8870 / www.mrpaintball.com                         $$$$$
*Lake Wohlford Road, Escondido*
(Going N. on Escondido Fwy [15], exit E. on Via Rancho Pky, which turns into Bear Valley, R. Valley Center Parkway, R. on Lake Wohlford Rd. Drive about 2.2 miles to the top of road, the entrance is on left.)

Armed with a semi-automatic paint gun and dressed in mask, goggles, and layers of clothing (to reduce the somewhat painful impact of the paintballs), you are now ready to play the wildly exhilarating and intense game of paintball. Teams are pitted against while running around the 100-acre outside playing area where hills, valleys, and trees are used for both offensive and defensive tactical maneuvers. Games last between fifteen to thirty minutes. Bring running shoes, a water bottle, lunch, and most of all - stamina.

**Hours:** Open daily from 8am - 5pm.

**Admission:** $45 for all-day play includes camouflage clothing, a semi-automatic marker, full face and head protection, all-day supply air for your gun, and 200 paintballs. Other equipment is also available for rent.

**Ages:** 8 years and up.

## PIRATE'S COVE
(619) 539-7474 / e-mail:giant-dipper@worldnet.att.net        $$
*West Mission Bay Drive and West Mission Boulevard, San Diego*
(Exit San Diego Fwy [5] W. on Sea World Dr. and follow the signs to W. Mission Bay Dr.)

At one end of BELMONT PARK (look under this section for more information) there are two buildings with wonderful pirate murals that comprise an indoor family playland called **Pirate's Cove.** One building has air hockey, a few video games, and kiddie rides. Downstairs, is an underground cave-like tunnel that connects the two Cove buildings. This second building, with costumed pirate mannequins, is where most of the swashbuckling action takes place. Here are the ball pits, soft play areas, obstacle courses, and big plastic tunnels and tubes that your mateys dream of! There is also a separate area for younger buccaneers to pillage, I mean play on. Note: Socks are required at Pirate's Cove.

**Hours:** Open in the summer Sun. - Thurs., 10am - 9pm; Fri. - Sat., 10am - 10pm. Open the rest of the year Mon. - Thurs., 10am - 7pm; Fri. - Sun., 10am - 9pm. Call first as hours fluctuate.

**Admission:** $6.50 for ages 3 to 12; $4.50 for children 2 years and under; two parents can play for free for each paying child. Note: If you come play here for just the last hour, admission is $3 per child. Ask about combo prices for Pirate's Cove and the kiddie rides at Belmont Park.

**Ages:** 6 months - 12 years.

# ROLLERSKATELAND AND LASER STORM ☀

(619) 562-3791                                                                                      $$

*9365 Mission Gorge Road, Santee*                                                    ♨

(Going N. on San Vicente Fwy [67], exit W. on Prospect Ave., R. on Cuyamaca St., L. on Mission Gorge Rd. Going S. on 67, exit W. on Woodside Ave., which turns into Mission Gorge Rd. Going E. on Fwy 52, go to the end, go E. on Mission Gorge Rd. It's behind Jack-in-the-Box.)

Take two opposing teams, arm them with vests and laser phasers, let them loose in a darkened arena with neon-colored partitions, and let the games begin! A dividing line separates the teams. When you shoot the "enemy," you deactivate their phaser. They have to go to the energy pod and reactivate it to get back into the game. Of course, if you get hit, you must do the same thing. A scoreboard keeps track of which team is ahead, and which team ultimately wins. Each exciting game lasts for about ten minutes. But just like potato chips, it's hard to stop at just one (game).

Roller skating is a separate activity from laser tag. Call for skate sessions.

**Hours:** Laser Storm is open Thurs., 6pm - 10pm; Fri., 6pm - 11pm; Sat., 10:30am - 11pm; Sun., 1:30pm - 7pm. Call for extended summer hours. To call to reserve the arena at other times and dates you must have at least eight players. Call for skate sessions.

**Admission:** Laser Storm costs $3.50 for the first game; $2.50 for additional games. Skate sessions vary in cost depending on the date and time. In-line skate rentals are an additional $3.

**Ages:** 5 years and up.

# SOLID ROCK (Poway) ☼

(619) 299-1124 / www.solidrockgym.com                                          $$$$

*13026 Stowe Drive, Poway*                                                          ♨

(Exit Escondido Fwy [15] E. on Poway Rd., R. on Pomerado Rd., L. on Stowe.)

See SOLID ROCK (San Diego) for details.

# SOLID ROCK (San Diego) ☼

(619) 299-1124 / www.solidrockgym.com                                          $$$$

*2074 Hancock Street, San Diego*

(Going S. on San Diego Fwy [5], exit at Old Town Ave., off the off ramp onto Hancock St. Going N. on 5, exit at Moore St., L. on Old Town Ave, L. on Hancock St.)

Experience the thrill and physical challenge (i.e. you'll get sweaty) of rock climbing in a safe, indoor, controlled atmosphere. Novice climbers can learn the basic skills and importance of a well-placed foot and/or hand, while experienced climbers will enjoy the opportunity to continue training by sharpening their skills. This is a great sport to introduce kids to because it builds confidence, physical fitness, and strategic thinking. (All this just by rock climbing - and we thought school was important!) Staff members are experienced climbers and are always around to instruct and encourage.

Multi-colored stones mark various routes on the walls, overhangs, and the bouldering cave. Although a child may be tentative at the beginning, by the end of the first session, he/she is usually literally climbing the walls, and having a great time doing it. So, if you're looking for a creative way to channel your child's excess energy, turn off the cartoons and come *rock* and roll on Saturday mornings! Note: Kids' Climb is open to all ages, however, parents of climbers 8 years and under are required to stay and work with their children. A party room is on the premises.

**Hours:** Solid Rock is open Mon. - Fri., 11am - 10pm; Sat., 9am - 9pm; Sun., 11am - 7pm. Kids Climb hours are Sat., 9am - 1pm; Sun., 3pm - 7pm. They are welcome to climb here at other times, but they need an adult who can belay them.

**Admission:** Kids Climb is $15 for non-members, $10 for members. It includes 4 hours of climbing, staff supervision, and all rental equipment. Climbing at the Rock costs $10, Mon. - Fri. before 5pm; $12, Mon. - Fri. between 5pm - 10pm, all day Sat., or all day Sun. You will need to bring a partner or belayer for climbing; bouldering you can do on your own. Full package rentals - shoes, harness, and chalk bag - is $6. Kids 16 years and under cost $10 a day, plus $3 for a harness. They need to wear tennis shoes and bring a partner to belay them.

**Ages:** 4 years and up.

# SURF AND TURF

(619) 481-0363

$$

*15555 Jimmy Durante Boulevard, Del Mar*

(Exit San Diego Fwy [5] W. on Via de la Valle, L. on Jimmy Durante Blvd.)

Next to this driving range are two, eighteen-hole, miniature golf courses. The courses are not as elaborately embellished as others we have played at, but there are enough mini structures, and twists and turns, to keep them interesting and fun. Note: Older kids might want to try out a bigger back swing at the driving range.

**Hours:** Open daily 7am - 9pm.

**Admission:** $4 for ages 3 and up - for as many rounds as you want to play.

**Ages:** 4 years and up.

# ULTRAZONE (San Diego)

(619) 221-0100 / www.playultrazone.com

$$$

*3146 Sports Arena Boulevard, San Diego*

(Going W. on Ocean Beach Fwy [8], exit before the end of the freeway S. on Midway Dr. / Mission Bay Dr., L. on Sports Arena Blvd.)

Come play laser tag - the tag of the future! Put on your vest, pick up your laser gun, and for fifteen minutes you'll play hard and fast. Laser tag is action-packed, and the thrill of the chase really gets your adrenaline pumping! This Ultrazone, with its dark, cave-like setting, is themed "Underground City." The multi-level city, or playing arena, is huge. Run up and down ramps; seek cover behind floor-to-ceiling walls; duck into partly-hidden doorways; and zap your opponents. Tip: The best time for younger kids to play is weekday afternoons and early evenings, or during the day on weekends. Older kids come out here in hordes at nighttime. See ULTRAZONE (Sherman Oaks) for more of a description.

**Hours:** Open Mon. - Thurs., 4pm - 11pm; Fri., 2pm - 2am; Sat., 11am - 2am; Sun., 10am - 11pm. Summer hours are Sun. - Thurs., 10am - 10pm; Fri. - Sat., 10am - midnight.

**Admission:** $6.50 a game. Sat. and Sun. from opening until 2pm is Kids Zone, where kids 11 years and under pay $5 per game.

**Ages:** 6 years and up.

# VERTICAL HOLD SPORT CLIMBING CENTER, INC. ☼
*$$$$*

(619) 586-7572 / www.verticalhold.com

*9580 Distribution Avenue, San Diego*

(Exit Jacob Dekema Fwy [805] E. on Miramar Rd., L. on Distribution Ave. Or, exit Escondido Fwy [15] W. on Miramar Rd., R. on Distribution Ave.)

Indoor rock climbing is rapidly becoming one of the fastest growing indoor sports in America. This physically challenging and mentally stimulating activity is a great way to redirect a child growing up in our couch potato/video game society. Vertical Hold has over 150 routes that are changed every few months. Climb vertical walls (of course!), overhangs, and chimney routes, or try your hand (and feet) at bouldering. At this rock climbing center, you need to bring your own belayer (i.e. the person who stays on the ground attached to your rope so if you should slip or fall, you won't fall far). So, in order for your child to climb or participate in the Kids' Climb, you or someone you bring with you, must be a certified belayer. Call about signing up for a belaying class, as well as a climbing class. Don't just crawl out from under a rock - go climb it!

**Hours:** Open Mon. - Fri., 11:30am - 10pm; Sat., 10am - 9pm; Sun., 10am - 8pm. Kids Climb is any three-hour time period on the weekends. Kids are welcome to climb at any other time, too, at the regular rate.

**Admission:** There are various fee structures to choose from. Weekend Kids Climb is $12 per child, which includes equipment rental. For those (adults or children) with their own equipment - $12 a day; $95 for 10 visits; or $6 per visit at lunchtime (between 11:30am - 1:30pm). Otherwise, it's $18 a day with equipment rental of a harness, rope, shoes, and chalk included in this price.

**Ages:** 5 years and up.

## VISTA ENTERTAINMENT CENTER / LASER STORM

(760) 941-1032  $$
*435 West Vista Way, Vista*
(Exit 78 Fwy N. on Melrose Dr., R. on W. Vista Wy.)

(Laser) lights! Action! Laser Storm is a quick, action-packed game of laser tag. The arena is designed with cardboard hanging partitions painted with neon-colored "gak" splats. There are no solid walls to hide behind, so you need to be constantly on your guard and ready to fire. The ten-minute games, played nearly in the dark, are played by shooting laser guns at the opposite team members' vests and/or at their base, to score points. When you are hit - not "if" because you will get hit - you'll be unable to shoot for just a few seconds while you are being recharged. Laser Storm might not be as elaborately set-up as other laser tag places, but it is less expensive and a lot of fun!

Score more fun when you bowl in the lanes just outside the Laser Storm doors. The Entertainment Center has a large bowling alley, a small video games room, a full-service snack bar, and a nice-sized nursery/childcare room.

**Hours:** Laser Storm is open Mon. - Tues. and Thurs., 6pm - 10pm; Fri., 6pm - midnight; Sat. - Sun., noon - 10pm. Hours do fluctuate. Call for open bowling times.

**Admission:** Call for a schedule of prices for Laser Storm. Costs vary from $1 per game on Dollarmania nights, to $3 per game, to $10 for a whole night of fun called "Fire Til' You Tire."

**Ages:** 5 years and up.

## WEEKEND WARRIORS

(619) 445-1217 / www.paintballfield.com  $$$$$
*25 Browns Road on the Viejas Indian Reservation, Alpine*
(Exit Interstate 8 N. on Willows, R. on Browns Rd.)

True to its name, you look like (and probably feel like) a warrior in this game of paintball. Suited up with a full, wrap-around face shield and a paint ball gun (and maybe even some camouflage clothing), you are ready to play a combination of Tag, Hide-and-Go-Seek, and Capture the Flag, at one of twelve outdoor "battlefields." Moving stealthily through the trees, using rocks as covers, you spy an opponent, then pull the trigger, and splat - he/she has been tagged (ouch!) with a paint ball and is out of the game. (Realize that this can happen to you, also.) Each game lasts about fifteen minutes. Strategizing and staying focused are key elements. (Oh yea, and having fun, too.) Your admission fee includes all day play, which is about fifteen games, and one tank of $CO_2$. Wear dark clothing that you don't care much about, and expect it to get very dirty. Ask about kids-only events. Tip: Paint ball is a great way to burn calories! Note: Next to the field is a full-service grocery store, two restaurants, and an R.V. park with a pool, showers, and Jacuzzi.

**Hours:** Open Sat. - Sun. from 8am - 4:30pm, and certain school holidays.

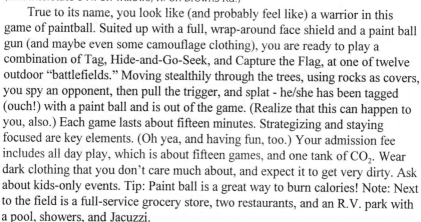

**Admission:** $20 field entrance fee per person. Gun rentals range from $10 - $15 and include a tank of $CO_2$, and full face shields. Paintballs cost $7 per 100. Spectators are $3. Prepaid groups of ten or more save a lot of money on entrance and rental equipment.

**Ages:** As young as 10 years old with a parent; 12 years and up on their own.

## WILD WOODY'S ADVENTURES IN PAINTBALL

(760) 941-0230 - reservations; (760) 765-1023 - field

*Highway 78, Julian*

(On Hwy 78, head 5 miles east past the town of Julian. The field is on the left hand side.)

$$$$$

      A simple explanation of paintball is that two opposing teams compete at a game similar to Capture the Flag. Add paintballs, however, a paintball gun (or marker), camouflage clothing, goggles, face mask, adrenaline, and 140 acres (six different fields) of shaded forest fields and hilly terrain, and this simple description takes on a whole new meaning. This intense game of hunter and the hunted is played while your heart is beating wildly, both from exhilaration and physical exertion. If you are hit with a paintball (splat), you are out of the game. A game is won when a player successfully returns the opponent's flag to his own team's flag station. Games usually last about twenty minutes, so six to ten games can be played in any given day. All games are refereed to insure player safety, and fair play. Tip: Wear pants, shoes with traction, and multiple layers of clothing to pad the sting of getting hit. Note: There is a campground one mile down the road from the paintball field. Overnight camping is $4 per person, or only $3 if you are a paintball player. Amenities include showers, full hook ups, barbecue pits, and a general store.

**Hours:** Open to the public Sat. - Sun. from 8am - 4:30pm. Open Mon. - Fri. for group play only.

**Admission:** $25 - $40 per day, depending on the type of equipment you want. A semi-automatic rifle is $20, 200 paintballs are $10, etc.

**Ages:** 12 - 17 year olds can play with prior arrangement. Children as young as 10 years old can play at kids' events and special games.

## CLUB DISNEY (Thousand Oaks)

(888) CLUB DIS (258-2347) or (805) 777-8000 / www.clubdisney.com

*120 South Westlake Boulevard, Thousand Oaks*

(Exit Ventura Fwy [101] N. on Westlake Blvd. It's on the corner of Westlake Blvd. and Thousand Oaks Blvd. in Westlake Village shopping center.)

$$$

      The name "Disney" is synonymous with "family fun." Club Disney, an indoor play site with lots of (Disney) character appeal, lives up to its namesake. Younger children can "plant" plastic carrots in the holes in Rabbit's garden, crawl through a log, or cuddle up with stuffed Tiggers for a honey of a storytime at Pooh 'N You. Goofy's game area offers no-tokens-needed games such as Duck-a-Puck (air hockey with Mighty Duck figures popping up to block your shot) and a giant board maze game. The Jungle Climber is a green-carpeted, multi-level climbing structure that kids can climb up, then use the slides to come down. Mickey's Circus is a toddlers' area with soft play blocks, a small merry-go-round, and a scale circus train to climb aboard. Applaudeville Theater features your children dancing with Mickey and Donald, interacting in an animated story time, or starring in a fashion show. The Mouse Pad has sixteen computer stations with educational games that challenges ages 3 to 103. In Animation Alley kids can use toy figures and computers to make their own stop motion animation film. Character Creations offers half-hour art classes. It gives children (and adults) the opportunity to actually learn about art as well as make their own *mouse*terpiece! A small, mirrored maze room is maddeningly fun to walk through.

Upstairs, Merlin performs magic shows throughout the day; a small room for adults only allows parents to relax on a couch or surf the Internet; and a mini-science station offers carnival-type distortion mirrors, a voice changer that makes you sound like a chipmunk or Darth Vader, and a photosensitive wall that will take your (temporary) picture, and more.

Club Disney also offers delicious Mickey Mouse-shaped food in their Club Cafe. The menu includes personal pizzas ($3.75), a bagel with cream cheese ($1.25), chicken strips with dip and fries ($3.50), and a to-die-for raspberry streusel ($2.75). Remember, you must wear socks to play inside the second happiest place on earth. And yes, of course, there is a gift shop! Also see CLUB DISNEY (West Covina).

> **Hours:**    Open Tues. - Wed. and Sun., 10am - 7pm; Thurs. - Sat., 10am -
> 8pm. Open in the summer one hour later. It's usually open on
> holiday Mon.
>
> **Admission:**  $8 per person for ages 2 years and up. Adults must be
> accompanied by a child.
>
> **Ages:**  1 - 14 years old.

## GOLF 'N STUFF    ☼

(805) 644-7132    *$$$*
*5555 Walker Drive, Ventura*    ⬛
(Exit Ventura Fwy |101| N. on Victoria Ave., take a quick L. on Walker St. The Golf 'N Stuff sign is visible from the freeway.)

If you and the kids are in the mood for a little golf 'n stuff, here's the place for you. There are two, **miniature golf** courses with windmills, a tower, and other fanciful buildings, to putt around on at $6 per round for adults; $5 for seniors; children 5 years and under play for free. **Indy cars** have a height requirement of 52", while **bumper cars** and **water boats** both have height requirements of 48". The cost per ride for any one of these three rides is $5. Inside, there are arcade games and a snack bar.

> **Hours:**    Open Sun. - Thurs., 10am - 11pm; Fri. - Sat., 10am - 1am.

**Admission:** Attractions are individually priced above or buy a pass that includes four rides, a round of miniature golf, and four arcade tokens for $15 per person.

**Ages:** 4 years and up.

## LAZERSTAR (Oxnard)

(805) 983-0333 / www.lazerstar.com        *$$$*

*921 E. Ventura Boulevard, Oxnard*

(Exit Ventura Fwy [101] N. on Rose Ave. and make an immediate L. on Ventura Blvd., which parallels the freeway.)

Reach for the stars at Lazerstar, a galactic adventure in laser tag. The entrance hallway is decorated with a moon and planets mural. The large, noisy, dark lobby has numerous video games, including virtual reality games (e.g. skateboarding, alpine racer, etc.), and arcade games, such as Wack-A-Mole and skee ball, along with a prize redemption center. The stool seats are on big, black coils, adding to the other-worldly atmosphere. A few smaller rooms, branching off the main lobby, are for eating or for hosting a party. The full-service snack bar sells hot dogs, pizza, etc.

Two teams, of up to twenty individuals each, compete against each other armed with laser guns and a lighted vest. The foggy arena, illuminated only by black lights, has ceiling, walls, and barriers that are painted with fluorescent markings and space-related murals. Because the arena is so large (over 5,000 square feet), with numerous obstacles, expect to run around a lot during your fifteen-minute game. Stalk, dodge, hide, and fire laser beams in an effort to score against your opponents, while having fun, of course. When your mission is completed, return to Mission Command Center to pick up your score sheet because it details who scored on who and how many times. Tip: Ask Lazerstar about their great deals for team parties and their various monthly specials.

**Hours:** Open Mon. - Thurs., noon - 10pm; Fri., noon - midnight; Sat., 10am - midnight; Sun., 10am - 10pm. Open in the summer and on holidays Sun. - Thurs., 10am - 10pm; Fri. - Sat., 10am - midnight.

**Admission:** $5.75 per player for one game; $3.75 for each additional game.

**Ages:** 5 years and up.

## SPACEPLAY

(805) 339-2200        *$*

*2855 Johnson Drive, Ventura*

(Exit Ventura Fwy [101] N. on Johnson Dr. It's in the Gateway shopping center, near Kids R Us and Toys R Us.)

Spaceplay is true to its themes - half of the building contains a *space*ious play area, and all of the dark blue walls have murals of planets, the moon, stars, astronauts, rocket ships, etc. The indoor play room, Spacetube City, has a lot of games, including video (mostly non-violent ones), arcade (air hockey, skee ball, and basketball), and games of chance. (Good luck winning these!) A fully-stocked prize redemption area awaits the more fortunate players. The colorful, two-story, main play structure has a maze of tunnels, plus ball pits, several slides, an obstacle course, a mini zip line, and a punching bag. The only problem I had was trying to find my kids when it was time to go - I had to look up at the overhead tunnels and try to get their attention, knowing that they would avoid me if at all possible. Benches are in here, too, for weary parents. A separate toddlers' section has a ball pit, small slides, and large foam alphabet squares. Note: Socks are required in both play areas.

A little haven in the midst of all the noise and U.F.K.'s (Unidentified Flying Kids) is the Parents' Quiet Room. This room, with a few comfortable chairs and some magazines, has a huge glass window so parents can readily see, but not hear, almost everything in the play area.

The other half of Spaceplay is a complete eating area. The Far Out Food full-service snack bar offers pizza ($9.95) and sandwiches - turkey, ham, chicken salad - ($4.95 each), plus salads, hot dogs, bagels, beverages, etc. There are plenty of tables to eat at, as well as a few kiddie rides and arcade games. A large party room is also available. Spaceplay answers the age old question, "What's in outer space?" The answer - "Fun!"

**Hours:** Open daily 9am - 9:30pm.
**Admission:** Mon. - Thurs., $2 for ages 1 - 15 years; adults are free. Fri. - Sun., $3 for ages 1 - 15 years; adults are free.
**Ages:** 1 - 13 years.

112

# GREAT OUTDOORS
## Botanical Gardens, Nature Centers, and Parks

Contrary to popular belief, Southern California cities consist not only of concrete buildings, but also of the great outdoors. So, come and explore the natural beauty of city life, and take a hike (with your kids)!

Tip: Passes to Orange County Regional Parks are available for $50 a year; $30 for seniors. For an additional $25, you'll also receive a pass that is good at most Orange County beaches. Call any Orange County Regional Park for more information.

## CHILDREN'S NATURE INSTITUTE

(310) 364-3591 / e-mail:chldnature@aol.com

*From Los Angeles through Ventura Counties.*

Children's Nature Institute provides guided walking tours for groups and families with babies, toddlers, and children up to 10 years old. With over sixty locations throughout the Los Angeles and Ventura counties, you're almost guaranteed to find a walk at a park near you. Some of the hikes are very easy, while others are longer and more strenuous. Tour guides usually encourage strollers, and they gear exploratory walks specifically towards kids. This is a tremendous opportunity for young children to be exposed to the beauty of nature, and to learn to respect the environment at a tender age. Note: Children (future leaders) who have gone on several Nature Adventures for Kids walks, can lead their peers, with adult assistance, on walks, too!

Bring your camera, sunscreen, and snacks, and enjoy the pitter patter of little feet next to yours on the nature trails!

**Hours:** The nature walks are given almost daily at various locations, and usually start at 10am.

**Admission:** $5 per family. Some parks also have parking fees.

**Ages:** Birth up to 10 years.

## SIERRA CLUB

(213) 387-4287 / www.sierraclub.org

*3345 Wilshire Boulevard, #508, Los Angeles*

Sierra Club's goals are to preserve our unspoiled wilderness, safeguard endangered species, and clean up our environment. One way they achieve these goals is to take people on hikes so that they, too, can experience nature at its finest, and be moved to protect it. You may sign up to become a Sierra Club member, or simply enjoy their hikes, many of which are geared specifically for children. *Tiny Trailblazer* newsletters come out three times a year and list the hikes for the upcoming months, including the meeting place, the length of the hike, and any "extra" activities. A one-year subscription is $6. All of the hikes are free! (We like free.) There are numerous Sierra Club chapters throughout Southern California. Call the above phone number for more information.

**Admission:** Free

**Ages:** Varies, according to the hike.

## FORT TEJON STATE HISTORIC PARK

(805) 248-6692 / www.forttejon.org

*Fort Tejon Road, Lebec*

(Exit Golden State Fwy [5] on Fort Tejon Rd. The park is on the W. side of the fwy, about 30 miles S. of Bakersfield.)

A long time ago, battles were fought, and the U.S. Dragoons were garrisoned at this fort. Near the entrance is very small museum with several informational panels and a few military uniforms. Come and explore the long barracks building, walk through the officers' quarters that displays war time memorabilia, and pretend to shoot the cannons at unseen enemies. Portions of the fort are still intact, such as a few foundational remains of buildings and a small cemetery. There are plenty of picnic tables and wide open grass areas, plus a few trails for hiking. Note: Primitive overnight camping is permitted here.

I highly recommend coming here when Living History Days and/or Civil War Re-enactments are presented. Living History Days activities include adobe brick making, playing old-fashioned games, participating in chores from days of yore, etc. Visitors will also see a blacksmith in action, open hearth cooking, military drills, and the everyday life of a soldier. During Civil War Re-enactment days, troops of the Union and Confederate armies are all authentically uniformed and equipped. Meet soldiers and civilians and tour their camps. See demonstrations of weapons and watch battle skirmishes at 10am, noon, and 2pm. Guided tours of the fort are given in between battles. Come see history in action!

**Hours:**  The fort is usually open daily from 9am - 5pm. Closed New Year's Day, Thanksgiving, and Christmas. Living History Days and Civil War Re-enactments are held on alternating months during the year, usually on Sun. Call for dates and times.

**Admission:**  $2 for adults; $1 for ages 6 - 12; children 5 years and under are free. Dogs are $1. Special programs cost $14 for a family (mom, dad, and kids under 18 years), or $5 for adults; $3 for ages 6 - 12; children 5 years and under are free. Camping is $10 a night for a family; $50 a night to rent the entire group campground.

**Ages:**  3 years and up.

## ABALONE COVE / SHORELINE PARK

(310) 377-1222 - info; (310) 377-0360 ex. 309 - reservations                    $$
*5907 Palos Verdes Drive South, Rancho Palos Verdes*
(Exit Harbor Fwy [110] W. on Pacific Coast Hwy., L. on Western Ave., R. on Palos Verdes Dr. S.)

This beautiful cove and park on the Palos Verdes Peninsula offer a variety of outdoor, educational guided tours and hikes. A two-hour tidepool tour is an exciting way to discover small creatures native to California waters. Wear shoes with good tread as you must first hike down a quarter of a mile, moderate "trail," then cross a cobblestone beach to get to the rocky tidepool. And remember - wet rocks are slippery rocks! Your guide will explain all about the animals you see and ones that you may gently touch. Look for sea stars, sea slugs, sea urchins, crabs, octopuses, and mussels, and scan the ocean for seals and sea lions. Tours are given on days when low tides are one foot above sea level, or lower. Tips: Wear sunscreen and bring a water bottle. You are also welcome to explore the tidepools on your own.

Two-hour habitat hikes include a good amount of hiking and information about the environment. Depending on the topic emphasized or studied, hikers will see and learn about coastal sage scrub, bluffs, active landslides, and an Indian site. Topics deal with native animals, geology, plants, ecology, and Indian use of natural resources, or any combination thereof. Picnic tables are available on the grounds.

**Hours:** Tours are given by reservation only and require a three week advance notice.

**Admission:** Parking is $5 per car; $15 per bus. Tours are $2 for adults; $1 for children 13 years and under; with a minimum of $15.

**Ages:** 6 years and up.

## APOLLO PARK ☼

*William Barnes Avenue, Lancaster*                                              !

(Exit Antelope Valley Fwy [14] W. at Ave. G, R. on William Barnes Ave. [across from 50th St. West], past the General Fox Airfield, into the park.)

This *space*ious park has three man-made lakes, named after the astronauts from Apollo XI: Lake Aldrin, Lake Armstrong, and Lake Collins. The lakes are stocked with trout, and while there is not a fee for fishing, you do need a California state fishing license if you are over 16 years of age. The park, though surrounded by the desert, is picturesque with its shade trees, bridges over portions of water, and plenty of run-around room. There is also a small playground. My kids were intrigued by the glass-enclosed, well-built mock-up of a command module. The placard describes the dedication of the park to the Apollo program. (Don't you love sneaking in a history lesson?) Tip: Bring bread to feed the relentlessly friendly ducks and geese. This ritual alone took us over half an hour!

**Hours:** Open daily from dawn to dusk.

**Admission:** Free

**Ages:** All

## ARBORETUM OF LOS ANGELES COUNTY ☼

(626) 821-3222 / www.mobot.org/aabga/member.pages/la_county.html        $$

*301 N. Baldwin Avenue, Arcadia*

(Going W. on Foothill Fwy [210], exit S. on Baldwin. Going E. on 210, exit E. on Foothill Blvd., R. on Baldwin.)

Do you have a budding horticulturalist in your family? Come visit this awesome arboretum and explore the more than 127 acres of plants and trees from around the world. The blooming flowers and the variety of gardens is astounding. We walked along the southern (and most interesting) route first. There are numerous paved pathways as well as several dirt pathways leading through trees, bushes, and jungle-like landscape which makes the walk an adventure for kids. Ducks and geese loudly ask for handouts at Baldwin Lake. (Look for the turtles in the lake's water.)

For your history lesson for the day, peek into the spacious Hugo Reid Adobe house where each room is furnished with period furniture. The adobe grounds are beautiful and reflective of the mid-1800's. Peer into the gracious Queen Anne "Cottage" for a glimpse of the past. You'll see mannequins dressed in old-fashioned clothes, elegantly furnished rooms, and a harp in the music room. The nearby immaculate Coach Barn has stalls ornately decorated with wood paneling and iron grillwork. Instead of horses, they now display farm tools, blacksmith tools, and a coach. Also see the Santa Anita Depot with a train master's office and railroad paraphernalia.

The lush greenery around the waterfall makes it one of the most enchanting spots in the arboretum. Walk up the wooden stairs for a panoramic view and "discover" a lily pond. Back down on Waterfall Walk you'll see a serene woodland area and rock-lined stream. I was utterly content to sit while the kids let their imaginations kick into gear and play. Colorful Koi fish are just around the "corner" at the Tule Pond.

The northern section has a few greenhouses with exotic flowers and plants. An African and Australian section at this end has an abundance of trees.

Peacocks are everywhere - strutting their stuff and calling out in plaintive-sounding wails. (Peacock feathers are available at the gift shop for $1 each.)

Picnicking is not allowed on the grounds, but there is a shaded, grassy area between the parking lots. Or, eat at the Peacock Cafe which has reasonably-priced food. Tip #1: Take a half-hour tram ride around and through the extensive arboretum, or get off at any one of the seven stops along the way and reboard at a later time. Trams run from 11am to 3pm, and passes cost $1.50 for ages 3 and up. Tip #2: It gets hot here during the summer, so bring water bottles (and look for the sprinklers to run through).

Wonderful, family-geared events are held here several times throughout the year. In the summer, Science Adventure Day Camps, which include classes on space and rocketry, magic, etc., are offered.

**Hours:** Open in the summer Mon. - Fri., 9am - 6:30pm; Sat. - Sun., 9am - 4:30pm. Open the rest of the year daily from 9am - 4:30pm. Closed Christmas.

**Admission:** $5 for adults; $3 for seniors, students with ID, and ages 13 - 17; $1 for ages 5 - 12; children 4 years and under are free. The third Tuesday of every month is free for everyone. Free parking. (Certain discounts for the arboretum are available through AAA.)

**Ages:** 2 years and up.

## BALBOA PARK (Van Nuys) / LAKE BALBOA

(818) 756-9743 - Lake Balboa and boat rentals; (818) 756-9642 - sports center
*6300 Balboa Boulevard, Van Nuys*
(Exit Ventura Fwy [101] N. on Balboa Blvd. It's between Burbank Blvd. and Sepulveda Blvd.)

Is there anything you can't do at the massive Balboa Park? It is very spread out: On the east side of the street are three golf courses; on the west side is an enormous field with sixteen soccer fields, four lighted baseball diamonds, sixteen lighted tennis courts (and a backboard), lighted basketball courts, and lots of open space and gently sloping hills.

Our favorite place to play is a little further north, just south of Victory Boulevard, at Balboa Lake. The huge playground has large flat rocks around its perimeters (which is almost all my boys need) and a few play areas for both toddlers and older kids. The play grounds feature slides, climbing apparatus (some with steering wheels), and wooden bridges, plus large (relatively speaking) model camels, elephants and turtles to climb on. The twenty-seven acre man-made lake, made from reclaimed water and patrolled by lifeguards, offers pedal boat rentals. The boats hold up to four passengers (with the smallest person weighing at least thirty pounds), and take some muscle power, but are a lot of fun. Bring some old bread for the always-hungry ducks swimming around here. Numerous walkers take advantage of the cement pathway that loops around the scenic lake - no bikes, blades, or skateboards are allowed.

Drive east through the park, past a golf course and you'll reach Anthony Beilenson Park. Its outstanding feature is a model aircraft flying field. Members of the San Fernando Valley Flyers club are often seen here, using (and fixing) their remote-controlled aircraft on a scale runway, and then flying them. See if you can tell the difference between the models and the real planes coming to and from the nearby Van Nuys airport.

**Hours:** Most parts of the park are open daily from sunrise to sunset. Pedal boat rentals are available daily during the summer from 10am - 6:45pm; available the rest of the year on weekends and holidays only from 10am - sunset.

**Admission:** Free to the park. Pedal boats are $7 a half hour; $10 an hour.

**Ages:** All

# BIBLICAL GARDEN

(562) 420-1311
*6201 E. Willow Street at St. Gregory's Episcopal Church, Long Beach*
(Exit San Diego Fwy [405] N. on Palo Verde Ave., L. on Willow)

This small garden plot grows over eighty of the 110 plants mentioned in the Bible. Some of the least common plants that bloom here include a caper bush, citron tree, and Rose of Phoenicia. Many of today's plant uses remain the same as they did in biblical days - food, healing, adornment, etc. Take a self-guided "tour," which is simply reading the placards that have the names of the plants and pertinent Bible passages. Tip: Have your kids look up various plants in the Bible, either before or after your outing, to see how many they can find.

**Hours:** Open Mon. - Fri., 8:30am - 3:30pm.

**Admission:** Free

**Ages:** 5 years and up.

# CASTAIC LAKE RECREATION AREA

(805) 257-4050 - lake information; (805) 257-2049 - boat rentals
*Ridgeroute Road and Lake Hughes, Castaic*
(Exit Golden State Fwy [5] E. on Lake Hughes. It's about 7 miles N. of Magic Mountain.)

There are so many ways to play in the great outdoors at the massive (8,000 acres) Castaic Lake Recreation Area. The lake and lagoon are stocked with trout and bass. A California state fishing license is needed if you're over 16 years old. All kinds of boating activities are available. A lifeguarded swimming area at the lagoon (available seasonally), picnicking, and playgrounds can all be found in the park. Ask about their Jr. lifeguard program. The scenery is beautiful with shade and pine trees, plenty of grassy areas, and of course, the lake. Nature trails, for both hiking and biking, are as short as one mile and as long as seven miles. The trails range from an easy stroll to rugged hikes. Maps are available. Come spend the night in sites reserved for RV and tent camping. However long you choose to visit, an escape to Castaic Lake fits all your recreational desires!

**Hours:** Open daily sunrise to sunset.

**Admission:** $6 per vehicle. Camping starts at $12 a night. A fourteen-foot aluminum, nine-horse-power boat rents for $24 for the first two hours, $6 an hour thereafter.

**Ages:** All

# CHARLES WILSON PARK

(310) 618-2930

*2100 Crenshaw Boulevard, Torrance*

(From San Diego Fwy [405], exit S. on Crenshaw Blvd. Going S. on Harbor Fwy [110], exit W. on Carson St., L. on Crenshaw Blvd. Going N. on 110, exit at 220th, L. on Figuroa St., L. on Carson St., L. on Crenshaw Blvd.)

This large, elongated park has a delightful playground for younger children, several baseball diamonds, grassy "fields," gently rolling hills lined with shade trees, stroller-friendly pathways that crisscross throughout, and a fountain in the middle. A hockey rink is available by reservation. On the first and third Sundays of each month, the Southern California Live Steamers Club offers free rides on their scale trains.

**Hours:** The park is open daily sunrise to sunset. Train rides are offered on the first and third Sun. from 11am - 3pm.

**Admission:** Free

**Ages:** All

# CHATSWORTH PARK

(818) 341-6595

*22360 Devonshire (South) or 22300 Chatsworth (North), Chatsworth*

(Exit Simi Valley/San Fernando Valley Fwy [118] S. on Topanga Canyon Blvd., R. on Devonshire for the south park, or R. on Chatsworth for the north park.)

There are two Chatsworth parks; a north and a south. The north park has shade trees, baseball diamonds with stadium lights, a play area, a basketball and volleyball court, and some pathways to explore.

My family is partial, however, to Chatsworth Park South. It has two tennis courts, a basketball court, a playground, open grassy areas, a community center building that offers lots of activities (including a wheelchair hockey league), a small natural stream running throughout, and picnic tables. Best of all, it has several hiking trails around the perimeter of the park with our favorite ones leading up to, through, and on top of the surrounding rocks! I love climbing rocks and my kids share this passion, so we think this park is "boulderdacious"!

At the southern end of the south park, at 10385 Shadow Oak Drive, is the historic Hill-Palmer House. Take a tour through the old house while visiting the park. It is open the first Sunday of every month from 1pm to 4pm, and admission is free.

**Hours:** The parks are open daily sunrise to 10pm.

**Admission:** Free

**Ages:** All

## CHESEBRO CANYON

(818) 597-9192

*Chesebro Road, Agoura Hills*

(Going E. on Ventura Fwy [101], exit at Agoura Rd., L. on Palo Comado Canyon Rd., R. on Chesebro. Going W. on 101, exit N. on Chesebro Rd.)

Hike on the numerous trails here to go through canyons, grasslands, and riparian areas. The road most traveled is the one immediately accessible, the Chesebro Canyon Trail. The hike starts off moderately easy along a streambed and through a valley of oak trees. A picnic area is about a mile-and-a-half from the parking lot. Stop here, or continue on to more strenuous hiking. You'll reach Sulphur Springs (almost another two miles), where the smell of rotten eggs will let you know you've arrived. This particular trail goes on for another mile through a variety of terrain. Several trails branch off and connect to the Chesebro Trail. Pick up a trail map at PARAMOUNT RANCH (see that entry in this section), which is down the road a bit, or call to have one sent to you.

**Hours:** Open daily sunrise to sunset.

**Admission:** Free

**Ages:** 3 years (for shorter hikes) and up.

## CHEVIOT HILLS RECREATION AREA

(310) 837-5186 - park; (310) 202-2844 - pool

*Corner of Pico Boulevard and Motor Avenue, Los Angeles*

(Going W. on Santa Monica Fwy [10], exit at National. Drive past National, up Manning and go R. on Motor Ave. Going E. on 10, exit N. on Overland, R. on Pico. Going S. on San Diego Fwy [405], exit E. on Pico.)

This large park really fits the bill of a recreation area with its basketball courts, baseball diamonds, tennis courts, and nice playground. During the hot summer months, when kids have played hard and need to cool off, they can take a dip in the municipal swimming pool.

**Hours:** The park is open Mon. - Fri., 9am - 10pm; Sat. - Sun., 9am - 7pm. Summer sessions for the pool are Mon. - Fri., 10am - 1pm and 2pm - 5pm; Sat. - Sun., 1pm - 5pm.

**Admission:** The park is free. Each swim session costs $1.25 for adults; 75¢ for kids 17 years and under.

**Ages:** All

## DENNIS THE MENACE PARK

(562) 904-7127

*9125 Arrington Avenue, Downey*  ⚏
(Exit Golden State Fwy [5] S. on Lakewood Blvd., L. on Gallatin Rd., L. on Arrington Ave.)

This park has nothing to do with the character, Dennis the Menace, but it has everything to do with fun, imagination, and Camelot. The age of chivalry is not dead as your kids become knights and ladies in King Arthur's court. A big cement castle is the main play structure, complete with an "upstairs," slides, and a wooden bridge for crossing over the pretend moat. Kids can also climb up a sea serpent, try pulling out the sword in the stone, or just play on the other equipment of slides and swings. Note: The play equipment here has not been updated for quite some time.

The front part of the park has huge shade trees and lots of grass. The community center building is open after school, and has board games and sports equipment to lend. This park has readily become a favorite.

**Hours:** Gates are usually open Mon. - Fri., 10am - 5pm; Sat. - Sun., 10am - 6pm. The community center is open daily during the summer, and the rest of the year Mon. - Fri., 3pm - 5pm; Sat. - Sun., 10am - 6pm.
**Admission:** Free
**Ages:** All

## DESCANSO GARDENS  ☼
(818) 952-4400 / www.descanso.com  $$
*1418 Descanso Drive, La Canada*  ⚏
(Exit Foothill Fwy [210] S. on Angeles Crest Hwy., R. on Foothill Blvd., L. on Verdugo Blvd., L. on Alta Canyada Rd., which turns into Descanso Dr.)

Descanso Gardens is over sixty acres of incredible beauty. It's not just a bed of roses here as lilacs, camellias, tulips, dogwood, etc., also bloom. Although flowers bloom here year round, you can call for a specific bloom schedule. A network of stroller-friendly trails wind through the grounds. One trail that is particularly delightful goes through a forest of California oaks. There are also open grassy areas to run around.

The Japanese garden is intriguing because of its unique maze-like layout. It also has ponds and a stream. Be on the lookout for squirrels, and land and water birds, as this is a haven for more than 150 species.

Take the forty-five-minute guided tram tour to see all of Descanso Gardens. Hop aboard the five-minute model train ride for a more kid-oriented trip. Either way, bring your camera and enjoy your fragrant outing. Food is available at a cafe daily from 9:30am to 3pm, at the Japanese Tea Garden on weekends, or bring your own and use the picnic grounds adjacent to the parking lot.

**Hours:** The gardens are open daily from 9am - 4:30pm. Closed Christmas. Tram tours are offered Tues. - Fri. at 1pm, 2pm, and 3pm; Sat. - Sun. at 11am, 1pm, 2pm, and 3pm. Train rides are available every Sat. and Sun.

**Admission:** $5 for adults; $3 for seniors; $1 for ages 5 - 12; children 4 years and under are free. On the third Tuesday of each month, admission is half price. The tram tour and train ride each cost $1.50 per person.

**Ages:** 2½ years and up.

# DEVIL'S PUNCHBOWL ☼
(805) 944-2743                                                              $
*28000 Devil's Punchbowl Road, Pearblossom*
(Exit Antelope Valley Fwy [14] E. on Ave S., R. on Pearblossom Hwy [138], R. on Longview, L. on Tumbleweed Rd. which turns into Devil's Punchbowl Rd.)

The "punchbowl" is a spectacular geological formation that looks like a huge, jagged bowl created from rocks. The 1,310-acre park consists of rugged wilderness rock formations along the San Andreas Fault, plus a seasonal stream. The hiking trails vary in degrees of difficulty. We hiked down into the punchbowl and back up along a looping trail in about half an hour. The terrain is diverse, ranging from desert plants to pine trees, as the elevation changes from 4,200 feet to 6,500 feet. Rock climbing is a popular sport here, whether you prefer climbing on boulders or scaling sheer rock walls.

The small nature center museum contains a few taxidermied animals and displays that pertain to this region. Outside the center, a few live birds, such as owls and hawks, live in cages. The park also offers picnic areas and equestrian trails, and is host to many special events throughout the year. Ask about school field trips, too.

**Hours:** Open sunrise to sunset.
**Admission:** $3 per vehicle.
**Ages:** 5 years and up.

# EARL BURNS MILLER JAPANESE GARDENS ☀
(562) 985-8885                                                              !
*Earl Warren Drive at California State Long Beach, Long Beach*
(Exit San Diego Fwy [405] S. on Bellflower, L. on State University Dr. Or, take Garden Grove Fwy [22] to the end, turn R. on Bellflower, R. on State University Dr. From State University Dr., go through the campus gates, turn L. on Earl Warren. The garden is on the L.)

This one-acre, beautiful, Japanese garden has two waterfalls, a meditation rock garden, a quaint teahouse (to look in), and a koi pond. Kids can help feed the koi weekdays at 8:30am and noon; Sundays at 12:30pm and 3pm. As you cross over the zig-zag bridge into the gardens, share with your kids that it was built in this shape to side-step spirits because, according to Japanese tradition, spirits can only travel in straight lines!

**Hours:** Open Tues - Fri., 8am - 3:30pm; Sun., noon - 4pm. Closed Mon. and Sat.
**Admission:** Free. There is metered parking (to your right) in Student Lot D on weekdays.
**Ages:** 3 years and up.

## EAST AND RICE CANYONS                                           ☼

(805) 255-2974                                                          !

*Off The Old Road, Newhall*

(Exit Golden State Fwy [5] on Calgrove and go W. back under the freeway, S. on The Old Road about 1 mile. The trailhead is S. of the entrance to Towsley Canyon, just past the Church of Nazarene - look for signs.)

    A year-round stream and a wide variety of plants and trees, line trails that lead hikers away from city life and straight into nature. The Rice Canyon trail is a little over two miles round trip and a relatively easy walk. However, it does go up hill towards the end. The trail follows along the stream and crosses over it a few times. If you smell petroleum, it's not coming from cars, but from natural oil seeps near the creek. This area was once part of an oil boom town. The East Canyon trail is almost four miles round trip. As you go steadily up in elevation, you'll pant harder, but you'll also see big-cone, Douglas-fir trees and vistas of the Santa Clarita Valley. Be on the lookout for wildlife such as deer, foxes, skunks, and an abundance of birds. Neither trail loops, so I hope you like the way you came, because you get the opportunity to see it all again! Also look up TOWSLEY CANYON in this section.

    **Hours:**   Open daily from sunrise to sunset.

    **Admission:**   Free

    **Ages:**   3 years and up.

## EATON CANYON COUNTY PARK                                        ☼

(626) 398-5420                                                          !

*1750 North Altadena Drive, Pasadena*

(Going W. on Foothill Fwy [210], exit at Sierra Madre Blvd.; the off ramp turns into Maple. Stay on Maple and turn R. on N. Altadena Dr. Or, going E. on 210, exit N. on Altadena Dr.)

    Located in the foothills of the mountains, this 184-acre wilderness park has several rugged dirt trails leading up into the mountains. For hardy hikers, take a trail up to Mt. Wilson, a "mere" ten-mile hike. Approximately two-thirds of this park was burned in a 1993 brush fire. As the slopes and flats continue to recover from the fire, new plant growth is restoring the park's beauty.

    There are shorter trails in the immediate vicinity of the nature center, which is temporarily housed in an on-site trailer. One such trail is only a quarter of a mile and has a self-guiding pamphlet (pick it up from the nature center) that helps identify the plants. The first, and most important, plant to recognize is poison oak.

    The Eaton Canyon Wash (river bed) is filled with rocks and is fun to explore - when it's dry, of course. Eaton Creek flows through the canyon, except during the summer months. Pretty, shaded, and almost hidden picnic areas are found just off the parking lot. Remember to B.Y.O.W. - Bring Your Own Water. The park offers many special events, such as free family nature walks which are given every Saturday from 9am to 11am.

    **Hours:**   Open daily sunrise to sunset.

    **Admission:**   Free, until the nature center is rebuilt.

**Ages:**    3 years and up

# EL DORADO EAST REGIONAL PARK

(562) 570-1771

*7500 East Spring Street, Long Beach*

(Exit San Gabriel River Fwy [605] W. on Spring St. El Dorado Park is on the N. side, the Nature Center on the S. side. If going E. on Spring, use the Nature Center entrance and drive around to park.)

El Dorado has 450 acres of lush green park with lots for kids to do! There are three fishing lakes, that have ducks clamoring for handouts; pedal-boat rentals at $7 per half hour - available seasonally; an archery range where targets are provided, but you must bring your own equipment; a model glider field; several playgrounds; a Frisbee golf course; four-and-a-half miles of biking trails, including access to the San Gabriel River cement embankment; and a one-mile, gasoline-powered scale train ride that runs in the summer, Tuesday through Sunday from 11am to 7:30pm. The rest of the year it runs Wednesday through Sunday, and holidays, from 10:30am to 4:30pm. The cost is $1.75 for ages 17 and up; $1.25 for ages 2 to 16. Call (562) 496-4228 for more information. Hayrides are also available in the park for $100 for up to ten people, $7.50 for each additional person, and a maximum of twenty-five people. Call (562) 865-3290 for information and reservations. Organized youth groups are invited to camp here overnight. You can be as active or relaxed as you want (or as the kids let you!) at El Dorado Park. Also see EL DORADO NATURE CENTER and EL DORADO PARK WEST.

**Hours:**    Open daily from 7am - dusk.

**Admission:**    $3 per vehicle Mon. - Fri.; $5 on Sat. - Sun. and holidays. Entrance fee is good for a same-day visit to the Nature Center located across the street. Annual passes are $35.

**Ages:**    All

# EL DORADO NATURE CENTER

(562) 570-1745

*7550 East Spring Street, Long Beach*

(Exit San Gabriel Fwy [605] W. on Spring St. El Dorado Park is on the N. side, the Nature Center is on the S. side. If going W. on Spring, use the park entrance and drive around to the nature center.)

The eighty-five-acre El Dorado Nature Center is part of the El Dorado East Regional Park. When crossing over the wooden bridge leading to the museum and trail-heads, look down to see the many ducks and turtles swimming in the water below.

The Nature Center Museum has skulls, antlers, and other artifacts to touch; bugs to look at under a magnifier; a few cases of live insects and reptiles; a display on feathers and wings; and a huge book depicting various animal habitats. Contact the Center for information on their many special programs, like the Turtle and Reptile Show, or summer camps.

Walk on a short, quarter-mile paved trail, or hike a two-mile, stroller-friendly dirt trail that goes under the pine trees. The longer trail winds around two lakes and a stream. I love being in God's beautiful creation! Picnicking is not allowed inside the Nature Center, but picnic tables and shade trees can be found outside the gates at the end of the parking lot. The Nature Center is truly "an oasis of greenery and woodland in the middle of Long Beach." Also see EL DORADO EAST REGIONAL PARK and EL DORADO PARK WEST.

**Hours:**    The trails and park are open Tues. - Sun. from 8am - 5pm. The museum is open Tues. - Fri., 10am - 4pm; Sat. - Sun., 8:30am - 4pm. The Nature Center is closed on Christmas.

**Admission:**    $3 per vehicle Tues. - Fri.; $5 on Sat. - Sun. and holidays. Entrance fee is good for a same-day visit to El Dorado Regional Park located across the street. Annual passes are $35.

**Ages:**    All

## EL DORADO PARK WEST

(562) 570-3225 - park; (562) 425-0553 - tennis courts

*2800 Studebaker Road, Long Beach*

(Exit San Gabriel River Fwy [605] W. on Spring St., L. on Studebaker.)

This city park is just around the corner from its neighbors, EL DORADO EAST REGIONAL PARK and EL DORADO NATURE CENTER. It features lots of grassy areas, picnic tables under shade trees, a pond with ducks, baseball diamonds, playgrounds, a large library, and fifteen tennis courts.

**Hours:**    Open daily sunrise to sunset. The tennis courts are open Mon. - Fri., 7am - 9pm; Sat. - Sun., 7am - 7:30pm.

**Admission:**    Free to the park. The tennis courts are $4 per hour during day light hours; $5 per hour after 5pm; and an additional $4 per hour if using lights.

**Ages:**    All

## EXPOSITION PARK

*Exposition Park, Los Angeles*

(Exit the Harbor Fwy [110] W. on Exposition Blvd., L. on Flower, L. on Figueroa. Or, exit Santa Monica Fwy [10] S. on Vermont, L. on Exposition, R. on Figueroa. Parking is available by entering the first driveway on the right.)

The expansive Exposition Park encompasses the AEROSPACE MUSEUM, CALIFORNIA AFRO-AMERICAN MUSEUM, CALIFORNIA SCIENCE CENTER, L.A. MEMORIAL COLISEUM and L.A. Sports Arena, NATURAL HISTORY MUSEUM OF LOS ANGELES, and 3D IMAX THEATER. (Look up capitalized attractions individually under the Alphabetical Index.) Up until now, most of park has simply been grassy areas surrounding these attractions. Exposition Park is currently undergoing development that is transforming it into a more family-oriented park. The perimeters of the park will be lined with trees and each of the four corners of Exposition Park will become distinct parks in their own right, with picnic table, barbecue grills, and playgrounds, as well as open grassy areas. A Community Center, with recreational facilities, will be located in the Southwest quadrant of the park. While paved pedestrian areas will provide easy access to and from the Coliseum, spacious lawns will provide a great place for picnics and tailgate parties.

The sunken Rose Garden, adjacent to the California Science Center, has always been a *scent*ral part of the park. Enjoy its seven acres of beauty where 16,000 specimens of 190 varieties of roses are cultivated. (I bet your kids didn't know there are so many different varieties.) The gardens are wonderful for walking, smelling the perfumed air, and picture taking, plus it's stroller accessible. Often on weekends, people of various nationalities have their wedding ceremonies in the garden. (We like looking at the wedding attire.)

    **Hours:**   Open daily.

**Admission:**   Free

    **Ages:**   3 years and up.

## FOX HILLS PARK

(310) 253-6650

*6161 Buckingham Parkway, Culver City*

(Exit San Diego Fwy [405] N. on Sepulveda Blvd., R. on Green Valley Circle. It's on the corner of Birmingham and Green Valley.)

    This attractive little park, surrounded on the street level by office buildings and condos, is tucked away on a hill and offers a pleasant respite from city life. The hillside is landscaped with flowers, bushes, and trees and has a packed-dirt jogging/walking trail winding all around it. Exercise equipment, such as pull up bars and rings, are along the track. For kids, and those who work nearby and have extended lunchtime, the top of the hill has a playground, sand volleyball court, a basketball court, several tennis courts, a large flat grassy area (baseball field!), climbing trees, and picnic tables. My boys enjoyed the playground with its slides, climbing structures, and a cement dolphin. When the recreation center building is open, the staff offers board games and sometimes arts and crafts activities.

    **Hours:**   The park is open daily from 7am - 10pm. The rec center building is open daily in the summer from 10am - 7pm. It's open the rest of the year, Mon. - Fri., 3pm - 6pm; Sat. - Sun., 10am - 6pm. The tennis courts are open park hours, except for 6am - noon on Wed., and Tues. from 3:30pm - 5:30pm.

**Admission:**   Free.

    **Ages:**   All

## FRANK G. BONELLI REGIONAL COUNTY PARK / PUDDINGSTONE LAKE

(909) 599-8411- park information

*120 East Via Verde, San Dimas*

(Take San Bernardino Fwy [10] or Orange Fwy [57] to the 210 Fwy, exit on Raging Waters Dr. It's just S. of RAGING WATERS.)

    This sprawling park is centered around the huge Puddingstone Reservoir, which is an ideal water hole for all your fishing and boating desires. A fishing license is required for those over 16 years old. Boat rentals, (909) 599-2667, are available daily during the summer and on weekends the rest of the year. Rental prices start at $15 an hour for a four-passenger boat. Life jacket rentals are an additional $5. You can also launch your own boat here. Jet skiing, fast boating, and water skiing are allowed on alternate days. If the fish are biting, your kids can catch bass, catfish, and trout. They'll also enjoy feeding the ducks and observing the wildlife. (We saw a heron and a crane, which my kids thought was pretty cool.) Picnic areas are plentiful with tables, barbecue pits, and playgrounds, too.

There are a few walking paths here, but you can really rein your children in with a horseback ride. Horse rentals are available Tuesday through Sunday from 9am to 4pm (later on weekends), for $20 an hour for adults; $15 for ages 7 to 12. Younger children can take a pony ride around the compound for $5. Call (909) 599-8830 for more information. The scenery along the equestrian trail changes and ranges from cacti to pine trees - only in California!

Just outside the park grounds, treat yourself and the kids to a relaxing time in a hot tub. (Or just indulge yourself after spending a day with the kids!) Choose from fifteen private, hilltop tubs. Tub rentals are available daily from noon to midnight for $22.50 an hour. Celebrate "Happy Hour" from 5pm to 7pm, when rentals are half price. Call Puddingstone Hot Tubs Resort at (909) 592-2222 for reservations. To reach the hot tubs, exit the 10 Fwy at Fairplex Drive, turn left on Via Verde Drive, right on Camper View Drive.

**Hours:** Open daily March 1 through October 31 from 6am to 10pm. Open November 1 through February 28, sunrise to 7pm. Boat rentals are available Fri., 7am - 4pm; Sat. - Sun., 6:30am - 4pm.

**Admission:** $6 per vehicle; $6 for a daily boat permit.

**Ages:** All

# FRANKLIN CANYON
(310) 858-3834
*Franklin Canyon, Los Angeles*
(From L.A., exit San Diego Fwy [405] E. on Sunset Blvd., L. on Beverly Dr. [past Beverly Glen Blvd.], follow signs "to Coldwater Canyon Drive" to the stoplight at Beverly Hills Fire Station #2, turn L. - staying on Beverly Dr. Go 1 mile to Franklin Cyn. Dr., turn R. and go 1½ miles to Lake Dr., and follow signs to the canyon. From the Valley, exit Ventura Fwy [101] S. on Coldwater Cyn. Dr., R. on Franklin Cyn. Dr. [cross over Mulholland Dr.] to the canyon.)

Franklin Canyon, almost 600 acres large, proves that there is more to Los Angeles than just skyscrapers. The lower canyon is the site of an old ranch house, which is now an office. A big green lawn and a few picnic tables are the only things down here. Follow the creek along the mile-and-a-half trail leading to the Upper Canyon, and the Nature Center. Inside the Sooky Goldman Nature Center are displays of animals that live in the canyon, a scale model of the Santa Monica Mountains, an interactive exhibit on Native Americans, and an exhibit on the importance of water conservation. For your tactile child, there are fossils, antlers, furs, bones, and even a few nests to touch.

This Center is also the headquarters of the William O. Douglas Outdoor Classroom, which is really the name for numerous, on-going, free nature programs. Docent-led tours are open for the general public on weekends, with titles like Incredible Edibles. There are programs for all ages that range from Babes in the Woods, which is a stroller-friendly walk on a paved trail, to Full Moon Hikes, geared for older kids to have a howling good time. Tours are available for school groups Tuesday through Friday, between 10am and noon.

The canyon has a variety of trees such as California live oaks, black walnuts, and sycamores. Wildlife here includes deer, bobcats, coyotes, rabbits, etc. The Upper Reservoir has reverted to a natural lake, and is a wetland area for herons and other waterfowl. Enjoy your day in the wilds of L.A.!

**Hours:**  The canyon entrance is open daily from dawn to dusk. The Nature Center is open daily from 10am - 4pm.

**Admission:**  Free

**Ages:**  All

# GREYSTONE MANSION AND PARK

(310) 550-4768

*905 Loma Vista, Beverly Hills*

(Exit Santa Monica Fwy [10] N. on Robertson Blvd., R. on Santa Monica Blvd., L. on San Vicente Blvd., L. on Sunset Blvd., R. on Mountain Dr., R. on Loma Vista. Look for park signs.)

Edward Doheny made an oil discovery that enabled him to become one of the world's largest oil producers. In 1927 he put a great deal of his wealth into constructing the fifty-five room Greystone mansion, designed in Gothic and neo-classical styles. It was built using mainly grey stones (hence the name), plus limestone facing, a slate roof, and seven magnificent brick chimneys. The basement used to house a bowling alley and billiards room. This multi-story, castle-like mansion is the epitome of opulence and, although you may not go into it, you are welcome to peer into the windows. Opened, iron gates at the end of a stone driveway lead to an outside porch that's made of marble. We looked in the windows at the elegant entry way and saw black and white checkered tiles, a gorgeous chandelier, elaborately carved wooden banisters, and several archways that are followed by incredibly long hallways. There isn't any furniture inside. Quite a few shows have been filmed here including episodes of *Murder She Wrote* and the movie, *Ghostbusters II*. Walk around to the front sundeck for a gorgeous view of Beverly Hills and the Los Angeles area.

Behind the mansion is a dungeon (according to my boys) built into the hillside. The adjacent, closed, control room has levers and a high voltage sign, which clinched the dungeon notion. Imagination definitely reigns here!

Tiered, lush gardens and extensive grounds lavishly landscaped into and around the hillside are immaculately maintained. Go up the stone steps or walk the pathways to see the acres of grassy areas, courtyards surrounded by trimmed hedges, shade trees, a few koi fish ponds, reflecting pools, fountains, and a few park benches. A highlight for my kids was simply running down the long, sloping stone driveway - then panting their way back up.

**Hours:** The park is open daily from 10am - 5pm.
**Admission:** Free
**Ages:** All

## GRIFFITH PARK

(213) 665-5188 / www.ci.la.ca.us/dept/RAP/grifmet/index.htm                  */$
*4730 Crystal Springs Drive, Los Angeles*

(Going N. on Golden State Fwy [5] or W. on Ventura Fwy [134], exit at Zoo Dr. and follow the signs. Going E. on 134 Fwy, exit S. on Victory Blvd., L. on Zoo Dr. Going S. on 5 fwy, exit S. on Western, L. on Victory Blvd. to Zoo Dr.)

The vast 4,200 acres of the eastern Santa Monica Mountains encompass wilderness areas, picnic areas, and children's attractions. There are numerous trails for hiking and horseback riding. Call or visit the Ranger's Station for trail information. One particularly interesting picnic area is the Old Zoo Picnic Area, on Griffith Park Drive, that has tables placed around obsolete caves and animal cages from the original zoo. Another standout picnic area is Park Center, near the merry-go-round, because it has playground equipment as well as picnic tables.

The children's attractions include (from the northern end of the park to the southern end): 1) Los Angeles Live Steamers - located west of the Victory Boulevard entrance to the park. (Also see TRAVEL TOWN under the Museums section.) This club offers free twelve-minute, large scale model train rides on Sundays from 11am to 3pm. Call (213) 669-9729 for more information. 2) Merry-go-round - located off Griffith Park Drive, south of the Zoo. The antique carousel offers rides daily in the summer and on weekends and holidays the rest of the year from 11am to 5pm. Rides are $1 per person. 3) Pony rides and covered wagon rides - located at the Los Feliz entrance to the park. Each ride is $1.50 per person and available Tuesday through Sunday from 10am to 4pm. 4) Train rides and simulator - located at the Los Feliz entrance to the park. The eight-minute, mini-train ride costs $1.25 for children and $1.75 for adults. The simulator, which simulates bobsledding, riding a roller coaster, or being in an airplane, costs $1.25 for adults and children. Both are open daily from 10am to 5pm. 5) Tennis courts, a soccer field, and a swimming pool - located at the Los Feliz entrance to the park. (The cross street is Riverside.) The pool is open mid-June to September, Monday through Friday, 2pm tp 6pm; Saturday and Sunday, noon to 3pm and 4pm to 7pm. Adults are $1.25 per session; kids 17 years and under are 75¢. Call (323) 644-6878 seasonally, for pool information. 6) Bird Sanctuary - located on Vermont Canyon Road, northeast of the Observatory. This verdant area has a short, stroller-friendly nature trail that crosses over a creek and loops around. A wide variety of birds flock here and make it their home. It's open daily from 10am to 5pm. 7) Ferndell - located near the Western Avenue entrance. This is a pretty spot to rest and picnic. Ferns and flowers growing along the brook make it an attractive, cool haven on hot days and nature trails take you into the heart of the park. A snack stand, open seasonally, is also available here.

There are refreshment stands located throughout the park, as well as two restaurants. Operating hours fluctuate. For other attractions located in Griffith Park, see AUTRY MUSEUM OF WESTERN HERITAGE, GRIFFITH OBSERVATORY AND PLANETARIUM, and LOS ANGELES ZOO.

**Hours:**   The park is open daily from 6am - 10pm.
**Admission:**   Free
**Ages:**   All

## HERITAGE PARK (Cerritos)

(562) 916-8570
*18600 Bloomfield, Cerritos*
(Exit San Gabriel Fwy [605] E. on South St., L. on Bloomfield.)

One if by land, two if by sea . . . The most unique feature of this noteworthy park is an island with a kid-size version of an old New England town. Cross the covered bridge and be transported back in time. (Not actually, it's just the atmosphere of the island.) This "town" has a replica of Paul Revere's house, a cemetery, and the North Church Tower, which has two slides coming out of it. (Creative parents can reinforce a Paul Revere history lesson here.) Next to the cement slide are rocks to climb up. Kids can pull themselves back up to the tower via a short tunnel that has an anchored rope through it. The town has little buildings with more slides in them, firehouse-like poles to slide down, and small cannons to sit on or "fire." A small replica of a British ship is harbored nearby. It's designed for pint-sized merchants to climb aboard. The island has a brook running through it and plenty of shade trees, so it is refreshingly cool even on hot days.

The ducks swimming in the "moat" surrounding the island are always looking for a handout, so be sure to bring old bread. Across the water are two wonderful play areas. One is for slightly older kids, and the other has scaled-down equipment for younger children. The park also has picnic tables, a few barbecues, basketball courts, large grass areas, climbing trees, and a baseball diamond with stadium-type benches.

**Hours:**   The park is open daily sunrise to sunset. The island is open September through May, Mon. - Fri., 2pm - dusk; Sat. - Sun., 11am - 5pm. During the summer it's open daily from 11am - 6pm.
**Admission:**   Free
**Ages:**   All

## HOPKINS WILDERNESS PARK

(310) 318-0668
*1102 Camino Real, Redondo Beach*
(Exit Harbor Fwy [110] W. on Sepulveda, which turns into Camino Real.)

Escape to the wilderness of Redondo Beach. This gated, eleven-acre, hilltop park has two streams running through it, two ponds, and a wonderful view of the city. Hike along the nature trail that will take you through California Redwood and pine trees; through a meadow - be on the lookout for butterflies and lizards;

and to the small waterfall and pond where turtles, crayfish, and bullfrogs have made their homes. Wilderness Park also has a campground and is a popular spot for local, overnight camping. Note: Wilderness protection is strictly enforced here.

**Hours:**   Open Thurs. - Tues. from 10am - 4:30pm. Closed Wed., New Year's Day, Thanksgiving, Christmas, and in bad weather. November through April the park closes at 4pm.

**Admission:**   The park is free. Tent camping (no stakes allowed) is $4 a night for non-resident adults (residents are $3); $2 a night for non-resident kids 17 years and under (residents are $1). Residency is proven by bringing a utility bill. Picnic tables and BBQ pits are available for campers.

**Ages:**   3 years and up.

## JOHNNY CARSON PARK

*Bob Hope Drive and Parkside Avenue, Burbank*

(Going W. on Ventura Fwy [134], exit N. at Hollywood Wy., go right at end of off ramp on Alameda Ave., R. on Bob Hope Dr. Going E. on 134, exit N. on Bob Hope Dr. It's across the street from NBC STUDIO TOURS and just down the street from WARNER BROS. STUDIOS VIP TOUR.)

Despite the proximity of the freeway, this pleasant park offers a refuge, of sorts, in downtown Burbank. Kids will enjoy the large grassy areas, small woods, climbing and shade trees, and stroller-friendly dirt pathways that run throughout the park. The Tonight Show Playground, for today's kids, has slides, swings, and climbing apparatus. Picturesque bridges go over what I first thought was a seasonal stream, but it is only a drainage "creek." Come enjoy a picnic here before or after you take the NBC or WARNER BROS. studio tours. (Both are listed under the Tours section.)

**Hours:**   Open daily.

**Admission:**   Free

**Ages:**   All

## KENNETH HAHN STATE RECREATION AREA

(323) 298-3660

*4100 S. La Cienega Boulevard, Los Angeles*

(Exit Santa Monica Fwy [10] S. on La Cienega Blvd., exit E. at the turnoff with signs for Kenneth Hahn.)

This spacious, 320-acre natural parkland in the heart of Baldwin Hills has hilly grasslands, forest areas, and several dirt hiking trails. It also features a large lake that is stocked with trout in the winter, and catfish, bluegill, and bass in the summer. Swimming in the water is not allowed. You may, however, feed the ducks who are always looking for a handout. There are seven picnic areas, complete with barbecue grills, for families to enjoy as well as a few scattered playgrounds, and basketball and volleyball courts.

**Hours:**   Open daily sunrise to sunset.

**Admission:** Free during the week; $3 per vehicle on the weekends and on county holidays.

**Ages:** All

## LADERA LINDA COMMUNITY CENTER
(310) 541-7073 - info; (310) 377-0360, ex. 309 - tour reservations          !/$
*3201 Forrestal Drive, Rancho Palos Verdes*
(Exit Harbor Fwy [110] W. on Pacific Coast Hwy., L. on Western Ave., R. on Palos Verdes Dr. S.)

This park features wilderness hiking trails, picnic areas, groves of shade trees, lots of wide open spaces, basketball courts, soccer and baseball fields, playgrounds, a game room, and a Discovery room. The small Discovery room has a few live animals, displays of rocks and fossils, photos of the area, and information regarding this area. Ask about the REACH programs for the developmentally disabled.

Two-hour, docent-led hikes offered by the center enable groups of kids, minimum ten, to explore the coastal habitat of the Palos Verdes Peninsula. Look out for and learn about coastal sage scrub, native trees, and wildflowers, as well as important critters such as lizards, butterflies, and birds. Hikes are moderately difficult, so bring a water bottle and wear sunscreen. The hike/tours can focus on a topic of your choice, such as plants, animals, fossils, or the geology of the area. A visit to the Discovery Room, with explanations about the exhibits, is included in your time here.

**Hours:** The park is open daily from dawn to dusk. The building is open during the summer Mon. - Fri., 1pm - 6pm; Sat. - Sun., 10am - 6pm. It's open the rest of the year Mon., Wed., and Fri. - Sun., 1pm - 5pm. Tours are set up by reservation.

**Admission:** Free to the park. Tours $2 for adults; $1 for children 13 years and under; with a $15 minimum.

**Ages:** All for the park; 7 years and up for the tours.

## LIBERTY PARK
(562) 916-8565          !
*19211 Studebaker Road, Cerritos*
(Exit San Gabriel River Fwy [605] W. on South Street, L. on Studebaker Rd.)

Experience the freedom at Liberty Park to do almost anything. The park offers long grassy areas to run around, three playground areas, picnic tables, barbeque pits, three picnic shelters, three sand volleyball courts, a 330-yard walking/jogging track, a softball field, a disc (Frisbee) golf course, outside exercise clusters equipped with pull up bars and more, and six lighted tennis courts. Tennis is free for Cerritos residents (show a driver's license or utility bill for proof of residency) and $5 per hour for non-residents. Inside the community building are four racquetball courts ($5 per hour for residents, $8 for non-residents); a weight room (free to residents, $2 per day for non-residents); and a Walleyball court (indoor volleyball that uses walls) on Monday nights ($10 per hour for residents, $15 for non-residents). Summertime offers the refreshing pleasures of a wading pool that has a water sprayer, Monday night family time at the movies ("G" rated), and Wednesday night family entertainment consisting of puppets, magicians, or storytellers.

**Hours:** Open Mon. - Fri., 9am - 10pm; Sat. - Sun., 9am - 6pm. Call for times for special programs.
**Admission:** Free to the park. Fees for activities are listed above.
**Ages:** All

## LIVE OAK PARK

(310) 545-5621
*Valley Drive N. and 21ˢᵗ Street, Manhattan Beach*
(Exit San Diego Fwy [405] W. on Rosecrans Ave., L. on Pacific Coast Highway, next R. on Valley Dr.)

This park is formed around a bend in the road and is divided into various, gated sections. The northern section has baseball diamonds, picnic tables, and some short, bent gnarled trees for climbing. One particular threesome of trees bends in and down so much that they form a kind of hideout. Other sections have playground equipment, soccer fields, places just to run and play, and tennis courts. The six courts are open daily from 7am to 9pm and cost $5 per court. Call (310) 545-0888 to make reservations. Parking is plentiful at the park.

**Hours:** Open daily from dawn to dusk.
**Admission:** Free
**Ages:** All

## MADRONA MARSH

(310) 32 MARSH (326-2774)
*3201 Plaza Del Amo, Torrance*
(From San Diego Fwy [405], exit S. on Crenshaw Blvd., R. on Carson St., L. on Madrona Ave., L. on Plaza Del Amo. Going S. on Harbor Fwy [110], exit W. on Carson St., L. on Madrona Ave., L. on Plaza Del Amo. Going N. on 110, exit at 220ᵗʰ, L. on Figuroa St., L. on Carson St., L. on Madrona Ave., L. on Plaza Del Amo.)

The Madrona Marsh hosts educational nature walks for kids (and adults) of all ages. During the hour, or so, guided tour you'll see and learn mostly about birds, plus ground animals and several varieties of plant life. Summer field study tours are also given. A mobile trailer Nature Center holds a few displays, and is open during scheduled walks. The forty-three acre marsh is located in the middle of an industrial section. If it's not big enough to make you feel like you've gotten away from it all, it's at least big enough to make you feel like you've gotten away from some of it.

**Hours:** The marsh is open sunrise to sunset to explore on your own. Guided walks are given the fourth weekend of every month, and field study tours are given at various times. Call for details.
**Admission:** Free; donations gladly accepted. Summer field study tours are $5 per person or $10 per family.
**Ages:** 6 years and up.

# MALIBU CREEK STATE PARK

(818) 880-0350 - park; (800) 444-7275 - camping reservations

*On Malibu Canyon Road, Calabasas*

(Exit Ventura Fwy [101] S. at Las Virgenes Rd., which eventually turns into Malibu Canyon Rd. S. The park is S. of Mulholland Hwy.)

Of the many hiking trails to choose from in the Santa Monica Mountains, one of our favorites is the Malibu Creek Trail. Starting at the broad fire road, veer to the right as the trail forks onto Cragg Road. The scenery keeps getting better the further in you hike. Oak trees shade part of the trail as you follow the high road along the creek. Man-made Century Lake is a great place to stop for a picnic, take in the beauty of your surroundings, and/or fish. This spot marks a four-mile round trip. Continue on an additional two miles (round trip) to the former M*A*S*H* set. Being here might not have any meaning for your kids, but they'll at least think the rock formation, named Goat Buttes and used in the opening scene of the show, is worth a "wow."

Malibu Creek Park has many other interesting things to see and do. A mile in from the parking lot is the Visitor's Center, which also has a small museum. Each room in the museum is different. One contains taxidermied animals, another contains M*A*S*H* memorabilia, and yet another is a room for school groups to work on craft projects.

Feel like taking a dip in cool, refreshing water? Just beyond the Visitor's Center, over the bridge and to the left, is a rock pool.

Take advantage of all that the park offers by spending a night or two here. Each of the sixty-two campsites, some of which are shaded, has a picnic table and charcoal-use fire pit. Eight people per campsite are allowed.

**Hours:** The park is open daily from 8am to sunset. The Visitor's Center is open Sat. - Sun. from noon - 4pm.

**Admission:** $5 per vehicle. Camping prices are seasonal, and start at $12.

**Ages:** 3 years and up.

# MATHIAS BOTANICAL GARDEN / FOWLER MUSEUM / U.C.L.A.

(310) 825-3620 - garden; (310) 825-4361 - Fowler Museum / www.fmch.ucla.edu

*U.C.L.A. Campus, Westwood*

(Exit San Diego Fwy [405] E. on Wilshire Blvd., L. on Westwood Blvd. to the information kiosk. Make sure you ask for a map. Parking lot 9 is the closest to the garden.)

Mathias Botanical Garden, located on the U.C.L.A. campus, gave us the feeling of being in a secret garden, with its stony pathways through a lush "forest" and a hidden dirt path along the small creek. Trails crisscross through cactus and various other plant sections, which are as interesting to study as they are beautiful.

We took a free shuttle to the north end of the campus to the Murphy Sculpture Garden, which has over sixty sculptures scattered around an open grassy area. My 11-year old summed it up best from a kid's perspective; "I thought this was supposed to be great art. How come it's just a bunch of naked people?"

The U.C.L.A. Fowler Museum of Cultural History is also on the north end of campus. The majority of the exhibits are sophisticated, but older kids might enjoy them. Call for a current schedule of exhibits showing in the gallery rooms. Inquire about their children's programs and family workshops.

I hope walking around the classic campus, with its huge old brick buildings and stately trees, planted some dreams in my children's minds of going to college. There are several places to eat lunch or grab a snack on campus, and since you've paid for parking, you might as well make a day of it!

**Hours:** The Botanical Gardens are open Mon. - Fri., 8am - 5pm; Sat. - Sun., 8am - 4pm. The Fowler Museum is open Wed. - Sun., noon - 5pm (open Thurs. until 8pm.) Both are usually closed on University holidays.

**Admission:** Free admission to the gardens. The Fowler Museum is $5 for adults; $3 for seniors; discounts are given to U.C.L.A. associated alumni; free to ages 17 and under. The museum is free every Thurs. Parking in U.C.L.A. is $5 for the day.

**Ages:** All for the Botanical Gardens; 8 years and up for the Fowler Museum.

# MAYFAIR PARK

(562) 866-4776 or (562) 866-9771 - park; (562) 804-4256 - pool (in season)

*5720 Clark Street, Lakewood*

(Exit Artesia Fwy [91] S. on Lakewood Blvd., L. on South St. It's on the corner of South and Clark Sts.)

Mayfair Park is a very fair park indeed! The two enclosed playgrounds have fun equipment for younger children. The best attractions (judging by my kids playing on them for a long time) are the wooden train to climb on and in, and a sand play area that has buckets attached to pulleys on the outside of a small climbing structure. Open grassy fields are plentiful here, plus there are basketball courts, tennis courts, baseball diamonds with lights and stadium seating, barbecue pits, a swimming pool, a wading pool, and an Express McDonald's that's usually open in the summer and during special events.

**Hours:** The park is open daily. The pools are open mid-May through mid-June, weekends only; open daily in the summer. Swim sessions are 1pm to 2:30pm and 2:45pm to 4:15pm. Call for extended nighttime hours.

**Admission:** Free to the park. Each pool session costs $1.25 for adults; 75¢ for children 17 years and under. The wading pool is free.

**Ages:** All

# MENTRYVILLE / PICO CANYON

(805) 259-2701 / www.scvleon.com/mentryville

*Pico Canyon Road, Santa Clarita*
(Exit Golden State Fwy [5] W. on Lyons Ave. which turns into Pico Canyon Road. Go about 3 miles, staying to the left at the Y intersection and when the road forks, up a bumpy, semi-paved road.)

Mentryville was once an oil boom town. Of the few old buildings that remain, the Felton schoolhouse, originally built in 1885, is the only one open to the public. Inside are wooden school desks, a pot bellied stove, blackboards, and a very small library room that no longer contains books. A dual-seat outhouse and a tire swing are just outside. Other structures on the grounds include Mr. Mentry's house, a barn and chicken coop, and a jail that was built just a few years ago for a movie. Picnic tables are set up under shade trees. A seasonal creek runs through this area. Take a short hike on a service road that is stroller/wheelchair accessible. The road leads to Johnson Park, a picnic spot featuring a replica of a wood oil derrick. Hike a bit further through the surrounding hills of Pico Canyon, past foundation remains and up to some overlooks. After a few miles the trail changes. Only experienced hikers should continue as the trail now contains several very steep and strenuous sections. Tip: Bring your own water.

Creative teachers can plan a field to Mentryville that incorporates activities such as a school lesson in the schoolhouse, making butter, taking a nature walk, etc. A park ranger will come to give the class a history talk about the area.

**Hours:** Open weekends from 8am - 6pm. Explore Pico Canyon on your own on these days as well. Short, guided tours of Mentryville are offered the first and third Sun. of each month between noon and 4pm. School groups may call to reserve a time during the week.

**Admission:** Free

**Ages:** All

# NEW OTANI HOTEL AND GARDENS

(213) 629-1200

*120 S. Los Angeles Street, Los Angeles*
(Exit Harbor Fwy [110] E. on 4th St., L. on Los Angeles. Or, exit Santa Ana Fwy [101] S. on Alameda, R. on 1st St., L. on Los Angeles.)

Amid the hustle and bustle of downtown Los Angeles, take a quick breather at the New Otani Hotel gardens. Ride the elevator up to the small, but beautiful, Japanese garden located just outside the Thousand Cranes Restaurant. The garden's waterfall give it a sense of serenity. We loved its unique location - on top of a roof! Enjoy your short break from the busy world not far below.

**Hours:** Open daily - hotel hours.

**Admission:** Free; metered parking is available.

**Ages:** 2 years and up.

# NORWALK PARK

(562) 929-5702

*12203 Sproul Street, Norwalk*

(Exit Santa Ana Fwy [5] S. on Pioneer Blvd., L. on Firestone Blvd., L. on San Antonio Dr., R. on Sproul.)

This park has a Nature Center located in the back corner, near the freeway. A little stream and benches under shade trees, make it a nice place to visit some farm friends. The animals, all in pens, include spotted goats, sheep, a donkey, pot-bellied pigs, geese, and steer.

The park itself is spacious with lots of open grassy areas, a playground for younger kids, tennis courts, basketball courts, and a small museum. The museum contains artifacts from early Norwalk, including pictures, a few articles of clothing, and some furniture. A pool, with a shallow end and a diving board at the deep end, is open seasonally. A snack bar is in the pool area.

**Hours:** The park is open daily sunrise to sunset. The Nature Center/mini-farm is open daily from noon - 3pm. Call for hours during the week when it is open by appointment for tours for younger children. Call for museum hours. The pool and snack bar are usually open daily mid-June through August. Swim sessions are daily from 1pm - 2:45pm and 3:15pm - 5pm. An additional Sunday session goes from 11am - 12:30pm.

**Admission:** Free. Swim sessions are $1 per person.

**Ages:** All

# ORCUTT RANCH HORTICULTURE CENTER ☀

(818) 883-6641                                                          !

*23600 Roscoe Boulevard, West Hills*

(Exit Ventura Fwy [101] N. on Valley Circle Ave., R. on Roscoe Blvd.)

The horticultural center was originally created in the early 1900's. A stroll through these nostalgic gardens is a delightful way to pass a half an hour or so. A short, wide, stroller-friendly, dirt trail leads into a grove of shady oak trees and through grounds that are lush with greenery and wildflowers. The adjacent pathway along Dayton Creek, which borders one side of the Ranch's perimeters, is not for strollers. It does have stone benches for resting and leads to a few bridges that extend over the water. (On the other side of the creek is a cozy picnic area.) Look for ancient live oaks throughout the ranch; one is over 700 years old (and still growing)! Also on the grounds are a picnic table in the small bamboo grove, a grassy picnic area near the gazebo, and more formal gardens consisting of maze-like hedges around the rose gardens. A statue of Father Serra is in the courtyard, by the fountain, near a small stone grotto. Note: Visitors may not walk through the adjacent acres of citrus trees.

The adobe building, once the Orcutt's home, is now used for park offices and group rental functions. A quick walk around and through the mostly unfurnished building allows you to see the Mexican-influence architecture and hand-painted, South-of-the-Border tiles.

**Hours:** The grounds are open daily from 8am - 5pm. Many private functions are held here, however, so call first. (But you would do that anyhow, right?) Docent-guided tours are given the last Sun. of the month, except July and August, from 2pm - 5pm.

**Admission:** Free
**Ages:** All

# PARAMOUNT RANCH

(805) 370-2300
*On Cornell Road, Agoura Hills*
(Exit the Ventura Fwy [101] S. on Kanan Rd., go ¾ of a mile and turn L. on Cornell Rd., drive 2½ miles to the ranch.)

Howdy partners! You've come to the right ranch if you're looking for some action. Western Town in Paramount Ranch was once owned by Paramount Studios and used as a western movie set. The "town" still stands. The most recent television show filmed here was *Dr. Quinn, Medicine Woman*. Walk the dusty roads and inspect the town buildings, from the outside. It all looks so real! The town even has a train depot and a quarter-mile, or so, of railroad track. Dress up your cowboy or cowgirl and bring your camera. Better yet, bring your video camera (and a script) and do your own western mini-movie.

There is a huge meadow next to the main part of town, with an old-looking church building, and a schoolhouse on the perimeter. There are a few picnic tables here, too. Free, guided walking tours that describe the set and history of the area are usually given on the first and third Saturdays of each month at 9:30am.

Down by the meadow is a wonderful, wooded trail that follows along a creek, and is only one-eighth of a mile round trip. If the kids are in the mood for hiking into the mountains, go up Coyote Canyon Trail, just behind Western Town. This uphill, three-quarters of a mile round-trip trail goes through green chaparral-covered canyons overlooking the valley. The picnic spot up here has a view that is worth the effort. The 5K Run Trail is longer, obviously. It traverses a variety of scenery from the Oak Restoration Area, through Western Town, and down near the creek. Ranger-led naturalist programs are also offered at the park. Call regarding the many special and seasonal events that the ranch hosts.

**Hours:** Open daily 8am - sunset.
**Admission:** Free
**Ages:** All

# PETER STRAUSS RANCH

(805) 370-2300
*3000 Mulholland Highway, Agoura*
(Exit Ventura Fwy [101] S. on Kanan Rd., L. on Troutdale Dr., L. on Mulholland Hwy.)

This sprawling park, once owned by actor Peter Strauss, goes for miles and miles, with great hiking trails amongst the chaparral and oak trees. One of the smaller trails is only a three-quarter-mile loop, but there are several other trails for more ambitious walkers.

**Hours:** Open daily from 8am - 5pm.
**Admission:** Free.
**Ages:** 4 years and up.

## PLACERITA CANYON NATURE CENTER AND PARK    ☼
(805) 259-7721                                                        $
*19152 Placerita Canyon Road, Newhall*                               ♨
(Exit Golden State Fwy [5] N. on Antelope Valley Fwy [14], S. on Placerita Canyon Rd.)

Placerita Canyon was the site of one of the first gold discoveries, small though it was, in California. In fact, the famed oak tree where gold was first discovered, "Oak of the Golden Dream," is just a short walk from the parking lot. There is a wealth of history and wilderness to be found at this Nature Center and park.

The Center has live animals such as snakes and lizards, on display outside. One of the rooms inside has exhibits regarding the circle of life - predators, prey, and plants. Other exhibits include equipment that monitors weather conditions; dirt samples comparing texture and content; and taxidermied animals. Another room has live snakes and spiders (in glass cases), and a touch table with nests, pine cones, and bones.

The hiking is great here, especially for more experienced hikers. Canyon Trail is a gradual climb, following along a stream. The left fork leads to the scout campground. The right fork leads to the Waterfall Trail, where yes, about two-thirds of a mile back, is a waterfall. Canyon Trail also hooks up to Los Pinetos Trail, which is a hardy, eight-mile hike.

A large picnic area on the hillside of the park is nestled in a huge grove of oak trees. Play equipment is here, although the main attractions are the beauty of the area, and a small hiking trail. Call to find out more about the Saturday nature hikes, animal demonstrations, astronomy club, and other special programs, like summer camps.

**Hours:**     Open daily 9am - 5pm.
**Admission:** $3 per vehicle.
**Ages:**      2 years and up.

## POINT FERMIN PARK                                         ☼
(310) 548-7756                                                        !
*807 S. Paseo del Mar, San Pedro*                                    ♨
(Take Harbor Fwy [110] to the end, turn L. on Gaffey St., L. on 9th St., R. on Pacific Ave. to the end, then R. on Paseo del Mar.)

This corner park has lots of green grassy areas, shade trees, and a few play structures. Its two best features are the wonderful view of the California coastline, and a nineteenth-century lighthouse. The lighthouse is not open for tours, but it is very picturesque, with a wide variety of flowers and other plants surrounding it. I mention this park mainly because its large size and its proximity to several fun places in San Pedro makes it ideal for picnicking.

**Hours:**     Open daily sunrise to sunset.
**Admission:** Free
**Ages:**      All

# POLLIWOG PARK

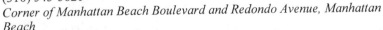

(310) 545-5621

*Corner of Manhattan Beach Boulevard and Redondo Avenue, Manhattan Beach*

(Exit San Diego Fwy [405] S. on Inglewood, R. on Manhattan Beach Blvd.)

This expansive park is wonderfully deceptive. The part seen from the street is beautiful, with a play area and lots of grass and trees. Some of the trees have low branches that beckon to climbers. There is also an exercise area, with wood benches and handles for pull-ups, sit-ups, etc. A huge portion of the lawn is graded for summer concerts in the park.

However, as you take the stroller-friendly pathway leading down toward the interior of the park, you'll discover some "hidden" delights, such as a pond where marshy reeds and ducks abound. (Signs ask that you don't feed the ducks.) Tip: Watch your children around the water as there are no guard rails. Kids, ages 6 to 12, have a play structure here that looks like Noah's Ark. This big boat was built with its middle pulled apart so kids can climb on it and slide down it, but hopefully not jump ship. Part of the ship was destroyed in a fire, but kids enjoy playing on it just the same. Younger kids, ages 2 to 5, have a playground designed especially for them with rope bridges, tires, slides, and swings.

**Hours:** Open daily from dawn to dusk.
**Admission:** Free
**Ages:** All

# PYRAMID LAKE

(805) 295-1245 - lake; (805) 257-2892 - bait shop

*Off Interstate 5, 20 miles N. of Santa Clarita Valley.*

(Exit Golden State Fwy [5] W. on Smokey Bear Road)

This huge, sparkling reservoir lake, surrounded by hills, offers a myriad of activities for families. Year-round boating, including waterskiing, canoeing, rowboating, and rubber rafting, is allowed. B.Y.O.B. (Bring Your Own Boat), as only aluminum fishing boats, which seat up to four people, are available to rent. Shaded picnic shelters and barbeques are near the docks. Some of the beach and picnic sites across the lake are reachable only by boat. Fish for seasonal bass, trout, catfish, crappie, and bluegill. A bait and tackle shop is on the grounds. A California state fishing license is required for those 16 years old or older. The waveless swim beach is open during the summer and is patrolled by lifeguards on the weekends. Outdoor showers are available here. Meander on trails along the lake, enjoy a picnic meal, visit the nearby VISTA DEL LAGO (see the Museums section), and/or camp at your choice of two campgrounds near the lake. Los Alamos Campground, two miles up the road, has room for ninety-three family units and three group units. Hard Luck Campground, on Piru Creek, has twenty-two family units.

**Hours:** The lake is open daily 6am - 8pm. The swim beach is open the same hours, seasonally.

**Admission:** $6 per vehicle, plus an additional $6 if you are bringing in your own boat. Fishing boat rentals start at $25 for the first two hours. Fishing poles are $5 for a half day. Camping is $10 per night. The swim beach costs $1 for adults; 50¢ for children 11 years and under, but only when a lifeguard is on duty. Swim at your own risk, for free, during the week when a lifeguard isn't on duty.

**Ages:** All

## RANCHO SANTA ANA BOTANIC GARDEN                    ☼

(909) 625-8767                                                                    $

*1500 N. College Avenue, Claremont*

(Exit San Bernardino Fwy [10] N. on Indian Hill Blvd., R. on Foothill. Go 3 blocks, then turn L. on College Ave.)

This eighty-six-acre botanic garden is beautiful in scope and sequence, and abundant with plants native only to California. Thousands of different kinds of plants grow in our state, so this garden covers a lot of ground with its giant sequoias, fan palms, California live oak, manzanitas, cacti, wildflowers, and more.

The numerous trails, many of which are stroller friendly, here afford good walking opportunities. Since the diverse vegetation attracts a wide variety of birds, bird lovers can pick up a bird check list at the gift shop, or join an organized bird walk on the first Sunday of each month. I don't know how much horticulture my kids take in when we visit botanic gardens, but it's a good introduction to the variety and importance of plant life, and a beautiful walk is always enjoyable.

**Hours:** Open daily from 8am - 5pm. Closed New Year's Day, Independence Day, Thanksgiving, and Christmas.

**Admission:** Free; donations of $2 per person or $5 per family are suggested.

**Ages:** 3 years and up.

## ROBERT E. RYAN PARK                    ☼

(310) 377-2290 - park site; (310) 541-4566 - city parks                    !

*30359 Hawthorne Boulevard, Rancho Palos Verdes*

(Exit Pacific Coast Highway [1] S. on Hawthorne Blvd. It's S. of Crest Rd., near Vallon Dr.)

From the parking lot of this nine-acre park, you get a glimpse of the California coastline, and on a clear day, Catalina Island. Steps lead down into the park itself. Note: Strollers and wheelchairs can take a ramp only a short distance down toward the park. The main play area is then accessible by going over a grassy slope.

The community center has some play equipment to check out, as long as you leave your driver's license in exchange. Play a game of basketball or baseball or romp around on the large, open, grassy areas. Set sail on a metal ship, with masts, that looks like something Columbus would have used for his explorations.

Shipmates can climb from stern to bow, go down a slide, and slide down a pole at the end of a gangplank. The playground also has climbing apparatus, swings, and slides, all in a big sand pit. Stroll under shade trees on cement pathways that go through a good portion of the park. Bring a sack lunch to enjoy at the picnic tables, or grill food at the barbecues.

**Hours:** Open July - Labor Day daily and on holidays from 10am - dusk. Open the rest of the year usually Mon. - Fri. and Sun. from noon - dusk; Sat., 10am - dusk. The parking lot is closed New Year's Day, Thanksgiving, Christmas Eve, and Christmas Day.

**Admission:** Free

**Ages:** All

# ROXBURY PARK

(310) 550-4761 - park; (310) 550-4979 - tennis
*471 S. Roxbury Drive, Beverly Hills*
(Exit Santa Monica Fwy [10] N. on Robertson, L. on Olympic. It's on the corner of Olympic and Roxbury.)

This beautiful park fits right in with its surroundings of well-manicured lawns and stately homes. Although it is off a main street, it still seems somewhat removed from city life. The park offers a wealth of activities to choose from such as tennis (four courts plus backboards), grass volleyball, basketball, baseball, and soccer. Along with a few picnic tables, barbecue pits, and some large shaded grassy areas, there is a good-sized playground. One of the wooden structures is designed for slightly older kids with a big slide to go down, bridges to cross, and ropes to climb. The other is designed with younger kids in mind. It has swings, slides, and fun cement shapes to crawl through.

**Hours:** Open daily from 7am - 11pm.

**Admission:** Free. Tennis courts are $6.50 an hour.

**Ages:** All

# RUNYON CANYON PARK

(213) 666-5004
*Fuller Street, Hollywood*
(Exit Hollywood Fwy [101] W. on Sunset Blvd., N. on Franklin St. all the way to the top.)

Hike the hills of Hollywood in the popular Runyon Canyon. The dirt trail starts off at an upward slant, leading past ruins where house foundations and a few chunks of wall still remain. We walked the scenic, mostly woodland, main trail all the way up the mountain, as it affords a spectacular view of the famed city. The hike is strenuous, going up and along the rim of the hills. The trail eventually levels off, then loops back down. The two-mile round trip hike is not stroller/wheelchair accessible. Nor is the slightly longer hike out to Mulholland. Bring water! Note: Look where you walk as this is a popular park for walking dogs. Guided hikes are given on the third weekend of each month. Inquire about the periodic full-moon hikes.

**Hours:** Open daily from dawn to dusk.

**Admission:** Free
**Ages:** 5 years and up.

## RUSTIC CANYON ☼

(310) 230-0137                                                   //$
*601 Latimer Road, Pacific Palisades*                            ♨
(Exit San Diego Fwy [405] W. on Wilshire Blvd., R. on 7th St. which turns into Entrada Dr., R. on Mesa Rd., L. on Latimer Rd.)

This pretty park is nestled in a somewhat secluded area of Pacific Palisades, but it's worth making the effort to visit here. Shade trees line the perimeter of a paved pathway that leads down into the park. A baseball field, basketball court, playground, grassy area, climbing trees (always a hit with this family), a wooden pyramid structure (to climb on and around), two picnic areas, and barbeque pits make up the central part of the park. Several tennis courts are located in one corner. Up near the parking lot is an older-style recreation center which offers a variety of classes. An adjacent, medium-sized community swimming pool is open seasonally.

**Hours:** The park is open daily sunrise to sunset. The pool is open the middle of June through Labor Day. Swim sessions are Mon. - Fri., 10am - noon and 1pm - 5pm; Sat. - Sun., 1pm - 5pm.
**Admission:** Free to the park. Swim sessions are $1.25 for adults; 75¢ for kids 17 years and under.
**Ages:** All

## SADDLEBACK BUTTE STATE PARK ☼

(805) 942-0662 / www.calparksmojave.com/saddleback             $
*17102 Avenue "J" East, Lancaster*
(Going N. on Antelope Valley Fwy [14], exit N. on 20th St. West, N. to Ave. "J." Going S. on Antelope Valley Fwy [14], exit E. on Ave. "J." It's quite a few miles out to the park.)

This state park is 3,000 acres of desert landscape, with Joshua trees scattered throughout and a huge granite mountain top, Saddleback Butte, jutting up almost a 1,000 feet above the valley. Several hiking trails are available here, including a two-and-a-half-mile trail that leads to the top of the Butte, and a view that makes the hike worthwhile. Springtime is particularly beautiful at the park because the wildflowers are in bloom. Near the entrance and park headquarters are several covered picnic areas, complete with barbecues. Please remember that desert weather is hot in the summer and cold in the winter, so dress accordingly. Overnight camping is available here. Saddleback is located just a few miles down the road from the ANTELOPE VALLEY INDIAN MUSEUM (look under the Museums section).

**Hours:** Open daily sunrise to sunset.
**Admission:** $5 per vehicle for day use. Camping is $10 per night.
**Ages:** 5 years and up.

## SAND DUNE PARK

(310) 545-5621
*At the corner of 33rd Street and Bell Avenue, Manhattan Beach*
(Exit San Diego Fwy [405] W. on Rosecrans Ave., L. on Bell.)
    This little park has a big surprise. While there is a small playground for younger children, the park is really beachy because of its steep wall of sand that is perfect for running, jumping, or rolling down. Here is a local's favorite tip: After it rains, take a snow sled down the hill!
    Wooden steps lead to the top of the hill. Behind the steps is a short "trail" in a small wooded area. With a little imagination this section becomes a jungle or a deserted island. Picnic tables and a few barbecue pits are also available. Parking is limited.
    **Hours:**    Open daily dawn to dusk.
    **Admission:**    Free
    **Ages:**    All

## SAN DIMAS COUNTY PARK

(909) 599-7512
*1628 Sycamore Canyon Road, San Dimas*
(From Foothill Fwy [210], take the 30 Fwy E. go N.W. on Foothill Blvd., R. on San Dimas Canyon Dr., up the hill to the park office.)
    Nestled in the foothills of the San Gabriel Mountains, adjacent to Angeles National Forest, is a wonderful county park/museum/wildlife sanctuary. The nature museum is small but comprehensive. It has live snakes, such as rosy boas and rattlesnakes; taxidermied animals, such as California gray squirrels, birds, and raccoons; and several small collections including rocks, arrowheads, insects, and butterflies.
    The outside wildlife sanctuary offers a caged home to several injured or non-releasable native animals. Hawks, heart-faced barn owls, and great-horned owls are part of the bird rehabilitation area; not part of the bird "rebellion" area as my son misread the sign. (Hmm - could be something to do with his childhood. . . ) Other live animals here include a deer, raccoon (his little paws were busily cleaning his food when we saw him), possum, a destunked skunk, fox, pheasants, and tortoises, plus many squirrels running around freely.
    A one-mile, self-guiding nature trail, begins in the oak woodland just behind the nature center building and loops around. There are several other trails to choose from which satisfy both novice and experienced hikers. There are plenty of picnic tables here under the cover of shady oak trees. Some of the picnic areas have barbeques. The area below the museum has a baseball diamond, a few playgrounds, and large grassy areas. An equestrian center is next to the park, and a portion of a long bike route goes through part of the park. Come visit the park on your own, or via a Jr. Ranger Program, offered through the park system. A visit to the San Dimas County Park is a great for temporarily escaping city life.
    **Hours:**    The park is open daily 8am - sunset. The nature center is open daily 9am - 5pm.

**Admission:** Free
**Ages:** All

# SANTA FE DAM RECREATIONAL AREA

(626) 334-1065
*15501 Arrow Highway, Irwindale*
(From San Gabriel River Fwy [605], exit E. on Live Oak Ave. which turns into Arrow Hwy. From Foothill Fwy [210], exit S. on Irwindale, R. on Arrow Highway.)

    Though located in the middle of an industrial section, city sounds fade away while at this enormous recreational area that sports a mountainous backdrop. Our first stop was at the nature center trail, at the northern end of the park. The rock-lined, three-quarter-mile looping trail is paved, level, and a delight to walk. Desert is the predominant theme. We observed an abundance of cacti and other plant life, and animals such as jackrabbits, lizards, roadrunners, and hummingbirds.

    The huge lake toward the entrance offers a nice-sized beach with a lifeguarded swimming area, and a small, water play area for children 52" and under. This area has a few slides and some climbing apparatus in shallow waters. Other attractions in the park include a playground; fishing - a California state license is required for those 16 years of age and older; quiet boating activities (no gasoline powered boats allowed), with rentals available; picnic facilities; and unpaved walking trails. This lakeside area, with its shade trees and acres of green grass, is vastly different from the northern desert area.

    Ready for a bike ride? Choose your route and go the distance all the way north to San Gabriel Canyon, or south to Long Beach, using various trails that go through this park. Parts of the trail are paved, while other parts are not.

**Hours:** Open sunrise to sunset. The swim beach and water play areas are open seasonally.
**Admission:** $6 per vehicle; $3 for a senior citizen's or a disabled person's vehicle. There is no extra charge to use the swim beach. The water play area, however, is $1 per person for each hour-and-a-half swim session.
**Ages:** All

# SANTA MONICA MOUNTAIN NATIONAL RECREATION AREA

(818) 597-9192
*30401 Agoura Road, #100, Agoura Hills*

    From the thousands of acres of mountains to the coastline beaches to the inland grounds, the enormous Santa Monica Recreation Area covers a major part of the wilderness and parkland in Southern California. This national park service publishes a quarterly calendar of events, which includes docent or ranger-guided programs, hikes, and educational "classes," as well as specific family activities. Come by, or call and ask a ranger to send you a booklet. Just some of the parks covered in this area include FRANKLIN CANYON, MALIBU CREEK STATE

PARK, MALIBU LAGOON STATE BEACH / ADAMSON HOUSE,
PARAMOUNT RANCH, PETER STRAUSS RANCH, RANCHO SIERRA
VISTA, and WILL ROGERS STATE PARK. (These parks are listed
individually in this section.)
**Hours:**  Open daily.

## SOUTH COAST BOTANICAL GARDENS                               ☼
(310) 544-6815 / parks.co.la.ca.us/south_coast_botanic.html     $$
*26300 S. Crenshaw Boulevard, Rolling Hills Estates*            ≛
(Exit San Diego Fwy [405] S. on Crenshaw Blvd. It's a few miles to Rolling Hills Estates.)
    This attractive, eighty-seven-acre garden is a breath of fresh air for Southern
Californians. It's planted with exotic trees, shrubs, and flowers from Africa and
New Zealand, and all over the world. There are several different specialty areas
here including a cactus garden, a rose garden (we love taking pictures of roses
here - such color and variety), and a Garden for the Senses. In the latter,
vegetation with unique fragrances, textures, and color schemes flourish. Stroll
along the cement and dirt pathways through the gardens, under shade trees, and
up and down the gently rolling hills and grassy areas. It feels good to be
surrounded by such beauty! Feed ducks at the man-made lake and look for koi,
turtles, heron, and other waterfowl who make their home here. Enjoy a half-hour
narrated tram tour on the weekend. Outside food can't be brought in, but a picnic
area is just outside the gates.
**Hours:**  Open daily from 9am - 5pm. The tram tour is available Sat. -
          Sun. at 11am, 1pm, and 3pm. The Gardens are closed on
          Christmas.
**Admission:**  $5 for adults; $3 for seniors and students; $1 for ages 5 - 12;
          children 4 years and under are free. Admission is free the third
          Tuesday of every month. The tram tour costs $1.50 per person.
**Ages:**  3 years and up.

## STONEY POINT                                                ☼
*Topanga Canyon Boulevard, Chatsworth*                          !
(Exit Simi Valley/San Fernando Valley Fwy [118] S. on Topanga Canyon Blvd. It's the
first big rock on your left.)
    Do you have a rock-climber "wannabe" in your household? Stoney Point is
a famous (at least locally) rock climbers' delight. Practice repelling on this small
mountain of stone, or just hike the trail up to the top. Either way, it can be an
exhilarating way to spend the day.
**Hours:**  Open daily sunrise to sunset.
**Admission:**  Free
**Ages:**  4 years and up to hike; your discretion about rock climbing.

## TEMESCAL GATEWAY PARK                                       ☼
(310) 454-1395                                                  $$
*15601 Sunset Boulevard, Pacific Palisades*                     ≛

(From Pacific Coast Highway [1], head N. on Temescal Canyon Rd., cross Sunset Blvd., into the park.)

This comely wilderness park is particularly pretty in the spring when the wildflowers are blooming profusely. Dirt trails meander throughout - up a hill, under shade trees, and over a seasonal creek. Picnic tables are here, too, so bring a sack lunch.

**Hours:** Open daily sunrise to sunset.
**Admission:** $6 per vehicle.
**Ages:** All

## TOWSLEY CANYON

(805) 255-2974
*24255 The Old Road, Newhall*
(Exit Golden State Fwy [5] on Calgrove and go W. back under the freeway, S. on The Old Road. Look for entrance signs.)

This beautiful mountain wilderness park contains some spectacular geological structures. First, visit the nature center located at Canyon View trailhead, which contains displays on the history of the park. These include old photographs, taxidermied animals, and artifacts from the days when this area was an oil boom town. A picnic area and restrooms are here, too. Hiking trails range from easy to difficult. The two-mile Canyon View loop trail is a mostly moderate hike with a few short, steep grades. The five-and-a-half-mile Towsley View loop trail has more strenuous grades. This trail, which hooks up to Wiley Canyon, parallels the creek as it goes past grassy areas, the Narrows (where there are unique rock formations), and old oil drilling grounds. Be on the lookout for seasonal wildflowers, valley and coastal live oak trees, and animals that share this habitat. The Wiley Canyon trail is two miles round trip and a fairly easy walk. Also see EAST AND RICE CANYON, listed in this section, as that park is just down the road.

**Hours:** Open daily from sunrise to sunset.
**Admission:** Free
**Ages:** 3 years and up.

## TREEPEOPLE / COLDWATER CANYON PARK

(818) 753-4600 or (818) 753-4631
*12601 Mulholland Drive, Beverly Hills*
(Exit Ventura Fwy [101] S. on Coldwater Cyn Ave., which merges with Mulholland Dr. near the park.)

Ever feel like our lease as earth's caretakers is up for renewal? And we might not get the contract again because we haven't done a very good job? If you and your kids are concerned about environmental issues, come visit the TreePeople. In a garage-type building, the Recycling Education Center shows how plastic, glass, and aluminum can be recycled and reused in clothing, fiberfill, etc. Kids can turn a crank to see a beautiful canyon transformed into a dirty landfill. Practical recycling tips are shown by neighbors Dirty and Desperate, who create waste by throwing out everything, versus Clean and Cool, who recycle everything possible and are earth-conscious shoppers. Visit the small garden, and the next exhibit building to see an urban forest map, nests, eggs, a photo display on bees, and even a little stage for putting on *tree*mendous productions. The adjacent compost pile is smelly, but a fascinating resource tool.

Hour-long, guided tours of the park include in-depth information about conservation, as well as the importance of planting trees in areas damaged by pollution. Children, 4 to 12 years, will play interactive games as they explore the environmental exhibits and hike the trails. Tour reservations are recommended as there is a limited number of people per tour.

Coldwater Canyon Park is beautiful, with large oak and California Bay Laurel trees shading the meandering trails. Most of the five miles of hiking trails are covered with sawdust and small broken twigs, making it bumpy for strollers. Picnic tables are available toward the park entrance.

**Hours:**      The park is open daily. Call to make a reservation for a
                TreePeople tour.
**Admission:**  The park is free, and the tours are usually free, too.
**Ages:**       6 years and up.

## VASQUEZ ROCKS

(805) 268-0840
*10700 East Escondido Canyon Road, Agua Dulce*
(Exit Antelope Valley Fwy [14] N. on Agua Dulce Canyon Rd., R. on Escondido Canyon Rd. Follow the signs along the way.)

This park became an instant favorite with my boys. The Ranger Station, housed in a barn with corralled horses outside, sets the mood for this all-natural, rustic park. Some of the unusual rock formations are almost triangular in shape, jutting practically straight up from the ground. They have ridges along their sides making them moderately easy to climb. The kids can climb until their hearts' content, or until your heart can't take them going up to the tops anymore. For those who don't like heights, there are several smaller rocks to conquer, and plenty of walking trails.

If you experience "deja vu" while here, it's probably because this park has been used in numerous commercials and films, such as *The Flintstones*, as well as westerns and science fiction thrillers. Tip: Call before you come because sections of the park are closed when filming is taking place.

Vasquez Rocks, named for an outlaw who hid among the rocks here, also contains Tatavian Indian sites and a seasonal stream. Be forewarned - drinking water is not available in the park. Camping for organized youth groups is allowed.

**Hours:**      Open daily 8am to sunset.
**Admission:**  $3 per vehicle.
**Ages:**       3 years and up.

## VINCENT LUGO PARK

(626) 308-2875

*Wells Street, San Gabriel*                                              ⛲

(Exit San Bernardino Fwy [10] N. on Ramona St., R. on Wells St.)

There are three great play areas immediately visible here: A small enclosed one for toddlers; one with a rocket structure to climb up and slide down; and another that is just fun. In the summertime a very small enclosed wading pool is open. A sand pit, lots of grassy running space, and picnic tables help classify this park as a good one.

According to my "park-smart" kids, however, the best part of the park is across the service road and to the south, almost hidden from sight. Children can play on the oversized cement sea creatures that have surfaced here, such as an octopus and whale. Shouts of, "this is the best!" came from my kids as they slid down the sea serpent that is wrapped around a lighthouse. Another giant sea serpent is curled around a rocky hill, which has a huge shade tree growing from it, plus a slide to go down. Like a chest filled with gold on the bottom of the ocean floor, this nautical park was a treasure of a find!

     **Hours:**   Open daily from 7:30am - 10pm.

  **Admission:**   Free

      **Ages:**   All

# WHITTIER NARROWS RECREATION AREA   ☼

(626) 575-5526             !

*Rosemead Boulevard and Santa Anita Avenue, South El Monte*  ⛲

(There are a few different entrances - Exit Pomona Fwy [60] N. on Rosemead Blvd. to the athletic facilities; exit S. on Santa Anita Ave. to the lake and park; exit S. on Peck, R. on Durfee to the nature center.)

Whittier Narrows will broaden your horizons with the scope of its recreational activities. This expansive 1,100-acre park offers something for every age, interest, and activity level in your family. The section of park on the northern side of the freeway is for the sports-oriented with sixteen lighted tennis courts, six soccer fields, seven baseball diamonds, an archery range, a trap and skeet shooting range, a model plane airfield, a model car track, playgrounds, bike trails, and a bicycle motocross (BMX) track - (626) 575-5521. Check out the adjacent AMERICAN HERITAGE PARK / MILITARY MUSEUM, listed under the Museums section.

Don't want to make waves? Visit the placid Legg Lake, (562) 434-6121, which is south of the freeway. At the time of this writing, the lake was drained, but expected to be filled up again soon. Pedal boat rentals are available here at $6 a half hour, or rent a rowboat for $9 a half hour. Boating activities are operational only on the weekends. Kids can have a "reel" fun time fishing here, too. The pretty parkland surrounding the lake has shade trees, large grass areas, and playgrounds.

For those who hear nature calling, the nature center is located at 1000 Durfee, (626) 575-5523. The center is small, but it has live frogs, snakes, and turtles as well as a few taxidermied animals. We saw cardinals and blue jays at the bird feeders just outside. There are miles of hiking and biking trails going through the trees, along a creek, and throughout the park. The particularly beautiful Lake Trail (three-and-a-half-miles long) loops around the lake and back toward the center. Ask about the center's hour-and-a-half guided school tours. Knowledgeable docents lead the kids on a hike, pointing out and explaining about the plants and animals seen along the way. Students will also listen to a ranger talk regarding the displays in the nature center building. Another tour option is taking a forty-five-minute tractor-drawn hayride around the area. The ranger talk is included in this tour, too. Bring a sack lunch to enjoy at the picnic site here. Note: Hayrides are available for individuals and families every Saturday, too, at 10am. Inquire about other park programs, too, such as the Jr. Ranger program for ages 7 to 12 years old.

**Hours:** The park is open daily from sunrise - sunset. The nature center is usually open Mon. - Sat. from 9:30am - 5pm, Sun., 11am - 5pm. Closed Christmas. Call to make tour reservations.

**Admission:** Parking is free on weekdays; $3 on weekends and holidays. Admission and parking are free at the nature center. The hiking tour is $10 total for up to sixty students. The hayride is $50 total for up to fifty children. The Sat. hayride is $2 for adults; $1 for children.

**Ages:** All

# WILDERNESS PRESERVE
(626) 355-5309
*2240 Highland Oaks Drive, Arcadia*
(Exit Interstate Fwy [210] N. on Santa Anita Ave., R. on Elkins Ave., L. on Highland Oaks.)

In the foothills of the mountains, and on the same street as residential housing, is a wilderness park/preserve. A short dirt trail through the shade trees loops around a large grassy area. Plenty of picnic tables are scattered among the woods. A picnic shelter with enough picnic tables for a busload, or two, is on the grounds, next to the kitchen facility that has two sinks, a freezer, a refrigerator, and an oven. This shelter area is available for group rental and also has a fire ring with amphitheater-type seating. Call before you come to ask if the Santa Anita creek, kept in check by controlling the water from the Santa Ana dam, is flowing. If so, get at least your feet wet - so refreshing on a hot summer's day. A swimming hole at the north end of the creek usually has three or four feet of water, regardless.

The nature center contains quite a few, glass-encased, taxidermied animals. We looked at barn owls, ravens, a gold eagle, black bear, mountain lion, coyote, raccoon, and lots more. The building also has a mounted insect collection and a few live snakes. Ask about the many classes that the park offers, including merit badge classes.

**Hours:** Open January - May and October - December on Fri. only from 8:30am - 4:30pm. Open the summer months and September, Mon. - Fri., 8:30am - 7pm. Weekend admission is by advanced reservation only.

**Admission:**  Free
**Ages:**  All

## WILLIAM S. HART MUSEUM AND PARK ☼

(805) 254-4584 - museum; (805) 259-0855 - park and camping  /  !
www.hart-friends.org; www.lam.mus.ca.us/hart
*24151 San Fernando Road, Santa Clarita*  ♨

See WILLIAM S. HART MUSEUM AND PARK under the Museums section.

## WILL ROGERS STATE HISTORIC PARK ☼

(310) 454-8212 / willrogerspolo.org/htm/wwstpark.htm  $$
*1501 Will Rogers State Park Road, Pacific Palisades*  ♨
(From Pacific Coast Highway, exit N. on Sunset Blvd., L. on Will Rogers State Park Rd.
From San Diego Fwy [405], exit W. on Sunset Blvd., R. on Will Rogers State Park Rd.)

"I never met a man I didn't like." These famous words were spoken by the "cowboy philosopher," actor, columnist, humorist, philanthropist, etc., - Will Rogers. His ranch house was deeded to the state, and is now a museum. It has been left virtually unchanged from when he lived here in the late 1920's. The rustic, wood-beamed living room features many Indian blankets and rugs, saddles, animal skins, a longhorn steer head over the fireplace, a wagon wheel "chandelier," Western statues, Will's boots, and furniture. You'll also see his library/drawing room, upstairs bedrooms, and an office, which are all simply and comfortably furnished, and decorated with a western flair, of course.

The Visitors Center shows a free, continuously playing twelve-minute film on Will Rogers, featuring some of his rope tricks. Also available at no cost is an audio wand tour. Borrow a wand and place it at the several designated locations throughout the park, and it will tell you information about that area.

Picnic tables are plentiful at the park. The huge grassy area is actually a polo field. Games are held on weekends April through September. So come, have fun, learn a little history about a fascinating man, and if you feel like horsing around, watch a polo match.

There are several trails leading through the park that connect with its "backyard" neighbor, the huge Topanga State Park. One of the most popular hikes is the two-mile loop to Inspiration Point which, on a clear day, gives an inspirational, breathtaking view.

**Hours:** The park is open daily from 8am - 6pm. Tours of the house are available every hour on the half hour from 10:30am - 4:30pm, staff and weather permitting.
**Admission:** $6 per vehicle. House tours and polo matches are free.
**Ages:** 5 years and up.

## ADVENTURE PLAYGROUND ☼

(949) 786-0854  !
*1 Beech Tree Lane, Irvine*  ♨

(Exit San Diego Fwy [405] S. on Jeffrey, which turns into University Dr., R. on Beech Tree. It's in the University Community Park.)

This park is a dream come true for children, as they are actually encouraged to play in the mud! They can go down a waterslide (i.e. a tarp-covered hill with a hose) into the mud, and ooze their way through an obstacle course. Tip: Call to make sure that the water is being turned on the day you plan to come - no water, no mud. Bring a change of clothes for the kids (and you). There is an outdoor shower.

Drier play equipment includes kid-size buildings and a big wooden climbing structure. Kids 6 years and older can add on to the little shanty town here. After completing a one-hour safety course (yea!) they are free to use the wood, hammer, and nails provided by the park to build onto existing forts, clubhouses, castles, etc. - whatever they imagine the structures to be. If your child is a regular here, he/she can stake a plot of land and construct his/her own building.

Some of the special classes offered (for a small fee) include Basic and Advanced Carpentry, Pioneer Cooking (campfire cooking), Mechanical Gadgetry, Jr. Archaeologist, etc.

Shade is scarce in Adventure Playground, but fun is not. Bring a picnic lunch to enjoy either in here or just outside the gates at University Community Park. This spacious grassy park has non-muddy playgrounds, a Frisbee golf course, and open areas for field sports and roller hockey, which is offered a few days a week.

Note: Close-toed shoes are required at Adventure Playground. The best times to come are after 2pm during the week or on Saturdays, as day campers often ~~invade~~ come play at this unique play area. Note: Look under the June Calendar section for details on the Adventure Playground in Huntington Beach. It is only open, however, for five weeks in the summer.

| | |
|---|---|
| **Hours:** | Open in the summer Tues. - Sat. from 10am - 5pm. Open the rest of the year, Tues. - Fri., 2:30pm - 5pm; Sat., 10am - 5pm. |
| **Admission:** | Free. Groups must call for reservations, and they are charged a minimal fee. |
| **Ages:** | 5 - 14 years. Note: Kids under 6 years must be accompanied by an adult at every activity. |

# ALISO AND WOOD CANYONS REGIONAL PARK   ☼

(949) 831-2791 or (949) 831-2790                                            $

*Alicia Parkway and Aliso Creek Road, Laguna Niguel*

(Exit San Diego Fwy [5] W. on Crown Valley Pky., R. on La Paz Rd., L. on Aliso Creek Rd., L. on Alicia Pky., R. on Awma. The entrance is 500 ft. S. of Alicia Pky. and Aliso Creek Rd.)

This regional park has 3,400 acres of wilderness sanctuary to explore by hiking or biking. You and your child will see everything that patience allows - coastal sage, chaparral, oak woodlands, open grassland meadows, canyons, and creeks, plus wildlife such as deer, possums, coyotes, bobcats, etc.

This huge park is like life, offering many paths to choose from. Take a trail from here into the adjacent Laguna Niguel Regional Park; ride the twelve-mile

Aliso Creek Bikeway, which basically follows along Alicia Parkway; or choose from several other paths. We walked the Aliso Trail. The first part is paved and rather bland, scenically speaking. As we reached the dirt pathway and went into the hills, the terrain and scenery became much more interesting. (Strollers and bikes can go here, but it does get a bit bumpy.) About a mile and half down the road is the Nature Center. It houses Indian artifacts, taxidermied animals, photographs of wild flowers in bloom, and maps.

There are numerous caves, or overhangs, throughout the park. A few are open to the public. Past the Nature Center, or Gate 2, is Cave Rock. Kids enjoy climbing up into Cave Rock, and sliding back down. Further back on the trail, is Dripping Cave, also called - and this has much more kid-appeal - Robbers Cave. Legend has it that bandits used this cave as a hideout after a robbery! At one time the holes inside supposedly had wooden pegs to hold their saddle bags, and bags of booty. Tell this to your kids and let their imaginations take over. If you have the time and energy, keep on going to Coyote Run, deeper into the heart of the park. Tip: Bring water!

Look up the ORANGE COUNTY NATURAL HISTORY MUSEUM, under the Museums section, for information on this museum that's located at the trailhead of the park.

**Hours:**      The park is open 7am to sunset. The Nature Center is open
                sporadically, whenever staffing is available.
**Admission:**  $2 per vehicle.
**Ages:**       2 years and up.

# ATLANTIS PLAY CENTER                                   ☼
(714) 892-6015                                            $
*9301 Atlantis Way, Garden Grove*                        ☷
(Exit the Garden Grove Fwy [22] S. on Magnolia, L. on Westminster, L. on Atlantis Way.
It's N. of the Garden Grove Park.)

This "lost island" park is quite a find. Atlantis Play Center is a wonderful, large, enclosed play area for kids of all ages. Several different playgrounds are scattered around the park that feature slides, tubes, swings, sand pits, etc., plus big, concrete aquatic creatures to play on. The sea-serpent slide is a favorite. The green rolling hills are perfect for picnicking. Numerous shade trees make the park surprisingly cool, even in the heat of the summer. A full-service snack bar is open daily during the summer, and usually on the weekends the rest of the year.

One of my boys' favorite things to do is to play in and amongst the bushes that go around the perimeter of the park. The bushes become hideouts, forts, a pirate's landing, etc. - a little imagination goes a long way!

Just outside Atlantis is the Garden Grove Park, with more play equipment and wide open grassy areas.

**Hours:**      Open in the summer Tues. - Sat., 10am - 4pm; Sun., noon - 4pm.
                Open the rest of the year Tues. - Fri., 11am - 4pm; Sat., 10am -
                4pm; Sun., noon - 4pm.
**Admission:**  $1 for ages 2 and older; children under 2 years are free.

**Ages:**   1½ - 12 years.

## BOLSA CHICA ECOLOGICAL RESERVE

(714) 846-1114 - interpretative center; (714) 897-7003 - tour info  /
www.goodtime.net/hbe/lohbe074.htm
*Warner Avenue, Huntington Beach*
(Exit San Diego Fwy [405] S. on Bolsa Chica Rd., R. on Warner Ave., L. on Pacific Coast
Highway. The reserve is opposite Bolsa Chica State Beach.)

This 530-acre, saltwater wetland reserve is home to a variety of plant and
waterfowl such as avocets, egrets, plovers, sand pipers, ducks, and terns. We also
saw herons, and a few brown pelicans that swooped down to scoop up fish. Bird
lovers should bring binoculars. Although the nesting and breeding islands are
protected by a chain link fence, you may cross over the wooden bridge to walk
along an easy and stroller-friendly, mile-and-a-half trail that loops through the
reserve, and partially along the highway. No bikes are allowed. My little
explorers especially liked walking down to inspect the water and its inhabitants,
a little closer than I felt comfortable with. Free, guided tours are given the first
Saturday of every month beginning at 9am.

A small Interpretative Center is housed in a trailer on the corner of the
reserve, at 3842 Warner Avenue and Pacific Coast Highway. Inside are local
ecology displays such as pictures of birds in the area; a rattlesnake skin; a
preserved stingray and leopard shark; a touch table; and information panels on
the value of wetlands. Interested in helping take care of this area? Clean-up
Saturday, where volunteers pick up trash and remove non-native plants, is held
the last Saturday of each month. Note: For more fun in the sun, BOLSA CHICA
STATE BEACH is directly across the street from the reserve. (See the Beaches
section for details.)

**Hours:**   The Reserve is open daily 8am to sunset. The Center is usually
open Tues. - Fri., 10am - 4pm. Call for weekend hours.
**Admission:**   Free
**Ages:**   All

## BOYSEN PARK / ANAHEIM TENNIS CENTER

(714) 991-9090 - tennis center
*975 S. State College Blvd., Anaheim*
(Exit Artesia Fwy [91] S. on State College Blvd. The park is at the intersection of State
College Blvd. and Wagner.)

Take off to this park whose main attraction is a large gray cement airplane.
The wings are tipped just enough so kids can climb up on them (wingwalkers!)
and into the instrumentless cockpit. Other park amenities include picnic tables, a
playground, baseball fields, and sand volleyball courts. The adjacent schoolyard,
available to use when school is not in session, has basketball courts, a few
scattered playgrounds, and more baseball diamonds. The park wraps around the
Anaheim Tennis Center. Get in the swing of things by playing on one of the
Center's twelve lighted courts and/or three ball-machine courts.

**Hours:** The park is open daily. The Tennis Center is open Mon. - Thurs., 8am - 10pm; Fri., 8am - 9pm; Sat. - Sun., 8am - 6pm.

**Admission:** The park is free. Tennis costs vary from $3 an hour for adults to $7 an hour, depending on the time of day. Children 11 years and under are $1.50 an hour.

**Ages:** All for the park; able to hold a racquet and play tennis for the Center.

## BROOKHURST COMMUNITY PARK

*2271 W. Crescent Avenue, Anaheim*
(Going S. on Santa Ana Fwy [5], exit S. on Brookhurst St., R. on Crescent. Going N., exit W. on La Palma Ave., L. on Brookhurst, R. on Crescent. From Crescent, turn R. on Ventura, which turns into Green Acre. The park is right there.)

Baseball diamonds, basketball courts, a few picnic tables, and barbecue pits are here, but more importantly, your kids can come to this park and walk on the moon! "Crater Park," our nickname for it, resembles the surface of the moon with play equipment inside crater-shaped areas. There are slides, swings, climbing structures, a rocket ship (for blasting off to parts unknown), and a big, white, cement walkway that interconnects the play areas. Being here almost eclipses playing at other parks.

**Hours:** Open daily sunrise to sunset.

**Admission:** Free

**Ages:** 2 years and up.

## CARBON CANYON REGIONAL PARK

(714) 996-5252
*4442 Carbon Canyon Road, Brea*
(Exit Riverside Fwy [91] N. on Imperial Hwy., R. on Valencia Ave., R. on Carbon Canyon Rd.)

Talk about recreational opportunities! Carbon Canyon is 124 acres big and offers everything for the sports-minded and fun-loving family. There are tennis courts, volleyball courts, horseshoe pits, softball fields, a huge open field for whatever other sport you feel like playing, and five great playgrounds scattered throughout the park.

Other activities include taking a hike to the ten-acre Redwood Grove; cycling on the one-and-a-half-mile paved trail; or riding the equestrian trail that accesses Chino Hills State Park. The beautiful four-acre lake in the middle of the park has two fishing piers, but it is not stocked. Bring suntan lotion and food, and have a great day.

**Hours:** Open November 1 through March 31 from 7am - 6pm. Open April 1 through October 31 from 7am - 9pm.

**Admission:** $2 vehicle entrance Mon. - Fri.; $4 on Sat. - Sun.; $5 on holidays.

**Ages:** All

## CARL THORNTON PARK

(714) 571-4200

*1801 W. Segerstrom Avenue, Santa Ana*

(Going E. on San Diego Fwy [405], exit N. on Fairview Rd., L. on Segerstrom Ave. Going S. on Costa Mesa Fwy [55], exit E. on Dyer Rd. which turns into Segerstrom Ave.)

The front part of this park is a huge open area, great for kite flying because the trees are short (at least right now). A small creek runs through this area, ending in a big pond that attracts a lot of ducks, geese, and sea gulls. (Don't get goosed by the geese!) For your sporting pleasure, there are also two baseball diamonds.

At the northeast corner of the park, accessible by paved pathways, is an enclosed "barrier free" playground. This means that it has special apparatus designed for disabled children. One of the swings can hold a wheelchair-bound child. A sand play area, with water fountains to make sand castles, is elevated for kids in wheelchairs. Other play areas are great for all kinds of kids, as there are slides, tunnels, and things to climb. Stone turrets give the playground a castle-like setting. A large grassy area is inside the enclosure for safe, run-around play.

**Hours:** Open daily from 8am - 10pm.
**Admission:** Free
**Ages:** All

## CASTLE PARK

(949) 552-4352

*Northwood Community Park, 4351 Bryan Avenue, Irvine*

(Exit Santa Ana Fwy [5] N. on Culver, R. on Bryan.)

The focal point of Castle Park is the big, fortress-like structure which is great for climbing on and around. It has slides, steps, and a rocky wall that completes the fortress image. The playground also has tire swings, a balance beam, slides, a wooden and cement pirate ship, and sand boxes.

The surrounding park has soccer fields, tennis courts, a basketball court, shuffleboard, a handball court, and baseball diamonds. You can check out play equipment, free of charge, at the information building.

**Hours:** The park and information building are open Mon. - Fri., 9am - 9pm; Sat. - Sun., 9am - 6pm.
**Admission:** Free
**Ages:** All

## CEDAR GROVE PARK

(714) 573-3325

*11385 Pioneer Road, Tustin*

(Exit Santa Ana Fwy [5] N. on Jamboree Rd., L. on Tustin Ranch Rd., R. on Pioneer Way. It's located at the intersection of Pioneer Way and Pioneer Rd.)

This park is unique in that it has play equipment for all ages, plus a half-circle basketball court. Starting at the parking lot, follow the winding pathway (reminiscent of a snake's trail), back to three interconnecting playgrounds which are geared for ages 2 to 5, 6 to 10, and 10 years and up. The toddler playground, built in the sand, has a wooden train to board, a castle play structure (complete with a drawbridge), a heavy-duty sand digger, and an area that has a few water spigots for making wet sand creations. Tip: Bring a change of pants for your child. Go over or under a wooden bridge to reach the next play area which is padded with dense foam. Kids can pretend to sail the seas on the wooden Adventure Ship, as well as play on the swings, wavy slides, monkey bars, rings, climbing structure, and cargo net. Older kids have their own, small, play area. It has several colorful metal ladders and geometric shapes for kids to climb on or across. (I wondered if the shapes had a particular function or purpose, but my imaginative kids just had a great time playing on them.) Other fun things here include trying to balance yourself on a rope ladder without it twisting you around and holding on to S-shaped poles as their bases spin around. Plenty of picnic tables line the playground's pathway.

The huge, adjacent grassy area has numerous cedar trees around its perimeters. Next to this is a grove of shady pine trees with picnic tables nestled underneath.

**Hours:**     Open daily sunrise to sunset.
**Admission:**   Free
**Ages:**       All

## CRAIG REGIONAL PARK

(714) 990-0271
*3300 North State College Boulevard, Fullerton*
(Exit Orange Fwy [57] W. on Imperial, L. on State College.)

124 acres and three separate playgrounds make this an ideal park for all ages. The upper area is hilly and woodsy, blessed with lots of pine trees. The lower slopes flatten out, with alder and willow trees. One of the playgrounds meets the ADA (Americans with Disabilities Act) Standards; one is geared towards little ones; and another is designed for slightly older kids, as it has steeper slides.

There are picnic gazebos, baseball diamonds, volleyball courts, tennis courts, racquetball courts, and a lake. Fishing is allowed in the lake, but it isn't stocked so bring your wiggliest worms. The Nature Center has dioramas depicting the changing environment of animals in Craig Park and the surrounding areas.

**Hours:**     Open daily April through October from 7am - 9pm. Open daily November through March from 7am - 6pm. The Nature Center is open Sat. - Sun. from 8am - 4pm.
**Admission:**   $2 per vehicle Mon. - Fri., $4 Sat. - Sun.; $5 on holidays.
**Ages:**       All

## CROWN VALLEY PARK

(949) 362-4350
*29751 Crown Valley Parkway, Laguna Niguel*

(Exit San Diego Fwy [5] W. on Crown Valley Parkway. The park is W. of La Paz Rd.)

This delightful park has something that will appeal to each member of your family. Several short trails wind through the hillside botanical garden. Some of the trails are cement, and therefore stroller-friendly (although uphill), and some are dirt paths with wooden steps. Hike up to the picturesque viewpoint and enjoy beautiful landscaping along the way. A playground at the base of the hill has swings, slides, and a wooden fun ship to climb aboard. Picnic tables are scattered throughout the park. Summer concerts are given on an outdoor stage with tiered seating on a grassy hill. At the top of another hill is a soccer field and baseball field. Between the park office and the adjacent Y.M.C.A. is a regulation-size swimming pool that is open year round to the public and for swim meets. Diving competitions also take place on the two low diving boards, two high dives, and a (really high) diving platform. Cement stadium seats are on one side of the pool. The canopied-covered wading pool is great for your little tadpoles. Finally, a three-quarter-mile bike path here connects to Laguna Niguel Regional Park. This park is a *crown* jewel in Laguna Niguel.

**Hours:**    The park is open daily from 6am - 10pm. The pool is open for public swim sessions year round Mon. - Fri., 1pm - 4pm; Sat. - Sun., noon - 4pm. It's open in the summer for an additional session Mon. - Fri., 9am - noon.

**Admission:**    Free to the park. Swim sessions are $2 for adults; $1.50 for seniors and children 2 - 12 years.

**Ages:**    All

# CRYSTAL COVE STATE PARK     ☀
(949) 494-3539     *$$*

*East Coast Highway, between Laguna Beach and Newport Beach, Laguna Beach*

(Take the San Diego Fwy [405] or the Costa Mesa Fwy [55] to the Corona Del Mar Fwy [73], which turns into MacArthur Blvd. Exit MacArthur Blvd. S. on East Coast Highway. A gated entrance is just opposite Newport Coast Dr. The visitor center and ranger station are farther down on Coast Hwy., on the L.)

This 2,800-acre, largely undeveloped state park encompasses everything from coastal and canyon areas on one side of the freeway, to three-and-a-half miles of sandy beach on the other side. The size of the park allows a variety of programs and fun things to do, such as guided tidepool tours (when the tide is low), whale watching, fishing, hiking, camping, mountain biking, or just enjoying the beach!

Environmental camping - meaning whatever you backpack in you take out - is an adventure in the "back country" of the park. The closest campsite is a four-mile hike. No open fires are allowed. With twenty miles of trails on relatively untouched land, hiking and/or camping here is a real opportunity to commune with nature! Pick up a map at the headquarters.

If you get hungry, the Crystal Cove Shake Shop, serving shakes (try their date shakes) and sandwiches, is across the way at 7408 Pacific Coast Highway, (949) 497-9666. It's open daily from 11am to 4pm.

**Hours:**     Open daily sunrise to sunset.
**Admission:**  $6 per vehicle. Camping is $10 a night per person Mon. - Fri.;
                $11 a night Sat. - Sun.
**Ages:**      All

# EISENHOWER PARK                                                ☼

(714) 744-2225                                                    !
*1045 E. Lincoln, Orange*                                        ♨
(Exit Costa Mesa Fwy [55] W. on Lincoln, R. on Oceanview, R. at Main to the park.)

Driving down Lincoln Boulevard, it's easy to miss Eisenhower Park, but it's worth looking for. This park has a stream running through it with almost irresistible stepping stones. You may fish in the lake, although it is not stocked. There are two small play areas for slightly older kids. One area is especially "cool" with a rocket ship play structure, wavy slides, swings, and a big sand area. This big park offers plenty of green rolling hills, plus a few scattered picnic tables and barbecue pits to make your day picnic perfect. Cement pathways make the entire park stroller accessible.

**Hours:**     Open daily sunrise to sunset.
**Admission:**  Free
**Ages:**      All

# EL CAMINO REAL PARK                                            ☼

(714) 744-2225                                                    !
*400 Main Street, Orange*                                        ♨
(Exit Orange Fwy [57] E. on Chapman Ave., L. on Main Street)

My monkeys (I mean kids) like this park mainly because of its two climbing structures. Both the large structure and the slightly smaller one look like tepees made out of rope ladders, so children can climb all around them and up to the top. Note: Although the bases are grounded and surrounded by sand, would-be stuntmen can still hurt themselves by being too daring.

The park also boasts of grassy rolling hills, picnic tables, barbecue grills, two cement volleyball courts, four tennis courts, two basketball courts, baseball diamonds, and a playground.

**Hours:**     Open daily sunrise to sunset.
**Admission:**  Free
**Ages:**      All

# ENVIRONMENTAL NATURE CENTER                                    ☼

(949) 645-8489                                                    !
*1601 16th Street, Newport Beach*
(Take Costa Mesa Fwy [55] S.W. to the end, continue on Newport Blvd., L. on 17th, R. on Irvine Ave., L. on 16th.)

This two-and-a-half acre nature center is an almost hidden gem that has been here for more than twenty-five years! Walking back to the trailhead, notice the rocks along the path containing imbedded fossilized shells. Although buildings are around the perimeters of this wooded area, you'll still feel like you're in the midst of nature while walking along the various crisscrossing trails. You'll see a cactus garden, pine trees, woodland trees, and a small rock-lined stream. You can purchase a pamphlet (25¢) at the center to help identify the various plants and animals found here.

The small nature center building has shelves and tables that contain rocks, shells, animals skins, turtle shells, skulls, feathers, and bird's nests, plus many nature-inspired craft ideas. My boys also liked seeing the live snakes, crickets, and lizards in here.

**Hours:** Open Mon. - Fri., 8am - 4pm; Sat., 8am - 3pm. Closed Sundays and school holidays.

**Admission:** Free

**Ages:** 2½ years and up.

## FULLERTON ARBORETUM

!/$

(714) 278-3579 - arboretum; (714) 278-2843 - house/museum / arboretum.fullerton.edu

*1900 Associated Road, Fullerton*

(Exit Orange Fwy [57] W. on Yorba Linda, L. on Associated Rd. [or Campus Dr.], onto California State Fullerton campus.)

This twenty-five-acre botanical garden is a delightful, verdant refuge, with flower-lined pathways, a small lake, a stream, and a few bridges. It's big enough to let the kids run loose a little. Take a whiff - the air is perfumed with the scent of roses, mint, and citrus. Garden benches offer a picturesque resting spot, underneath shade trees in the midst of the plants and flowers. Idea: Have your kids dress up and bring your camera for some potentially great shots in a garden setting.

An 1894 Victorian Heritage House, that was the home and office of the first physician in Orange County, is also on the grounds. Older kids will appreciate a tour through the house that has turn-of-the-century furnishings.

There are many special events going on at Fullerton Arboretum throughout the year, including Science Adventure programs, volunteering opportunities, and much more. Please call for details.

**Hours:** The Arboretum is open daily from 8am - 4:45pm. Closed New Year's Day, Thanksgiving, and Christmas. The house is open for tours Sun. from 2pm - 4pm. Call to make an appointment for other days and hours. The house is closed for tours in January and August.

**Admission:** The Arboretum has a donation box by the entrance gate. The house tour is a $2 for adults; $1 per child.

**Ages:** All

## GENERAL THOMAS F. RILEY WILDERNESS PARK

$

(949) 459-1687

*30952 Oso Parkway, Coto De Caza*

(Exit San Diego Fwy [5] E. on Oso Parkway, N. on Coto De Caza. It's 6 ½ miles off the freeway.)

This hilly wilderness preserve is a sanctuary for native wildlife - coyotes, mountain lions, raccoons, mule deer, a multitude of birds, etc. It's comprised of hills with protected sagebrush, oak trees, and other plant life, plus a pond and seasonal creek. Rugged dirt trails (stroller occupants would have a bumpy ride) loop throughout the park and visitors are asked not to stray from them. Although housing developments border part of the park, miles of undeveloped canyons, tree groves, and Santa Ana Mountain peaks can still be seen from the viewpoints.

Take a self-guiding nature hike, or sign up for a guided walk or program. The park makes a wonderful outdoor "classroom" and offers students of all ages firsthand knowledge about the environment. Some of the programs offered include merit badge classes, which could include a topical game and craft; Bat Habits, which includes a slide show and short hike into bat country; Star Watch, designed for viewing and learning about the stars and moon; Jr. Rangers, which is a six-week, springtime class; special classes for toddlers; and more. Most of the programs have a minimal fee.

The small nature center contains a few taxidermy animals and a game that kids can take on the trail to help them identify objects they find along the way. A few picnic tables are under shade trees in front of the nature center. Note: The rangers are very friendly and dedicated to enabling children to learn more about the wilds of Orange County.

**Hours:** Open daily 7am - sunset.
**Admission:** $2 parking fee.
**Ages:** 3 years and up.

# HART PARK

(714) 744-7272
*701 Glassell Street, Orange*
(Exit Garden Grove Fwy [22] N. on Glassell.)

Stone walls add to the beauty of this spacious park. The northern section has lots of picnic tables and barbecue pits, a playground, trees to climb, a few tennis courts (although kids were roller skating on them when we visited), a sand volleyball court (or, for younger kids, a sandbox with a net), and a swimming pool.

The southern section has a large open grassy area lined with trees, plus soccer fields and a few baseball diamonds. One of the diamonds has stadium seating and lights.

**Hours:** The park is open daily from 8am - 10pm. The pool is open in the summer daily, with swim sessions at 1pm - 2:15pm and 2:30pm - 3:45pm. It's also open Wed. from 7pm - 8:15pm.
**Admission:** The park is free. Each swim session costs $1.50 for adults; $1 for ages 17 and under.
**Ages:** All

## HERITAGE PARK (Irvine)

(949) 724-6750 - Youth services center; (949) 559-0472 - Aquatics Complex
*14301 Yale Avenue, Irvine*
(Going S. on Santa Ana Fwy [5], exit S.W. on Culver Dr., L. on Walnut Ave., L. on Yale Ave. Going N. on 5, exit S.W. on Jeffrey Rd., L. on Walnut Ave., R. on Yale Ave.)

Heritage Park is forty-five acres huge - the city's largest community park. The wooden water tower slide is almost as tall as a real water tower - whoosh on down!! There are two terrific playgrounds here. One has a pirate ship with bridges, slides, and a ropes obstacle course - kid heaven!

The center area has a beautiful lake (with ducks) to skate or stroller around, and lots of grassy, gently rolling hills to play on. There are also basketball courts, twelve lighted tennis courts, and four lighted fields for organized sports play. The community youth services center, library, and the IRVINE FINE ART CENTER (look under the Arts and Crafts section) are adjacent to the park. The Heritage Park Aquatics Complex is just around the corner. Two of their pools are open for recreational swim in the summer.

**Hours:** The park is open daily. The pools are open daily in the summer Mon. - Fri., 1pm - 3pm; Sat. - Sun., 1pm - 4pm.
**Admission:** The park is free. Swimming costs $1.50 for adults; $1 for ages 18 and under.
**Ages:** All

## HILLCREST PARK

*Brea Boulevard, Fullerton*
(Exit the Riverside Fwy [91] N. on Harbor Blvd., R. on Brea Blvd., R. into the park.)

For some Fullerton fun, try Hillcrest Park. This huge hilly park has a winding road throughout, with parking lots in several different spots along the way. We saw some creative kids using cardboard to slide down a hill, which probably isn't great for the grass, but it looked like fun. Hillcrest has a few woodland areas with dirt paths for hiking. There are also some play areas, picnic tables, and barbecue pits. The wooden structure at the base of the hill, on Lemon Street, is in the shape of a ship.

**Hours:** Open daily.
**Admission:** Free
**Ages:** All

## HUNTINGTON CENTRAL PARK / SHIPLEY'S NATURE CENTER

(714) 960-8847
*Golden West Street, Huntington Beach*
(Exit San Diego Fwy [405] S. on Golden West St. It's between Slater and Ellis Ave.)

There are many options to lose yourself, temporarily of course, in this gigantic park: Fish at the un-stocked lake, which is tucked in the corner; let the kids go wild on the playgrounds; ride bikes along the cement pathways that crisscross all over; enjoy the sports fields; play the Frisbee golf course on the west side of Golden West Street; see a weekend polo match or horse show at the Equestrian Center (call [714] 848-6565 for details); check out books from the huge library off Talbert Street (see HUNTINGTON BEACH CENTRAL LIBRARY under the Potpourri section); play at Adventure Playground for summertime fun (see the June Calendar section for details); or go for a nature walk at Shipley's Nature Center at the northern end of the park.

We turned the easy, fifteen-minute walk around Shipley's Nature Center into over an hour of delightful exploration. The dirt trail, which is not stroller-friendly, leads around a pond that supports diverse animal life - frogs, turtles, and butterflies. We hiked the trail through tall grass, to the pine trees, and looped back around to the small Nature Center building. Inside the building are a few taxidermied animals and other natural exhibits.

If you'd like to have breakfast (or lunch) in the park, eat at ALICE'S BREAKFAST IN THE PARK. (Look under the Edible Adventures section.)

**Hours:** The park is open daily sunrise to sunset. The Nature Center is open sporadically.

**Admission:** Free

**Ages:** All

# IRVINE LAKE

(714) 649-9111
*4501 Santiago Canyon Road, Orange*
(Exit Costa Mesa Fwy [55] E. on Chapman, R. on Santiago Canyon Rd.)

Casting around for fun places to go with your little fisherman? The huge Irvine Lake is stocked seasonally with a variety of fish such as bass, trout, catfish, crappie, and bluegill. There is a five fish limit per person. A smaller, almost-guarantee-you'll-catch-something Catch Out Pond (stocked with trout) is also here. Conveniently, a bait and tackle shop are also on the grounds. No fishing license is needed. Most boat rentals are available on the weekends only, including motorboats - $40 for the day, $27 after noon; rowboats - $28 for the day; and pedalboats - $8 for a half hour, $12 for an hour. Overnight camping for organized groups is available. (It's ideal for those who enjoy fishing in the wee hours of the morning, but don't want to actually be on the road that early.) For those kids who get antsy after quietly fishing for a while, there is a three-and-a-half-mile nature trail that goes around the lake.

**Hours:** Open daily from 6am - 5pm. Summer twilight hours are Fri. - Sat., 2pm - 11pm. (Hours do fluctuate.)

**Admission:** Fishing is $13 for adults; $11 for seniors; $7 for ages 4 - 12; children 3 years and under are free. The rates include the entrance fee and up to five fish. Call about twilight rates. Entrance other than fishing is $3 per person. Ask about overnight camping for organized youth groups.

**Ages:** 4 years and up.

# IRVINE REGIONAL PARK

(714) 633-8074

*1 Irvine Park Road, Orange*

(Exit Costa Mesa Fwy [55] E. on Chapman, N. on Jamboree, which ends at Irvine Regional Park.)

Entire days can be spent exploring all there is to see and do at this 477-acre regional park. The middle area is "carved out," with lots of grass for picnic areas, playgrounds, and baseball diamonds. Toddlers through about 8 years old can ride ponies around a track that is open Tuesday through Sunday from 10am to 4pm during the summer and on weekends only from 10am to 4pm the rest of the year. Rides are $2.50 each. Kids 8 years and older can take a guided horseback ride inside the park, Wednesday through Sunday for $20 an hour. Call Country Trails at (714) 538-5860 for further horse back riding rental information. More fun can be had with pedal boat rentals, which are available weekends from 10am to 5pm at $7 per half hour. Bike rentals are available weekends from 10am to 5pm at $10 per hour for side-by-sides. Ten-minute, scale model train rides around the park are available daily from 10am to 4pm, at $2 per person. This is a fun little trip!

The Interpretive Center, (714) 289-9616, has taxidermied animals to look at; skulls, furs, and animal pelts to touch; a grinding rock to try out; plus displays and information about the wilderness part of the park. Biking, hiking, and equestrian trails are plentiful in Irvine Regional Park with creeks, sagebrush, and animals throughout. Rangers are available for school and scout tours. See ORANGE COUNTY ZOO, under the Zoos and Animals section, as it's located inside the park.

**Hours:** Irvine Park is open daily April through October from 7am - 8:45pm. It's open the rest of the year daily from 7am - 5:45pm. The Nature Center is usually open Sat. - Sun. from 11am - 3:45pm.

**Admission:** $2 per vehicle, Mon. - Fri., $4 on Sat. - Sun; $5 on holidays.

**Ages:** All

# LAGUNA LAKE PARK

*Lakeview Drive and Clarion, Fullerton*

(Exit Riverside Fwy [91] N. on Euclid, R. on Lakeview Dr.)

Leaping frogs! This lake is literally covered with large lily pads. In contrast to my earlier thinking, I now know that parks don't require a playground to make it "good." It simply must have kid-appeal, and this one does. The dirt path around the long lake is bike and stroller friendly. The marshy reeds are a great place for dragonfly hunting. Bring bread for the ducks, bait for your fishing pole, and enjoy this unusual park. Barbecue pits and picnic tables are here, too.

**Hours:** Open daily sunrise to sunset.

**Admission:** Free

**Ages:** All

## LAGUNA NIGUEL REGIONAL PARK

(949) 831-2791 - park; (949) 362-3885 - fishing
*28241 La Paz Road, Laguna Niguel*
(Exit San Diego Fwy [5] W. on Crown Valley Pky., R. on La Paz.)

   This park is 236 acres of adventures waiting to be had. It offers volleyball courts, horseshoe pits, tennis courts, bike trails, an area for flying remote-controlled airplanes, toddler-friendly playgrounds, open grass areas, barbecue pits, and picnic shelters, plus a forty-four acre lake for fishing and boating. No fishing license is required. The lake is seasonally stocked with catfish and bluegill, with a limit of five fish per person, per day. Bass are strictly catch and release. Fish from the floating docks or rent a boat at $8 an hour. A bait and tackle shop are conveniently located on the park grounds. The shop rents poles for $6 a day. The park tends to get crowded on weekends and holidays, so get an early start!

**Hours:** Open daily April through October from 6am - 9pm. Open daily November through March from 6am - 6pm.

**Admission:** $2 per vehicle Mon. - Fri.; $4 on Sat. - Sun.; $5 on holidays. A day use fishing permit costs $10 for adults; $8 for seniors; $4 for ages 4 - 16; children 3 years and under are free.

**Ages:** All

## MILE SQUARE PARK

(714) 962-5549
*Warner Avenue and Euclid Street, Fountain Valley*
(Exit San Diego Fwy [405] N. on Euclid St.)

   Mile Square Park has everything you need for a full day of family fun. There are picnic areas with barbecue grills, bike trails, baseball fields, a hobby area for flying model planes and rockets, blacktop for racing cars, and four playgrounds. One of the playgrounds is on an island in one of the lakes. Kids can take the bridge across and have fun climbing up and down the tower. You may fish in the two man-made lakes - no license is needed unless your child is over 16 years old. Duck food is available to purchase for $1 a bag, in case you forgot to bring your own.

   Get physical on the weekends with various pleasure rentals - surrey bikes are between $12 to $22 an hour, depending on the number of passengers; peddle boats are $12 an hour; and funcycles or tandems are $6 an hour.

**Hours:** Open daily in the summer from 7am - 9pm. Open daily the rest of the year from 7am - 6pm.

**Admission:** $2 per vehicle Mon. - Fri; $4 on Sat. - Sun.; $5 on holidays.

**Ages:** All

## OAK CANYON NATURE CENTER

(714) 998-8380
*6700 Walnut Canyon Road, Anaheim*

(Exit Riverside Fwy [91] S. on Imperial Hwy, L. on Nohl Ranch Rd., L. on Walnut Canyon. It's next to the Anaheim Hills Golf Course.)

This rustic Nature Center is a fifty-eight-acre natural park nestled in Anaheim Hills. Surrounded by such beauty, it doesn't seem possible that there is a city nearby. Take a delightful, easy hike along the wide pathways along the stream and through the woods that boast of huge oak and other shade tress. Or, opt for more strenuous hiking on the six miles of trails offered here. No bikes or picnicking are allowed so that the animals and plants that consider this canyon their home can continue to live here unharmed.

The good-sized, Nature Center building houses live critters, plus several trays of mounted butterflies and other insects. The small stage area is great for putting on shows using the animal puppets.

The Nature Center offers many different programs. One-hour programs for preschoolers like Feed the Critters, or Mudpies and Stone Soup include a guided nature walk and related activities. The fee is $3 per child. For ages 4 to 6, Tykes on the Go is a once-a-month, two-hour program that may include a guided nature hike, live animal demonstrations, and/or a related craft. The fee is $5 per child. Every Saturday morning a family program is offered that incorporates learning about nature with doing a craft together. This program is usually free. On Wednesday evenings throughout the summer, Nature Nights for families begin at 7pm with a twilight walk through the canyon. A formal presentation is given at 7:30pm at the outdoor amphitheater. Ask about their summer day camps.

**Hours:**   Open daily from 9am - 5pm.
**Admission:**   Free
**Ages:**   All

# O'NEILL REGIONAL PARK
(949) 858-9365
*30892 Trabuco Canyon Road, Trabuco Canyon*
(Exit Santa Ana Fwy [5] N.E. on El Toro Rd., R. on Live Oak Canyon Rd., which turns into Trabuco Canyon Rd.)

As we explored parts of this over 2,000-acre park, I kept thinking of how absolutely gorgeous it is. O'Neill Park is a canyon bottom and so filled with trees, it's like being in a forest. A creek runs throughout, creating lush greenery. The abundant nature trails are mostly hilly dirt trails, though a few are paved "roads."

The playground has a log cabin-like building with slides and swings and such around it. Inside the small Nature Center are taxidermied animals around the perimeter of the room. A few tables in the middle display skulls, furs, and rocks to touch. The park also has beautiful campgrounds.

**Hours:**   The park is open daily from 7am to sunset. The Nature Center is usually open Sat. - Sun. from 2pm - 4pm.
**Admission:**   $2 per vehicle on Mon. - Fri.; $4 on Sat. - Sun; $5 on holidays. Camping starts at $12 a night.
**Ages:**   All

## PETERS CANYON REGIONAL PARK

(714) 538-4400

*Canyon View Avenue, Orange*

(Exit Costa Mesa Fwy [55] E. on Chapman., R. on Jamboree, R. on Canyon View.)

My boys and I have decided that this huge, 354-acre undeveloped park is for rugged hikers. The lake by the parking lot is one of the most scenic spots here. The narrow dirt trails are lined with sage scrub, grassland areas, and willow and sycamore trees. The upper Lake View Trail guides you through the reservoir, while the lower East Ridge Trail provides a panoramic view of the canyon and the surrounding area.

**Hours:**   Open daily from 7am - sunset.

**Admission:**   Free

**Ages:**   5 years and up

## RALPH B. CLARK REGIONAL PARK

(714) 670-8045

*8800 Rosecrans Avenue, Buena Park*

(Exit Santa Ana Fwy [5] N. on Beach Blvd., R. on Rosecrans.)

This sixty-five-acre park is one of the most aesthetically pleasing parks we've seen. It has all the things that make a park great - a lake to fish in, ducks to feed, tennis courts, horseshoe pits, three softball fields, a baseball diamond, volleyball courts, and a few small playgrounds. Take a short hike around Camel Hill, or let the kids climb on the small, ironically named, Elephant Hill. A paved bicycle trail goes all around the perimeter of the park.

The Interpretative Center has a working paleontology lab where kids can look through a big window and observe the detailed work being done. The Center also houses a twenty-six-foot Baleen whale fossil; a skeletal saber-tooth cat "attacking" a skeletal horse; fossils of a ground sloth and a mammoth; a model of a T. rex; shells; and more.

Kids really dig the marine fossil site across the street where a *bone*afide paleontologist conducts "Family Fossil Day" four times a year. This three-hour class is geared for youngsters 6 years and up. They can practice their ~~paleontologistical paleontologisting~~ bone-digging skills, bring the fossils back to the lab at the Interpretive Center to study and classify, and perhaps do a related craft. The price for the field trip is simply the price of admission to the park.

**Hours:**   The park is open November 1 to March 31 from 7am - 6pm; April 1 to October 31 from 7am - 9pm. The Interpretative Center is usually open Tues. - Fri., 12:30pm - 5pm; Sat. - Sun., 10am - 4:30pm.

**Admission:**   $2 vehicle entrance Mon. - Fri.; $4 on Sat. - Sun.; $5 on holidays.

**Ages:**   All

## RANCHO MISSION VIEJO LAND CONSERVANCY

(949) 489-9778

*Ortega Highway, San Juan Capistrano*
(Exit San Diego Fwy [5] E. on Ortega Hwy. [74]. It's about 5.1 miles.)

The Land Conservancy manages a 1,200 acre wilderness reserve in the coastal foothills. They offer an incredible array of special programs to the general public and to school groups that give intimate glimpses into the wilderness of Orange County. Programs include guided nature walks, bird watching (and finding), wildlife workshops, astronomy nights, owl outings, bat walks, butterfly classes, butterfly counting (for research purposes), trail maintenance, and much more. The programs are given by trained docents, or professionals in that field of study. What a wonderful opportunity for kids to become aware of wildlife, and what they can do to help protect it.

**Hours:** Call for program hours or to receive a calendar of events.
**Admission:** Depending on the program, the fees range from free to $8.
**Ages:** Varies, depending on the program.

# RONALD W. CASPERS WILDERNESS PARK
(949) 728-0235
*33401 Ortega Highway, San Juan Capistrano*
(Exit San Diego Fwy [5] E. on Ortega Hwy. It's over 7 miles down the road.)

Orange County's largest park is massive, and mostly wilderness. The over thirty miles of hiking trails, ranging from an easy walk to strenuous, mountain-man hikes, are only available when hiking with a ranger or a park docent. (This really is a wilderness park, with all of the implied dangers, and beauty.) There is, however, plenty to do. For instance, enjoy a barbecue under shade trees; play on the large wooden playground with swings and slides, surrounded by trees; check out the Nature Center that has a few taxidermied animals and hands-on activities; hike the mile-and-a-half paved trail; and/or walk around the wooded day use area. There are numerous camp sites here.

**Hours:** Open daily sunrise to sunset. Rangers are available on the weekends at 9:30am and sometimes in the afternoon to hike the trails.
**Admission:** $2 per vehicle Mon. - Fri.; $4 Sat. - Sun; $5 on holidays. Camping is $12 a night.
**Ages:** All

# SANTIAGO OAKS REGIONAL PARK
(714) 538-4400
*2145 North Windes Drive, Orange*
(Exit Costa Mesa Fwy [55] E. on Katella, which turns into Villa Park, then into Santiago Canyon Rd., L. on Windes, to the end.)

Get back to nature at this 350-acre park that has beautiful hiking and equestrian trails that connect to the Anaheim Hills trail system. Take a short path along the creek leading to a waterfall at the dam, or travel more rugged terrain into the heart of the park. Be on the lookout for animals such as lizards, squirrels, deer, and birds. Mountain lions have been seen on rare occasion, too.

A favorite activity here is cooking breakfast over the charcoal barbecues early in the morning, while it's still quiet and cool. A small playground and a few horseshoe pits round out the facilities under a canopy of oak trees. The small Nature Center has taxidermied animals, pictures, and a few hands-on activities. Free, ranger-led tours are given on the weekends beginning at 10am.

**Hours:** The park is open daily from 7am - sunset. The nature center is open daily from 8am - 4pm.

**Admission:** $2 per vehicle Mon. - Fri., $4 Sat. - Sun.; $5 on holidays.

**Ages:** All

## TEWINKLE PARK

(714) 754-5300

*970 Arlington Drive, Costa Mesa*

(Exit San Diego Fwy [405] S. on Fairview, L. on Arlington.)

This fifty-acre park has something for everyone. There is a play area with a big tire to climb on, volleyball courts, baseball fields, and a utility field.

I think nature-loving kids will enjoy this park most. A stream goes around a good portion of it, with ducks and geese having a swimmingly good time. They also populate the small lake. A hike up the hill yields the treasure of a pond in a small, forest-like setting. This park is cool, even on a hot day.

**Hours:** Open daily dawn to dusk.

**Admission:** Free

**Ages:** All

## TUCKER WILDLIFE SANCTUARY

(714) 649-2760

*29322 Modjeska Canyon Road, Modjeska*

(Exit Costa Mesa Fwy [55] E. on Chapman, which turns into Santiago Canyon Rd. Turn R. on Modjeska Canyon Rd., drive about 2 miles, veer to the right at the fork.)

Tucker Wildlife Sanctuary is tucked in the mountainside at the end of a long and winding road. The Nature Center has a small, one-room museum with live snakes, lizards, and turtles. It also contains taxidermied animals and a touch table with skulls, fossils, and bird's nests.

There are several short - one-fifth or so of a mile - nature trails to walk. Along the Riparian Woodland Trail you'll find a small pond, a few caged animals, and an enclosed observation porch. The porch, located over a creek, has birdseed scattered on it so kids can sit and readily observe wild birds. The hummingbirds, attracted by the brightly-colored sugar water in their feeders, are our favorites. There are picnic tables along the trail.

**Hours:** Open daily from 9am - 4pm. Closed Christmas.

**Admission:** $1.50 donation requested per person.

**Ages:** All

## TURTLE ROCK NATURE CENTER

(949) 854-8151

*1 Sunnyhill Drive, Irvine*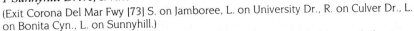
(Exit Corona Del Mar Fwy [73] S. on Jamboree, L. on University Dr., R. on Culver Dr., L. on Bonita Cyn., L. on Sunnyhill.)

This small, five-acre nature preserve has both a desert habitat and pine trees, so the stroller-friendly trail is partially in the sun and partially in the shade. A ranger here said that going around a little pond, over a few bridges, and looping back around takes "ten minutes if you don't see anything, thirty minutes if you follow the trail guide. The longer you're here, the more you'll learn."

Inside the Center, a quiz board lights up if the right answer button is pushed. Kids can also reach in discovery boxes to feel for animal pelts or bones. Visit the small Animal Room (50¢) to see live snakes, bunnies, turtles, crows, and a raccoon. Note: The animals on exhibit do change. Find out why the animals are here and what we can do to take better care of their homes. The room is open every hour on the hour between 11am to 3pm.

The surrounding park has tennis courts, a basketball court, sand volleyball courts, and a playground, plus a nature trail that goes over a creek.

**Hours:** The nature center is open Mon. - Sat. from 10am - 4pm. In the summer, it is also open Sun. from noon - 4pm. The park is open daily sunrise to sunset.
**Admission:** Free
**Ages:** 2 - 13 years.

## UPPER NEWPORT BAY ECOLOGICAL RESERVE AND ☼ REGIONAL PARK

(949) 640-6746 / www.members.home.net/unbn                    *!/$$*

*600 Shellmaker, Newport Beach*
(Take Costa Mesa Fwy [55] S.W. to end, which turns into Newport Blvd., L. on W. Coast Hwy., L. on Jamboree Rd., L. on Backbay Dr. to Shellmaker. Or, from Corona Del Mar Fwy [73], exit S.W. on Jamboree R., R. on Backbay Dr. to Shellmaker.)

This reserve, a remnant of a once-extensive wetland, is part of an endeavor to conserve wildlife in the Upper Bay. Although surrounded by urban development, the bay and small islands are home to hundreds of waterfowl, sea critters, and a variety of plants. The reserve is ringed by roads, but only hikers, bikers, and boaters have access inside the reserve. Introduce your children to the valuable natural resources that God originally put on the earth by involving kids in a variety of interactive and interpretive programs offered here. As you "Canoe the Back Bay," you'll see herons, egrets, and numerous other birds. This program is available every Saturday and costs $13 per person. Campfire Programs are offered the first, second, and third Saturday of each month at 7:30pm, with hot chocolate and marshmallows provided. This is a wonderful family time that could include skits, stories, a speaker, songs, or games. Free walking tours are given on the first and third Saturday of each month at 9am. All this plus kayak tours, youth fishing programs, and shark studies are mere samplings of what the reserve has to offer.

**Hours:** Hours vary, depending on the program.
**Admission:** Prices vary, depending on the program.

**Ages:** 3½ years and up.

# WHITING RANCH WILDERNESS PARK
(949) 589-4729

*Santiago Canyon Road, Portola Hills*

(Exit San Diego Fwy [5] E. on Lake Forest, go 5 miles and turn L. on Portola Pky., R. on Market, first driveway on the left. Or, from Lake Forest, turn R. on Portola Pky., L. on Glenn Rd. and into the large dirt parking area. This section leads into Serrano Canyon.)

"Real" hikers can explore the hills of Trabuco Canyon via Whiting Ranch Wilderness Park. Follow the trails through forested canyons, along streams, and past huge boulders. A moderate hike starts at the Borrego Trail and leads to the Red Rock Canyon trail, which is five miles round trip and loops back around. Note: This trail is more easily reached from the Market Street entrance. The scenery is outstanding. The size and beauty of this park offers the opportunity to enjoy some good, back-to-nature time with your kids.

**Hours:**      Open daily 7am - sunset.
**Admission:**  $2 per vehicle.
**Ages:**       5 years and up.

# WILLIAM R. MASON REGIONAL PARK
(949) 854-2490

*18712 University Drive, Irvine*

(Exit San Diego Fwy [405] S. on Culver Dr., which turns into University Dr.)

This 350-acre park is great for children of all ages. There are three different playgrounds with modular plastic equipment like tunnels, slides, swings, forts, etc. Fishing is allowed in the lake, but be forewarned - it isn't stocked. Lots of ducks, geese, and other birds will vie for food, so bring those bread crumbs. Come enjoy the over two miles of paved bike and walking trails.

**Hours:**      Open daily November through March from 7am - 6pm. Open
                daily April through October from 7am - 9pm.
**Admission:**  $2 per vehicle Mon. - Fri.; $4 Sat. - Sun.; $5 on holidays.
**Ages:**       All

# ARLINGTON PARK
(909) 715-3440

*Van Buren Boulevard, Riverside*

(Exit Riverside Fwy [91] N. on Van Buren Blvd. It's just past Magnolia, on the W. side of the street.)

This nice corner park has an older style playground and well-used shuffleboard courts. It also has basketball courts, tennis courts, barbecue pits, and a swimming pool.

**Hours:**      The park is open daily. The pool is open in the summer Mon. -
                Sat. from 1pm - 5pm; plus Tues. and Thurs. from 6pm - 8pm.
**Admission:**  Free to the park. Swim sessions are $2.25 for adults; $1 for ages
                6 - 17; 75¢ for children 5 years and under.
**Ages:**       All

# CALIFORNIA CITRUS STATE HISTORIC PARK

(909) 780-6222
*Van Buren Boulevard at Dufferin Avenue, Riverside*
(Exit the Riverside Fwy [91] S. on Van Buren Blvd., L. on Dufferin Ave. into the park.)

The park, with its acres of citrus groves, captures the spirit of Riverside's slogan, "The land of citrus and sunshine." The main section is beautifully landscaped, and has a big, grassy area for running around or for picnicking.

There are two, mile-long hiking trails. The Arroyo Trail goes through a wooded area and creek bed, up towards the dam. The Knolls Trail takes the high, non-shady road, past Grower's Mansion (a soon-to-be restaurant) towards the dam. Neither trail is very strenuous; just good, short nature hikes. Don't forget to stop and smell the oranges along the way!

   **Hours:**  The park is open daily from 8am - 5pm.
   **Admission:**  Free
   **Ages:**  2 years and up.

# FAIRMOUNT PARK

(909) 715-3440 - park; (909) 715-3406 - boathouse
*Off Market Street Riverside*
(Exit Pomona Fwy [60] S. on Market St., R. on Locust St.)

This lush park has a lot to offer. The huge playground has swings, slides, bridges, and lots of other fun things. The surrounding grassy area is large, with plenty of shade trees and picnic tables. With all this, plus tennis courts, basketball courts, and horseshoe pits, kids can play here all day! The park's rose garden is located at the corner of Redwood and Dexter drives.

Take a very windy drive around the lakes, and watch out for the ducks - they're everywhere! Don't forget your fishing poles as you can stop almost anywhere to fish, including from a small, horseshoe-shaped pier. A fishing permit is required. Pedal boat and rowboat rentals are available seasonally. An adult picture I.D. is required for deposit and children 12 years and under must be accompanied by an adult.

The Information Center is open on weekends from 10am to 5pm and has exhibits of local history and environmental projects. You'll have a better than fair day at Fairmount Park!

   **Hours:**  The park is open daily sunrise to 10pm. The boathouse is open weekends only from 10am - 5pm. Note that hours do fluctuate.
   **Admission:**  Free. Boat rentals are $5 per half hour.
   **Ages:**  All

# HIDDEN VALLEY WILDLIFE AREA

(909) 785-7452
*At the west end of Arlington Avenue, Riverside*
(Exit Riverside Fwy [91] N. at La Sierra, keeping L. as it turns in to Arlington.)

Aptly named, this 1,300-acre wildlife area is indeed off the beaten path. There are several options to see at least parts of this "park": Drive along the ridge to see vast expanses of treeless stretches that are close to the road, and wooded areas that are further back into the park; hike along the numerous trails and view the wildlife closer up; or horseback ride, which is obviously a popular option judging from the number of horse trailers we observed.

As Hidden Valley is located along the Santa Ana River, much of the wildlife encouraged and seen here are migratory birds. There are many ponds, too, as you'll discover if you hike into this sprawling park. A small Nature Center is up the road a bit.

**Hours:** Open daily from 7am - 4:30pm. The Nature Center is open Tues. - Sat. by appointment.

**Admission:** $2 for adults; $1 for children 12 years and under. There is a box near the entrance, so admission is on the honor system.

**Ages:** 4 years and up.

# HUNTER PARK
(909) 715-3440
*Corner of Columbia and Iowa, Riverside*
(Exit Riverside Fwy [215] E. on Columbia Ave. It's just N. of 91/60/215 Jct.)

Hunter Park is comprised mostly of grassy playing fields. Its best feature occurs on the second and fourth Sunday of each month when scale model train rides are offered. Kids love taking a ride on the track that encircles the park.

**Hours:** Steam train rides are on the second and fourth Sunday from 10am - 3pm.

**Admission:** Free

**Ages:** All

# JENSEN-ALVARADO RANCH HISTORIC PARK
(909) 369-6055
*4307 Briggs Street, Riverside*
(Exit Pomona Fwy [60] S. on Rubidoux Blvd., R. on Mission St., L. on Riverview Dr., L on 42nd St., R. on Briggs St.)

This historic site brings the history of the 1880's to life. Costumed docents are on hand to demonstrate farm chores like butter churning, livestock care, and outdoor cooking. The front part of the park is a large, fairly treeless area, with picnic tables. Rusty old farm equipment lines the main pathway. The corral and animal pens, with a few horses, sheep, chicken, and other ranch animals, are located next to the Jensen-Alvarado Ranch House. Behind the house was a winery; it's now a small museum. Inside is period furniture, plus wine-making presses, barrels, and other equipment.

A two-and-a-half-hour school tour includes all of the above, plus hearing a living history presentation; participating in hands-on demonstrations such as making ice cream or tortillas; and maybe, feeding the animals. Tour reservations begin the first week of September; openings are usually filled by the end of the month. (Also, check the September Calendar section for the Cornelius Jenson Birthday Celebration.)

**Hours:**    Open September 15 through June 30, Tues. - Fri. for school and large groups only, by reservation. Open to the public September through June on Sat. from 10am - 4pm. Closed on holidays.

**Admission:**    Sat. admission is $3 for adults; $1.50 for kids 12 years and under. School tours are $4 per child; $1 for adults.

**Ages:**    6 years and up.

## LAKE PERRIS STATE RECREATION AREA

(909) 940-5603 - general info; (909) 657-2179 - marina; (909) 940-5656 - Home of Wind Indian Museum

*17801 Lake Perris Drive, Perris*

(Exit Escondido Fwy [215] E. on Cajalco Expressway/Ramona Expressway, L. on Lake Perris Dr.)

Come for at least a day of play at the popular Lake Perris! This gigantic, man-made lake supports a multitude of water activities. (It's hot out here, so you'll need them.) For your boating pleasure, choose from four- or six-seat passenger boats, ranging from $19 to $54, or pontoon boats, ranging from $40 to $180 a day. Waterskiing is available, if you bring your own boat. Fish at the lake and catch a big one, or at least try to. A license is required for those over 16 years. There are seven (!) swim beaches, each with a playground and barbecue pits. The three waterslides add a little zip to your day, at a cost of $5 per person per two-hour session, or $8 for all-day water fun.

Drier activities include picnicking, hiking, biking (a nine-mile trail goes around the lake), rock climbing, and a visit to the small, regional Indian museum. The museum contains stuffed animals, displays on native plant life, exhibits of Indian art, and a beautiful view of the lake out the glass windows. What more could nature-loving kids want?! Camping! There is so much to do at Lake Perris, that you'll want to spend a night, or two, here.

**Hours:**    The recreation area is open in the summer, 6am - 10pm; open the rest of the year 6am - 8pm. The marina is open 6am - 8pm year round. The waterslides are open daily in the summer from 11am - 4pm; open weekends only in April through mid-June and September through October from 11am - 4pm. The museum is open Wed., 10am - 2pm; Sat. - Sun., 10am - 4pm. School tours of the museum are given Tues. and Fri. by reservation only.

**Admission:**    $6 per vehicle. Tent camping is $15 a night; RV camping is $22 with hook-ups - prices include vehicle admission. Waterslides and boat rentals are priced above.

**Ages:**    All

## LAKE SKINNER COUNTY PARK

(909) 926-1505 - recorded info.; (909) 926-1541 - park ranger; (800) 444-7275 -camping reservations.

*Rancho California Road, Riverside County*

(Exit Temecula Valley Fwy [15] N.E. on Rancho California Rd.)

Here's the skinny on Lake Skinner. The main attraction is fishing, either from a boat, or from the shore. A California state license is required. Day permits are $5 for adults; $4 for children 12 years and under. The well-equipped marina offers all sorts of fishing supplies as well as a cafe/restaurant, for those who didn't have much luck catching their own meal. Other activities include hiking, picnicking, playing on the small playground, overnight camping, and seasonal swimming in the pool.

**Hours:** The park is open daily 6am - dusk. Fishing is available daily from 6am - dark. The pool is open daily in the summer from 11am - 6pm.

**Admission:** $2 for adults; $1 for children 12 years and under. The pool is an additional $1 per person. Tent camping is $12 a night; RV camping is $17 a night.

**Ages:** All

## LOUIS ROBIDOUX NATURE CENTER

(909) 683-4880
*5370 Riverview Drive, Riverside*
(Exit the Pomona Fwy [60] S. on Rubidoux Blvd., R. on Mission St., L. on Riverview Dr. As Riverview turns into Limonite Ave., turn L., staying on Riverview.)

This nature park is wonderful for kids who have an adventuresome spirit. A grouping of big rocks in front of the nature center is fun for climbers. A pond is at the trailhead of Willow Creek Trail, which is an easy, half-mile loop to walk around. Other pathways veer off in all directions, allowing some real hiking excursions. Walk along a tree-lined creek; explore the woodlands and water wildlife along the Santa Ana River; or go farther into the Regional Park system along the horse trail that has extensive chaparral. No biking is allowed, and only off-road strollers will make it. Pick up a self-guided trail map, which also has nature questions for kids to answer.

The main building, or Interpretive Center, houses live animals such as snakes, and taxidermied animals, plus an extensive butterfly and insect collection. Kids are welcome to touch the various animals pelts; use the discovery boxes that contain skulls, seeds, or feathers, etc.; or just play with the puzzles. As with most nature centers, special programs are offered throughout the year. Note: The trail by the parking lot leads into RANCHO JURUPA REGIONAL PARK (look just a few entries down).

**Hours:** The park and trails are open daily, sunrise to sunset. The Interpretive Center is open to the public on Sat. from 10am - 4pm. With advanced reservations, it is open Tues. - Fri. for school groups and other large groups.

**Admission:** Free

**Ages:** All

## MOUNT RUBIDOUX

*Off Buena Vista Drive, Riverside*

(Exit Riverside Fwy [91] W. on University Ave., R. on Redwood Dr., L. on Buena Vista Dr. Just S. of the Santa Ana River, turn in where you see a small green picnic area and park at the base of the mountain.)

For kids who enjoy a somewhat rugged hike, climbing Mount Rubidoux is a great adventure. The steep trail winds around the hill that is barren except for boulders and cacti. Reaching the top is a climax. There are rocks to climb on, and on a clear day, the panoramic view of the San Gabriel and San Bernardino Mountains is beautiful. On the western slope of the hill, watch vintage planes take off and land at Rubidoux's Flabob Airport. Hiking here in the summer gets hot, so bring a water bottle. Plan on about an hour-and-a-half round trip. The bike trail at the base of the mountain goes a few miles back to Martha McClean/Anza Narrow Park and beyond.

**Hours:**  Open daily.
**Admission:**  Free
**Ages:**  It depends how far up you want to hike!

# RANCHO JURUPA REGIONAL PARK

(909) 684-7032
*4800 Crestmore Road, Riverside*
(Exit Pomona Fwy [60] S. on Rubidoux Blvd., L. on Mission Blvd., R. on Crestmore Rd., about 1 mile.)

This huge mountain-wilderness park, which is part of the even bigger Santa Ana River Regional Park system, provides a delightful escape from the city. The three-acre lake is beautiful. It is stocked with trout in the cooler months and catfish in the summertime. Fishermen (and women) 16 years and older must have a state fishing license. Near the lake is a big, wooden play structure with slides, swings, and monkey bars. Enjoy a day (or two or three) here by camping in one of the eighty camp sites that are slotted in a big, open space near one end of the lake. Horseshoe pits are located over here, too.

On the other side of the main lake are a few smaller lakes, big grassy open spaces for baseball or whatever, plenty of picnic tables, and barbecue pits. Enjoy an easy hike along the river trail to the adjoining LOUIS ROBIDOUX NATURE CENTER (see a previous entry in this section), where more trails, an Interpretive Center, and rocks to climb on await your kids.

**Hours:**  Open daily from 8am - 8pm. Call for extended summer hours.
**Admission:**  $2 per person for ages 13 and up; $1 per person for children 12 years and under. Dogs are $2 each. Fishing is $5 for ages 16 and older; $4 for ages 6 - 15; children 5 years and under fish for free with a paid adult. A campsite with one vehicle and two people costs $16. Each additional person is $1; up to six people allowed in one campsite. Group rates are available.
**Ages:**  All

# SANTA ROSA PLATEAU ECOLOGICAL RESERVE

(909) 677-6951
*Clinton Keith Road, Murrieta*

(Exit Interstate 15 W. on Clinton Keith Rd. You'll see entrance signs. Another trailhead is located further down the road, where Clinton Keith turns into Via Volcano.)

From riparian stream sides to basalt-capped mesas, this gigantic reserve covers the gamut of topography. Trails range from one mile to five miles round trip. Depending on which one you choose, you'll hike through oak woodlands, acres of grasslands, chaparral, up the Santa Ana mountains, and down to creek beds. Look for treefrogs and turtles in the water, and ground squirrels, woodpeckers, hawks, horned lizards, etc., along the wooded pathways. Pick up a trail map from the visitors' center at 22115 Tenaja Road.

**Hours:** Open daily sunrise to sunset. The visitors' center is open Sat. - Sun., 9am - 5pm.
**Admission:** $2 for adults; $1 for children 2 - 12 years.
**Ages:** 3 years and up.

# UNIVERSITY OF CALIFORNIA AT RIVERSIDE BOTANIC GARDENS
(909) 787- 4650
*University of California, Campus Drive, Riverside*
(Exit Moreno Valley Fwy [215] E. on University Ave. to the entrance of the campus, follow Campus Dr. to parking lot 13.)

Riverside's climate ranges from subtropical to desert to mountains all within forty acres and five miles of hilly trails! A gently sloping walkway provides access to the gardens main areas for wheelchairs and strollers. Explore the botanic gardens to see rose gardens, fruit orchards, an herb garden, saguaros, barrel cacti, pine trees, giant sequoias, and so much more.

Besides the diverse plant life, numerous animals share this habitat. Be on the lookout for bunnies, lizards, squirrels, snakes, coyotes, and numerous bird species. A main trail loops around, and is walkable in forty-five minutes. At the far end of the trail is a pond supporting more wildlife such as frogs, turtles, dragonflies, and koi. A dome-shaped building made of cedar that houses a "living fossils" collection, and a greenhouse are more discoveries you'll make along the way.

Come with your kids to enjoy the beauty of the gardens, and/or come for an educational field trip. Ask for a self-guiding tour booklet such as *Outdoor Classroom* or *Deserts of the Southwest*, which will greatly enrich your day of exploring and learning.

**Hours:** Open daily from 8am - 5pm. Closed New Year's Day, Independence Day, Thanksgiving, and Christmas.
**Admission:** Free; donations appreciated.
**Ages:** All

# CUCAMONGA-GUASTI REGIONAL PARK
(909) 481-4205
*800 North Archibald Avenue, Ontario*
(Exit San Bernardino Fwy [10] N. on Archibald Ave.)

Guasti Regional Park offers seasonal catfish and trout fishing at its nice-sized lakes. Pedal boat rentals are available in the summer. The playground has a tire swing, monkey bars, and cement tubes with holes to climb through, plus open grassy areas for running around.

During the summer have some wet fun by going down the two waterslides and/or swimming in the pool. You can also just beach it on the sandy area around the pool and grassy area beyond that. A snack bar, open seasonally also, sells hot dogs, burritos, chips, ice cream, etc., and is located next to the bait shop - make sure you choose the right food place for you!

**Hours:** The park is open Fri. - Wed. from 7:30am - 5pm. (Closed on Thurs.) Call for extended summer hours.

**Admission:** $5 per vehicle weekdays; $6 per vehicle on weekends and holidays. Pedestrians are $2. Fishing permits are $5 for ages 8 years and older; $2 for 7 years and under. Pedal boat rentals are $5 a half hour, and available in the summertime only. Swimming is $3 for 4 years and older, plus the entrance fee. An all-day swim and waterslide pass costs $8, plus the entrance fee.

**Ages:** All

# GLEN HELEN REGIONAL PARK

(909) 880-2522

*2555 Glen Helen Parkway, San Bernardino*

(Exit San Bernardino Fwy [215] S. on Devore Rd., which turns into Glen Helen Pky. Or, exit Ontario Fwy [15] N.E. on Glen Helen Pky.)

This 1,340-acre park is worth the drive. It offers an assortment of year-round fun, such as fishing in the sizeable lake (a license is needed for those over 16 years old), volleyball courts, playgrounds, campgrounds, and lots of trails for hiking up and down the mountain. Favorite summer activities include renting pedal boats, swimming in the half-acre lagoon, sunbathing on the surrounding beach area, and slip-sliding down the two waterslides. Replenish your energy at the nearby snack bar. Camping is available so you can enjoy the park longer. Note: See the April Calendar section for details about the annual Renaissance Pleasure Faire held here.

**Hours:** Open Mon. - Fri., 7:30am - 5pm; Sat. - Sun., 7:30am - 6pm. The park is open for extended hours in the summer. Water activities are open Memorial Day through Labor Day, Wed. - Sun. from 10am - 5pm.

**Admission:** $5 per vehicle, or $2 for pedestrians. All-day swimming is $2, plus the entrance fee. All-day swimming and use of waterslides is $4 per person, plus the entrance fee. Pedal boat rentals are $5 for a half hour and are available on weekends only. Camping starts at $10 a night.

**Ages:** All

# JURUPA HILLS REGIONAL PARK / MARTIN TUDOR

(909) 428-8360

*11660 Sierra, Fontana*
(Exit San Bernardino Fwy [10] S. on Sierra Ave.)
Jurupa Hills is another terrific park nestled into a rocky mountainside. It has a great wooden playground for slightly older kids, with wavy slides, a big spiral slide, swaying bridges, and swings. The playground is just outside the water play area. A 418-foot long, gently winding waterslide helps cool off sweaty bodies during the hot summer months. There is also a pool with a small slide. The lower level of the park has a grassy picnic area, along with a baseball diamond, and a few swings.

**Hours:** The park is open daily 10am - dusk. The pool and slide are open weekends only May and September; daily in the summer from 11am - 6pm.
**Admission:** $2 per vehicle. An additional $5 per person includes admittance to all the water activities.
**Ages:** All

## LAKE GREGORY
(909) 338-2233
*Crestline*
(From Hwy 18, go through Crestline and follow signs to Lake Gregory. It's about 7 miles off the hwy.)
Crestline is a little mountain town that crowds usually just pass through on their way to stay at Lake Arrowhead or Big Bear. Lake Gregory, toward the east end of Crestline, is a large, beautiful lake with clear blue water and a stretch of white sandy beach. It's nestled in the San Bernardino mountains and surrounded by pine and oak trees. One section of the waveless water is roped off for swimmers and paddle boarders, and is patrolled by lifeguards. The long, thin paddle boards rent for $2 a half hour and must be handled with some degree of finesse if you want to stay topside. Another fun aquatic option is a 300-foot-long, twisting waterslide that ends in a small pool. Barbecue pits and picnic tables are available at the swim beach. You may bring in ice chests, but no glass containers or alcohol. A snack bar is here, too.
The rest of the lake is open year round for boating and fishing. The on-site bait and tackle shop rents poles. Rowboat rentals are available for $5 an hour, with a $10 minimum, plus a $25 deposit. Seasonal boat rentals include canoes, kayaks, and windsurfers. Pedal boats, which seat four people, and Aqua Cycles, big-wheel-type water cycles that seat two people, both use pedal power and rent for $6 a half hour, each. They are available daily in the summer, and on the weekends through October.

**Hours:** The lake is open daily sunup to sundown for fishing. The swim beach and waterslide, and most boating activity is open daily Memorial Day through Labor Day from 10am - 5pm.
**Admission:** $3 for ages 4 and up for the swim beach; children 3 years and under are free. In addition to the entrance fee, an all-day waterslide pass is $6; five rides on the slide is $4. Fishing is free.
**Ages:** All

## MOUNT BALDY TROUT PONDS                                      ☼

(909) 982-4246                                                  $$$

*Mount Baldy Road, Mount Baldy Village*

(Exit San Bernardino Fwy [10] N. on Monte Vista Ave., which turns into Padua Ave., R. on Mount Baldy Rd. It's about 11 miles past Montclair.)

   No waders are needed to catch fish at this delightful fishing spot up in the mountains. The clear, spring water ponds are surrounded by shady oak trees. The first pond stocks fish 13" through 18"; the second holds smaller fish, 9" through 13". The fish are abundant here, so chances are your young fisherboy/girl will make at least one catch of the day! All fish caught must be kept and paid for. After you've caught your fill, or the kids need more action, take a hike through the woods on the surrounding trails. During the summertime, enjoy a refreshing dip in the nearby stream.

   **Hours:**    The ponds are open Sat., Sun., and holidays (including week-long school holiday breaks) from 9am - 4:30pm. Additionally, they are open July through August, Tues. - Sun., 10am - 4pm. Note: You must be here at least a half hour before closing time. Closed Thanksgiving and Christmas.

   **Admission:** $1 if your bring your own pole; $2 to rent a pole. Price includes bait, cleaning, and packing fish in ice. You may share poles. Fish prices range from $1.95 for 9" to $14.95 for 18".

   **Ages:**     3 years and up.

## PRADO REGIONAL PARK                                          ☼

(909) 597-4260 - park information; (909) 597-5757 - horse rentals.     $$

*16700 S. Euclid Avenue, Chino*

(Exit Riverside Fwy [91] N. on the 71, N. on Euclid [or the 83], just south of Pine Ave. From the Pomona Fwy [60] exit S. on the 83.)

   This is another, has-it-all regional park! Besides the three softball diamonds, two soccer fields for tournament games or family fun, and year-round fishing at the huge lake (over 16 years old needs a license), there are four playground areas. One playground has assorted cement shapes to climb up and through, while the others have newer equipment with more traditional activities.

   For those of you with delicate noses, you have correctly detected the nearby presence of horses, cattle, and sheep, as this is farm country. There are herds and ranches all up and down Euclid Street. The Prado Equestrian Center is located at the northern end of the park. Children 7 years old and up can take a one-hour, or more, ride on a trail through the park and to the basin. Kids 2 to 7 years can be led inside the arena for a minimal charge.

   Get physical on the weekends in the summer by renting a row boat, pedal boat, or aqua cycle. There is a special area for radio-controlled boats, too. A snack bar is also open in the summer. The paved street that winds all around the park will have to suffice for most skating or hiking desires. Across Euclid Street, the park also has trap and skeet fields.

   If you like it here so much that you don't want to go home, stay and camp.

The campgrounds are at the far end of the park and are nice-looking. While a few of the sites have small shade trees, the majority of the campsites are near barren, gently sloping hills.

**Hours:**   The park is open daily from 7:30am - 5pm and open extended hours during the summer. Boat rentals are available in the summer only. Horseback riding is available Tues. - Sun. from 8am - 5pm.

**Admission:**   $5 per vehicle during the week; $6 on weekends. Pedestrians are $2. Boat launches are $2. Fishing, ages 7 and older, is $5 a person; $2 for children 6 years and under. Horseback riding is $20 an hour for the first hour; $5 an hour for the second. Pedal boats rentals are $5 for half hour; aqua boats are $6 for half hour; and rowboats are $5 an hour Mon. - Fri.; $7 an hour Sat. - Sun., with minimum rental hours required. Camping starts at $15 a campsite.

**Ages:**   All

# YUCAIPA REGIONAL PARK

(909) 790-3127

*33900 Oak Glen Road, Yucaipa*

(Exit San Bernardino Fwy [10] N.E. on Yucaipa Blvd., L. on Oak Glen Rd. It's W. of the Oak Glen apple orchards.)

Nestled in the rocky San Bernardino Mountains is this huge, beautiful oasis of a park offering year round fun. Fish in any one of the three, very large, picturesque lakes to catch seasonal bass, trout, or catfish. A fishing license is required.

During the summer months, get in the swim of things in the one-acre swim lagoon, and/or go for the two long waterslides! White sandy beaches frame the water's edge, with grassy areas just beyond them. A few steps away is a full-service snack bar, plus pedal boat and aqua cycle rentals. A wonderful playground is right outside the swim area. Another playground, designed specifically for disabled children, is across the way.

RV and tent camping is available for those who really want to get away from it all for a weekend or so. The grassy areas, trees, and mountains are a scenic setting for the camp sites. There are plenty of picnic tables and shelters, as well as barbecue pits. Hiking is encouraged on either paved trails or along the few dirt pathways. (See OAK GLEN / APPLE PICKING & TOURS, under the Edible Adventures section, for nearby places to go.)

**Hours:**   The park is open daily from 7:30am - 6pm. Swimming is available Tues. - Sun. from 10am - 5pm in the summer.

**Admission:** $5 per vehicle Mon. - Fri.; $6 per vehicle Sat. - Sun. and holidays. Pedestrians are $2. A fishing license is needed for those over 16 years - available here for $9.20. Fishing is $5 a day for ages 8 and older; $2 for ages 7 and under, plus park admission. Entrance to the swim lagoon is $3 per person for kids 4 years and up, plus park admission. An all-day waterslide and swim pass is $8 per person, plus park admission. Pedal boat and aqua cycle rentals are $6 for a half hour. Camping prices range from $11 to $17 per night, for up to four people.

**Ages:** All

## AGUA CALIENTE SPRINGS COUNTY PARK

(619) 694-3049 - park; (619) 565-3600 - reservation
*39555 Great Southern Overland Stage Route of 1849, Agua Caliente Hot Springs*
(From 8 Fwy head east to Ocotillo, N. on Imperial Hwy [S2]. It's about 25 miles to the park. From Route 78 head east through Julian, S. on S2.)

For a more therapeutic take on life, come visit Agua Caliente Springs County Park. It features a big, glass-enclosed pool with water temperature maintained at 102 degrees as it is fed by underground hot mineral springs. Ahhhh - feels so good! However, only kids 14 years and up and adults may use the indoor pool. (There are permanent residents on the grounds who live here for health reasons). The fifteen-foot by thirty-foot shallow outdoor pool is fun for children to use, though.

The park also has a general store, shuffleboard courts, horseshoe pits, play areas, over 140 campsites, and hiking trails. There are several trails to choose from, including a half-mile loop called Ocotillo Ridge Nature Trail and a more arduous two-and-a-half-mile trail called Moonlight Canyon Trail. The park is pretty and parts of it are lush with lots of plants and trees fed by the natural springs running throughout. Look for the many species of birds, and other wildlife, that call it home.

**Hours:** The park is closed for the summer. It is open Labor Day through Memorial Day, Mon. - Thurs., 9:30am - 6pm; Fri. - Sun., 9:30am - 9pm. The indoor pool is open daily for day use and campers from 10am - 5:30pm. It is also open campers only, Mon. - Thurs., 8am - 10am; Fri. - Sun., and holidays, 5:30pm - 8:30pm. The outdoor pool is open daily 8am - sunset for all ages.

**Admission:** $2 per vehicle for day use. Use of the pools are included in this fee. Camping costs between $10 (tents) - $16 (full hook-ups) a night. There is an additional $3 fee for camping reservations.

**Ages:** 3 years and up

## ANZA BORREGO STATE PARK

(760) 767-5311 - state park; (760) 767-4684 - wildflower hotline; (800) 444-7275 - camping reservations.

*Anza Borrego*

(From San Diego - Exit 8 Fwy N. on San Vicente Fwy |67|, L. on 79 |about 10 miles|, R. on S-2, L. on Montezuma Valley Rd. |S-22| into Borrego Springs, L. at first stop sign, Palm Cyn Dr., which dead ends into the Visitors Center. Look for the flagpole as the Visitors Center building is hidden. From Escondido Fwy |15| exit E. Rt.79 through Warner Springs, S. on S-2, then look at the directions from San Diego for the park entrance. From San Diego Fwy |5|, exit E. on 78 Fwy to Julian. Take 78 E. out of Julian, N. on Yaqui Pass Rd. |S-3| into Borrego Springs, L. on Palm Canyon Dr. |S-22|, stay on Palm Canyon to the end.)

This massive state park is over 600,000 acres of living desert, which includes sand, rocks, mountains, palm trees, flowers, oases, bighorn sheep, lizards and much more. The following description merely touches on a few of the activities and places that this park has to offer. Remember that this is a desert and the temperatures can reach over 125 degrees during the summer - always bring water!!! Nighttime temperatures can drop drastically, no matter what time of year, so be prepared for anything!

As with any major park, your best bet is to start at the Visitors Center. Get familiar with the park by watching the slide show that is presented upon request, and looking at the exhibits such as taxidermied animals and photographs. Be sure to pick up trail guides and a map.

Anza Borrego has some of the most incredible scenery in Southern California and although much of it can be seen by driving through the park, the really awe-inspiring vistas and landscape can only be seen by hiking. Within the park, take your choice of hiking trails which range from easy loops to arduous "mountain man" trails. One of the most popular hikes is a one-and-a-half-mile nature trail from the Borrego Palm Canyon campground up through Borrego Palm Canyon. The end of the trail is a sight for sore eyes (and hot bodies) - a refreshing waterfall with a pool! Parking is available near the trail entrance for $5 per vehicle.

There are several campsites available in this gigantic park, including one for campers with horses. Tip: Try to choose a site that has some shelter from the desert winds that blow in seemingly at random. Prices for camping run the gamut from the $5 per vehicle entrance fee for back country camping to $22 a night, depending on location and facilities. For more information call the park office at the number above.

See the previous entry, AGUA CALIENTE SPRINGS COUNTY PARK, as it located at the southern part of Anza Borrego park, as well as OCOTILLO WELLS STATE VEHICULAR RECREATION AREA under the Transportation section.

**Hours:**     The park is open 24 hours a day, 365 days a year. The Visitor's Center is open Labor Day through Memorial Day daily from 9am - 5pm. It is open in the summer on weekends and holidays only, from 9am - 5pm.

**Admission:** $5 per vehicle for day use. Camping prices range from $5 - $22 a night.

**Ages:**      3 years and up.

## BALBOA PARK (San Diego)

(619) 239-0512 - This Visitors Center number gives a listing of the museums and information about upcoming events.

*Balboa Park on the Prado, San Diego*

See BALBOA PARK (San Diego) under the Museums section.

## CUYAMACA RANCHO STATE PARK / LAKE CUYAMACA

(760) 765-0755 - park; (800) 444-7275 - camping reservations; (760) 765-0515 - lake

*12551 Highway 79, Descanso, San Diego County*

(Exit 8 Fwy N. on Hwy. 79, about 9 ½ miles up; or exit Hwy 78 [from Julian] S. on Hwy. 79.)

Retreat from the buildings, noise, and general busyness of city life to this outstanding state park with its 25,000 acres of pristine wilderness - a balm to the mind and soul. Take in the forests, grassy meadows, streams, peaks, and valleys that this park has to offer. There are over 120 miles of hiking trails and forty miles of biking trails along the fire roads and access roads. As the terrain varies, hiking trails vary in their degree of difficulty. Be on the lookout for birds, mule deer, lizards, coyotes, etc. Pick up a trail map (50¢) at the park headquarters. While at the headquarters, go through the adjacent museum, which features Native American artifacts, and other exhibits regarding the history and the plant and animal life of this area. The once-prosperous Stonewall Mine site now has just a few pieces of mining equipment to see, as well as the opening to the shaft behind a fence. There are some photographs of the mine nearby.

Seasonal changes at this altitude of 4,000 feet are often drastic and beautiful: Autumn bursts on the scene with its rich colors of gold, red, and orange; winter brings a white blanket of snow; spring explodes with a profusion of brilliant wildflowers; and summer offers refreshment, by sitting near a stream, under a canopy of trees.

Want to go horseback riding through the mountainside, but don't own a horse? Call Holidays on Horseback riding stables, (619) 445-3997, and enjoy a one-and-a-half-hour ($25 per person) or two-hour ($35 per person) excursion. Rides are given between 9:30am to 2:30pm, and riders must be at least 6 years old. Call to make a reservation.

Beautiful campgrounds in the park, and some near rivers, are available for families at either Paso Picacho or Green Valley. You can hike to waterfalls from the latter campground. The cost is $15 per night, maximum eight people per campsite. Most of the camp grounds have picnic tables, fire rings, and heated showers (25¢). Paso Picacho also has a few one-room cabins available for $30 a night. Camp with your horse at specific campgrounds for $19 a night.

Fishing or boating at Lake Cuyamaca, (760) 765-0515, is another way to enjoy this area. Motorboat rentals are $25 a day *oar* rent a row boat at $12 a day. Fishing permits are $4.75 for adults (a California license is also required); $2.75 for kids 8 to 15 years; children 7 years and under are free. Depending on the

season (and your luck), you can catch trout, catfish, bass, bluegill, and crappie.
The lake is at the northern end of the park.

**Hours:** The park is open daily sunrise to sunset. The gift shop and
museum are open Fri. - Mon., 10am - 4pm. Fishing and boat
rentals are available daily from 6am - 6:30pm. Call for extended
summer hours.

**Admission:** $5 per vehicle for day use of the park; dogs are $1 each. There
are several scenic turn-outs off Hwy. 79 that offer picnic tables
and hiking trails.

**Ages:** 2 years and up.

# IMPERIAL SAND DUNES

(760) 337-4400

*On Highway 78, E. of Brawley, near the city of Glamis, San Diego*

(Exit State 78, between Highway 111 and Highway S34, near the city of Glamis, which
is near the borders of Mexico and Arizona. North of the 78 is the dunes wilderness;
south is open for off-road vehicles.)

The expansive Imperial Sand Dunes, also referred to as the Algodones
Dunes, extend for over forty miles - almost as far as the eye can see. They
change in appearance from smooth surfaces to rippling waves, depending on the
prevailing winds. They conjure up images of science fiction flicks, or of a lone
sunburnt person clothed in rags crawling across them desperately crying out,
"water, water!" Tip: Bring your own water.

Stop off first at the Osborne Overlook, located two miles east of Gecko
Road along SR78. Here you'll see a great view of the dunes and the surrounding
Imperial Valley. The appropriately named "wilderness" area is north of the 78,
between Ted Kipf Road and the Coachella lands. A viewing area is two miles
north of Glamis along Ted Kipf Road. Awe-inspiring dunes are towards the west
side, while the east side has mostly smaller dunes and washes. The region is open
for you to walk, run, jump, and roll down the dunes. Horseback riding is also
allowed. Note that summer temperatures can rise to 110 degrees, so the most
favorable months to visit are between October and May. Bring your sunglasses,
camera, and a bucket and shovel.

The area south of the highway is open for tent and RV camping, off-
highway vehicles (OHVs), and all-terrain vehicles (ATVs). Dune buggies are not
readily available for rent, so you must bring your own vehicle. Camping is
primitive, and trash must be packed out. For more information and an area map,
call the BLM (i.e. Bureau of Land Management) at the above number.

**Hours:** Open daily sunrise to sunset.

**Admission:** Free

**Ages:** It depends on how far you want to hike, or if you are content
with just playing in the sand.

# KIT CARSON PARK / ESCONDIDO SPORTS CENTER

(760) 741-4691 - park; (760) 839-5425 - sports center                *!/$$*

*Bear Valley Parkway, Escondido*

(Exit Escondido Fwy [15] E. on Via Ranch Pky which turns into Bear Valley Pky.)

Come to where the action is! This "state-of-the-art" sports center is located in the heart of Kit Carson Park. It has a arena soccer with bleachers, a roller hockey arena, a 20,000 square-foot skate park, and a pro shop and concession stand. The outdoor, fully lighted, skate park is complete with variously-sized ramps, a full street course with roll ins, and a bowl with a ramp. The skate park is for skaters as well as bikers. Bring your own equipment, or borrow a helmet, elbow pads, and knee pads from the park at no charge, but know that it is first come, first served. Sign up for leagues, camps, and/or skate sessions, or just come to watch the action.

Kit Carson park has 185 undeveloped acres and 100 developed acres. It's very family-friendly with plenty of picnic tables, barbeque pits, green grassy areas for running around, a few playgrounds (plus one just for tots), nine ball fields (some with stadium seating), tennis courts, soccer fields, an amphitheater, a fitness course, a fitness trail with markers, and hiking trails. Whew! This park handily accommodates all of your family's different activities.

**Hours:** The park is open daily from dawn to dusk. Call for hours on the various sporting center activities. Skate sessions are Mon. - Fri., 4pm - 6:30pm and 7pm - 9:30pm; Sat. - Sun., 9am - 12:30pm, 2pm - 5:30pm, and 6pm - 9:30pm. Hours are extended in the summer. The first session on Wed. and Sat. is for kids 6 - 12 years only. The second session on Wed. and the last session on Sun. is for bikers only.

**Admission:** The park is free. Skate/bike sessions are $10 per session. Year memberships are available at $15 per person, which brings the cost of each session down to $4 during the week, $6 on weekends.

**Ages:** All for the park. 6 years and up for some skate sessions.

# LA JOLLA INDIAN RESERVATION CAMPGROUND / TUBING ON SAN LUIS REY RIVER

(760) 742-1297

*Route 76, on the La Jolla Indian Reservation, Pauma Valley*

(Exit Escondido Fwy [15] E. on Rt. 76 and up about 25 mountain miles. It's 100 yards N. of Segnme Oaks Rd., R. at the Texaco Gas Station.)

Come to the campground just for the day, or spend a night or two here in the lush, semi-wilderness of the foothills of the beautiful Palomar Mountains. Hike amongst the beautiful foliage along the San Luis Rey River; climb the rocks on the river banks; try your luck at fishing; or wade in the river waters.

For more wet thrills, go inner tubing down the river. Cruise down the two mile stretch, which takes about an hour, as many times as you want throughout the day. Parts of the river are idyllic, while other parts are a bit more exciting (and bumpy). Old army troop transportation trucks will pick you up at the end of the run and bring your family back to the starting point. Be prepared for this adventure by wearing a hat, tee shirt, sunscreen, and sneakers (for painlessly stepping on the rocks on the river bottom). B.Y.O.T. (Bring Your Own Tube) or rent an inner tube here for $5. Tip: Tie your inner tube to your child's so you can stay together!

Almost all of the camping sites are located right by the river. (The water can be soothing or loud, depending on how you interpret its sound.) Chemical toilets are scattered throughout the camp, and hot showers are available at designated places. Campfires are allowed. Firewood, tackle, supplies, and food are available at the small Trading Post on the grounds.

**Hours:** Open sunrise to sunset. Tubing is available daily during the summer from 8am - 6pm.

**Admission:** $9 per vehicle for day use for up to four people. Additional passengers are $1 per person. River tubing is included in this price. Tube rentals are $5. Camping is $13 per vehicle for tent campers; $18 for R.V.s.

**Ages:** 4 years and up

# LAKE POWAY RECREATION AREA / CLYDE E.    ☼
# REXRODE WILDERNESS AREA

(619) 679-5466 - general info; (619) 486-1234 - boat concession                    $
*Lake Poway Road, Poway*

(Exit Escondido Fwy [15] E. on Rancho Bernardo Rd. Go about 4 miles, then turn L. on Lake Poway Rd., and go up the hill.)

The fish are usually biting at the stocked Lake Poway. Depending on the season, reel in catfish or rainbow trout. Looking for something fun to tackle on summer nights? Try night fishing from Memorial Day through Labor Day on any Thursday, Friday, and/or Saturday night from 4pm to 11pm. Boats rentals available here are: rowboats - $10 a day; motorboats - $15 a day; paddle boats - $8 an hour; and canoes - $8 an hour.

The 400 acres surrounding the lake are the Clyde Rexrode Wilderness Area, named after Poway's first mayor. There are miles of trails to choose from, including a scenic three-mile loop around the lake, which takes about an hour. This trail is great for sturdy walkers and can be used by mountain bikers, too. More rugged trails include the two-and-a-half-mile hike up to Mt. Woodson, and trails leading down into Blue Sky ecological reserve. Scenery ranges from sage bush to large trees. Be on the lookout for wildlife such as red-tail hawks, raccoons, and even deer. This wilderness area offers an escape from city life.

**Hours:** The park is open daily 7am - sunset. The lake is open for fishing and boating, Wed. - Sun. from sunrise to sunset.

**Admission:** Entrance to the park is free during the week. Sat., Sun., and holidays, non-residents pay $4 per vehicle. Daily fishing permits are $4.50 for adults; $2 for ages 8 -15 years; children 7 years and under may fish off an adult permit.

**Ages:** 3 years and up.

## MISSION BAY PARK                                              ☼
*San Diego*                                                      !/$
(Exit San Diego Fwy [5] W. on Clairemont Dr. to drive the Mission Bay loop - go S. on E. Mission Bay Dr. to Sea World Dr. to Mission Bay Dr. [or N. on Ingraham St.] to Grand Ave.)

Mission Bay Park is not a singular bay or park like the name implies - it is thousands of acres of incredibly beautiful vistas, and of beaches, water, pathways, playgrounds, grassy areas, and various attractions. Generic things to do include jogging, cycling, in-line skating, swimming, picnicking, fishing, kayaking, sailing, pedal boating, paddle boating, and camping. Park at any one of the scenic spots you see along Mission Bay Drive, or Ingraham Street, and enjoy. Hot spots include: <u>Pacific Beach</u>, just north of Mission Beach on Mission Boulevard - a favorite hang out for surfers, swimmers, joggers, etc.; <u>Fiesta Island</u>, just northeast of Sea World, and <u>Vacation Isle</u>, on Ingraham Street north of Sea World Drive - both have numerous biking trails, delightful picnic areas, and a few playgrounds; <u>South Mission Beach</u> and <u>North Mission Beach</u>, both along Mission Boulevard - popular beaches for swimming and laying out; and <u>De Anza Cove</u>, on E. Mission Bay Drive - a nice area for swimming.

A few helpful names and phone numbers in the Mission Bay area include: Campland on the Bay, (619) 581-4200, for camping; Hamel's Action Sports Center, which is a building shaped like a castle, (619) 488-5050, for rentals of bikes, skates, boogie boards, etc.; San Diego Sailing Center, (619) 488-0651, for rentals of sailboards and kayaks; and Windsport Kayak & Windsurfing Center, (619) 488-4642, for kayak and windsurfing rentals.

Attractions listed separately in Mission Bay Park are: BELMONT PARK, PIRATE'S COVE, SAN DIEGO VISITOR INFORMATION CENTER, SEA WORLD, and TECOLOTE SHORES PLAY AREA.

**Hours:**     Open daily
**Admission:** Free
**Ages:**      All

## MISSION TRAILS REGIONAL PARK
(619) 668-3275                                                    !
*One Father Junipero Serra Trail, San Diego*
(There are several entrances to the park. From Mission Valley Fwy [8], exit N. on Mission Gorge/Fairmount and go 4 miles N. on Mission Gorge Rd. The Visitor and Interpretive Center entrance is on the L. between Jackson Dr. and Golfcrest Dr., on Father Junipero Serra Trail. From Route 52, exit S. when it ends on Mission Gorge Rd. If visiting the Old Mission Dam area, the Old Mission Dam entrance is about ½ mile down Mission Gorge Rd. The Visitor and Interpretive Center is about 2 miles further down Mission Gorge Rd. See directions from Fwy 8.)

This massive, almost 6,000-acre recreational area is comprised of several major areas and points of interest: 1) Lake Murray - At the southern part of the park is a beautiful, stocked lake that allows fishing and boating activities from 5:30am to 5pm on Wednesdays, Saturdays, and Sundays between November and Labor Day. A paved trail goes around the lake. Picnic tables are also available; 2) Cowles Mountain - Hiking is the main sport here. For an outstanding 360 degree view of the city, take the one-and-a-half-mile trail (about two hours) to the top of the mountain; 3) Old Mission Dam Historic Area - This is a starting point for several hikes. Picnic tables are here, too. People of all abilities can go on a self-guided paved pathway from the parking lot to the footbridge across the San Diego River, lush with foliage. Further along is the gorge with rock cliffs. Press buttons along the trail to listen to explanations of the area. Take a longer hike, too. So many trails - so little time!; 4) East Fortuna Mountain - This area offers some of the most diverse environments of the park. Check out some of the canyons! The smallish Kumeyaay Lake, accessible from Father Junipero Serra Trail, is fun for shoreline fishing. A relatively flat one-and-a-half-mile trail goes around the lake; 5) West Fortuna Mountain - You can hike or mountain bike up plateaus and series of canyons; 6) The Visitor and Interpretive Center - This architecturally beautiful building blends in with the natural rock setting of the park, and is a great starting place for an adventure. Pick up trail guides, program information, and/or enjoy some interactive exhibits inside. Kids gravitate to the Indian faces carved from "rocks." Several touch screens offer information about the park - where to go, and all about the plants and animals. Every thirty minutes the small theater presents a film on the park. Walk to the upper story of the center amid bird and animal sounds. See ancient volcanic rock and a great view of your surroundings. Outside the center is a small stage and rocks that are almost irresistible for kids to climb. The kids sweated (I glowed) as we hiked on the moderate looping trail around the Visitors Center, which took us a good hour. Our mission is to come back to Mission Trails and experience more of what it has to offer!

**Hours:** The trails and park are open daily sunrise to sunset, although the car entry gates are open from 9am - 5pm. The Center is open daily from 9am - 5pm. Closed on Christmas.

**Admission:** Free

**Ages:** 3 years and up.

## OLD POWAY PARK

(619) 679-4313
*14134 Midland Road, Poway*

See OLD POWAY PARK, under the Potpourri section, for details.

## PALOMAR MOUNTAIN STATE PARK / PALOMAR OBSERVATORY

(760) 742-2119 - observatory; (760) 742-3462 - state park; (800) 444-7275 - camping reservations.

*S6, Palomar Mountain*

(Exit Escondido Fwy [15] E. on Pala Rd. [Route 76], L. [ N.E.] on S6 about 26 miles up the mountain to the observatory.)

Up in the Palomar Mountains, at the end of a long and winding road, is the Palomar Observatory. A short hike up to the observatory allows you to see the famed 200" Hale telescope. But forewarn your children - you can only look <u>at</u>

the telescope which is housed behind glass panes; you cannot look through it. The telescope is magnificent in size and scope and seeing it is almost worth the drive here! The small one-room museum displays outstanding photos of star clusters, galaxies, and clouds of glowing gas. It also shows a continuously running video about the workings of the telescope and about our universe.

Just a few miles down the road is Palomar Mountain State Park. If you're planning on coming to the observatory, I suggest making the park a destination, too, as just walking around the observatory and museum took us only half an hour. Palomar Mountain General Store, (760) 742-3496, is at the junction of S7 and S6, making it a natural stopping place before going on to the park. The store has a bit of everything, including fossils, gems, Indian jewelry, and artifacts.

Continue about three miles on S7 to reach the park. At 2,000 acres, this Sierra Nevada-like park is incredibly beautiful. You'll find several hiking trails through the scenic mountainside. The Boucher Hill Lookout trail, for instance, is a looping two-mile hike with marvelous vistas. Fishing is available at Doane Pond, which is stocked with trout regularly. There is a five fish limit per day, and those 16 years old and older need a California state license. The park also provides areas for picnicking and overnight camping. Thirty-one family campsites have fire rings, picnic tables, and coin-operated hot showers. Call the ranger station (park office) for more information.

**Hours:** The museum and the observatory are open daily 9am - 4pm. The state park is open sunrise to sunset.

**Admission:** Free to the observatory and museum. A $5 vehicle entrance fee is charged for day use of the park. Overnight camping is $15 weekdays; $16 on weekends, for a maximum of 8 people, 1 vehicle. Additional vehicles are $5.

**Ages:** 8 years and up for the observatory and the museum; ages 3 and up for the park.

# QUAIL BOTANICAL GARDENS

(760) 436-3036

*230 Quail Gardens Drive, Encinitas*

(Exit San Diego Fwy [5] E. on Encinitas Blvd., L. on Quail Gardens Dr. There are signs along the way.)

We didn't see any quail on our visit to the Quail Botanical Gardens, but we did see (and hear) woodpeckers plus a variety of other birds such as wrens, finches, scrub jays, and hermit thrushes. The thirty landscaped acres here include desert, exotic tropical, palm, bamboo, and native California plants. The lush foliage; the incredible array of flowers; the meandering trails (some dirt, some paved); the beautiful waterfall; and the benches under shade trees, all invoked the sensation of visiting a secret garden. Some of our highlights included seeing the Sausage Tree, with its large and very heavy pods that really do resemble sausages; walking up to the Overlook Pavilion for a 360-degree view of the gardens, mountains, ocean, and surrounding community; and taking pictures of the unique flowers. Our favorite flowers were the white and yellow upside-down bellflowers. Strolling around the botanical gardens is a delightful way to spend the day!

**Hours:**  Open daily 9am - 5pm. Closed New Year's Day, Thanksgiving, and Christmas.

**Admission:** $5 for adults; $4 for seniors; $2 for ages 5 -12; children 4 years and under are free.

**Ages:**  2 years and up.

## RANCHO VISTA SPORTS PARK AND COMMUNITY RECREATION CENTER

(909) 694-6410                                                          !/$

*30875 Rancho Vista, Temecula*

(Exit Temecula Fwy [15] E. on Rancho California Rd., S. on Ynez Rd., L. on Rancho Vista)

Have a ball at this terrific sports park! It has twelve ball fields, seven soccer fields, lots of open grassy areas for running around, two great playgrounds, shade trees, picnic shelters, and barbecue grills. The one-acre, concrete skateboard park has ramps, rails, etc., which make it fun and challenging. The roller hockey rink has some open time, though it is used mostly by leagues. The indoor gym offers basketball, and can be set up for volleyball. Keep your cool in the twenty-five-meter outdoor swimming pool that has a diving board and a waterslide. There is also a shallow pool just for tots. The Teen Center is a great place for 12 - 18 year olds to hang out. It offers pool, air hockey, Carom, Nintendo, and more. This park offers everything active kids need - my boys would be very happy living there!

**Hours:**  The park is open sunrise - 10pm. Skateboard sessions are 2½ hours long: Mon. - Fri., between 1pm - 9pm; Sat., between 10am - 9:30pm; Sun., between 1pm - 6:30pm. The roller hockey rink is usually available for open play Mon. - Fri. before 4pm. After 4pm and on weekends, it is booked for leagues. The pool is open weekends only in April, May, September, and October from 1pm - 5pm. During summer months it's open Mon., Wed., Fri., 2pm - 5pm; Sat. - Sun., 1pm - 5pm. The Teen Center is open Mon. - Fri., 2pm - 8:45pm during school hours. Weekends and off-school hours, it's open noon - 8:45pm.

**Admission:** The park is free. Skateboard sessions cost $2 for residents; $5 for non-residents. Bring your own equipment, or rent everything needed for $5. Pool sessions for residents are $2.25 for adults; $1.75 for ages 8 - 17; $1 for kids 7 years and under. Pool rates for non-residents are $3 per person. The Teen Center asks that a resident card be purchased - $1 for a year's membership.

**Ages:**  All ages for the park. Skateboarders under 7 years must be accompanied by an adult. Kids must be between 12 - 18 years to hang out inside the Teen Center.

# SAN PASQUAL BATTLEFIELD STATE HISTORIC PARK

(619) 220-5430

*15808 San Pasqual Valley Road (SR78), San Pasqual*

(Going S. on San Diego Fwy [5], or Escondido Fwy [15], exit E. on Hwy 78, turns into San Pasqual Valley Rd. Going N. on 15, exit E. on Via Rancho Pkwy., turns into Bear Valley Rd., R. on San Pasqual Rd., turns into Via Rancho Pkwy., go to end, R. on San Pasqual Valley Rd. It is just E. of San Diego Wild Animal Park)

This is the site of the worst (i.e. bloodiest) battles in California in the Mexican-American War. Kids need to know this fact for its historical significance, and because it will make their visit here more exciting. The grounds have picnic tables and a quarter-mile, looping trail. The visitors center overlooks the battlefield, which is actually across the highway, on private land. The small center has interpretive panels, a few uniforms, weapons, and a ten-minute video entitled *Mr. Polk's War*. Living History Days are held the first Sunday of each month from 11am to 3pm. Docents are dressed in period costume and do old-fashioned chores, crafts, etc. Periodically, you can also see a cannon being fired. Note: The battle is re-enacted in December.

**Hours:** The park is open Sat. - Sun. and holidays, 10am - 5pm. Guided school tours are given during the week, by appointment.

**Admission:** Free

**Ages:** 6 years and up.

# SANTEE LAKES REGIONAL PARK AND CAMPGROUND

(619) 448-2482

*9040 Carlton Oaks Drive, Santee*

(Take the 52 Fwy E. to the end, go E. on Mission Gorge Rd., L. on Carlton Hills Blvd., L. on Carlton Oaks Dr. Going N. on San Vicente Fwy [67], exit W. on Prospect Ave., R. on Cuyamaca St., L. on Mission Gorge Rd., R. on Carlton Hills Blvd., L. on Carlton Oaks Dr. Going S. on 67, exit W. on Woodside Ave., which turns into Mission Gorge Rd., R. on Carlton Hills Blvd., L. on Carlton Oaks Dr.)

This regional park is like a mini-resort. It has campgrounds, a swimming pool (for campers only), a general store, laundry facilities, a recreation center, playgrounds, and several lakes for boating and fishing. The lakes are seasonally stocked with trout, catfish, bluegill, and bass. No swimming is allowed in the lakes. A California state fishing license is required and available for purchase at the park entrance. Full hook-up campgrounds start at $22 a night for two people; $1 for each additional person. Primitive campgrounds, open Friday and Saturday only, are available for $15 a night for two people; $1 for each additional person. Each campsite has a picnic table and barbeque pit. Today's a great day to get away to Santee!

**Hours:** The park and fishing are open Mon. - Thurs., 8am - sunset; Fri. - Sun., 6am - sunset. The pool is open seasonally.

**Admission:** $2 per vehicle during the week; $3 per vehicle on the weekends. Fishing permits are $4 for adults; $2 for ages 7 - 15; children 6 and under fish for free. Camping prices are listed above.

**Ages:** 2 years and up.

## SOUTH CLAIREMONT RECREATION CENTER / POOL

(619) 581-9924 - recreation center; (619) 581-9923 - pool        !/$
*3605 Clairemont Drive, Clairemont*

(Going N on San Diego Fwy [5], exit W. on Balboa Ave., L. on Clairemont Ave. Going S. on 5, exit S. on Mission Bay Dr., L. on Garnet, turns into Balboa Ave., L on Clairemont Ave.)

This large community park offers various activities for families to enjoy. Green grassy areas and scattered picnic tables provide a picnic atmosphere, while the older-style playground, complete with hopscotch, slides, swings, and climbing apparatus, provides the fun. Check at the community center building for special classes, programs, and events. There are also two tennis courts and a good-sized, outdoor swimming pool that is open year round. During the week only half of the pool is open for public use because the swim team uses the other half. On weekends, the whole pool is open for the public to use.

**Hours:** The park is open daily sunrise to sunset. The pool is open Mon. - Fri., 10am - 3:45pm (shallow end only); Sat. - Sun., 11am - 3pm (whole pool).

**Admission:** The park is free. Swimming sessions cost $2 for adults; $1.50 for kids 15 years and under.

**Ages:** All

## TECOLOTE SHORES PLAY AREA

*West Mission Bay Drive, San Diego*        !

(Exit San Diego Fwy [5] W. on Clairemont Dr., L. on E. Mission Bay Dr., past the Hilton.)

Head for some big time fun at the large Tecolote Shores Play Area. This wonderful playground has a great combination of old and new equipment. In the main area, with its sand-covered grounds, there are slides, swings, and cement turtles to climb on (and under). Other sections include aquatic cement creatures, a pirate ship, mini-obstacle ropes course, bridges, and various other climbing apparatus. There are plenty of picnic tables and grassy areas here, too. As the playground is right on the bay, the view is beautiful. Tip: There aren't many tall trees here, at least right now, so this is a great place to fly a kite.

**Hours:** Open daily sunrise to sunset.

**Admission:** Free

**Ages:** All

## TIJUANA ESTUARY and VISITORS CENTER / BORDER FIELD STATE PARK

(619) 575-3613 - Estuary and Visitors Center                                      !
*301 Caspian Way, Imperial Beach*
(Exit San Diego Fwy [5] W. on Coronade Ave., which turns into Imperial Beach Blvd., L.
on 3$^{rd}$ St., L. on Caspian Wy.)

First things first - an estuary is: "The wide part of a river where it flows near the sea; where fresh water and salt water mix." (That's why this book is called "Fun and *Educational* . . .") The Visitors Center has several wonderful interactive exhibits. One of our favorite displays were ordinary-looking, black and white sketched pictures of habitats that magically revealed brightly colored birds, insects, fish, and other animals when viewed through a polarized filter. The touch table contains snake skin, nests, skulls, and a dead sea turtle. The food chain is portrayed through pictures and graphs. Beneath the Sand exhibit entails pressing the bill of bird puppet heads into holes in various levels of "sand." A light on the side panel displays what birds with shorter beaks, that reach only shallow levels, eat (insects and plant seed), compared to what birds with longer beaks, that can reach deeper levels, eat (crabs and worms). A small theater shows, upon request, films such as *Timeless River* and *Tide of the Heron*.

Eight miles of walking trails are interspersed throughout the reserve. Ask for a map at the center, as there are different entrance points. Some of the trails follow along the streets, while others go deeper into the coastal dunes and near the Tijuana River. Be on the lookout for terns, egrets, herons, curlews, etc., and other wildlife. On a very short loop around the center, my boys and I saw interesting plants and birds, plus thirteen bunnies! Take a guided walking tour to learn more about the flora and fauna at the estuary, or sign the kids up for one of the numerous programs available. The Jr. Ranger Program, for students kindergarten through sixth grade (under 6 years old must be accompanied by a parent), is offered every Thursday from 3:15pm to 4:45pm. During the program kids will enjoy a walk, earn patches or buttons, and/or make a craft - all free of charge!

Just south of the estuary is Border Field State Park, which borders Mexico. A marker shows the United States - Mexico boundary. The cliffs provide an awesome view of the ocean, and of the whales during whale-watching season, which is January through March. You can even see some of Tijuana from here, including a bullfighting ring. Picnic tables, grassy areas for running around, and pathways for hiking into parts of the estuary are all parts of the park.

An exciting way to see more of the park is by taking a horseback ride on the beach. Wear long pants, a windbreaker, and close-toed shoes before saddling up for a two or three-hour adventure. Call Sandi's Rental Stables, located at 2060 Hollister Street, at (619) 424-3124. The stables offers other rides too, such as going on the wildlife trail in the estuary, or mounting up for a Chuckwagon Meal Ride. Although children 4 years and up may join in a horseback ride, younger children may also take a pony ride around the parking lot.

**Hours:**     The Visitors Center is open daily from 10am - 5pm. Closed
            Thanksgiving and Christmas. The stables are open every day.
**Admission:**  Free to the Visitors Center. Horseback riding starts at $20 an
            hour; $10 for a half-hour pony ride around the parking lot.

**Ages:**   3 years and up.

## TORREY PINES STATE RESERVE                                    ☼
(619) 755-2063                                                     $
*Torrey Pines Park Road, La Jolla*
(Exit San Diego Fwy [5] W. on Del Mar Heights Rd., L. on Camino Del Mar, turns into North Torrey Pines Rd., R. on Torrey Pines Park Rd. past the beach and up the hill.)

The Torrey pine tree grows only in this reserve - no where else in the whole world! My kids were impressed with this fact and by the beauty of the park. Our favorite trail was the Guy Fleming Trail. It's an easy loop, only two-thirds of a mile, and incredibly scenic through the trees out to a cliff overlooking the ocean. Tip: Hold on to younger children! Other trails include the half-mile, Parry Grove looping trail; the two-thirds-of-a-mile, Razor Point Trail with dramatic views of gorges; the steep, three-quarters-of-a-mile (one way), Beach Trail which ends at the San Diego - La Jolla Underwater Park; and the two, demanding, Broken Hill Trails.

The Visitors Center shows a short film that gives an overview of the reserve - just ask to see it. The exhibits here offer good visual information regarding the plants and animal wildlife of the reserve. On display are taxidermied raccoons, skunks, and birds; a pine cone display; a pine needle display; and more. We appreciated Torrey Pines Reserve for its glorious nature trails and its breath of fresh air! A lifeguarded State Beach is right below the reserve for those who are into sand and surf.

**Hours:**   Open daily from 8am - sunset.
**Admission:**   $4 per vehicle.
**Ages:**   3 years and up.

## VOLCAN MOUNTAIN NATURE PRESERVE                               ☼
(760 )765-0650                                                     !
*Near the intersection of Wynola and Farmers Roads, Julian*
(On Hwy 78, just N. of town, take Main St., which becomes Farmers Rd. Turn R. at the 4-way intersection, then take an immediate L. The entrance is on your R.)

The three-mile trail up the mountain encompasses spectacular wilderness scenery. You'll pass through meadows, high chaparral, and forests of oak and pine, to eventually reach a 360 degree panoramic view of the surrounding area, including the Salton Sea.

**Hours:**   Open daily sunrise to sunset.
**Admission:**   Free
**Ages:**   3 years and up.

## WILLIAM HEISE COUNTY PARK                                      ☼
(619) 694-3049 for information; (619) 565-3600 for camping           $
reservations.
*Frisius Road, Julian*
(From Hwy 78, take Pine Hills Rd. south for 2 miles, then head east on Frisius Rd. for another 2 miles. It's 4 miles south of Julian.)

Consider this forest-like park a family destination. With eight miles of hiking trails to choose from, there is bound to be a trail, or two, suitable for each member of the family. Select an easy pathway that leads through a cedar forest, a moderate trail that goes through canyon live oak, or choose a rugged trail for more experienced hikers.

Over forty tent sites, sixty RV sites, and two cabins with electricity and a few furnishings, provide overnight camping in this beautiful area. The campgrounds have piped-in water, showers, barbeques and fire rings, and a playground. The one-room cabins each have a fireplace and sleep up to six people.

**Hours:** Open daily 9am - 5pm.

**Admission:** $2 per vehicle. Camping is $14 a night. The cabins are $30 a night.

**Ages:** All

# CHANNEL ISLANDS NATIONAL PARK

(805) 658-5730 - National Park; (805) 642-7688 - recorded information for Island Packers; (805) 642-1393 - Island Packers reservations / www.isle.net/~ipco

*The park headquarters is at 1901 Spinnaker; Island Packers is at 1867 Spinnaker Dr., Ventura*

(Going S. on Ventura Fwy [101], exit S. on Harbor Blvd. Going W. on 101, exit S.W. on Seaward Ave., L. on Harbor Blvd. From Harbor, go R. on Spinnaker Dr., all the way to the end. There are also departures from Oxnard Harbor Channel Islands.)

The Channel Islands comprise eight islands off Southern California, five of which make up Channel Islands National Park and marine sanctuary. Prepare your kids for a half or whole day excursion to an island by first obtaining information from the park service. The islands were originally the home of Chumash Indians. Then, hunters came and killed certain otter, seal, and sea lion species almost to extinction. Finally, ranchers settled here. Some parts of the islands are still privately owned. It's important to emphasize to your child that Channel Islands is a national preserve, so "take only memories, leave only footprints."

Climate on the islands is different from mainland climate, even during the summer. The harsher conditions have produced various terrains within the relatively small parcels of land from sandy beaches to rocky hills. Cruise to the islands and explore nature at her best and wildest. Kids get especially excited about seeing the numerous seals and sea lions that are plentiful because they breed on many of the islands. Be on the lookout for blue sharks and dolphins. Once on an island, be on the lookout for some unusual birds, and animals like the island fox. Bring jackets and your camera; wear sneakers; pack a water bottle; and have a terrific outing!

Here is a very brief overview of the islands (enough to whet your adventuring appetite), along with cruise prices from Island Packers:

**Anacapa** - This is the closest island to Ventura, only fourteen miles away. It is five miles long. On East Anacapa, climb up the 153 steps to a sweeping panoramic view. Enjoy a small visitor's center and nearly two miles of hiking trails. There is no beach here, but swimming is allowed at the landing cove on calm summer days, as is scuba and skin diving. Picnicking is welcomed. This is one of the most popular islands to visit. Round-trip takes about seven hours, including about three hours on the island. Adult fare is $37; children 12 years and under are $20. A half-day cruise around the island, with no island landing, is about three-and-a-half hours long. Whale watching is offered on this cruise from the end of December through the month of March. Adult fare is $21; children 12 years and under are $14. Take an express run - a five-hour day, including two hours on the island, for $32 for adults; $20 for kids. On days of low tide, visit the tide pools at West Anacapa. The price for this cruise is the same as an all-day cruise.

**Santa Cruz** - At twenty-four miles long, this is the largest island off California. Topography varies from sea caves and steep cliffs to rolling hills and grasslands. Offered year-round, round-trip takes eight to nine hours, including about three-and-a-half hours on the island. Adult fare is $42; children 12 years and under are $25. Overnight camping here is $54 for adults; $40 for children 12 years and under.

**Santa Rosa** - This island is fifteen miles long and, although eighty-five percent of it is grasslands, there are still canyons, volcanic formations, and fossil beds that vary the landscape. There is plenty to see and do here for those who thrive on being in the midst of nature. Offered April through November, round-trip takes about twelve hours, including about four hours on the island. Adult fare is $62; children 12 years and under are $45. Overnight camping is $80 for adults; $70 for children 12 years and under.

**San Miguel** - This eight-mile-long island has beaches and an incredible number of seals and sea lions. The most popular destination here is the Caliche Forest (i.e. mineral sand castings), which is a three-and-a-half-mile hike from the beach. Be prepared for strong winds, plus rain and fog any time of the year. The varying island terrains reflect the assault of weather upon San Miguel. Weekend camping, offered May through November, and round-trip transportation costs $90 for adults; $80 for children 12 years and under. Day trips leave only from Santa Barbara, and entail spending the night before on the boat. The day visits to San Miguel, offered April, and June through October, are recommended for hardier kids.

**Santa Barbara** - This is the smallest island, only 640 acres, and is the farthest away from mainland Ventura. It has steep cliffs, a small "museum," and hiking trails. There are no shade trees on the island, so load up with sunscreen. Round-trip, offered April through November, takes about eleven hours, including about four hours on the island. Adult fare is $49; children 12 years and under are $35. Camping is $75 for adults; $65 for children 12 years and under.

     If you prefer to fly, check out Channel Islands Aviation, (805) 987-1301, located in the Camarillo Airport. Following a half-hour scenic flight over Anacapa and Santa Cruz Islands, you'll land on Santa Rosa Island and be here for about five and a half hours. A ranger drives around the island where you'll see a century-old cattle ranch and other island highlights. You can hike around a bit, have a picnic lunch (which you supply), and explore more of the island before you fly back to Camarillo. Adult fare is $98 round trip; children 2 to 12 years cost $78.

Also check out CHANNEL ISLANDS NATIONAL PARK VISITOR CENTER under the Museums section, and VENTURA HARBOR and VILLAGE under the Piers and Seaports section.

**Hours:** Listed under each island.
**Admission:** Listed under each island.
**Ages:** 6 years and up.

# CONEJO CREEK NORTH LIBRARY PARK
(805) 495-6471 - park; (805) 449-2660 - library
*1401 E. Janss Road, Thousand Oaks*
(Exit the 23 Fwy E. on Janss Rd.)

Around the back of the library, near the freeway, is a long strip of land that is a delightful park. Trees block the view of the freeway, and some of its sound. A rock-lined creek runs through most of the park. (My boys could spend hours playing just here, and getting a little wet.) There are also walkways, a few nice playgrounds, sand volleyball courts, picnic shelters, grassy areas, shade trees, an ornamental fountain, and quite a few bridges, one of which leads directly to the library. A visit to the library and/or adjacent senior/teen community center can round out your trip.

**Hours:** Open daily sunrise to sunset. The library is open Mon. - Thurs., 10am - 9pm; Fri., 10am - 6pm; Sat., 10am - 5pm; Sun., 1pm - 5pm.
**Admission:** Free
**Ages:** All

# CONEJO VALLEY COMMUNITY PARK and BOTANIC  GARDEN
(805) 495-2163
*1300 Hendrix Avenue, Thousand Oaks*
(Exit Ventura Fwy [101] N. on Lynn Rd., R. on Gainsborough Rd.)

This nature park is delightful in size and scope. There are acres and acres of green rolling hills, and a creek running throughout. The creek, by itself, is a major attraction. My boys loved looking for crawdads and, of course, stepping on the rocks, with the possible thrill of slipping and getting a bit wet. Almost a full day's adventure can be had by climbing the gnarled, old oak trees. There are cement pathways throughout the park, making much of it stroller accessible. The ambiance here is peaceful, unless you bring your kids, of course!

The upper field sports a baseball diamond, while a basketball court is across the way. A playground is located in front of the community center building. A covered picnic area with barbecue pits is also available here.

The Botanic Garden is bigger than it first appears. One short path traverses through a variety of landscapes, looping around and covering most of the garden. Another nature trail goes up and around the hillside, following a creek through oak and willow trees before looping back around. I don't know how much actual plant knowledge my kids gained from our garden walk, but I'm always hopeful that just spending time in such an environment will help them develop an appreciation for the beautiful gift of nature.

**Hours:** The park is open daily from dawn to dusk. The community center is open Mon. - Fri., 9am - 7pm; Sat., 9am - 4pm; Sun., noon - 4pm.

**Admission:** Free

**Ages:** All

## LAKE CASITAS RECREATION AREA

(805) 649-2233

*11311 Santa Ana Road, Ventura*

(Exit the Ojai Fwy [33] E. on Casitas Vista Rd., R. on Santa Ana Rd. It's at the junction of Route 150 and Santa Ana Rd.)

Main attractions at this beautiful lake have traditionally been fishing, biking, and camping. The bait and tackle shop, (805) 649-2043, has boats for rent. A four-passenger aluminum motor boat is $25 an hour and a ten-passenger pontoon boat is $50 an hour. No waterskiing is allowed. A fishing license is needed for those 16 years and older. A day license is available here for $9.70. Bike on the five miles or so of paved trail, and a few dirt paths, that run throughout the park. Cycles for Rent, (805) 652-0462, is located just inside the recreation area. Bike rentals start at $7 an hour for a mountain bike and $10 an hour for a tandem. Campsites range from basic tent camping to full RV hookups. Each site has a picnic table and fire ring.

Beat the summer heat with the lake's Blue Heron Water Playground, designed for children 12 years and under. Kids on the upper end of this spectrum, however, will probably find this wading pool too tame. (The park is hoping to expand its water attractions to accommodate more age groups.) This spacious, colorful water play area has six slides, chutes, climbing structures, wheels to turn to adjust the water spray, anchored squirt guns, and water spurting out of its pipes - all in only eighteen inches of water. Several lifeguards patrol the pool. Although children squeal loudly while they play, the roar of the water is louder. Parents can cool off in the water or relax on the adjacent grassy areas that surround this aquatic playground. Note: If your younger child is not quite potty trained, swim diapers are available to purchase here for $10. The water is tested throughout the day and if someone has used it instead of the restrooms, the play area will be shut down for the day for cleaning. Pay for sessions in one-hour increments, or for all-day play. The pool can accommodate up to 200 visitors.

**Hours:** The lake and most amenities are open daily from sunrise to sunset. The water playground is open on weekends only in May, September, and October from 10am - 5pm. It is open daily during the summer from 10am - 7pm. Sessions are at 10am, 11:20am, 12:40pm, 2pm, 3:20pm, 4:40pm and 6pm.

**Admission:** Entrance to the lake is $6.50 per vehicle; $11.50 with a boat. Camping prices range from $14 - $32.50, depending on the site and time of year. For walk-ins (i.e. those not paying the vehicle entrance fee), the water playground costs $3 per person per session or $10 per person for all day. If you have paid a day-use entrance fee for the park or are a camper here, you receive four complimentary sessions. Additional sessions are $1 per person per session or $5 for an all-day pass. Prices are subject to change.

**Ages:** 1 - 12 years for the water playground; 3 years and up for the rest of the park.

# LIBBEY PARK

*Ojai Avenue [or Highway 150]), Ojai*
(Enter directly off either Ojai Ave. [150], where Signal is the nearest cross street, or from Ojai Ave., turn S. on Montgomery St.)

This sprawling park is really a combination of several kinds of parks. The playground area, accessible from Ojai Avenue, is terrific. It has heavy-duty, plastic tubes to crawl through, and suspension bridges to cross, plus slides and swings. Kids love squishing the wonderfully fine sand between their bare toes. A thirty-five-foot long talking tube is mostly underground, with just the funnel-shaped ends above ground, at kid-level. Have your child talk into one end while you listen at the other.

An abundant number of tennis courts are here, some with stadium seating as this is the home of an annual spring tournament that attracts the country's top-ranked collegiate players. The half-dome-shaped Libbey Bowl has graded seating for concerts, or for your young stars to make their (pretend) debut.

Further back, or entering from Montgomery Street, is the nature section of the park. Kids naturally gravitate to the creek that is surrounded by glorious old oak and sycamore trees. For just a little while, you'll feel refreshingly removed from civilization. The OJAI VALLEY NATURE TRAIL, listed later in this section, also begins (or ends) here. Tip: Top off your time with a visit to the ice cream store across Ojai Street, in the Antique Mall.

**Hours:** The park is open daily from dawn to dusk.

**Admission:** Free

**Ages:** All

# MORANDA PARK

(805) 986-6555
*Moranda Parkway, Port Hueneme*
(Exit Ventura Fwy [101] S. on Ventura Rd., L. on Port Hueneme Rd., R. on Moranda Pky.)

This hilly green park is spread out and diverse with eight tennis courts, two softball fields, horseshoe pits, a sand volleyball court, a basketball court, and a nice playground. A path goes around and through the park making it a great place to stroll, jog, or bike. Stop to play, or have a picnic while exploring Oxnard and Ventura!

**Hours:** Open daily from dawn to dusk.
**Admission:** Free
**Ages:** All

## OJAI VALLEY NATURE TRAIL

(805) 654-3951
*Ojai*
(The trail begins or ends at LIBBEY PARK or Foster County Park, which is along Ventura Ave., Hwy. [33].)

This nine-mile paved trail is great for strollers, bikes, horses, or just walking. Although the pathway follows along the major street of Ventura Avenue, oak and sycamore trees adorn it, making it pretty, while also shading a good portion of it.

**Ages:** All

## RANCHO SIERRA VISTA / SATWIWA INDIAN CULTURE CENTER

(805) 370-2300
*Potrero Road, Newbury Park*
(Exit Ventura Fwy [101] S. on Campino Dos Rios/Wendy Dr. about three miles, R. on Potrero about 1 mile.)

The chaparral-covered hillsides and oak and sycamore trees make this an ideal place for some great hiking and/or picnicking. The Satwiwa Loop Trail branches out from the center and loops back around. If you continue straight on the trail before looping back, you'll cross a stream several times and eventually reach a waterfall. Other trails from the center hook up to Pt. Mugu State Park.

Come on a Sunday to the Satwiwa Native American Culture Center, located in the park, to listen to a traditionally-dressed, Native American tell stories, or to watch a craft demonstration. The Center also has Chumash exhibits such as gourds, pictures, and text. Outside, there are picnic tables and a Chumash round dwelling made of willow and tule.

**Hours:** The park is open daily from dawn to dusk. The Culture Center is open weekends during the summer, and Sun. the rest of the year, from 10am - 5pm.
**Admission:** Free
**Ages:** 8 years and up.

## WILDWOOD REGIONAL PARK

(805) 381-2741
*W. Avenue de los Arboles, Thousand Oaks*

(Exit Ventura Fwy [101] N. at Lynn Rd., L. at Avenida de los Arboles, all the way to the end.)

Take a walk on the wild side at Wildwood Regional Park. The narrow, dirt trails and service roads are great for real hiking. There are two major trail heads that lead to an extensive trail system for hikers, bikers, and equestrians. Come prepared by bringing water bottles, sunscreen, and backpacks with food for designated picnic areas. Although hiking downhill is easy, plan twice as much time for the hike back up.

Some highlights along the somewhat shorter trails, which are still an almost all day event, include Indian Cave, with re-created Indian rock drawings; the Nature Center; Little Falls; and Paradise Falls, which is a forty-foot waterfall that you'll hear before you actually reach it. As you walk along the creek or throughout the chaparral and woodlands, be on the lookout for wildlife, such as mule deers or lizards.

Hike here during the spring months and you'll see an abundance of wildflowers. I encourage you to get a trail map, as different routes have different highlights that you'll want to explore. The park offers wonderful, fun, and educational programs like Saturday Night S'Mores, Full Moon Hikes, and Outdoor Experiential Workshops. Enjoy nature, almost in your backyard!

**Hours:**     Open daily from dawn to dusk.
**Admission:**  Free. Some of the programs cost between $3 - $4.
**Ages:**     4 years and up. Kids will tire easily.

# MALLS

This section is not to tell you necessarily where to go shopping, but rather to inform you of free kids' clubs, programs, events, and "shoppertainment" features that your local mall has to offer. Be entertained, enjoy, and create - and maybe get a little shopping in, too!

# EAGLE ROCK PLAZA - KIDS CLUB

(323) 256-2147

*2700 Colorado Boulevard, Los Angeles*

(Exit Ventura Fwy [134] S. on Harvey Dr., immediate L. on E. Wilson Ave., which becomes W. Broadway, which turns into Colorado Blvd.)

One-hour shows feature comedy, juggling, singers, dancers, or even real reptiles! Come to the lower level center court and join in the fun.

**Hours:** Every Wed., at 11am, except the month of December.

**Admission:** Free

**Ages:** 1 ½ - 6 years.

# FALLBROOK MALL - WEDNESDAYS ARE FOR KIDS CLUB

(818) 340-5871

*6633 Fallbrook Avenue, West Hills*

(Exit Ventura Fwy [101] W. on Ventura Blvd., R. on Fallbrook Ave.)

Every week a different, forty-five-minute children's performance is featured near the food court. Performances can include music, storytelling, or anything else that's fun and entertaining. On the third Wednesday of every month, the show is presented in front of Discovery Zone. Afterward, all children registered with the club are invited into Discovery Zone at no charge! Note: The only thing you need to do to register your child is fill out a registration form.

**Hours:** Every Wed. at 11am, from January through October.

**Admission:** Free

**Ages:** 1 ½ - 10 years.

# THE GALLERIA, AT SOUTH BAY - KIDZ PLAY

(310) 371-7546

*1815 Hawthorne Boulevard at Artesia Boulevard, Redondo Beach*

(Exit San Diego Fwy [405] W. on Artesia Blvd. The show is held at the Picnic Place Stage, Level Three.)

Twice a month kids can come to the Galleria and enjoy an hour of entertainment such as stories, puppets, an animal show, or a sing-along, presented near the food court. Make new friends as you and your child become regulars!

**Hours:** The shows are given the first and third Tues. of each month at 10:30am, except the month of December.

**Admission:** Free

**Ages:** 1½ - 6 years.

# GLENDALE GALLERIA

(818) 240-9481 / www.glendalegalleria.com

*Colorado Boulevard and Central Avenue, Glendale Galleria, Glendale*

(Exit Golden State Fwy [5] E. on Colorado Blvd.)

This mall often hosts special events, programs, and displays. Past happenings have included Radio Disney's sponsoring of interactive booths and auditioning kids for emcee spots, and a re-creation of the set from the movie *Babylon 5: Thirdspace*, which included a props display, touch screens, and even star appearances. Call for a current schedule.

**Hours:** The mall is open Mon. - Fri., 10am - 9pm; Sat., 10am - 8pm; Sun., 11am - 7pm. Call for special program dates and times.
**Admission:** Free
**Ages:** Varies with programs offered.

## LAKEWOOD CENTER MALL - A2Z KIDZ CLUB

(562) 531-6707
*200 Lakewood Center Mall, Lakewood*
(Exit Artesia Fwy [91] S. on Lakewood Blvd.)

The first 225 kids are invited to participate in a fun, usually seasonal craft, like decorating a Father's Day barbecuing apron in June, or sand buckets in August. It's a great club to belong to because kids love to make projects, and all the materials are supplied for free! There are also member discounts on various products and restaurants in the mall. As an added benefit, the mall mails your child a certificate redeemable for a few little birthday presents during the month of his/her birthday. Note: Make sure your child is registered with the club by simply filling out a registration form.

**Hours:** The club meets the second Tues. of every month from 4pm - 7pm. Call for holiday availability.
**Admission:** Free
**Ages:** 3 - 12 years.

## MEDIA CITY SHOPPING CENTER - KID CITY

(818) 566-8617
*201 E. Magnolia Boulevard, Burbank*
(Exit Golden State Fwy [5] E. on Burbank Blvd., R. on 3rd St., R. on Magnolia.)

Kids gather together on Thursdays on the first level at Macy's Court for an hour of puppetry, music, storytime, etc.

**Hours:** Every other Thurs. at 10:30am, except the month of December.
**Admission:** Free
**Ages:** 1 ½ to 6 years.

## NORTHRIDGE FASHION CENTER - NFC KIDS KLUB

(818) 885-9700
*At Tampa Avenue and Nordhoff Street, Northridge*
(From San Diego Fwy [405], exit E. on Nordhoff St. From Ventura Fwy [101], exit N. on Tampa Avenue.)

Become a NFC kid and get in on all the fun! Forty-five-minutes of storytelling, singing, dancing, or even short plays are on the morning's agenda. The Klub also gives its young members discounts at participating mall stores, and a free gift on their birthday.

**Hours:**    The first and third Thurs. of each month at 10:30am in Bullock's
              Court.
**Admission:** Free
**Ages:**     2 - 12 years.

# PUENTE HILLS MALL - CREATIVE KIDS CLUB

(626) 965-5875
*449 Puente Hills Mall, Industry*
(Exit Pomona Fwy [60] S. on Azusa Ave. Mall is immediately on left.)
    This kids club features a forty-five-minute interactive show of magic,
storytelling, music, or whatever fun entertainment various groups perform.
**Hours:**    First and third Tues. of each month at 10:30am.
**Admission:** Free
**Ages:**     2 - 8 years.

# SANTA MONICA PLACE - KIDS WORLD

(310) 394-5451
*395 Santa Monica Place, Santa Monica*
(Exit Santa Monica Fwy [10] N. on Lincoln Blvd, L. on Colorado. Mall is on R.)
    Forty-five minutes of live theater, or other types of showy productions, are
put on for children on the third level in the community room.
**Hours:**    Fri. at 11am and 1pm, during the summer only.
**Admission:** Free
**Ages:**     2 - 9 years.

# SOUTHBAY PAVILION - LI'L SHOPPERS CLUB

(310) 327-4822
*Avalon Boulevard, Carson*
(Exit San Diego Fwy [405] at Avalon Blvd. The club meets at Center Court.)
    Encourage your little shoppers to join the Li'l Shoppers Club. Children
enjoy the forty-five-minute shows put on by some great children's entertainers.
**Hours:**    Every Thurs. of the month at 6pm, February through November.
**Admission:** Free
**Ages:**     1½ - 8 years.

# STONEWOOD MALL - KIDS' CLUB

(562) 861-9233
*251 Stonewood Street, Downey*
(Exit San Gabriel River Fwy [605] W. on Firestone Blvd., R. on Lakewood Blvd., R. on
Stonewood St.)
    Join Kids' Club, held in the fountain court, for one hour of fun and
entertainment. The shows feature singers, dancers, puppets, or magicians. What a
great family outing! Register your children for the club and they will receive a
free gift on their birthday.
**Hours:**    Every Thurs. at 6pm, except the month of December.

**Admission:** Free
**Ages:** 1½ - 8 years.

## THIRD STREET PROMENADE                                           ☼
*3ʳᵈ Street, Santa Monica*                                        !/$$
(Exit Santa Monica Fwy [10] N. on Lincoln Blvd., L. on Wilshire Blvd. Park wherever you can.)

This three-block pedestrian walkway is a fascinating outdoor mall experience. It rates an A+ for people-watching as the international mix of people, converging here from the nearby Los Angeles International Airport, make it a cultural adventure. Nighttime and weekends bring out performers who want to show off their talents, however glorious or dubious they might be. We've seen and heard African drum playing, tap dancing, folk songs, acrobatics, men acting like robots, clowns making balloon animals, and an Organ grinder monkey begging - all within the span of an hour. Benches are plentiful, so if you really enjoy some of the entertainment, sit down and watch. A plethora of artsy and unique stores and boutiques, plus movie theaters line the "street." Vendor carts are along the sidewalks. Choose from a multitude of restaurants that range from upscale to grab-a-bite, or snack at a bakery or ice cream shop. A few fountains, featuring dinosaurs spouting water, complete the eclectic ambiance at the promenade. If you haven't gotten enough shopping in, at the other end of the promenade is Santa Monica Place, which is three levels of indoor shopping and 140 stores. Note: The Tide Shuttle runs a loop from Main Street to Third Street Promenade every fifteen minutes at a cost of 25¢ per person.

**Hours:** Open daily 10am - 6pm. Open for extended hours in the summer.
**Admission:** Free, but bring spending money.
**Ages:** All

## TOPANGA PLAZA - FAMILY FUN NIGHT                                ☀
(818) 594-8740                                                      !
*6600 Topanga Canyon Boulevard, Canoga Park*                       ♨
(Exit Ventura Fwy [101] N. on Topanga Canyon Blvd.)

Families can enjoy free shows for an hour and a half every Friday night at the mall. Past shows and activities have included clowns, mall bingo, karaoke, hulas, and a 50's dance night.

**Hours:** Every Fri. night at 7pm, except the month of December.
**Admission:** Free
**Ages:** All

## VALENCIA TOWN CENTER - KIDSTOWN                                 ☀
(805) 287-9050                                                      !
*24201 W. Valencia Boulevard, Valencia*
(Exit Golden State Fwy [5] E. on Valencia Blvd. Kidstown is usually held in the Sears Court.)

Kidstown comes to town every other Thursday morning by the Sears court. Join in the forty-five-minute show of puppetry or song and dance - it's all interactive fun for young kids.

**Hours:** Every other Thurs. morning at 10:30am, March through November.
**Admission:** Free
**Ages:** 1½ - 6 years.

## WESTSIDE PAVILION - KIDS' CLUB

(310) 474-6255
*10800 W. Pico Boulevard, West Los Angeles*
(Exit San Diego Fwy [405] E. on Santa Monica Blvd., R. on Westwood Blvd., Mall is on corner of Westwood and Pico. Or, exit Santa Monica Fwy [10] N. on Overland Ave. The mall is on corner of Overland and Blythe Ave.)

Parents and kids can enjoy a half hour together on Wednesday nights at Westside Pavilion. Shows can consist of puppetry, magicians, musicians, and more.

**Hours:** Every Wed. night at 6pm, except the month of December.
**Admission:** Free
**Ages:** All

## BREA MALL - KIDS IN RESIDENCE

(714) 990-BREA (2732)
*1065 Brea Mall, Brea*
(Exit Orange Fwy [57] W. on Imperial Highway, at State College.)

Kids in Residence is several arts and entertainment programs under one name. Free, hour-long shows are performed once a month that vary in context. They can include sing alongs and movement songs, storytelling, puppetry, an animal show with live reptiles, and more. What a fun way to enjoy entertainment with your child!

The arts program includes educational and creative workshops conducted by professional artists and college art students. Workshops feature working with a variety of media such as watercolors, oils, acrylics, pastels, poster paints, markers, and stencils. Classes are offered after schools and on Saturdays, depending on the age of the participant and style of art being studied. Registration is often required. Art exhibitions of the student's work is held throughout the year and selected artwork is used in the mall's marketing, such as participant-designed Christmas cards. Note that high schoolers can learn the art and history of mural-making under the tutelage of a professional muralist. The in-mall mural projects are seasonally themed, and what a way to have their work displayed! Art workshops are given for ages 3 through adults. Call for a specific program information or pick a complete schedule at the mall information booth.

**Hours:** Shows are the first Tues. of every month at 10:30am, except the month of December. Call for or pick up a program of year round art workshops.
**Admission:** Free for all shows and all workshops.

**Ages:**   1½ - 8 years old for the shows; ages 3 years and up for the art
workshops.

# IRVINE SPECTRUM CENTER

(949) 789-9180                                                                    !/$

*At the junction of the 405 and 5 Fwy, Irvine*

(Going S. on Santa Ana Fwy [5], exit W. on Alton Pky. At the end of the off ramp, go
straight into the Spectrum. Going N. on 5, exit W. on Alton Pky. Going S. on San Diego
Fwy [405], exit N. on Irvine Center Dr., R. on Pacifica.)

Just two of our favorite stores in this outside mall include a gigantic Barnes
and Noble Bookstore and Out Takes, which takes your picture in your choice of
computer-generated scenes. For interactive fun, try Sega City, (949) 727-1422 -
a large video arcade with simulator rides and virtual reality games; or Nascar
Silicon Motor Speedway, (949) 753-8810. Nascar has twelve, incredibly realistic
racing car simulators geared for teens on up as the jolting motion and virtual
power of the cars make them hard to manage. The center also has a Dave &
Busters, an eatery/arcade/virtual game play place for adults. Hungry? Choose
from four outstanding restaurants - Bertolini's, Champps Americana, P. F.
Chang's China Bistro, or Wolfgang Puck. A wonderful food court is also here,
complete with a Ben and Jerry's Ice Cream, and a sweet shop. As usual, kids
enjoy the simple pleasures, like playing (and getting wet) on the turtle statues in
the fountain outside the food court. See EDWARDS IMAX 3D THEATER,
under the Shows and Theaters section, for information on the 3D theater here.

**Hours:**   Open daily 11am - 11pm.

**Admission:**   Technically free.

**Ages:**   All

# MALL OF ORANGE - KIDS KORP

(714) 998-0440                                                                       !

*2298 N. Orange Mall on Tustin Avenue, Orange*

(Exit Costa Mesa Fwy [55] E. on Lincoln, L. on Tustin Ave. Or, exit [55] Fwy, E. on
Katella, R. on Tustin.)

Kids Korp. is a club where the first 300 kids can decorate themed crafts with
their parents. It's designed for kids and parents to spend some fun time together,
to encourage your child's creativity, and to take home a seasonal memento, like a
Father's Day baseball cap or a Halloween tote bag. Members also receive
coupons for special values on meals and merchandise at participating Mall of
Orange stores.

**Hours:**   The club is usually held on Tues. from 4pm - 7pm, except the
month of December. Call for dates.

**Admission:**   Free

**Ages:**   3 - 12 years.

# WESTMINSTER MALL - VIK (VERY IMPORTANT KID) CLUB

(714) 898-2550 / www.westminstermall.com

*Bolsa Avenue and Golden West Street, Westminster*

(Exit San Diego Fwy [405] at Golden West St.)

The Westminster Mall offers two great deals for families - a kids' club, and periodic, special exhibits. Calling all younger children for the VIK club - come and enjoy a forty-five-minute show of magic, storytelling, puppets, or sing alongs at the club. Afterwards, each child receives a small treat.

The special exhibits are presented at various times throughout the year. For instance, in celebration of Project Earth, giant sea creatures (up to forty feet long!) came alive via dinamation - they roared and thrashed their tails. Other exhibits in conjunction with this theme included a display from Sea World's wild arctic, weekend stage shows, and a rivers and oceans wetlands exhibit. Who knew that malls could be so fun and educational?!

**Hours:**    The show is presented on the first Thurs. of every month at 5:30pm, except the month of December.

**Admission:**    Free to both type of events.

**Ages:**    1½ - 8 years for the club; all ages for the exhibits.

# GALLERIA AT TYLER - KIDSTRAVAGANZA

(909) 351-3110

*Tyler Street, Riverside*

(Exit Riverside Fwy [91] N. at Tyler St.)

It's show time Tuesdays at Macy's Court. Weekly performances can include some name-brand entertainers such as Joanie Bartels, who brings song and dance to her audiences, and the Bob Baker Marionettes, plus magic shows, kids comedy acts, and more.

Make it a point to stop by the KIDstravaganza Craft Corner, located in the Terrace Cafes Food Court near Del Taco, on Thursdays where each week a new craft project is introduced. All of the materials and instructions for the crafts are free and are designed to take your little artist about fifteen minutes to create. Past projects have included a butterfly plant marker, sun visor, flower pot, tote bag, etc.

The Galleria often has special fun and educational exhibits near the food court. A past summer exhibit was colorful butterflies in "flight" that were 400 times their actual size. Each had an information marker that told interesting facts about that species.

**Hours:**    Kidstravaganza is only offered in the summer. Shows begin every Tues. at 11am and the every Thurs. Craft Corner is open from 1pm - 4pm. Call for information on their year round special exhibits.

**Admission:**    Free to all of the above.

**Ages:**    2 - 11 years

# ONTARIO MILLS MALL

(909) 484-8300 / www.ontariomillsmall.com

*One Mills Circle, Ontario*
(Exit San Bernardino Fwy [10] N. on Milliken Ave., R. on 4th St. or exit Ontario Fwy [15] W. on 4th St.)

Ontario Mills is California's largest outlet mall with over 200 outlet, speciality, and off-price retail stores. It has become a tourist destination and even houses a California State Visitors' Center that is stocked with numerous free brochures and maps. The mall also offers "shoppertainment." There are several movie theaters, including an EDWARDS IMAX 3D movie theater (see the Shows and Theaters section) and an UltraScreen Theater - a giant, six-story screen which uses a large-format projection system for both 2D and 3D capabilities. The movies we have seen in the latter two theaters incorporate both spectacular scenery and the capability to immerse the viewer in the film.

Other entertainment offered at the mega mall includes AMERICAN WILDERNESS ZOO AND AQUARIUM (look under the Zoos and Animals section); GameWorks, an almost surrealistically-decorated virtual reality and Sega Genesis game and arcade center; and Dave & Buster's, a combination restaurant/bar and game/arcade center geared for adults.

The food court is fancifully decorated with large, colorful, inflated foods. Other eating experiences here include delicious food in unique surroundings are Wolfgang Puck's Cafe, RAINFOREST CAFE (Ontario) (look under the Edible Adventures section), and Wilderness Grill, which is adjacent to American Wilderness Zoo and Aquarium. The Grill's mountain-lodge decor is reminiscent of log cabin days of early America. Menu choices include Wild Turkey Sandwiches, served with apple-cranberry mayonnaise, and Dirt Apple Bacon Burgers, served with Dirt Apple Onion Jam, plus pastas, fresh fish, beef dishes, and salads. Prices range from $8 to $17. Kids' meals cost $5.25 for a choice of pasta, pizza, chicken tenders, or a burger, plus a beverage.

**Hours:** The mall and most attractions are open Mon. - Sat., 10am - 9:30pm; Sun., 10am - 8pm.

**Admission:** Technically, free.

**Ages:** All

## HORTON PLAZA

(619) 238-1596 - plaza; (619) 236-1212 - San Diego Visitor's Bureau / www.hortonplaza.com

*324 Horton Plaza, San Diego*
(Going S. on San Diego Fwy [5], exit W. on Ash St., L. on 4th Ave. Going N. on 5, exit S. on 6th Ave., R. on Broadway.)

This outdoor mall is seven city blocks of shopping, dining, and entertainment. Colorful and unique architecture, with buildings designed at various, odd angles, contain over 140 places to shop. Favorite kid-friendly stopping places include FAO Schwarz (a gigantic toy store), the Nature Company, and the Disney Store. Other attractions are the numerous movie theaters and over twenty places to dine, including PLANET HOLLYWOOD. (See the Edible Adventure's section.) Stop by the visitor's bureau to pick up a coupon booklet, information, and/or maps on the area.

**Hours:** Open Mon. - Fri., 10am - 9pm; Sat., 10am - 7pm; Sun., 11am - 6pm.
**Admission:** Technically, free.
**Ages:** All

# PLAZA BONITA MALL - KIDS CLUB
(619) 267-2850
*3030 Plaza Bonita Road, National City*
(Exit Jacob Dekema Fwy [805] E. on Bonita Rd., L. on Plaza Bonita Rd.)
Have some fun while making new friends at the Kids Club at Plaza Bonita. Free, hour-long, weekly entertainment could include puppet shows, toe-tapping music, storytelling, and/or singing. Each club "meeting" starts with Kid Aerobics or jazzercise. Meet in the Center Court near J. C. Penney.
**Hours:** Every Wed. at 3:30pm
**Admission:** Free
**Ages:** 1 -10 years.

# PLAZA CAMINO REAL MALL - KIDS' CLUB
(760) 729-7927
*El Camino Real at the Plaza Camino Real Mall, Carlsbad*
(Exit San Diego Fwy [5] E. on 78 Fwy, R. on El Camino Real)
Come join in the Kids' Club fun at the Center Court, lower level, at Plaza Camino Real. Clubs usually begin with an action warm-up of Kid Aerobics or jazzercise. Free, forty-five-minute, weekly entertainment can include laughing with kids' comedians, dancing, singing, storytelling, and general silliness.
**Hours:** Every Tues. at 10am, except the month of December.
**Admission:** Free
**Ages:** 1 - 10 years.

# THE OAKS - OK KIDS CLUB
(805) 495-2031
*222 W. Hillcrest Drive, Thousand Oaks*
(Exit Ventura Fwy [101] N. on Lynn Rd., R. on Hillcrest.)
A variety of half-hour shows are presented every week at the lower level court. Shows could include marionettes, singers, dancer, magicians, etc.
**Hours:** Every Thurs. at 10:30am, except the month of December.
**Admission:** Free
**Ages:** 1 ½ - 7 years.

## MUSEUMS

While children are (almost) never too young to start appreciating art, there is a whole new world of kid-friendly museums that captivates their imaginations, hearts, and even their hands! A few tips about museums:
• Exhibits rotate, so be flexible in your expectations.
• If you really like the museum, become a member. You'll reap benefits such as being invited to members-only events, receiving newsletters; etc.
• You can $ee L.A. or you can ¢.E.E. L.A.! The Cultural Entertainment Events card (C.E.E. L.A.) is an incredible way to explore nineteen top museums, including AUTRY MUSEUM, GEORGE C. PAGE, LOS ANGELES CHILDREN'S MUSEUM, KIDSEUM, NATURAL HISTORY MUSEUM OF L.A., PETERSEN AUTOMOTIVE, RICHARD NIXON LIBRARY AND BIRTHPLACE, and more for only $40 a year for your family! (A family is defined as four to six members; up to three generations.) This card also offers 50% off major sporting events, and theater and concert venues. Call (818) 957-9400 for more details.
• If you're looking for a special gift, most museum gift shops carry unique merchandise that is geared toward their specialty.
• Museums offer a wide array of special calendar events. Get on mailings lists!
• Take a tour! You and your kids will learn a lot more about the exhibits.
• May 18th is International Museum Day. Many museums offer free admission and/or they sponsor a family day of arts and crafts activities.

# AIR FORCE FLIGHT TEST CENTER MUSEUM ☼

(805) 277-8050 / www.edwards.af.mil
*Edwards Air Force Base, Kern County*
(Exit the Golden State Fwy [5] N. on the Antelope Valley Fwy [14] Fwy. Exit [14] E. on
Edwards/Rosamond and drive for a few miles.)

Edwards Air Force Base is the premier site for flight research and flight
testing. You'll drive by a huge dry lake which is the main landing site. The
museum, at least for now, is located in two places on the base compound. Kids
can walk around the fourteen, or so, aircraft on display on the corner of
Rosamond Boulevard and Lancaster Boulevard. The planes vary in design,
shape, size, and maneuverability. Some of the planes currently on display
include A-12, B-52D, T-33A, and an F-104A.

The small, indoor, storefront museum is temporarily located on Payne
Avenue. A larger, permanent facility is being built next to where the planes now
reside. The museum is packed with memorabilia fitting for the birthplace of
supersonic flight. One section is dedicated to "Mach Busters," the men who
broke sound barriers, including, of course, Chuck Yeager. It shows and tells how
planes (and men) were tested for this significant breakthrough. The "First Flights
Wall" is a model display of the more than 100 aircraft that completed their first
flight at Edwards AFB. Other items on exhibit include aircraft propulsion
systems, life support equipment, photographs, flight jackets, and personal
memorabilia. Ask to see the film on the history of Edwards and on flight testing.
While here, check out the NASA DRYDEN FLIGHT RESEARCH CENTER
tour and/or the AIR FORCE FLIGHT TEST CENTER tour, listed under the
Tours section. Important note: There is a Burger King and Baskin Robins just
down the street. Also note that the Aerospace Walk of Honor, in downtown
Lancaster between 10th Street W. and Sierra Highway, displays biographical
plaques that honor forty aviation pioneers.

**Hours:**      Open Tues. - Sat. from 9am - 5pm.
**Admission:**  Free
**Ages:**       6 years and up.

# BORAX VISITOR CENTER ☼

(760) 762-7432
*Borax Road, Boron*
(Exit Highway 58 N. on Borax Rd. This facility is E. of Edwards Air Force Base.)

Borax isn't something that my family normally spends a lot of time thinking
about. However, visiting this center made us realize how widely this mineral is
used. As you drive past the active mine (and past the sign that states the speed
limit as 37 ½ m.p.h.), you'll see what appears to be a little city, complete with
buildings, trucks, and Goliath-type machines used to extract and process the
borax. This area supplies nearly half the global need for the mineral!

Up the hill is a state-of-the-art visitors' center. Outside are original twenty
mule team wagons, with harnessed mule statues, that were once used to haul the
ore over 165 miles through desert and rocky terrain. Inside is a large sample of

kernite, a type of borate ore, plus a pictorial history of the Borax company, and an exhibit that shows the process of raw ore being transformed (crushed, actually) into fine dust. The "Borax at Home" display shows examples of everyday staples made from borax, including glass, ceramic glazes, detergent, shaving creams, and plant fertilizer. For products closer to a child's heart, the display features footballs, Play Doh™, and nail polish. Borax is also added to commodities to make them sparkle, including toothpaste and fireworks. An adjacent room shows continuously running videos of Borax commercials starring Ronald Reagan, Dale Robertson, Clint Eastwood, and others. The front room (or back room) has an all-glass wall for an unobstructed view of the entire open pit mine. School tours of the center are given, and fun, supplemental materials are available to aid learning. Don't forget to stop off at the TWENTY MULE TEAM MUSEUM (look at the next entry), just down the road.

**Hours:** Open October through April daily from 8am - 4pm. Open May through September daily 8am - 6pm. Closed major holidays and during inclement weather.
**Admission:** $2 per vehicle.
**Ages:** 4 years and up.

## TWENTY MULE TEAM MUSEUM                                    ☼
(760) 762-5810                                                                      !
*Twenty Mule Team Road, Boron*
(Exit Highway 58 S. on Boron Ave., R. on Twenty Mule Team Rd. The city of Boron is N.E. of Edwards Air Force Base.)

This small-town museum is built around its claim to fame - the Twenty Mule Team wagons. Beginning in 1883, these wagons were used for five years to haul borate ore 165 miles through the desert and rocky outcroppings, from Death Valley to the Mojave railhead. The museum displays the history of the surrounding area from the late nineteenth century up to the present day via enlarged photographs, a continuously running video, and four small rooms that contains artifacts. Some of the items on exhibit include samples of kernite and borate ore (components of Borax); mining equipment, such as replica scale mine cars, and caps that held candlesticks and lamps; models of planes tested at Edwards Airborne Base; clothing worn during the turn-of-the-century; and handcuffs and prison garb from the nearby Federal prison.

Stroll around outside to see more exhibits, such as rusty agricultural and mining equipment, a large granite boulder with holes (because it was used for drilling contests), water pumps, an ore bucket, a surrey, and a miner's shack to peer into. There is also a shade area with a few picnic tables. Make sure to visit the nearby BORAX VISITOR CENTER, listed in the above entry.

**Hours:** Open daily 10am - 4pm
**Admission:** Free; donations appreciated.
**Ages:** 4 years and up.

## ADAMSON HOUSE and MALIBU LAGOON MUSEUM ☼

(310) 456-8432 - museum; (818) 880-0363 - lagoon tour                    !/$
*23200 Pacific Coast Highway, Malibu*
(It's on P.C.H., W. of Malibu Pier, near Serra Rd.)

The Adamson House, and its adjacent museum, is on beautifully landscaped grounds just a few feet away from the Malibu Surfrider Beach and lifeguard station, and Malibu Lagoon - definitely beach front property. The outside of the house and the fountains integrate the colorful Malibu tiles in their design. We wandered around the grounds on flagstone walkways that wove through grassy lawns, beneath shade trees, along several gardens (including a rose garden), past a pool that was once filled with salt water from the ocean, and to the chain-link fence which marks the house boundaries. Here, just a short distance from the pier, we watched surfers do their thing.

The small museum features exhibits pertaining to the history of Malibu including cattle brands, arrowheads, maps, fossilized shells, and numerous photographs. I liked the Malibu Colony of Stars' pictures of Robert Redford, Bing Crosby, Clara Bow, Joan Crawford, etc. Ask for a tour, or explanations, regarding the history of the railroad, the dam, the movie colony, and more.

The two-story house was built in 1929, and the rooms can be seen on a one-hour, guided tour. Adults and older children will appreciate the bottle-glass windows, hand-painted murals, additional tile work (especially in the kitchen), furnishings, and unique decor.

There isn't any direct access to the lagoon (i.e. the parcel of water and land that is a haven for various bird species) from the house. You can get to this area by walking or driving over the bridge and down Cross Creek Road. We observed pelicans, herons, sandpipers, etc., coming in for a landing before taking to the skies once again. Visit here on your own or make tour reservations to educate your kids (and yourself) about the waterfowl, ecology, the area's Chumash Indian past, and more. The lagoon programs are given by a state park ranger. Note: Although the beach is accessible by going through the museum parking lot, the waters are for surfers only. If your kids want to go swimming, head a short distance south to Malibu Pier.

**Hours:** The house and museum are open Wed. - Sat. from 11am - 3pm. The last house tour begins at 2pm. Call for information on lagoon tours and programs.

**Admission:** The small museum is free. The house tour costs $2 for adults; $1 for ages 6 - 17; children 5 years and under are free. Lagoon tours cost $6 per vehicle for parking. Parking in the museum lot costs $2 per vehicle. Some free street parking is available.

**Ages:** 2 years and up for the house grounds and lagoon; 7 years and up for the house tour and museum.

## ADOBE DE PALOMARES

(909) 623-2198                    $
*491 East Arrow Highway, Pomona*

(Exit San Bernardino Fwy [10] N. on Towne Ave., L. on Arrow Hwy.)

This thirteen-room restored adobe was originally built in 1854. A guided tour of the house includes seeing authentic period furniture, as well as cooking utensils (how did they live without so many technical doohickeys?!), tools, antique clothing, and children's toys. The grounds are lovely. Adjacent to the Adobe is Palomare Park, so bring a picnic lunch and enjoy some running around space.

> **Hours:** Open Sun. from 2pm - 5pm
> **Admission:** $2 for adults; $1 for children 12 years and under.
> **Ages:** 6 years and up.

## AEROSPACE MUSEUM

(213) 744-7400
*Exposition Park, Los Angeles*
(Exit Harbor Fwy [110] W. on Exposition Blvd., L. on Flower, L. on Figueroa. Or, exit Santa Monica Fwy [10] S. on Vermont, L. on Exposition, R. on Figueroa.)

This building is hard to miss with a jet fighter perched precariously on its top! The atmosphere is uplifting with planes, such as the 1902 Wright Flyer; jets, such as the Northrop T-38 jet trainer; and a space capsule, the Gemini II, all suspended from the ceiling in mock flight. Catwalk-like ramps add to the airy feeling. Educating the public on flight technology is accomplished through several interactive displays. Kids have hands-on fun designing their own computer-generated jet fighter and learning the principles of aerodynamics using a control stick. Space Station Earth has video displays to monitor our weather and the weather on Venus or Jupiter. A weather station on the roof of the museum shows the collected data, such as temperature, humidity, barometric pressure, etc., on the first floor in the museum.

There are many fascinating space exhibits here including a darkened room with a big screen movie that explains how we reach for the stars. Kids will glean even more information about our universe on a school tour here, plus they'll get a closer look at the DC-3 and DC-8 planes parked outside the museum.

A wonderful way to round out your day is to have a picnic and visit one of the other attractions in this complex - CALIFORNIA AFRO-AMERICAN MUSEUM, CALIFORNIA SCIENCE CENTER, EXPOSITION PARK, LOS ANGELES MEMORIAL COLISEUM, NATURAL HISTORY MUSEUM OF LOS ANGELES, and 3D IMAX THEATER. (Look under the Alphabetical Index to find these attractions.)

> **Hours:** Open daily from 10am - 5pm. Closed New Year's Day,
> Thanksgiving, and Christmas.
> **Admission:** Free. Parking is $5.
> **Ages:** 3 years and up.

## AFRICAN AMERICAN FIREFIGHTER MUSEUM

(213) 744-1730
*1401 S. Central Avenue, Los Angeles*

(Exit Santa Monica Fwy [10] N. on Central Ave. It's on the corner of Central and 14<sup>th</sup> St.)

    This small, beautiful museum is set in a Los Angeles neighborhood. It chronicles the history of black firefighters by honoring them and their white colleagues who pushed for integration. The walls and reference books contain photographs and stories that tell of the once-segregated station. For instance, although black and white men battled fires and fought side-by-side to save lives, they couldn't cook or eat together. African Americans even slept in beds designated "black beds." Exhibits include a fire engine, uniforms, boots, fire extinguishers, badges, helmets, and other mementos.

    **Hours:**   Open the second and fourth Sun. of each month from 1pm - 4pm.
    **Admission:**   Free
    **Ages:**   5 years and up.

## AMERICAN HERITAGE PARK / MILITARY MUSEUM

(626) 442-1776  / www.members.aol.com/tankland/museum.htm     *$$*
*1918 N. Rosemead Boulevard, South El Monte*
(Exit Pomona Fwy [60] N. at Rosemead Blvd. The entrance is on the R. side of the street, at the northern part of WHITTIER NARROWS RECREATION AREA.)

    Attention! Over 125 pieces of equipment, representing all branches of the United States Military, can be found at this outside museum. The collection contains vehicles and weapons from World War II, and the Korean and Vietnam wars. It includes Jeeps, amphibious trucks, ambulances, helicopters, cannons, gun turrets, and thirty-ton Sherman tanks. The vehicles can be looked at, but not sat on or touched.

    To the untrained eye it looks like a random compilation of old military equipment. And it is. However, some pieces are in the process of being restored, and some have been used in movies and T.V. shows. The volunteers are knowledgeable and know many of the "inside" stories about the vehicles. Idea: This is an ideal setting if your kids are studying any of the wars and want to make a video.

    **Hours:**   Open Sat. - Sun. from noon - 4:30pm. Open Wed., Thurs., and Fri. for groups by appointment. Closed on rainy days.
    **Admission:**   $4 for adults; $3 for seniors and military; $2 for ages 10 - 16; 50¢ for ages 5 - 9; children 4 years and under are free.
    **Ages:**   4 years and up.

## ANGELS ATTIC

(310) 394-8331     *$$*
*516 Colorado Avenue, Santa Monica*
(Exit Santa Monica Fwy [10] N. on 5<sup>th</sup> St., R. on Colorado Ave.)

    Picture a quaint Victorian house filled with beautiful collectable dolls and doll houses. Now, add a warm, inviting atmosphere and you've got Angels Attic. This 1895 Queen Anne-style house/museum has antique toys, dolls, and over sixty doll houses. Each doll house is complete, and the architectural style and furnishings reflect the era in which it was built - a mini-history lesson. Although little hands may not touch, little eyes will enjoy looking, especially since most exhibits are at eye level. Tea time, with homemade cake and cookies, is also available with advanced reservations and an additional $7.50 per person.

At Christmas time, the outside of Angels Attic is decorated and so is every doll house - truly a mini-extravaganza. Don't miss Santa's Workshop in miniature, with reindeer, Santa and Mrs. Claus, and over 130 elves completing the festive scene.

The small gift shop sells doll house accessories and books and magazines related to collecting miniatures and dolls.

**Hours:** Open Thurs. - Sun. from 12:30pm - 4:30pm.
**Admission:** $6.50 for adults; $4 for seniors and students; $3.50 for children 11 years and under.
**Ages:** 5 years old and up.

## ANTELOPE VALLEY INDIAN MUSEUM ☼

(805) 946-3055 - museum; (805) 942-0662 - state park / $
www.calparksmojave.com/avim
*Avenue "M", between 150th and 170th Streets East, Lancaster*
(Exit Antelope Valley Fwy [14] E. on Ave. "K", R. on 150th St. East, L. on Ave. "M". Or exit Pearblossom Highway [138] N. on 165th St. East, turns into 170th St., turn L. on Ave. "M".)

Built into and around rock formations of the Mojave Desert, the outside of this Indian museum looks incongruously like a Swiss Chalet. The inside is just as unique. Once the home of artist Howard Edward, portions of the interior (e.g. walls, ceilings, and flooring) are composed of boulders. My kids' reaction was simply "WOW!" The large, main room is lined with Kachina dolls on the upper shelves and painted panels of the dolls on the ceiling. (The Hopi People believed that Kachina dolls brought rain.) The unusual furniture and the support beams are made from Joshua trees. A connecting room has several glass-cased displays of pottery shards that were once used for money and jewelry; cradle-boards; baskets; and various items made from plants, such as yucca fiber sandals.

Kids love climbing up the narrow stony steps into a large display room, which is "carved out" of rock. Exhibits here include arrowheads, whale bone tools, shells, whale ribs, harpoons, and weapons. Go back down a few of the steps. Stop. Look up. You'll see Indian dioramas and re-created cave paintings.

Outside, you'll pass by a series of small cottages that were once used as guest houses. Your destination is Joshua Cottage, a place that has some hands-on activities for kids. They can grind corn with stone mortars and pestles, try their hand at using a pump drill to drill holes, and "saw" with a bow drill to create smoke. Kids can even learn how to make a pine needle whisk broom. (The brooms may not have much practical use now-a-days, but it's a fun and educational project.) Docents will gladly explain the use of various seeds and other plant parts. The small adjacent room is a gallery that's also used for educational programs.

The museum is part of the California Department of Parks and Recreation. Enjoy an easy half-mile nature walk on the trails through the buttes and desert just behind the Indian Museum. A guidebook (50¢) explains the fourteen Native American symbols on the posts along the trail.

**Hours:** Open from the middle of September through the middle of June on Sat. - Sun. from 11am - 4pm. Tours are available Tues., Wed., and Thurs. by appointment.

**Admission:** $3 for adults; $2 for ages 12 - 18; children 11 years and under are free.

**Ages:** 5 years and up.

## AUTRY MUSEUM OF WESTERN HERITAGE

(213) 667-2000 / www.autry-museum.org

*4700 Western Heritage Way, in Griffith Park, Los Angeles*

(Going N. on Golden State Fwy [5] or W. on Ventura Fwy [134], exit at Zoo Dr. and follow the signs. Going E. on 134, exit S. on Victory Blvd., L. on Zoo Dr. Going S. on 5, exit S. on Western, L. on Victory Blvd. to Zoo Dr. The museum is across the parking lot from the L. A. Zoo.)

The cowboy lifestyle lassos our imagination. Bryce, my middle son, wants to become a cowboy missionary (yes, he is special), so this museum really spurred on his desire, at least regarding the cowboy part of his career choice. It will also delight fans of the Old West with its complete array of paintings, clothing, tools, weapons, and interesting artifacts. Movie clips and videos throughout the museum highlight specific areas of this romanticized period. In the Spirit of Imagination Hall, a big hit is sitting on a saddle and making riding motions to become part of an old western movie showing on a screen behind the rider. My kids particularly enjoyed the small, Children's Discovery Gallery, where they dressed up like cowboys, played with toys in a re-created town-home attic, "washed" clothes and put them through a wringer, and sat on a lifelike horse statue.

The entire museum is interesting and stroller-friendly, but you do have to keep your kids corralled, as most of the exhibits are not hands-on. Saturday programs, for ages 6 to 12, are more interactive with storytelling, games, and even sing alongs. Ask about their weekly summer history classes for kids. A cafe is on the grounds, as is a wonderful, large, grassy picnic area.

**Hours:** Open Tues. - Sun. (and certain Mon. holidays) from 10am - 5pm. Closed Thanksgiving and Christmas.

**Admission:** $7.50 for adults; $5 for seniors and ages 13 - 18; $3 for children 2 - 12 years old. (Certain discounts available through AAA.) (See C.E.E. L.A. for membership savings, pg. 213.)

**Ages:** 4 years and up.

## CALIFORNIA AFRO-AMERICAN MUSEUM

(213) 744-7432 / www.caam.ca.gov

*600 State Drive, at Exposition Park, Los Angeles*

(Exit the Harbor Fwy [110] W. on Exposition Blvd., L. on Flower, L. on Figueroa. Or, exit Santa Monica Fwy [10] S. on Vermont, L. on Exposition, R. on Figueroa. Parking is available the first driveway on the R. It's located in the same building complex as the CALIFORNIA SCIENCE MUSEUM.)

This museum portrays the works of Afro-American artists documenting the Afro-American experience in this country. The rotating exhibits are interesting to people of all races. The exhibits we saw were various playhouse-size houses and work environments made from recycled materials, along with photographs, and various sculptures. Another room contained lots of Western artifacts, and the fascinating history of James Beckwourth, an explorer, trapper, and businessman who lived from 1798 to 1866. See the nearby AEROSPACE MUSEUM, CALIFORNIA SCIENCE CENTER, EXPOSITION PARK, NATURAL HISTORY MUSEUM OF LOS ANGELES, LOS ANGELES MEMORIAL COLISEUM, and 3D IMAX THEATER. (Look up the attractions listed individually in the Alphabetical Index.)

**Hours:** Open Tues. - Sun. from 10am - 5pm. Closed New Year's Day, Memorial Day, Thanksgiving, and Christmas.
**Admission:** Free. Parking costs $5.
**Ages:** 5 years and up.

## CALIFORNIA HERITAGE MUSEUM

(310) 392-8537
*2612 Main Street, Santa Monica*
(Take Santa Monica Fwy [10] W. almost to the end, exit S. on 4<sup>th</sup> St., R. on Pico, L. on Main.)

This two-story house/museum is hard to miss with its giant cowboy sign out front! A grassy lawn welcomes picnickers. Inside, the downstairs living room is cozy and rustic-looking. I like the antler candelabras on the mantel. The dining room atmosphere is more elegant as the table is set with fine china. The restored kitchen is the one Merle Norman originally used to cook-up her cosmetic recipes. (From such humble beginnings . . . )

The upstairs is redecorated each time a new exhibit is installed. Note: The museum is usually closed between installations. Often the exhibits are aimed at appealing to the younger generation. Past themes have focused on cowboys, guitars from all over the world, children's books and illustrations, and model trains. Call for information on the current display.

**Hours:** Open Wed. - Sat., 11am - 4pm; Sun., 10am - 4pm.
**Admission:** $3 for adults; $2 for seniors and students; children 11 years and under are free.
**Ages:** 5 years and up.

## CALIFORNIA SCIENCE CENTER

(323) SCIENCE (724-3623) / www.casciencectr.org
*700 State Drive, Exposition Park, Los Angeles*

(Exit Harbor Fwy [110] W. on Exposition Blvd., L. on Flower St., L. on Figueroa. Or, exit Santa Monica Fwy [10] S. on Vermont, L. on Exposition, R. on Figueroa. Parking is available in the second driveway on the R.)

Hanging from a very high ceiling that connects the IMAX Theater to the Science Center are hundreds of various-sized gold balls dangling on wires: an intriguing mobile. Inside, the lobby is dominated by another science-oriented piece of art - a fifty-foot, kinetic unfolding structure, suspended by cables and designed by an artist-engineer. The first floor contains the museum store, which has an extensive selection of science experiments, kits, books, etc. It also has a McDonald's (which gets extremely busy during lunch hours), and the less-crowded MegaBites eatery. A sit-down restaurant, the Rose Garden Cafe, is located on the third floor.

The second floor was our favorite. The west wing, titled World of Life, is packed with exhibits that pertain to human and animal lives. Look closely at cells via a microscope and a video. Crank a knob to watch how a model's digestive system unravels to stretch over eighteen feet. Watch a movie of an actual heart transplant as it is beamed onto a statue patient. Drive a simulator car to experience the difference in driving sober and driving drunk. See preserved fetuses in jars ranging from a few weeks old to nine months. View a movie on conception (suitable for older children). Sit on a clear, no-butts-about-it chair filled with over 200 cigarettes and watch a movie on lung cancer. Press buttons to match real hearts on display to their recorded heartbeats, from the huge elephant's to the medium-sized cow's to the tiny mouse's. Look at real brains - human, monkey, and rat. Learn about the basic needs of plants and animals through other interactive displays.

Tess, the reclining, fifty-foot human figure, comes to "life" in a great, fifteen-minute presentation in the BodyWorks room in the west wing. A large movie screen above her head stars a cartoon character who helps Tess explain how her body parts work together to keep her system in balance (i.e. homeostasis). Periodically, her muscles, organs, and circulatory system are illuminated by fiber optics. An adjacent Discovery Room allows younger children to put on puppet shows, and look at small, live animals such as frogs and mice.

The east wing, or Creative World, features communication exhibits. In the hallway, astronaut "wannabes" can pay $5 to be strapped in a Space Docking Simulator; a spinning sphere where participants virtually attempt to retrieve a satellite. Inside the large Creative World room, visitors can play virtual volleyball; whisper into a parabolic dish and have someone across the room hear them; type in telephone or television messages that are then relayed by satellite; play air drums and digitize the sound; construct buildings using scale model parts and then subject them to the shake, rattle, and roll of an earthquake via a shake table; build archways using Styrofoam blocks to learn about the strength of compression; and more. There are several large and small screen videos in both east and west wings that offer enticing and entertaining visual bits of information, although they are often not accompanied by written or verbal data.

Part of the third floor is a continuation of Creative World, focusing on transportation. Fans that blow wind to move model sailboats and a solar-paneled car are a few of the exhibits. The Discovery Room has a play house and game activities that enable younger children to learn more about the displays throughout the center. The west room features special rotating exhibits. It was a geography room when we visited. Kids learned about people, customs, plants, and unique geological formations from all over the world, via interactive displays.

Ever want to join the circus and try the high-wire act? Here's your chance. For $3, you can pedal a weighted bike across a cable wire that is forty feet above the ground. Although you're strapped in and safety netting is in place, it is still a slightly scary venture, especially when the staff person tilts the bike before pushing it across the cable wire!

Future plans for the Center include an enormous aquarium that will feature animals and eco systems ranging from the coral reef to the tropical rain forest. You'll be able to walk underneath a glass tunnel while sharks and schools of fish swim above your head. Learning about tides, currents, islands, and ice formations will occur in innovative ways. The final major exhibit will have the small task of examining the universe utilizing models, equipment, instruments, and lots of visuals. Suspended air and space craft will provide a setting for a flight training center. An on-site science and math public elementary school and educational resource center are also in the works.

Ask about the numerous special classes and programs offered for children and adults. For instance, audience-participatory shows, including *Science Comes Alive* are presented for various age groups. Another program, called Think Science!, sends teachers supplemental materials and activities, for a modest fee, on specific topics related to science and technology. Call the education department at (213) 744-7444 for a schedule of programs and for more information.

Tips: 1) School kids come in busloads on weekday mornings, so several exhibits require waiting in line to view or use during these peak hours. Therefore, consider either arriving early to watch an IMAX movie and explore the grounds and other nearby museums first, or come in the early afternoon. 2) Avoid restaurant lunch lines by packing a lunch. There are several shaded grassy areas for picnicking. 3) Locker rentals are available on the first floor. Note: The Center is stroller/wheelchair accessible. Check out the nearby AEROSPACE MUSEUM, CALIFORNIA AFRO-AMERICAN MUSEUM, LOS ANGELES MEMORIAL COLISEUM, NATURAL HISTORY MUSEUM OF LOS ANGELES and 3D IMAX THEATER. (Look under the Alphabetical Index to find each listing.)

**Hours:**  Open daily from 10am - 5pm. Closed New Year's Day, Thanksgiving, and Christmas.

**Admission:**  Free. Parking is $5 per vehicle.

**Ages:**  3 years and up.

# CAROLE & BARRY KAYE MUSEUM OF MINIATURES ☼

(323) 937-MINI (6464) / www.museumofminiatures.com            $$$
*5900 Wilshire Boulevard, Los Angeles*
(Exit Santa Monica Fwy [10] N. on La Brea, L. on Wilshire.)

Where can you see the Doge's Palace, the Chateau De Fontainebleau, and
the Vatican under one roof? At this museum, which houses "the biggest little
collection of miniatures in the world." The displays range from one-room
dioramas to relatively huge houses and castles. Most of the exhibits have step-
stools, so children can see every little thing. The first floor gallery has replicas of
the above-mentioned buildings and each one has furnishings, wallpaper,
chandeliers, silverware, etc., complete to the minutest detail. A bakery shop has
tiny little cakes and other pastries so real looking that you can almost taste 'em.
On a grand (but still small) scale is an exquisite Victorian village.

The second floor has a lot of kid-appeal. Ships, cars, airplanes, and trains
each have a display area to themselves. The Titanic model is comprised of
75,000 toothpicks and lots of Elmer's glue - what a hobby! For those who still
think that miniatures are just for girls playing with doll houses, check out Old
West Town with its cowboys and Indians. Action figures in other displays
include samurai warriors, Batman, RoboCop, and more.

Carnival Nights depicts a pier scene, complete with a "big" Ferris wheel,
and real fish swimming underneath it! A collection of First Ladies, from Martha
Washington to Barbara Bush, are in reproductions of their Inaugural Ball gowns.
Just a few other highlights include: knights in shining armor; King Tut's tomb; a
miniature violin workshop inside an actual violin; a sea captain, his equipment,
and nautical carvings inside an old-fashioned brass diving helmet; and a display
of microscopic wonders. There is too much to mention here because 14,000
square feet is maximum coverage for miniatures! If all this makes you long for a
Lilliputian lifestyle, check out the gift shop. You'll find everything you need to
furnish and decorate your miniature dream house - you can even buy the house.

**Hours:**      Open Tues. - Sat., 10am - 5pm; Sun., 11am - 5pm.
**Admission:**  $7.50 for adults; $6.50 for seniors; $5 for students 13 - 21 years;
              $3 for ages 3 - 12. Parking is 50¢ an hour on the street, $5 for the
              day at a lot across the street, or $1.20 an hour (which is the
              validated price) for parking under the Mutual Benefit building
              next to the museum.
**Ages:**      6 years and up.

# THE DRUM BARRACKS CIVIL WAR MUSEUM    ☼

(310) 548-7509 / www.sanpedro.com/spcham/champint/drmbrks.htm     $
*1052 Banning Boulevard, Wilmington*
(Exit Harbor Fwy [110] E. on Pacific Coast Highway, R. on Avalon Blvd., L. on "L" St., R.
on Banning Blvd.)

The year is 1861 and the Civil War has broken out. Although most of the
fighting was done in the east, troops from Camp Drum, California fought on the
Union side. Your forty-five-minute tour of the medium-sized

barracks/house/museum starts in the library research room. The first video is six minutes long and tells the history of Camp Drum through re-enactments, with a costumed character narrating. Do your kids enjoy a good mystery? The second video features the Drum Barracks in an episode of *Unsolved Mysteries*. Apparently, a few good ghosts from the Civil War still hang out here. Needless to say, my kids heard "ghostly" noises throughout the rest of our visit.

The parlor room is where the officers entertained. Besides period furniture, it also has a stereoscope, which is an early Viewmaster™, to look through. Q: Why didn't people smile for photographs back then? A: Many people had bad teeth, plus it took half an hour to take a picture.

The hallway shows a picture of the Camel Corps. which is a regiment that actually rode camels. It also has a flag from an 1863 battlefield - have your kids count the stars (states). Upstairs, the armory room has a few original weapons, like a musket and some swords. A rotating exhibit up here has displayed a hospital room with beds, old medical instruments, and a lifelike mannequin of a wounded soldier; a quarter master's quarters; etc. The officer's bedroom has furniture, personal effects, and old-fashioned clothing. Q: Why did women usually wear brown wedding dresses? A: You'll have to take the tour to find out!

**Hours:** Tours are given Tues. - Thurs. on the hour between 10am - 1pm; Sat. - Sun, between 11:30am - 2:30pm.
**Admission:** $3 per person.
**Ages:** 5 years and up.

# EL MONTE HISTORICAL MUSEUM
(626) 580-2232
*3150 North Tyler Avenue, El Monte*
(Exit San Bernardino Fwy [10] S. on Santa Anita, L. on Mildred St., L. on North Tyler Ave. It's on the corner, next to El Monte School.)

A visit to this adobe-style museum offers fascinating glimpses into the history of the United States, as well as the history of the pioneers of El Monte. There is plenty to see and learn to keep young people's interest peaked, even though no touching is allowed. Items in the numerous glass displays are labeled, making it easy to self-tour. However, I highly recommend taking a guided tour, given for groups of ten or more people, so your family doesn't miss out on the many details and explanations of the exhibits.

My kids were captivated by the hallway showcasing Gay's Lion Farm, which was a local training ground in the 1920's for lions used in motion pictures. The photos depict the large cats interacting with people in various circus-type acts. There are also several adorable shots of lion "kittens." A lion's tail and teeth are on display, too. The Heritage Room, toward the back, looks like an old-fashioned living room with antique furniture and a piano, plus cases of glassware, ladies' boots, and clothing. The walls are lined with pictures of walnut growers and other first-residents of El Monte.

The Pioneer Room has wonderful collections of typewriters, lamps/lanterns, dolls, toys, books, bells, quilts, army medals, and Bibles. It also contains ornate swords, a flag (with two bullet holes in it) from the battlefield at Gettysburg, a piece of the Berlin wall, George Washington's lantern, and an actual letter written by the Father of our Country who, by the way, had nice handwriting! The Frontier Room is equally interesting with early-day policeman and fireman hats, police badges and guns, a 1911 Model T, a wall of old tools, early Native American artifacts, and a re-created old-time law enforcement office.

The huge Lexington Room is sub-divided into smaller, themed "rooms" such as a turn-of-the-century schoolroom with desks, maps, and schoolwork; an old-time general store filled with shelves of merchandise; a barber shop with a chair; a music shop with ukuleles, violins, a Victrola, and more; and a dressmaker's shop with beautiful dresses, sewing machines, elegant hair combs, and beaded handbags. Most of the rooms also have period-dressed mannequins. This section of the museum also contains re-created rooms that would have been found in a house of the early 1900's such as a parlor, bedroom, kitchen, and library. Each room is fully furnished and complete to the smallest detail. The El Monte Historic Museum - "The end of the Santa Fe Trail" - offers a window to the world!

For further study, or just for the joy of reading, the El Monte Public Library is only a few buildings down. Directly across the street from the museum is a park. This pleasant corner park offers plenty of picnic tables and shady oak trees, plus a few slides and some metal transportation vehicles to climb on.

**Hours:** Open Tues. - Fri., 10am - 4pm; Sun., 1pm - 3pm. Open on Sat. by appointment.
**Admission:** Free
**Ages:** 5 years and up.

# FORT MACARTHUR MILITARY MUSEUM

(310) 548-2631- museum; (310) 548-7705 - Angels Gate Park /
www.ftmac.org
*3601 S. Gaffey Street, San Pedro*
(Exit Harbor Fwy [110] S. on Gaffey St. Drive almost to the end of Gaffey, then R. through the gates on Leavenworth Dr., past Angels Gate Park.)

This concrete World War II coastal defense battery building really fires up kids' imaginations as they walk the grounds and tour rooms filled with big artillery guns, cannons, mines, uniforms, pictures, and other war memorabilia. Military history is important to learn, but my boys really loved running through the underground corridors! Starting at the Gun Pit, it's a slightly scary thrill to run from one end of a long narrow darkish tunnel to the other end, then climb up stairs, through an open trap door, and into the Plotting Room. Now this is adventure!

A sixteen-minute video shows recoil guns shooting and the history of this museum. In the small Decontamination Room my kids pretended they had come in contact with poisonous gas and stepped on an air pump to blow it off, just like the soldiers of old. Only then could they enter the Communications Room, which has fascinating old radios and transmitters behind glass. Store Room 2 has riveting pictures of battleships being blown up. The pictures also tell stories of soldiers' bravery and hardships. The Barracks Display shows the inside of a soldier's (small) room and typical army articles.

Talking through the elaborate speaking tube system keeps kids busy for a long time, as someone speaks through one end while someone else tries to find the receiving end. Don't forget to take the steps up to the top of the defense building where one of the hideouts, used by lookouts with guns to watch for incoming, attacking ships, is still open to spy from. Picnic tables on the rooftop of the small souvenir shop make a picnic here special. (Check the July Calendar section for Old Fort MacArthur Days war re-enactments.)

Just east of the museum, on a hill in Angels Gate Park, sits the seventeen-ton Korean Friendship Bell set in a traditional, Korean-style pagoda. Let the kids run loose to enjoy the grassy knolls. There are a few pieces of climbing apparatus and a basketball court, too. Since it's a fairly treeless area, it's also ideal for kite flying. On a clear day the coastal view is gorgeous, and you can see Catalina Island.

> **Hours:** The museum is open Sat. - Sun. from noon - 5pm. It's open for tours, with advanced reservations, Tues. and Thurs. from noon - 5pm. Docent tours are offered Sat. - Sun. at 1pm and 3pm. The park is open daily from sunrise to 6pm.
>
> **Admission:** Free; donations gladly excepted.
>
> **Ages:** 2 years and up, though younger ones will have to be careful not to yell in the corridors, where noise reverberates off the cement walls. The walls are marked "Quiet please" in an attempt to keep the noise level at a minimum.

## THE GAMBLE HOUSE                                                    ☀

(626) 793-3334 / bcf.usc.edu/~bosley/gamble.html                      $
*4 Westmoreland Place, Pasadena*
(Exit Foothill Fwy [210], near where it intersects with the Ventura Fwy [134], W. on North Orange Grove Blvd., turn R. into the Gamble House)

Wood, and the way various types are crafted and blended, is the primary focus of the Gamble House. Teak, maple, cedar, redwood, and oak were used in the furniture, cabinetry, paneling, carvings, and exterior walls in a way that represents the best of the Arts and Crafts movement from the turn of the century. Not that kids care about these details, but they are impressed by the natural beauty of the rooms, original furnishings, and terraces. A one-hour guided tour explains the history of the house, the era in which it was built, and the architecture's harmonious use of wood and natural light in the home in accord with its environmental surroundings. Highlights, besides the use of wood, include the appealing open porches (used as sleeping porches), and the Tiffany glass throughout. Note: The house is not stroller/wheelchair accessible.

The outside grounds are classy looking, with beautiful landscaping, rolling green lawns, and a brick walkway and driveway.

**Hours:**      Open Thurs. - Sun. from noon - 3pm. It is closed on major
                holidays.
**Admission:**  $5 for adults; $4 for seniors; $3 for students with I.D.; children
                11 years and under are free.
**Ages:**       6 years and up.

# GENERAL PHINEAS BANNING RESIDENCE MUSEUM ☼
# AND PARK
(310) 548-7777  / www.banning.org                                    $
*401 E. M Street, Wilmington*
(Exit Harbor Fwy [110] E. on Pacific Coast Highway, R. on Avalon Blvd., L. on M St.)

This huge Victorian residence museum, where the founder of Wilmington
once lived, is reflective of the Banning family lifestyle in the 1800's. The hour-
and-a-half guided tours are best suited for older children as there is much to see,
but not to touch. First, in a room below the main house, you'll watch a film that
gives a history of the family and this era. Next, you'll walk through the photo
gallery and past a display of brilliant cut glass.

Inside the house, each of the seventeen rooms are beautifully decorated with
period furniture and eclectic art work. (Note: The house is completely decked
out at Christmas time and looks particularly splendid.) Check out the hoof
inkwell in the General's office. Get the kids involved with the tour by asking
them questions like, "What's missing from this office that modern offices have?"
(Answer - a computer, a fax machine, etc. Surprisingly, a copy machine *is* here.)
The parlor doubled as a music room and contains a piano, violin, and small
organ as well as an unusual-looking chair made out of buffalo hide and horns.
Other rooms of interest are the children's nursery; the bedrooms - one has a
unique hat rack made of antlers, while another has a stepping stool that is
actually a commode; and the kitchen with its pot-bellied stove and all of its
gadgets. (Obviously some things never change.) Request to see the Stagecoach
Barn, a fully-outfitted, nineteenth-century working barn with real stagecoaches.
Ask your children if they can figure out what some of the tools were used for.

School groups are given tours that include the one-room schoolhouse, with
its old-fashioned desks, slates, and McGuffy primers. Kids don an apron or
ascot, get a math or English lesson from that time period, and play games of
yesteryear.

The museum is situated in the middle of a pretty, twenty-acre park that has a
small playground, a few picnic tables, a rose garden, eucalyptus trees, giant
bamboo trees, and grassy areas.

**Hours:**      Touring hours are Tues. - Thurs. at 12:30pm, 1:30pm, and
                2:30pm; Sat. - Sun. at 12:30pm, 1:30pm, 2:30pm, and 3:30pm.
**Admission:**  $3 per adult; children 12 years and under are free.
**Ages:**       7 years and up.

# GEORGE C. PAGE MUSEUM / LA BREA TAR PITS ☼
(323) 934-PAGE (7243)  / www.tarpits.org                           $$$

*5801 Wilshire Boulevard, Los Angeles*                                   ⛪

(Exit Santa Monica Fwy [10] N. on Fairfax, R. on Wilshire Blvd, L. on Curson St.)

Kids boning up on becoming paleontologists will really dig this place. First, take them to see the fifteen-minute movie, *Treasures of the Tar Pits*. It gives an interesting overview and explains that the fossils they'll see in the museum have been excavated from the pits, just outside.

The George C. Page Museum has over thirty different exhibits including saber-tooth cats, an imperial mammoth, dire wolves, mastodons, bison, giant ground sloths, and a variety of birds and plants. (Forewarn your kids that dinosaurs had been extinct for many years before the tar pit entrapments occurred, so the only thing here on dinosaurs is a short film.) The exhibits are comprised of fossils, skeletons, and lifelike murals, plus an animated model of a young mammoth. Kids can pit their strength against the force of asphalt by pulling on glass enclosed cylinders stuck in the sticky stuff. The futility of this effort makes it easier to understand why animals, of any size, couldn't escape the tar pits.

Other highlights include the La Brea Woman, whose image changes continuously, via optical illusion, from a skeleton to a fleshed-out figure; the wall display of over 400 dire wolf skulls; and watching, through the huge windows of a working paleontologist's laboratory, the on-going process of cleaning, studying, and cataloging newly excavated fossils. Kellan, my oldest son, wanted to become a paleontologist until he saw how tedious the work can be. I'm encouraging him to keep an open mind. Toward the exit is a room devoted to the theory of evolution.

Outside, enjoy a walk around the twenty-three acres of beautifully landscaped Hancock Park, otherwise known as the La Brea Tar Pits. The pits are comprised of asphalt that has seeped to the surface to form sticky pools in which the animals got trapped and died. There are several active tar pits in the park, with hundreds more having been dug out and filled in. For two months during the summer, you can see real excavation work going on at Pit 91. Note: If all else fails, kids will have a great time rolling down the hills outside the museum and climbing on the statues!

**Hours:** Open daily in the summer from 10am - 5pm. Open the rest of the year Tues. - Sun. from 10am - 5pm. Closed New Year's Day, Thanksgiving, and Christmas.

**Admission:** $6 for adults; $3.50 for seniors and students with ID; $2 for ages 5 - 12; children 4 years and under are free. (Certain discounts available through AAA.) The museum is free to everyone on the first Tuesday of the month. Parking in the lot behind the museum is $6, with validation, or try parking on 6th Street directly behind the museum, for free. (See C.E.E. L.A. for membership savings, pg. 213.)

**Ages:** 3½ years and up.

# THE GETTY CENTER / J. PAUL GETTY MUSEUM    ☼

(310) 440-7300 / www.getty.edu          *$*

*1200 Getty Center Drive, Los Angeles*

(Exit San Diego Fwy [405] W. on Getty Center Drive. It is just N. of Interstate 10.)

Everything you've heard about the Getty Museum is true! Your adventure begins with a four-and-a-half-minute tram ride up a winding track that seemingly hugs the edge of the road. You may also hike up the 1.9 mile road, but you'll get enough exercise walking around the Getty.

The architecture of the museum is stunning - it elicited several exclamations of admiration from my kids. The all-white marble structures can also be blinding, so bring sunglasses. Once inside the lobby, make your first stop at one of two theaters that show a ten-minute orientation movie regarding the Center. Next, invest $2 for an audio guide that suggests special stops for families, and describes over 250 works in a total of six and a half hours. Simply press the number on your tape machine that corresponds to the number near the work of art to hear commentary and interviews regarding that specific piece.

Stroll down the courtyard toward the boulder fountain as you aim for your next destination, the Family Room. This small room contains several child-oriented art books, a computer for finding out more art information, and five costumes for children to try on that are originally depicted in paintings found in the Getty. Note: Kids will find these particular paintings in the museum and think it's cool that they dressed up like that, too! You can check out a game kit from the Family Room that enables your kids to go from mere observers to interactive participants in the galleries. Make up your own activities, too, such as having your children imitate portrait poses, or encourage them to be on the lookout for paintings with bridges or dogs or the color red.

The four Art Information rooms, staffed with knowledgeable volunteers, are worthy of your time. One shows step-by-step depictions of how bronze statues are made using wax moldings. It also has samples of crushed rocks, plants, insects, charred human bones, and copper corrosion that were used for color in illuminated manuscripts. Another room has easels, paper, colored pencils, and still life objects for aspiring artists to use for drawing their own masterpiece. As pictures can be displayed here for the day, you can truthfully boast that your child had a picture hanging at the Getty.

Now it's time to actually see the world-renown art. Forgive me for not going into detail here about the works - they are too numerous and grand. Suffice to say that the five, multi-level galleries feature paintings, sculptures, drawings, photography, and decorative arts (e.g. elegant gold-gilded furniture, tapestries, vases, etc.) in natural-light conditions, which enhance the beauty of the work. My boys were fascinated with the overhead sun panels that automatically adjust to let in the right amount of light. Many of the works have stories about the pieces printed alongside them, making them more interesting than just being another pretty picture. A separate, darkened room features medieval, illuminated (i.e. hand-painted) manuscripts with still-vivid colors painted on vellum (i.e. sheep skin). From Van Gogh to Rembrandt to Renoir, the Getty has something to please every palette.

Hardwood floors and elevators make the Center stroller/wheelchair accessible, although the doors that connect the galleries are heavy to push and pull open. As the Getty is on a hill, the several terraces offer magnificent vistas from Mt. Baldy to Catalina to the surrounding Beverly Hills area. We particularly liked the cactus garden on top of a building outside the South Pavilion. Another outside attraction is the tiered, maze-like, central garden which you may walk in and around.

Hungry visitors have several options. Two cafeterias have both indoor and outdoor seating, and serve a variety of prepacked cold or hot lunche and dinner items for an average of $6. The on-site restaurant is an elegant, sit-down dining experience, and entrees range from $8 to $22. You may also bring a lunch to enjoy at the large picnic area by the base of the tram ride. It has grassy green lawns and numerous covered picnic tables. This last choice entails taking the electric tram down to the parking lot and then back up to the museum.

Here are a few tips to make your day more memorable: 1) Consider pre-purchasing (through the Getty bookstore or elsewhere) *A is for Artist*, a Getty Museum pictural alphabet book that inspires children to be on the lookout for certain works of art. (Familiarity, in this case, breeds pleasurable recognition.) Or, buy *Going to the Getty* by J. otto Seibold and Vivian Walsh, a book that gives a solid and fun overview of the museum, as well as a look at a few pieces in particular. 2) Look for fossils embedded in the Getty walls, particularly at the plaza where the tram arrives. 3) Pre-warn your children to stand 6" to 12" away from the art. There are no ropes in front of the pieces, and while the security guards are friendly, they are also insistent. 4) A free coat/bag check is available in the entrance hall. 5) Going outside, just to another building, is almost unavoidable, so if it's raining bring an umbrella. 6) Wear comfortable walking shoes! 7) Parking reservations are required and are often filled for months at a time. You may arrive here, however, without reservations, by bike, taxi, or bus. MTA bus No. 561 and the Santa Monica Blue Bus No. 14 stop at the entrance. Those arriving without reservations may encounter long lines and are not guaranteed admission due to site capacity limitations.

Our eyes were glazed over when we left the Getty, but our minds and hearts were filled with wondrous works of art.

**Hours:**     Open Tues. - Wed., 11am - 7pm; Thurs. - Fri., 11am - 9pm; Sat. - Sun., 10am - 6pm. Closed Mon. and major holidays.
**Admission:** The museum is free. Parking is $5 per vehicle.
**Ages:**      3 years and up.

# GORDON R. HOWARD MUSEUM / MENTZER HOUSE ☼
(818) 841-6333                                                                    $

*The Museum is located at 115 N. Lomita Street, Burbank; the Mentzer House is connected to the museum by a walkway, but its address is 1015 West Olive Avenue, Burbank*

(Exit Ventura Fwy [134] N. on Victory Blvd., L. on Olive Ave. Or, exit Golden State Fwy [5] W. on Olive Ave. to the House: N. on Lomita St. to the Museum)

Make sure to save a Sunday afternoon to come and explore the Gordon Howard Museum. The hallway has old toys and dishes on display, plus a drawing room and a music room. The salon contains wedding dresses, old dresses (that are now back in style), and a stunning 1898 dress with beads and lace, plus ladies boots, jeweled hat pins, and dolls.

The Historical Room is large and filled with interesting slices from Burbank's past. Along one wall are glass-enclosed rooms, each one complete with furniture and period-dressed mannequins. Look into the rooms, pick up an old-fashioned telephone receiver, press a button, and listen to stories about Dr. Burbank (does that name ring a bell?), a family-owned winery, a 1920's hotel lobby (when $1 paid for a room!), a country store, and the *Jazz Singer*, Al Jolson. Other exhibits in this room include military uniforms, flags, and other war memorabilia; a display devoted to Lockheed, comprised of numerous pictures and model airplanes; a tribute to Disney featuring animation cells, photographs, and posters; an ornate desk used by Spanish noblemen; and more.

The Vehicle Room is packed with lots of antique "stuff," such as an old switchboard, tools, parking meters, a huge Gramophone, a hotel telephone booth, fire hats, etc. It also showcases classic cars in mint condition, and several vintage vehicles including a 1922 Moreland Bus, a 1909 Ford horseless carriage with a crank, and a 1949 fire engine with a huge target net that my kids thought was a trampoline. The small upstairs gallery has pictures and paintings as well as a complete collection of old cameras. A video on the history of Lockheed is shown at 1:10pm and again at 2:30pm.

Follow the walkway from the museum courtyard to the reconstructed Mentzer House, which was originally built in 1870. On your walk-through tour you'll see two bedrooms, a dining room, and a living room containing period furniture, plus old-fashioned items such as a phonograph, an old telephone, a vacuum cleaner, etc. The kitchen has a beautiful coal stove, china dishes, and cooking gadgets.

Right next door is the Olive Recreation Center, easily identified by the model F-104 Starfighter in the front. The park has picnic tables and a playground, plus tennis and basketball courts.

**Hours:**     Open Sun. from 1pm - 4pm.
**Admission:**  $1 donation per person is requested.
**Ages:**      5 years and up.

# GRIER MUSSER MUSEUM
(213) 413-1814
*403 S. Bonnie Brae Street, Los Angeles*
(Exit Harbor Fwy [110] W. on 3rd St., L. on Bonnie Brae. The house/museum is in a L.A. neighborhood, with parking behind the building.)

This thirteen-room, two-story, green and rust-colored Queen Anne-style house/museum was built in 1898. It was the Grier Musser family home. Since the tour guides are family relatives, they know and share the history and interesting stories of the memorabilia. The house is literally packed with personal ~~stuff~~

treasures accumulated over the years. The front parlor contains an original chandelier, Delph plates, a grandfather's clock, and other antiques. The family room has a 1950's television set, a piano, and a fainting couch for women who did just that. The dining room's fireplace is decorated with ornate tiles and beautifully carved wood work. The kitchen has a wood-burning stove, a gas stove, a beaded chandelier from the 1915 Exposition Fair, dishes from the Depression era, a collection of cookie jars, kitchen gadgets, and china cabinets filled with original boxes of Ivory Soap, Morton's Salt, etc. At the foot of the stairs is a red velvet chaperone's seat. While a gentleman courted his lady love, a chaperone would sit out of the way, but within eyesight.

An upstairs study contains a desk, grandma's diploma from high school, and a pictorial history of the Red Cross, plus a closet full of nursing uniforms from WWII. The master bedroom and adjoining bedroom have maple furniture, and closets full of hats, dresses, and boots. The children's bedroom is filled with toys, stuffed animals, dolls, and dollhouses. The dresser displays old bottles and hairbrushes as well as a more unique sign of the past - a container of leg makeup from WWII. Women would put this makeup on their legs to make it look like they were wearing nylons - seams and all. The sundeck is a favorite room for kids because of the numerous games and toys, and extensive Disney collection. Open the printer drawers to see even more treasures, such as jewelry.

Using the maid's stairway, go down to the basement to see pictures of the family and the Los Angeles area, and an extensive postcard collection from around the world. A visit here makes you wonder if maybe you should have kept that bottle cap collection, or at least your great grandfather's fishing pole.

**Hours:** Open Wed. - Fri., 1pm - 4pm; Sat., noon - 4pm.

**Admission:** $5 for adults; $3 for seniors and students; $2.50 for ages 5 - 12; children 4 years and under are free.

**Ages:** 5 years and up.

# GRIFFITH OBSERVATORY AND PLANETARIUM

(323) 664-1191 / www.griffithobservatory.org

*On the slope of Mount Hollywood, in Griffith Park, Los Angeles*

(Exit Golden State Fwy [5] W. on Los Feliz Blvd., take Hillhurst Ave. N. past the Greek Theater to the Observatory.)

The Observatory is one of the best places to get an overview of the city on a cloudless day, and to view the city lights and stars on a clear night. Coin-operated telescopes are here to get that "closer" look that kids insist they need. The largest public telescope in California is available to use (for free) every clear evening in the summer from dusk to 9:45pm. It's available the rest of the year Tuesday to Sunday from 7pm to 9:45pm. Call the Sky Report, (213) 663-8171, for twenty-four-hour recorded information.

The Hall of Science in the Observatory has some fascinating and interactive exhibits that explore astronomy and the physical sciences. The West Hall emphasizes light and stars. The solar telescope allows viewing of the sun, through filters, on clear days, so kids can actually see sun spots or solar flares.

Have the kids step on a scale and see how much they would weigh on Mars or Jupiter. (The moon scale is my personal favorite.) The computer terminals have astronomy quiz games like astronomer's hangman, etc.

The East Hall's emphasis is on more down-to-earth sciences. The weather exhibit has an earth and moon globe, plus a seismograph exhibit where kids can stomp on the floor and measure their own "earthquake." The space telescope here is one-fifth the size of the Hubble. Out on the rotunda, kids enjoy the huge Foucault pendulum that knocks big pegs over, illustrating the rotation of the earth. Note that the observatory has limited handicapped accessibility. (See GRIFFITH PLANETARIUM AND LASER SHOWS, in the Shows and Theaters section, for show information.)

**Hours:** Open daily in the summer 12:30pm - 10pm. Open the rest of the year Tues. - Fri., 2pm - 10pm; Sat. - Sun., 12:30pm - 10pm.
**Admission:** Free
**Ages:** 4 years and up.

# GUINNESS WORLD OF RECORDS MUSEUM
(323) 463-6433
*6764 Hollywood Boulevard, Hollywood*
(Exit Hollywood Fwy [101] W. on Hollywood Blvd.)

There are over 3,000 facts, feats, and world records told about and shown at this very Hollywood museum, so there is something to astounded all ages. See life-size models, pictures, videos, and special effects of the tallest, smallest, most tattooed, most anything, and everything. (The kids should be great at Trivial Pursuit after this visit.) We were enthralled with the domino exhibit, which shows a video of an incredible domino run.

Prep your children before their visit: Q. - Do you know who holds a record for the most fan mail in one day? A. - Mickey Mouse. He received 800,000 letters one day in 1933. Q. - What animal had the smallest brain in proportion to his body? A. - Stegosaurus. Q. - What was the longest length a human neck was stretched using copper coils? And why? A. - Fifteen and three-quarter inches. I don't know why, though. Watch some fascinating footage of intriguing and bizarre facts about our world and the people and animals in it: *The Human World, The Animal World, Planet Earth, Structures and Machines, Sports World,* and a salute to *The World of Hollywood.*

**Hours:** Open daily 10am - midnight. Closed major holidays.
**Admission:** $9.95 for adults; $6.95 for ages 6 - 12; children 5 years and under are free. Combination tickets with HOLLYWOOD WAX MUSEUM (see this entry in this section) are $14.95 for adults; $8.95 for ages 6 - 12.
**Ages:** 4½ years and up.

# HACIENDA HEIGHTS YOUTH SCIENCE CENTER
(626) 854-9825
*16949 Wedgeworth Drive, Hacienda Heights*

(Exit Pomona Fwy [60] S. on Azusa, R. on Pepper Brook, R. on Wedgeworth. It's located in classroom 8 at the Wedgeworth Elementary School.)

The Youth Science Center functions as a museum and a classroom. Actually, the museum is in a classroom decorated with colorful, informative posters, at Wedgeworth Elementary School. Although it's not state-of-the-art, a lot of science is contained in this room: A sand pendulum creates patterns depending on how you swing it; a heat-sensitive, liquid crystal display leaves colored impressions when touched; a Jacob's ladder of electricity is on display; a cow's heart and a pig embryo are in jars; a case of fossils and drawers of butterflies and other insects can be examined; and a tank with fish in it shares shelf space with a few other live critters like snakes, frogs, tortoises, a tarantula, and a scorpion. Also here are computer stations with game cartridges, Geo Safaris, puzzles, books, construction toys, and numerous scientific videos to borrow. The retail store area is a small space packed with rocks, shells, science books, and experiments.

For a minimal fee, children can attend classes like "The Great Paper Airplane Race," where they'll learn about aerodynamics and wind, while making and flying paper airplanes. Several field trips, such as nature hikes and tours, are offered throughout the school year. A terrific array of science-related classes, from model rocket-building to hands-on, physical science, are available during the summer. Call for a schedule.

**Hours:** Open in the summer, Mon. - Fri. from 8am - noon. Open during the school year on Sat. from 10am - 2pm.
**Admission:** Free
**Ages:** 4 years and up.

# THE HATHAWAY RANCH MUSEUM

(562) 944-6563 / www.alumni.caltech.edu/~remy/HRM/HRM.html
*11901 East Florence Avenue, Santa Fe Springs*
(From Santa Ana Fwy [5] or San Gabriel River Fwy [605] exit E. on Florence Ave. The driveway is just east of Pioneer Blvd.)

Drive up the driveway and into the past where great grandma Nadine Hathaway still lives on the premises of this five-acre ranch. Dogs bark their greeting outside the small visitor's center that houses saddles, old pictures, a collection of irons, etc. Check out the 1930's machine shop next door, filled with tools, tractor pistons, and even some working lathes.

All of the antiques on display in the house/museum have been accumulated from three generations of Hathaways; things used until they couldn't be fixed, and kept because the family couldn't bear to throw anything away. (So, if I start saving all my "stuff" and my children's stuff, someday their children could open up a museum!) The first room inside the museum is a fully furnished living room. The adjacent kitchen contains a coal and a wood burning stove, ice box, old baby buggy, high chair, and a myriad of labeled gadgets such as butter molds, old graters, etc. A 1920's girl's bedroom holds dolls, pictures of movie stars from that era, tennis racquets, etc. Another bedroom displays Nadine's grandmother's wedding dress, feather boas, and more. Upstairs is a hideaway

room that kids immediately want duplicated in their own homes. The small
"secret" room now holds model trains and old-fashioned toys. A bedroom holds
dresses from different eras including a prom dress, plus fur coats, shoes, hats,
and sewing machines. The hallway has a display of once-stylish hats and beaded
handbags. The "military room" is packed with personal belongings from several
wars. It contains uniforms, medals, a forty-eight star flag, a Civil War hat, and a
WWII helmet. See history close up!

The grounds are equally fascinating - so much machinery in one place! If
your group is small, a golf cart is used to show you around. If your group is
larger, or you come on a Sunday, a tractor wagon is used. You'll see and learn
about old John Deeres, combines, numerous tractors, oil well engines, gas
shovels, old trucks, farming equipment, a wagon originally used on the Oregon
Trail, a steam roller, a filling station with gas pumps, and lots more. Though it
may resemble a large junkyard, much of the machinery is in the process of being
restored. While on the ranch grounds you'll also see ducks and chickens, a
garden growing of its own accord, and more old farm equipment.

**Hours:** The grounds are open Mon. - Tues., Thurs. - Fri., from 11am -
4pm. The museum is open and a tour of the grounds is available
the first Sun. of the month from 2pm - 4pm. Call to make an
appointment if you're interested in a tour during the week.
**Admission:** A donation of $1 per person is appreciated.
**Ages:** 4 years and up.

# HERITAGE JUNCTION HISTORIC PARK

(805) 254-1275
*24101 San Fernando Road, Santa Clarita*
(Take Golden State Fwy [5] to Antelope Valley Fwy [14], exit N. on San Fernando Rd.)

A steam locomotive is on the tracks out in front of this restored, late 1800's
train station/museum. Inside the museum are photographs, information, and
artifacts that show and tell the history of this valley, including the Spanish era,
the petroleum and mining areas, and its rich film history. Several other buildings,
in various stages of restoration, comprise the rest of the junction. You can walk
back and peek in through the windows of the little red school house, the Ramona
chapel, and the Edison house. On the first Sunday of the month, you may take a
tour through the small Kingsbury house that contains nineteenth-century
furniture. We weren't here long, but it was an interesting, historical stop. Note:
The junction park is right next to the WILLIAM S. HART MUSEUM AND
PARK. (Look under the Museums section for more details.)

**Hours:** Open Sat. - Sun., 1pm - 4pm. Open for school tours during the
week.
**Admission:** Free
**Ages:** 6 years and up.

# HERITAGE PARK (Santa Fe Springs)

(562) 946-6476 / www.santafesprings.org/historic.htm

*12100 Mora Drive, Santa Fe Springs*
(Exit San Gabriel River Fwy [605] E. on Telegraph Rd., past Pioneer, R. on Heritage Park Dr. to the end.)

Heritage Park is like a breath of fresh air among the historical parks. Its six acres of beautifully landscaped grounds make any length visit here a pleasure. The high-ceilinged, wood Carriage Barn, which holds turn-of-the-century exhibits, is a must-see. Two carriages from horse and buggy days take the center floor. Behind glass is a large display of period clothing, including a wedding dress, plus dolls, toys, and books. The small touch and play area has clothing to try on, an old telephone to dial (not touch tone), and a few other articles to play with. Inventing a Better Life display features old phonographs, typewriters, bikes, roller skates (not in-line skates), plus cameras and other equipment. It's interesting to see how the inventions of yesteryear benefit us today.

Grab a bite to eat at The Kitchen, an outside, full-service snack bar. It's open Monday through Friday from 8am to 3pm. The average cost of a sandwich or salad is $4. Or, bring your own lunch, and enjoy the garden setting with beautiful old shade trees and wooden picnic tables. A walk-through aviary has parakeets, canaries, etc. A small window to an archeological pit shows excavated trash like cattle bones, pottery, etc. There are remain sites marking original fireplace and basement foundations, but kids cannot go down in them to explore. A hedge around the beautiful formal gardens gives way to an old fig tree with huge roots that are irresistible for kids to climb on. An immaculate wood-paneled tank house, once used to store water, is at the far end of the park. On a school tour, kids can go inside the tank house and walk up the crisscross stairs to the top, then go outside, and take in the view.

I can't emphasize the beauty of this park enough. It's clean, green, and the walkways throughout make every area accessible. Ask about the park's special programs throughout the year, including a Pow Wow in November.

Just outside the park gates are three restored railroad cars on a track. Take a tour of the engine car and ring the bell, then go through the caboose and see where coal was stored. Look for a Native American "village" to open soon. It will feature a thirty-foot (in diameter) dome structure made from tule and willow branches. Exceptional, two-hour, school tours of Heritage Park include lots of historical information, presented in a kid-friendly way, plus hands-on activities. Tours are free.

**Hours:**    The park is open daily from 7am - 10pm. Railroad exhibit and Carriage Barn hours are Tues. - Sun., noon - 4pm. School tours are given between 9am - noon, Wed. and Thurs. Call for a reservation.

**Admission:**    Free

**Ages:**    All

# HERITAGE SQUARE MUSEUM
(626) 796-2898 / www.heritagesquare.org                                 *$$*
*3800 Homer Street, Highland Park*

(Exit Pasadena Fwy [110] S. on Avenue 43. Take an immediate R. on Homer St.)

This little "town" behind a gate at the end of a residential street has eight houses, a carriage barn (used for storage), a church building, and a train depot. The elegant Victorian homes, originally built between 1865 to 1914, have been relocated here and are in various stages of restoration. Each one has a different architectural style. One is white with columns, almost colonial-looking, while another is green, gingerbreadish in style, and has a brick chimney. The octagon-shaped house is the most unique-looking house here. Its unusual configuration makes it interesting to look at as well as walk through.

Only on the one-hour guided tours can you go through some of the homes. The last house on the tour is the only one furnished. The grassy grounds are ideal for picnicking.

**Hours:** Open Fri., 10am - 3pm; Sat. - Sun. and holiday Mon., 11:30am - 4:30pm. Guided tours are given Sat. - Sun. at noon, 1pm, 2pm, and 3pm.

**Admission:** Friday admission is free, but only the grounds are open. Admission to the buildings and the grounds on weekends and holiday Mon. is $5 for adults; $4 for seniors and ages 13 - 17; $2 for ages 7 - 12; children 6 years and under are free.

**Ages:** 6 years and up.

# HOLLYWOOD BOWL MUSEUM

(323) 850-2058 / www.hollywoodbowl.org
*2301 N. Highland, Hollywood*
(Exit Hollywood Fwy [101] at Highland and follow signs to Hollywood Bowl.)

While at the Hollywood Bowl for a concert, or if you're in the area, stop by the Hollywood Bowl Museum. This 3,000 square foot museum offers a history of the Bowl via displays of musical instruments and pictures of performers and conductors. Touch screens show concerts featured at the Bowl. The second story has rotating exhibits focusing on various aspects of music. A music education program is offered for school groups where kids learn about music, as well as try their hands at playing some instruments. The program specifics change from season to season.

**Hours:** Open during the summer daily from 10am - 8:30pm. Open the rest of the year Tues. - Sat. from 10am - 4:30pm. It's also open during intermission on concert evenings.

**Admission:** Free. Parking is free.

**Ages:** 7 years and up.

# HOLLYWOOD ENTERTAINMENT MUSEUM

(323) 465-7900 / www.hollywoodmuseum.com
*7021 Hollywood Boulevard, Hollywood*
(Exit Ventura Fwy [101] E. on Hollywood Blvd.)

The main room in this entertaining museum is done up dramatically in true Hollywood style with movie posters, old movie cameras, microphones, lighting equipment, a Hollywood time line, and video screens that show the history and background information of particular exhibits. Listen to Walt Disney talk about animation, or see Buster Keaton in action. Other exhibits include the armor, sword, and helmet from *Ben Hur*; a gown worn by Marilyn Monroe; a Max Factor display showing stars at their most glamourous; and the opportunity to become a Star Trek character, via a mirrored reflection. A central screen intermittently shows a montage of film clips and/or a mini-documentary. The stage below the screen has a model of the town of Hollywood built into the floor and covered with plexiglass so you can walk on it. Note: Flash photography is not allowed in the museum.

Take the behind-the-scenes tours which are included in your admission price. One enables you to see a prop room filled with masks, desks, stuffed animals, clocks, sports equipment, musical instruments, etc., plus closets stuffed with costumes and outfits categorized by color and season. *Star Trek* fans (and others) can beam aboard the Enterprise's bridge, sit in the captain's chair, and watch clips from the original and *Next Generation* series. Picard's ready room is also here. Look closely at the diagrams and technical jargon on the display panel in the hallway. You'll see a hamster on a wheel, "slippery when wet" signs, and sayings such as, "In space no one can hear you scream." The cameras never shot close enough to catch these details! Another Trekker room follows, with masks and items that would be found on a Klingon vessel. For a change of scenery, walk through the entire original *Cheers* bar, where everybody knows your name.

The second tour is a fascinating Foley Room. Station one shows how sound effects bring life to motion pictures. Horses clopping, kissing, even putting on a leather jacket are all sounds later incorporated into a film using a variety of creative props, such as trash can lids, etc. Kids (and adults) can try out their new-found knowledge at station two where a silent clip is shown once, and then again. The second time the audience is invited to add dialog and use the doorbell, typewriter, telephone, etc., at the proper spots. The clip is played for a third time with the (hilarious) results recorded.

Other intriguing, interactive tours that are currently not included in the admission price involve recording at the Recording Studio, and editing film in the Editing Suite. The museum also offers school programs to students who are interested in learning about the entertainment industry.

The museum is located in a complex with a theater and several shops and restaurants. It is also in the heart of Hollywood's Walk of Fame, so look down to see the stars' names adorning the sidewalks. Just a few blocks down is Disney's El Capitan Theater, the famous Mann's Chinese Theater (with stars' handprints and footprints), plus other Hollywood museums and activities.

**Hours:** Open Tues. - Sun. from 10am - 6pm. Open daily in the summer the same hours. Closed most major holidays.

**Admission:** $7.50 for adults; $4.50 for seniors and students; $4 for ages 5 - 12; children 4 years and under are free. Metered parking is available wherever you can find it, or park for $2 around the corner on Sycamore Street.

**Ages:**   6 years and up.

# HOLLYWOOD WAX MUSEUM

(323) 462-5991
*6767 Hollywood Boulevard, Hollywood*
(Exit Hollywood Fwy [101] W. on Hollywood Blvd.)
Hundreds of celebrities from the world of television, movies, sports, politics, and religion are presented in waxy lifelikeness, surrounded by appropriate and realistic settings. Kids will enjoy "seeing" their favorite stars like Sylvester Stallone as Rambo, Clint Eastwood dressed in his "make my day" attire, Dorothy and her companions in the Wizard of Oz, Kareem Abdul Jabbar, Elvis, and hundreds more. A permanent exhibit here includes over 100 original movie costumes such as Christopher Reeve's *Superman*, Esther Williams' bathing suit, etc. A word of caution: There is a House of Horrors which might frighten younger children, though thankfully it has a separate loop.

**Hours:**   Open Sun. - Thurs., 10am - midnight; Fri. - Sat., 10am - 2am. Closed major holidays.

**Admission:**   $8.95 for adults; $8.50 for seniors; $6.95 for ages 6 - 12; children 5 years and under are free. Combination tickets with GUINNESS WORLD BOOK OF RECORDS (see this entry in this section) are $14.95 for adults; $8.95 for ages 6 - 12.

**Ages:**   4 years and up.

# HOLYLAND EXHIBITION

(323) 664-3162
*2215 Lake View and Allesandro Way, Los Angeles*
(Heading S. on Golden State Fwy [5], exit R. on Fletcher Dr., make a quick L. on Riverside Dr., R. on Allesandro St., R. on Oak Glen Pl. [across a bridge], R. on Allesandro Way. The house is on the corner of Lake View and Allesandro. Heading N. on [5], exit at Stadium Way, quick L. on Riverside Dr., L. on Allesandro St. Then follow the above directions.)
Wow! I could take this tour at least three more times and still not see and learn everything this museum has to offer! The Holyland Exhibition is an inconspicuous two-story corner house that was built in the late 1920's. It contains an incredible collection of priceless Egyptian and biblical items. The two-hour tour is not hands on. It does involve a lot of listening and learning. An incredibly well-informed, costumed docent will take you first to the tapestry-rich Bethlehem/Egyptian room which, like all the rooms, is not large, but packed with artifacts. You'll feel transported to a different time and country. Some of the items explained in depth are the 2,600-year-old mummy case; the hand-made brass art pieces and plates; papyrus; shoes made of camel hide and ram skin; headdresses; and a lunch bag made of goat skin. Each item is presented with its history and its biblical connection. You'll also see jewelry, engraved leather goods, a 2,000-year-old lamp, and much more.
The Bible Art and Archaeology Room has stones, shells, pottery, spices, etc., from Nazareth, Bethlehem, the Jordan River, and surrounding areas. You'll

view the type of large thorns used in Christ's crown of thorns; a big chunk of salt called Madame Lot; a very comprehensive family tree detailing lineage from Adam to Jesus; the kind of stones crushed and used for pitch on Noah's ark; a picture of Mt. Ararat where *ark*eologists believe the ark landed; and a re-created Ark of the Covenant. Make sure your tour guide explains how Mr. Futterer, the museum founder, went on an expedition to find the ark and how this was the basis for the movie *Raiders of the Lost Ark.* (This will definitely spark your children's interest.) Again, amazing amounts of Bible references are given with the presentation of each article.

While sitting on oriental rugs around low tables, you're served small samples of Holy Land refreshments - a taste of Israel. The Jerusalem Bazaar is a gift shop with souvenirs (and great teaching materials) made of olive wood, mother-of-pearl, etc., at bargain prices. The Damascus Room has an intricate game table inlaid with mother-of-pearl that took fifty man-years to make - kids may not play games on it! The room also contains beaded lamps, musical instruments, a camel saddle, animal skin (to write on), and many unique pieces of furniture. With all that I've just written, I've barely scratched the surface of what this museum features. So, come, take a trip to the middle east, via the Holyland Exhibition, and learn about its peoples and customs. The interdenominational museum is frequented by Christians, Jews, Muslims, and people of various other faiths.

**Hours:** The museum is open to tour seven days a week, including holidays and evenings. Call at least a week ahead of time, and choose the most convenient time for your group of at least ten or more.

**Admission:** $2.50 for adults; $2 for ages 2 - 16 years.

**Ages:** 6 years and up.

## THE HOMESTEAD MUSEUM                                              ☼

(626) 968-8492 / www.homesteadmuseum.org                            !
*15415 E. Don Julian Road, City of Industry*
(Exit Pomona Fwy [60] N. on Hacienda Blvd., L. on Don Julian Rd.)

The Homestead Museum resides on six acres of land. A major portion of the property is an open, grassy area between the main group of buildings and the old mausoleum. A shady picnic area is here, too. A one-hour guided tour, starting at the water tower, will take you behind the gates. Kids will see and learn about the history of the United States, and about California in particular. They'll learn, for instance, that our state was once Mexican territory, and how that influence has factored in the development of our culture. They will also learn about the Art and architecture of the 1830's through the 1930's.

The tour goes into the two residences on the premises. The Workman adobe home has no furniture inside, but outside are a few artifacts that kids can touch. The Temple house is spacious with twenty-five rooms, mostly furnished in 1920's decor. Kids will also get information about the onsite pump house, tepee, and mausoleum.

**Hours:** Open Wed. - Sun., 1pm - 4pm. Tours are given on the hour. Open for tour groups, minimum ten people, at other times throughout the week. Call for a reservation. Closed major holidays and the fourth weekend of every month.
**Admission:** Free
**Ages:** 6 years and up.

## HUNTINGTON LIBRARY, ART COLLECTIONS AND ☼ BOTANICAL GARDENS

(626) 405-2125 / www.huntington.org                                    *$$*
*1151 Oxford Road, San Marino*
(Exit Foothill Fwy [210] S. on Sierra Madre Blvd., R. on California, L. on Allen Ave.)

The Library houses one of the world's greatest collections of rare books, manuscripts, and documents including a Gutenberg Bible; Ellesmere Chaucer, *The Canterbury Tales*; Benjamin Franklin's autobiography, in his own handwriting; original works by Whitman and Dickens; and letters written by George Washington, Thomas Jefferson, and Abraham Lincoln.

The Huntington Art Gallery is the epitome of opulence. This mansion contains sculptures, rare tapestries, miniatures, period furniture, and famous paintings, including Gainsborough's *Blue Boy*. Watch the interesting, thirteen minute video about this painting first, then see if you can find some of the hidden elements in the painting. Get kids involved with observing the paintings by pointing out the ones with children and ones with different styles of dress. Tell them stories about the subjects. For instance, sweet-faced *Pinkie* died soon after her portrait was finished, and the boy in *Lavina, Countess Spencer and her son Viscount Althorp* was one of Princess Diana's great great (great, etc.,) grandparents. This is a gentle way to introduce children to some truly great works of art.

The botanical gardens are comprised of twelve separate, amazing gardens that cover 150 acres of the 200-acre estate. As Lisa Blackburn, a museum associate says, "The gardens . . . have wide open spaces and vast rolling lawns; great for running, somersaulting, cartwheeling, shrieking, and releasing all that boundless energy that is sometimes stifled in traditional museum settings." There are waterfalls, lily ponds, koi, ducks, turtles, and frogs to capture kids' attention - almost more than can be seen in one day. The Desert Garden has, again to quote Lisa, "twelve acres of some of the most bizarre, colorful, creepy-crawly plants that a child could imagine." Another favorite garden is the Japanese garden, which is a quarter-mile west of the main entrance. This has a traditionally furnished Japanese house, stone ornaments, an old temple bell, a moon bridge, and a bonsai court. My little Tarzans said the best part of coming to the Huntington, though, is hiding in the bamboo groves in the Jungle Garden.

Picnicking is not allowed on the grounds. However, a special treat for you and your daughter, as it's not really a boy's cup of tea, is to dress up and sip English tea in the Rose Garden Tea Room, (626) 683-8131. Prices for the variety of finger sandwiches and delightful English desserts are $11 for adults, $5.50 for children 9 years and under. A restaurant is on the grounds, too. Ask about the numerous special classes and programs.

**Hours:** Open in the summer Tues. - Sun. from 10:30am - 4:30pm. Open the rest of the year Tues. - Fri., noon - 4:30pm; Sat. - Sun., 10:30am - 4:30pm. Self-guiding tour brochures are available. Garden tours depart Tues. - Sun. at 1pm. Closed major holidays.

**Admission:** $8.50 for adults; $7 for seniors; $5 for students with ID; children 12 years and under are free. Admission is free the first Thurs. of every month.

**Ages:** 4 years and up.

## INTERNATIONAL PRINTING MUSEUM                                                      ☼

(714) 523-2070 or (714) 529-1832 / www.gamall.com/museum                              $$
*315 Torrance Boulevard, Carson*
(Exit Harbor Fwy [110] E. on Torrance Blvd)

A visit to this museum helps kids to understand the history and importance of the printed word, and how printing presses changed the world of reading. Visitors will see a working wooden press from 1750, printing artifacts, and demonstrations of bookbinding and papermaking. They will also have the opportunity to fold their own book as a keepsake. This facility, opening in January 1999, offers a general tour for the public and specific tours for groups up to fifty people. As a parent and a readaholic, I appreciate all that this fine museum has to offer, especially the presentations that encourage kids to realize the joy of reading.

Two, ninety-minute group tours, which also include a general museum tour, are the Pages of Invention: The Communication Tour, and Pages of Freedom: The Constitutional Convention. The Invention tour is a fascinating journey that begins thousands of years ago when the Chinese first invented paper and "wrote" on it using carved blocks of wood. Children continue traveling to the period when Egyptian scrolls were written on papyrus, then on to the time of Gutenberg's wonderful contribution of the printing press. Students learn about the tools of the trade while listening to anecdotes and information on bookbinding. They also learn about the time it took to make a hand-written book (three to five years); the price; the increase in availability of books to the common people because of the press; and a lot more. A costumed appearance by Benjamin Franklin - well, not the real one, but one who is a dead ringer - then follows. Utilizing slides and equipment, Ben explains his numerous inventions and discoveries, such as electricity, an unsteady chair (i.e. rocking chair), markers called milestones, etc. Eager audience members participate in experiments that demonstrate static electricity and electricity generated through a replica 1750 electro static generator. He regales listeners about his life in Colonial America and encourages children to get educated by reading. The Freedom tour is a re-enactment of the Constitutional Convention. Divided into thirteen groups (colonies), students use pre-written cards to debate foundational issues such as representation taxation, election of the president, and slavery. Ben

Franklin presides over the meeting which ends with the colonies signing the Constitution. This is an outstanding, experiential history lesson/tour!

If your group comprises more than fifty students, reserve a History in Motion: A Museum on Wheels presentation, where the museum comes to your site. Host a slightly expanded version of the Inventions tour, or invite just Ben Franklin for a fifty-minute presentation/"show."

**Hours:** Open to the public Fri. - Sat., 10am - 4pm. Open for groups by reservation.

**Admission:** $7 for adults; $5 for seniors and ages 8 - 16; children 7 years and under are free. In-house group tours are $125 for up to 25 people; $5 per person over that number. The traveling tours, for up to 150 students, are a flat fee of $500 for the two-hour presentation; $350 for the talk with Ben.

**Ages:** 5 years and up.

## JAPANESE AMERICAN NATIONAL MUSEUM ☼ $$
(213) 625-0414  / www.lausd.k12.ca.us/janm
*369 E. 1st Street, Los Angeles*
(Exit Harbor Fwy [110] E. on 1st St. Or, exit Hollywood Fwy [101] S. on Alameda, R. on 1st St. It's on the corner of 1st St. and Central Ave. in Little Tokyo.)

During World War II, more than 120,000 people of Japanese ancestry, most of whom were American citizens, were incarcerated in American relocation/concentration camps from 1941 to 1946. This museum is dedicated to preserving the memory of that time period, and learning from it. There are two buildings to this one museum. They are located across the street from each other in Little Tokyo.

One building contains the Legacy Room, which displays photographs of Japanese families, the Japanese-American time line, uniforms, and scale models of the layout of the camps. In addition, there are personal belongings and works of art, like wood carvings whittled while the carver was in a concentration camp. The second floor shows a forty-five-minute collage of homemade movies called *Something Strong Within*. This film documents the harsh conditions of every day life in the camps. Rotating displays here touch upon various aspects of Japanese culture, whether the exhibits focus on art or Sumo wrestlers.

The other building, opening in 1999, will have seven exhibit rooms, two large classrooms, a central hall (to rent out), and a water and stone garden outside. The exhibit rooms will hold rotating displays, varying from art exhibits, to the history of Japanese Americans, etc. Permanent exhibits include fragments and remains of the wooden barracks.

The Japanese American Museum also has computers for kids to play history games, or to learn how to compose a Haiku poem. A craft table is available, too, where volunteers show visitors how to create origami art.

**Hours:** Open Tues. - Sun., 10am - 5pm (open Thurs. until 8pm). Closed New Year's Day, Thanksgiving, and Christmas.

**Admission:** $6 for adults; $5 for seniors; $4 for ages 6 - 17; children 5 years and under are free. Admission is free the third Thurs. of every month.
**Ages:** 7 years and up.

# KENNETH G. FISKE MUSICAL INSTRUMENT MUSEUM
(909) 621-8307 / cucpo.cuc.claremont.edu/fiske
*Fiske Museum, in Claremont College, Claremont*
(Exit San Bernardino Fwy [10] N. on Indian Hill Blvd., R. on 4th St. The College is at the corner of 4th St. and College Way. The museum is on the lower level of the Bridges auditorium.)

This museum is like music to your ears. The three galleries contain a comprehensive collection of over 400 rare, historic, and ethnic musical instruments. The instruments on display, ranging from the 1600's to the twentieth century, include exotic drums, Civil War bugles, and player pianos. On the half-hour tour, the curator explains the various instruments and even plays a few of them. This museum can be instrumental in teaching your kids about music!
**Hours:** Call for an appointment.
**Admission:** Free; donations accepted.
**Ages:** 7 years and up.

# KIDSPACE
(626) 449-9143 / www.kidspacemuseum.org
*390 S. El Molino Avenue, Pasadena*
(Take Pasadena Fwy [110] to end, R. on California Blvd., L. on El Molino. Or, exit Foothill Fwy [210] S. on Lake Ave., R. on Del Mar, L. on El Molino.)

As soon as your kids enter this great participatory museum they will immediately get immersed in the professions and activities offered as they sit behind a desk at a "TV studio" and become newscasters; dress up as firefighters and man (or woman) the hoses and ladders, which are (thankfully) attached to walls; learn how they get things letter-perfect at the Post Office by playing Postmaster; get sand between their toes at the beach play area; and play in, on, and under the indoor treehouse play area, called Critter Caverns. There is also a dress-up area, a computer room, and a zone by the frame of a house for future builders and construction workers to practice their skills. Your shoppers or cashiers-in-the-making have a mini-market with baskets, food, and a (play) cash register. Little ones have a wonderful area just for them that offers various things to do.

Saturday and Sunday craft times, for ages 5 and up, are weekend bonuses. During the week, "No Nap" storytelling and craft times are offered for toddlers. The museum also features many special programs, exhibits, and workshops throughout the year. We have thoroughly enjoyed school field trips here as students learn about insects (or other subject matter) in depth, complete a related craft project, and play.

**Hours:** Open in the summer Sun. - Thurs., 1pm - 5pm; Fri. and Sat.,
10am - 5pm. Open the rest of the year Tues., 1:30pm - 5pm;
Wed. - Fri. and Sun., 1pm - 5pm; Sat., 10am - 5pm. Closed Mon.
Open for school tours during the week, with advanced
reservations.

**Admission:** $5 for ages 3 and up; $3.50 for seniors; $2.50 for children 1 - 2
years old. (Certain discounts available through AAA.) School
tours are $2.50 per person. Admission is free on the last Mon. of
every month (except October), from 5pm - 8pm.

**Ages:** 1½ - 11 years old.

## THE LEONIS ADOBE                                                        ☼

(818) 222-6511                                                             $
*23537 Calabasas Road, Calabasas*
(Exit Ventura Fwy [101] S. on Valley Circle Blvd. and take a quick R. onto Calabasas Rd.)

Step back over 100 years in time when you visit the Leonis Adobe. The
restored buildings help kids to picture the wealthy ranchero as it once was. The
rustic grounds, complete with grape arbors, old farm equipment, windmills, and
a corral containing longhorn cattle, horses, sheep, and goats, enhance the
yesteryear atmosphere. Officially Los Angeles' Historic Cultural Monument No.
1, the adobe was once owned by Miguel Leonis, a Basque who led a very
colorful life, and Espiritu, his Native American wife. Both the museum and its
owners have a rich and fascinating history that kids will enjoy hearing.

The Visitor's Center has a few glass-cased displays of mannequins dressed
in period clothing. Outside, a huge, 600-year-old oak tree dominates the grounds.
You are welcome to explore the barn, complete with wagons and buggies; a
blacksmith's shop that is outfitted with saddles and tools; and the adobe. The
bottom story of the adobe has a kitchen with a wood-burning stove and other
old-fashioned kitchen implements; a pantry for preserving and drying food (kids
like the hanging cow with fake blood); and a dining room - notice the dirt floors.
Upstairs is the Leonis' elegant bedroom that has a red velvet bedspread over the
canopy bed, plus ladies' boots, and leather trunks. You'll notice that the hallway
floor tilts at a downward angle, slanting away from the house. It was built like
that to ensure that rains would run away from the walls, not seep into them. The
Juan Menendez (bed) Room has a ghost story associated with it. (Every good
historical home has at least one such story!) Also up here is an office, complete
with desk, ledger, and guitar. Elsewhere on the ranch grounds are penned
turkeys, ducks, and chickens; a covered beehive oven which was used for baking
bread; and steps leading up to the tank house, or worker's bedroom. The Leonis
Adobe is a classy reminder of the relatively brief, but pivotal Mexican/California
era.

Just a short walk eastward, past the Sagebrush Cantina restaurant, is the
small, but beautiful Calabasas Creek Park. It offers a pleasant picnic area and
respite with a rose garden out front, wrought-iron benches throughout, massive
shade trees, and bridges over the duck pond. The only drawback to this serene

scene is the ever-present freeway noise.

**Hours:** The Leonis Adobe is open Wed. - Sun. from 1pm - 4pm.

**Admission:** $2 for adults; $1 for children 12 years and under.

**Ages:** 4 years and up.

## LOMITA RAILROAD MUSEUM

(310) 326-6255 / www.lomita-rr.org

*250<sup>th</sup> Street and Woodward Avenue, Lomita*

(Exit Harbor Fwy [110] W. on Pacific Coast Hwy., R. on Narbonne, R. on 250th St.)

Stop, look, and listen! This small, re-created, turn-of-the century train depot is as charming to look at - with its decorative wrought iron, gingerbread molding, and brick patio - as it is to tour. Inside the depot museum/souvenir shop, visitors will see various train memorabilia such as an old-time station agent ticket office, scale model train cars, telegraph equipment, locomotive whistles, marker lights, an exhibit of railroad ties, and glass cases filled with photographs and more artifacts. Hanging from the ceiling and the walls is a collection of hand-lanterns.

Outside, on real train tracks, are two railcars: An all-wood, 1910 Union Pacific "bobber" (i.e. caboose) to look around in and a 1902 Southern Pacific Steam locomotive with a cab that the kids can climb in and let their imaginations go full steam ahead. Note that the valves and handles are labeled with explanations for their use, but they are not for touching.

The museum annex park is just across the street. This pretty little grassy spot, with a few picnic tables under shade trees, boasts a real wood box car and a 1923 Union Oil tank car that are for display purposes only..

**Hours:** Open Wed. - Sun. from 10am - 5pm. Closed Thanksgiving and Christmas.

**Admission:** $1 for adults; 50¢ for children 12 years and under.

**Ages:** 1 ½ years and up.

## LOS ANGELES CHILDREN'S MUSEUM

(213) 687-8800 / www.lacm.org

*310 N. Main Street, Los Angeles*

(Exit Hollywood Fwy [101] S. on Alameda, R. on Temple St., R. on Los Angeles St. It's in the Los Angeles Mall.)

In the midst of skyscrapers, the city of angels has a very kid-friendly building with over fifteen main exhibits - the Los Angeles Children's Museum. City Streets will rev up the engines of your child's imagination as he/she "drives" the front end of a bus, "rides" on a real police motorcycle, and, for a really hot time, dresses up in a firefighter's uniform. The Mars play area has a rocket ship to climb on, a sand box to play in, and space-related interactive activities. The Recording Studio has real equipment to your child's talent. (Buy a tape for blackmail, I mean to cherish, for $1.) My oldest gleefully took the microphone in hand and proceeded to tell some really bad knock-knock jokes, but **he** had a good time. The Videozone has "blue screen" technology so kids can choose any back drop, from the moon to the ocean, to dress up, and act out stories (or whatever) and have it taped for posterity. (You may buy the tape for $2.) Studio time fills up fast, so sign your kids up as soon as you get to the museum. In the $H_2O$ area kids will get their hands wet, but it's O.K. - they're learning about water! Shadow Box, where a light flashes and takes a "picture" of your body (or body parts) against the wall, and the small Cave of the Dinosaurs are also terrific.

On the second floor, kids can create take-home treasures from the Loft craft area and paper products from the Pulp Factory. Weekends are extra fun as different programs such as storytelling, mini-productions, etc., are offered. Don't be fooled by the name *Children's* Museum - adults have a great time here, too.

**Hours:** Open in the summer Mon. - Fri., 11:30am - 5pm; Sat. - Sun., 10am - 5pm. Open the rest of the year, Sat. - Sun., 10am - 5pm. Reservations for groups of ten or more are also available at other times throughout the school year. Closed major holidays.

**Admission:** $5 for ages 2 and up; children under 2 years are free. Parking ranges from $5 - $15 and is available at the Los Angeles Mall (Los Angeles Street and Temple) daily; Lot 7 Municipal Parking (San Pedro Street and Temple) on weekends only; and Lot 2 Municipal Parking (Temple and Alameda) weekdays only. (See C.E.E. L.A. for membership savings, pg. 213.)

**Ages:** 2 - 13 years old.

# LOS ANGELES COUNTY MUSEUM OF ART and ☼ L.A.C.M.A. WEST

(323) 857-6000 / www.lacma.org                                    *$$$*
*5905 Wilshire Boulevard, Los Angeles*
(Exit Santa Monica Fwy [10] N. on Fairfax Ave., R. on Wilshire.)

Art, according to Webster, is: "The use of the imagination to make things of aesthetic significance; the technique involved; the theory involved." This leaves the interpretation of what constitutes art wide open! The Los Angeles County Museum of Art is composed of five buildings, plus the Bing Center of theater and movies for older audiences. Each building features a different style of art.

The Anderson building is a favorite with its twentieth-century art, which translates as "anything goes." We started in the *Garage* (our title for the exhibit). Open the door to this walk-through exhibit, and it's like being in your grandfather's garage. It's crammed with old, rusted tools hanging up on the walls, other storage-type incidentals, and a car that needs more work than it will ever get. (I can now tell my husband that our garage is not a mess - it's art.) Throughout the Anderson building, kids are attracted to and puzzled by the larger-than-life sculptures, abstract paintings on gigantic canvases, and common objects that express artistic creativity, like a kitchen sink, or an arrangement of cereal boxes. Two particularly eye-catching pieces are the life-size, faceless monks sitting around in a circle, and *The Black Planet*, which is a huge black disc with long strands of black tubing (think Cajun spaghetti) coming out of it.

In contrast, the Ahmanson Building has more traditional works of art from

Medieval European, the Romantic, and the Renaissance periods. Classic paintings and portraits hang in various galleries throughout the stately, three-story building. Gilbert gold and silver pieces, such as elaborate bowls, candelabras, etc., are on display here, as are incredibly detailed, inlaid stone pictures. Other exhibits include Korean, Chinese, and American art.

The Pavilion for Japanese Art is architecturally unique, inside and out. It houses mostly paintings and a few sculptures in a serene, natural-light setting. The Samurai warrior statue, dressed in eighteenth-century black chain mail armor, gets our vote for the most interesting exhibit here. The stairs spiral downward, toward the small waterfall and pond on the lowest level.

The Hammer Building specializes in photography, impressionism, and prints. The permanent and temporary exhibits here portray another medium of artistic endeavor.

The L.A.C.M.A. West, on the corner of Fairfax and Wilshire, is adjacent to the huge, central museum. It has an art deco front, and only the first floor of the multi-story building is open to the public. There are three major galleries here. One houses exhibits from the SOUTHWEST MUSEUM's collection (look up this museum under this section) that focuses mainly on textiles, pottery, and baskets. Displays do rotate. Another gallery rotates exhibit pieces from the central art museum's massive permanent collection, and showcases traveling exhibits. One of the most interesting galleries for kids is the third gallery. This huge space, dubbed "the experimental gallery" is used as an educational and interactive room for children. It's first exhibit was called, Body & Soul: Art and the Afterlife in Egypt and SubSaharan Africa. Linking the central museum to the art museum West are museum-run retail stores and a cafe. (Does this mean there is an art to shopping?)

Although many docents are on hand to insure that nothing is touched, the atmosphere is not stifling. Contact the museum about educational and family tours, and art classes that are offered throughout the year. For your information, a cafe, serving great food, is in the courtyard. Enjoy walking around the museum's spacious backyard, Hancock Park. Ask about concerts and presentations at the amphitheater here.

**Hours:** Open Mon., Tues., and Thurs., noon - 8pm; Fri., noon - 9pm; Sat. - Sun., 11am - 8pm. Closed Wed., Thanksgiving, and Christmas. School tours are often given in the morning hours.

**Admission:** $7 for adults; $5 for seniors and students; $1 for ages 6 - 17; children 5 years and under are free. Parking costs $5 in the lot at the S.E. corner of Wilshire Blvd. and Spaulding, or at Hancock Park at Sixth St. and Curson Ave. Admission is free on the second Tuesday of each month, except for ticketed events.

**Ages:** 6 years and up.

# LOS ANGELES MARITIME MUSEUM

(310) 548-7618 / www.sanpedrochamber.com/champint/lamartmu.html     *$*
*Berth 84, San Pedro*

(Take Harbor Fwy [110] to the end. It turns into Gaffey St. Turn L. on 9$^{th}$, L. on Harbor Blvd. It's at the foot of 6$^{th}$ St.)

If you have older children who dream of sailing the oceans blue, they will enjoy walking through the six galleries of this maritime museum, which is housed in an old ferry building. There are hundreds of ship models to look at, ranging from real boats to ones inside a bottle. (How do they do that?) An impressive twenty-one-foot scale model of the Queen Mary and two cut-away models, of the Titanic and Lusitania, give your kids the inside scoop on ocean liners.

A highlight is the Amateur Radio Station where your child might be able to talk to someone on the other side of the world.

**Hours:** Open Tues. - Sun. from 10am - 4:30pm. Closed New Year's Day, Thanksgiving, and Christmas.

**Admission:** $1 donation for adults.

**Ages:** 5 years and up.

# MINI CAKE MUSEUM

(626) 793-7355

*434 N. Lola Avenue, Pasadena*

(Exit Foothill Fwy [210] N. on Allen Ave., R. on Villa, R. on Lola. It is a house in a residential district. Look for the mailbox that looks like a tiered wedding cake.)

The Mini Cake Museum is not a museum of miniature cakes, but a museum in a relatively small, two-story house that features cakes and the art of cake decorating. You'll first watch an eight-minute movie showcasing some of the 200 cakes in the museum, as well as the techniques that make them unique. Frances Kuyper - founder, curator, artist, and cake-maker extraordinare - will then point out museum highlights and show you around. The downstairs has a working kitchen, as Frances still teaches the "how to's" of cake decorating, and glass-encased cupboards that contain a variety of cakes from all over the world. Just a few of the special techniques on display here are air brushed portraits and realistic-looking flowers created from gumpaste icing. I was enthralled with the elegant, lacy wedding cakes, while my kids were drawn to the more fanciful cakes such as a dinosaur, a castle, and a coral reef with fish.

The three, small rooms upstairs function as a reference room (it has over 1,000 books), a guest bedroom for traveling teachers, and a video room. The latter has autographed pictures from Mary Pickford, Carol Channing, Sonja Henie, and others, that were given to Frances as a "thank you" for portraits she sketched of them when she was a young girl. If your kids are already interested in baking, then a visit to this museum is just icing on the cake.

**Hours:** Open (almost) daily, by appointment only.

**Admission:** Free. Or, take a tour that includes a cake demonstration, so you can have your cake and eat it too, for $5 per person - minimum ten people.

**Ages:** 5 years and up.

## MISSION SAN FERNANDO REY DE ESPAÑA ☼
(818) 361-0186                                                                *$$*
*15151 San Fernando Mission Boulevard, Mission Hills*
(From San Fernando Valley Fwy [118] exit N. on Sepulveda Blvd., R. on San Fernando
Mission Blvd. Going N. on San Diego Fwy [405], exit E. on San Fernando Mission Blvd.
Going S. on 405, exit E. on Rinaldi St., R. on Sepulveda Blvd., L. on San Fernando
Mission Blvd.)

What was life like in the early days of California? Take a self-guided tour of
one of my family's favorite missions to find out. Mission San Fernando Rey,
founded in 1797, was the seventeenth mission in the chain of outposts along the
coast of California. It has a beautiful, large courtyard, with a small sundial at the
north entrance, and west gardens that are surrounded by numerous rooms. These
rooms lead to small, alcove rooms - what delightful exploration! The Museum
Room is a good place to begin as it's filled with old photos (including one of a
bathroom that looks like a small indoor pool), statues, bows and arrows, peace
pipes, a bell collection, and several more artifacts. The Madonna Room is
fascinating as it contains over 100 representations of the Madonna, each depicted
by different nationalities and cultures. From simplistic versions to ornate ones,
there are Chinese, African, and Indian Madonnas, plus one that looks like a
prairie woman, another like an Eskimo, etc.

Other rooms and items of interest we saw include a hospice that held beds
made with rope supports (pre-box springs); simply furnished bedrooms; plain
wooden tables and chairs; the Convent, where meat was hung to dry; mission
vestments; a library containing shelves of very old books including a colorful,
hand-illuminated liturgical book with large Gothic lettering; brick ovens; and
pipe organs. The workshop and weaving rooms are interesting because they hold,
respectively, blacksmith tools, saddles, and scythes, and a large wooden loom
with cowhide chairs. The church, which still holds regular worship services, has
adobe walls and an ornately decorated altar with gold-leaf overlay. A small
cemetery behind the church opens into a huge, neighboring cemetery. In the
midst of all this history, my boys loved seeing the many peacocks that wandered
the grounds. They even "discovered" a few roosters that were tame enough to
pet.

Brand Park, once a part of the mission, is just across the street. This grassy
park has lots of shade trees, plenty of picnic tables, and running around space,
but no playground. It also has vats where mission wines were once produced.

**Hours:** Open daily from 9am - 4:30pm. Closed Thanksgiving and
Christmas.
**Admission:** $4 for adults; $3 for seniors and ages 7 - 15; children 6 years and
under are free. Admission to Brand Park is free.
**Ages:** 5 years and up.

## MISSION SAN GABRIEL ARCHANGEL �»
(626) 457-3048                                                                *$*
*537 West Mission Drive, San Gabriel*
(Exit San Bernardino Fwy [10] N. on Del Mar Ave., L. on West Mission Dr.)

Located in the Mission District, California's fourth mission is aptly nicknamed "Queen of the Missions." The graceful buildings and pleasant grounds transport you back to 1771, when the mission was founded. They also offer a wonderfully visual way to learn about California's Spanish/Mexican heritage.

In the midst of the cactus garden are tanning vats, with a placard describing the tanning process. Walk up a few stone steps to see four large holes in the ground, which were once the soap and tallow vats. The San Gabriel Mission supplied soap and candles to most of the other missions. There are several fountains and statues distributed throughout the mission gardens. In the cemetery, for instance, is a life-size crucifix - a memorial to the 6,000 Indians buried on the grounds.

The Mission Church is still in use. The wall behind the altar is eye-catching as it is ornately decorated. The small baptismal room is equally impressive. Next to the church, the small and somewhat dark museum contains only a few articles that were of interest to my kids - big, old books covered in sheepskin dating from 1489 and 1588, and a Spanish bedroom set. Knowing that the museum was once a series of rooms, such as sleeping quarters, weaving rooms, and carpenter shops, made it a bit more interesting for my children.

Located in the center of the mission is the Court of the Missions. Models of each of California's twenty-one missions, varying in size and layout, but similar in style, are on display here. Vaya con Dios! (Go with God!)

**Hours:** Open daily from 9am - 4:30pm. Closed Easter, Thanksgiving, and Christmas.

**Admission:** $4 for adults; $3 for seniors; $1 for ages 6 - 12; children 5 years and under are free.

**Ages:** 5 years and up.

# MUSEUM OF CONTEMPORARY ART / GEFFEN CONTEMPORARY

(213) 626-6222 / www.moca-la.org                                                    *$$$*

*250 South Grand Avenue, Los Angeles*

(Going W. on Hollywood Fwy [101], exit S. on Grand Ave. Going E. on 101, exit E. on Temple St., R. on Grand Ave.)

The elegant Museum of Contemporary Art (MOCA), located on top of a plaza, presents rotating exhibits of eclectic art work - paintings, sculptures, photos, etc. This type of museum is a fun one to bring kids to as an introduction to art because the pieces are unusual, imaginative, and sometimes puzzling. Idea: After visiting the museum, have the kids come home and create their own contemporary or abstract piece of art. As we looked at the huge paintings on canvas, my boys and I took the liberty of renaming several pieces. (I think some of their title choices were more apropos than the ones the artists chose.) This involved the kids in studying the art and enhanced our visit here. Downstairs in the museum is a reading room with several books, many geared for children, that pertain to the Art and artists currently featured at the MOCA.

A satellite building of MOCA, the Geffen Contemporary, is located one mile away at 152 North Central Avenue in Little Tokyo. The Museum of Contemporary Art is actually one museum in two buildings!

**Hours:** Open Tues. - Sun. from 11am - 5pm (Thurs. until 8pm). Free public tours are given at noon, 1pm, and 2pm. Closed New Year's Day, Thanksgiving, and Christmas.

**Admission:** $6 for adults; $4 for seniors and students with I.D.; children 11 years and under are free. Thurs. from 5pm - 8pm is free admission. Paid admission is good for both locations of the museum, if visited on the same day. Parking in the plaza costs about $5.

**Ages:** 6 years and up.

## MUSEUM OF FLYING                                                   ☼

(310) 392-8822 / www.mof.org/mof                                      $$

*2722 Donald Douglas Loop, North, Santa Monica*                       ⚏

(Exit Santa Monica Fwy [10] S. on Bundy Dr., R. on Ocean Park Blvd., L. on 28th St. It's adjacent to the Santa Monica Airport.)

Ready to take-off to a place where the sky is the limit? This airy museum has three stories of vintage aircraft, models, and air-related exhibits. Take the catwalk-like stairs to the second level, which has an observation window overlooking the airport. Kids can listen to the control tower via the headphones. My boys liked the mock-up of a war-briefing room up here, too.

Some of the planes are maintained in flight-ready condition. In fact, a hangar door is open for kids to watch WWII planes and other small aircraft taxiing, flying, and landing on the runway. Want to feel the jolting of a "real" flight? Take a simulator ride for $2. If you've always wanted to be a tactical fighter, but have a desk job, then become a pilot for a half-hour in a simulated flight on a FA-16 for $20.

A replica of the Voyager, which flew non-stop around the world in 1986, is on display at the entrance to Airventure. So is a slightly older flying model - a Pterodactyl. Airventure is designed just for kids as they can sit in a real Vietnam War-era helicopter, pilot the controls at a real cockpit, and play in various pretend planes. Workshops for kids ages 5 and older are offered on the weekends. Call for specific times and details.

Tip: Propel yourself over to the adjoining DC3 RESTAURANT (look under the Edible Adventures section) for their Jr. Jet program. It allows adults to eat at a nice restaurant while kids eat in a separate area and then go down and enjoy supervised play at the museum.

**Hours:** Open Wed. - Sun. from 10am - 5pm.

**Admission:** $7 for adults; $5 for seniors; $3 for ages 3 -17; children 2 years and under are free.

**Ages:** 3 years and up.

## MUSEUM OF LATIN AMERICAN ART

(562) 437-1689 / www.molaa.com

*628 Alamitos Avenue, Long Beach*

(Exit Long Beach Fwy [710] E. on Anaheim St., R. on Alamitos)

This museum has a nicely laid out main gallery and surrounding gallery rooms. Rotating exhibits feature art, sculpture, and paintings by Latin American artists. The museum regularly hosts hands-on art workshops for children, usually geared for ages 6 and up, that tie in with the present exhibit. Explore Latin American culture and heritage while experiencing its art. Note: The gift shop is filled with wonderful, cultural items to purchase.

  **Hours:**     Open Tues. - Sat., 11:30am - 7:30pm; Sun., noon - 6pm.
  **Admission:**  $3.50 for adults; $2.50 for seniors; $2 for students; children 12 years and under are free.
  **Ages:**      6 years and up.

## MUSEUM OF NEON ART

(213) 489-9918

*501 W. Olympic, Los Angeles*

(Exit Harbor Fwy [110] E. on 9th St., R. on Grand Ave. It's on the corner of Olympic and Hope, with the entrance on Hope. Free underground parking is available at the Renaissance Tower on Grand Ave., just N. of Olympic Blvd.)

For an enlightening experience, bring your kids to the Museum of Neon Art. Only here can you see Mona Lisa's smile really light up. Walk through the rainbow arch and into the warehouse-like rooms that display rotating exhibits of artists who use kinetic and electric art as an outlet for their creative endeavors. In other words, there are some funky-looking, 3D reliefs and sculptures in here! Most of the pieces are fragile, but some of them have buttons to push that make parts light up or move around.

Just outside the museum is Hope Grant Park, which is the front lawn to the Fashion Institute of Design and Merchandise. This haven of greenery in the middle of downtown Los Angeles is a welcome respite. It has a small playground, a few picnic tables, a mosaic clock tower, colorful mosaic art forms, and a large fountain with steps around its perimeter that kids love to climb.

  **Hours:**     The museum is open Wed. - Sat., 11am - 5pm; Sun., noon - 5pm. On the second Thurs. of each month, the museum is open until 8pm. The park is open daily from 7am - 6pm.
  **Admission:**  $5 for adults; $3.50 for seniors and students; children 12 years and under are free. Admission is free on the second Thurs. of every month from 5pm - 8pm. The park is free.
  **Ages:**      4 years and up.

## THE MUSEUM OF TELEVISION AND RADIO

(310) 786-1000

*465 N. Beverly Drive, Beverly Hills*

(Exit Santa Monica Fwy [10] N. on Robertson, L. on Wilshire, R. on Beverly Dr. Or, exit San Diego Fwy [405] E. on Santa Monica Blvd, R. on Beverly Dr. Two hours of free valet parking, with validation, is available under the museum, just off Little Santa Monica Blvd.)

Tune in to the Museum of Television and Radio, which houses the ultimate collection of broadcasting programs. Inside the upscale, contemporary-looking building are various rooms to watch and listen to shows, with just the touch of a button. The lobby has rotating exhibits of art, mementos, storyboards, costumes, sets, etc. The Radio Listening Room is just what its name implies. The room is quiet as visitors use headphones to choose from five preset radio channels. A sampling of the rotating selections can include comedy, rock 'n roll, history of radio, witness to history (e.g. historic speeches), etc. There is also a fully equipped radio station in here to do live broadcasts. Next door, watch a pre-selected show in the fifty-seat Screening Room, or watch a film in the 150-seat Theater Room. Call to see what's playing.

Use the upstairs computer library to select your choice of radio or television show. For example, key your television selection into the computer, then view it in the adjacent Console Room. This room has individual monitors, and family consoles which accommodate up to four people. Your child is in couch potato heaven here, able to choose his own television programs from literally thousands of titles available.

Some of the benefits of this museum include viewing (and listening to) historic shows both for school-aged children and for researchers. Ready access to programs is also great if you just want to choose a favorite show. Call for information on special children's events.

**Hours:** Open Wed. - Sun. from noon - 5pm (open Thurs. until 9pm). Closed Mon., Tues., New Year's Day, Independence Day, Thanksgiving, and Christmas.
**Admission:** $6 for adults; $4 for seniors and students; $3 for children 12 years and under.
**Ages:** 6 years and up.

## MUSEUM OF TOLERANCE / SIMON WEISENTHAL CENTER ☼

(800) 900-9036 or (310) 553-8403 / www.wiesenthal.com            $$$
*9786 W. Pico Boulevard, Los Angeles*
(Exit San Diego Fwy [405] E. on Santa Monica Blvd., R. on Glen Blvd., L. on Pico.)

The Simon Wiesenthal Center's Beit Hashoah Museum of Tolerance is unique in its format of numerous technologically advanced, interactive major exhibits, and in its focus on personal prejudice, group intolerance, the struggle for civil rights in America, and the Holocaust. After orientation, enter through the door marked Prejudiced or the one marked Unprejudiced to begin your journey in the American Experience/Tolerancenter. A computer exhibit of the L.A. riots asks visitors for a personal profile - age, gender, ethnicity - then asks thought-provoking questions about social justice and responsibility. In a mock 50's diner visitors use a monitor to answer questions about personal

responsibility regarding drinking, drugs, etc. A replicated courtroom, called
Crime and Punishment, allows students to serve on juries that examine global
crimes. You'll also be riveted and affected by the sixteen-screen video Civil
Rights Wall, an interactive U.S. map that discloses 250 hate groups in America,
an intense movie called *Genocide*, and a short walk through the Whisper Gallery.
Voices in here whisper racial slurs and derogatory remarks, and then encourage
you to think twice about the words you use.

The Holocaust "tour" begins as you print out a child's passport. You then
witness a series of chronological vignettes, while listening to narration that
explains the events leading up to the Holocaust. This factual and emotional forty-
five-minute tour is one of the most informative and visual ways to begin to
understand what happened. After walking through a replica of the gates of
Auschwitz, your tour culminates in the Hall of Testimony, where you'll discover
the fate of the child whose passport you hold.

The second floor of the museum contains a multimedia learning center with
over thirty work stations. Numerous films - on Anne Frank, Harriet Tubman,
Helen Keller, etc. - are available for viewing. Also housed here are original
letters of Anne Frank, a bunkbed from a concentration camp, and medical
instruments. Holocaust survivors speak here several times throughout the day.
The third floor displays rotating exhibits. Call for a current schedule. The fourth
floor has a cafeteria. Note: Cameras are not allowed in the museum.

On alternating Sundays at 2pm, a one-hour musical and/or interactive play is
presented for children 5 years and up. This is a lighter version of the museum's
focus of encouraging kids to think about how they treat their friends, and other
people. Admission to the show is $6 for adults; $4 for ages 5 to 12.

**Hours:**        Open Mon. - Thurs., 10am - 4pm; Fri., 10am - 3pm; Sun.,
                  10:30am - 5pm. Closed Sat., Thanksgiving, Christmas, and
                  Jewish holidays.

**Admission:**    $8 for adults; $6 for seniors; $5 for students with ID; $3 for
                  children 3 - 10 years. Free validated underground parking is
                  available on Pico Blvd.

**Ages:**         10 years and up - it is too intense for most younger children.

# MY JEWISH DISCOVERY PLACE

(323) 857-0072 / e-mail:museum@mjdp.org
*5870 W. Olympic Boulevard, West Los Angeles*
(Exit Santa Monica Fwy [10] N. on Fairfax Ave., R. on Olympic. It's in the Westside
Jewish Community Center. Parking is available in the structure behind the Center, on
Olympic Blvd., and on San Vicente.)

Shalom and welcome to this colorful, completely hands-on museum,
developed for kids to have fun while learning about Jewish history, customs,
values, holidays, folklore, traditions, heros, and music, as well as Shabbat, Israel,
and the Hebrew language. Oy!

Some of the exhibits and things to do include boarding the Discovery
Airplane, that has real cockpit controls, to watch a video of a flight to Israel; 3-2-
1 Blast Off, a room with glow-in-the-dark stars, where black light is used to

illuminate symbol puzzles (and white clothing) and the touch and feel objects in the discovery box; an activity center for arts and crafts; an Improv Theater, which is a stage and costume center; a seven-foot by sixteen-foot Torah; a miniature model synagogue; a Hebrew letters rubbing table; and lots of changing exhibits in playhouse-size rooms. Some of the exhibits have included You and Me and Discovery, a room to learn about people with special needs. The room contained a braille typewriter, a wheel chair, several pairs of glasses, a vibrating bed (an alarm clock for people who are deaf), and wall posters of sign language. Where We Grew Up, an area representing early L.A., included a small diner with play food (bagels, etc.), as well as hats, pictures of local politicians and athletes, and a little market with more food, a cash register, etc. Family Trees provided tools to make a family tree - on the computer, on paper, and even on a quilt piece. It also had story books and maps.

**Hours:**     Open Tues - Thurs., 12:30pm - 4pm; Sun., 12:30pm - 5pm.
              Closed for national holidays and Jewish holidays.
**Admission:** $3 for adults; $2 for ages 2 - 7; children under 2 year are free.
**Ages:**      2 - 12 years.

## NATIONAL HOT ROD ASSOCIATION MOTORSPORTS ☼ MUSEUM

(909) 622-2133                                                                  *$$*
*1101 W. McKinley Avenue, Pomona*
(Exit San Bernardino Fwy [10] on Fairplex, R. on McKinley. It's adjacent to Pomona Raceway.)

To see some really hot wheels, visit this stylish hot rod museum that showcases over sixty, very cool cars in mint condition. The cars chronicle the colorful history of drag racing, from its days as an illegal street activity to its current status as a major spectator event. Some of the legendary cars on display include Kenny Bernstein's 1992 Budweiser King Top Fuel Dragster, the first car to break the 300mph barrier in NHRA competition; Warren Johnson's 1997 GM Goodwrench Pontiac Firebird, the first Pro Stock machine to break the 200 mph barrier; "Big Daddy" Don Garlits' 1971 Swamp Rat 14, the first successful rear-engine dragster; and the "Bean Bandit" dragster from the early 1950s; plus Indy roadsters, midgets, and much more. With all of this inspiration, what kid (or man) wouldn't dream of being behind the wheel of any one of these cars and racing towards the finish line?!

Glass cases that run almost the length of the museum contain trophies, photographs, helmets, driving uniforms, etc. Murals and paintings decorate the other walls. Don't be a drag; race to this museum.

**Hours:**     Open Wed. - Sun. from 10am - 5pm.
**Admission:** $5 for adults; $3 for ages 6 - 15; children 5 years and under are free.
**Ages:**      3 years and up.

# NATURAL HISTORY MUSEUM OF LOS ANGELES COUNTY  ☼

(213) 763-3466 / www.nhm.org.                                                *$$$*
*900 Exposition Boulevard, Los Angeles*
(Exit the Harbor Fwy [110] W. on Exposition Blvd., L. on Flower, L. on Figueroa. Or, exit Santa Monica Fwy [10] S. on Vermont, L. on Exposition, R. on Figueroa. Metered parking is available on the street across from U.S.C., or park in the lot on Menlo Blvd.)

This museum has a lot of a little bit of everything. Four long halls show North American, African, and exotic mammals mounted in a backdrop of their natural habitat (i.e. huge dioramas). The gigantic walrus, buffalo, and elephant are the most impressive. Take a walk through time in the American history rooms. They contain early vehicles, such as tractors, stagecoaches, and a streetcar; mannequins dressed in period clothing; early weapons; and other pioneer artifacts. An adjacent, outstanding rock and mineral collection includes fluorescent minerals (that shine neon colors under black light), and rocks that are so brilliant in color or so oddly shaped that they look unreal. Some of our favorite exhibits at the museum are the dinosaurs in the Din-O-Scovery room. On display, in life-like poses, are some of the massive animals in skeletal form, while others are fleshed out, so to speak. Other exhibits on this floor include a real mummy; a preserved, unusually long, and flat-looking fish - the oarfish; a Megamouth shark; and a room devoted to pre-Columbian archaeology.

The second floor has an entire wing devoted to our fine feathered friends. There are taxidermied penguins, vultures, ostriches, ducks, turquoise cotingas (guess what color they are?), and more. Pull out the drawers of the cabinets in the hallway to see a variety of feathers and bird eggs. A large part of the ornithology (study of birds) exhibit is interactive. Turn a disk to get a magnified view of wings, feathers, and bones. Step on a scale to see how much just your bones weigh - they make up 17% of your body weight. Exit through a dark rain forest that resounds with bird noises. Another room upstairs presents an in-depth look at marine life via murals, mounted animals, and information.

"Hands-on" is the motto at the wonderful Discovery Center. This includes putting on puppet shows; making rubbings from fossilized shells (you'll take home a lot of these papers); playing on computers; going for a fossil dig at the small sandpit; and touching rocks, shells, bones, and skulls of an alligator and polar bear. Kids can also touch (or wrap themselves in) skins of deer, fox, skunk, opossum, sheep, etc. There are live animals in here, too, such as iguanas, toads, a python (he gets fed once a week), and fish. Forty different Discovery Boxes offer different activities with varying degrees of difficulty. "Sharks" simply has shark teeth and fossil vertebrae to look at and study, plus books on sharks to read. "Native Games" gives directions and materials to play with walnut shells, dice, Indian darts, etc. "Listen Up" is a game where the same objects that are in clear jars are also in black jars. Shake them, listen, and then match the sounds and the jars.

Just up the stairs is the Insect Zoo, which has cases swarming with live insects! Show no fear (or disgust) in front of your kids - some of the little buggers are quite interesting. You'll see scorpions, millipedes, tarantulas, beetles, and more (than you've ever wanted!).

The museum also features wonderful rotating exhibits, usually downstairs. "Cats, Mild to Wild," featured house cats to lions in dramatic pictures, interactive animated figures, etc. Call to see what is currently showing. Also, ask about the museum's numerous, in depth field trips, for various age groups, as well as their special events held on site.

Picnic tables and lots of grassy areas surround the museum. Also see the nearby AEROSPACE MUSEUM, CALIFORNIA AFRO-AMERICAN MUSEUM, CALIFORNIA SCIENCE CENTER, EXPOSITION PARK, LOS ANGELES MEMORIAL COLISEUM, and 3D IMAX THEATER. (Look up the attractions listed individually under the Alphabetical Index.)

**Hours:** Open Mon. - Fri., 9:30am - 5pm; Sat. - Sun., 10am - 5pm. Closed New Year's Day, Thanksgiving, and Christmas.

**Admission:** $6 for adults; $3.50 for seniors and students; $2 for ages 5 - 12; children 4 years and under are free. (Certain discounts are available through AAA.) Special exhibits raise the admission price a few dollars. The first Tues. of every month is free admission day. Parking in the lot costs $5. (See C.E.E. L.A. for membership savings, pg. 213.)

**Ages:** 2½ years and up.

## PASADENA HISTORICAL MUSEUM / FEYES ☼ MANSION

(626) 577-1660                                                        $

*470 West Walnut Street, Pasadena*

(Exit Foothill Fwy [210], near where it turns into Ventura Fwy [134], W. on West Walnut St., L. on N. Orange Grove Blvd., and turn L. into the first driveway past the mansion on the corner.)

Pasadena's stately heritage landmark mansion/museum showcases gracious living at the turn of the century. A one-hour guided tour allows visitors to see original memorabilia and furnishings which came from all over the world. Some of the highlights downstairs include several clocks, such as the grandfather clock in the foyer that has rotating, colored-glass slides of early Pasadena; old-fashioned utensils in the kitchen (my boys needed an explanation about the rug beater); china in the butler's pantry; numerous volumes of books in the hallway and office; the solarium; fine, wooden tables and chairs; and chests in the living room and studio ornately finished with tortoise shell, ivory, and mother-of-pearl. The stories about the artifacts are intriguing, especially the legend of flying carpets, which is thought to come from prayer rugs supposedly endowed with magical powers. A prayer rug is located in the studio.

The elegantly-decorated master bedroom and a child's bedroom are upstairs. So are a few bathrooms, which always appeal to kids.

A few small rooms adjacent to the lower level gift shop hold old tools, a piano, an old bike with one large front wheel, a collection of old cameras, and several military uniforms. The grounds are beautifully landscaped and steps lead down to the research library and the Finnish Folk Art Museum, just next door. Pasadena is a city with rich cultural history that is well represented by this mansion/museum.

**Hours:** Open Thurs. - Sun., 1pm - 4pm. Tours are given every hour on the hour.

**Admission:** $4 for adults; $3 for seniors; free for children 12 years and under.

**Ages:** 6 years and up.

## PETERSEN AUTOMOTIVE MUSEUM

(323) 930-CARS (2277) / www.petersen.org/petersen

*6060 Wilshire Boulevard, Los Angeles*

(Exit Santa Monica Fwy [10] N. on Fairfax, R. on Wilshire.)

*$$$*

The driving force behind this 300,000 square foot, state-of-the-art museum is dedication to the art, culture, and history of the automobile. Streetscape, on the first floor, takes you on a chronological walk through time via cars, from horse and buggy, vintage automobiles, and an exhibit of gas pumps, to prototypes, solar-powered, and other, futuristic-type cars. Each car is displayed in its own walk-through setting, complete with asphalt, manholes, sidewalks, fake plants - whatever surroundings fit the car - as well as mannequins dressed in period outfits. Sounds, like birds chirping where a Model T is "Stuck in the Mud," help children enter into the spirit of the lifestyles represented here. Kids can climb aboard the trolley car used in old Laurel and Hardy movies, although other cars on this floor are not hands-on.

The second floor has six galleries, including a terrific collection of hot rods, roadsters, race cars, and classics in prime condition. A glitzy Hollywood Gallery stars cars that were featured in movies and television shows, and/or that were owned by celebrities. Biking enthusiasts will appreciate the adjacent Otis Chandler Motorcycle Gallery. However, the ultimate in kid-cool is putting on a helmet and getting behind the wheel of a real Indianapolis 500 race car!

The third floor, the Discovery Center, will really get kids revved up with its 6,500 square feet of motor vehicle interaction! They can ride on a real Highway Patrol car, complete with sirens blaring and flashing lights. Have your children dress up in a motoring duster, cap, and scarves and "drive" a Model T. A Sparklett's water truck contains plastic jugs filled with a variety of games, puzzles, costumes, and construction toys all pertaining to the car motif. A play area is set up for toddlers to race mini-cars around on tracks and play mats. Older kids can get behind the wheel of a virtual reality simulator called Driver's Ed. (Now I know why they don't allow 11 year olds to have a license!) Another large room is for the mechanically minded. It has a giant dashboard, which visitors can manipulate; a display that traces the route an engine takes to come to life, from ignition to the voltage regulator; and other learning stations that allow kids to push, pull, steer, or observe different facets of how a car actually works. Our favorite exhibit is Power of the People. This car seat, on huge wheels, can actually be moved across the room when you (and some strong-legged friends) push down on oversized pistons that pop up at regular intervals. (Fun, but tiring.) Take a pencil Treasure Hunt, sign up for a Kids' Pit Crew class, and/or ask about the other special activities and classes Petersen offers for kids. Know that a visit here will definitely accelerate your child's interest in cars!

**Hours:** Open Tues. - Sun. from 10am - 6pm. The Discovery Center closes at 5pm.

**Admission:** $7 for adults; $5 for seniors and students with ID; $3 for ages 5 - 12; children 4 years and under are free. Enter the museum parking structure from Fairfax - $4 for all-day parking. (See C.E.E. L.A. for membership savings, pg. 213.)

**Ages:** 5 years and up.

# POINT VINCENTE INTERPRETIVE CENTER AND ☼
# PARK

(310) 377-5370                                                                    $

*31501 Palos Verdes Drive W., Rancho Palos Verdes*

(From Pacific Coast Highway [1] in Redondo Beach, turn S. on Palos Verdes Dr. W. and drive the winding coastal road just past Hawthorne Blvd. Turn R. into the park. Or, exit Harbor Fwy [110] W. on Anaheim, L. on Palos Verdes Dr. N., L. on Crenshaw to end, L. on Hawthorne to end, L. on Palos Verdes Dr. W. Or, exit San Diego Fwy [405] S. on Crenshaw, go to the end, L. on Hawthorne to end, L. on Palos Verdes Dr. W.)

This small museum has a variety of natural wonders on display, such as fossils of ocean animals, a side-by-side comparison of fossilized shells with recent shells of the same type, and taxidermied animals such as the great horned owl, a gray fox, and a peacock.

Whales are the main focus here as this is a prime site for whale watching. The museum has an overhead model of a gray whale, a continuously running video on whales, and a telephone so kids can literally listen to the call of the whales. There is a small enclosed area upstairs and an outside area that are good spots to either watch the whales as they migrate, January through March, or just to see a terrific view of the coastline. The Point Vincente Lighthouse is close by and on foggy days, you'll hear the horn blast its warning signal.

A quarter-mile paved trail winds around the Interpretive Center and the few picnic tables that are here. If your family is in a hiking or biking mood, there is a three-mile, or so, narrow dirt trail leading from the Center and looping back around. This main pathway and its offshoots are alternately flat and hilly, so be prepared for some real exercise! Have a whale of a time at this small museum and at the park.

**Hours:** The Center is open daily in the summer from 10am - dusk. It's open daily the rest of the year from 10am - 4:30pm. Closed New Year's Day, Thanksgiving, Christmas Eve, and Christmas Day. The park is open daily from dawn to dusk.

**Admission:** The museum entrance fee is $2 for adults; $1 for seniors and ages 4 - 14; children 3 years and under are free. There is no admission for the surrounding park and trails.

**Ages:** 2½ years and up.

# QUEEN MARY

(562) 435-3511 / www.queenmary.com                                    $$$$

*Pier J, Long Beach*

(Take Long Beach Fwy [710] S. to the end, R. on Queen's Way Bridge and follow signs.)
      Cruise over to Long Beach Harbor to see the Queen, Queen Mary I mean -
one of the largest luxury passenger liners ever built. Take a one-hour guided
Behind-the-Scenes tour and learn about the ship's fascinating history. Only on
this tour can you see the dining room/ballroom, boiler room, and an original first
class suite. Younger children, however, will get antsy. We thoroughly enjoyed
our self-guided Shipwalk tour. Starting on the lower decks, we watched a video
called, *The Queen Mary Story* about its construction, maiden voyage, and service
during WWII. The Hall of Maritime Heritage, a small museum, displays
navigating instruments, ship models, and pictures and stories of famous doomed
ships, including the Titanic. Everything in the engine room is clearly marked,
making it easy to explain the machinery's function to youngsters. The last
remaining propeller on the ship is in an open-top, propellor box in water. It looks
like a shark fin at first; and tell your kids that the life-size diver is just a model.
We toured the bridge, the wheel house where officers were quartered, and the
state room exhibits. A highlight for my boys was playing on the gun turrets on
the bow of the ship, as they fought off invisible enemies.
      The wooden upper decks are great for ~~running~~ strolling around. Note: As an
older ship, there are many narrow staircases, but not many ramps on board.
Elevators enable those using strollers or wheelchairs to get from deck to deck.
      Queen Mary's Seaport, adjacent to the ship's berth, has the Queen's
Marketplace for your shopping and dining pleasures. There are also several fine
shops and restaurants on the ship, that run the gamut from very elegant and
expensive to family-style and family priced. Tip #1: For a ~~cheap~~ inexpensive
family date, come on board after 6pm (during the school year) when there isn't
an admission charge, only a parking fee. Although the stores and many parts of
the ship are not open then, some restaurants are open, it's fun for kids to walk
around, and the sunsets are beautiful. Don't miss the ship! Tip #2: Watch the
fireworks on board the Queen Mary on Saturday nights at 9pm during the
summer. (Or, watch them for free from a nearby vista point.) Tip #3: Remember,
that you can sleep on board the Queen Mary, as it functions as a floating hotel,
too. See SCORPION, under this section, and LONG BEACH AQUARIUM OF
THE PACIFIC, under the Zoos and Animals section, for information on these
nearby attractions.
      **Hours:**   Open daily from 9am - 9pm in the summer. Open the rest of the
             year daily 10am - 6pm.

**Admission:**   General admission is $13 for adults; $11 for seniors; $8 for ages 4 - 11; children 3 years and under are free. General admission plus the behind-the-scenes guided tour, is $20 for adults; $16 for seniors; $12 for children ages 4 - 11 years; children 3 years and under are free. (Ask about AAA discounts.) Parking is $3 for the first half hour; $6 for all day. Beat parking prices by catching the free Passport shuttle that runs from downtown Long Beach to the Queen Mary.

**Ages:**   3 years and up.

## RANCHO LOS ALAMITOS                                            ☼
(562) 431-3541                                                    !
*6400 E. Bixby Hill Road, Long Beach*
(Exit San Diego Fwy [405] S. on Palo Verde Ave. to the end. Go through the gated entrance [tell the gate employee you are going to the museum], L. on Bixby Hill.)

This beautiful, historic ranch appeals to kids of all ages. The barn has several horse stalls, a few of which have been converted into small rooms, or self-contained history lessons. They display photographs, animal pelts, branding irons, and (our favorite) a suspended horse harness, showing how a horse was hooked up to help plow. Other buildings of particular interest, in this area, contain a blacksmith shop filled with old tools, and a room with lots of saddles and branding irons. A ranch is not complete without animals, so goats, sheep, chickens, ducks, and Shire horses are in outside pens.

An hour-long tour includes going inside the adobe ranch house. It's always fun to try to guess the name and use of gadgets in old kitchens. The bedroom, library, music, and billiards rooms are interesting to older children.

The front of the house has a garden and two, 150-year-old Moreton Bay fig trees with huge roots. An Artifacts Room is open at certain times so kids can touch - that's right - artifacts! Ask about the rancho's terrific school tours.

**Hours:**   Open Wed. - Sun. from 1pm - 5pm. Tours are offered on the half hour. School tours are given at various times throughout the week. Call to make reservations. The rancho is closed on holidays.

**Admission:**   Free; donations appreciated.

**Ages:**   3 years and up for the outside grounds; 6 years and up for a tour of the house.

## RANCHO LOS CERRITOS                                            ☼
(562) 570-1755                                                    !
*4600 Virginia Road, Long Beach*
(Exit San Diego Fwy [405] N. on Long Beach Blvd., L. on Roosevelt, then make a quick R. on Virginia Rd.)

This picturesque historic rancho is situated almost at the end of Virginia Road. The visitors center has a clever exhibit of big puzzle pieces representing different eras with pictures and information on them, that attempt to fit together

pieces of our past. The information is interesting and some of the window-type
"pieces" offer glimpses into the past by displaying old pottery, equipment, and
other artifacts.

The perimeter gardens are beautifully landscaped around a grassy center
area. There is also a huge old Moreton Bay fig tree with tremendous roots. A
one-hour tour takes you through the house which is furnished as it was in the late
1870's. This is a terrific way to see and learn about our Mexican-California
heritage. Kids can more easily relate to the bigger picture of state history when
they explore a small part of it.

School group tours include hands-on fun, such as candle-dipping and
playing old-fashioned games. They also have the opportunity to do chores, such
as butter churning and washing clothes, the way they were done years ago. The
tour might also include seeing a blacksmith's demonstration.

Ask for a Kids' Activity Treasure Hunt, where young visitors use pencil and
paper as they look for particular items throughout the museum - it makes a visit
here that much more interesting. Bring a sack lunch as there are picnic tables on
the grounds. Ask for a schedule of the Rancho's special family events - they are
great. (See Mud Mania in the August Calendar section.)

**Hours:** Open Wed. - Sun. from 1pm - 5pm. Guided tours are given on
the weekends only on the hour. School tours are given on Wed.
and Thurs., from 9:30am - noon.

**Admission:** Free; donations appreciated.

**Ages:** 7 years and up.

# RAYMOND M. ALF MUSEUM  ☀
(909) 624-2798 / mail.lightside.com/~webb/Alf/AlfHome.html  $
*1175 W. Baseline Road, Claremont*
(Exit the San Bernardino Fwy [10] N. on Towne Ave., L. on Baseline Rd., R. up the hill. It
is part of the Webb Schools.)

Make no bones about it, this unique museum displays dinosaur skeletons
and skulls, plus fossils and archaeological finds from all over the world. As you
enter this circular museum you'll see Footprints in the Sands of Time, an
unusually large rock slab containing numerous reptile footprints that is
reportedly 250 million years old. Kids can try the Indian stone mortar and
pestles, once used for grinding meal. Next to the display on Egyptology is a skull
cast of a Purussaurus, an animal with jaws that are almost as big as the upper part
of my body. The touch table has mastodon tusks, vertebrae, rocks, and a
fossilized turtle shell, which is surprisingly heavy.

Head toward the hallway to see quite a display of stuffed animal heads,
including buffalo, mountain lions, and lots of members of the deer family. The
exhibits downstairs consist mainly of trackways, which are rock slabs with
castings of dinosaur, camel, horse, and bear-dog footprints. The trackways are
displayed on the walls, and around the room, under glass-encased coffee tables
(albeit, priceless ones).

Good-sized rock and mineral specimens, like geodes and petrified wood, abound, as do fossils such as mammoth molars, and fern imbedded in rock. Have your kids look at the rocks on the table near the exit and take the "test" - do they know which is a fossil and which is a mineral?

This museum is great for older kids who are interested in paleontology, or for younger ones to just see the sheer size of some of the animals from long ago. Month-long research expeditions, which combine fossil collecting and camping, are available for high school students during the summer.

**Hours:** The museum is open Mon. - Thurs., 8am - noon and again from 1pm - 4pm. It is also open the first Sun. of each month from 1pm - 4pm. Closed major holidays.

**Admission:** $1 for ages 5 and up. Addmission is free every Wed.

**Ages:** 4 years and up.

## RIPLEY'S BELIEVE IT OR NOT! MUSEUM (Hollywood) ☼
(323) 466-6335                                                                         $$$
*6780 Hollywood Boulevard, Hollywood*
(Exit Hollywood Fwy [101] W. on Hollywood Blvd.)

See the description under RIPLEY'S BELIEVE IT OR NOT! MUSEUM (Buena Park). This museum displays nearly 300 unusual and amazing items and facts collected from around the world.

A few doors down is Mann's Chinese Theater, where many past and present stars have left their imprints in the concrete courtyard in front of the theater. See if your child can fill his favorite star's shoes!

**Hours:** Open Sun. - Thurs., 10am - 10pm; Fri. - Sat., 10am - 11pm.

**Admission:** $8.95 for adults; $7.95 for seniors; $5.95 for ages 5 - 12; children 4 years and under are free. Certain discounts are available through AAA.

**Ages:** 5 years and up.

## SCORPION                                                                            ☀
(562) 435-3511 / www.queenmary.com                                                     $$$$
*1126 Queens Highway, Long Beach*
(Take Long Beach Fwy [710] S. to the end, R. on Queen's Way Bridge and follow the signs to the Queen Mary, as it is docked adjacent to the famous ship.)

Do your kids like to play spy? The 300-foot-long Scorpion, technically known as the Povodnaya Lodka B-427, is a Soviet-built, Foxtrot-class submarine that is docked here for five years. In service for twenty-two years, it was once equipped with low-yield nuclear torpedoes. (That information alone makes it interesting to kids.) It was assigned mainly to gather intelligence on Allied naval activities. Now a tourist attraction, the Scorpion triggers spy game ideas, at least with my kids, as well as being a vessel of education and intrigue. Note: You may view the submarine, topside, without going on a tour.

Before you board, go into a holding room that contains labeled artifacts from the sub, such as an emergency escapes suit, flags, pressure gauges, manuals in Russian, etc. Get your feet wet, so to speak, by watching a thirteen-minute re-enactment video on the history of the submarine and its "warriors beneath the waves."

Your actual tour inside the Scorpion is self-guiding, with a Russian-accented narration piped into each compartment. Begin by going down a narrow staircase to the forward torpedo room. The room contains six torpedo tubes and replicas of the warheads once loaded inside them. Then, think thin and squeeze through several porthole-style hatches, walk down narrow hallways, and look into (through glass-covered doorways) very small sleeping quarters, a control room, a dining room, the galley, and various other rooms. The tour has its own momentum as there is not a lot of room for the people behind you to pass. Visitors can peer through a periscope to the outside world, push the numerous buttons, and turn the wheels on board. My boys would have liked to stay down here for hours. Down another staircase is the engine room filled with gadgets that helped churn the water to power the sub. The last stop on your tour is the aft torpedo room which held four torpedoes. It is a relatively short tour for your money, but it is historic and fascinating.

Note that strollers aren't allowed on the Scorpion, nor may you carry children on the tour. If you get claustrophobic, this isn't the place to be. Ladies, stepping through hatch openings and down narrow ladders doesn't lend itself to wearing dresses or heels.

See ENDANGERED SPECIES ECOPARK, LONG BEACH AQUARIUM OF THE PACIFIC, QUEEN MARY, and SHORELINE VILLAGE under the Alphabetical Index for attractions in the immediate vicinity.

**Hours:** Open daily 9am - 9pm.

**Admission:** $10 for adults; $9 for seniors, military personnel, and ages 4 - 11 years; children 3 years and under are free. Parking is $3 for the first half hour, then it jumps to $6 for the day. Take a free Passport shuttle from downtown Long Beach to save on parking fees.

**Ages:** 4 years and up.

## SHERIFFS TRAINING AND REGIONAL SERVICES (STARS) CENTER

(562) 946-7081

*11515 South Colima Road, Whittier*

(Going N. on Santa Ana Fwy [5], exit N. on Carmenita Rd., R. on Leffingwell, L. on Colima. Going S. on 5, exit E. on Imperial Hwy., L. on Colima.)

This 5,000 square foot museum depicts the history of the Los Angeles County Sheriffs Department from 1850 through the present day. A classic 1938 Studebaker police car can not be touched, but kids can "ride" on the police motorcycle and push a button to make the red lights flash. (I hope this won't bring back any bad memories!)

A westernized room has a replica of a nineteenth-century sheriff's office, complete with a model sheriff and a prisoner behind bars. The Vice Exhibit showcases how different carnival-type games can be rip-offs, as well as illegal.

The back room, which can be bypassed, contains a gun case, a display of gang weapons, and graphic scenes of some infamous cases.

Another room contains an entire helicopter. It also has the side of a Search and Rescue helicopter mounted on a wall, with a dangling child mannequin that's being air-lifted in a basket. The live-video footage shows the awesome job that Search and Rescue teams perform.

Outside, a wall too filled with plaques memorializes officers killed in the line of duty. For your information: Every May a memorial ceremony is held here that commemorates the lives of peace officers who have died in the line of duty in L.A. County in the past year. This moving ceremony, attended by numerous officers, families of slain officers, and government officials, is also open to the public.

**Hours:** Open Mon. - Fri. from 9am - 4pm. Closed on major holidays.
**Admission:** Free
**Ages:** 5 years and up.

# SKIRBALL CULTURAL CENTER                              ☼

(310) 440-4500 / www.skirball.com                        *$$*
*2701 N. Sepulveda Boulevard, Los Angeles*
(Exit San Diego Fwy [405] on Skirball Center Dr.)

This Cultural Center tells the story of the Jewish people, from post-biblical days and journeys, to present day life in America. The exhibits of Jewish heritage include ancient and modern artifacts, photographs, Art, film, and video screenings all housed in a building beautifully designed with archways and high-ceilings. The variety of the unique Torah mantles and Hanukkah lamps on display is outstanding. One of our favorites is the menorah with each of its eight branches fashioned like the Statute of Liberty.

The Coming to America room features a reproduction of the hand and torch of the Statue of Liberty at seventy percent of full scale. It's huge! This room also contains documents from past United States Presidents that supported non-discrimination. The Lincoln display has a lifemask of his face (i.e. a mold of his actual face), which is one of only six ever made.

In the Discovery Center, geared for ages 8 and up, kids can uncover the wonders of the archaeological world. Upstairs is a re-creation of a dig site, a hands-on tool area, and a great computer game called "Dig It." The stairway is lined with lamps behind glass displays. The downstairs has a reproduction of a tomb in a rock; displays that show the new condition of an animal or object, and then its remains after years have gone by; and over twenty "discovery" game boxes containing great activities that reinforce the concepts presented. Kids can also learn about the history of writing and try different forms of it at the rubbing table. Students on school tours will gain a tremendous amount of insight into the archaeological world as docents teach and guide them through the Discovery Center. They'll also go outside where they can excavate roads, walls, an alter, etc., at a small mock dig site.

As you enter and exit the Skirball Center you'll see, etched in stone, words

fit for everyone - "Go forth . . . and be a blessing to the world." (Genesis 12: 1 -
3)

**Hours:**      Open Tues. - Sun., noon - 5pm. Closed Mon.
**Admission:**  $8 for adults; $6 for seniors and students; children 11 years and
            under are free.
**Ages:**       7 years and up.

## SOUTHWEST MUSEUM                                                 ☼

(323) 221-2164 / www.southwestmuseum.org                            *$$*
*234 Museum Drive, Highland Park*
(Exit Pasadena Fwy [110] N.E. on Avenue 43, R. on Figueroa St., L. on Ave. 45, R. on
Marmion Way, L. on Museum Dr.)

There are three ways to enter this museum on a hill: One is an
unadventurous walk up the driveway; another is walking up the steep Hopi trail,
which is a stone stairway. Catch your breath at the top, and take a look at the
view of the city and beyond. The third is walking (running) through a 250-foot
tunnel - which echos every footstep and shout - burrowed into the museum
hillside. It's lined with twenty Indian dioramas. From here, take the elevator up
into the museum.

The Southwest Museum collection represents Native American cultures
from Alaska to South America. The two-story building has displays of Indian
clothing, some of which are decorated with elk's teeth or bone; costumes; boots;
beautifully beaded moccasins; an extensive collection of baskets; rabbit-skin
blankets; weapons; turquoise and silver craft jewelry; early baby snugglies
(cradleboards); musical instruments such as a flute, drum, and rattle; and
Kachina dolls, which are supposedly rain-bringing spiritual beings. The exhibits
are mostly behind glass.

A rotating exhibit room had, for example, Spirit Horses, the entrance of
which was a simulated cave, with horses painted on its walls. The room itself,
which doubles as a (small) auditorium, had statues of horses, paintings of horses,
a mural of horses, beautiful saddles, etc. *Neigh* doubt about it, this room
embodied the American Indian legend that the horse is a spiritual gift of the
gods.

Another room has an eighteen-foot Cheyenne tepee (just to look at), and a
big rock with reproduced pictographs. Kids can crawl through a doorway (think
dog door) that has photographs on the other side. Also on display in this room
are headbands, arrowheads, bows, and rattles made of cocoons and rattlesnakes.
Outside, an archeological dig site is a bit further up the hill. A small botanical
garden is in the front of the museum.

How do you learn more about Native Americans? An extensive research
library on the museum grounds is open to the public Wednesday through
Saturday, from 1pm to 5pm. If you're looking for a place to picnic, just drive
north on Figueroa Street to Highland Park. Check out LOS ANGELES
COUNTY MUSEUM OF ART, under this section, which has a satellite building
of the Southwest.

**Hours:** Open Tues. - Sun. from 10am - 5pm. Closed major holidays.
**Admission:** $5 for adults; $3 for seniors and students; $2 for ages 7 - 17; children 6 years and under are free.
**Ages:** 5 years and up.

## S. S. LANE VICTORY

(310) 519-9545 / www.lanevictoryship.com

*Berth 94, San Pedro*

(Exit Harbor Fwy [110] or Vincent Thomas Bridge on Harbor Blvd. Cross Harbor Blvd. onto Swinford St. and follow signs to Berth 94.)

This forty-five-year-old ship served as a cargo ship during World War II, the Korean War, and the Vietnam War. The large Victory ship is not only seaworthy, but it is also a museum, with one-hour tours given by retired merchant marines. We sensed adventure, though, and decided to explore the ship unaccompanied.

You and your kids will get ship-shape by climbing up and down ladders from the bridge and crew's quarters to the radio room, and into the huge engine room. The multi-level engine room is a bit spooky, with the noises and bulky machinery, but this added to the excitement of being on our own.

Guns and superstructures make the decks interesting to investigate. (Tell your kids that they are on a poop deck - it will make your outing a big hit!) Below deck, the ship's museum room features memorabilia such as flags, whistles, photographs, and cannons. The Gift Shoppe sells wonderful nautical items from clothing to medals to model ship kits. Batten down the hatches and be sure to wear tennis shoes for your ship-to-shore adventure.

A few times a year the S.S. Lane Victory hosts an all-day cruise to Catalina where a "Nazi spy" is discovered on board. Nazi fighters are soon attacking the ship, but American aircraft come to the rescue. The mock aerial dogfight uses blanks, but the World War II planes are real. This is more exciting than any Hollywood movie! The cruise also includes continental breakfast, live music, and a buffet luncheon. The cost is $100 for adults; $60 for kids 15 years and under.

**Hours:** Open daily from 9am - 4pm.
**Admission:** $3 for adults; $1 for ages 5 - 15; children 4 years and under are free. Parking is free for the first two hours.
**Ages:** 5 years and up.

## TOURNAMENT HOUSE / THE WRIGLEY GARDENS

(626) 449-4100 / www.tournamentofroses.com

*391 S. Orange Grove Boulevard, Pasadena*

(Take Pasadena Fwy [110] N. to the end, where it turns into Arroyo Pky., L. on California, R. on Orange Grove. Going W. on Foothill Fwy [210], exit S. on Fair Oaks, R. on Colorado, L. on Orange Grove. Going E. on 134, exit E. on Colorado, R. on Orange Grove.)

The Tournament House, more aptly referred to as a mansion, is used throughout the year as the meeting headquarters for committees, float sponsors, and practically everything else associated with the annual Tournament of Roses

Parade. Once owned by Wrigley, of the chewing gum fame, each room is simply, but elegantly furnished. The downstairs contains a spacious living room, a library, meeting rooms, and the Eisenhower bathroom - so named because when he was Grand Marshall, he got stuck in here and no one knew where he was (even the Secret Service agents).

The second floor is interesting to kids who have some knowledge and interest in the Rose parade and Rose Bowl games. Each former bedroom is dedicated to various elements of Tournament of Roses' traditions. The Rose Bowl Room showcases pennants and football helmets from Rose Bowl teams, plus photographs, trophies, and other memorabilia dating back to the first game in 1902. The Queen and Court Room is femininely decorated to allow the reigning Queen and her Court, who attend over 100 events a year, a place to recuperate. A display case in here features past winners' crowns, tiaras, and jewelry. The Grand Marshall's Room shows photographs of past Grand Marshals like Bob Hope, Shirley Temple Black (do your kids know who she is?), Hank Aaron, Walt Disney, Charles Schultz, etc. Out in the hallway is an impressive 240-pound sterling silver saddle - heigh ho, Silver, away! The President's Room has pictures and other mementos of past presidents of the Rose Parade, plus models of the current years winning floats. You are also invited to watch an interesting fifteen-minute behind-the-scenes film on how the floats and parade are put together.

The beautifully-landscaped grounds have a fountain surrounded by one of the rose gardens. Another huge rose garden at the north end also blooms seasonally.

**Hours:**     Tours of the house are given February through August, on Thurs. from 2pm - 4pm. The grounds are open throughout the year except December 31 - January 2.

**Admission:**  Free

**Ages:**     7 years and up.

# TRAVEL TOWN

(213) 662-5874 / www.ci.la.ca.us/dept/RAP/grifmet/index.htm
*5200 Zoo Drive, Los Angeles*
(Going N. on Golden State Fwy [5] or W. on Ventura Fwy [134], exit at Zoo Dr. and follow the signs. Going E. on 134, exit at Forest Lawn Dr., L. on Zoo Dr. Going S. on 5, exit S. on Western, L. on Victory Blvd. to Zoo Dr. It's near the L. A. Zoo.)

"All aboarrrrrd!" This wonderful outdoor "town" has a "trainriffic" atmosphere. There are real boxcars, a few cabooses, and some steam locomotives to climb into (but not on top of). Grassy areas invite you to rest (one can always hope), play, and/or picnic. A scaled model train takes you for a ride around the small town - $1.75 for adults, $1 for seniors, $1.25 for kids 12 years and under.

Inside the buildings are old-fashioned carriages, wagons, period automobiles, and early fire-fighting equipment. It's tempting to touch the vehicles, but don't give in to temptation. Note: Live Steamers, located just west of Travel Town, offers free, twelve-minute rides through a part of Griffith Park on Sundays from 11am to 3pm.

For a listing of other things to do in this area see AUTRY MUSEUM OF
WESTERN HERITAGE, GRIFFITH PARK, GRIFFITH PARK
OBSERVATORY, and LOS ANGELES ZOO listed separately in the
Alphabetical Index.
    **Hours:**   Open April through October, Mon. - Fri., 10am - 5pm; Sat. -
              Sun. and holidays, 10am - 6pm. Open November through March,
              Mon. - Fri., 10am - 4pm; Sat. - Sun. and holidays 10am - 5pm.
              Closed Christmas.
  **Admission:**  Free; donations appreciated.
     **Ages:**  2 years and up.

## VISTA DEL LAGO VISITORS CENTER  ☼

(805) 294-0219                                                          !
*Vista de Lago, Gorman*
(Exit Golden State Fwy [5] on Vista del Lago. It is 20 miles north of Santa Clarita Valley
and 5 miles S. of Gorman.)

Overlooking Pyramid Lake is a hexagon-shaped building showcasing
California's liquid gold - water. This surprisingly interesting museum features
many educational and interactive exhibits that show the State Water Project's
water supply and delivery systems throughout California. Step on special scales
in the first room and find out how much of your body is comprised of water
(60%), and how much you actually weigh. Visual displays show the amount of
water needed daily to grow and process food, manufacture household items, do
laundry, etc. Video presentations and information panels point out that although
water is abundant in the north, most of the population is in the south, so we need
ways to transport it down. At the "Big Lift," visitors can turn a crank to lift up a
full bucket of water, which translates into learning how much energy it takes for
a pumping plant to lift water over the mountains. Learn how water is treated
before it is delivered to homes and how it is tested for quality. Thirsty yet? Go
with the flow by playing the computer games and using the touch screens in each
of the seven display rooms. The theater room shows several short films, ranging
from five to seventeen minutes, that show various aspects of water, for instance
*Water for Farming*, *Save Water*, and *A Visit to the Feather River Hatchery*.
Educators take note: Not only can the videos be rented, but there is a lot of
information given here on a field trip. Pamphlets, comic book-style booklets,
teacher's guides and lots more add to a guided tour of the facility.

The Visitors Center is a great place to quench your child's desire to learn
about irrigation, flood control, and water conservation. Tip: After your visit here,
enjoy the rest of the day at PYRAMID LAKE (look under the Great Outdoors
section), where you can boat, fish, swim, picnic, hike, and even camp.
    **Hours:**   Open daily 9am - 5pm. Closed New Year's Day, Thanksgiving,
              and Christmas.
  **Admission:**  Free
     **Ages:**  4 years and up.

## WELLS FARGO HISTORY MUSEUM

(213) 253-7166                                                                   $

*Wells Fargo Center, 333 S. Grand Avenue, Los Angeles*
(Exit Harbor Fwy [110] E. on 3rd St., R. on Grand.)

Discover the Old West in the middle of downtown Los Angeles. The history
and development of the West (and of Wells Fargo) is laid out like booty in this
museum. Highlights include an 100-year old stagecoach, which kids may not
climb on; a replica stagecoach, that they are welcome to climb in; a replica of an
1850's agent's office; a mining display with yes, real gold; a gold miner's
rocker; a telegraph machine to try out; photographs; and a twenty-minute film
that depicts the hardships of a journey taken in 1852 from St. Louis to San
Francisco. Buy a pan and some gold here so kids can try their hand at working a
claim in their own backyard!

    **Hours:**     Open Mon. - Fri. from 9am - 5pm. Closed bank holidays. Tours
                      are available with advanced reservations.
  **Admission:**   Free. Parking starts at $4 on Hope and 3rd Sts.
      **Ages:**     4 years and up.

## THE WESTERN HOTEL MUSEUM

(805) 723-6260                                                                   !

*557 W. Lancaster Boulevard, Lancaster*
(Going N. on Antelope Valley Fwy [14], exit N. on 20th St. West, R. on Ave J, L. on 10th
St., R. on Lancaster Blvd. Going S. on Antelope Valley Fwy [14], exit E. on Ave. J, L. on
10th St., R. on Lancaster Blvd.)

This small, quaint Western Hotel/Museum has been restored to look like it
did when it was originally built in the late 1800's, when room rentals were only
$1 a day. The downstairs has a few bedrooms and a parlor that contains old
furniture, a wheelchair, and a phonograph that belonged to the last owner,
Myrtie Webber. Kids are interested in hearing some of the stories about her, and
are impressed that she lived until she was 110 years old! (She doesn't look a day
over 70 in her photographs.)

Upstairs is a dinosaur/fossil/artifacts room; a life-size diorama of early
Antelope Valley residents and housing facilities, which translates as Native
Americans and their huts; a furnished office; and Myrtie's bedroom, which
displays some of her clothing and hats, along with her bedroom furniture. The
highlight for my boys was seeing the vivid black-and-white pictures of jack
rabbit hunts. The rabbits were hunted, corralled, and then clubbed to death.
Although it is not a pretty sight, it is an interesting slice of Lancaster history.

    **Hours:**     Open Fri. - Sat. from noon - 4pm.
  **Admission:**   Free
      **Ages:**     4 years and up.

## WESTERN MUSEUM OF FLIGHT

(310) 332-6228 / www.wmof.com                                                    $

*12016 S. Prairie Avenue, Hawthorne*

(Exit San Diego Fwy [405] E. on El Segundo, L. on Prairie. It's in the Hawthorne airport, on the corner of Prairie and 120th.)

A rendition of "Off we go, into the wild blue yonder, flying high into the sky. . ." goes through one's mind when visiting this museum. The Western Museum of Flight "houses" between twelve to fifteen rare planes like the YF23A, YF17, a flyable Freedom Fighter, and an exact replica of the first controlled aircraft, an 1883 glider. Most of the planes are outside, braving the elements, although several are inside the hanger. The ones inside are being restored, so kids have the opportunity to see this process. Also in the hanger are displays of engines, model planes, medals, leather helmets and jackets, and other memorabilia from WWI and WWII. This museum is for the more serious students of flight. For those interested in doing aeronautical research, an extensive library is available. Call for more details.

**Hours:** Open Tues. - Sat. from 10am - 3pm.
**Admission:** $3 for adults; $2 for children 12 years and under.
**Ages:** 6 years and up.

# THE WHITTIER MUSEUM ☿

(562) 945-3871 !
*6755 Newlin Avenue, Whittier*
(Exit San Gabriel River Fwy [605] E. on Whittier Blvd., L. on Philadelphia, L. on Newlin. It's on the corner of Philadelphia and Newlin.)

Journey back in time to the early days of Whittier, circa 1900. Stroll along a wonderfully re-created, full-size Main Street. The Victorian style is predominate in both the store and home fronts, and in the fully-furnished, walk-through rooms. A stereoscope and an old-fashioned stove and bathtub are some of our favorite items. Authentically-dressed mannequins all around make the visitors feel a part of this era.

The next few rooms feature an outhouse, a water pump that kids can actually try, photos, murals depicting early Whittier as a farming community, a tractor, old farm tools, and a big model of an oil derrick. Sitting on old church pews, kids can watch a video that shows the history of Whittier. The transportation room has photos, an encased display of old medical instruments and medicine vials, plus a doctor's buggy, a racing plane, and a replicated front end of the historic Red Car. Walk up through the Red Car and into the children's room filled with hands-on delights, such as old typewriters, adding machines, telephones, and a switchboard. There are also old-fashioned toys to play with and clothes for dressing up. The Library Room is an archival room housing documents on the history of Whittier. Upstairs is a large gallery room with changing exhibits. Call to see what's currently showing. Kids enjoy walking through history at this museum.

**Hours:** Open Sat. - Sun. from 1pm - 4pm. Group tours are also given Tues. - Fri., by appointment.
**Admission:** Free
**Ages:** 3½ years and up.

# WILLIAM S. HART MUSEUM AND PARK

(805) 254-4584 - museum; (805) 259-0855 - park and camping  /
www.hart-friends.org
*24151 San Fernando Road, Santa Clarita*
(Take Golden State Fwy [5] N. to Antelope Valley Fwy [Hwy 14], exit W. on San
Fernando Rd., approximately 1½ miles to the park, after the railroad tracks.)

William S. Hart was a famous western star of the silent films - a bit before my time. His Spanish, colonial-style home is now a museum. It is a short, but tough hike up a winding trail to reach the house/museum on the hill. Note: Seniors and physically disabled people can get a pass from the park ranger to drive up the side street to the house. The half-hour guided tour of his home is quite interesting, as the house is filled with western and Indian art and furnishings. Kids can look at, but not touch, the saddles, guns and other weapons, forty-pound buffalo coat, bear skin rug, stuffed buffalo head, paintings, and western movie memorabilia.

The park covers over 265 acres, with almost 110 acres set aside for wilderness area. Herd of buffalo roam the grounds (which definitely adds to the Old West ambiance), within an enormous fenced-in enclosure. Many deer consider this area home, too. Hiking and nature trails through chaparral and woodland start behind the museum, and loop back around. Primitive camping is available here, too. A large picnic area is located next to the barracks, which contain period artifacts. A smaller area is behind the "farm." Purchase some animal feed to entice the barnyard animals - sheep, ducks, horses, burros, and cows - to come within petting distance.

Hey pardners, ask about "Cowboy Sleepovers and Night Hikes" held on special days throughout the year. Crafts, ranch-type activities, and learning about Native American lifestyles are just part of the program. Call for dates and information and ask about other special events.

**Hours:** Hart park is open daily from 7am - sunset. The museum is open in the summer Wed. - Sun. from 11am - 3:30pm. It's open the rest of the year Wed. - Fri., 10am - 12:30pm; Sat. - Sun., 11am - 3:30pm. Docent-led tours are given every half hour. The museum is closed New Year's Day, Thanksgiving, and Christmas.
**Admission:** Free
**Ages:** All

# ANAHEIM MUSEUM

(714) 778-3301
*241 S. Anaheim Boulevard, Anaheim*
(Exit Santa Ana Fwy [5] E. on Lincoln Ave., R. on Anaheim Blvd.)

This small museum is housed in Anaheim's restored 1908 Carnegie Library building. The upstairs room displays show the growth of Orange County's oldest city from an orange grove and grapevine-producing society to the opening of Disneyland in 1955 to the present. There are photos, a model of Disneyland, and a display of old tools and machines, as well as orange crate labels.

Downstairs is a small, children's gallery that features rotating, hands-on exhibits such as puppets, toys, musical instruments, and games. It reminds me of a culturally-aware kindergarten classroom, but there are also workshops for older kids.

**Hours:**  Open Wed. - Fri., 10am - 4pm; Sat., noon - 4pm.
**Admission:**  Donations appreciated.
**Ages:**  2 years and up.

## BOWERS KIDSEUM

(714) 480-1520 / www.bowers.org
*1802 N. Main Street, Santa Ana*
(Exit Santa Ana Fwy [5] S. on Main St. It's located on the corner of Main and 18ᵗʰ St., just South of the Bowers Museum of Cultural Art. And yes, the building was a bank at one time.)

Kidseum is a hands-on, cultural museum designed to assist kids, ages 6 to 12, develop an appreciation of art and the ways of life in African, Asian, and Native American cultures. Cross over the short (symbolic) bridge from the lobby into the main gallery. Your kids will love trying on unusual masks from around the world; playing unique musical instruments, like deer hoof shakers, African drums, and string instruments; and dressing up in a wide variety of ethnic costumes in the theater area.

The Time Vault, which was an actual bank vault, has an incredible mural on the wall. Kids can "saddle up" on the workbench horses in here or grind pretend corn with a stone mortar and pestle. Playing games from foreign lands; working on geography puzzles; and putting on your own puppet show at the small theater - all this is available at Kidseum!

Afternoons and weekends at the museum is a time for telling tales, storytelling tales, that is. The storytelling room also brings to life Asian tales in January, in celebration of the Chinese New Year; African tales in February to celebrate Black History Month; etc. Stop by the Art Lab, which is usually open about the same hours as the museum, where kids can paint, color, learn how to make Indian rain sticks, experiment with sand art, etc. Most activities are included in the price of admission. School tours here are my favorite combination of hands-on fun and learning. Kidseum proves that learning about other cultures can be exciting!

Note: The Bowers Museum, located just down the street at 2002 N. Main Street, is the parent museum of Kidseum. It contains carvings, pictures, and other art work from African, Asian, and Native American cultures. Older kids might appreciate a walk through the galleries. As admission is reciprocal with Kidseum when visited on the same day, why not visit both?!

**Hours:**  Open in the summer Wed. - Fri., 2pm - 5pm; Sat. - Sun., 10am - 4pm. Open the rest of the year Sat. - Sun., 10am - 4pm. Call to make a reservation to take a tour during the week.

**Admission:**   $6 for adults; $4 for seniors and students; $2 for ages 5 - 12; children 4 years and under are free. There is reciprocal admission with the Bowers Museum if both are visited on the same day. (See C.E.E. L.A. for membership savings, pg. 213.)

**Ages:**   3 - 13 years. Young children will enjoy the hands-on quality of this museum, though signs do ask for a gentle touch.

# CHILDREN'S MUSEUM AT LA HABRA

(562) 905-9793  / www.lhcm.org
*301 S. Euclid Street, La Habra*
(Exit Artesia Fwy |91| N. on Euclid.)

$$
This museum, housed in a renovated Union Pacific Railroad Depot, has a child's interest at heart. Out front dinosaur print trackways of a stegosaurus and tyrannosaurus, a sand bed where visitors can make their own tracks, and a replica nest containing unhatched "dino" eggs. Youngsters can also count the rings on a six foot diameter tree slab. Inside, a small Science Station encourages hands-on exploration with a Dino Dig (i.e. digging in sand for "fossils"), pendulum and marker pictures, and a few science experiments. The adjoining room has a carousel to ride, a mini-market for shopping, and the front end of an Orange County Transit bus to practice driving skills. The next room has wonderful, interactive, changing exhibits. Past themes have included "Cowboys and the Wild West," which featured western gear to try on, a wooden horse with a saddle, and a guitar to strum on the range; and "Would You Look At That?" which featured fun with lenses, light, and optical equipment. This room is always enlightening! Do you hear trains chugging, clanging, and whistling as they come around the mountain? A connecting room contains a large model train layout. The train room then leads to the nature room. Listen to the sounds of nature (e.g. birds chirping, etc.) as you look at the taxidermied wildlife, such as bears, mountain lions, a raccoon, and a wart hog. Hanging on the wall are stuffed animal heads of deer, moose, and buffalo. A touch table in here has fur and skulls. A bee observatory gets the kids all a-buzz.

Quiet on the set! The dress-up area, with its stage, numerous costumes (including several fireman uniforms), and even prepared scripts, inspires future actors and actresses. The lighting booth, with all of its working buttons, is perfect for aspiring directors. The playroom, for children 5 years and under only, has a fake tree to climb, a little puppet theater, a play castle, and a small, separate play room for very little ones. Just outside the museum is a train caboose that is open to walk through at certain times.

On Saturdays, the museum hosts special programs such as craft projects, storytelling, or shows for kids to enjoy and participate in. Call for a schedule of events.

Portola Park is located just behind the museum. It's open daily and features a playground, baseball fields, and tennis courts, plus picnic tables and barbecue grills.

**Hours:** Open Mon. - Sat., 10am - 5pm; Sun., 1pm - 5pm. Closed major
holidays.
**Admission:** $4 for ages 2 years and up; children under 2 years are free.
**Ages:** 1½ - 12 years.

## DISCOVERY MUSEUM

(714) 540-0404 / www.discoverymuseumoc.com
*3101 W. Harvard Street, Santa Ana*
(Exit San Diego Fwy [405] N.E. on Warner Ave., L. on Fairview, L. on Harvard.)
Travel back to Victorian times as you visit the Kellogg House (i.e.
Discovery Museum), built in 1898. Tours begin in the parlor where kids can play
a pump organ, crank an old telephone, listen to music played on an Edison
talking machine, and look through a stereoscope - an early version of the
modern-day View Master™. The kitchen has wonderful gadgets that kids can
learn about as well as touch. The wood dining room is oval-shaped with cabinets
specially made to bend with the curves, like the inside of a ship. The twisted,
wooden staircase got "cool" raves from all the kids. Upstairs, children play a
game that teaches them the parts of a Victorian house. The master bedroom is
now a room to dress up in authentic Victorian clothing, with beautiful dresses for
the girls and dapper coats and vests for the boys. The hats are great, too. The
children's room has old-fashioned toys to play with. Kids may sit at the one-
room, schoolhouse desks and write with chalk on the slate boards.

Outside, on the back porch, children can practice *real* chores like "washing"
clothes on a scrub board and drying them with the clothes wringer. Sometimes
visitors are invited to make their own butter or learn how to play Victorian-era
games. After the official tour, kids are welcome to go back and explore their
favorite rooms, with parental supervision, of course.

Toward the back of the property is a small nature trail, an interpretative
center with a few live animals (e.g. snakes, insects, turtles, etc.), and hands-on
displays such as bones and animal skins. Coming soon are heavenly exhibits,
including a turn-of-the-century astronomical site containing a 16" telescope built
in 1908, star charts, and interactive activities.

Enjoy a picnic lunch in the Gazebo area. A working blacksmith's shop is
open on the third Sunday of the month, and sometimes on Thursdays.
Demonstrations are given here, such as crafting candlesticks out of iron. Once a
month the museum offers special events, such as American Indian Day, or a
themed tea, where kids are invited to make crafts and participate in topical
programs. Call for a schedule and for pricing. Each Sunday, from October
through May, brings a special family activity such as storytelling, a craft,
blacksmith demonstrations, or a nature hike. This activity is included in your
admission price.

Of all the historical homes we've toured, and we've been through quite a
few, this one has earned one of the highest ratings from my boys. Most houses,
while beautiful and worthy of a tour, are understandably hands off. The
Discovery Museum has hands-on activities, plus the docents gear the tour

towards youngsters, both in the tour length and the way the information is
presented. Come here and let your kids touch history!

**Hours:**  Open Wed. - Fri., 1pm - 5pm; Sun., 11am - 3pm. Open Sat. for
special events only. Call to book a school tour or scout outing
during the week.

**Admission:**  $4 for adults; $3 for seniors and ages 3 - 12; children 2 years and
under are free.

**Ages:**  3 years and up.

## DISCOVERY SCIENCE CENTER

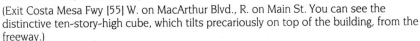

(714) 540-2001 / www.go2dsc.org.                                        *$$$*
*2522 Main St., Santa Ana*
(Exit Costa Mesa Fwy [55] W. on MacArthur Blvd., R. on Main St. You can see the
distinctive ten-story-high cube, which tilts precariously on top of the building, from the
freeway.)

This high-caliber science center has over 100 hands-on experiments and
displays throughout its eight major exhibits areas: Human Perception, Quake
Zone, Dynamic Earth, Principles of Flight, Human Performance, Space
Exploration, Exploration Station, and KidStation. For instance, the Bed of Nails
is a large wooden table with 3500 sharp steel nails embedded in it. Visitors can
lie down on the on the bed and not get hurt, due to the equal distribution of body
mass. (May your kids never complain about an uncomfortable mattress again!)
See yourself in a "new light" inside a room with a camera that takes real time
pictures of your movements. Watch your image reflected on a screen in vivid
colors and lights. If you can't get enough of the real California quakes, enter the
Shake Shack, a room with a platform that simulates major and minor quakes.
Walk through an eight-foot-tall artificially generated tornado and even redirect
its pattern. Use wind to blow sand into dunes or other formations. Create a
cloudy day (inside!) by pushing on large rings around a cloud machine which
then form various-sized clouds. Experience what you would weigh on the moon
or Mars by hoisting yourself up on a properly weighted pulley system. You are
also invited to create an animated movie, participate in live science shows, climb
a rock wall, log on to the over twenty computer terminals, and so much more.
Don't forget to catch a show at the 3D Laser Theater!

In the space-themed KidStation, designed for children five years old and
younger, kids can suit up as an astronaut, turn and "repair" gears at the Gear
Wall, converse through the Talk Tubes, race balls down a slide at the Ball Run,
fingerpaint electronically (a lot less messier than the real thing), bop around in
the soft play area, play with space-age toys, and read books about the stars and
planets.

Ask about the numerous special programs offered here, including a "Meet
the Scientists" series, science camps, scout programs, etc. The Discovery Science
Center unites education with entertainment in an appealing format for this
generation.

**Hours:**  Open daily 10am - 5pm. Closed New Year's Day, Easter, Fourth
of July, Thanksgiving, and Christmas.

**Admission:**   $8 for adults; $6 for seniors and ages 3 - 17 years; children 2
years and under are free. Shows at the 3D Laser Theater are $2
per person.
**Ages:**   2 years and up.

## DOLL AND TOY MUSEUM                                                         ☼

(714) 527-2323                                                                  $
*1238 S. Beach Boulevard, Anaheim*
(Exit Artesia Fwy |91| S. on Beach Blvd. Or, exit Garden Grove Fwy |22| N. on Beach.
The museum is in Hobby City, 2 miles S. of Knott's Berry Farm.)
　　Take a walk down memory lane as you go through this museum. It contains
a personal collection of the owner's over five thousand rare and antique dolls
from around the world, all housed in a half-scale model of the White House
(making the museum easy to spot). Some of the more kid-recognizable dolls
include Cupie dolls, Star Wars figures, and an extensive Barbie collection. This
small museum is for the special child who can resist the touching urge. The
attached shop buys, sells, and repairs old and modern dolls. They also carry a
line of doll clothes, shoes, wigs, hats, and books. (Look up the adjacent
attractions - ADVENTURE CITY and HOBBY CITY, listed separately in the
Alphabetical Index.)
**Hours:**   Open daily from 10am - 6pm.
**Admission:**   $1 for adults; 50¢ for senior citizens and children 12 years and
under.
**Ages:**   3 years and up.

## FULLERTON MUSEUM CENTER                                                     ☼

(714) 738-6545 - museum; (714) 738-3136 - tour info  /                          $
www.ci.fullerton.ca.us/museum
*301 N. Pomona Avenue, Fullerton*
(Exit Riverside Fwy |91| N. on Harbor Blvd., R. on Commonwealth, L. on Pomona. It's
on the corner of Wilshire and Pomona.)
　　This cultural museum has two small galleries with rotating exhibits that
often have terrific kid-appeal, plus a video that explains more about what is
currently showing. Past exhibits have included The Nature of Collecting, which
featured different collections ranging from *I Love Lucy* paraphernalia to pencil
sharpeners and old radios; Touchable Sculptures, with over seventy touchable,
lifecast sculptures of contemporary and historic figures such as George Bush,
Clint Eastwood, and Dizzy Gillespie; and Anne Frank, a re-creation of the life
and times of Anne Frank through photographs and facsimiles of her diary, plus
commentary.
　　One-and-a-half-hour school tours are given that include an in-depth tour of
the museum and a hands-on activity that correlates to the current exhibit.
　　Super Saturdays are year round family workshops, held on one Saturday a
month from 1:30pm to 3pm. The art activity is geared for kids ages 5 through 9.
Super Tuesdays are held on most Tuesdays during the summer, from 9:30am to

11am. The activities are geared for kids ages 8 to 12 years. These culturally-themed and/or art workshops, like Secrets of Pharaoh, Papermaking, International Christmas Tree Ornaments, or Day of the Dead, include an interesting lesson followed by a related craft. Reservations are needed.

**Hours:** The museum is open Wed. - Sun. from noon - 4pm; open Thurs. until 8pm.

**Admission:** $3 for adults; $2 for students; children 12 years and under are free. The workshops cost $6 per person. Tours are $2 for ages 12 years and up; $1 for children 11 years and under. Adult chaperones are free.

**Ages:** 5 years and up.

# HALL OF FAME MUSEUM
(714) 990-4131

*2000 Gene Autry Way, Anaheim*
(Exit Santa Ana Fwy [5] N. on State College Blvd. It's at the Edison Field - Angels Stadium.)

Check out who's who in the Orange County Sports Hall of Fame, located at Gate 6 on the south side of the Edison Field Angels stadium. Come see the Mighty Ducks Wing, California Angels Wing, and Orange County Olympians section. The sports world, including tennis, volleyball, off-road racing, football, basketball, boxing, baseball, golf, swimming, etc., is represented here in over 1,000 photographs and displays of sports events and personalities. You'll see signed sports memorabilia including footballs, jerseys, hockey sticks, baseball bats, etc.; Olympic gold and silver medals; busts of baseball greats; trophies and awards such as Phil Neven's Golden Spike Award; autographed bowling pins; Gary Carter's shin guards; etc. This museum will score points with your young sports fans.

**Hours:** Open by appointment.
**Admission:** $1 per person.
**Ages:** 5 years and up.

# HERITAGE HILL HISTORICAL PARK
(949) 855-2028

*25151 Serrano Road, Lake Forest*
(Exit San Diego Fwy [5] N.E. on Lake Forest Dr., L. on Serrano. It's on the corner. Parking is available in the adjacent shopping center.)

Heritage Hill consists of several restored historical buildings in a beautiful gated setting. Four buildings are open to tour that reflect part of Orange County's heritage. The Serrano Adobe dates from 1863 and has furniture from the late nineteenth-century. The Bennet Ranch House, built in 1908, reflects a ranching family's lifestyle from the early twentieth century. St. George's Episcopal Mission, built in 1891, has many of its original interior furnishings. El Toro Grammar School was built in 1890. It is a favorite with kids because it has school books from that era, as well as desks and other school-related items. The

Historical Park has a few picnic tables on the grounds.

Two school tours are offered. The third grade tour is one-and-a-half hours long, costs $2 per person, and is designed for ten to seventy students. Groups go through each house and do an activity in each, such as grinding corn in the adobe, etc. In the school house, they participate in a mini school session. The fourth grade tour is two hours long and cost $3 per person. Seventeen to thirty-five students participate in hands-on lessons in the school house. Learning was never so interesting! Reservations for tours are required.

If your kids need more running around space, visit Serrano Creek Park, just behind Heritage Hill. Serrano is a long, narrow, wooded park with a paved walkway and a creek running through it. The big wooden play structure, which looks like a clubhouse, has a bridge, slides, and some huge tires to climb on.

**Hours:**   Heritage Hill is open Wed. - Sun., 9am - 5pm. Guided tours are the only way to see the interior of the buildings. The tours are given Wed. - Fri. at 2pm; Sat. - Sun. at 11am and 2pm. School groups can make reservations for tours at other times throughout the week. Closed major holidays.

**Admission:**   Donations. School tours are $2 a person.

**Ages:**   6 years and up.

# HISTORIC GEORGE KEY RANCH

(714) 528-4260 / www.oc.ca.gov/pfrd/hbp/keyranch.htm      $$
*625 W. Bastanchury Road, Placentia*

(Exit Riverside Fwy [91] N. on Orange Fwy [57], E. on Yorba Linda Blvd., L. on Placentia Ave., L. on Bastanchury. Parking is not permitted on the grounds, but on the adjacent streets of Gilman Circle or Key Drive.)

Orange groves, originally planted in 1893, once covered most of the George Key Ranch. On your guided tour here you can still see two remaining acres of producing orange trees. Your one-a-half-hour tour begins with a brief video of the Key family. Then walk through the Key house to see the family furnishings and old photographs; the Kitchen Collection building, which has an extensive collection of kitchen items, dating from the 1890's to the 1940's, that all came from local ranch houses; a workshop shed that contains artifacts related to ranch life, such as a squirrel and gopher smoker, a drill press, an avocado picker, and an alfalfa/grass chopper for making chicken feed; and a blacksmith and carpentry shop which holds smithing and carpentry tools as well as implements used in picking and packaging oranges. The yard contains a variety of old farm equipment and machinery such as plows, harrows, spreaders, seeders, orchard heaters, a citrus spray rig, and even wagons from the early 1900's. Enjoy a stroll along the brick-lined garden and bring a sack lunch to enjoy at the picnic tables here.

Ask about the ranch's special programs, such as the Civil War Brass Band and the California Battalion - a concert of military music and camp songs with the President and Mrs. Lincoln in attendance; the summer concert series; Open House, where docents in period dress demonstrate old-fashioned crafts; scout programs; ranch clean up programs; and more.

**Hours:** Open only for guided tours, by appointment. Tours are limited to thirty people and are usually given on Fri. mornings for school groups and Fri. afternoons for adults. Note: There is presently no handicapped access.
**Admission:** $4 per person.
**Ages:** 6 years and up.

# HUNTINGTON BEACH INTERNATIONAL SURFING ☀
# MUSEUM
(714) 960-3483 / www.surfingmuseum.org                          $
*411 Olive Avenue, Huntington Beach*
(Exit San Diego Fwy [405] S. on Ellis Ave., veer L. past Beach onto Main St., R. on Olive near end of Main.)

Surf's up at this small museum that celebrates surfing and surf culture, from its roots in Hawaii to the present day. Get in the mood with beach music playing in the background. Feel like catching a wave? Check out some of the famous and unique surfboards here, like the Batman board and a surfboard made in three pieces. There are also trophies, clothes, and photographs to look at. The Surfer's Walk of Fame, honoring eleven people, is just down the street.

**Hours:** Open June through Labor Day daily noon - 5pm. Open the rest of the year, Wed. - Sun. from noon - 5pm.
**Admission:** $2 for adults; $1 for kids; children 6 years and under are free.
**Ages:** 6 years and up.

# LAUNCH PAD                                                    ☀
(714) 546-2061                                                   !
*3333 Bear Street, Suite 323, Costa Mesa*                        ▦
(Exit San Diego Fwy [405] N. on Bristol St., L. on Sunflower, L. on Bear St. It's on the 3rd floor of the Crystal Court at South Coast Plaza, next to Macys.)

The Launch Pad is scheduled to close in the year 2000 as it was intended to be a preview facility for the gigantic and impressive DISCOVERY SCIENCE CENTER, which is now open. (Look up the Center under this section for details.) The Pad is a small, hands-on, science museum for kids with numerous featured attractions, including a Bubble Wall, created out of dipping a long rod in bubble solution; Angular Momentum, that looks like a one-person merry-go-round - this is not for those with a tendency toward motion sickness; a "morphing" station that transforms human faces into animal ones, via a computer; and displays using lights, lasers, and illusions. Younger kids will take particular delight in a room just for toddlers with soft foam blocks, bubbles and telephones that really work (inside the room only). Stop in at the gift store as it offers an array of fun and educational experiments, toys, etc.

**Hours:** Open Mon. - Fri., 10am - 9pm; Sat., 10am - 7pm; Sun., 11am - 6pm.
**Admission:** Free
**Ages:** 2 years and up.

## MARCONI AUTOMOTIVE MUSEUM FOR KIDS

(714) 258-3001         *$*

*1302 Industrial Drive, Tustin*

(Exit Cost Mesa Fwy [55] E. on Edinger Ave., R. on Red Hill Ave., R. on Industrial Dr.)

The front hallway of this classy museum is lined with gleaming motorcycles. The museum is for kids in that money raised through it is donated to children's charities. Also, unlike many vintage car museums, there aren't any ropes around the cars and kids are encouraged to (gently) touch the cars on display and peer through their windows. The museum features the private collection of Dick Marconi's automobiles, which are kept in mint condition. He owns seventy-two-plus cars and over thirty of them are housed here at any given time. The cars vary in style, shape, and color. His collection includes a 1929 Ford Model "A" Cariolet, a 1937 Ahrens-Fox Fire Engine, a 1954 green Chevrolet, a 1973 canary-yellow convertible Ferrari Daytona Spider (once owned by Cher), a restored 1964 Corvette Sting Ray, and a jet-black 1989 Lamborghini Countach, plus seventeen racing Ferraris, an assortment of motorcycles, and a few kid-size cars. Marconi's prized possession is the last car Mario Andretti drove to victory at the 1993 Phoenix International Raceway. It is signed by Andretti. My boys' favorite was the rather colorful car completely decoupaged with magazine covers featuring boxing champions. Racing flags, trophies, drivers' jumpsuits and helmets, and a huge, shining silver horse constructed out of old car bumpers complete this museum.

**Hours:** Open Mon. - Fri. from 9am - 5pm by appointment only. You may call as little as a few hours before you would like to visit.

**Admission:** $5 for adults; children 12 years and under are free.

**Ages:** 5 years and up.

## MISSION SAN JUAN CAPISTRANO

(949) 248-2048 (Dial ext. 2047 for educational information.) /   *$$*
www.missionsjc.com

*Between Camino Capistrano Street and El Camino Real, San Juan Capistrano*

(Exit San Diego Fwy [5] W. on Ortega Hwy. [74]. It's on the corner of Ortega and Camino Capistrano.)

The Mission, founded in 1776, is thirteen acres of historic stone buildings and beautifully landscaped gardens, courtyards, and walkways. It's easy to see why the San Juan Mission was considered "the Jewel of the Missions." There are many "parts" to the Mission, so there is something to interest almost any age child. It's a history treat for school kids as they visit and "experience" the early Native American, Spanish, and Mexican lifestyles, depicted in separate rooms. Walk through rooms that contain murals such as Indians hunting, and artifacts such as bone weapons. The Soldiers' Barracks room looks "lived in," just as it did many years ago. It contains life-size models of soldiers and their (few) possessions. Note: Outside, behind the barracks, are some picnic tables.

The extensive grounds are a maze of pathways. The Central Courtyard, the cemetery, the areas of on-going archaeological excavation, and the industrial center are all interesting. For instance, tanning vats in the industrial center were used to turn animal skin into sellable leather, while the ovens were used to turn animal fat into candles, soap, and ointments.

The Mission has two churches. One is the Serra Chapel, the oldest building in California, where mass is still regularly performed. The glittery baroque altar, made of gold leaf overlay, is eye-catching. The Great Stone Church, once a magnificent cathedral, was destroyed by an earthquake in 1812. Scaffolding is around the ruins, holding up the remaining walls while the church awaits restoration.

Mission San Juan Capistrano offers several special, educational activities such as Saturday at the Mission. This program, offered during the school year, is held on the first Saturday of the month from 9am to 11:30am. It's geared for kids ages 6 to 12. A topic is introduced and then reinforced, either with a related craft, by playing games, or even by participating in a simulated, archaeological dig. Living History Day occurs on the last Saturday of each month from 10am to 2pm. Authentically costumed docents become living historians. Talk with them to find out about mission life "firsthand."

If you're looking for somewhere fun to eat, RUBY'S (see the Edible Adventures section) is across the street and up the stairs at the shopping district. This 1940's diner has a train going around overhead, red vinyl seats, and kids' meals that are served in a forties-style, cardboard car. Afterwards, take a walk around Camino Capistrano (street). It has many interesting stores with truly unique merchandise. Idea: Take a train into town and really make a day of your visit here! The train depot is only two blocks away from the Mission. (See the March Calendar section for the Fiesta de las Golondrinas. Also look up JONES FAMILY MINI FARM under the Zoos and Animals section.)

**Hours:** Open daily from 8:30am - 5pm. Closed Good Friday afternoon, Thanksgiving, and Christmas.

**Admission:** $5 for adults; $4 for seniors and ages 3 - 12; children 2 years and under are free. Saturday at the Mission is $10 per participant.

**Ages:** 5 years and up.

## MOVIELAND WAX MUSEUM

(714) 522-1154 / www.movielandwaxmuseum.com
*7711 Beach Boulevard, Buena Park*
(Exit Artesia Fwy [91] S. on Beach Blvd. It's 1 block N. of Knott's Berry Farm.)

Over 400 movie and television celebrities are immortalized in wax, posed in the settings that made them famous. To insure authenticity, almost every measurement and picture angle imaginable is taken of the star before the sculptor begins his work. Often times the costumes and props adorning the wax figure, and its surrounding settings, are personally donated by the stars.

Kids who are film buffs will probably get more out of this museum, but almost any age child enjoys "seeing" Dorothy and the whole *Wizard of Oz* gang; Robin Williams as Mrs. Doubtfire; and Michael Jackson dressed from his video *Bad*; as well as Whoopi Goldberg, *Star Trek* crew members, Superman, the Little

Rascals, and many more. Special lighting, sound effects, and animation are also used throughout the museum to enhance the realism of the exhibits. Halfway through the museum, you are routed through a gift and candy shop and small arcade area. Here you have the choice of whether to go through the Chamber of Horrors or bypass it. (The Chamber of Horrors, which holds scary and sometimes gross figures, could frighten younger children.)

**Hours:** Open Mon. - Fri., 10am - 6pm; Sat. - Sun., 9am - 7pm.
**Admission:** $12.95 for adults; $10.55 for seniors; $6.95 for ages 4 - 11; children 3 years and under are free. (Certain discounts available through AAA.)
**Ages:** 4 years and up.

## NEWPORT HARBOR NAUTICAL MUSEUM

(949) 673-7863 / www.newportnautical.org                                    *$*
*151 East Coast Highway, Newport Beach*
(Take Costa Mesa Fwy [55] to end, where it turns into Newport Blvd., L. on E. 17th St., R., at end, on Dover Dr., L on E. Coast Hwy., on Newport Bay)

This beautiful, paddlewheel riverboat, now harbored in Newport Bay, looks like it just came down the Mississippi River. Our visit here wasn't long, but it was interesting. An upstairs room is devoted to glass-enclosed model ships. The huge (for a scale model) Fort Victoria is displayed in the center. The U.S.S. Missouri model, built in remembrance of the men who served on her and for the WWII peace treaty which was signed on board, is complete with men and little cannons, plus waves under the bow and stern. Other outstanding models were crafted from sterling silver, intricately carved wood, and bone. In the hallway is a captain's wheel with beautiful stained glass panels - spin it gently. Elegantly displayed exhibits in the other upstairs room consist of artifacts from early California. My boys particularly liked the bowl made from whale vertebrae and the necklace made from fish bones. Downstairs is a wall display of ships in a bottle and a small seashell exhibit. You can also watch a short, grainy, homemade video taken during a real hurricane in Newport Beach in 1939.

If you've worked up an appetite, dine at the classy Riverboat Cafe & Dinner House located on board. It's open Tuesday through Friday from 11am to 9pm, and weekends from 7am to 9pm, and offers good food at reasonable prices. For example, Chinese Chicken Salad is $7.25; burgers, turkey, and ham sandwiches average $6.50; Filet Mignon is $19.95; and Seafood Pasta is $17.95.

**Hours:** The museum is open Tues. - Sun. from 10am - 5pm.
**Admission:** $4 for adults; $1 for ages 3 - 12; children 2 years and under are free.
**Ages:** 6 years and up.

## NEWPORT SPORTS COLLECTION

(949) 721-9333 / e-mail:nscf@earthlink.net                                   *!*
*620 Newport Center Drive, Suite 125, Newport Beach*

(Exit San Diego Fwy [405] S. on Jamboree Rd., L. on Santa Barbara, L. on Newport Center Dr. It's in Fashion Island, in the lower level of the Northern Trust Bank building. Call to reserve one of the two allotted parking spaces near the museum.)

Name a sport, any sport. Almost any one that you can think of is represented in this 5,000 square-foot, ten-room, sports museum. The hundreds of game-used and game-worn equipment and clothing on display include jerseys, shoes, hockey sticks, basketballs, footballs, etc. An Olympic room here contains Olympic memorabilia and paraphernalia.

The Newport Sports Collection Foundation is the non-profit organization who own and operate this facility. It also puts on programs where athletes come in and speak to kids about staying in school and staying off drugs. Call for more information about this program, but come by and see the sports collection any time.

**Hours:**   Open Mon. - Fri., 8am - 6pm; Sat., 9am - 1pm.
**Admission:**   Free
**Ages:**   5 years and up.

# OLD COURTHOUSE MUSEUM

(714) 834-3703
*211 Santa Ana Boulevard, Santa Ana*
(Exit Santa Ana Fwy [5] S. on Main St., R. on Civic Center Dr. Although the address is on Santa Ana Blvd., metered parking is on Civic Center Dr.)

Order in the court! Older kids interested in the history of our legal system, or in seeing what an actual courtroom looks like, will enjoy visiting the oldest courtroom in Southern California. Built in 1901, this huge, red sandstone building contains three floors of Orange County history. The bottom floor has glass cases of archaeological artifacts, such as fossils and bones. The second floor, which is the entrance, has two displays containing information about the museum and the court of law.

The third floor is your ultimate, and most interesting, destination. It features a turn-of-the century courtroom, jury room, and judge's chambers, plus a court reporter's room that has original transcribing machines, a candlestick telephone, and an old roll-top desk. My boys and I role-played a bit here so they could get a feel for how the court system is set up. The museum, which is a room of changing exhibits, is across the way from the Superior Courtroom. Past exhibits have included displays of sheriff's badges, war posters, a mock-up of a 1940's living room, World War II artifacts from Orange County, etc. A visit to the Old Courthouse Museum is a good beginning for future lawyers. I rest my case.

**Hours:**   Open Mon. - Fri. from 9am - 5pm. Guided tours are available Tues. from 10am - 2pm, and by appointment.
**Admission:**   Free
**Ages:**   6 years and up.

# ORANGE COUNTY DENTAL SOCIETY MUSEUM

(714) 634-8944 / e-mail:ocdsexec@aol.com
*295 S. Flower Street, Orange*

(Exit Orange Fwy [57] E. on Chapman Ave., R. on Flower St.)

This small museum doesn't floss over America's early dental period. It contains several old dental chairs, including an 1855 wooden chair with a straight back and a spittoon - no running water on this device; an 1876 velvet, rose-colored chair with fringe and a spittoon; and a modern-day chair with all the amenities. The glass-enclosed display shelves are lined with old dental tools that made me wince just to look at them, such as extraction forceps, clamps for separating teeth, and small saws. My 8-year old commented, "I'm going to brush my teeth ten times a day from now on!" We also saw a lot of false teeth, porcelain shade guides (used to match teeth for bridge work or capping), metal swagging sets (for making gold crowns), a buffalo horn mallet (used before plastic), and numerous steel instruments - some made with ivory and some with mother-of-pearl handles. The crowning jewel here is in a silver trinket box - a partial denture of four of George Washington's ivory teeth! You are welcome to explore the museum on your own, as everything is labeled, or ask for further explanations across the hall at the Dental Society. This museum is something you can really sink your teeth into!

**Hours:** Open Mon. - Thurs., 8am - 3pm; Fri., 8am - 1pm.
**Admission:** Free
**Ages:** 4 years and up.

## ORANGE COUNTY MARINE INSTITUTE ☼

(949) 496-2274 / www.ocmi.org                                    $
*24200 Dana Point Harbor Drive, Dana Point*
(Exit San Diego Fwy [5] N. on Pacific Coast Highway, L. on Dana Point Harbor, all the way to the end of the road. It's a part of Dana Point Harbor/Mariner's Village.)

The Orange County Marine Institute's main purposes are to teach about maritime history and about the marine environment. It offers wonderful classes and outings, such as the Bio-Luminescence cruise. This two-and-a-half-hour night cruise highlights glowing worms, glow fish, and plankton. The cost is $20 for adults, $14 for kids 12 years and under. Children must be at least 4 years old for the cruises. Other cruises include Let's Go Squidding, Marine Mammal Exploring (which includes whale watching in season), etc. Classes include tidepool hikes and more.

If, however, you are coming just to see the Institute, there are relatively few things here to look at besides the great gift shop that has educational toys, books, and games. One tank has an octopus. The back room has a touch tank, where a docent holds a starfish or a lobster for your child to touch. Overhead is a skeleton of a gray whale.

Behind the Institute is a small park overlooking the harbor, with rock jetties and a few picnic tables. The historic Tallship "Pilgrim" is moored in front of the building. (See the September Calendar section for the terrific annual Tallships Festival.) School groups are offered a variety of tours that incorporate different aspects of ship and marine life. Make the Institute a stopping point during your visit to Dana Point, or better yet, go on an Institute outing. (See DANA POINT HARBOR under the Piers and Seaports section.)

**Hours:**     The Institute is open daily from 10am - 4:30pm. The touch tank
is open Sat. - Sun. from 10am - 4:30pm. Tours of the ship are
usually given on Sun. from 10am - 2:30pm. Call for school group
tours. Everything is closed on major holidays.
**Admission:** Free; donations appreciated.
**Ages:**      3 years and up.

## ORANGE COUNTY NATURAL HISTORY MUSEUM

(949) 487-9155  / www.ocnha.mus.ca.us

*28373 Alicia Parkway, Laguna Niguel*

(Exit San Diego Fwy [5] W. on Alicia Parkway, cross Aliso Creek Rd., R. on Awma. It is
located in a spacious trailer by Gate One at Aliso and Wood Canyons Regional Park.)

   This terrific trailer museum has exhibits of fossils and seashells, and an
extensive butterfly and moth collection. It also has a skeleton of a dolphin, the
tooth of a great white shark, whale bones, and the remains of Waldo, a walrus or
a sea lion. Children may touch the animals bones and pelts. Many taxidermied
birds are on display - some in flight and others lying down - including owls,
hummingbirds, quail, a scrubjay, warbling, etc. Other stuffed native animals are
a coyote, raccoon, opossum, badger, and more. Make tracks of the wildlife by
using life-size paw print stamps in a box of dirt. Live lizards, toads, and several
kinds of snakes, including a huge rattlesnake, take up residence here in glass
cases. Look for fossils in the pile of rocks here, and look at some of the shells
recently gathered from Shellmaker Island and surrounding areas. Kids can take a
pencil safari where they are given a list of things to find and check off. Picnic
tables are just outside the trailer under a few shade trees. See ALISO AND
WOOD CANYONS REGIONAL PARK, under the Great Outdoors section, for
details on exploring the adjacent wilderness park.

   Micropals is one of the many programs offered and sponsored through this
museum. It is taught by a geologist and allows kids to extract specimens, process
samples, and go on field trips while learning about the world of
micropaleontology. Call for more information about this and other programs.

**Hours:**     Open Wed. - Sun. from 11am- 5pm.
**Admission:** $1 for adults; 50¢ for children 12 years and under. Parking is $2.
**Ages:**      3 years and up.

## RICHARD NIXON PRESIDENTIAL LIBRARY AND
## BIRTHPLACE

(714) 993-3393  / www.nixonfoundation.org                          *$$*

*18001 Yorba Linda Boulevard, Yorba Linda*

(Exit Orange Fwy [57] E. on Yorba Linda. Or, exit Riverside Fwy [91] N. on Imperial Hwy
[90], L. on Yorba Linda.)

   This museum/library/grave site/rose garden features nine acres of galleries
and gardens, plus the restored birthplace of - here's a quiz - what number
president? (The answer is at the end of this description.) Bring a pencil and
request a Children's Treasure Hunt to encourage your kids to become more

involved with the exhibits in the museum. They'll search for objects like the Presidential Seal, the Woody Station Wagon Nixon used for campaigning, and the piano he practiced on in his younger years.

The theater presents a twenty-eight-minute movie, documenting Richard Nixon's political career. It's a great introduction to who he was, both personally and presidentially. There are several videos and touch screens throughout the museum showing different aspects of his life, including the Kennedy/Nixon debates, footage from his speeches, a tribute to Pat Nixon, and a presidential forum with over 300 questions to choose from. I was surprised at how interested my kids were in all of this.

The exhibit of ten, life-size statues of world leaders (some of whom were very short) is impressive. Touch screens offer comments and biographical summaries on the leaders. Gifts of State are unique treasures to look at. My oldest son, however, thought the pistol from Elvis Presley was the coolest gift. Other pieces of history include a big chunk of the Berlin Wall; the presidential limo that at various times held Johnson, Ford, Carter, and Nixon; a re-creation of the White House's Lincoln Sitting Room; numerous photographs; Nixon's daughters' wedding dresses; and the Watergate Room. In the latter room, excerpts of the "smoking gun" tape can be heard through headsets. A pictorial and descriptive time line of this historic event takes up an entire wall. Tip: At the very least, know how to explain the term "impeach" to your kids. Two-hour, free guided tours are given Monday through Friday for fourth through twelfth graders, with advanced reservations.

Walk outside, through the First Lady's beautiful rose gardens (which look prettier in bloom), to the home where Nixon was born. A tour of the small house only takes fifteen minutes. Richard Nixon was, by the way, our thirty-seventh President.

**Hours:** Open Mon. - Sat., 10am - 5pm; Sun., 11am - 5pm. Closed Thanksgiving and Christmas.

**Admission:** $5.95 for adults; $3.95 for seniors; $2 for ages 8 - 11; children 7 years and under are free. (Certain discounts are available through AAA.) (See C.E.E. L.A. for membership savings, pg. 213.)

**Ages:** 6 years and up.

# RIPLEY'S BELIEVE IT OR NOT! MUSEUM (Buena ☼ Park)

(714) 522-7045  / www.movielandwaxmuseum.com/rip.html                  *$$$*
*7850 Beach Boulevard, Buena Park*
(Exit Artesia Fwy [91] S. on Beach Blvd. It's just N. of Knott's Berry Farm.)

As a reporter, Robert Ripley traveled all over the world visiting over 200 countries and meeting with Kings and Queens, Cannibal Chieftains, and tribesmen to collect interesting, humorous, and bizarre items and facts. There are hundreds of pictures, life-size models, special effects, statues, and assorted odd artifacts throughout the museum. My son, Bryce, summed up the exhibits best by saying, "They're kind of cool and kind of gross."

The "native" section is a little eerie and includes a real shrunken head. The Asian section contains a model of a Chinese man who had two sets of pupils in each eye, and a man who held a real burning candle *in* his head, among others exhibits. (Truth can definitely be stranger than fiction.)

The next section has unusual, rather than weird, displays, such as a sculpture of Marilyn Monroe made from over a quarter of a million "real" dollars (that will make your child's mouth drop open); a miniature violin, which is only five-and-a-half inches long, yet it can actually be played; and a complete landscape scene painted on a potato chip. Two of my favorite exhibits here are a rendition of the Last Supper done with 260 pieces of toast (varying from barely toasted to burnt), and the huge portrait made out of dyed clothes dryer lint. How do people think of these things, and why?

Videos show amazing feats such as unusual body contortions, swallowing razor blades, etc. (Don't try these activities at home.) Trivia buffs can really study up here. Toward the end of the museum are a few graphic "bloody" exhibits to bypass. Word of warning: If you take an inquisitive child who can't read the explanations, be prepared to read a lot of information and answer a lot of questions!

**Hours:**    Open Mon. - Fri., 11am - 5pm; Sat. - Sun., 10am - 6pm.
**Admission:**  $8.95 for adults; $6.95 for seniors; $5.25 for ages 4 - 11; children 3 years and under are free. (Certain discounts available through AAA.)
**Ages:**    5 years and up.

# WESTMINSTER MUSEUM / HISTORICAL PARK

(714) 891-2597
*8612 Westminster Boulevard, Westminster*
(Exit Garden Grove Fwy [22] S. on Magnolia St., R. on Westminster. It's the gated historic park on the S. side of the street.)

Like many other cities who want to preserve their roots for future generations, the city of Westminster has a historical museum. It houses displays from its founding in 1870, to the present day. The museum building, which looks like a converted auditorium, has exhibits, mostly in glass cases, set up in chronological groups. Each grouping has a number that corresponds to an information sheet which explains the memorabilia, thus making for an easy self-guided tour. If you prefer, a docent will explain articles more fully and allow children to touch just a few items - this is a mostly "eyes-on" (as opposed to hands-on) museum. Some of the more interesting items to see include a very small 1897 child's bed; an old stove, washboard, butter churn and other kitchen implements; an antique, wind-up phonograph that still works; old-fashioned ladies' hats and clothing; a collection of dolls from around the world; war posters; and the head of a water buffalo.

Four other buildings grace the park's grounds. A California Crazy, or Shutter Shack, is a little, picture-perfect "store" that looks like a camera. (It was once used for dropping off and picking up film.) A docent will take you through the other buildings. The small, restored McCoy-Hare House was the community's first drugstore as well as a home. The front room contains a pump organ, plus shelves filled with jars of medicine, bolts of fabric, and sundries. The adjacent living room has some period furniture and clothing. Next, walk through the Wayne Family Farmhouse to see the parlor, which holds a 1749 grandfather's clock and a piano; a dining room, with its table set with china; the bedroom that contains a bed (people were much shorter back then!) and a ceramic pot (i.e. port-a-potty); and the kitchen with its stove and old-time telephone. A sink wasn't necessary as water and garbage were simply thrown out the back door to feed the plants and the chickens, respectively. The adjacent large barn contains saddles, large farm equipment, a wooden sugar beet wagon, and tools. Everything is well-labeled. Walk into the part of the barn that has two fire engines and an antique paramedic "van." Kids may climb into the cab of the 1952 white fire engine and "drive" around.

A few grassy areas and a picnic table on the premise complete this park.

**Hours:** Open to the public the first and third Sunday of each month from 1pm - 4pm. School groups may call to book a tour during the week.

**Admission:** Free

**Ages:** 5 years and up.

## CALIFORNIA MUSEUM OF PHOTOGRAPHY                    ☼

(909) 784-FOTO (3686) / www.cmp.ucr.edu                                 $

*On Main Street, the pedestrian walkway, Riverside*

(Exit Riverside Fwy [91] W. on University Ave. Park and walk to the pedestrian walkway.)

Expose your kids to the photographic arts at the unique, three-story California Museum of Photography. The main level has rotating photo exhibits, with an emphasis on various photography styles or photographers, such as Ansel Adams. The back area houses a collection of cameras, including working miniature cameras (my boys refer to them as "spy" cameras), old-fashioned cameras with the drape cloth, a Spiderman camera, and one that is part of a radio-controlled car! If you feel like taking up another sport, surf the Internet here.

Take the spiral stairs up to the mezzanine terrace, which is a catwalk-like hallway gallery. The top floor focuses on kids with its small, interactive gallery. Children can use the Zoetropes to draw pictures and spin them around in a drum, creating moving images - animation! The next exhibit proves that not all shadows are black as the images shadowed here produce a rainbow of colors. Use the next display to visually explain to kids how the aperture of a camera is similar to the pupils in their eyes. Have them look into a light and watch in the mirror as their pupils enlarge or contract, according to the amount of light entering in. The Shadows Room temporarily imprints body outlines on the photosensitive wall when a light flashes. Camera Obscura is a small, dark room with a tiny hole of light that projects an upside down image of the outside scene on its wall. This is a visual demonstration of how a camera lens works. Kids will get a wide angle view of photography at this Museum!

**Hours:** The museum is open Wed. - Sat., 11am - 5pm; Sun., noon - 5pm.

**Admission:** $2 for adults; $1 for seniors and students; children 12 years and under are free. Every Wed. is free admission day. "First Sunday," occurring on the first Sunday of the month from October to June, offers free admission from 1pm - 4pm at this and nearby museums in Riverside.

**Ages:** 3 years and up just to look at things; ages 5 and up will begin to really appreciate it.

# GILMAN HISTORIC RANCH and WAGON MUSEUM    ☼
(909) 922-9200                                                      $

*On Wilson Street and 16ᵗʰ Street, Banning*

(Exit San Bernardino Fwy [10] N. on San Gorgonio, L. on Wilson, R. on 16ᵗʰ.)

Wagons, ho! Take the dirt road back to the Gilman Historic Ranch and Wagon Museum, and explore life as it was over 150 years ago. Over fifteen wagons from yesteryear are inside the museum including chuck wagons, stagecoaches, and prairie schooners. Some of the wagons are hitched to large wooden horses. Learn how our pioneer ancestors traveled across the country, and hear about the hardships that they endured. Also on exhibit are saddles, a bedroom set with a ladies' riding habit and surrey, and Indian artifacts.

The adjacent ranch has a few historic buildings, shaded picnic grounds, and hiking trails. Some of the trails go across the creek and to the upper reservoir, while others go deeper into the canyons. Be on the lookout for rabbits, deer, and other wildlife.

School groups, with a minimum of twenty students, can take two-hour tours, which include a tour of the museum and grounds, a nature hike, and doing hands-on activities. The activity choices are making a mobile, creating a brand (out of a rubber stamp), or panning for gold (and getting some real gold flakes to take home). Enjoy your day reliving the past! (Look up Mountain Man Days under the October Calendar section.)

**Hours:** The museum and grounds are open to the public Sun., March through November, from 10am - 4pm. Tours for school groups are offered throughout the week by reservation.

**Admission:** $2 for adults; $1 for children 11 years and under. Tour prices range between $3 - $5.50 per participant, depending on the activity involved.

**Ages:** 5 years and up.

# HERITAGE HOUSE    ☼
(909) 689-1333                                                      $

*8193 Magnolia Street, Riverside*

(Exit Riverside Fwy [91] N. on Adams St., R. on Magnolia St. It's on the N. side of the street.)

Heritage House is a beautiful Victorian house built in 1892. It is fully restored and filled with elaborate, turn-of-the-century furniture. Adding to its charm is the wrought iron fence in front, the well-kept grounds, the backyard windmill, and the barn complete with clucking chickens.

Your older children will appreciate the half-hour guided tour as they see and learn about a different era and style of living. Kids can look through the stereo-optic, which is an early version of today's View Master™ and view a unique, old music box. Explaining the Edison phonograph is a lot harder now that record players are also a thing of the past! The formal oak stairway leads upstairs to the master bedroom. You'll also find the office/library with trophy animal heads and a bearskin rug, and the servant's quarters up here. Heritage House graciously displays the life of an affluent citrus grower.

The last Sunday of every month is Living History Day, when the past comes to life in the present. Docents dress up as from the late 1900's owner and have a (pretend) party. Talk to the hostess, maid, cook, and guests to learn about customs from this time period. Call about the House's other special events.

**Hours:** Open Thurs - Fri., noon - 3pm; Sun., noon - 3:30pm. Closed July through Labor Day, except for regular Sun. hours.
**Admission:** Suggested donations are $1 for adults; 50¢ for kids.
**Ages:** 7 years old and up.

## JURUPA MOUNTAINS CULTURAL CENTER / EARTH ☼ SCIENCE MUSEUM

(909) 685-5818 / www.dreamsoft.com/jmcc                                    !/$$
*7621 Granite Hill Drive, Riverside*                                         ⛪
(Exit Pomona Fwy |60| S. on Pedley Rd., L. on Mission Blvd., L. on Camino Real, under the freeway.)

This center is a rock hound's paradise where kids can either start or add to their rock collection. The main building is a gigantic warehouse with an incredible array of rocks, minerals, dinosaur skeletons, and fossils of all sizes and quality, for display and purchase.

The adjacent Earth Science Museum has outstanding rocks, minerals, fossils, and Indian artifacts displayed according to classification. The large crystals, geodes, carbons, etc., are worthy of a few "oohs" and "aahs." The collection of ancient and modern Native American artifacts includes tools, weapons, a wonderful arrowhead exhibit, an 1100 year-old corn cob, and costumes, in particular, a beautiful fringed and beaded wedding dress. Products, like Borax, are shown in their commercial form next to their original mineral form. Other unique exhibits are the florescent exhibit, which literally highlights rocks with luminescent characteristics; the space exhibit, which includes moon rocks; and the ivory exhibit, which has examples of intricately carved scrimshaw. Note: The outside of the building is comprised of petrified wood and fossils.

If your kids want to take home their own, hand-picked treasures, go Rock Collecting at the Dinosaurs. This drop-in, family field trip starts at the magnetic rock, proceeds to the small petrified wood "forest," and has several other stops along the way, with kid-appropriate explanations about the fascinating plants and rocks you'll see. (I finally understand that fossil simply means, "something that was once living.") The destination, dinosaur mesa, has eight, giant, non-scary, kid-made dinosaurs. The highlight of the excursion is sorting through the huge spread of rocks and rock chips strewn at the dino's feet, and picking out twelve to take home! Egg cartons are provided. Crystals, jasper, malachite, petrified wood, amethyst, chrysocolla, etc., are some examples of what can be found here. Back at the warehouse/store, you can label each of your treasures, with a geologist's help if needed.

Another great drop-in field trip is Kids' Fossil Shack, geared for ages 6 and up. Kids will learn about fossils, and then clean and prepare one to take home. This is, obviously, a more sit-down activity, but another great way to combine hands-on education and fun.

The Jurupa Cultural Center offers a wide variety of school group and scout programs, such as gold panning, a tour of the Crestmore Mine, lapidary workshops, creating an Indian pictograph, archaeology, and lots more. The Center also offers periodic Pow Wows and Renaissance Fairs, as well as week-long classes of Nature School in the summer that range from hiking and survival, to dinosaurs and fossils.

**Hours:** The warehouse store is open Tues. - Sat. from 8am - 4pm. The Earth Science Museum is open Tues. and Thurs., noon - 4pm; Sat., 8am - 4pm. Both are closed on national holidays. Rock Collecting at the Dinosaurs is held every Sat. from 9am - 10:30am and again from 1:30pm - 3pm, weather permitting. During inclement weather, inquire about other Sat. afternoon outings. Kids' Fossil Shack is held Sat. from 10:30am - noon.

**Admission:** Entrance to the warehouse store is free. The Earth Science Museum is $1.50 for adults; $1 for seniors and ages 2 - 12. Rock Collecting at the Dinosaurs and Kids' Fossil Shack are $4 per person, each event. No reservations are needed. School tours start at $4 per participant. Call for specific information and a class schedule.

**Ages:** 3 years and up.

# KIDZONE - RIVERSIDE YOUTH MUSEUM                      ☼
(909) 683-3800 / www.kidzone.org                          $$
*3800 Main Street, Riverside*                              ≡
(Exit Riverside Fwy [91] S. on University. It's on the corner of University and Main St., the latter of which is a pedestrian mall.)

Kids need a place to call their own and KidZone is it! The huge, rectangular room is divided into colorful sections with various interactive machines, games, and exhibits. Each one emphasizes a particular educational aspect. Note: Some exhibits do rotate.

The first section has a computer that "morphs" human faces onto animals or objects. It also contains a giant kaleidoscope, and a momentum machine, where you spin around and around and around. Next, walk through a (fake) volcanic mountain with "lava" flowing out, hear and feel it erupt every twenty minutes, or so, and watch a video on volcanos. The short mountain tunnel exits at a mock archeological site. Put on a hard hat, dig in the sand pits, and use a paint brush to uncover pottery fragments and bones. "Drive" a material recovery car, which is used as an aid in learning about recycling. Hop on a police motorcycle complete with a radio, buttons to push, and a helmet. Practice rescuing techniques in a fully-equipped paramedic car with lights, sirens, and a two-way radio that is connected to the police motorcycle and to the nearby kid-size medical office. The office has official white lab coats for all visiting "doctors," as well as a stethoscope, human body models, scales, etc. A toddlers' play area has a little playground, construction toys, and a place to draw. All ages will be challenged in the shape room, where geometric pattern pieces and 3D polyhedra await someone to put them together. The (make believe) KKID TV station allows future anchormen and women to sit behind a newscaster's desk and watch themselves on a TV monitor. (Note: All those funny faces they're making also show on a monitor at the entrance to the museum.)

Guests will be *powerfully* impacted by the energy section, where they can try on repairmen equipment; learn about transformers; push buttons connected to objects in a doll house to see how much electricity is used by a computer, TV, lamp, etc.; pedal a bike which then pumps water from a well; pull levers to make water go through pipes, and filter through a re-created treatment plant; and measure how much water a family uses doing everyday activities.

Kids are also invited to play wheelchair basketball, blow bubbles, look at a compost bin, create a take-home craft, stare at a life-size Allosaurus skeleton, and shake with an earthquake that registers 7.0 on an earthquake platform. Special workshops are offered for families, and some just for parents. The museum brochure says it all: "KidZone is not a 'museum'; it's a 'do-seum' and doing is what learning is all about."

**Hours:** Open Tues. - Fri., 10am - 5pm; Sat. - Sun., 10am - 4pm.
**Admission:** $4 per person; children under 2 years are free. Admission and craft activities are free from 1pm - 4pm on "First Sunday," a program which occurs the first Sunday of the month from October through June. Note: Other museums in Riverside are also free on this day.
**Ages:** 1½ to 13 years.

# MARCH FIELD MUSEUM

(909) 697-6600
*16222 Interstate 215, March Air Force Base*
(Exit Moreno Valley Fwy [215] E. on Van Buren Blvd.)

A P-40 Warhawk stands guard at the entrance of March Field Museum, which is the proud home to one of the most extensive collection of military aircraft and aviation artifacts in the United States. The walkway is lined with airplane engines, plus a jeep that kids can get into and "drive" around. Outside, over forty historic airplanes are on display, from the smaller F-84 to the massive

296 MUSEUMS - RIVERSIDE COUNTY

B-52 to the sleek SR-71. Kids are welcome to look at the planes, but not to climb in them.

Inside, the huge hanger displays everything possible pertaining to the Air Force. Airplanes, such as a biplane trainer, have landed in here, as have exhibits of flight uniforms, photographs, model planes, engines, medals, weapons, and equipment from both World Wars, Korea, Viet Nam, the Cold War, and Desert Storm. This museum defines the word "comprehensive!"

*The March Field Story* and other informative films are available for viewing with prior notice. Although the only touchable activity for kids is to strap themselves into a flight training chair, they really enjoy the museum, particularly your pilots-in-training.

**Hours:** Open daily from 10am - 4pm. Closed New Year's Day, Easter, Thanksgiving, and Christmas.

**Admission:** $5 for adults; $2 for ages 5 - 12 years; children 4 years and under are free.

**Ages:** 3 years and up.

# MISSION INN / MISSION INN MUSEUM

(909) 784-0300 - Inn; (909) 788-9556 - museum / www.missioninn.com    $$
*3649 Mission Inn Avenue, Riverside*
(Exit Riverside Fwy [91] W. on University Ave., R. on Orange St., L. on Mission Inn Ave.)

Is it a European castle? Not quite, but this elegant, old, sprawling Inn is beautiful to look at and tour. The hour-and-a-half tour shows much of its eclectic architecture and furnishings. Mediterranean style, emphasized in the colorful tiles, spiral columns, and bells, is incorporated with an Oriental influence, such as a hotel kitchen chimney in the shape of a pagoda, plus other unique touches. Only through the tour can you see all four wings of the hotel with highlights including the gilded eighteenth-century altar in the wedding chapel; the music room; the Court of Birds (there are no actual birds still here, but the stories about them capture the imagination); the Taft Chair, that seats up to five kids at one time; and the open-air, five-story spiral staircase in the rotunda, which is quite grand looking. If your kids are interested in architecture or hearing about the Inn's history, they will enjoy the tour. If not, at least take a quick walk through the grounds.

The small museum is located on the pedestrian walkway, next to the Inn's gift shop. Frank Miller, the Inn's builder, had an international collection that reflected his tastes. Housed in the museum are a scale model of a pagoda, encased figurines, artifacts, and photos. The most appealing exhibit to kids has old-time barber shop chairs (not to sit in) with mirrors and hair cutting instruments. A tape of old-timers reminiscing adds to the display's atmosphere.

**Hours:** The Inn is a functioning Inn so it is open daily. Tours are given Mon. - Fri. at 10:30am and 2pm; Sat. - Sun. from 10am - 3pm, approximately every hour. The Museum is open daily from 9:30am - 4pm.

**Admission:** You can walk around the hotel at no charge. The tour costs $8 for adults; children 11 years and under are free. The Museum is $2 per person.

**Ages:** 8 years and up.

## ORANGE EMPIRE RAILWAY MUSEUM

(909) 657-2605
*2201 South "A" Street, Perris*

See ORANGE EMPIRE RAILWAY MUSEUM, under the Transportation section, for details.

## RIVERSIDE MUNICIPAL MUSEUM

(909) 782-5273 - museum; (909) 788-2747 - educational tours
*3580 Mission Inn Avenue, Riverside*
(Exit Riverside Fwy [91] W. on University Ave., R. on Orange St., L. on Mission Inn)

This museum contains a wealth of information and fun for both kids and adults. The natural history exhibits are a natural place to start. Push a button and the taxidermied mountain lion crouched on the ledge "roars." Other stuffed animals are also posed in animated positions. For instance, a baby bobcat is batting at something and a skunk is doing a handstand on its front paws. The geology area has a nice display of rocks and minerals, plus a section on earthquakes. The paleontology exhibits have a saber-tooth cat skeleton, some fossilized elephant tusks (they are huge!), and a few dinosaur bones. The anthropology section has displays of Indian clothing, musical instruments, hunting weapons, and a few dioramas. The local history display features missions, cowboys, tools, and guns, plus machinery and crate labels of citrus growers.

The upstairs sometimes has rotating displays. We saw exhibits that emphasized Mexican heritage, with ethnic costumes, etc. The hallway is lined with small botanical dioramas. A favorite room is the small Nature Laboratory. Kids can inspect shells and bugs under a microscope. They can also dissect owl pellets. There is a small sea display with preserved sea horses, and a few live reptiles in here, too - snakes, lizards, and turtles -, and. The entire museum rates high on kid-interest! In a program called "First Sunday," free arts and crafts activities are offered on the first Sun. of each month, October through June, from 1pm to 4pm. Other museums in Riverside offer free admission and/or arts and crafts on this Sun., too.

**Hours:** The museum is open Mon., 9am - 1pm; Tues. - Fri., 9am - 5pm; Sat., 10am - 5pm; Sun., 11pm - 5pm. The Nature Laboratory is open Wed., 2pm - 4:30pm; Sat., 1pm - 3pm.

**Admission:** Free

**Ages:** 2 years and up.

## WORLD MUSEUM OF NATURAL HISTORY

(909) 785-2209

*4700 Pierce Street in Cossentine Hall on the campus of La Sierra
University, Riverside*
(Exit Riverside Fwy [91] S.W. on Magnolia, R. on Pierce. Enter on Campus Dr. from the
intersection of Pierce St. and Sierra Vista Ave. Park at the end of Campus Dr. in parking
lot F on weekends. If you've made arrangements for a special tour, ask the curator to
get a parking permit for you.)

This quality museum is tremendous in its comprehensive scope of minerals,
and freeze-dried animals. Full-grown and young animals are displayed according
to species. The old and new world primates - or monkeys, gorillas, and chimps -
all look so life like! The size and variety of the Crocodiles of the World is
impressive. We had not heard of at least half the ones featured here. The Indian
Gavial is especially unique with a snout that resembles a long, thin saw blade.
The numerous types of turtles were similarly astounding. They range from the
very small to the gigantic alligator snapping turtle. Snakes of the World boasts
another record-breaking variety, ranging from boas, pythons, and common
garters, to venomous snakes and even a two-headed snake. Other reptiles,
including a huge Komodo dragon, are also on display. Birds from all over the
world are represented here, such as pelicans, flamingoes, penguins, an imperial
eagle, and a blue-hued hunting green magpie. Some of the more unusual animals
on display are the flat-headed cat (which, not surprisingly, has a very flat head),
bats (one is just the size of a pin), an armadillo, a kangaroo, and an Indian rhino.

An outstanding collection of rocks and minerals are grouped, in one section,
according to color. These include large specimens of amethyst, malachite, etc.
Other groupings include meteorites, fluorescent minerals, geodes, and huge slabs
of petrified wood. There is also a large display of sphere balls or, in kidspeak,
"cool-looking bowling balls." Part of this display shows the progression of a
chunk of raw rock to a cube and then to the finished, sphere product. A fine
display of Indian artifacts, such as arrowheads and headdresses, is also
noteworthy. The World Museum of Natural History is a gem of a place!

**Hours:**     Open Sat. from 2pm - 5pm, or weekdays by appointment. Tours
          are welcome.
**Admission:** Free; donations gladly accepted.
**Ages:**     2 years and up.

# THE AIR MUSEUM "PLANES OF FAME"
(909) 597-3722 / www.planesoffame.org                               *$$$*
*7000 Merrill Avenue, Chino*
(Exit Riverside Fwy [91] N. on the 71, N. on Euclid [or the 83]. Exit Hwy 83 R. on Merrill
Ave., R. on Airport Way.)

For some *plane* old fun, come see the over 100 vintage aircraft (some of
which are flyable) that have landed here, including one of the only air-worthy
Japanese Zeros in the world. Every Saturday and Sunday a B-17 Bomber lands
at the Air Museum and, for a $1 donation, your child can sit in it and "fly."

Outside the north hanger (i.e. the Tom Friedkin Hanger) is the plane that
crashed (and obviously never recovered) from the movie *Waterworld*. Other
planes, parts of planes, and military vehicles are stationed here. Inside the hanger

are Japanese aircraft from WWII. Some of them are "flying" around overhead, while others are grounded. My boys were drawn to the "Wild Grinning Face of the Green Dragon Unit" - a nose of a plane that has machine guns and is decorated with a fire-breathing dragon painted on its side. This building also displays airplane engines and small models of Japanese army aircraft, plus news clippings regarding Pearl Harbor.

The Bob Pond Hanger has more colorful and historic aircraft to look at. In the midst of such classic planes, what really grabs my children's attention, however, is the cartoon characters on the sides of the planes (e.g. Goofy at bat).

Part of the Jim Maloney Display Hanger is a restoration work area. Kids who are aeronautically inclined will be in their element here, although they cannot touch anything. Children are welcome, however, to touch and play in the hands-on aviation room in this hanger. They can climb into three experimental planes and play pilot. They can also practice their mechanical skills by "using" rivet guns and drills, plus taking apart (and putting together) parts of an engine. This hanger also displays gun turrets, cockpit control panels, uniforms, and the most model aircraft we've ever seen in one place!

It's a short drive around the corner to the Fighter Jets Museum and Space Exhibit. The Bell X-1 was used in the movie, *The Right Stuff* and was the first plane to break the sound barrier. Other planes here have descriptions that are equally informative, though some are a bit technical. The Space Exhibit currently has a full-size model of the Apollo 13 capsule, along with posters, photos of astronauts, and rockets blasting off - all underneath a ceiling painted to look like a starry, nighttime sky. Future plans include a cockpit with real control panels, fueled by imagination, and more space-related displays.

The Air Museum is in the Chino airport, so kids can experience the thrill of seeing planes take off and land. If you get hungry, pilot your way to Flo's Cafe, which is also on airport grounds.

**Hours:** Open daily from 9am - 5pm. Closed Thanksgiving and Christmas.
**Admission:** $8.95 for adults; $1.95 for ages 5 - 11; children 4 years and under are free.
**Ages:** 3 years and up.

# A SPECIAL PLACE
(909) 881-1201
*315 E. Fourth Street, Ontario*
(Exit Hwy 30 S. on Waterman, R. on Highland, R. into Harrison to park.)

A Special Place is ideal for younger children who delight in hands-on activities. (That should include all of the younger population!) Outside, a covered cement patio enhances disability awareness via a wheelchair maze (those corners are tough!); a swing for kids in wheelchairs; braces to try on; crutches to use; and even prostheses to touch. Your children will get a feel for what it's like to be mobile in different ways. Also out here is western gear, such as boots, cowboy hats, and a few saddles so kids can ride the range.

Inside, two rooms are divided into sections. The drama area has face painting and costumes. It's a hot time in the old town when kids dress up as firefighters and climb up (and down) the fireman pole. The schoolroom area has a few old-fashioned school desks and a thirteen star flag. (See if your kids notice this and know how many stars are on our flag today.) There is also a working traffic light here to play Red Light, Green Light.

Along the back wall is a wonderful aquatic mural, plus fish and turtle aquariums, and even a cage of birds. Kids can turn a handle at an Edison display to try to generate enough electricity to power a light bulb. At the puppet theater, children make the puppets come to life.

Another section is set-up like a mini-Kaiser clinic, with an X-ray machine, infant incubator, and blood pressure machine. Prepare your child to go to the doctor or to become one! The Shadow Room is always fun. When the light flashes, kids love posing to leave a temporary shadow of their body on the photo-sensitive wall.

The museum is small, but it has a great variety of interactive things to do, making it a special place, indeed.

**Hours:** Open Mon., 1pm - 5pm; Tues. - Thurs., 9am - 1pm; Fri., 9am - 5pm; Sat., 11am - 3pm. Call for extended summer hours.

**Admission:** $2 per person; children 2 years and under are free. The first Sat. of each month is free for grandparents who are accompanied by a paying child.

**Ages:** 6 months to 10 years.

## GRABER OLIVE HOUSE

(909) 983-1761 / www.inland.net/graberolives

*315 E. Fourth Street, Ontario*

(Exit San Bernardino Fwy [10] S. on Euclid, L. on Fourth St.)

This is an unusual pit stop for kids. On the grounds are a small museum, an olive processing plant, a gift shop, and the owner's house, whose Victorian-style living room doubles as a tea room and etiquette classroom for kids and adults. The one-room museum shows a pictorial history of olive processing. It also has an eclectic mix of antiques such as a big wooden olive grader, a Singer sewing machine, a sausage stuffer, etc.

Take a short tour around the working olive plant. The "on-season" is mid-October through December, when the machinery and workers are in full production. Walk into the grading room, where olives are sorted by size and quality, and peer into the enormous olive vats. The boiler room, where olives are sterilized, the canning machine, and the labeling machine are all interesting to look at. A ten-minute video, that shows the history of the packing plant, is also available to watch.

The gift shop is very classy with etiquette videos, stationery, delicious jams, and elegant candies. (The chocolate-covered cherries are to die for!) Kids can sample a Graber olive, which might mean more to them after a tour.

**Hours:** Open Mon. - Sat., 9am - 5:30pm; Sun., 9:30am - 6pm. Make a
reservation for a guided tour.
**Admission:** Free
**Ages:** 5 years and up.

## LINCOLN MEMORIAL SHRINE

(909) 798-7636 - Shrine; (909) 798-7632 - Heritage Room at the Smiley
Public Library / www.aksmiley.org
*125 W. Vine Street, Redlands*
(Exit San Bernardino Fwy [10] S. on Hwy 38 [or Orange St.], R. on Citrus Ave., L. on
Eureka St. It's behind the Smiley Public Library.)

"Fourscore and seven years ago. . ." begins the Gettysburg Address. If your
older children are studying our revered sixteenth president, but can't make it to
Washington D.C., bring them to the Lincoln Memorial Shrine. The central,
octagon-shaped building is devoted to Lincoln memorabilia and contains books,
letters and documents about and from Lincoln, plus Civil War photos, bullets
found on battlefields, officers' uniforms, medals, and a lifemask (i.e. an exact
likeness of a person via a mold) and handcast of Abraham Lincoln. Mementos
from his assassination include his cuff links and a strand of his hair. The wings
on either side of the shrine display Civil War artifacts such as swords, an 1863
Springfield rifle, hardtack, documents, models, and pictures of Abraham Lincoln,
Robert E. Lee, and Ulysses S. Grant.

Come view the materials here on your own. Better yet, make a tour
reservation and benefit from knowledgeable docents who explain the exhibits in
more detail and who ask thought-provoking questions. Exhibits at the memorial
rotate because the small shrine cannot contain the 3,000-plus manuscripts and
other items in the archives. Note that the buildings are inscribed with excerpts
from Lincoln's inaugural addresses and various other speeches.

**Hours:** Open Tues. - Sat., 1pm - 5pm. Closed holidays except for
Lincoln's birthday. Small group tours can be arranged for
morning hours.
**Admission:** Free
**Ages:** 7 years and up.

## MOJAVE RIVER VALLEY MUSEUM / DANA PARK

(760) 256-5452 - museum; (760) 256-5661 - park
*Corner of Barstow Road and Virginia Way, Barstow*
(Exit Mojave Fwy [15] N. on Barstow Rd.)

This little museum is full of interesting artifacts and displays. My boys liked
hearing the story and seeing the bones of a headless horseman, found astride his
horse. The rock and minerals on display include nice specimens of arrowheads,
quartz, calate, and black and gold forms of chalocopyrite, plus fluorescent
minerals that glow neon colors under black light. Other glass-encased exhibits
are an eclectic mixture, such as lanterns, irons, rug beaters, pottery, clothing, a
collection of glass insulators used by telegraph companies, etc. Kids can try their

hand at grinding corn with stone mortar and pestle. They can also touch various animal skins, a turtle shell, bones, pinecones, rocks, and cotton. Short nature films are available to watch upon request. Call to arrange a field trip, and students will not only learn a lot about local history, but they can pan for real gold (and keep it!). Classes are usually taught by Mr. Walker, an archeology instructor at the college. The outside of the museum has large mining equipment around its perimeters - ore carts, picks, etc. Across the street is the small Centennial Park, which is actually an extension of the museum. It has a caboose, an army tank, and a mining display, which are representative of the three industries that helped formed Barstow.

Dana Park is just across Virginia Way. It has picnic shelters, some grassy hills to roll down, a playground, and an indoor community swimming pool that is open year round. Call (760) 255-4431 for pool information.

**Hours:** The museum is open daily 11am - 4pm. The pool is open daily from 1pm - 5pm.

**Admission:** Free to the museum, though donations are appreciated. The pool is $2 per person, per session.

**Ages:** 3 years and up.

# MUSEUM OF HISTORY AND ART, ONTARIO

(909) 983-3198
*225 S. Euclid Avenue, Ontario*
(Exit the San Bernardino Fwy [10] S. on Euclid, L. on Transit. It's on the corner.)

The Museum of History and Art captures the flavor of historic Ontario. The hallway leading toward the history section is lined with local school children's art work. The small museum's history galleries feature artifacts from citrus groves and industry, such as a replica of a Graber olive grader and a citrus smudge pot, which was used to warm trees. Other displays, mostly behind glass, include an old-fashioned kitchen exhibit; an iron collection; a section of photographs, uniforms, and information on WWII; and old machinery such as a typewriter and switchboard.

The art rooms contain changing exhibits of local and regional artists, as well as student work. Set in a Mediterranean-style building with a big fountain out front, the museum is a pleasant way to learn more about local roots.

**Hours:** The museum is open Wed. - Sun. from noon - 4pm.

**Admission:** Free

**Ages:** 6 years and up.

# RAINS HOUSE - CASA DE RANCHO CUCAMONGA

(909) 989-4970
*8810 Hemlock Street, Rancho Cucamonga*
(Exit San Bernardino Fwy [10] N. on Vineyard. It's 2 blocks N. of Foothills Blvd., on the corner of Vineyard and Hemlock, in a residential area.)

Built with bricks in 1860, this restored rancho residence has an open courtyard. Tours are given of the beautiful grounds, and through the historical home to see period furniture in the bedrooms, living rooms, etc. Docents recount stories about the people who once lived here. Their lives were like soap operas, complete with affairs, murders, buried treasure, etc. - kids love this (and they are learning history!) Ask about the special events that the Rancho hosts, such as Old Rancho Days, etc.

**Hours:** Open Wed. - Sat., 10am - 5pm; Sun., 1pm - 5pm.
**Admission:** $1 donation per person.
**Ages:** 6 years and up.

# ROY ROGERS - DALE EVANS MUSEUM ☼
(760) 243-4547 / www.royrogers.com    $$$
*15650 Seneca Road, Victorville*
(Exit Mojave Fwy [15] W. on Roy Rogers Dr. and circle 'round to the museum. You'll see it from the freeway.)

The Roy Rogers - Dale Evans Museum is easy to spot from the freeway. It looks like a fort, and has a larger-than-life statue of Roy's horse, Trigger, out front. Step into the museum and step back to a simpler time when cowboys were heroes and family morals were admired and desired. Although you, and certainly your kids, might be too young to remember when Roy Rogers and Dale Evans were household names and he reigned as "King of the Cowboys," this museum is fascinating to all ages. It is an extensive collection of personal memorabilia that is incredibly well-displayed and delightful to explore.

Roy saved a lifetime of things and turned them into a museum. Family albums and celebrity photos abound. There are also many cases of trinkets, letters, and other items sent by fans, including lots of signed sports paraphernalia. After the Roy Rogers Show went on the air, Roy's likeness began appearing on everything from cereal boxes to comic books to lunch boxes, etc. He endorsed almost every kind of child's toy imaginable including cap guns, lassos, rings, hobby horses, and more. A sample of these items are on display here. My middle son (and cowboy "wannabe") loved seeing all the guitars, glitzy saddles, spurs, Western statues, numerous pairs of boots, and the fancy western duds that both Roy and Dale wore. At the kiddie corral, three sturdy wooden horses and a blue sky backdrop make for a great "ride 'em, cowboy!" photo opportunity.

One of the most popular displays features the taxidermied Trigger (Roy's beloved horse), Buttermilk (Dale's horse), and Bullet (the "wonder dog"). There are many more stuffed animals on exhibit including an exotic black Russian Boar, a mountain lion, an albino skunk, and an albino raccoon. Roy was a game hunter, at a time when it was politically acceptable. His collection also includes mounted baboons, a zebra leg stool, a monkey rug, and an elephant feet foot stool. He also amassed a number of guns, pistols, and rifles - some with extravagant handles.

We enjoyed the Story Theater which shows a film, several times a day, of the family sharing memories of growing up with Roy and Dale, plus movie clips. It's like watching a professional (and entertaining) home video. The back room contains vehicles that are special to the family, including a horse-drawn carriage and a car with show guns mounted on the hood. The outside center courtyard has more displays of large game - an elephant's head, a polar bear, etc., as well as Native American displays. The latter includes feather headdresses, beaded clothing, rugs, and more. I'll close this entry with an inevitable, "Happy trails to you."

**Hours:** Open daily 9am - 5pm. Closed Easter, Thanksgiving, and Christmas.

**Admission:** $7 for adults; $6 for seniors and ages 13 - 16; $5 for ages 6 - 12; children 5 years and under are free.

**Ages:** 3 years and up.

## SAN BERNARDINO COUNTY MUSEUM

(909) 307-2669 / www.co.san-bernardino.ca.us/museum

*2024 Orange Tree Lane, Redlands*

(Exit San Bernardino Fwy [10] N. on California St., R. on Orange Tree Ln.)

Spend a day at the incredible San Bernardino County Museum where the hallway exhibits are just as fine as the ones in the exhibit rooms! The distinctive half-dome attached to the main building is the Fisk Gallery of Fine Arts. The Hall of History and Anthropology is down the ramp from the main level. Here you'll find a covered wagon and a Wells Fargo stage coach, along with period clothing. The Anthropology section has Indian artifacts, such as arrowheads and painted rock art.

The hallway going to the Upper Level is lined with exhibits such as old-time medicine bottles, fossilized mammoth tusks, the bones of a ground sloth, and a saber-tooth cat skull. The other side of the hallway is a wonderful prelude to the Upper Level, displaying taxidermied birds and bird eggs. The eggs vary in size from very large elephant bird eggs to very small hummingbird eggs.

If your kids show any interest in ornithology, the study of birds (calling each other bird brain doesn't count), they will be fascinated by the entire Upper Level. The Hall of Water Birds takes you on flights of fancy, although with taxidermied birds you won't get very far. See if your kids can correctly match the birds to their eggs, which are also on display throughout the room. The next wing, Hall of Land Birds, displays birds and eggs according to regional habitat. Look for the "awww, so cute" hatchling exhibit. I have never seen so many birds flocked together.

A large stuffed California Condor guards the entrance to the Upper Dome Gallery. This gallery has rotating exhibits of art work.

An absolutely dazzling display of rocks, minerals, and gemstones line the hallway toward the Lower Level. The doors in the hallway lead out to the Discovery Hall, but we'll come back to that. Continue down the ramp into the Hall of Mammals. The walls in here are lined with fossilized animal bones, horns, and teeth. Bug collectors will be bug-eyed at the comprehensive collection of mounted insects of all sizes, shapes, and colors. Also along the walls are dioramas of smaller taxidermied animals and reptiles, such as spotted skunks, possums, and turtles. The Hall of Mammals is unique in that it also has exhibits of larger taxidermied animals, such as a polar bear, an Alaskan brown bear, a mountain lion, a bison, and a gigantic moose. My kids were really impressed by the sheer size of some of the animals.

Outside, between the main building and the Discovery Hall, is a patio area designed just for kids. (Check out the F-105 jet just around the corner.) The displays include a mining car carrying "explosives" on track toward a tunnel and a full-size caboose and steam engine that are sometimes open to climb aboard. Picnic tables are here for snack attacks.

The Discovery Hall is a learning center that has small, live mammals, such as bunnies and bats, and reptiles, such as iguanas, a boa, and other snakes. Kids can touch fossils, animal furs, and casts of bones and dinosaur fossils. The hall also has aquariums.

The Elsie Munzig Special Exhibit Hall has terrific, changing, usually interactive displays. A past exhibit was rather batty - Masters of the Night - The True Story of Bats. It included entering through the portals of a gothic castle, seeing videos, touching models of bats, and literally hanging around in a bat cave.

A one-hour, Saturday Morning Family Fun program is usually held every Saturday. It's designed to educate the entire family about a particular topic or animal in a fun, hands-on manner. The programs are free with general museum admission. Ask about special events, classes, and tours.

**Hours:** Open Tues. - Sun. from 9am - 5pm. The Discovery Hall is open Tues. - Thurs. from 10am - 1pm; Fri., 10am - 4pm; Sat. - Sun., 1pm - 4pm. The whole museum is closed New Year's Day, Thanksgiving, and Christmas.

**Admission:** $5 for adults; $4 for seniors and students; $3 for ages 5 - 12; children 4 years and under are free. Admission prices are sometimes temporarily raised when the exhibit hall has a special exhibit.

**Ages:** 2 years and up.

## TEMECULA MUSEUM / TEMECULA - OLD TOWN

(909) 676-0021                                                                       !/$

*Front Street and Moreno Street, Temecula*

(Exit Temecula Valley Fwy [15] W. on Rancho California Rd., L. on Front St. to Old Town, or L. on Moreno St. to the museum at Sam Hicks Park.)

Mosey on over to Old Town Temecula and enjoy an hour or so shopping along Main Street. This western strip of town looks and feels authentic, right down to its bootstraps. The many unique-looking stores with specialty gift items for sale make it an alluring place to shop, even with children.

The museum is located on a corner park - Sam Hicks Park - that has a small playground, and a large rock inscribed with the names of pioneers. The museum is an interesting glimpse into Temecula's past. The tools, household goods, guns, saddles, army equipment, etc., on display, portray life on the local ranches and frontier towns. A six-foot by nine-foot diorama depicts the city of Temecula, circa 1914. There are also Native American artifacts, plus memorabilia from Erle Stanley Gardner, the author of the Perry Mason stories and a one-time resident of Temecula.

**Hours:** Open Wed. - Sun. from 11am - 4pm. Main Street shopping is open daily, usually from 10am - 6pm.

**Admission:** By donation

**Ages:** 5 years and up.

## ANTIQUE GAS & STEAM ENGINE MUSEUM, INC.

(800) 5-TRACTOR (587-2286) or (760) 941-1791 /
www.ziggyworks.com/~museum
*2040 North Santa Fe Avenue, Vista*

(Exit San Diego Fwy [5] N. on San Luis Rey Mission Exwy [76], continue on Mission Ave. Or, from Escondido Fwy [15], exit W. on Pala Rd [76], which turns into Mission Ave. From Mission Ave. go S. on N. Santa Fe Ave. From Vista Fwy [78], exit N. on Melrose Dr., R. on W. Bobier Ave., L. on Santa Fe Ave.)

California has a museum for almost any interest. This one answers the age-old question, "Where do engines go when they run out of gas (or steam)?" The forty-acre, mostly outdoor museum, has hundreds of tractors, combines, gas and steam engines (that's a given from the name of the museum), horse-drawn carriages, and equipment used in mining, oil drilling, construction, agriculture, and more. The machines have been (or are in the process of being) restored to working condition. In fact, some of the equipment is used to help farm the adjacent lands. Walk around on your own; ask one of the volunteers for a tour; or better yet, come to a demonstration usually held on the third and fourth weekends of June and October. At these Threshing Bees and Antique Engine & Tractor Shows, watch or take part in planting, harvesting, household chores, early American crafts, blacksmithing, log sawing, parades, square dancing, etc. It's a good ol' time!

Some of the museum's collection is housed in structures resembling a small town. Featured buildings include a huge (and complete) blacksmith and wheelwright shop, a farm house with parlor, a sawmill, a one-third scale train with a telegraphers office, and a barn. There are picnic tables here and even a small playground with two small, stationary tractors to climb on. The museum is interesting to visit anytime, but it's exciting to visit at exhibition time!

**Hours:** Open daily from 10am - 4pm.

**Admission:** Free, except for special events that usually cost $6.

**Ages:** 4 years and up.

## BALBOA PARK (San Diego)

(619) 239-0512 - This Visitors Center number gives a listing of the museums and information about upcoming events. /
www.balboapark.org
*Balboa Park on the Prado, San Diego*

(Going S. on Cabrillo Fwy [163], exit N. on Park Blvd. Going S. on San Diego Fwy [5], exit at Ash St. / "A" St., L. on "A" St., L. on Park Blvd. Going N. on 5, exit W. on "B" St., R. on Park Blvd. Once on Park Blvd. turn L. on Presidents Way to get to the museums.) This massive 1,158-acre park is the cultural and recreational heart of San Diego. Numerous programs and seasonal events are held here - see the Calendar section in the back of the book and/or call for a schedule of events. The park has shade trees, grassy areas, picnic areas, and playgrounds located at Pepper Grove Picnic Area on Park Boulevard, which is south of the San Diego Zoo, and located at the north end of Balboa Drive. Morley Field Sports Complex, located off Morely Field Drive in the northeastern section, has twenty-five public tennis courts available for $4 per person for all day use. Call (619) 295-9278 for reservations. It also has a fitness course; boccie ball, Italian sport similar to lawn bowling; a velodrome; a fly-casting pool, with free lessons on Sunday mornings; an archery range; baseball diamonds; a frisbee golf course; playgrounds; picnic areas; and a swimming pool that is open seasonally. Swim sessions cost $2 for adults, $1.50 for seniors and children. Call (619) 692-4920 for more information. Call (619) 692-4919 for more information regarding the sports complex.

Balboa Park is home to a majority of the city's museums, as well as the world famous SAN DIEGO ZOO (look under the Zoos and Animals section). Individual museum entries are found under this section, listed by their official titles: MINGEI INTERNATIONAL FOLK ART MUSEUM, MUSEUM OF PHOTOGRAPHIC ARTS, MUSEUM OF SAN DIEGO HISTORY, REUBEN H. FLEET SCIENCE CENTER, SAN DIEGO AEROSPACE MUSEUM, SAN DIEGO AUTOMOTIVE MUSEUM, SAN DIEGO HALL OF CHAMPIONS SPORTS MUSEUM, SAN DIEGO MODEL RAILROAD MUSEUM, SAN DIEGO MUSEUM OF ART, SAN DIEGO MUSEUM OF MAN, and SAN DIEGO NATURAL HISTORY MUSEUM. Passports can be purchased to visit eleven museums for $21 for adults. Passes can be bought at the Visitors Information Center and are good for one week from the date of purchase. Below is a list of which museums are free on particular Tuesdays: First Tuesday: S.D. Natural History (permanent exhibits only), Reuben H. Fleet Science Center, and S.D. Model Railroad; Second Tuesday: Museum of Photographic Arts, Museum of S.D. History, and S.D. Hall of Champions Sports Museum; Third Tuesday: Japanese Friendship Garden, Mingei International Folk Art Museum, S.D. Museum of Art (permanent exhibits only), and S.D. Museum of Man; Fourth Tuesday: Cottages and Hall of Nations films, such as *Children Around the World* (11am to 3pm), House of Pacific Relations International, S.D. Aerospace Museum, and S.D. Automotive Museum.

The park also offers many other attractions that are worthy of mention. The beautiful, latticed **Botanical Building** is located at the north end of the lily pond next to the San Diego Museum of Art. It has (labeled) tropical and subtropical plants on display. It is open Friday through Wednesday from 10am to 4pm. Admission is free. The **Timken Museum of Art** is located next to the Visitors Center. Housed here are collections of works by European Old Masters, eighteenth- and nineteenth-century American paintings, and Russian icons. It is open Tuesday through Saturday from 10am to 4:30pm; Sunday, 1:30pm to 4:30pm. Admission is free. The **Japanese Friendship Garden** is a Japanese-style house with a main room that has a traditional table set with (fake) Japanese food. Children must stay on the short path leading to the small garden. If you are interested in seeing this room and garden, come here when admission is free, on the third Tuesday of the month, as admission is otherwise $2 per person. Free outdoor concerts are given on the famous **Spreckels Pipe Organ** every Sunday from 2pm to 3pm, plus on Mondays from 8pm to 9:30pm during July and August. The organ is located in an architecturally beautiful building set in a huge half circle. My kids think the steps here are a great place for picnicking. The **Spanish Village Art Center**, (619) 233-9050, is just north of the San Diego Natural History Museum. The "village" has retained its old-world charm with its Spanish architecture and colorful courtyard tiles and flowers. The thirty-five art studios and galleries include woodcarvings, sculptures, and gems and minerals, for show and sale. Oftentimes, the artisans demonstrate their craft which makes the Spanish Village Center an intriguing stop for slightly older kids. The **House of Pacific Relations**, (619) 234-0739, is located behind the United Nations Building, across from the Spreckels Organ. The "House" is comprised of fifteen cottages representing thirty-one nationalities. Exhibits in each cottage pertain to specific ethnic groups. Music and dance programs are held on Sundays from 2pm to 3pm from mid-March through October 31. The cottages are open Sundays from 12:30pm to 4:30pm and on the fourth Tuesday from noon to 3pm. Admission is free. Two other kid-friendly attractions are the **miniature train ride** and the **merry-go-round**. Both rides are located south of the Zoo and north of the Spanish Village Center. They operate weekends and holidays only from 10:30am to 5:30pm. The train ride costs $1.25 per person. The old-fashioned carousel has horses and other animals to ride on, and offers a chance to grab at the gold ring. Rides cost $1 for all ages. There are many theaters and places to eat within Balboa Park, too.

At any time during your visit to the park, you are welcome to hop aboard the Balboa Park Tram. This free, intra-park transportation system can take you from Presidents Way and Park Boulevard, up to the carousel, through where the museums are, and up north to 6th Street and the MARSTON HOUSE (look under this section for more details). It makes several stops along the way, so you can catch it coming or going. It operates daily from 10am to 4pm, with extended hours in the summer. Plan to visit Balboa Park many times, as you obviously cannot see it all in one, two, or even three days!

**Hours:** The park is open daily. The Visitors Center is open daily 9am - 4pm. Individual attractions are listed separately.

**Admission:** Entrance to the park is free. Individual attractions are listed separately.

**Ages:** All ages for the park. Individual attractions are listed separately.

# BUENA VISTA AUDUBON NATURE CENTER
(760) 439-BIRD (2473)

*2202 South Coast Highway, Oceanside*
(Exit San Diego Fwy [5] W. on Vista Way, L. on South Coast Highway. It is just N. of the Buena Vista Lagoon.)

This museum is not just for the birds! The exhibits inside this small building consist mainly of taxidermied birds (some in flight) such as a pelican, a great blue heron, a red-tailed hawk, a colorful yellow western tanager, and more. A stuffed owl has a mouse in its beak and a pellet at its feet that contains partially digested animal parts. Other mounted animals on display include a bobcat and a possum. The touch table has a raccoon skin, petrified wood, and whale bones, among other things. Look through a kid-level window on the central display to see fish "swimming" underneath. A book corner for children has a nice selection of nature books to read. Other items of interest are the fish tank with catfish (it's easy to see where they got their name), a small rock and mineral display, and a live tarantula.

Outside, take a walk through the marshy reeds out to the lagoon. This area is home to a wide variety of birds. Guided field trips are one of the best ways to really learn about the abundant wildlife at Buena Vista. Migrate over to the picnic tables which are available to make your day just ducky!

**Hours:** Open Tues. - Sat., 10am - 4pm; Sun., 1pm - 4pm.
**Admission:** Free
**Ages:** 3 years and up.

## CALIFORNIA SURF MUSEUM

(760) 721-6876 / www.surfmuseum.org
*223 North Coast Highway, Oceanside*
(Exit San Diego Fwy [5] W. on Mission Ave., R. on North Coast Hwy.)

Surfing is the heart of the Southern California beach culture. This small museum aims to preserve the history and lifestyle of surfing so it won't be wiped out. It displays a good selection and wide variety of surfboards. To the inexperienced eye, some might look simply like thick boards, but I'm learning that there is more to the board than meets the eye. Exhibits rotate yearly and have included a tabletop wave, a Hawaiian hut made of palm leaves that paid homage to surfing's roots, and lots of photographs and information regarding surfing.

**Hours:** Open daily 10am - 4pm.
**Admission:** Free; donations gladly accepted.
**Ages:** Surfer dudes 8 years and up.

## CAMP PENDLETON

(760) 725-5569 - general information; (760) 725-5710 - rancho tour information; (760) 725-2660 - amphibious museum
*Oceanside*
(Exit San Diego Fwy [5] W. at Harbor Dr. / Vandegrift Blvd. onto the base.)

Driving on I-5 between Orange County and Oceanside, it's hard to miss the sprawling Camp Pendleton. This military training camp is one of the largest, especially for amphibious training. My boys like the thought of being on a real marine base, so taking a "windshield tour" (i.e. driving around in here) was a (quick) treat for them. Camp Pendleton is also on an historical site where early Spanish explorers traveled. For a more detailed understanding of this time period, tour the on-site Rancho Las Flores and the nineteenth-century Santa Margarita adobe ranch house. The houses retain the essence of yesteryear in both landscaping and interior furnishings. Advanced registration is needed and your group must comprise of twenty or more people.

The Amphibious Vehicle Museum is located at the southern end of Camp Pendleton at the Del Mar basin. There are many military vehicles around the area, but the most interesting in the museum are the six L.V.T.'s (Land Vehicle Tracks) - amphibious vehicles used in combat. These relics from WWII are accompanied by war mementoes such as uniforms, weapons, personal artifacts, etc. You may ask to watch the video on the history of the L.V.T.'s. You'll need to show your driver's license and vehicle registration at the main gate.

**Hours:**    Drive through Camp Pendleton Mon. - Fri. from 7:30am -
              4:30pm. Call for rancho and adobe house tours. The Amphibious
              Museum is usually open Tues. - Sat. from 9am - 4pm.
**Admission:** Free
**Ages:**     6 years and up.

## CARLSBAD CHILDREN'S MUSEUM

(760) 720-0737  / www.museumforchildren.org
*300 Carlsbad Village Drive, #102, Carlsbad*
(Exit San Diego Fwy [5] W. on Calsbad Village Dr.)

After my oldest son understood that we were not going to Carl's Bad Children's Museum, his dread turned into anticipation and we all had a great time. Set sail for adventure and catch some pretend fish while skippering a real boat (at least the front end of one), surrounded by a wall with a sea mural. Use a cart to hold all your items while shopping at the well-stocked Kid's Marketplace. The cashier can use the real cash register, with fake money. Things are positively medieval when your kids play at the large replica castle. Girls dress up and turn into princesses (temporarily) while boys (and girls) suit up to become knights in shining (plastic) armor. My oldest son simply declared himself king and ordered everyone else around. Mirror Magic, a room with carnival-type "funny" mirrors, kept the kids busy for a long time. Who would have thought they could make that many faces?! Also, try playing mirror tic-tac-toe. On reflection, it's harder than it seems. Every week Creative Corner provides your child with a new art project to create and take home. Aprons are available for those with messier instincts. At the science area, test a hand battery, watch a solar-powered train go around a track, and stand in the center of a bubble that's as tall as you are. There are a few computers in the museum and a small area for toddlers that has books, toys, and a puppet theater.

The Children's Museum is located in Carlsbad Village Faire, directly across from the Status Chocolates Shop, a sweet stop. The fountain in the middle of the

Plaza has reclining chairs around it making it a delightful place to rest, unless your child falls in the water!

**Hours:** Open Sun., Tues. - Thurs., noon - 5pm; Fri. - Sat., 10am - 5pm. Closed Mon. It's open in July and August daily from 10am - 5pm.

**Admission:** $3.50 for ages 2 years and up.

**Ages:** 1½ years - 11 years.

## CHILDREN'S MUSEUM SAN DIEGO, MUSEO DE LOS NIÑOS

(619) 233-KIDS (5437)                                                                      $$
*200 West Island Avenue, San Diego*
(Exit San Diego Fwy [5] S. on 1ˢᵗ St., R. on Broadway, L. on State, L. on Island.)

The museum's emphasis is "to be a hands-on, minds-on experiential learning environment for people of all ages" and "to be truly bi-national, recognizing Tijuana and Mexico as neighbors." The exhibits here, designed by artists, are all arts and humanities focused.

There are very few permanent exhibits in this innovative children's museum that is housed in a warehouse. They include the Art Studio, which is a place to create wonderful art projects, and it is the home of a 1952 Dodge pick-up truck that kids can paint, repaint, and paint again; the Improv Theater, which is a dress up and stage area; and Cora's Rain House, which is a giant tin house featuring a recreated rain forest and recycled water. It is designed for kids to come in and express their thoughts or emotions by talking, drawing, or writing. Mi Casa es Tu Casa is a semi-permanent exhibit. Kids enter a room and, via virtual reality and video machines, are "transformed" into characters on a screen. Kids in a museum in Mexico City have the same sort of set up and the characters in the two nations are able to interact with each other on screen. Isn't technology incredible?!

The temporary exhibits are all hands-on and great fun. Just a few of the past exhibits include building a prefab house with hammer and nails; the story of making candy told in pictorial renderings; a giant, floor checkerboard, played by using huge red and black foam pillows; and Pop Art featuring life-size super heroes and other cool guys. Call to see what is currently being featured, although kids will thoroughly enjoy whatever it is. A small park, good for picnicking, is located diagonally across the street from the museum.

**Hours:** Open Tues. - Sun. from 10am - 5pm.

**Admission:** $5 for ages 2 and up; $3 for seniors. There is limited free parking. Paid parking is available at Front and Island St. The SAN DIEGO TROLLEY (look under Transportation section) also stops at the museum.

**Ages:** 2 years and up.

## CORONADO BEACH HISTORICAL MUSEUM

(619) 435-7242

*1126 Loma Avenue, Coronado*
(Exit San Diego Fwy [5] W. on 75 and cross over the Coronado Bridge, L. on Orange Ave., R. on Loma Ave. The toll is $1 to Coronado and the return trip is free. If you are car pooling, cross the bridge using the right lane, at no charge.)
    This quaint house contains exhibits depicting the early history of the seaside village of Coronado. Half of the downstairs displays rotate. A past favorite was "Toys and Treasures of a Coronado Childhood," which featured antique toys and furniture, books, games, clothing, and photographs from yesteryear. Note: The museum closes temporarily in between displays. The permanent exhibits include photographs and information on the Hotel Del Coronado, the Navy, the ferry, and tent city. There is also memorabilia such as vintage clothing, jewelry, and a few other items.
    **Hours:**    Open Wed. - Sat., 10am - 4pm; Sun., noon - 4pm.
    **Admission:** Free
    **Ages:**    7 years and up.

## FIREHOUSE MUSEUM

(619) 232-3473 /
www.globalinfo.com/noncomm/firehouse/Firehouse.HTML
*1572 Columbia Street, San Diego*
(Going N. on San Diego Fwy [5], exit at the first exit after Cabrillo Fwy exchange, turn L. on 6$^{th}$ St. at end of off ramp, R. on Ash St., R. on State St., L. on Date St., L. on Columbia. Going S. on 5, exit at Ash / "A" St., go R. at end of off ramp on Ash St., R. on State St., L. on Date St., L. on Columbia.)
    Have a hot time in downtown San Diego by visiting the Firehouse Museum! Housed inside an old fire station, the museum features ten fire engines from different time periods. Also on display are several antique pieces of fire-fighting equipment such as a water pump and steamer, helmets, axes, and speaking trumpets through which chiefs would shout their orders, plus other items like a telephone switchboard, etc.
    **Hours:**    Open Thurs. - Fri., 10am - 2pm; Sat. - Sun., 10am - 4pm.
    **Admission:** $2 for adults; children 12 years and under are free. The first Thurs. of every month is free admission day.
    **Ages:**    4 years and up.

## GASKILL STONE STORE MUSEUM

(619) 478-5707
*31330 Highway 94, Campo*
(Exit 8 Fwy [45 miles from downtown San Diego] S. on Buckman Springs Rd., 10.5 miles to Hwy. 94, bear right [1.5 miles] to the store on the corner.)
    This small museum is exactly as its name implies - a museum created from an old store built with stones in 1885. The exhibits in the room consist of a stocked, old-fashioned general store; a small, turn-of-the-century kitchen; tools; appliances; and lots of photographs and documents. The back room, once used for storing food and other items, is a man-made cave blasted from rock. Upstairs is a military room with mannequins in uniforms, plus photographs and

information about this area's military region. A stream runs in front of the museum and a woods surrounds it. Just around the corner is the SAN DIEGO RAILROAD MUSEUM. (See the Transportation section for more details.)

**Hours:** Open weekends and selected holidays from 11am - 5pm.
**Admission:** $2 for adults; children 12 years and under are free.
**Ages:** 7 years and up.

## GUY B. WOODWARD MUSEUM OF HISTORY ☼

(760) 789-7644                                                                    $
*645 Main Street, Ramona*
(From San Diego Fwy [5] or Escondido Fwy [15], take 78 Fwy E. to Ramona, L. on Main St. [also 78]. From 8 Fwy, take San Vicente Fwy [67] N. Stay on Hwy 67 to Ramona, which turns into Main St.)

A complex of buildings make up this small, early western museum "town." The museum contains the heritage (and furnishings) of the older citizens of Ramona. The main house has roped-off rooms to look into including a turn-of-the-century doctor's office with a bloodied mannequin patient on the bed, and a collection of early medical instruments and vials; a beautifully decorated parlor, which is a combination of living room and music room, with mannequins dressed in period clothing; a library; a bedroom; and a kitchen that is packed with irons, dishes, butter churns, and other implements. The screened in back porch is set up like a bedroom - my kids were ready to move in!

The downstairs used to be a wine cellar, and the temperature is still cool here. The conglomeration of "stuff" now stored and displayed here includes Civil War artifacts, such as uniforms and cannon balls; a collection of cameras; a turkey-feather cape; a six-foot long Red Diamond Rattlesnake skin; Native American artifacts, such as stone mortar and pestle, and pottery; a hair perming machine that looks like something out of a science fiction film; a Casey Tibbs memorial exhibit dedicated to this World Champion rodeo rider; and more. Gift shop items can also be found down here.

The outside courtyard has a stage wagon - no springs makes for a bumpy ride! A red barn houses an old medicine car (an RV prototype). The long garage contains a 1920's tractor, old buggies, an antique fire engine, fire fighting equipment, and lots of old tools, such as saws and wheat scythes, in neat rows on the walls. Just around the corner is a Honey House which contains beekeeping equipment. A narrow Millinery Shoppe features a doll collection, real mink stoles, outrageous feather hats, and a few beaded dresses. Other buildings here include a real jail; an outhouse; a re-created Post Office; a Hobby Room, which is really a catch-all room filled with old typewriters, bottles, and one of the first T.V. sets; a Bunkhouse where cowboys used to live; a Tack Room with dusty, rusty saddles; and a Blacksmith Shop complete with all the tools of the trade. Farm machinery is displayed all around the cluster of buildings. See if your kids can recognize washing machines, butter churns, the large incubator, a cream separator, a machine for bottling milk, etc.

This unique museum is more than a glimpse into the past - it is a good, long, and interesting look into our ancestors' way of life. While you're here, enjoy a

stroll around historic Old Town Ramona, located on both sides and across the
street from the museum.
   **Hours:**     Open Fri. - Sun. from 1pm - 4pm. Closed the month of
                  September.
   **Admission:** $3 for adults; 50¢ for children 12 years and under.
   **Ages:**      5 years and up.

# HERITAGE OF THE AMERICAS MUSEUM                                         ☼
(619) 670-5194                                                            $
*2952 Jamacha Road on Cuyamaca College, El Cajon*
(Going W. on 8 Fwy, exit S. on 2nd St./Jamacha Rd. [Hwy 54], continue on Jamacha Rd.,
R. on Cuyamaca College Dr. W. Going E. on 8, exit S. on Fwy 125, exit S. on Spring St.,
immediately get on 94 Fwy E., continue on to end, turns into Campo Rd., L. on
Jamacha Rd., L on Cuyamaca College Dr. W. It is on the Cuyamaca College campus.)
   This museum makes learning about our heritage much more exciting than
simply reading about it in a history book. Four different exhibit halls branch off
diagonally from the reception desk. The Natural History Hall contains rocks and
minerals, including a lodestone (i.e. a hunk of rock with a magnetic
"personality") with nails sticking out from it. The meteorite display is out of this
world. Other favorite items in this wing include a fossilized turtle shell, a T-Rex
tooth, an Allosaurus claw, trilobites, a rattlesnake skin, a prehistoric bee trapped
in amber, shells, coral, and seahorses. The many taxidermied animals include a
leopard, deer, coyote, and the head of a cape buffalo.
   The Archaeology Hall contains an incredible arrowhead collection, gathered
from all over the world, and from different periods of time. Some of them are
practical, while others are more ornamental. Other displays in glass cases include
stone artifacts, such as hoes and ax heads; Mayan treasures of stone and clay;
necklaces made of jade, quartz, and amethyst; and various forms of money, such
as shells and copper. Weapons, of course, are always a hit with my boys.
   The Anthropology Hall showcases impressive Native American articles such
as eagle feather headdresses, ceremonial costumes, and exquisitely beaded
moccasins, gloves, and vests. More intriguing, however, are the elk tooth and
eagle claw necklaces; the beaded mountain lion paw bag; the knife made from a
blackfoot bear jaw; the shark tooth sword that looks like a small chain saw; and
dance rattles made out of turtle shells and trap door spiders' nests. This section
also displays tomahawks, guns from the Old West, and a buffalo robe.
   The Art Hall features Western art with cowboys and Indians portrayed in
drawings, paintings, photographs, and sculptures. Four different pamphlets are
available that give details about exhibits in each of the halls. This hilltop
museum also has two small gardens with picnic tables, plus a stunning 360-
degree view.
   **Hours:**     Open Tues. - Fri., 10am - 4pm; Sat., 1pm - 5pm. Closed selected
                  holidays.
   **Admission:** $3 for adults; $2 for seniors; $1 for students with I.D.; children
                  11 years and under are free.
   **Ages:**      5 years and up.

# HERITAGE WALK / GRAPE DAY PARK

(760) 743-8207 !

*321 North Broadway, Escondido*

(Exit Escondido Fwy [15], E. on Hwy 78, R. on Broadway)

Grape Day Park has a charming ambiance created by a rose garden, large grassy areas, shade trees, picnic tables, Victorian buildings, a restored train depot, and a unique playground. The small playground has colorful metal configurations that look like interlocking tree branches to climb up, under, and through. It also has a small play structure that resembles the top of a space ship, with enough room at the flat top for just one person to sit - a natural setting to play King of the Hill. The park has horseshoe pits, too. Equipment can be checked out weekdays from 8am to 4pm. (Parental supervision is required.)

The five buildings that comprise the museum complex of Heritage Walk were relocated here in 1976, and are open to the public. They are: 1) Escondido's first library; 2) A quaint, completely furnished, two-story 1890's house with a living room, parlor, and kitchen, plus four small bedrooms upstairs; 3) A 1900's barn with a 1890's popcorn wagon, a 1935 winery truck, a working printing press, and more; 4) A blacksmith's shop which holds demonstrations when it's open; and 5) An 1888 Santa Fe Depot. The two-story depot building is nice-looking and interesting to explore. Some highlights include a train master's office, a working telegraph station (send a message to someone!), a stuffed grizzly bear, and displays of conductor's hats, dining plates once used on trains, etc. The depot also has a real train car that can be toured. It contains a model train set with an historic layout that makes tracks around realistic looking landscape. A tank house and a small herb garden can also be seen on the short walk around Heritage Walk. The park is a fun place for kids to play, but bring them sometime to see the museum part of it, also. Call for tour information.

**Hours:** The park is open daily sunrise to sunset. The museum is open Thurs - Sat. from 1pm - 4pm. It is closed Thanksgiving weekend, and all major holidays.

**Admission:** Free; donations for Heritage Walk are appreciated.

**Ages:** All for the park; ages 5 and up for the museum.

# JULIAN PIONEER MUSEUM

(760) 765-0227 $

*2811 Washington Street, Julian*

(From San Diego Fwy [5] or Escondido Fwy [15], take 78 Fwy E. to Julian. 78 is Washington St. in Julian. From the 8 Fwy, take 79 N. to Julian, at 78 Jct. turn left on Main St., L. on Washington St.)

If I were to clean out my grandparents' and great-grandparents' attics, closets, garages, etc., I would probably find many articles similar to what is inside this pioneer museum. The wide assortment of items here include carriages, guns, saddles, tools, eyeglasses, mining equipment, rocks, bottles, clothing, arrowheads, a ceremonial Indian costume, kitchen implements, a metal bathtub, a pot-bellied stove, an American flag (with forty-five stars), and lots of old, handmade lace. My favorite exhibit was a machine from a 1930's beauty shop. It was supposed to perm hair, but with the wires and rods sticking out all over the mannequin's head, it looks more like something from a science fiction film! Bring a lunch and enjoy a picnic on the tables outside this quaint museum.

Julian is a charming town with unique shops along Main Street. Your kids will enjoy a stop-off at the Julian Drugstore, located at the corner of Main Street and Washington Street, to enjoy an ice cream at its old-fashioned soda counter. Also see EAGLE MINING COMPANY, under the Tours section, to take a tour of a real gold mine.

**Hours:** Open December - March, Sat. - Sun. from 10am - 4pm. Open April - November, Tues. - Sun. from 10am - 4pm. Closed New Year's Day, Thanksgiving, and Christmas.

**Admission:** $1 for adults; children are free.

**Ages:** 5 years and up.

# JUNIPERO SERRA MUSEUM / PRESIDIO PARK

(619) 297-3258

*2727 Presidio Drive, San Diego*

(Going E. on Mission Valley Fwy [8] exit S. on Taylor St., L. on Presidio Dr., and L. again to stay on Presidio Dr. Going W. on 8, exit at Hotel Circle/Taylor St. [the exit before Morena Blvd.], go straight off the off ramp and curve over fwy, R. on Taylor St., L. on Presidio Dr., and L. again to stay on Presidio Dr.)

Located just above OLD TOWN SAN DIEGO AND STATE HISTORIC PARK (see entry in this section), picturesque Presidio Park has green rolling hills and lots of old shade trees. Follow the signs and walk along the Old Presidio Historic Trail and you'll be walking in the footsteps of settlers from centuries ago.

On a hilltop in the park sits the mission-style Junipero Serra Museum. It was built in 1929 to commemorate the site where Father Junipero Serra and Captain Gaspar de Portola established California's very first mission and fortified settlement. Outside the museum is an old wine press. Inside, the first floor contains 400-year-old Spanish furniture, some of which is quite elegant. Second story exhibits include clothing, weapons (such as a cannon and cannon balls), art, and housewares that belonged to Native American and early Spanish/Mexican residents. There is also a room dedicated to the founder, Father Serra, that contains personal belongings and items given to him. A seven-minute video is shown throughout the day that describes San Diego's beginnings. Upstairs, in a bell-like tower, look through the windows for an unparalleled view of San Diego.

Can you dig it? During the summer, archaeological students work the site adjacent to the museum, unearthing artifacts and putting them on display. Several hundred people lived within the walls of the presidio during its sixty-year existence, so there are many "treasures" still left to uncover. The site is open year round to look at and into.

**Hours:**   The park is open daily sunrise to sunset. The museum is open during the summer Tues. - Sat., 10am - 4pm; Sun., noon - 4pm. It's open the rest of the year Fri. - Sun., 10am - 4:30pm. Tours for eight or more people can be given at other times. Call for a reservation.

**Admission:**   The park is free. The museum is $3 for adults; children 12 years and under are free.

**Ages:**   The museum is best suited for ages 7 and up.

# MARINE CORPS RECRUIT DEPOT COMMAND   ☼
# MUSEUM

(619) 524-6038 - museum; (619) 524-8727 - graduation info                                !
*In the Marine Corps Recruit Depot on Pacific Highway and Witherby Street, San Diego*
(Going S. on San Diego Fwy [5], exit at Old Town Ave., off the off ramp onto Hancock St., R. on Witherby St. Going N. on 5, exit at Moore St., L. on Old Town Ave, L. on Hancock St., R. on Witherby St. You must show a valid driver's license to enter the base. The museum is directly across from the guard entrance.)

The first thing my kids noticed were the Japanese 70mm Howitzers outside the museum. Inside, the downstairs California Room displays numerous paintings of war, including battles involving Native Americans, blue coats verses grey coats, etc. The hallway has photos of movies and television shows that have featured Marines. An on-going, twenty-minute narrated film is presented in the small theater. It shows all the different phases of Marine training, from boot camp to graduation. Naturally, the "coolest" parts of it, according to my boys, were the army maneuvers where rounds and rounds of ammunition were shot, and the nighttime target practice where spots of light were seen when the guns were fired. After the movie my youngest son, with his eyes shining, declared, "I want to be a Marine!" The Visitor's Lounge looks like a large living room with couches and chairs. Around the perimeter of the room are exhibits such as helicopter and ship models, various military hats, and small models of physical fitness courses that make me tired just looking at them.

Upstairs the rooms are filled with military memorabilia. The extensive exhibits include uniforms, swords, medals, grenades, posters, pictures, flags, mannequins dressed in camouflage, rocket launchers, jeeps, police motorcycles, a collection of knives (including machetes and bayonets), and a room devoted to guns and ammunition. The China Room focuses on American Marines in Peking. It contains a lot of documents and news articles from this time period, plus photos, traditional Chinese military dress, and a canon.

The museum encompasses the history of the Marines from its inception 222 years ago, through WWI and WWII, and up to the present day. Always looking for "a few good men and women," the Marine Corps maintains a museum that is historically important, and that will enlist your child's attention.

Forty-four Fridays out of the year the Marine Corps holds a brief "morning colors ceremony," where the flag is raised and the *National Anthem* is played. It begins at 8am sharp. At 9:50am, a "pass and review" parade, mini band concert, and graduation ceremony commence. The public is welcome to attend one or both ceremonies. Call for specific dates.

**Hours:** Open Mon. - Fri., 0800 - 1600 (8am - 4pm); Sat., 1000 - 1400 (10am - 2pm).

**Admission:** Free

**Ages:** 5 years and up.

# MARITIME MUSEUM

(619) 234-9153 / www.sdmaritime.com

*1306 North Harbor Drive, San Diego*

(Going N. on San Diego Fwy [5], exit at the first exit after Cabrillo Fwy exchange, turn L. on 6th St. at end of off ramp, R. on Ash St. Going S. on 5, exit at Ash / "A" St. Go W. on Ash St. The museum is at the end of Ash St., on Harbor Drive.)

"I saw a ship a-sailing, a-sailing on the sea; and, oh! it was all laden with pretty things for thee!" (An old rhyme.) The three historic ships that comprise the Maritime Museum - the Star of India, the Berkeley, and the Medea - are laden with wonderful, nautical artifacts. The 1863 Star of India is beautiful to behold with its intricate-looking rigging, interesting figurehead, and polished wooden exterior. Inside, kids can look out the portholes; check out the very narrow bunks that once held emigrants; look at the old tools and display of knots; and marvel at the variations of ships in bottles. Not only are the ships unique, but the shapes of the bottles vary, too. Our favorite was the ship in a lightbulb. The fifteen-minute video, *Around Cape Horn* is a bit dry, though it depicts action at sea. Top board is the captain's cabin (which is small enough to give me claustrophobia), a few passengers' cabins (which passengers had to furnish themselves), a dining room, and the chart room.

The 1898 ferryboat, Berkeley, contains a number of fascinating model ships and yachts. A model ship construction and repair shop is on board, and we watched a builder at work. He told us a model takes an average of five years to complete! Such detailed work! One section of the Berkeley has a whaling gun on exhibit and displays of fish (mostly tuna) and fisheries. Downstairs is the engine room which you can explore on your own. The room is intriguing with its huge machinery and gears, narrow walkways, and slightly spooky ambiance. Also below deck is a room showcasing memorabilia from America's Cup. The triple expansion steam engine is put to work and demonstrated at various times throughout the day.

Cross over the bridge from the Berkeley to the 1904 steam yacht, Medea, which is a very small vessel. Peek into the elegant, Edwardian-decorated smoking room and into the galley that contains a coal-burning stove, big copper pots, and a wooden ice box. All in all, we had a merry time at the Maritime Museum.

**Hours:** Open daily from 9am - 8pm. Open one hour later in the summer.

**Admission:** Admission includes all three ships - $5 for adults; $4 for seniors and ages 13 - 17; $2 for ages 6 - 12; children 5 years and under are free. (Ask about AAA discounts.)

**Ages:** 5 years and up.

## MARSTON HOUSE

(619) 298-3142                                                                               $$
*3525 7th Avenue, San Diego*

(Going S. on San Diego Fwy [5], exit S. on Kettner Blvd., L. on Laurel St., L. on 6th Ave.,
R. on Upas St. It's at the end of Upas St. on 7th Ave. Going N. on 5, exit N. on 6th Ave.,
R. on Upas St. Going S. on Cabrillo Fwy [163], exit S. on 6th Ave., L. on Upas St.)

This 1905 mansion was built to provide "function, simplicity and good
design." (For an interesting contrast, compare its practical exterior and interior
designs to the much more elaborate VILLA MONTEZUMA JESSE SHEPARD
HOUSE , which is listed in this section.) The sixteen various rooms, covering
four floors, are decorated in American Arts and Crafts, oriental, and Native
American styles. What a fun and different way to learn the many facets of
American history! This tour is better for older kids who can appreciate the
lifestyle changes that occurred during the early twentieth century.

**Hours:** Open Fri. - Sun. from noon - 4:30pm

**Admission:** $5 for adults; $2 for ages 6 - 17; children 5 years and under are
free.

**Ages:** 8 years and up.

## MINGEI INTERNATIONAL FOLK ART MUSEUM

(619) 239-0003  / www.mingei.org                                                            $$
*Balboa Park, San Diego*

(Going S. on Cabrillo Fwy [163], exit N. on Park Blvd. Going S. on San Diego Fwy [5],
exit at Ash St. / "A" St., L. on "A" St., L. on Park Blvd. Going N. on 5, exit W. on "B" St.,
R. on Park Blvd. Once on Park Blvd. turn L. on Presidents Way to get to the museums.)

"Min" is the Japanese word for "all people"; "gei" means "art," so mingei
translates as "art of all people," or folk art. A child's enjoyment of this folk art
museum depends on the current exhibits. We saw many tapestries, handcrafted
furniture, and beautiful pieces of jewelry. Past exhibits have included toys and
dolls from around the world, Mexican folk art, the horse in folk art, etc. Call
first, or go on the third Tuesday of the month when admission is free. The
museum's gift shop offers colorful and unique items. (See BALBOA PARK [San
Diego] in this section for a listing of all the museums and attractions within
walking distance.)

**Hours:** Open Tues. - Sun. from 10am - 4pm.

**Admission:** $5 for adults; $2 for ages 6 - 17; children 5 years and under are
free. Admission on the third Tuesday of every month is free.
Passports for 11 museums in Balboa Park are available for $21
for adults at the Visitors Center, and are good for one week from
the date of purchase.

**Ages:** 8 years and up.

## MISSION BASILICA SAN DIEGO DE ALCALA

(619) 281-8449                                                                               $
*10818 San Diego Mission Road, San Diego*

(Going W. on Mission Valley Fwy [8], exit N. on Mission Gorge Rd., L. on Twain Ave.,
which turns into San Diego Mission Rd. From Escondido Fwy [15], exit E. on Friars Rd.,
R. on Mission Gorge Rd., R. on Twain Ave., which turns into San Diego Mission Rd.)

Father Junipero Serra came to California on a mission - to start missions.
The Mission San Diego de Alcala was the first church in California, founded by
the Padre in 1769. As with a visit to any of the twenty-one missions, coming here
brings the past vividly back to life. The church is long and narrow and, of course,
housed in an adobe structure. The gardens here are very small, but pretty. The
Padre Luis Jayme Museum, named after the missionary who was killed here by
an Indian attack, contains some interesting excavated artifacts such as flintlock
pistols, swords, buttons, and pottery. Other exhibits here include vestments, old
photos, and small dioramas of all the missions. The monastery ruins have partial
walls and the outlines of where the padres living quarters, the library, and other
rooms once stood. Tip: Read the pamphlet about the mission as you explore it,
because knowing its history makes it much more interesting for kids.

**Hours:** Open daily from 9am - 5pm. Closed Easter, Thanksgiving, and
Christmas.

**Admission:** $2 for adults; $1 for seniors and students over 12 years; 50¢ for
children 11 years and under.

**Ages:** 7 years and up.

# MISSION SAN ANTONIO DE PALA

(760) 742-3317                                                                     $

*Pala Mission Road, Pala*

(Exit Escondido Fwy [15] E. on Pala Rd. [Route 76], go about 6 miles, then N. on Pala
Mission Rd. into the town of Pala)

This mission, founded in 1816, is the only remaining Spanish California
Mission to continue in its original purpose of proselytizing and serving Native
American Indians. The adjacent school is for Native American children and the
gift shop is run by Native Americans. The small mission is located on an Indian
Reservation, a fact that greatly enhanced its value in my children's eyes.

The museum part of the mission consists of two small wings. One contains
arrowheads, pottery, clothing with intricate beadwork, the Padre's small
quarters, and an altar. Hand-carved religious figures and the Southwestern-style
painted ceilings are eye-catching. The other wing is the Mineral Room,
showcasing nice specimens of jasper, petrified wood slabs, and amethyst. The
room also has a marine display that includes a stuffed puffer fish, corral, huge
shells, and a giant clam shell.

The small back courtyard has a nicely landscaped garden, an altar, and a
fountain with Koi. The old bell tower is around the side of the mission, next to
the cemetery.

**Hours:** Open Tues. - Sun., 10am - 3:30pm. Closed most major holidays.

**Admission:** $2 for adults; $1 for children 12 years and under.

**Ages:** 6 years and up.

## MISSION SAN LUIS REY DE FRANCA

(760) 757-3651                                                                              $

*4050 Mission Avenue, Oceanside*

(Exit San Diego Fwy [5] N. on San Luis Rey Mission Exwy [76], continue on Mission Ave. Or, from Escondido Fwy [15], exit W. on Pala Rd [76], which turns into Mission Ave.)

Founded in 1798, this mission has been nicknamed "King of the Missions" because it is the largest of the twenty-one missions. It is also one of the most interesting. The extensive grounds cover nearly six and a half acres, though not all of it is open to the public. The first series of rooms contain several glass-encased displays that document the history of the mission. Next, is the Friar's small bedroom with a knotted rope bed, and monks' robes. (Twenty-one Franciscan monks still live here in a separate section of the mission.) The weavery and work rooms have a loom, spinning wheel, and implements for leather tooling, respectively. The kitchen contains pots, pans, a brick oven, and glassware typical of the Mission period. The next few rooms display embroidered vestments, statues of angels and the Madonna, and other religious art work. The big Mission Church is gorgeous. Exit the church through the Madonna Chapel into the cemetery which contains a large wooden cross to commemorate the 3,000 Indians buried here.

The grounds are equally interesting to explore. Large grassy areas, with plenty of picnic tables, are outside the mission's front doors. Just past this area are ruins of soldiers' barracks. Further down, toward the street, is an ornate stone arch and a tiled stairway that lead to an old mission laundry area and large sunken garden. The garden looks like it was left over from Babylonian times; once elegantly landscaped, but now overgrown. Mission San Luis Rey de Franca is a great one to cover for those fourth grade mission reports!

**Hours:** Open daily 10am - 4:30pm. Closed New Year's Day, Thanksgiving, and Christmas.

**Admission:** $3 for adults; $1 for ages 8 - 14; children 7 years and under are free.

**Ages:** 5 years and up.

## MOTOR TRANSPORT MUSEUM

(619) 233-9707 or (619) 756-1543                                           $

*31949 Highway 94, Campo*

(Exit Fwy 8 [45 miles from downtown San Diego] S. on Buckman Springs Rd. 10.5 miles, R. on Hwy. 94.)

Museum is almost too formal a word for this truck yard, although it is accurate in the sense that it holds a collection of over 150 antique transportation vehicles. This museum-in-process is on the grounds of the historic Campo Feldspar Mill, which was built in 1929 to mill feldspar mined in nearby Hauser Canyon. (Feldspar was ground and processed into porcelain.) It displays mostly trucks and buses, plus a few fire-fighting vehicles. About fifteen of the vehicles are restored and inside the old nine-story building, while the others are outside. The few exhibits inside are photos, literature, and memorabilia relating to trucks.

Ask about programs for older kids who like to work with their hands, such as a mechanic's workshop. Keep on trucking.

**Hours:**   Open April through November, on the second Sat. of each month from noon - 5pm. Call for more information, or to ask about other times to visit the museum.

**Admission:**   Donations accepted.

**Ages:**   5 years and up.

## MUSEUM OF CONTEMPORARY ART (La Jolla)

(619) 454-3541 / www.mcasd.org

*700 Prospect Street, La Jolla*

(Exit San Diego Fwy [5] W. on La Jolla Village Dr., L. on Torrey Pines Rd., R. on Prospect Pl., which turns into Prospect St.)

I admit two things about contemporary art museums: 1) I enjoy visiting them, and 2) I don't always "get" the art on exhibit. I've learned not to step on things lying on the floor or to touch anything, even things as seemingly innocuous as a pole in the center of the room - it could be an exhibit. Displays here rotate quarterly, so there are new eclectic paintings, sculptures, photos, and other pieces to figure out every few months.

Our favorite past exhibits include a room-size metal spider carrying a nest of eggs; toddler-size figures made out of wax in various stages of melting because of the heat lamps directed on them; the "Reason for the Neutron Bomb," which had 50,000 match tips glued onto nickels on the floor, each one representing a Russian tank; and a darkened room with a large church bell which, when my kids pulled on the rope, triggered a hologram of the Virgin Mary and baby Jesus to appear.

Borrow an audio tape (and player) at the front desk that explains the current exhibits. The M.C.A. offers free school group tours with titles such as Art and Creative Writing, Meaning and Wonder of Art, etc. Pick up a free children's guide (pamphlet) at the reception desk about discovering contemporary art. It asks thought-provoking questions, and gives kids things to do and look for. By the way, the view of the coastline from the museum is spectacular. Also see the following entry, MUSEUM OF CONTEMPORARY ART, San Diego.

**Hours:**   Open Tues. - Sat., 10am - 5pm (Wed. until 8pm); Sun., noon - 5pm.

**Admission:**   $4 for adults (also good for the downtown San Diego location for 3 days from date of purchase); $2 for seniors, military with I.D., and students; children 11 years and under are free. Admission is free on the first Sun. and Tues. of every month.

**Ages:**   6 years and up.

## MUSEUM OF CONTEMPORARY ART (San Diego)

(619) 234-1001 / www.mcasd.org

*1001 Kettner Boulevard, San Diego*

(Going S. on San Diego Fwy [5], exit at "A" St. and go straight off the off ramp on 10<sup>th</sup> St., R. on Broadway to Kettner. Going N. on 5, exit W. on "J" St., R. on 12<sup>th</sup>, L. on Broadway to Kettner. It's at Broadway, right by the metro. Parking is hard to come by.)

This artsy-style building sets the right mood for your visit to San Diego's contemporary art museum. What kinds of materials are used in the art that you're looking at? Traditional materials, like paint? Or nuts, bolts, wires, or other improbable materials? These are a few of the questions listed in the (free) children's guide on discovering contemporary art, which is found at the reception desk. The guide helps your child become more involved with the art, and enables him/her to understand the artist's vision in creating their work. Contemporary art is fun because it is eclectic. Some art pieces might be as unusual as a box of cereal, while other paintings, sculptures, and/or photos are a more daring combination of design, light and texture. This small museum, which has quarterly rotating exhibits, is a branch of the main M.C.A. in La Jolla.

**Hours:** Open Tues. - Sat., 10am - 5pm; Sun., noon - 5.
**Admission:** $2 for adults, $1 for seniors, military with I.D., and students; children 12 years and under are free. Admission is half-off the La Jolla location with each paid admission at this location. Admission is free on the first Sun. and Tues. of every month.
**Ages:** 6 years and up.

## MUSEUM OF CREATION AND EARTH HISTORY

(619) 448-0900 / www.icr.org
*10946 Woodside Avenue North, Santee*
(Take the 52 Fwy E. to the end, go E. on Mission Gorge Rd, L. on Carlton Hills Blvd., L. on Carlton Oaks Dr. Just past the intersection at Magnolia, the road forks at a stop sign; go L. on Woodside Ave. North. The museum is ¼ mile on the L. From San Diego - Exit 8 Fwy, N. on San Vicente Fwy [Hwy. 67], L. on Riverford Rd., L. at light, L. again under fwy, L. onto Woodside Ave. North. The museum is ¼ mile on the L.)

Genesis 1:1: "In the beginning, God created the heavens and the earth." This walk-through creation museum, a part of the Institute of Creation Research, is a richly visual way of seeing how the earth and its inhabitants have developed. Each phase of the earth's history is graphically represented by murals, photographs, models, audio sounds, Biblical references, questions to ponder, and lots of technical information. Start at the beginning, of course, and proceed through to modern day. Day four (when the sun, moon, stars, and planets were created) is the first dramatic depiction of the unfolding wonders of our universe. This room is basically dark, with spotlights on stunning photos of the planets, constellations, and our sun. Each photograph is accompanied by factual explanations. Entering the room for days five and six is like entering a small jungle. Greenery abounds alongside a few cages of small live animals such as birds, fish, snakes, and mice. Accompanied by Psalm 139 ("I am fearfully and wonderfully made. . .") an entire wall shows models of man, his inner workings, diagrams, and pictures of families.

Continue on, and see the fall of man, illustrated by bones, decay, and the sound of crying; a wood-paneled room with a mural depicting Noah's ark,

complete with storm sounds and lightening flashing; a room with touchable walls
that are layers of the earth, plus a replicate of Mt. St. Helens' volcano that you
can walk through; a blue hallway representing the Ice Age with icicles hanging
overhead, and models of woolly mammoths; an Egyptian room with a scale
model of the enormous Tower of Babel taking center stage; the Stone Age room;
the room of civilization immortalizing (so to speak) Greek and Roman cultures;
and finally, the hallway of modern man, including pictures and philosophies of
evolutionists and creationists. The Museum of Creation is the ultimate,
interactive time line.

Each of the rooms offers various free pamphlets that discuss the ideas and
facts presented throughout the museum. Guided tours are available for groups,
with reservations. Once-a-month classes are also available for upper elementary
and older students who wish to delve into creation research and Biblical learning
and understanding. The classes and the museum are geared for slightly older
children as a lot of the information is very technical, however, the incredible
visuals make quite an impact on any age.

**Hours:** Open Mon. - Sat. from 9am - 4pm. Closed holidays.
**Admission:** Free
**Ages:** 5 - 9 years for the visual enjoyment; 10 years old and up to
understand the technical information.

# MUSEUM OF PHOTOGRAPHIC ARTS

(619) 238-7559  / www.mopa.org                                            $
*Balboa Park, San Diego*
(Going S. on Cabrillo Fwy [163], exit N. on Park Blvd. Going S. on San Diego Fwy [5],
exit at Ash St. / "A" St., L. on "A" St., L. on Park Blvd. Going N. on 5, exit W. on "B" St.,
R. on Park Blvd. Once on Park Blvd. turn L. on Presidents Way to get to the museums.)

Your shutterbugs will appreciate this large gallery that features changing
exhibits of photographic works. Some exhibits zoom in on portraiture work or
the history of American photography, while others focus more on pictures taken
from all over the world. We enjoyed comparing styles and choice of subjects, as
well as just the artistry in the pictures. Free, guided tours are given Sundays at
2pm. (See BALBOA PARK [San Diego] in this section for a listing of all the
museums and attractions within walking distance.)

**Hours:** Open daily from 10am - 5pm.
**Admission:** $4 for adults; children 11 years and under are free. Admission on
the second Tues. of every month is free. Passports for 11
museums in Balboa Park are available for $21 for adults at the
Visitors Center, and are good for one week from the date of
purchase.
**Ages:** 7 years and up.

# MUSEUM OF SAN DIEGO HISTORY

(619) 232-6203                                                         $$
*Balboa Park, San Diego*

(Going S. on Cabrillo Fwy [163], exit N. on Park Blvd. Going S. on San Diego Fwy [5], exit at Ash St. / "A" St., L. on "A" St., L. on Park Blvd. Going N. on 5, exit W. on "B" St., R. on Park Blvd. Once on Park Blvd. turn L. on Presidents Way to get to the museums.)

This museum presents the history of San Diego, from the 1850's to the present, via numerous photographs, plus maps, works of art, costumes, household goods, furniture, and other artifacts. An authentic stagecoach is the first item you'll see and it sets the mood for your visit here. We always enjoy seeing history and understanding more about our ancestors' way of life. (See BALBOA PARK [San Diego] in this section for a listing of all the museums and attractions within walking distance.)

**Hours:**   Open Tues. - Sun. from 10am - 4:30pm. Open also the second Tuesday of each month.

**Admission:**   $5 for adults; $4 for seniors; $2 for ages 6 - 17; children 5 years and under are free. Admission the second Tues. of every month is free. Passports for 11 museums in Balboa Park are available for $21 for adults at the Visitors Center, and are good for one week from the date of purchase.

**Ages:**   5 years and up.

# OLD TOWN SAN DIEGO AND STATE HISTORIC PARK                ☼

(619) 220-5422 - Robinson Rose House and park ranger                          !/$
*Taylor, Juan, Twiggs, and Congress Sts., Old Town, San Diego*
(Going S. on San Diego Fwy [5] [just south of Interstate 8] exit E. [across the bridge] on Old Town Ave., L. on San Diego Ave. or L. on Congress St. Going N. on 5, exit at Moore St., R. on Old Town Ave., L. on San Diego Ave. or Congress St. Parking is available on the streets if you arrive early, or at several parking lots.)

Old Town is a six-block, closed-to-through-traffic area, bound by Taylor, Juan, Twiggs, and Congress streets. The places mentioned below encompass this area, plus the immediate, walkable vicinity.

Old Town is a wonderful conglomeration of unique shops, scrumptious places to eat, vintage houses, museums, and a Mexican bazaar, all located along dirt "roads" that are closed to automotive traffic, and paved sidewalks. It's a town you'll want to revisit to make sure you experience all it has to offer. San Diego is the site of the first permanent Spanish settlement on the California coast, thus it shares a similar historical significance with Jamestown, the first English settlement on the East Coast. Old Town contains many original and restored buildings from San Diego's Mexican period before 1846, and the early California period. A day here is a combination of history lessons and fun shopping! The route for the attractions listed below starts at the Robinson Rose House - the park headquarters - then proceeds east, south, and north before looping back around. Most of the attractions are open daily from 10am to 5pm; shops are usually open until 9pm. Admission is free, unless otherwise noted. All historic buildings are closed on January 1, Thanksgiving, and Christmas. Free maps of the area are available at the park headquarters, in many of the stores in Old Town, and in local hotel lobbies. Free walking tours that cover all of the old buildings, not just the more kid-friendly ones I've listed here, are offered daily at 2pm beginning at Robinson Rose House.

ROBINSON ROSE HOUSE is located at 4002 Wallace Street, on the other side of the parking lot from Taylor Street. This 1853 adobe structure houses the park headquarters and has walking tour maps available for purchase. It also has a few exhibits, such as photo murals and a scale model of Old Town as it appeared in the mid 1870's.

OLD TOWN PLAZA is located directly in front of the Robinson Rose House. This area is essentially a large grassy area for kids to run around, with olive, fig, cork, and eucalyptus trees providing beauty and shade. A large fountain is in the middle of this park and there are plenty of benches for weary travelers (or shoppers).

The row of stores across from the Plaza are in reconstructed buildings dating from around 1830. Just a few of our favorite stores in Old Town include Miner's Gems and Minerals, Toler's Leather Depot, The Mexico Shop, and of course the ice cream and candy shops! Old Town is truly a shopper's delight.

COLORADO HOUSE/WELLS FARGO MUSEUM is located on San Diego Street in the heart of Old Town. This museum has the appeal of the Old West, with a Concord Stagecoach prominently displayed in the center. Other exhibits include a colorful wall display of Wells Fargo featured in comic books, trading cards, and even a board game; rocks with gold, gold coins, and bags of gold found in treasure boxes; mining tools; Old West posters; and more. A video shows and describes this time period and the history of Wells Fargo.

CASA DE MACHADO Y STEWART is located almost directly behind the Colorado House/Wells Fargo Museum. This plain-looking adobe is an exact replica of the original house, complete with a dirt walkway leading to it. The brick-floored house contains few furnishings; a dining table, shelves with dishes and pottery, a sparsely furnished bedroom, and some tools. Just beyond the front porch is a beehive oven and open fire stoves, evidence of the outdoor cooking that pioneers once employed.

MASON STREET SCHOOL is located on Mason Street, diagonal to the Casa de Machado y Stewart. This 1865 red schoolhouse is a child's favorite historical stop in Old Town. It was the first public schoolhouse in San Diego and retains its old-fashioned ambiance with twenty school desks, a school bell, flags, a chalkboard, a wood-burning stove, the dunce's corner (and cap), and old pictures and books. It's open daily from 10am to 4pm.

THE DENTAL MUSEUM is located on San Diego Avenue, in front of the schoolhouse. Kids will enjoy a quick peek at the past here as they see a dentist chair, instruments, and even some molds of teeth.

SAN DIEGO UNION BUILDING is located on San Diego Avenue. The first edition of the San Diego Union came off the presses here way back when. Now, kids can see an old Washington handpress (printing press), typeset letters and tools, and the adjacent small newspaper office.

WHALEY HOUSE - See WHALEY HOUSE, in this Museums section, for details. It's an interesting museum! Take a quick peek into the Old Town Drug Store Museum, located behind this museum. Kids can see an old-time pharmacy containing bottles, patented medicines, and a mortar and pestle.

HERITAGE PARK, (619) 565-3600, is located north of the Whaley House, on Harvey and Juan Streets. This group of buildings is enchanting to simply look at. Each of the seven Victorian houses now serve other functions: The Sherman Gilbert house, our favorite, was built in 1887 and is now the Old Doll Shoppe, offering dolls, dollhouses, miniatures, and ornaments for sale; the Christian House is now a bed and breakfast; etc.

THE MORMON BATTALION VISITOR CENTER, (619) 298-3317, is located on Juan Street. An informative tour guide will show your family around this small center. The first thing we noticed was a statue as tall as the biblical Goliath - he *really* was tall! Kids can hold a sun-baked adobe brick and learn its historical significance. They'll also learn how people placed copper pennies in an oven (an alternative way of baking bricks) until the pennies began to melt, at 2,000 degrees. This meant the oven was hot enough to bake bricks (and lots of other things, too!)
    Although the 500 men (and women and children) of the Mormon Battalion never fought a battle, the 1846 volunteer unit marched 2,000 miles across country to San Diego to help fight in the Mexican/American war. Their arduous trail blazing efforts and accomplishments are re-enacted in an interesting fifteen-minute film. The diorama adjacent to the screen is occasionally spotlighted to emphasize portions of the movie. After the film, we were led into another room and shown huge paintings of Jesus during various times of his ministry. As our tour concluded, we were offered a Book of Mormon and asked if we could have someone call on us regarding the Mormon religion. The visitor center is open daily 9am to 9pm. Admission is free.

SEELEY STABLES is located on Calhoun Street. This huge, reconstructed barn contains several exhibit stalls. The saddles, bells, and harnesses, plus at least ten stagecoaches and carriages, are great visual aids for picturing the past. Free slide shows are presented in the downstairs theater throughout the day, so come and rest, and learn a little history. The upstairs loft has more exhibits of the wild, wild west, such as branding irons, spurs, more saddles, a Mexican cowboy hat, and furniture including an unusual chair made out of steers' horns. A native

American display features Kachina dolls, a feather headdress, and baskets. Other exhibits up here include an old-fashioned slot machine, a roller organ, an antique telephone, a case of model horses, and a child's room with toys.

The backyard of the stables is an open courtyard with early farm equipment around its perimeters, plus several more carriages and stagecoaches in glass-cased enclosures. Also back here, or accessible from Mason Street, is THE BLACK HAWK LIVERY STABLE AND BLACKSMITH. This large blacksmith workshop holds demonstrations every Wednesday and Saturday from 10am to 2pm. Kids might see the hot fires help bend pieces of metal into horseshoes or heavy chains, or they might hear a hammer clank against the anvil to create a sword or branding iron. The stable room is filled with finished pieces and tools.

GEORGE JOHNSON HOUSE is located on Calhoun Street, near Mason Street. This small building has a room to walk through - it took us maybe five minutes. It displays archaeological findings of the area such as bottles and pottery, plus tools of the trade and pictures showing the painstaking work of excavation and cleaning.

BAZAAR DEL MUNDO, (619) 296-3161 / www.bazaardelmundo.com, is located on the corner of Juan and Wallace Streets. This gaily decorated traditional Mexican courtyard is festive in appearance and atmosphere. Mariachi bands play, costumed dancers entertain occasionally, and the colorful storefronts and wares beckon shoppers of all ages. Our favorite shops here include Geppetto's, a wonderful toy store; Just Animals, for the wild (and tame) at heart; Creations and Confections, specializing in old-fashioned candies, chocolates, and party supplies; La Panaderia, serving delectable Mexican breads and pastries, including churros; and Treasures, a store that carries gifts and crafts from exotic lands. If your tummy is saying, "tengo hambre" (that's Spanish for "I'm hungry"), sample and savor some of the culinary delights at any one of the several restaurants here.

Look up JUNIPERO SERRA MUSEUM / PRESIDIO PARK (see the entry in this section), located just north of Old Town.

**Hours:**     Most "attractions" open daily 10am - 5pm.
**Admission:**   Free, but bring spending money. See individual listings.
**Ages:**      4 years and up.

# RANCHO BUENA VISTA ADOBE

(760) 639-6164
*640 Alta Vista Drive, Vista*
(Exit 78 Fwy, N.E. on Sunset Dr. / Escondido Ave., R. on Alta Vista Dr.)

Situated between residential homes is the Rancho Buena Vista, an historic adobe home built circa 1850. Take a forty-five minute tour of the gracious home to learn about this time period and the lifestyles of the rancheros. Part of the tour is a ten-minute video presentation, which helps present-day youth better understand the past. You'll see the living room, kitchen, bedrooms, etc., that contain period furniture, and other Mexican-California memorabilia. Ask about Adobe Days (living history programs) for children as well as field trips, camps, and classes. Viva la historia!

**Hours:** Open usually Wed. - Sat., 10am - 3pm; Sun., 12:30pm - 3pm. Closed all major holidays, during inclement weather, and special events.

**Admission:** $3 for non-Vista resident adults; $2 for Vista resident adults and for seniors; $1 for students; 50¢ for children 12 years and under.

**Ages:** 7 years and up.

## REUBEN H. FLEET SCIENCE CENTER ☼
(619) 238-1233 / www.rhfleet.org                                                      $$$
*Balboa Park, San Diego*
(Going S. on Cabrillo Fwy [163], exit N. on Park Blvd. Going S. on San Diego Fwy [5], exit at Ash St. / "A" St., L. on "A" St., L. on Park Blvd. Going N. on 5, exit W. on "B" St., R. on Park Blvd. Once on Park Blvd. turn L. on Presidents Way to get to the museums.)

This huge Science Center is a fascinating place for hands-on exploration, experimentation, and discovery. There are numerous permanent exhibits throughout several gallery rooms, including a submarine periscope that literally goes through the roof to view the outside world; a fully operational amateur radio station; a build and play area for children ages 2 to 6; carnival-style "funny" mirrors; a virtual tour through the heart in Heartflight, where the beat goes on; and a multitude of experiments. Signals is an exhibit with forty-five interactive components that demonstrate the many ways that people transmit information. Kids practice communication skills by sending Morse code messages, phone images, and the alphabet that's relayed via lights and then displayed digitally (i.e. like the inner workings of a computer). Other ways to communicate include transmitting sound through a microphone into wave forms displayed on a monitor, and flashing lights and/or symbolic flags to send coded messages.

Changing exhibits have included Brain Games - playing with giant checker and chess sets, and testing your skill at probability and math games; Sport - exhibits that get you physically moving as you pitch, fish, row, and climb; and Structures - an area where you can build suspension bridges, monuments, or other architectural wonders.

The Omnimax theater screen looks like an inverted golf ball. One-hour films are shown that are ten times the size of those in regular movie theaters, therefore drawing you into the intense action on the screen, whether it's traveling to the ocean depths, through the human body, or hurtling down ski slopes. (Warning: For those prone to motion sickness, the swirling images can make your stomach queasy.) Past shows have included a cosmic view of the universe in *Cosmic Voyage*, and a behind-the-scenes tour of Hollywood's action films in *Special Effects*. Other stellar productions include various planetarium shows where the stars, constellations, and planets can be seen, night or day.

Take a jolting, five-minute ride on SciTours, a simulator, which holds up to twenty-three people. Riders must be at least 40" tall and children under 10 must be accompanied by a parent. Changing shows have included *Journey to Mars*, as well as other space-oriented themes.

Tip or warning: The gift shop appeals to all ages who are even slightly scientific or hands-on oriented. *Star Trek* fans, in particular, will have a field day here. (See BALBOA PARK [San Diego], in this section, for a listing of all the museums and attractions within walking distance.)

**Hours:** The Center and Omnimax theater (with shows almost hourly) are open daily 9:30am - 6pm. Closing times vary. Hours are extended in the summer.

**Admission:** Science Center exhibit entrance is $5 for adults; $4 for seniors; $3 for ages 3 - 12; children 2 years and under are free. Simulator rides are an additional $2 per person. Admission to a show and to the exhibits is $8 for adults; $7 for seniors; $5 for ages 3 - 12. Admission to the exhibits is free on the first Tues. of every month. Passports for 11 museums in Balboa Park are available for $21 for adults at the Visitors Center and are good for one week from the date of purchase.

**Ages:** 4 years and up.

## SAN DIEGO AEROSPACE MUSEUM

(619) 234-8291  / www.aerospacemuseum.org
*Balboa Park, San Diego*
(Going S. on Cabrillo Fwy [163], exit N. on Park Blvd. Going S. on San Diego Fwy [5], exit at Ash St. / "A" St., L. on "A" St., L. on Park Blvd. Going N. on 5, exit W. on "B" St., R. on Park Blvd. Once on Park Blvd. turn L. on Presidents Way to get to the museums.)

Take to the skies in this marvelous museum that visually chronicles the history of aviation from the dawn of flight through the age of space travel. The first few rooms, formally titled the International Aerospace Hall of Fame, give homage to the aero-engineers, pilots, and aviation founders that didn't fly off course in their vision for creating aircrafts and the aerospace industry. The hall is filled with photos, plaques, and medals of these aviation heroes. Portraits of Armstrong, Aldrich, and other astronauts, especially, caught my children's eyes. An Apollo XI display features a replica of the plaque left on the moon, the box used to collect lunar samples, and more.

The next rooms are packed with exhibits of early flying machines and models of inventors such as gliders, "birdmen" who used bicycle tires, bi-planes, and the Wright Brother's flyer, plus narrated videos that show pictures of early flying attempts. Consecutive eras are also well defined and enhanced with colorful wall murals, period-dressed mannequins, and other fine details. Wood-paneled rooms, complete with sandbags and army netting, house WWI and WWII planes and other memorabilia such as helmets, goggles, and uniforms. The flying aces and the fighter planes that served them, including the Spad, the Nieuport, Spitfires, Hellcats, and Zeros, are well represented. In between wars, the U.S. Mail service was introduced. Displays here include a Curtiss JN-4 *Jenny*, wall posters of stamps blown up in size that commemorate aviation, and a replicated 1918 mail office. Kids love the next exhibits of barnstormers and pictures of daredevils using planes to entertain. These showmen of the air are doing headstands on wings, transferring from a plane to a speeding car, etc.

The next series of rooms honor women aviators, house engines and propellers, and display lots of model airplanes. Enter a pilot's ready room to watch the film *Sea Legs*. The armed forces are saluted with their contributions and a scale model of the U.S.S. Yorktown, and the U.S.S. Langley - the Navy's first carrier.

Enter the Jet Age with the F-4 Phantom, and the spy plane, the Blackbird. This exciting time period is followed by the Space Age. This last set of rooms feature bulky astronaut uniforms, capsules, modules, a moon rock, and more. An adjacent theater room showcases the history of model making.

Soar to new heights as you and your children explore the Aerospace Museum! Tours of the aircraft restoration facility are available upon request. (See BALBOA PARK [San Diego], in this section, for a listing of all the museums and attractions within walking distance.)

**Hours:** Open daily from 10am - 4:30pm. Closed Thanksgiving and Christmas.

**Admission:** $6 for adults; $5 for seniors; $2 for ages 6 - 17; active duty military and children 5 years and under are free. Admission on the fourth Tues. of every month is free. Passports for 11 museums in Balboa Park are available for $21 for adults from the Visitors Center, and are good for a week from the date of purchase.

**Ages:** 4 years and up.

# SAN DIEGO AUTOMOTIVE MUSEUM
(619) 231-2886                                                         *$$*
*2080 Pan American Plaza, San Diego*
(Going S. on Cabrillo Fwy [163], exit N. on Park Blvd. Going S. on San Diego Fwy [5], exit at Ash St. / "A" St., L. on "A" St., L. on Park Blvd. Going N. on 5, exit W. on "B" St., R. on Park Blvd. Once on Park Blvd. turn L. on Presidents Way to get to the museums.)

Jump start your child's interest in automobiles at this museum that has more than eighty vehicles on display. Most of the gleaming cars are in a line and readily viewable. Some of the vintage automobiles are on display in appropriate settings, such as a fifties car in front of a backdrop of a drive-through. Classics here range from old-fashioned Model A's to futuristic-looking DeLoreans. Other favorites include a 1948 Tucker "Torpedo" (only fifty-one were ever built), a 1934 convertible Coupe Roadster, a 1955 Mercedes Benz (300SL Gullwing), a 1957 Chevrolet, and Packards from 1929 to 1936. Prototypes, model cars, a race car, a re-created mechanics shop complete with tools, and an engine room for those who want the inside scoop on cars, are also found at this museum. "Gentlemen, start your engines" applied to my boys as they raced over to see the over forty motorcycles on display. They were particularly elated by the Harley Davidsons, the Indian Chief, and an army cycle. (See BALBOA PARK [San Diego], in this section, for a listing of all the museums and attractions within

walking distance.)
> **Hours:** Open daily from 10am - 4:30pm. Open in the summer one hour later.
> **Admission:** $6 for adults; $5 for seniors; $2 for ages 6 - 15; children 5 years and under are free. Admission on the fourth Tues. of every month is free. Passports for 11 museums in Balboa Park are available for $21 for adults at the Visitors Center, and are good for one week from the date of purchase.
> **Ages:** 6 years and up.

# SAN DIEGO HALL OF CHAMPIONS - SPORTS MUSEUM

(619) 234-2544 / e-mail:sdhoc@socal.wanet.com

*Balboa Park, San Diego*

(Going S. on Cabrillo Fwy [163], exit N. on Park Blvd. Going S. on San Diego Fwy [5], exit at Ash St. / "A" St., L. on "A" St., L. on Park Blvd. Going N. on 5, exit W. on "B" St., R. on Park Blvd. Once on Park Blvd. turn L. on Presidents Way to get to the museums.)

Give your sports fans something to cheer about by taking them to the Hall of Champions. Over forty different sports are represented in this eye-catching museum, including baseball, basketball, hockey, boxing, table tennis, surfing, racing, boating, soapbox derby, and a beach game called over-the-line. The exhibits showcase athletes, like Ted Williams and Bill Walton, and teams, like the Padres, all associated with San Diego - what a winning city this is! You'll see photographs, statues outfitted in sports attire, videos, trophies, and lots of sports equipment such as uniforms, balls, and even a racing boat and a motorcycle. The theater presents continuously running sports films and clips, mostly bloopers, which kids love. (See BALBOA PARK [San Diego], under this section, for a listing of all the museums and attractions within walking distance.)
> **Hours:** Open daily from 10am - 4:30pm.
> **Admission:** $3 for adults; $2 for seniors; $1 for ages 6 - 17; children 5 years and under are free. Admission on the second Tues. of every month is free. Passports to 11 museums in Balboa Park are available for $21 for adults at the Visitors Center, and are good for one week from the date of purchase.
> **Ages:** 5 years and up.

# SAN DIEGO MODEL RAILROAD MUSEUM

(619) 696-0199

*Balboa Park, San Diego*

(Going S. on Cabrillo Fwy [163], exit N. on Park Blvd. Going S. on San Diego Fwy [5], exit at Ash St. / "A" St., L. on "A" St., L. on Park Blvd. Going N. on 5, exit W. on "B" St., R. on Park Blvd. Once on Park Blvd. turn L. on Presidents Way to get to the museums.)

You won't have to railroad your children into coming to this museum. Just one of the things I learned here was the difference between model trains and toy trains. (Hint: The way they operate and the way they look are very different.) The museum houses the largest operating model railroad exhibits in America.

Kids (and short adults) can step up onto platforms to get a closer look at the several huge layouts. Watch scale model trains make tracks through and around authentically landscaped hillsides and miniature towns that are complete with scale cars, trees, and people. Some of the exhibits depicting the development of railroading in Southern California include the Tehachapi Pass, the Cabrillo and Southwestern, and a Civil War era live steam locomotive. One of our favorites is the Pacific Desert Line, which has a model train going through a town, citrus groves, and a gorge, all of which can be seen by looking through real train car windows!

Kids will have the most fun in the Toy Train Gallery, which features Lionel O Gauge trains and more. Turn knobs, push buttons, and pull back on throttles to operate trains, make signal crossers flash, windmills turn, and toy trucks haul "rocks" to a loading dock. A wooden Brio train set for younger children completes this interactive and at*track*tive room. As the railroad museum is always in the process of re*modeling*, it is fun and different every time you visit. (See BALBOA PARK [San Diego], under this section, for a listing of all the museums and attractions within walking distance.)

**Hours:** Open Tues. - Fri., 11am - 4pm; Sat. - Sun., 11am - 5pm.
**Admission:** $3 for adults; $2 for seniors and students; children 14 years and under are free. Admission on the first Tues. of every month is free. Passports for 11 museums in Balboa Park are available for $21 for adults at the Visitors Center, and are good for one week from the date purchased.
**Ages:** 2 years and up.

## SAN DIEGO MUSEUM OF ART

(619) 232-7931 / www.sdmart.com *$$*
*Balboa Park, San Diego*
(Going S. on Cabrillo Fwy [163], exit N. on Park Blvd. Going S. on San Diego Fwy [5], exit at Ash St. / "A" St., L. on "A" St., L. on Park Blvd. Going N. on 5, exit W. on "B" St., R. on Park Blvd. Once on Park Blvd. turn L. on Presidents Way to get to the museums.)

This ornately-edificed building primarily features European, American, Asian, and Twentieth-century art. As with any art museum, my children's interest was sparked by having them look for differences in artistic styles or color, and looking at various choices of subject. Kids need to somehow participate with the art to enjoy it. My boys were intrigued most by the statues, especially the fighting Minotaur. The small Image Gallery room has touch screens that introduce and teach children (and adults) more about the paintings and sculptures throughout the museum. (Anything to do with computers draws this generation's interest!) Although the museum has more appeal for older children, Sunday Family Days are geared for ages 4 years and up. These programs focus on a particular aspect or image of art, (e.g. finding dogs in paintings), followed by a game and/or a related craft. Call for dates, times, and prices. Tip: If you're not sure your children will enjoy this museum, come on the third Tuesday of the month, when admission is free. (See BALBOA PARK [San Diego], under this section, for a listing of all the museums and attractions within

walking distance.)
>**Hours:** Open Tues. - Sun., 10am - 4:30pm. Closed Mon. (except Labor
>Day), New Year's Day, and Christmas.
>**Admission:** $7 for adults; $5 for seniors; $4 for military with I.D.; $2 for ages
>6 - 17; children 5 years and under are free. Admission Fri. - Sun.
>is $1 more for all paying age groups. Admission on the third
>Tues. of each month is free to view the permanent collection.
>Passports for 11 museums in Balboa Park are available for $21
>for adults at the Visitors Center, and are good for one week from
>the date of purchase.
>**Ages:** 8 years and up.

## SAN DIEGO MUSEUM OF MAN   ☼

(619) 239-2001 / www.museumofman.org                              $$

*Balboa Park, San Diego*

(Going S. on Cabrillo Fwy [163], exit N. on Park Blvd. Going S. on San Diego Fwy [5],
exit at Ash St. / "A" St., L. on "A" St., L. on Park Blvd. Going N. on 5, exit W. on "B" St.,
R. on Park Blvd. Once on Park Blvd. turn L. on Presidents Way to get to the museums.)

"You've come a long way, baby!" is the best way to rephrase this museum's
theme of our ancestors' growth, change, and accomplishments into modern day
man. The first floor exhibits that we saw (they do rotate) consisted of tapestry
hangings, a weaving demonstration, and plaster casts of stone monuments
engraved and dedicated to deities. Toward the stairs is a huge, stuffed mountain
gorilla and displays on primate evolution. Upstairs, the theory of evolution theme
continues with lots of visuals. There are skeletons of apes and man side by side
to compare and contrast; a theoretical time line; and life-size models depicting
what some scientists believe early man looked like. Warning: Many of the
models are naked (and very hairy). Peoples of the Southwest are represented by
displays of pottery, Kachina dolls, and jewelry. Hunters are represented by
displays of weapons, tools, and foods. Our favorite exhibits, pertaining to this
latter category, were the rabbit skin blanket, eagle feather skirt, shoes from
fibers, and a quiver made out of a raccoon. Ancient Egypt is *tut*ilating with a
real mummy, dating from around 330 B.C., plus coffin masks covered with
symbols of Isis, and exotic jewelry.

The hands-on Children's Discovery Center sometimes rotates its theme. We
"experienced" Ancient Egypt by dressing up in appropriate clothing and
headwear, building pyramids with blocks, trying our hand at hieroglyphics, and
playing ancient games - all in a replicated noble's home. On weekends, for an
additional $3 fee, your children can also participate in a take-home, themed craft.
(See BALBOA PARK [San Diego], under this section, for a listing of all the
museums and attractions within walking distance.)
>**Hours:** Open daily from 10am - 4:30pm.

**Admission:** $5 for adults; $3 for ages 6 - 17; children 5 years and under are free. Admission on the third Tues. of every month is free. Passports for 11 museums in Balboa Park are available for $21 for adults at the Visitors Center, and are good for one week from the date purchased.

**Ages:** 5 years and up.

## SAN DIEGO NATURAL HISTORY MUSEUM ☼

(619) 232-3821 / www.sdnhm.org                                   $$$

*Balboa Park, San Diego*

(Going S. on Cabrillo Fwy [163], exit N. on Park Blvd. Going S. on San Diego Fwy [5], exit at Ash St. / "A" St., L. on "A" St., L. on Park Blvd. Going N. on 5, exit W. on "B" St., R. on Park Blvd. Once on Park Blvd. turn L. on Presidents Way to get to the museums.)

*Naturally*, this is a favorite museum for kids to visit! A good portion of the first floor of the museum features first class, interactive exhibits that are changed three times a year. We saw a wild and woolly exhibit with elephants, woolly mammoths, and mastodons. Knowing that elephants (and their ancestors) are the largest land animals still didn't quite prepare my kids for the impact of seeing the towering life-size models. Touching re-created hair, trunk, and feet was unique, as was seeing a live Asian elephant close up (outside, in the "backyard") and learning about its anatomy. Another favorite past exhibit was on dinosaurs.

The Hall of Minerals has amazing specimens, including petrified logs, a huge jade boulder, and a gigantic amethyst geode. Walk through a re-created mine tunnel and see "holes" that showcase garnets, topaz, and other rocks and minerals. Try the crystal radio and hear how it works. Touch a meteor that is out of this world. Observe fluorescent rocks and glowing minerals. Experiment with radioactive rock. See rainbows through special crystals using a polarizing filter. Don't let the earthquake exhibit shake you up!

Downstairs, a Discovery Lab allows kids to see and even touch live animals, such as snakes, as well as look through a microscope at animal fur, skin, etc. Huge walk-through dioramas with caves depict the southwestern desert. Some of the taxidermied animals on this floor include cougars, coyotes, gold eagles, birds, and saber tooth cats. One wall has a beautiful array of butterflies - some have fantastic fluorescent colors. There are also numerous fossils, including those of dinosaurs. Dive into the next few rooms that contain models and stuffed sea creatures such as sea lions, stingrays, dolphins, sharks, and a pilot whale. Also on display are the menacing jaws of a shark, plus skeletons, a gigantic whale fin bone, and a whale skull.

The museum offers many classes, tours, family programs, camp outs, and even camp-ins! Call for a schedule. (See BALBOA PARK [San Diego], under this section, for a listing of all the museums and attractions within walking distance.)

**Hours:** Open daily 9:30am - 4:30pm. Open in the summer one hour later. Closed New Year's Day, Thanksgiving, and Christmas. During special exhibits, daily museum hours are extended - 9am - 6pm.

**Admission:**  $6 for adults; $5 for seniors; $3 for ages 6 - 17; children 5 years and under are free. Special exhibits can cause prices and hours to fluctuate, so always call first. In between special exhibits, admission is half-price for all ages. Admission is free on the first Tues. of every month to the permanent exhibits; half price to the special exhibits. Passports for 11 museums in Balboa Park are available for $21 for adults at the Visitors Center, and are good for one week from date of purchase.

**Ages:**  3 years and up.

## SAN DIEGO RAILROAD MUSEUM

$$$

(619) 595-3030
*Highway 94, Campo*

See SAN DIEGO RAILROAD MUSEUM under the Transportation section.

## STEPHEN BIRCH AQUARIUM-MUSEUM

$$$

(619) 534-FISH (3474)
*2300 Expedition Drive, San Diego*

See STEPHEN BIRCH AQUARIUM-MUSEUM under the Zoos and Animals section.

## VILLA MONTEZUMA JESSE SHEPARD HOUSE

$$

(619) 239-2211
*1925 "K" Street, San Diego*
(Going S. on San Diego Fwy [5], exit E. on Imperial Ave, L on 20th St., L. on "K" St. Going N on 5, exit E. on "J" St., R. on 20th St., R. on "K" St.)

Built and designed in 1887 for celebrated author, spiritualist, and musician, Jesse Shepard, this two-story house is by far one of the most interesting and ornamental Victorian houses we've ever seen. The outside is beautiful with its steep roofs, gables, turrets, and bay windows. The rooms inside are paneled with redwood and walnut, and are decorated with intricate wood carvings and moldings. The ceilings are elegantly embossed. There are numerous, gorgeous stained glass windows throughout that depict Beethoven, Mozart, a knight, the Greek poetess Sappho, and more. The furnishings are equally elaborate, and even though much of the furniture is not originally from this house, it is from the same time period. Older kids will enjoy the hour-and-a-half tour. They'll see the large music room, the drawing room, and the downstairs kitchen and laundry room which are filled with "labor saving" devices such as an early washing machine, vacuum cleaner, kitchen gadgets, etc. Upstairs are the bedrooms that, in keeping with the rest of the house, are also stylishly decorated. My 11-year old and I were fascinated by the house, but were bewildered as to why Jesse Shepard designed such a masterpiece and incurred the city's expense to construct it only to live in it for two years! Personally, I could live here for a lot longer.

**Hours:**  Open Sat. - Sun. from noon - 4:30pm. Group tours are available Tues. - Sun. by reservation.

**Admission:**  $5 for adults; $2 for ages 6 - 17; children 5 years and under are free.

**Ages:**  8 years and up.

# WHALEY HOUSE

(619) 298-2482 / www.san.rr.com/whaley                                      *$$*
*2482 San Diego Avenue, San Diego*
(Going S. on San Diego Fwy [5] [just south of Interstate 8] exit E. [across the bridge] on Old Town Ave., L. on San Diego Ave. or L. on Congress St. Going N. on 5, exit at Moore St., R. on Old Town Ave., L. on San Diego Ave. or Congress St. It's on the corner of San Diego Ave. and Harvey St.)

Built in 1847, this two-story brick house/museum is definitely worth touring. It has served in the community as a residence, store, theater, and courthouse, and is filled with numerous early California artifacts. The first room you're ushered into, the courthouse room, is fascinating. As you listen to the ten-minute tape explaining the history of the house and this time period, look around. Behind the railing is an old wooden judge's desk, and chairs for the jury. Along one wall is a bookshelf given to Ulysses S. Grant on his inauguration, and an 1860 lifemask (only one of six in existence) of Abraham Lincoln. Display cases in this room feature documents, spurs, pistols, Spanish helmets and swords, clothing, and ornate hair combs and fans. An early copy machine, a letter press, a handmade U.S. flag from 1864 (how many stars does it have?), plus pictures and portraits of George Washington, Abraham Lincoln, Ulysses S. Grant, and Robert E. Lee are also here.

The kitchen, with all of its gadgets, is downstairs, as is the beautifully decorated parlor, and a small music room that contains a spinet piano used in the movie, *Gone With the Wind*. There are several bedrooms upstairs that can be viewed through the protective glass in the doorframes. The bedroom behind the staircase has a decorative wreath, framed on the far wall. It is made from the Whaley girls' hair gathered from hairbrushes and then braided - something to keep the family busy on pre-television nights. The children's bedroom has dolls and toys, while the other bedrooms contain a soldier's dress uniform, mannequins clothed in elegant, ladies' dresses, a lacy quilt covering a canopy bed, and period furniture. The Whaley House is also one of two authenticated haunted houses in California. I highly recommend taking a guided tour, so you don't miss out on any of the background information. Ask about guided school tours.

Exit through the backdoor into a small, picturesque, tree-shaded courtyard. A quick peek into the Old Town Drug Store Museum allows kids to see an old-time pharmacy containing bottles, patented medicines, and a mortar and pestle. Push a button to hear more of the building's history. See OLD TOWN SAN DIEGO, in this section, for details about other attractions in this immediate area.

**Hours:**  Open daily from 10am to 4:30pm. Closed October through May on Tues.

**Admission:**  $4 for adults; $3 for seniors; $2 for ages 5 to 17 years; children 4 years and under are free.

**Ages:**   7 years and up.

# ALBINGER ARCHAEOLOGICAL MUSEUM

(805) 648-5823  / www.vcmha.org

*113 E. Main Street, Ventura*

(Going W. on Ventura Fwy [101], exit N. on California Ave., L. on Main St. Going S.E. on 101, exit S. on Olive, L. on Main. It's on the N. side of the street.)

This small, one-room museum has a collection of archaeological finds spanning thirty-five centuries that have been uncovered from this site. Arrowheads, bottles, milling stones, bone whistles, and more are on display. When the kids have seen their fill, which was pretty immediate with my younger ones, head out the back door and look at the site of an actual dig. The foundations of an original Mission (church) are clearly marked here. My kids were more interested after I explained what we were looking at, and how archaeologists found the remains. (Digging in dirt is a popular pastime with our family, too.)

The enticing stone steps back here lead, disappointingly, to a small street, but at least we got in some exercise.

**Hours:**   Open June through August, Wed. - Sun., 10am - 4pm. Open September through May, Wed. - Fri., 10am - 2pm; Sat. - Sun., 10am - 4pm. Closed New Year's Day, Easter, Thanksgiving, and Christmas.

**Admission:**   Free; donations appreciated.

**Ages:**   6 years and up.

# CARNEGIE ART MUSEUM

(805) 385-8157 - exhibit info.; (805) 385-8171 - tour and class info.  /   $

www.vcnet.com/carnart

*424 South "C" Street, Oxnard*

(Exit Ventura Fwy [101] S. on Hwy 1 [or Oxnard Blvd.], R. on 4$^{th}$ St. It's on the S. side of the street.)

I mention this small, beautiful museum mainly because of the kid-friendly workshops offered. (Tell your kids the building is done in neo-classical design, though they'll just think the columns look really neat.) I take my kids through art museums, explaining what I can and hoping that some understanding and appreciation for art will take root. However, I think the best way to reach and teach our kids is through guided tours and hands-on workshops.

In a group tour here, kids learn about a particular style, artist, or medium, depending on the current exhibit. Then, they create their own art projects in a workshop taught by a local artist. Reservations are needed. Carnegie occasionally offers family classes, too.

Come see the permanent and rotating exhibits of paintings, photographs, and sculptures at this Museum. Have your children draw a picture of their outing!

**Hours:**   Open Thurs. - Sat., 10am - 5pm; Sun., 1am - 5pm. Closed during public holidays and during installation of new exhibits.

**Admission:**  $3 for adults; $2 for seniors and students; $1 for ages 6 - 16; children 5 years and under are free. The museum is free from 3pm - 6pm on Fri.
**Ages:**  6 years and up.

## CASTLE EARTH CHILDREN'S MUSEUM
(805) 583-5243  / e-mail:castlee@gateway.net
*77 Tierra Rejada Road, Unit A, Simi Valley*
(Exit Ventura Fwy [101] N. on Hwy. 23, R. on Tierra Rejada. Or, exit Hwy. 118 S. on Madera South, R. on Tierra Rejada. The museum is in a shopping complex next to Chuck E. Cheese and K Mart.)

This unusual warehouse-converted-to-museum is part zoological, and part scientific interactive experiments and activities. The eclectic decor includes muted primary-colored walls with a few murals, lots of informational posters, and several stuffed animals. The first section of the museum, although small, is aromatic as it contains caged live animals - a tree squirrel, chickens, iguanas, a cat, a python and other snakes, rats, bunnies, tortoises, and a variety of birds, including a macaw. This informal "zoo" allows your child to pet or hold many of the animals - very cool.

The owner/curator has combined his scientific knowledge and his desire to educate children with lots of research to produce the second portion of the museum, which consists mostly of "homemade" science experiments. A small tank shows how the moon (represented by a ball with a lever) controls the tides by making the water level rise and fall. Fossils are unearthed by "digging" through window boxes filled with sand. Various-sized bean bags can be balanced on a T-scale. Portions of a board, covered with a poster of planets, will light up if you answer the questions underneath it correctly. In small booths around the perimeters, you can make a Zoetropes (i.e. drawings that spin around in a special drum to create animation); look through a microscope; go fishing with magnets, which makes learning more attractive; listen for sound vibrations by playing a guitar, xylophone, and wind chimes, and by pumping air through wood pipes; and more. Most of the exhibits are well labeled. Parents will need to read much of the information to younger children, but kids will like the hands-on displays no matter what age they are. Other activities and displays include an extensive insect and butterfly collection, a dress up area, a puppet show stage (with movie theater seats), plastic and wooden dinosaur skeletons, skull and human body models, a wheelchair to sit in, construction blocks, a reading corner, and eight computer stations with educational software.

Our favorite activity is the scavenger hunt. Thirteen different questionnaires, with five multiple-choice questions each, ask questions such as, "Stick bug (or walking sticks) eat. . . ?" and "This planet is 318 times smaller than Jupiter?" The answers are found throughout the museum. Note: Adult assistance is often needed. For each completed sheet your child brings to the staff, he/she earns points that can be turned in for prizes. Talk about motivation to learn! My over-achievers had to complete all thirteen sheets, which took them almost an hour. (I'm sure they did so because they love to learn, not because they could "buy" bigger prizes with more points!)

Castle Earth also offers a party room, group tours (with a minimum of fifteen children), and after-school workshops on Fridays (3pm to 6pm) pertaining to animal care and science experiments.

**Hours:**  Open Mon. - Sat., 11am - 6pm.
**Admission:**  $3 for adults; $5.50 for ages 3 - 12 years; children 2 years and under are free. School tours are $4 per student; adult chaperones are free. After-school workshops are $15 per child, per session.
**Ages:**  1½ years to 12 years.

## CEC-SEABEE MUSEUM

(805) 982-5163 / www.cbcph.navy.mil
*Located on 23rd Street in the Naval Construction Battalion Center, Port Hueneme*
(Exit the Ventura Fwy [101] S. on Ventura Rd., then just S. of Channel Islands Blvd. turn R. on 23rd Ave. through the gates of the military base. The museum has a statue of a huge bee with a machine gun outside the entrance.)

This huge museum is dedicated to documenting, preserving, and maintaining public awareness of the contributions of the Seabees and Civil Engineer Corps. The mission statement is formal sounding, but the museum is incredibly rich with fascinating exhibits. There are life-size models and statues of men and women depicted in scenes of battle and peacetime, wearing authentic uniforms and costumes from around the world. Displays of weapons, medals, banners, photos, and equipment, such as gas masks, represent all facets of a Seabee's life in action.

Another wing has model boats and an underwater diving exhibit with small, model scuba divers. Kids can touch a full-size, old-fashioned diving suit and helmet. Wonderful dioramas, such as a Seabee's amphibious landing and establishment of camp, can be easily seen, thanks to viewing platforms.

The Cultural Artifacts section is interesting because of the number of exhibits and international content. On display are unusual musical instruments; foreign currency and coins; tools; Indian weapons, beadwork, drums, and other artifacts; an Alaska exhibit; a China exhibit; and so much more! Although nothing here is hands-on, my kids were captivated by the variety and uniqueness of the items. Each exhibit brought a yell of, "Hey, come over here and check this out!" It's the kind of museum, because of its size and the scope of displays, that you can visit again and again.

**Hours:**  The museum is open Mon. - Fri. , 0800 - 1630 (8am - 4:30pm); Sat. 0900 - 1630 (9am - 4:30pm); Sun., 1230 - 1630 (12:30pm - 4:30pm). Closed federal holidays, Easter, and the week between Christmas and New Year's Day.
**Admission:**  Free
**Ages:**  4 years and up.

## CHANNEL ISLANDS NATIONAL PARK VISITOR CENTER

(805) 658-5730 / www.nps.gov/chis                                                    !
*1901 Spinnaker Way, Ventura*
(Going W. on Ventura Fwy [101], exit S.W. on Seaward Ave., L. on Harbor Blvd., S. on
Spinnaker. Going E. on 101, exit S. on Seaward Ave. which turns into Harbor Blvd, R.
on Spinnaker - all the way to the end.)

The Channel Islands Visitor Center is worthy of a trip in itself. You'll pass
by beaches and stores (see VENTURA HARBOR and VILLAGE under the Piers
and Seaports section), but pacify the kids with a, "we'll stop there on the way
out." The Center is a good combination of museum, store, and resource center.
The kids will head straight for the indoor tidepool (not a touch tank), which
offers an up-close look at sea stars, anemones, and other small, ocean creatures.
Other eye-catching displays are the taxidermied animals (some of the birds are in
flight), and a topographical model of the islands. My boys also enjoyed sifting
sand in the mini-sand pit and grinding pretend meal with a Chumash Indian stone
mortar and pestle.

The twenty-five-minute movie, *A Treasure In the Sea,* is shown throughout
the day, and is a fun way to learn more about sea life. Tidepool talks are
available on weekends as are free Ranger programs that offer an in-depth look at
a particular animal or habitat. (Also look under CHANNEL ISLANDS
NATIONAL PARK in the Great Outdoors section.)

**Hours:** Open Mon. - Fri., 8:30am - 4:30pm; Sat. - Sun., 8am - 5pm.
Extended summer hours.
**Admission:** Free
**Ages:** 2 years and up.

## CHUMASH INTERPRETIVE CENTER / OAKBROOK  ☀
## REGIONAL PARK

(805) 492-8076 / www.designplace.com/chumash                              $
*3290 Lang Ranch Parkway, Thousand Oaks*
(Exit Hwy 23 E. on Avenida De Los Arboles, R. on Westlake, then the first L. on Lang
Ranch Parkway.)

Long ago, the Chumash Indians occupied this area of land, which is now
Ventura County, and other surrounding areas. A small, one-room, Interpretive
Center features artifacts representative of the Chumash way of life. Pictures and
native paintings decorate the walls. Some local plants, and the way they were
used, are on display, such as yucca fibers braided into ropes, and sticks fashioned
into weapons. Rabbit and bear furs can be touched, while other exhibits are
behind glass. My kids liked the musical instruments, such as drums and rattles,
and I admired the jewelry made out of beads. Outside, kids can see a replicated
Chumash village. If kids can handle the one-and-a-half-mile walk, hike back to
see the centuries-old pictographs, or rock paintings, visible from the
caves/overhangs. (The pictographs might not look like much to kids, but their
symbolism and preservation is important to Chumash heritage.) Sign up for a
guided nature walk, given on Saturdays at 1pm and Sundays at 2pm. Ask for the
dates of the Pow Wows held here.

School or group tours are two hours long, very informative, and one of the most effective ways to really see and understand what the Center has to offer. The first hour consists of a slide presentation on the history of the Chumash, an explanation of the exhibits and making handcrafts to take home. The second hour is a guided walk through the park and archaeological preserve, from a Chumash perspective. You'll learn about their way of life; inspect a re-created Chumash village complete with a large ap (i.e. roundhouse), two smaller aps, and a sweat lodge; and hear how different plants and trees were used. As an alternative, the second hour could be a wildlife presentation, learning about the native animals, and how to live with and respect them.

The park itself is beautiful, and can be visited without going into the Interpretive Center, although they do ask that you sign in. There are picnic tables, shady oak trees, and miles of hiking trails.

**Hours:** The Center is open Tues. - Sat. from 10am - 5pm. The park is open daily from dawn to dusk.

**Admission:** $3 for adults; $2 for ages 5 - 12; children 4 years and under are free. Tours are $3 per child; adults are free. Entrance to the park is free.

**Ages:** 7 years and up for the Center.

## CONFEDERATE AIR FORCE WORLD WAR II AVIATION MUSEUM

(805) 482-0064 / www.avdigest.com/caf/caf.html
*Ubank Street, Camarillo Airport, Camarillo*
(Exit Ventura Fwy [101] S. on Las Posas Rd., R. on Pleasant Valley Rd.)

Five World War II aircraft are on display at this relatively small museum. Some in flyable condition and some are in the process of being restored. See a Japanese Zero fighter, a Curtiss C-46 transport, a Grumman F8F-2 fighter, a North American SNJ navy trainer, and a B-25 Mitchell bomber. Kids can climb in the cargo airplane and the fighter jet. The docents are affable, knowledgeable, and ready to impart aviation facts whenever asked. All of the artifacts on exhibit date from WWII and include helmets, flags, airplane parts, etc. Outside, children may climb on a cannon that was originally from an aircraft carrier. As the museum is adjacent to the airport, you'll want to spend some time watching small planes take off and land. Tip: At the end of the air field is Freedom Park, so bring a sack lunch.

**Hours:** Open Tues., Thurs., and Sat., 10am - 4pm. Guided tours are given on request.

**Admission:** Free

## EARTH SCIENCE MUSEUM

(805) 642-3155 or (805) 646-5976
*5019 Crooked Palm Road, Ventura*
(Exit Ojai Fwy [33] R. on Shell Rd., L. on Ventura Ave., L. on Crooked Palm Rd.)

This small museum is run by the Gem and Mineral Society and is open by appointment only. The "dinosaur petting zoo" consists of wonderful casts of dinosaur skulls, bones, and teeth that kids can touch. Other casts and real fossils include a ground sloth, mammoth tusk, sauropod ribs, skull of a cave bear, and lots more. The displays include nice pieces of various rocks and minerals, such as geodes, agates, etc; locally found fossils, including shells, eggs, and bird tracks; petrified wood; and lots of informational posters. Everything not behind glass can be handled. Tours are tailored toward your children's ages and attention spans, and the facts dispensed are fascinating. (i.e. A saber-tooth cat is not a tiger because it had no stripes.)

> **Hours:** By appointment.
> **Admission:** Free
> **Ages:** 4 years and up.

## GULL WINGS CHILDREN'S MUSEUM ☼

(805) 483-3005                                                          $$

*418 W. Fourth Street, Oxnard*

(Exit Ventura Fwy [101] S. on Hwy 1 [or Oxnard Blvd.], R. on 4th St.)

Children's museums strive for the right combination of fun and education. Gull Wings has achieved a delightful balance of these goals. The long building has sectioned off "rooms," each one focusing on a different theme. The first room is a delightful toddlers' play area. The next one is for future geologists or paleontologists. It contains rocks, fossils, and skulls to look at and/or touch. (The saber-tooth cat is a particular favorite). Kids can use a microscope to study other elements. This room also teaches engineering principles through play with wooden gears.

My kids played doctor and patient in the next room for over an hour. This complete medical room has gowns, a surgery table with play instruments, an X-ray set up, wheelchairs, and crutches. For hands-on health and science learning, there are plastic models of the body with removable parts, and cloth dolls that kids can unlayer to reveal muscles, bones, and organs.

Further back in the museum is a mini-market with shopping carts, a cash register, and bins of "food" for your little shoppers. A puppet theater allows storytellers to express themselves in creative ways. For more "let's pretend," kids can dress-up in elegant gowns, cowboy attire, or firefighter's or sailor's uniforms, etc. Backdrops and props, like a fire hydrant and a boat, help complete the scenes your kids act out. Face painting and an Art Nook bring out the creative genius in your offspring. Enter another dimension when you enter the Galaxy Room. This room is black lit with painted stars on the ceiling and "music of the universe" playing.

Other highlights include playing with a wooden train set, an at*track*tion for kids of all ages, taking temporary shadow pictures against a photo-sensitive wall, and "driving" a kid-proofed Saturn car. Young drivers can get behind the wheel, shift gears, turn on headlights and, via a plexiglass hood, see the inner workings of an engine. A side door panel is also clear. Critter Corner has a few live animals that children can pet or hold, including turtles, garter snakes, a rat, and a guinea pig.

Ask about the numerous craft and educational classes, storytelling hours, and special family nights. For your own craft supplies, purchase recycled materials at the museum's Resource Roundup store.

**Hours:**  Open Tues. - Sun. from 10am - 5pm.
**Admission:**  $3.50 per person; children under 2 years are free.
**Ages:**  1 to 13 years.

## MISSION SAN BUENAVENTURA
(805) 643-4318 / www.anacapa.net/~mission
*211 E. Main Street, Ventura*
(Going W. on Ventura Fwy [101], exit N. on California Ave., L. on Main St. Going S.E. on 101, exit S. on Olive, L. on Main. It's on the N. side of the street.)

Built in 1792, and ninth in the chain of California missions, San Buenaventura exudes old-world charm. Although the mission is readily seen from the street, a tour through the rooms and grounds offer a better picture of life during this historical time period. You'll see a small courtyard, artifacts from mission days in the several rooms, and even a small cemetery around the side. Groups, with a minimum ten people, can take guided tours, for a minimal fee. The tour includes information about the mission's past inhabitants and doing a thematic craft project.

**Hours:**  Open Mon. - Sat., 10am - 5pm; Sun., 10am - 4pm.
**Admission:**  $1 for adults; 50¢ for children 16 years and under.
**Ages:**  6 years and up.

## OJAI VALLEY HISTORICAL SOCIETY AND MUSEUM
(805) 640-1390
*130 W. Ojai Avenue, Ojai*
(Take State Hwy 150 into Ojai. The road turns into Ojai Ave.)

This museum, located inside an old chapel, has a mission - keeping historic Ojai alive by preserving the valley's cultural and natural heritage. Since most of the exhibits are encased in glass, my kids did a lot of nose pressing. They smudged up the cases containing Chumash Indian artifacts such as arrowheads, beadwork, and rattles made from turtle shells and sea shells. The simulated archaeological pit was interesting, too. Another exhibit area with a lot of kid-appeal is the taxidermied animals, some of which can actually be touched. The stuffed animals on our hit parade include the black bear and the more unusual, platypus and bat. The museum also has a fine collection of taxidermied snakes.

Some of the fossils featured here include a big sea snail and an even bigger rock with at least a dozen sand dollars imbedded in it. (The buck stops here!) The museum has a fairly extensive shell collection, too. I only hope we can remember some of their names the next time we go to the beach.

**Hours:**  Open Wed. - Sun. from 1pm - 4pm.
**Admission:**  $2 for adults; children 12 years and under are free.
**Ages:**  3 years and up.

# OLIVAS ADOBE HISTORICAL PARK                                          ☼

(805) 644-4346                                                          !

*4200 Olivas Park Drive, Ventura*

(Going S. on Ventura Fwy [101], exit S. on Harbor Blvd., L. on Olivas Park Dr. Going N.W. on 101, exit S. on Victoria, R. on Olivas Park Dr.)

The Olivas Adobe is a restored, two-story, adobe home built in 1847. It is representative of the rancho period in California's history. The residence has bedrooms, a living room, and a kitchen to look into that are furnished just as they were over 100 years ago. The grounds are beautifully landscaped. The open courtyard, containing a Chumash Indian oven and some farming equipment, gives younger ones some running-around space. A small exhibit building, across from the rose garden, contains items that relate to this particular time period, such as saddles, pictures, and ranching equipment. While this is not an all day visit, kids enjoy the opportunity to "see" the past.

> **Hours:**      The grounds are open daily from 10am - 4pm. The Adobe, and
>                 tours of it, are available on Sat. and Sun., between 10am - 4pm.
> **Admission:** Free
> **Ages:**       6 years and up.

# RONALD REAGAN PRESIDENTIAL LIBRARY AND          ☼
# MUSEUM

(800) 410-8354 or (805) 522-8444 / www.lbjlib.utexas.edu/reagan        $

*40 Presidential Drive, Simi Valley*

(Exit the Simi Valley/San Fernando Valley Fwy [118] S. on Madera Rd., R. up the hill on Presidential Dr.)

The massive, Spanish-style Ronald Reagan Library and Museum is alone on a hilltop. Remember those books that you read about kings and queens and their treasures? Walk down the hallway lined with incredible gifts from heads of states and feel like those storybook pages have come true. Treasures range from an exquisite hand-beaded blouse for the First Lady to an intricately carved, ivory-handled sword that has a gold sheath inlaid with jewels, for the President.

Reagan's heritage and love of the West is evident throughout the museum. One room, in particular, is dedicated to the American west with displays of elaborate saddles, boots, spurs, statues, and an eye-catching cowboy hat with a real rattlesnake head on the band. Even the full-size replica of the Oval Office, which reflects each President's personal style, is decorated with western art.

Two theaters show twenty-minute-plus videos of the Reagan years that include inauguration speeches, tearing down the Berlin wall, and a remembrance of the Challenger crew. My kids were thoroughly captivated by the footage.

The next few galleries depict Reagan's road to the presidency via movie posters, uniforms, costumes, documents, and lots of photos. My oldest child was also impressed by a large nuclear cruise missile on display that was once deployed in Europe. One room contains signed sports paraphernalia. Another displays gifts that range from the elegant to the homemade, such as a jellybean-painted cane, and the Presidential Seal crafted from 6,500 silver nails - what a great kid's project this would make! There are pictures of Nancy Reagan, some of her gowns, and a whole wall devoted to her "Just Say No" campaign.

There are numerous touch screens throughout the museum so kids can learn about Reagan's views on issues by letting their fingers "do the walking." Visitors can become members (albeit temporarily) of Reagan's cabinet while sitting around a table in a re-created White House Room. His image and responses are shown on a big screen in the room. Travel to the Geneva Convention and witness a historic meeting between Gorbachev and Reagan as their images are projected on the screen above the chateau's fireplace.

Out back is a huge, decoratively spray-painted, chunk of the Berlin wall. Note that the gift shop has great aids for teaching history. A Marie Callender's cafe is on-site, and is open the same hours as the museum.

**Hours:** Open daily from 10am - 5pm. Closed New Year's Day, Thanksgiving, and Christmas.

**Admission:** $4 for adults; $2 for seniors; children 15 years and under are free.

**Ages:** 5 years and up.

## SANTA PAULA TRANSPORTATION MUSEUM

(805) 933-0076
*851 E. Main Street, Santa Paula*
(Exit the 126 Fwy N. on State Route 150 [or 10th St.], L. on Main St.)

Over twenty vintage vehicles are on display in this museum located in the quaint town of Santa Paula. A partial listing of the vehicles includes a stagecoach, surrey, 1922 Union Oil truck, 1927 Model T, 1935 Packard Super 8, 1936 Topper Car and Trailer (actually used in the movie, *Topper*), 1960 Cadillac Coupe de Ville, and 1971 Foyt Coyote (Indianapolis Race Car). The vehicles, kept in mint condition, show how the mode of transportation has progressed throughout the years. Note: Don't miss the SANTA PAULA UNION OIL MUSEUM, just down the street.

**Hours:** Open the first Sun. of each month from 10am - 1pm.

**Admission:** Free

**Ages:** 5 years and up.

## SANTA PAULA UNION OIL MUSEUM

(805) 933-0076
*1001 E. Main Street, Santa Paula*
(Exit the 126 Fwy, N. on State Route 150 [or 10th St.]. The Museum is on the N.E. corner of 10th and Main St.)

The Union Oil Museum is housed in the original headquarters of the Union Oil Company. The interior and exterior of the 1890 building has meticulously been restored to its original luster. Upon entering, kids can punch a keepsake time card in an old time card machine. The walls are covered with great pictures and murals regarding the history and technology of the oil industry.

Quite a few of the exhibits are interactive, such as the Lubricity Exhibit.

Kids can turn the gears and see how much easier the figures on bicycles can pedal when the gears are oiled. They can push a button and watch a model rig "drill" for oil through the layers of the earth. With a touch of a button, the Centrifuge Exhibit spins to separate water and other substances from crude oil. A few touch screens here impart interesting information about how the oil industry affects so many aspects of our lives.

Since geology is vital to finding oil, several terrific geological displays are in the museum. Some of the fossils on display include shells, dinosaur bones, and shark teeth.

The upstairs, which can only be seen by a half-hour guided tour, is interesting to older kids. There are restored offices, bedrooms, a kitchen, and fireplaces with ornate tiles around them. A walk-in safe looks like a secret, hidden room.

Walk through the main building and outside to reach the Rig Room. Kids can see a huge cable rig in action as the engine turns the sand wheel that turns the band wheel that moves the wooden walking beam and the huge drill bits! I hope you feel like we did when we visited the museum - like we struck oil!

**Hours:**  Open Wed. - Sun. from 10am - 4pm. Tours of the upstairs are conducted only Fri. - Sun. from 11am - 2:30pm. Closed major holidays.

**Admission:**  Free to the museum. The tour of the upstairs costs $2 for adults; $1 for children 17 years and under.

**Ages:**  4 years and up.

## STAGECOACH INN MUSEUM                                    ☼
(805) 498-9441                                                      $
*51 S. Ventu Park Road, Newbury Park*
(Exit the Ventura Fwy [101] S. on Ventu Park Rd.)

This beautiful 1870's hotel and stagecoach stop is both interesting and educational, and seen only by guided tour. The downstairs consists mainly of the parlor, dining room, and kitchen. The furniture, decor, and history are interesting to older kids, but younger kids get antsy.

Upstairs, however, it is a different story. A small "cowboy" bedroom has a saddle, bear skin rug, and other western paraphernalia. The Chumash Indian room has a collection of fossils, beadwork, and pictures. Another room has an extensive butterfly and bug collection in glass cases. The Music Room has an old-fashioned, elegant feel to it as antique violins, other instruments, and vintage clothing are fashionably displayed. A child's room is filled with toys of yesteryear (no Nintendo!), and a bed that Todd Lincoln slept in. (I hope kids won't ask, "Who's that?") Oooooo - a man named Pierre was supposedly shot here and his ghost still haunts the Inn. Now, the Inn becomes fascinating to kids!

Outside the hotel, take a short nature trail that leads to other historic points of interest. The Carriage House contains stagecoaches, while further around the bend are the Pioneer Newbury House and the Spanish Adobe House. Both are open to tour. The Chumash Indian Hut and a beehive oven are also interesting.

Explain to your kids that the oven is named for its design, not for cooking bees.

When the kids have seen all they want, head out to the small Stagecoach Park above the Inn. It's easier to drive to the park than to walk, as the entrance is on another street.

**Hours:** The Inn is open Wed. - Sun. from 1pm - 4pm. The Carriage House is open only on Sun. from 1pm - 4pm.

**Admission:** $3 for adults; $2 for seniors; $1 for ages 5 - 12; children 4 years and under are free.

**Ages:** 5 years and up.

## STRATHERN HISTORICAL PARK AND MUSEUM

(805) 526-6453                                                                        *S*

*137 Strathern Place, Simi Valley*

(Exit Simi Valley/San Fernando Valley Fwy [118] S. on Madera Rd., R. on Strathern Place.)

This outside museum is several historical buildings inside a gated, park-like setting. Start your one-hour guided tour at the visitor's center. Learn about the early days of Simi by first watching a twenty-minute tape about the Valley's history. Some of the exhibits in here include maps and, a little more exciting, beekeeping equipment such as smokers and hoods. Next, walk through one of the very first local colony houses. Though the inside decor is from the 1930's, the building itself still retains its earlier, original charm. An adobe house, built in the early 1700's, displays an owner's furnishings from the 1950's. The Strathern House, which is a Victorian house built in 1893, has antique treasures throughout including furniture, clothing, and a pump organ.

The library contains some fossils, as well as books. The enclosed barn has eight stalls with different exhibits in each, such as kitchen gadgets, early laundry equipment, an old-fashioned switchboard, Chumash Indian artifacts, farm machinery, and old automobiles such as a truck, a tractor, and a Ford Model A. Another barn contains more farm equipment - hay wagons, etc. Around the perimeters of the historical park are pieces of old (rusted) farming equipment, which adds to the rustic ambiance.

**Hours:** Open to the public Sat. - Sun., 1pm - 4pm and Wed., 1pm - 2pm for tours, weather permitting. Open for school tours upon request.

**Admission:** $2 for adults; $1 for students.

**Ages:** 5 years and up.

## VENTURA COUNTY MARITIME MUSEUM

(805) 984-6260  / e-mail:vcmm@aol.com                                                *S*

*2731 South Victoria Avenue, Oxnard*

(Exit Ventura Fwy [101] S. on Victoria St. The museum is located at Channel Islands Harbor at the corner of Victoria St. and Channel Islands Blvd.)

Explore the seas without leaving port! This good-sized, nautical museum has original paintings, and various sizes and styles of model ships behind glass cases.

What detail! Marine artists from the 1700's to the present have their eye-catching work on display throughout the museum. If your child has the patience, or desire, a docent will gladly explain local nautical history, which gives more meaning to the exhibits.

**Hours:**    Open in the summer daily from 11am - 5pm. Open the rest of the year, Thurs. - Mon. from 11am - 5pm.

**Admission:**  $3 for adults; $1 for children 11 years and under.

**Ages:**    4 years and up.

## VENTURA COUNTY MUSEUM OF HISTORY AND ART ☼

(805) 653-0323 / www.vcmha.org                                                $

*100 E. Main Street, Ventura*

(Going W. on Ventura Fwy [101], exit N. on California Ave., L. on Main St. Going S.E. on 101, exit S. on Olive, L. on Main. It's on the S. side of street.)

This museum is a great introduction to art for children. The paintings and dioramas are beautiful, and the variety of exhibits is even better. As we followed along the building's circular layout, we saw a wonderful display of fossilized shells and bones. The outside patio area has an impressive collection of large farm machinery. Chumash Indian stone mortars and pestles are out here for kids to try. A section of the museum is set up chronologically, showing the beginnings of Ventura County, featuring Chumash artifacts, to the New West, represented by a 1910 car, an old vacuum cleaner, washer, etc.

The George Stuart Gallery room displays part of his over 200 historical figures. Marie Antoinette, American patriots, etc., are one-quarter life-size (three inches to the foot). The intricate art work and attention to detail makes the finished figures very lifelike. My kids were most intrigued with the models and pictures that explained how Mr. Stuart designs and constructs his figures. They now want to attempt to make similar figures at home.

The museum is well laid out and the kids enjoyed most of the exhibits - a good start for laying a foundation of art appreciation!

**Hours:**    Open Tues. - Sun. from 10am - 5pm.

**Admission:**  $3 for adults; children 16 years and under are free.

**Ages:**    4 years and up.

# PIERS AND SEAPORTS

It ap*pier*s that walking around seaport villages, looking at boats, fishing off piers, taking a cruise, and maybe going on some rides, is a delightful way to spend a few hours with your child!

## FISHERMAN'S VILLAGE

(310) 823-5411    !/$

*13755 Fiji Way, Marina Del Rey*

(Take Marina Fwy [90] to the end, L. on Mindanao, L. on Lincoln, R. on Fiji Way.)

   This turn-of-the-century, New England-themed shopping and boating complex is located on the main channel of the Marina Del Rey harbor. It offers pier fishing and boat rentals. (See MARINA BOAT RENTALS under the Transportation section.)

   I still say the best things in life are free, or relatively inexpensive. It's fun just walking along the pier, looking at the boats, maybe grabbing a snack, and feeling the ocean breeze.

   **Hours:**     The Village is open Sun. - Thurs., 9am - 9pm; Fri. - Sat., 9am - 10pm.
   **Admission:** Free. Two-hours of free parking with validation.
   **Ages:**      All

## PORTS O' CALL VILLAGE

(310) 831-0287    !/$

*Berth 77, San Pedro*

(Exit Harbor Fwy [110] S. on Harbor Blvd. and follow the signs.)

   This picturesque village with seventy-five shops and restaurants has cobblestone streets, making it an interesting stroll. Harbor tours are available (see the Transportation section), as are Adventure Helicopter rides. Five-minute helicopter rides are $20 - flight time and prices go up from there - and available on weekends and holidays. Call (310) 547-3419 for more information. Tip: The electric, green trolley has several stops in San Pedro, with Ports O' Call being one of them. Take the trolley to LOS ANGELES MARITIME MUSEUM, S. S. LANE VICTORY (both listed under the Museums section), or around town. At 25¢, this is a fun, mini-adventure. Note: The trolley doesn't run on Tuesdays or Wednesdays.

   **Hours:**     Most shops are open daily from 11am - 6pm. Restaurants are open later in the evenings. Shops and restaurants are open longer in the summer. Closed Christmas.
   **Admission:** Free, but bring spending money.
   **Ages:**      All

## REDONDO BEACH INTERNATIONAL BOARDWALK / KING HARBOR

(310) 318-0648    $

*Where Torrance Boulevard meets the sea, Redondo Beach*

(Exit San Diego Fwy [405] S. on Western, R. on 190th St. which turns into Anita St., L on Pacific Coast Highway, R. on Torrance.)

   This is no ordinary pier, but a fascinating place to explore with your family! Starting at the north end of the harbor, come hungry because enticing food smells waft through the air. Choose from egg rolls, gyros, hamburgers, or pizza as the international restaurants run the gamut from grab-a-bite to elegant. We munched as we watched the ducks and boats in the water, and soaked up the ambiance.

Stop off at Quality Seafood - it's like a mini-sea-zoo with tanks of live crabs, lobsters, shrimp, and shellfish. You cannot entirely avoid the Fun Factory which is a huge, under-the-boardwalk, amusement center. It has over 200 video, arcade, and carnival-style games, plus kiddie rides, which adds up to a lot of noisy stimulus. Come up for a breather 'cause right next "door" is the Marina Boat Ride, open on weekends and holidays. Enjoy a half-hour boat ride for $3 for ages 4 and up, $1 for children 3 years and under, children 2 years and under are free. While out at sea look for the colony of sea lions that usually hangs around.

Back on the cement, horse-shoe shaped pier, have your kids look down at the various sea etchings, including blue whales and sting rays. Try your luck at fishing off the pier. The gift shops on the older, wooden boardwalk offer a variety of merchandise for sale. Check out the store Shark Attack. Not only does it sell shark teeth, sea shells, etc., but for an additional $1.50 for adults, $1 for kids 10 years and under, you can go past the curtain and see a sixteen-and-a-half foot, taxidermied, great white shark.

Last, but not least, there are rock jetties here. Deeming them fairly safe for the kids to walk on, my husband and I won the coveted, "you guys are the greatest!" award from our children. Ah, the simple pleasures.

Look for nearby Whaling Wall. This incredible mural of the California gray whale, painted by marine artist, Wyland, decorates the massive wall of the Redondo Generating Station building located on Harbor Drive at Herondo Street. It's worth a drive by, or a stop and stare.

**Hours:** Most restaurants are open daily for breakfast, lunch, and dinner. Most of the stores and attractions are open daily from 10am - 6pm.

**Admission:** Parking is 50¢ for each 20 minutes; $5 maximum on weekdays; $10 maximum on weekends.

**Ages:** All

# SANTA MONICA PIER

(310) 458-8900 / www.pacpark.com                                    $$
*Foot of Colorado Boulevard, Santa Monica*
(Exit Santa Monica Fwy [10] N. on 4ᵗʰ St., L. on Colorado Blvd. It dead ends at the pier.)

This renowned wooden pier offers a lot to do, as well as just soaking up the beach atmosphere. There are food stands, restaurants, and great shops that carry a little bit of everything. Peek in the fresh fish store as it has tanks of live lobsters, crabs, and other shellfish. Or, go fishing off the pier to catch your own fresh meal. Rent a pole for $3 an hour at the bait and tackle shop at the end of the pier.

A major kid-attraction on the pier is PACIFIC PARK. (See the Amusement Parks section.) A food court is near the amusement park to service your tummy.

The Playland Arcade draws kids like a magnet with its video and arcade games. A friendly warning: Weekends can be almost overwhelmingly crowded here.

Discover a place where touchable tidepool life is teeming under the boardwalk at the U.C.L.A. OCEAN DISCOVERY CENTER. (See the Zoos and Animals section.) Santa Monica beach offers plenty of long stretches of beach, great surf, and several playgrounds.

Feel like going for a ride? A twenty-mile bike path goes through Santa Monica, from the north at Wills Rogers State Beach to the south at Torrance Beach. If you forget your wheels, call Sea Mist Rentals at (310) 395-7076. They also have in-line skates and boogie boards for rent.

Hours:      The stores are usually open 10am - 6pm year round. Open extended hours in the summer.

Admission:  Free to the pier. Parking can be hard to find. Parking on the pier is $3 for the first two hours, with a vendor validation, or maximum $7.

Ages:       2 years and up.

## SHORELINE VILLAGE
(562) 435-2668  / www.shorelinevillage.com
*407 Shoreline Village Drive, Long Beach*
(Take Long Beach Fwy [710] to the end, E. on Shoreline Dr., R. on Shoreline Village Dr.)

This turn-of-the-century coastal "village" has specialty shops and places to eat, including Parker's Lighthouse Restaurant, a multi-story "lighthouse" on the water's edge. There is also the all-important ice cream shop and candy stores. Located in the village, too, is ENDANGERED SPECIES ECOPARK. (Look under the Zoos and Animals section.) Weekday mornings are a great time to enjoy serenity here. Stroll along the walkways and/or take the cement pathway all the way to the LONG BEACH AQUARIUM OF THE PACIFIC (look under the Zoos and Animals section), and even beyond to a grassy park. Catch a water taxi to the Aquarium, the QUEEN MARY, or SCORPION. (Look under the Museums section for the latter two, which are just across the water.)

Hours:      The stores are open daily, usually from 10am - 6pm. Open extended hours in the summer.

Admission:  Free. Parking is free for the first two hours with validation and a minimum $3 purchase. It is $1 for every half hour after that; $6 maximum.

Ages:       2 years and up.

## BALBOA PIER
*Main Street, Balboa*                                                    !/$
(Take Costa Mesa Fwy [55] to the end, which turns into Newport Blvd., which turns into Balboa Blvd., R. on Main St. to end for the pier.)

Enjoy the miles of sandy beach for sunning and surfing; fish from the pier just for the fun of it; or grab a bite to eat at the small RUBY'S Diner at the end of the pier. (See the Edible Adventures section.) Peninsula Park is on the east side of the pier. This grassy park, shaded only by palm trees, has barbeques, picnic tables, and even a small playground. See BALBOA FUN ZONE, under the Family Pay and Play section, located just across the road, and combine both attractions for a full day of fun.

**Hours:** Open daily.
**Admission:** Free. Parking in the lot costs about $3.
**Ages:** All

## DANA POINT HARBOR - DANA WHARF / MARINER'S ☼ VILLAGE

(949) 496-10945                                                                    !/$
*34675 Street of the Golden Lantern, Dana Point*
(Exit San Diego Fwy [5] N. on Pacific Coast Highway, L. on Dana Point Harbor Dr./ Del Obispo St., L. on St. of the Golden Lantern.)

Dana Point Harbor has beaches, tidepools, a seaside shopping village, boat rentals, picnic areas, and more. Entering the Street of the Golden Lantern, Dana Wharf is to your left, and Mariner's Village is to your right. Activities on the Wharf side include shopping, whale-watching cruises, and boat fishing. Call Dana Wharf Sportfishing, (949) 496-5794 for more information. The Village offers many specialty shops, from Indian jewelry to seafaring items. Food choices range from the elegant to the quick bite, plus ice cream and candy shops, of course. Your young sailor can watch boats of all sizes, shapes, and colors sail in and out of the harbor and up and down the coast.

At the western end of the harbor, next to the Orange County Marine Institute, is Dana Cove Park, or "Baby Beach." There are a few picnic tables here overlooking the bluffs, rock jetties to climb on, and a waveless beach. Enjoy the day with your family day at Dana Point, whatever you choose to do! (See DOHENY STATE BEACH PARK, under the Beaches section, and ORANGE COUNTY MARINE INSTITUTE, under the Museums section, for other things to do here.)

**Hours:** Most shops are open daily from 10am - 6pm. Open extended hours in the summer.
**Admission:** Parking is free.
**Ages:** All

## OCEANSIDE PIER AND HARBOR ☼

(760) 721-1101 - Visitor's Information Center                    !/$
*At the end of Pier View Way at Pacific Street, Oceanside*
(Exit San Diego Fwy [5] W. on Mission Ave., R. on Pacific St., L. on Pier View Wy.)

The Ocean Beach Pier is the longest pier in San Diego County, and the majority of it is made from wood planks. It stretches out over the ocean almost 2,000 feet, or twenty minutes of walking, depending on the age of your youngest child. Don't want to walk? There is a Ruby's Scooby Doo golf-cart-like shuttle available for a mere 25¢ each way. The spacious RUBY'S Diner (see the Edible Adventures section) at the end of the pier is a 40's diner serving great all-American food at good prices in a very kid-friendly atmosphere. Another pier-related activity is fishing. It doesn't require a license, so reel 'em in! A bait and tackle shop has pole rentals available. The other end of the pier (the land end) offers a McDonald's restaurant, an outdoor amphitheater (used for in-line skating when concerts aren't in session), a playground with wooden climbing structures, sand volleyball courts, and, of course, miles of surf and sand.

Breeze on over to the Oceanside Harbor, just a few streets north of the pier. The Harbor offers your choice of boat rentals at Harbor Paddle Sports, including kayaks, jet skis, sailing, and sportfishing boats. Come on in, the water's fine for swimming and surfing. On the beach are sand volleyball courts, a playground for the younger set, and picnic areas with barbecues and covered cabanas. The Cape-Cod-like stores and restaurants entice the shoppers (and the hungry) to indulge.

I would be remiss if I didn't mention the famous Dog Beach, located a few miles south of the pier. Furry visitors from all over come to romp and play frisbee on this two-mile stretch of beach. Tip: Watch where you walk.

      **Hours:**     Most restaurants are open daily 10am - 6pm. Open extended hours in the summer.

  **Admission:**     Spending money.

       **Ages:**     All

## SEAPORT VILLAGE

(619) 235-4014 / www.spvillage.com

*800 West Harbor Drive at Kettner Boulevard, San Diego*

(Going S. on San Diego Fwy [5], exit W. on Ash St., L. on 4$^{th}$, R. on Broadway to the end, then L. on Harbor Dr. Going N. on 5, exit S. on 6$^{th}$ Ave., R. on Broadway to the end, then L. on Harbor Dr.)

This delightful harbor-side shopping area is in an expansive, beautiful, park-like setting. There are three themed plazas here representing early California, a New England fishing village, and the Victorian era. There are several wonderful restaurants to choose from as well as numerous places for snackers to eat. Along its boardwalk and cobblestone "streets" the Village offers over sixty-five unique shops, including Magnet Max, Miner's Gems and Minerals, and Fantasy World of Toys. Kids will enjoy riding the 100-year-old carousel located in the West Plaza. The carousel is open daily from 10am to 9pm. Rides cost $1 each for ages 4 years and up; children 3 years and under ride for free with a paid adult. See CINDERELLA'S CARRIAGE, under the Transportation section, for another way to see the village.

      **Hours:**     Open daily 10am - 9pm. Open in the summer one hour later.

  **Admission:**     Technically free. Parking for two hours is free with a validation of any purchase. Otherwise, it's about $1.50 an hour.

       **Ages:**     All

## CHANNEL ISLANDS HARBOR VILLAGE

*At the corner of Victoria Avenue and Channel Islands Boulevard, Oxnard*

(Exit Ventura Fwy [101] S. on Victoria Ave.)

Stroll and shop the day away in this quaint-looking, Victorian harbor village. While some stores cater to your taste buds, others have great gift-giving items for sale. Kids enjoy walking the village "streets" and taking in the sights. Stop in at the VENTURA COUNTY MARITIME MUSEUM (look under the Museums section) sometime before you ship out.

**Hours:** Most stores are open daily from 10am - 6pm.
**Admission:** Free
**Ages:** All

## VENTURA HARBOR and VILLAGE

(805) 644-0169 / www.venturaharborvillage.com !/$
*1559 Spinnaker Way, Ventura*
(Going W. on Ventura Fwy [101], exit S.W. on Seaward Ave., L. on Harbor Blvd. Going S. on 101, exit S. on Harbor Blvd. From Harbor Blvd., go R. on Spinnaker Dr.)

This harbor has a lot to offer. The picturesque "village" has over thirty unusual gift shops and restaurants. Come for lunch, or just dessert! Enjoy a stroll around and look at the boats, or take a ride on the merry-go-round at $1 a ride.

Your family can take a cruise (this is always such a treat for kids), walk on the rock jetties located down toward the Channel Islands Visitor Center, and/or play at the Marina Cove play area which has a slide, swings, and a miniature Spanish galleon ship to board, plus sand dunes. By the way, the rock jetties are not for the faint of heart or for really young kids, as part of the "walkway" on the rocks is washed away. Bring your fishing poles if you have the time and patience. The beach is here, too, of course, along with picnic areas and barbecues. Enjoy your day here with all there is to do and *sea*! (Also see CHANNEL ISLANDS NATIONAL PARK under the Great Outdoors section, and CHANNEL ISLANDS NATIONAL PARK VISITORS CENTER under the Museums section).

For cruise information, see BAY QUEEN HARBOR CRUISE under the Transportation section. If you want to experience the thrill of "really" flying like a bird, and you weigh at least 80 pounds, try parasailing with Blue Edge company, (805) 684-0022. The cost is $55 for a ten-minute ride. Passengers may accompany parasailers on the boat for $10. The boat ride out in the ocean and back takes about an hour.

**Hours:** Most stores are open daily from 10am - 6pm. The merry-go-round is open Mon. - Thurs., 10am - 7pm; Fri. - Sun., 10am - 9pm.
**Admission:** Free, but bring money.
**Ages:** All

## VENTURA PIER

*Harbor Boulevard, Ventura* !
(Going W. on Ventura Fwy [101], exit S.W. on Seaward Ave., L. on Harbor Blvd. Going S. on 101, exit S. on Harbor Blvd.)

The pier's real attraction is that it is the longest wooden pier in California, and the sunsets here are kid-approved! The playground and beautiful long stretch of sandy beach doesn't hurt, either.

**Hours:** Open daily.

**Admission:** Free

**Ages:** All

# POTPOURRI

The dictionary defines potpourri as: "A miscellaneous mixture; a confused collection." This accurately defines this section!!! You'll find a little bit of everything here, so pick through and have fun.

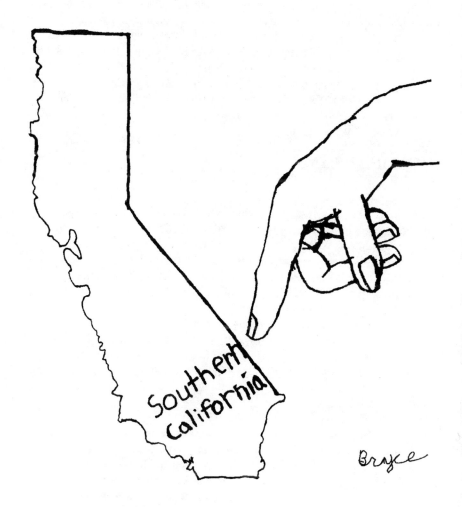

## ALLIED MODEL TRAINS

(310) 313-9353 / www.alliedmodeltrains.com                    *!/$*

*4411 S. Sepulveda Boulevard, Culver City*

(From the N., exit San Diego Fwy [405] on Washington Blvd. and turn L. at the end of the off ramp, L. on Culver Blvd., R. on Sepulveda. From the S., exit 405 L. on Culver Blvd., R. on Braddock Dr. It's on the corner of Sepulveda and Braddock.)

Chug on over to the world's largest model railroad store to pick up anything one could possibly use or need for trains, tracks, villages, etc. Allied caters to the casual hobbyist and the diehards and everything in between. Their stock includes ¼-inch-tall Z-gauge people, to Thomas the Tank, to collector's items costing thousands of dollars. We like to gaze at the multitude of marvelous displays. Streets, towns, even entire worlds (well, not quite) are on exhibit with working trains, lights, and animated scenes. Kids may need to be lifted up to see some of them. If you aren't enamored with trains when you first come through the doors, I bet you'll at least be tempted to buy a layout by the time you leave.

**Hours:**    Open Mon. - Thurs. and Sat., 10am - 6pm; Fri., 10am - 7pm.
**Admission:**    Free
**Ages:**    3 years and up.

## CATALINA ISLAND

(310) 510-1520 - Visitors Bureau / www.catalina.com                    *$$$$$*

*across the water!*

Catalina Island is a resort in the truest sense of the word. It's twenty-one miles long, eight miles wide, only twenty-two miles from the mainland, and packed with all sorts of things to see and do. The main town, Avalon, has an abundance of shops and restaurants along the beach and harbor. Come here to fish in the deep blue sea; take a glass bottom boat ride; go horse-back riding, hiking, or camping on the untamed side of the island; take an Island safari, where kids thrill at seeing real buffalo; or just enjoy the beach and all the water activities, such as swimming, snorkeling, canoeing, etc. Catalina has a quaint ambiance and is a wonderful family day trip or weekend excursion. I highly recommend ordering the 100-page Visitors Guide as it has *all* the information you could possibly want about Catalina. (Call the Visitors Bureau at the above number to order it.) The following are highlights and names and numbers to get you started.

How much time you have in Catalina will dictate what you should do. Consider taking a tour or two as you'll see more of the island. Both Catalina Adventure Tours, (310) 510-2888 and Discovery Tours, (310) 510-8687 or (800) 322-3434, offer numerous and diverse tours at comparable prices. (Prices quoted are from Adventure Tours.) Get acquainted with Catalina by taking a forty-five-minute, narrated city tour to see the Wrigley estate, the city streets, and an unparalleled view of the harbor while hearing about Catalina's history - $8.50 for adults; $7.50 for seniors; $4.25 for children ages 2 to 11. A longer city tour includes a stop at the Botanical Garden and Wrigley Memorial - a nice spot to walk along the pathways - $17.50 for adults; $15 for seniors; $9 for children.

The two-hour inner island tour is one of my favorites, although younger kids get antsy. You'll see canyons to coastlines, plus wild bison and maybe wild turkeys and foxes. A stop at Airport-in-the-Sky is good for stretching your legs, watching small planes land and take-off, trying a buffalo burger at the Buffalo Springs Station, and visiting the (free) Nature Center, (310) 510-0954. This tour costs $19.50 for adults; $18 for seniors; $9.50 for children. Adventure Tour offers a four-hour Land and Sea Tour that takes you all around the island by bus, including a stop over at the beach for an hour, then takes you back to Avalon by boat - $75 for adults; $55 for kids. Discovery Tours offers a narrated three-and-a-half-hour tour to see the Airport-in-the-Sky and to the Pacific side of Catalina where a visit to El Rancho Escondido, refreshments, and an Arabian horse performance are part of the deal - $29.50 for adults; $26 for seniors; $14.75 for kids.

There are several cruise and water taxi options, at about $3 per person, if you want to see Catalina from the water. The two tour companies also offer forty-minute, narrated glass-bottom boat rides, which are *clearly* one of the best ways to see the many varieties of fish and underwater gardens off the coast of Catalina. Aboard the Sea View, via Adventure Tours, you can even feed fish through specially designed tubes and watch the feeding frenzy. (It's just like the dinner table at home!) Night excursions are also available. Prices for the Sea View glass-bottom boat tour are about $9 for adults; $7.50 for seniors; and $4.75 for children. The Undersea Tour, via Discovery Tours, is given onboard a semi-submersible boat - $22 for adults; $19.25 for seniors, $11 for children. Inquire about Discovery Tours flying fish tours (yes, the fish really do fly) and cruises out to seal rock. Each excursion costs $8.50 for adults; $7.50 for seniors; $4.25 for children. Combo tour packages are available.

There are a myriad of other water activities to choose from, too, besides the obvious choice of swimming. Ocean Rafting Trips, (310) 510-0211, offers half-day and full-day voyages to explore coves, beaches, and sea caves. The voyages, which optionally include snorkeling, too, start at $45 per person. Take a guided kayak excursion with Catalina Island Expeditions, (310) 510-1226. A two-hour guided tour, which is really a natural history field trip, is two-plus miles of kayaking - $34 for adults; $16.50 for children 11 years and under. Parasailing, (310) 510-1777, offers the thrill of flying - ten minutes air time - for $45 per person. The flying and boat ride takes about an hour total. Additional passengers only in the boat are $10 each.

Dryer, land activities are fun, too! Go on a guided horseback ride, via Catalina Stables, (310) 510-0478, through the mountains to see the unspoiled countryside, and a great view of Avalon. Children must have previous riding experience, and rides start at $20 for half-an-hour. Get it in gear and rent a bike at Brown's Bikes, (310) 510-0986, to explore the island. Take an open jeep tour of the rugged inland with Jeep Eco-Tours, (310) 510-2595, starting at $65 per person for a two-hour ride. Play a beautiful and challenging miniature golf course at Golf Gardens, (310) 510-1200 - $5.50 for adults; $3 for children 7 years and under. Arcade and video games can be found at Mardi Gras Arcade in the Metropole Market Place. They can also be found on the beach at Avalon Arcade, along with pool and air hockey. There are two other noteworthy short stops: The small Catalina Island Interpretive Center, (310) 510-2514, which has mostly pictorial and informational displays, such as a marine mural with buttons to push to listen to whale sounds and a large kelp mural with text, plus rocks that were found on the island. The Center is open daily 10am to 4pm, and admission is free. The Catalina Island Museum, (310) 510-2414, is located in the famous Casino building. (If you take a tour of the building, admission to the museum is included). The museum has a wall with trophy fish such as Marlin, a few models of ships, old switchboards, and informational and photographic displays of the island's history. It's open daily 10:30am to 4pm. Admission is $1.50 for adults; $1 for seniors; 50¢ for children 5 to 11 years old.

   To really get away from it all, explore Catalina by hiking and/or camping. Seaside camping is at Two Harbors Campground, which is a quarter-mile from the small town of Two Harbors. The town is at the isthmus, down the coast quite a bit from Avalon. It's like being in another part of the world. This is a popular camping site because of its accessibility and water activities. Camping prices range from $18.50 to $36 per site for two people, depending on the site location. For a small cabin that sleeps four, or a tepee that sleeps up to six people, prices begin at $60 a night for two people. (Additional people cost extra.) For your information, a two-hour bus drive from Avalon to Two Harbors is $20 one way. Parson's Landing Campground is remote, located at the complete opposite end of the island from Avalon. Camping here costs $15.50 for one person ($22 for two people), which includes a bundle of wood and a few gallons of water. It is beautiful, and suitable for older kids who like to backpack. Little Harbor Campground is on the other side of the island from Avalon. The campground is near two sandy beaches under small, but somewhat shady, palm trees. Prices start at $9 per night, per person. It is accessible by taking a shuttle bus. Blackjack Campground, situated among a grove of pine trees, away from the water, toward the interior of the island, is for hardy campers. The surrounding area is great for hiking. Camping sites start at $7.50 per person, per night. Hermit Gulch Campground is the only campground in Avalon. Families can tent or tepee camp here. This is getting-away-from-it-all camping, but not too far away. With your own tent and other equipment, camping is $10 per adult and $8 per child, per night. A six-person tepee, or a small cabin, is $38 a night, mid-week, for two people, or $52 per night on the weekends. An additional $8.50 per person is charged no matter what day of the week you visit. Reservations are always recommended, and are necessary in July and August. For more information regarding campgrounds and for reservations, call Santa Catalina Island Company at (888) 510-7979.

   Note: Catalina's busiest season is the summer. September, however, provides balmy weather and travel discounts abound.

   Channel crossing time takes anywhere from one to two hours, depending on the point of departure and type of boat. Some numbers to call for cruise information, with various points of departure, are: *Catalina Channel Express*,

(800) 315-7925, which departs from Dana Point, Long Beach Harbor, and San Pedro. The just-over-one-hour cruise costs $36 for adults, $32 for seniors, $27 for ages 2 to 11. All-day parking is $8. *Catalina Cruises*, (800) CATALINA (228-2546), departs from Long Beach Harbor. The two-hour cruise costs $25 for adults, $22.50 for seniors, $20 for ages 3 to 11, $2 for children 2 years and under. All-day parking is $7.50. *Catalina Passenger Service*, (949) 673-5245 / www.catalinainfo.com, departs from Balboa. The hour-and-fifteen-minute cruise costs $36 for adults, $33 for seniors, $20 for ages 3 to 12, $2 for children 2 years and under. All-day parking is $7. If time is of the essence, take a fifteen-minute helicopter ride with *Island Express Helicopter Service*, (310) 510-2525 / www.islandexpress.com, which departs from Long Beach or San Pedro - $66 one way for all ages.

**Admission:**   Prices given above.
**Ages:**   All

## CHINATOWN                                        ☼
(323) 721-0763                                       !/$
*In between Hill Street and North Broadway, Los Angeles*
(Exit Pasadena Fwy [110] N. on Hill St.)

Instead of digging a hole to China, hop in the car and drive to Chinatown. Walk along Hill Street and North Broadway to meander through the red and gold decorated stores here (faux palace architecture), or immerse yourself in this Far East experience by entering the pedestrian plaza through a large Chinese-style gate with a sign that announces "Chinatown." Take along a few coins to toss at the wishing well inside that has signs directing you to throw your money at appropriate desires: love, health, wealth, etc. (And may all your wishes come true!) Among the open air booths and stores with neon signs, your kids will see touristy stuff as well as authentic Chinese items such as Chinese-style silk dresses, fortune cookies, live chickens in cages, barbecued ducks hanging in windows, robes with dragons embroidered on them, chopsticks, and lots more. The herb shops are fascinating, and many people swear by the concoctions. The bakeries are tantalizing. Hungry for something more substantial? Give your taste buds (and stomach) a surprise by trying ostrich, fried large intestines, or other unusual fare. Or, stop in at the Golden Dragon Restaurant at 960 N. Broadway for a traditional dim sum brunch. If you come on the weekends, your three-course meal, which begins at 12:30pm, is accompanied by a forty-minute magic show at 1:30pm. The cost of the food and show is $12.50 for adults; $6 for kids 11 years and under. Call the above number for reservations. Enjoy your cultural adventure!

**Hours:**   Most stores are open daily from 10am - 6pm, or so.
**Admission:**   Free, but bring spending money.
**Ages:**   All

## EL PUEBLO DE LOS ANGELES HISTORICAL       ☼
## MONUMENT / OLVERA STREET

(213) 628-1274                                                    *$$$*

*125 Paseo de la Plaza #400, Los Angeles*
(Going W. on Santa Ana Fwy [101], exit N. on Alameda, L. on Paseo de la Plaza. Going
E. on 101, exit N. on Los Angeles St., which turns into Paseo de la Plaza.)
   This attraction is not a single monument, but the oldest part of the city of
Los Angeles. It contains twenty-seven historic buildings, eleven of which are
open to the public, and four of those are restored as museums. A traditional
Mexican-style plaza and Olvera Street are also here. Tip: Read up a little on the
history of this area, as it will make your visit here more meaningful.
   The plaza is the central hub. Usually a docent is on hand giving out maps
and other information. If not, check the Visitors' Center at Sepulveda House,
which is mentioned a few paragraphs down. The circular plaza has some
interesting statues to look at. Across the way is the **Firehouse Museum**. Inside is
a restored, old fire engine that was once hooked up to a horse. The walls are
decorated with different fire hats. Next door is the **Docent Center**. This is the
starting point for two free tours. One is a one-hour, guided walking tour of the
highlights of El Pueblo Monument. This is best suited for fourth graders and up.
It is offered Tuesday through Saturday at 10am, 11am, noon, and 1pm.
Reservations are required for groups, but not individuals. The second tour is a
two-hour guided bus tour, for families and/or school-aged kids. Note that buses
are provided. The tour covers the central city and points of historic interest.
Stopping along the way depends on the docent giving the tour. It starts at 10am
on the first and third Wednesdays of each month. Reservations are required. Call
(213) 628-1274 for more information on the tours, and to make reservations.
   **Olvera Street** is one of the oldest streets in Los Angeles. In 1930 it was
closed to through traffic and reborn as a Mexican marketplace. It is very
commercial and a definite tourist attraction, but it still conveys the flavor of old
Mexico. Enjoy a walk down the brick-paved "street" to look at the colorful
displays, watch a glassblower at work, see candles being dipped, hear strolling
mariachi bands, and munch on bakery goods. There are inexpensive and
expensive Mexican handicrafts to purchase both inside the stores and at the
center stalls. Note: Kids love the variety of candy that is conveniently placed at
their grabbing level.
   Olvera Street offers four full-service restaurants. A favorite one is La Luz
del Dia, located toward the entrance, because the food is good and kids can
climb the ornately tiled steps and peer into the kitchen to see tortillas being made
by hand.
   **The Sepulveda House**, which also houses the Visitors' Center, is a few
doors down from the entrance on the west side of Olvera Street. You can also
enter it from Main Street. It has an encased display of Mrs. Sepulveda's
bedroom, and her kitchen as it appeared in the late 1800's. The small Visitors'
Center carries gift items, maps, etc. Inside a curtained room is an eighteen-
minute film, *Pueblo of Promise* about the early history of Los Angeles. (My kids
actually watched and enjoyed the movie.) The small gallery around the corner
has some interesting artifacts from the area.
   **The Avila Adobe** is located almost directly across from the Sepulveda

House. This is the city's oldest building, constructed in 1818. It has rooms to walk through that reflect the style of a wealthy ranch owner in the 1840's. Some of the more interesting items include a child's bed that used rope and cowhide instead of box springs, a wooden bathtub, and a Chinese shawl that was used as a bedspread. The Courtyard, a packed-dirt patio, was used as a kitchen because most of the cooking was done outside. We enjoyed the side trip here, and learned a little along the way.

As you walk around this historic area, enjoy soaking up the atmosphere of a different country while so close to home!

**Hours:** Olvera Street is open daily in the summer from 10am - 10pm. Open the rest of the year from 10am - 7pm. The Sepulveda House is open daily from 10am - 3pm. The Avila Adobe is open daily from 9am - 5pm. The Firehouse Museum is open Tues. - Sun., from 10am - 3pm.

**Admission:** The entrance to everything is free. Parking is available at a number of lots that charge between $5 - $10 for the day. The one on Main St., between Hope and Arcadia, charges $7.50 for the day. Some of them are quite a walk to the plaza.

**Ages:** 3 years and up in general; 7 years and up for the tours.

## FOREST LAWN MEMORIAL PARK (Glendale)

(323) 254-3131 / www.forestlawn.com
*1712 South Glendale Avenue, Glendale*
(From Glendale Fwy [2], exit N. on San Fernando Rd, R. on S. Glendale Ave. From Golden State Fwy [5], exit N. on Glendale Ave, turns into Brand Blvd., R. on San Fernando Rd., L. on Glendale Ave.)

Most of the Forest Lawn Memorial Parks have outstanding works of art. This Forest Lawn features stained glass and oil paintings. The Hall of Crucifixion contains one of the largest religious oil paintings ever created. It's 45-foot by 195-foot and titled *Crucifixion*. The *Resurrection* painting is a close runner up in size and impact, at 51-foot by 70-foot. The small, on-site museum contains stained glass pictures, coins mentioned in the Bible, and statues. Be sure to take your kids on the "tour" in the mausoleum to see a magnificent stained glass depiction of *The Last Supper*.

**Hours:** The museum is open daily 10am - 5pm. The paintings and *The Last Supper* stained glass masterpiece can be seen daily on the half-hour and hour, respectively.

**Admission:** Free

**Ages:** 5 years and up.

## FOREST LAWN MEMORIAL PARK (Hollywood Hills)

(818) 241-4151 / www.forestlawn.com
*6300 Forest Lawn Drive, Los Angeles*
(Exit Ventura Fwy [134] S. on Forest Lawn Dr. It's W. of Griffith Park.)

A cemetery might seem like an odd addition to this book, but Forest Lawn has several impressive art pieces and tributes to American history. There is a huge memorial and statue of George Washington, as well as larger-than-life commemorations of Abraham Lincoln and Thomas Jefferson. A 30-foot by 165-foot tiled mosaic graces the outside of the Hall of Liberty building. The colorful, chronological, mosaic scenes of freedom depict the surrender of General Cornwallis, the crossing of the Delaware, Betsy Ross making the flag, and the signing of the Declaration of Independence. Inside the hall is a replica of the Liberty Bell, models of famous early Americans in period costumes, and a continuously running film regarding the founding of our country called *The Birth of Liberty*. A small Museum of Mexican History is adjacent to the Hall of Liberty. It contains pictures, statues, models, clothing, and artifacts from Mayan, Aztec, and other Indian and Mexican cultures.

**Hours:**    Open daily from 9am - 6pm; closed during private services.
**Admission:**    Free.
**Ages:**    6 years and up.

## LOS ANGELES AIRPORT OUTING

(310) 646-2911 - Lot B, shuttle info; (310) 670-3093 - Proud Bird
*Los Angeles Airport, Los Angeles*
(From Imperial Fwy [105] take the Aviation exit, turn L. on Imperial, an immediate R. on Aviation, R. on W. 111ᵗʰ St. and into parking lot "B.")

This conglomeration of things to do makes for a fun, and relatively inexpensive, outing. After parking your car in parking lot B, either walk next door and grab a bite to eat at the Proud Bird restaurant, or take a free shuttle to the airport.

The Proud Bird has several airplanes out front, including a P-38 Lightning, P-51 Mustang, and BellXI. Inside, the restaurant has airplane-type decor, and there is a great view of the airplanes flying low overhead as they arrive and depart LAX. Adult entree lunches include blackened chicken, grilled salmon, hamburgers, and club sandwiches. Prices range from $4.95 to $8.95. Dinner choices include catfish, salmon, shrimp, chicken, ribs, and lobster. Prices range from $12.95 to $24.95. The kids' menu has grilled cheese sandwiches, hamburger, or chicken strips for $4.95. Their meals include an ice-cream cone, but beverages are extra.

After deciding which airline terminal to be dropped off at, take a free shuttle to LAX. Fun things to do at the airport include: buying lunch, or packing a snack to munch on; shopping at the stores, which often have touristy items, but sometimes have unique gifts items, too; watching planes land and take off; making up stories about the people involved with tearful reunions or departures; exchanging American money for foreign currency; dreaming about where your family could go on vacation (this is referred to as a mind trip); creating an educational field trip regarding the airport; etc! ENCOUNTER RESTAURANT (look under the Edible Adventures section) is just a walk across the very busy street. Besides the expensive food and out-of-this-world decor, this building has a free elevator ride up to an observation deck. Tip: At night the view is quite pretty with all the twinkling lights. Take the shuttle (which my kids consider a fun adventure in itself - go figure) back to parking lot B. I hope you had a nice trip!

**Hours:** Shuttles run 24 hours a day, every 20 minutes. The Proud Bird is open for lunch Mon. - Sat., 11am to 2:30pm; open for brunch Sun. from 9am - 2:30pm; open for dinner Mon. - Sat., 4pm to 10pm. Most of the airport shops are open daily from 10am - 6pm.

**Admission:** Parking in lot B is free for the first two hours; $1 for each 2 hour period, or increment thereof; or $5 for each 24 hour period. Bring spending money if you want.

**Ages:** 4 years and up.

## MRS. NELSON'S TOY AND BOOK SHOP

(909) 599-4558                                                              !/$

*1030 Bonita Avenue, La Verne*

(Exit Foothill Fwy [210] E. on Bonita Ave.)

Mrs. Nelson has a delightful selection of books, educational toys, games, puzzles, tapes, and arts and craft supplies. Storytelling, followed by a related craft, is offered on Tuesdays at 10am, and again on Saturdays at 11am, unless a special program is being offered. A few times a year, you are invited to bring your picnic blankets and enjoy a free sing-along or dance-along concert. Sign up to receive a quarterly newsletter that gives dates and times for these activities as well as workshop information, author book signings, etc.

**Hours:** Open Mon. - Thurs. and Sat., 9am - 6pm; Fri., 9am - 7pm; Sun., 11am - 5pm.

**Ages:** 2 years and up.

## NATURALIZATION CEREMONY

(213) 741-1151 / www.lacclink.com                                          $$

*1201 S. Figueroa Street, Los Angeles Convention Center, Los Angeles*

(Going N. on Harbor Fwy [110], exit E. on Pico Blvd., L. on Figueroa. Going S., exit at Olympic Blvd., turn L. at end of off ramp on Blaine St., L. on 11th St., R. on Figueroa.)

Naturalized citizens must meet three requirements: be lawful permanent residents of the United States; have lived here for at least five years; and pass a written citizenship test. Many applicants study our history so intensely that they know it better than those of us who have lived here all our lives.

The naturalization ceremony usually takes place once a month, and as several thousand people can be inducted at one time, it can take a few hours. After green cards are turned in and the applicants seated, each one is given a congratulatory letter from the White House and a small American flag to wave after the swearing in. A district judge pounds the gavel and administers the Oath of Citizenship in which the almost-new citizens renounce any foreign allegiance and promise to uphold the Constitution. Next on the agenda, an INS representative gives a short speech, a patriotic song is sung (with not many dry eyes in the audience), and a short video shows a sweeping overview of America.

Ta da - new American citizens have been born! Finally, Certificates of Citizenship are handed out.

I mention this ceremony as an outing because I think older kids who are studying the Constitution or immigration might be interested in seeing this process and perhaps even catch a little national fever. Note that the public is welcome, but they must sit or stand near the back of the huge hall.

**Hours:** Call for dates.
**Admission:** $6 for parking
**Ages:** 10 years and up.

## ROSE HILLS MEMORIAL PARK

(562) 699-0921

*3900 S. Workman Mill Road, Whittier*

(Exit San Gabriel River Fwy [605] E. on Rose Hills Rd., L. on Workman Mill Rd. to the East Park.)

This is one of the world's largest memorial parks. The east park features a three-and-a-half-acre rose garden with more than 750 varieties. We enjoyed their fragrance as well as their names: Iceberg, The Doctor, Las Vegas, Confetti, Mister Lincoln, Summer Fashion, etc. The west park has a small, traditional Japanese garden with a meditation house, lake, and a bridge that add to the serene beauty. Again, as with FOREST LAWN (see previous entries in this section), perhaps this is an odd addition to this book, but can be an enjoyable (and obviously different) place to go.

**Hours:** Open daily from 8am - 5pm. Open extended hours in the summer.
**Admission:** Free
**Ages:** 4 years and up.

## STORYOPOLIS

(310) 358-2500

*116 N. Robertson Boulevard, Plaza A, Los Angeles*

(Exit Santa Monica Fwy [10] N. on Robertson. Storyopolis is on the E. side of the street, in the Plaza, just N. of 3rd St.)

This unique store offers a perfect way to introduce children to art and to encourage a love of reading. Half of Storyopolis has rotating, book-related exhibits. We saw original art work by illustrators of children's books. The art was displayed at kids' eye level. Each book, from which the illustrations were inspired, was on a stand in front of its appropriate picture(s). My 8 year-old budding artist and I first read excerpts from the book and then matched the framed art work to illustrations in the book. He remarked that it gave him the idea to write and illustrate his own book so that "maybe people can see my work here, too."

The other half of this medium-sized store has a cozy reading area and a terrific selection of children's books, with an emphasis on the arts. Storyopolis regularly hosts children's story-times, craft projects, author-signings,

presentations, and special events. Call for a schedule of events.
> **Hours:** Open Mon. - Sat., 10am - 6pm; Sun., 11am - 4pm.
> **Admission:** Free
> **Ages:** 4 years and up.

## UNIVERSAL CITYWALK ☼

(818) 622-4455 / www.mea.com/citywalk                    $$
*Universal Center Drive, Universal City*
(Heading NW, exit Hollywood Fwy [101] N. at Universal Center Dr. Heading SE on
Hollywood Fwy [101] exit R. on Lankershim Blvd., L. on Cahuenga, L. on Universal
Center Dr. It's right next to UNIVERSAL STUDIOS HOLLYWOOD.)

CityWalk is an outdoor mall built in theme-park style with fantastic stores, unique restaurants, and unusual entertainment. Everything here, from the larger-than-life neon signs to the oversized, Disneylandish-decorated storefronts is done with spectacular Hollywood flair, and that's just the outside of the buildings! On weekend nights, live entertainment, like jugglers and magicians, add to the carnival-like atmosphere.

Listed here are some of the outstanding attractions along the walkway: •Outside the **Hard Rock Cafe**, is a gigantic neon guitar. Inside this restaurant, dedicated to the preservation of rock 'n roll, a car spins on a pedestal in the middle. Guitars, costumes, posters, and personal items from famed musicians decorate the walls. (See HARD ROCK CAFE under the Edible Adventures section.) •Across the way from the Cafe is an eighteen-screen movie theater, and **Imaginater**, a simulator ride. Shake, rattle, and roll your way through a five-minute ride of Space Race, the Devil's Mineride, and other film adventures. Imaginater is open Sunday through Thursday from 10am to 8pm, and Friday through Saturday from 10am to 1am. Kids must be at least 42" tall to ride. Each ride costs $5. •**Lighthouse Beach** is an outdoor snack bar (fish 'n chips - $9.95, cheeseburgers - $5.95, chili cheese fries - $3.95) with tables in the sand. Kick off your shoes 'cause "life's a beach." •**Sam Goody** has a giant neon gorilla (think King-Kong) hanging on its sign. Inside, kids like the constant music, the enormous wall posters, going up the grated stairs to the Coffee Cafe, and walking over the bridge to check out the mini-museum that has signed Beatles photos, a Judy Garland letter, record plaques, and costumes of famous performers. •Look out for the water fountain in the center circle of CityWalk, where water spouts up at unexpected times. •Two terrific kids' bookstores, **Upstart Crows Nest** and **Golden Showcase**, are decorated as I dream a really large children's room should look like. •**Hollywood Freez Way** lures people in with Hagen Daz ice cream. Its entrance sign has the front end of a car crashed through it, upside down. •**P. T. Copperpot** is an old-fashioned confectionery with everything sweet imaginable. • On the storefront of **Things From Another World** the back half of a spaceship, which is still emitting smoke, is all that remains from a crash landing. •Watch the ocean in motion outside **The Wave** store. Whew - the extravagant gimmicks alone are worth the price of parking! •An outdoor ice-skating rink is here November through February. Other months, concerts and other special events are offered. • At the end of CityWalk, check

out COUNTRY STAR and MARVEL MANIA restaurants, listed in the Edible
Adventures section, and UNIVERSAL STUDIOS HOLLYWOOD, listed in the
Amusement Parks section.
    You can experience practically all of Hollywood at CityWalk - all at one
time! Note: Weekend nights are a bit overwhelming for younger children.
    **Hours:**      Most stores and restaurants are open Sun. - Thurs., 11am - 9pm;
                    Fri. - Sat., 11am - 11pm.
    **Admission:**  Free. Parking, in a lot also shared by Universal Studios
                    Hollywood, is $7. Valet parking is $4 for the first two hours with
                    validation; $1.50 for each half hour after that.
    **Ages:**       2 years and up.

## WAYFARERS CHAPEL

(310) 377-1650
*5755 Palos Verdes Drive South, Palos Verdes*
(Exit San Diego Fwy [405] S. on Crenshaw Blvd., and stay on this street into the city of
Palos Verdes; turn R. on Crest Rd., L. on Hawthorne to the end, L. on Palos Verdes Dr.
It's about 2 miles on the L.)
    This unique, relatively small church, is nicknamed the "Glass Church" and
built almost entirely of glass and stone. It is nestled in some overgrown trees and
looks to be almost a part of them. It was designed by Lloyd Wright, son of Frank
Lloyd Wright. The church is built on a bluff overlooking the Pacific Ocean,
surrounded by redwoods and gardens. The chapel is unique and charming, and
the landscaping is beautiful. This is a short stop off, so look up POINT
VINCENTE INTERPRETATIVE CENTER, REDONDO PIER, or SOUTH
COAST BOTANICAL GARDENS - listed separately in the Alphabetical Index -
for other things to do in this area.
    **Hours:**      Open daily from 9am - 5pm. Church functions take precedence
                    over public accessibility.
    **Admission:**  Free
    **Ages:**       5 years and up.

## DISNEYLAND HOTEL

(714) 956-6425  / www.disneyland.com
*1150 W. Cerritos Avenue, Anaheim*
(Going S. on Santa Ana Fwy [5], exit W. on Ball Rd., L. on West St., R. on Cerritos. Going
N. on 5 , exit W. on Katella, R. on West St., L. on Cerritos. It's across the street and on
W. side of Disneyland.)
    If a day at the "Magic Kingdom" doesn't fit into your budget or energy
level, come spend an hour or two at the magic hotel. One section of the lobby
contains a collection of Disney memorabilia, while around the corner is a huge
wall collage displaying trinkets from Disneyland's past. (Remember "E" ride
tickets?)
    The eastern part of the hotel complex has shops filled with every kind of
Disney paraphernalia imaginable. Numerous painted backdrops around the
grounds that feature scenes from Disney's newest movie releases offer great

photo opportunities. A real treat for your kids is a meal at GOOFY'S KITCHEN, BREAKFAST WITH MINNIE, or PRACTICALLY PERFECT TEA WITH MARY POPPINS - all described under the Edible Adventures section. Enjoy a mini-adventure by taking the monorail round trip from the hotel through Tomorrowland and back - $3 per person; kids under 2 years are free. Make sure to tell your children that you're not actually stopping in Disneyland.
Disney delights in the back courtyard include the waterfalls. Your kids will thrill at walking down the stony steps (this part is not stroller accessible), and going behind the waterfalls. It does get loud down here for younger ones because of the roar of the waterfall, and it is a little wet, as it's real water (not animated) that spritzes the pathways. After sunset, the underwater lights turn the waterfalls into a rainbow of cascading colors. Back on the surface, check out the koi pond. Call the hotel to find out what time the koi feedings are. Further back, remote-controlled race cars are $2 a race. Want to indulge in the sweeter pleasures of life? Stop for an ice-cream cone at Castle Sundries - $1.75 for a single scoop.
At 7:30pm and 9:30pm during the spring and summer, and at 7:30pm the rest of the year (call to verify times), experience the highlight of a nocturnal visit to the hotel - a free, twenty-minute, Fantasy Water show, located by the fish pond. The dramatically lit water fountains dance, sway, and pulsate to classic and rock versions of Disney tunes. During summer nights, from this same spot, at 9:30pm, look between the hotel buildings to see a dazzling fireworks display put on by Disneyland Park; a terrific way to end your evening with a bang!
From the end of November through the beginning of January celebrate the ho-ho-holidays with lavish decorations, strolling carolers in Dickens-style dress, and a visit with Santa Claus.
**Hours:**    The hotel is open daily.
**Admission:**    Parking is $2 per hour; $15 maximum.
**Ages:**    All

## DOLL CITY U.S.A.
(714) 750-3585
*2080 South Harbor Boulevard, Anaheim*
(Exit Santa Ana Fwy [5] S. on Harbor. Or, exit Garden Grove Fwy [22] N. on Harbor. It is the 3rd signal S. of Disneyland.)
This is an interesting store and worth visiting if you have a doll buff in the family. There are hundreds of dolls and accessories here, ranging from $3.99 to $15,000. There are dolls for the serious collector, or for anyone who just needs "someone" to hug.
**Hours:**    Open Mon. - Sat. from 10am - 6pm.
**Ages:**    2½ years and up.

## HOBBY CITY
(714) 527-2323
*1238 S. Beach Boulevard, Anaheim*
(Exit Artesia Fwy [91] S. on Beach Blvd. Or, exit Garden Grove Fwy [22] N. on Beach Blvd. It's 2 miles S. of KNOTT'S BERRY FARM.)

What did you collect when you were a kid? Hobby City offers twenty-three different hobby, craft, and collector's shops to get your youngster started (or add to) his/her hobby habit. The "city" also has a restaurant, a Doll Museum (see DOLL AND TOY MUSEUM under the Museums section) and an amusement park just for younger children (see ADVENTURE CITY under the Amusement Parks section). Hobby City is very kid-friendly - it even has a small picnic area.

Some of the more kid-oriented shops include the Cabbage Patch Shop, The Bear Tree (in the shape of a tree trunk), Prestige Hobbies & Models (airplanes, ships, cars, etc.), The Little Depot (for all your model train needs and wants), The American Indian Store, Baseball Card Shop, Miniatures, Stamps, Coins, and Treasure Cove (for those hard to find craft supplies). Happy hobbying!

**Hours:**   Most stores are open daily from 10am - 6pm.

**Ages:**   3 years and up.

# HUNTINGTON BEACH CENTRAL LIBRARY and ☼ CULTURAL CENTER

(714) 842-4481                                                              !
*7111 Talbert Avenue, Huntington Beach*
(Going N. on San Diego Fwy [405], exit N. on Euclid St., L. on Talbert Ave. Going S. on 405, exit S. on Beach Blvd, R. on Talbert Ave.)

When is a library more than just a place to peruse books? When it is the Huntington Beach Central Library! This multi-level facility is delightful to visit. Kids are captivated by the huge center fountain inside and the spiraling paved walkway that encircles it. The fountain is loud, especially on the lower level, in contrast to the normal quiet tones associated with a library. The bottom floor has vending machines and tables and chairs for eating, reading, and/or studying. Look up and see returned books being transferred to be re-shelved via a metal conveyor belt. (Only kids notice this sort of thing.)

One side of the main floor has an incredible number of books organized on several levels within the library. A map is available to help you find your topic of interest. There are even a few small art galleries in this wing.

Just outside the Children's Room is a circular aquarium - look for the eel. The Children's Room has a large selection of books. It also contains a reading area, a toddlers' section, a wooden frame of a boat for tots to play in, and a big screen monitor that intermittently shows children's films. The adjacent Tabby Storytime Theater, which is used for storytelling events, and a media/computer room make this library complete. Pick up a calendar listing of children's events, or call (714) 375-5107 for children's programing information.

The Huntington Beach Playhouse is located on the lower level. Several, mostly adult-oriented performances, are given throughout the year. Children's productions are occasionally offered here, although usually given in the upstair theater room. These can include marionette and puppet shows, musicals, etc.

HUNTINGTON CENTRAL PARK (look under the Great Outdoors section) surrounds the library. Directly behind the library is a trail leading down to a pond. Acres of trails, rolling green hills, shade trees, and picnic areas are all here to enhance your day. For summertime fun, check out Adventure Playground (see the June Calendar section), just up the hill from the library.

**Hours:**    The library is open Mon., 1pm - 9pm; Tues. - Thurs., 9am - 9pm; Fri - Sat., 9am - 5pm. Call for hours for special events, and for the shows.

**Admission:**    Free to the library, although it is $25 a year if you are a non-resident and want to check books out.

**Ages:**    All

## INDEPENDENCE HALL

(714) 220-5244 - Adventures in Education tour information /      *$$*
www.knotts.com/advinedu/advinedu.htm

*Beach Boulevard, Buena Park*

(Exit Artesia Fwy [91] S. on Beach Blvd. It's right across the street from KNOTT'S BERRY FARM.)

This full-size reproduction of Independence Hall houses, among other things, a replica of the Liberty Bell. Press a button to hear a prerecorded history message about the bell. See the (replicated) room where the Declaration of Independence was signed. Every half hour, a twenty-minute "show," called *Storm in Philadelphia*, is presented. It consists of sitting in the darkened room while candle lights flicker, listening to voices debate the adoption of the Declaration of Independence. The gift shop here has patriotic memorabilia to purchase. Tip: Bring a dime to put in the machine to watch the miniaturized Spirit of '76 army march around.

Group tours are available, such as the half-hour, Adventures in History tour. The two-hour, Our Early American Heritage tour, has a costumed docent explain the history of our revolutionary times, and students meet with Benjamin Franklin and Patrick Henry. The latter tour requires a minimum of twenty-five people and costs $4 per person. Call the above phone number for information on the over twenty tours offered through Independence Hall and KNOTT'S BERRY FARM.

The surrounding park area has a pond with ducks, shade trees, and grass - perfect for picnicking.

**Hours:**    Open daily from 9am - 5pm.

**Admission:**    Free. $6 for parking.

**Ages:**    5 years and up.

## SOUTH COAST STORYTELLERS GUILD

(949) 496-1960      *!/$$$*

*1551 Baker Street #A, Costa Mesa*

(Exit San Diego Fwy [405] S. on Harbor Blvd., R. on Baker St.)

"It is an ancient art, yet it is ever new." (Heinrich Heine) What marvels have been passed down from generation to generation through the ancient art of storytelling! For parents and other educators who aspire to become better storytellers, help is at hand. The Guild offers a wealth of information via one-to-three-hour workshops, story swaps, special classes for kids, children's storytelling teas and crafts, and in-house use of their resource library. The library contains a few thousand story books, plus several reference books. One fairly complete resource book is *The Parent's Guide to Storytelling,* by Margaret Read MacDonald, which explains general guidelines and simple techniques, and includes nineteen stories. The best advice given to me here for obtaining terrific (and inexpensive) selections of stories was, "Look up section 398.2 at your local library for folk tales, fables, and fairy tales." The Guild also sells a Storytelling Kit that contains books, curriculum, etc., for $125. Ask the Guild for their complete set of guidelines, available at a nominal fee, for starting an ImagUtelling Club at your local school or church, or for a group of your children's friends. For more storytelling helps, call Knott's Berry Farm Adventures in Education, at (714) 220-5244, or the National Storytelling Association, at (800) 525-4514, which produces *Storytelling Magazine.*

There are about sixty Guild members. Several of them perform at various locations around the Southland, such as bookstores, museums, schools, children's shelters, and libraries. They also sponsor the annual Southern California Story Swapping Festival. Call for the date and time. So many tales to tell, so little time!

**Hours:**    The Guild office is open Sun. from 10am - 1pm. Call for a schedule of activities. The office is usually closed during the summer months.

**Admission:**  Story swaps are a $2 donation; workshops usually run about $20; and teas are usually $10 per participant.

**Ages:**    8 years and up.

## CALICO GHOST TOWN

(800) TO CALICO (862-2542)

*36600 Ghost Town Road, Yermo*

(Exit Mojave Fwy [15] N. on Ghost Town Rd. It's about about 10 miles E. of Barstow. There are plenty of signs to direct you.)

Once upon a time, a rich vein of silver was found in a mine underneath some multi-colored mountains. Word about the strike spread like wildfire, and pretty soon there were 5,000 people, of twenty different nationalities, living in and around this mining town. The town was called Calico because the varied minerals that created the different colors of the mountains were "purty as a gal's Calico skirt." Between 1882 and 1907, the 500 mine claims produced eighty-six million dollars worth of silver and forty-five million dollars worth of borax. Then, the price of silver dropped. And the boom town went bust. Thankfully, the story doesn't end here.

Nowadays, this authentic western town has twenty-three unique shops and restaurants (including an ice cream parlor) on both sides of the wide, dirt, main road that snakes up the mountain - put your walking shoes on. Some of the current shops are even housed in original buildings. Topping our list of favorite shops are the rock and fossil shop, the leather works, and an 1890's general store.

There are several other attractions here. Gun fights break out every hour on the half hour starting at 10:30am. Visit the re-created schoolhouse at the end of the road, and an authentically-dressed schoolmarm will gladly teach your kids what going to school was like in the olden days. There is a sturdy wooden teeter-totter and swing outside the schoolhouse. If you want to know more about the town's history, take a free guided tour offered daily at 10am, noon, and 2pm. The Mystery Shack is a small house of optical illusions where water rolls uphill, a broom stands up at an angle without falling over, etc. Before you walk through Maggie Mine, a real silver mine, look at the mining tools on display, such as a stamp mill, ore cart, re-created assay office, and more. Just inside the mine is a display of rocks and minerals mined from these parts, including fluorescent ones that glow in neon colors when the lights are turned off. Take the short walk through the mine, which has mannequin miners in action and audio explanations of the mining process. The Odessa Railroad is simply an eight-minute train ride on a narrow-gauge railcar. It takes you around part of a mountain where you'll see small cave-like openings that were front doors to miners' homes. On your ride you'll learn that the huge pile of "tailing," from the Silver King Mine, still contains six million dollars worth of silver ore, but it would cost nine million dollars to process. Oh well! Sharpshooters can test their skill at the shooting gallery, and gold diggers can pan for real gold. Look at and into the house made of bottles - it's the ultimate in recycling.

Call for a schedule of special events, such as a Civil War Re-enactment (President's Day Weekend), Hullabaloo Festival (Palm Sunday weekend), Calico Days (Columbus Day Weekend), etc. Oh, and do explain to your kids that the term, "ghost town" doesn't mean that there are ghosts here, but just that the town went from being inhabited to being deserted.

Tent, RV, or cabin camping is available just below the town. The sites are small, but the surrounding area makes it especially attractive for kids because there are (small) caves all over. In fact, seeing and even going into a few caves, was one of the things my children liked best about Calico. If you have a four-wheel drive vehicle, head for the hills to explore some of the hiking trails (and mineral deposits) in this area.

**Hours:** Open daily from 9am - 5pm. Closed Christmas.
**Admission:** Entrance is $6 for adults; $3 for ages 6 - 15; children 5 years and under are free. Annual family passes are $24 for up to four members of the family. The Mystery Shack and Odessa Railroad train ride are each $2 for adults; $1 for ages 6 - 15; children 5 years and under are free. A walk through Maggie's Mine is $1 per person. Gold panning is free. The Shooting Gallery is $1 for 20 shots. The schoolhouse, shootouts, guided tours, and tram ride up the hill from the parking lot, are free.
**Ages:** All

# LIVE OAK CANYON CHRISTMAS TREE FARM
(909) 795-TREE (8733)

*32335 Live Oak Canyon Road, Redlands*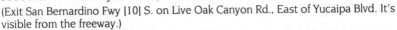
(Exit San Bernardino Fwy [10] S. on Live Oak Canyon Rd., East of Yucaipa Blvd. It's visible from the freeway.)

This huge (at least in my city eyes) family-operated farm yields bushels of fun in various seasons. A large, covered produce stand sells fresh local vegetables, fruits, honey, and other goodies. A petting zoo is on the grounds and is open the same hours as the farm. Admission is free. Walk in to pet and look at goats, sheep, pigs, donkeys, ponies, chickens, and ducks. Bring 25¢ to purchase feed from the machines. May through August are months ripe for blackberry picking. The farm offers fifteen different varieties! Tips: Wear gloves or be very careful of the thorns; bring a water bottle, because it's hot and you don't want to get dehydrated; and remember that the pretty purple color doesn't usually come out of clothing. If you can't eat all the berries right away, freeze them. This is a berry good outing!

Another great time to visit is in the fall. Tractor and mule-drawn hayrides are usually given during the fall/winter season and are free. A craft fair is presented twice during the fall/winter season. Call for dates. Bring a sack lunch, or purchase food from a refreshment stand that's set up during the fall, and eat at the numerous picnic tables scattered under shade trees. School tours of the farm are given by request. The pumpkin patch features acres and acres of pumpkins to be picked from the vine, as well as numerous pre-picked pumpkins that are watched over by a hundred scarecrows. Choose from giant pumpkins (and make pies for everyone in the neighborhood), regular pumpkins, and sweet white pumpkins. Wagons are available to help tote your load. An on-site store sells decorative fall items such as gourds (thousands of them), Indian corn in all colors, corn stalks, scarecrows, pumpkin carving supplies, etc. A major attraction is climbing onto and tunneling through a giant hay "castle." Hundreds of bales of hay are staggered on top of each other, with flags at the top and a maze burrowed through the bottom layers. Weekends bring special events such as musicians, pony rides, and other entertainment.

Come join in the festivities celebrated here around Christmas time. Warm yourself by a large fire pit, visit with Santa Claus (on certain weekends), listen to carolers (usually on the weekends), say thanks for the free candy cane, and enjoy the free hay bale maze, hay rides, and petting zoo. Walk among a twenty-five acre forest of home-grown Monterey Pines, Sierra Redwoods, and Aleppo Pines. Choose your own Christmas tree here (and have a worker cut it down) or purchase a fir tree shipped fresh from Oregon. A tented gift shop sells fresh wreaths, garland, and other decorations and gift items.

**Hours:**     The farm is open seasonally, so please call first. Berry picking is usually May through August. The pumpkin patch opens the end of September and runs through October. The Christmas season begins mid-November and runs through to a few days before Christmas. When the farm is open, the hours are usually daily from 9am - 6pm.

**Admission:**     Free, but bring spending money.

**Ages:**     All

# ARCO OLYMPIC TRAINING CENTER

(619) 482-6222

*1750 Wueste Road, Chula Vista*

(Exit San Diego Fwy [5] E. on "L" St., turns into Telegraph Canyon Rd., turns into Otay Lakes Rd. Turn S. on Wueste Rd.)

This incredibly beautiful facility is nestled in a mountain range by the blue waters of Otay Lakes. The 150-acre campus is the training grounds for future Olympians (and other athletes) as they prepare for the thrill of victory. Throughout the day, the visitors' center shows a free six-minute video, plus a longer twenty-minute film titled, *Once In A Lifetime.* The movies are great motivators to get you in the spirit of the Olympic games! The gift shop is first class.

Free guided tours of the facility are offered, or just take a detailed map and stroll along the paved Olympic Path on your own. The path slices through the center of the facility. It is elevated so you get a bird's eye view of the sports being played on both sides, including soccer, field hockey, tennis, track and field, cycling, and archery. Water sports, such as rowing, canoeing, and kayaking can also be observed from this vantage point. Visitors are asked to stay on the path, which is nine-tenths of a mile each way, as it winds through the training center.

Future sport venues in development are an aquatics center; a gymnasium for volleyball, basketball, and other indoor sports; and baseball diamonds. The facility also has athlete housing, an athlete dining area, a medical facility, etc. Call ahead to see which athletes are currently training here because seeing them in action makes the center come alive!

**Hours:** Open Mon. - Sat., 9am - 4pm; Sun., noon - 5pm.
**Admission:** Free
**Ages:** 6 years and up.

# CABRILLO NATIONAL MONUMENT

(619) 557-5450 / www.nps.gov/cabr

*Located at the southern end of Point Loma, on Cabrillo Memorial Drive, San Diego*

(Take Ocean Beach Fwy [8] to the end, L. on Sunset Cliffs Blvd, L. on Nimitz Blvd., S. on 209. Follow the signs.)

In 1542 Juan Rodriguez Cabrillo sailed into San Diego Bay and claimed it for Spain. A huge statue of Cabrillo, commemorating his epic voyage along the western coast of the U.S., resides on the tip of the peninsula at this national park. Press the button near the monument to hear the history of Cabrillo and the bay area.

Older kids will appreciate the exhibit hall in the building behind the monument. Displays include maps and drawings of the areas Cabrillo and other explorers "discovered"; lots of written information; examples of food eaten on board ship like dried fish, hardtack, etc.; and models of ships. The adjacent Visitors' Center offers pamphlets, film programs, and guided walks of this area, plus a book shop and an incredible view.

Before walking out to Point Loma Lighthouse, which was used from 1855 to 1891, listen to its history by pressing an outside storyboard button. We listened to it in Japanese and German [as well as English] - just for the fun of it. Kids think it's great to actually climb up the spiral staircase inside the refurbished lighthouse. The odd-shaped bedrooms are fully furnished with period furniture and knickknacks, as is the small living room, kitchen, and dining room. The entrance to the top floor is closed by a grate, but you can look through it and see the huge light that was a beacon to so many sailors.

Take the Bayside Trail, about three kilometers round trip, to walk further out to the point. Along the way look for remnants of a coastal artillery system used during both world wars. The trail goes down through a coastal sage scrub "forest." Topside of the trail, behind plexiglass, is a whale overlook. From late December through March, catch a glimpse of the gray whales during their annual migration southward. Audio information is, again, available at the touch of a button. (This time we listened to explanations in French and English.) Even if you don't see a whale, the view is spectacular.

From this viewpoint, look down to see the rocky marine environment of the tidepools. A driveable road from the monument leads down to them. Check with a park ranger for dates and times of low tides. Exploring tidepools is always a wondrous adventure for my kids. See and touch (but don't bring home) sea stars, anemones, and limpets, and be on the lookout for crabs and even octopus. Tip: Be sure to bring your camera, wear rubber-soled shoes (the rocks get slippery), and keep a close eye on your little ones! Ask about guided school tours for the tidepools and the monument park.

**Hours:** Open daily from 9am - 5:15pm.
**Admission:** $5 per vehicle; seniors are free.
**Ages:** 3 years and up.

# FARMERS MOUNTAIN VALE RANCH
(760) 765-0188                                                                    !/$
*4510 Hwy 78, Julian*
(Off Hwy 78, 2 ½ miles east of Santa Ysabel)

This ranch is a delightful stop. The small store offers delectable home-made goodies, such as jams and jellies, fresh ice cream, fruit, and pies. The kids will enjoy the small petting farm, with llamas, goats, pigs, turkeys, pheasants, and ducks. Feed is available to purchase. You are invited to walk around the ranch, through the rose garden and on the walking trails on the property. Short tours of the facility are given to groups of at least ten or more to see a cider press, apple peeler, water wheel, and duck pond. U-Pic apple picking is offered at nearby orchards.

**Hours:** Open daily September - May from 9am - 5pm. Open weekends only the rest of the year from 9am - 6pm.
**Admission:** Free; bring money for the store.
**Ages:** All

## GEMS OF PALA MINERAL SHOP
(760) 742-1356 / www.mmmgems.com                                          *$$*
*Magee Road, Pala*
(Exit Escondido Fwy [15] E. on Route 76, just past the cut-off to the town of Pala, L. on Magee Rd. Near corner of Pala & Magee.)

Located on the Pala Indian Reservation, the Gems of Pala offers a flawless selection of rocks and minerals. Both raw and polished emeralds, amethyst, opals, tourmaline, and more, can be found inside this small store. Outside, large bins hold chunks of rocks for sale. The gemstones come mostly from the nearby Stewart Mine, as well as from other mines all over the world. You can no longer go into the mine, but it is still worked regularly, and buckets of mine run are sold at the store. Purchase a two or five gallon bucket to dump and sift through on tables just outside the store, or at home. (First, watch a four-minute video that tells you how to do it, and what to look for.) Kids will be delighted with almost anything they find, although the jackpot is finding tourmaline. This precious stone comes in a rainbow of colors, with pink being the rarest, thus the most highly prized color. The mine also produces kunzite, morganite, lepidolite, etc. (The store owners can answer any rock-related questions you may have.) Whether you come to browse or buy, your rock-lovers will appreciate the variety of minerals on display. Call first to make sure mine run is available, if this is your goal.

**Hours:**    The store is open Thurs. - Sat.,10am - 4pm; Sun., 11am - 3pm.
**Admission:**    Buckets of mine run cost $10, $25, or $50 per, depending on where it was extracted within the mine. Other rocks and minerals are sold at various prices.
**Ages:**    3 years and up.

## OLD POWAY PARK
(619) 679-4313 - park; (619) 486-4575 - Hamburger Factory                  *!/$*
*14134 Midland Road, Poway*
(Exit Escondido Fwy [15] E. on Camino del Norte, R. on Midland Rd.)

This charming park is set up like a small historic, western village, complete with its own train depot. The two-acre grassy park boasts of shade trees, a gazebo, picnic tables, barbeques, crisscrossing pathways, and bridges over the creek. Come during the week to simply enjoy the park. Come on a weekend, however, for some action, because that's when the "town" is open and everything comes to life! Regular weekend activities include a farmer's market on Saturday mornings, arts and crafts booths, tours through the museum and house, and train rides. The small Heritage Museum has glass-encased displays from olden times in Poway such as pictures, clothing, a guitar, glassware, a piano, etc. The small Nelson House contains a turn-of-the century, fully furnished kitchen, living room, music room, and bedrooms. The blacksmith's shop puts on demonstrations of its craft on the third and fourth Saturdays of each month. Last, but not least, take a short ride around town on a genuine steam engine train, or one of the other train cars. Take a look into the train barn which houses the steam engine, a 1938 Fairmont Speeder, ore cars, and a 1894 Los Angeles Yellow Trolley. Don't forget to check out the many special events that go on here throughout the year!

Bring a picnic lunch, or enjoy good old American food at the on-site Hamburger Factory. The Factory has wood-paneled walls that are decorated with buffalo heads, steer skulls, etc., giving it a rustic ambiance. The restaurant is open daily for breakfast, lunch, and dinner. Kids' meal, starting at 11:30am, include hamburger, chicken nuggets, a hot dogs, or a grilled cheese sandwich. Meals come with fries and a drink for an average of $4.

**Hours:**      The park is open daily. Rail cars operate Sat., 10am - 4pm; Sun., 11am - 2pm. - closed the second Sun. of each month. The museum and Nelson House are open Sat., 9am - 4pm; Sun., 11am - 2pm. Attractions are closed on Christmas. The restaurant is open Sun. - Thurs., 6am - 8pm; Fri. - Sat., 6am - 9pm.

**Admission:**  The park is free. Train rides vary from $1 to $2 for adults depending on the rail car; children 12 years and under are 50¢. Donations are requested for the museum and Nelson House.

**Ages:**       All

# SAN DIEGO BAY FERRY / OLD FERRY LANDING ☼

(619) 234-4111                                                                    $$

*1050 North Harbor Drive at the Broadway Pier in downtown San Diego, and the Ferry Landing Marketplace in Coronado*

(Going S. on San Diego Fwy [5], exit W. on Ash St., L. on 4th, R. on Broadway to end. Going N. on 5, exit S. on 6th Ave., R. on Broadway to end.)

Take a fifteen-minute ride over to Coronado (and back) on the San Diego Bay Ferry. Enjoy the Ferry Landing Marketplace on the Coronado side with its Victorian-style shopping and eating complex. Bike, blade, or walk along the waterfront paved pathways. You can also romp in the grassy lawns along the pathways, or sunbathe on the beach. A farmer's market is held on the island on Tuesdays from 2:30pm to 6pm. If you want to go to Hotel Del Coronado, take the Coronado trolley, (619) 427-6438, from the landing. It runs approximately every hour from 9:20am to 6pm, with a few stops along the way. The trolley costs 50¢ a ride. Or, enjoy a scenic walk to the hotel (one-and-a-third miles), though it might get a little long for younger children. See HOTEL DEL CORONADO under the Tours section. Also see SAN DIEGO HARBOR EXCURSION, under the Transportation section, for longer, and more scenic, boat rides.

**Hours:**      The ferry departs from the pier every hour on the hour, Sun. - Thurs., 9am - 9pm; Fri. - Sat., 9am - 10pm. It leaves Coronado every hour on the half hour, running the same hours.

**Admission:**  $2 for adults (one way); children 3 years and under are free; bikes are an additional 50¢. Parking at the Broadway pier is $1 per hour; $3 maximum.

**Ages:**       All

## SAN DIEGO VISITOR INFORMATION CENTER

(800) 892-VALU (8258) or (619) 276-8200 / www.sandiego.org                 !

*2688 East Mission Bay Drive, Mission Bay*

(Exit San Diego Fwy [5] W. on Clairemont Dr., into the Visitor Center.)

I don't normally mention visitor centers as attractions, although they are always a good source for maps and brochures. This one, however, is located right on the bay so both the scenery and the actual building are picturesque. There are basketball courts just outside the center, plus picnic tables, a small playground, and a paved biking/walking trail. Just down the street is the TECOLOTE SHORES PLAY AREA. (See this entry under the Great Outdoors section.)

Inside the center you'll find a wealth of information on things to do in San Diego (actually it's all covered in this book!), plus maps, and discount coupons on attractions and hotels. This center and another, larger San Diego visitors center, at (619) 236-1212, carry a free coupon booklet that offers discounts on hotels, main attractions around San Diego, harbor cruises, trolley rides, restaurants, and more. Call for information on receiving it through the mail.

**Hours:** Open daily 9am - 5pm. Closed Thanksgiving and Christmas.

**Admission:** Free

**Ages:** All

## SUMMERS PAST FARMS

(619) 390-1523 / www.soapmaking.com/farm.htm                 !/$

*15602 Olde Highway 80, Flinn Springs*

(Exit 8 Fwy N. on Dunbar Ln., L. on Olde Hwy. 80.)

Experience a genteel way of life (yes, even with kids) at Summers Past Farms. Although the Farm is not large, its beautifully-landscaped gardens, blooming with a variety of flowers and herbs, almost ensure a delightful (and fragrant) *thyme* here. The plants are both for show and sale. One of the small gardens has a little creek with a bridge over it. There is a grassy area with trees, trellises, and white wrought-iron benches.

One of the retail shops, housed in a big red barn, offers potpourri, wreaths, baskets, teas, essential oils, lotions, dried and fresh flowers, etc. Craft classes are available. The other shop is Ye Old Soap Shoppe offering a wide variety of *scent*sational herbal soaps. Pick up a free sample (I chose Lavender/French Vanilla), and maybe you'll even get to see (and smell) the owner mixing essences for his soaps. You may purchase soap-making supplies, or a complete soap-making kit that includes <u>everything</u> you need to make twenty-eight aromatic bars for about $65.

**Hours:** Open Wed. - Sat., 8am - 5pm; Sun., 10am - 5pm.

**Admission:** Free

**Ages:** 5 years and up.

# TIJUANA, MEXICO                                    ☼
(across the border.)                                 $$$$

Hola! Come spend the day in a foreign country without the European price tag (or luxuries, majestic sights, etc.). There are several ways you can arrive at and enter into Mexico: 1) Drive into Mexico; 2) Take a tram from downtown San Diego to the border, and then take a taxi or walk across; or 3) Drive your own car almost to the border, park on this side of it, and then walk or take a shuttle across. Following are more details about the above options: Option 1 - If you drive into Mexico you must buy Mexican automobile insurance because American insurance doesn't mean anything over there. The border town of San Ysidro has several places to purchase Mexican insurance. The cost depends on the coverage you are buying and the value of your car. A few other things to take into account if you drive into Mexico: You will experience lines getting into and especially getting out of Mexico in the afternoon - it's rush hour traffic (actually this occurs no matter what mode of transportation you use); parking can be a problem (I mean challenge); and if you think that Los Angeles drivers are scary - you ain't seen nothing yet! For those who like to live life on the edge - drive into Tijuana. Option 2 - Take a trolley into Mexico from downtown San Diego, which costs $1.75 one way for ages 6 years and older. Trolleys run every twenty minutes, from 5am to midnight. You can pick one up at the corner of First and Broadway at the Transit Store, or call (619) 233-3004 for more locations and information. There is paid parking available (about $6 for the day) at the downtown location; parking is free at Old Town San Diego. The trolley takes you to the border where you can walk across the bridge or take a taxi into Mexico. It's a long walk from the border, about a mile, to the main shopping area in Tijuana. Even if you walk into Tijuana, you might consider taking a cab or shuttle out because you'll be carrying shopping bags, and your children will be tired (and so will you!). Taxis are plentiful, but determine exactly where you are going first, and decide on a price before you get into the cab. The fare is usually $5 to Avenida Revolucion. Option 3 - This was our personal choice, and it was fairly hassle-free. We parked on this side of the border at Border Station Parking - signs off the freeway direct you to the huge parking lots - which was $6 for all-day parking, and attendants are on duty twenty-four hours. Tip: Just behind Border Parking are factory outlet stores. Then we took a Mexicoach shuttle ($1 per person), which runs every half hour, from the parking lot into the heart of the oldest Tijuana shopping district - Avenida Revolucion, which is seven blocks of tourist-shopping heaven. You may buy up to $400 of duty free goods in Tijuana.

Shopping along Avenida Revolucion is an experience. The numerous small shops have goods almost overflowing onto the sidewalks that practically scream at your children to buy them. Vendors are constantly hawking their wares, enticing you, begging you, to come into their store. Be tough. Tips to keep in mind when shopping: 1) Don't feel obligated to buy just because you asked the price. 2) I can almost guarantee that you will see that exact same item at least ten more times. 3) Never pay the original asking price. Bargaining is expected. As a rule of thumb, pay around half (or a little more) of the asking price. Be willing to go higher if it's something you really want or can't live without. (Decide beforehand how much the item is worth to you.) Haggle if you want it, but be prepared to walk away in order to get a better price, or if it isn't the price you want. 4) Prepare your children beforehand that they won't always get the item being bargained for, if the price is still too high, etc. Lastly, and most importantly - 5) Teach your children to not say, "I love it - I must have it!"

Merchandise that appeals most to kids includes leather vests, hats, boots, purses, gold and silver jewelry, kids' guitars, gaudy ceramic figurines, watches, blankets, ponchos, and knickknacks. The more mature shopper will enjoy leather goods and jewelry, too, as well as perfumes, pharmaceutical supplies, clothing, and more. On every street corner you'll find the touristy-looking carts hooked up to donkeys (painted to look like zebras) along with gaudy sombreros available for you to wear while having your picture taken - $5 for a Polaroid, $1 with your own camera. (Our pictures turned out nice!)

There are other places to shop in Tijuana besides Avenida Revolucion. Try Avenida Constitucion, which is the next street over, and Plaza Rio Tijuana Shopping Center - near the Cultural Center - which has a few major department stores and specialty shops. The latter is a long walk, or a short drive, from Avenida Revolucion.

We walked around downtown Tijuana, just beyond the shopping district. Tijuana has been cleaned up and renovated in certain areas, but we also saw a lot of poverty, broken sidewalks, and people setting up shop in much less healthy environments than would be allowed in the States. It was an eye-opener for my kids. And, since they couldn't read any of the signs, it gave them an understanding of how difficult it is for foreigners in America to get around. Tip: Bring your own water, still.

There are several nearby attractions in Tijuana. Note: The 01152 number designates making an international phone call; (66) is the area code; the other digits are the actual phone number. **Bullfights** at Plaza Monumental de Playas, near the border, and on Agua Caliente Blvd. Fourteen fights are held May through September on Sunday afternoons. Tickets range from $15 - $38. Call 01152 (66) 80-1808 or (619) 232-5049 for more info. **Centro Cultural Tijuana** at Paseo de los Heroes y Mina. The art gallery wasn't that exciting to my kids, but the Centro also has a planetarium/Omnimax theater. (The shows, of course, are in Spanish.) Call 01152 (66) 84-1111 for more info. **Hipodromo Caliente** at Blvd. Agua Caliente y Tapachula. Greyhound races takes place here and there is a small zoo on the grounds. Call 01152 (66) 81-7811 for more info. **Jai Alai** at Avenida Revolucion at Calle 7. The beautiful old building has a Jai Alai player out front, showing kids what to expect. The fast-moving court game is played with a ball and a long, curved wicker basket strapped to the player's wrist. Games are played on various days and at various times. Tickets range from $2 to $5. Call 01152 (66) 85-2524 or (619) 231-1910 for more info. **Mexitlan** at Calle 2 and Avenida Ocampo. This city-block-long attraction houses about 200 scale models of Mexico's most important monuments, buildings, churches, plazas, archaeological sites, etc. This is a great way to get an overview of the country. Open May through October, Wed. - Fri., 10am - 6pm; Sat. - Sun., 9am - 9pm. Open November through April daily 10am - 5pm. Admission is $3 for adults; children 11 years and under are free. Call 01152 (66) 38-4101 or (619) 531-1112 for more info. **Mundo Divertido** (Family Entertainment Center) at Paseo de los Heroes y Jose Ma. This Family Fun Center offers the same fun, and at comparable prices, as the Family Fun Centers in the States - miniature golf, batting cages, bumper boats, go karts, video and arcade games, and amusement rides such as a roller coaster and a kiddie train. Call 01152 (66) 34-3213 for more info. **State Park Jose Maria Morelos Y Pavon** at Blvd. Insurgentes 16000. This state park has grassy lawns for picnicking and a Creative Center for children that offers an aquarium, a theater, and games. Call 01152 (66) 25-2469 for more info. **Q-Zar** at Via Oriente Local #9. This indoor laser tag arena is huge and located at the shopping Mall of Puerto Amigo. Phone 01152 (66) 83-6183 for more info. **Wax Museum of Tijuana** at Calle 1 near Avenida Revolucion. This museum is home to over sixty waxy, lifelike historical figures and movie stars such as Mikhail Gorbachev, Emiliano Zapata, Elvis Presley, Marilyn Monroe, and Christopher Columbus. It's open daily from 10am - 10pm. Admission is $3 for adults; $2 for ages 6 to 12; children 5 years and under are free. Call 01152 (66) 88-2478 for more information.

**Hours:** Most shops are open 10am - 8pm.

**Ages:** 5 years and up.

## BART'S BOOKS

(805) 646-3755                                                          *!/$*

*302 West Matilua, Ojai*

(Exit State Highway 150 [or Ojai Ave.] N. on Canada, L. at Matilua. It's on the corner of Matilua and Canada.)

This unique, outdoor, used bookstore is worth at least a browse-through, weather permitting. Your reader-child will delight in this big, Bohemian-style store. It's like exploring an old, comfortable (albeit roofless) house, except that most of the "rooms" are created by bookshelves. There are hundreds of books here on every subject, including a small, but packed, children's section. Sit down on an assortment of benches and chairs, or in a recliner by a fireplace, and peruse your purchase.

Books that are on shelves facing the outside of the store are available for purchase any time of day or night. The trusting (or hopeful) store sign reads: "When closed please throw coins in slot in the door for the amount marked on the book. Thank you." The atmosphere here is worth the trip.

**Hours:** Open Tues. - Sun. from 10am - 5:30pm.

**Admission:** Free

**Ages:** All readers.

## SHOWS AND THEATERS

How about a day (or evening) at the theater? The listings here range from theaters that have productions specifically for children, to planetarium shows, to musical extravaganzas!

## 3D IMAX THEATER

(213) 744-2014 / www.casciencectr.org  *$$$*

*Exposition Park, Los Angeles*

(Exit the Harbor Fwy [110] W. on Exposition Blvd., L. on Flower, L. on Figueroa. Or, exit Santa Monica Fwy [10] S. on Vermont, L. on Exposition, R. on Figueroa. It's adjacent to the California Science Center. Parking is available the first driveway on the right.)

Moviegoers can enjoy both traditional and 3D film formats at this large screen, IMAX Theater. In the 3D format, the use of polarized glasses, a surround sound system, and the seven-story high, ninety-foot-wide screen shows films that take you and your child on wonderful adventures. You'll explore the depths of the ocean and swim with fish (watch out for the sharks); river raft through the Grand Canyon; enter the world of outer space; etc., and feel like you've actually experience whatever is on the screen, without ever leaving your seat. "Edutainment" is what this theater all about! See nearby attractions listed individually in the Alphabetical Index: AEROSPACE MUSEUM, CALIFORNIA AFRO-AMERICAN MUSEUM, CALIFORNIA SCIENCE CENTER, EXPOSITION PARK, LOS ANGELES MEMORIAL COLISEUM, and NATURAL HISTORY MUSEUM OF LOS ANGELES.

**Hours:** Call for show titles and show times. Shows run daily from 10am - 8pm.

**Admission:** 2D movies are $6.25 for adults; $4.25 for seniors and ages 4 - 12; $3.75 for students 13 - 21; children 3 years and under are free. 3D movies are $7.25 for adults; $5.25 for seniors and ages 4 - 12; $4.75 for students. Parking is $5.

**Ages:** 3 years and up.

## AHMANSON THEATER

(213) 628-2772 / www.taperahmanson.com  *$$$$$*

*Music Center, North Grand Avenue at Temple Street, Los Angeles*

(Going S. on the Pasadena Fwy [110], exit N. on Hill St., R. on Temple St., L. on Grand. Going N. on the 110, exit E. on 4th St., L. on Olive St., go to end, L. on First St., R. on Grand. Going N. on Hollywood Fwy [101], exit W. on Grand. Going S. on 101, exit E. on Temple, R. on Grand.)

The theater puts on world-class, big-name, mainstream productions, many of which are terrific for the whole family.

**Hours:** Call for show dates and times.

**Admission:** Varies, depending on the show.

**Ages:** 5 years and up.

## BEN BOLLINGER'S CANDLELIGHT PAVILION

(909) 626-1254 / www.candlelightpavilion.com  *$$$$$*

*455 W. Foothill Boulevard, Claremont*

(Exit San Bernardino Fwy [10] N. on Indian Peak Rd., L. on Foothill Blvd.)

This family-owned, elegant dinner theater serves gourmet cuisine along with its ninety-minute, professional musical productions. Families dress up in their Sunday best, and sit down in padded booths with linen tablecloths, or larger groups may sit at equally nice, long tables. Tiered seating is available on the main floor, or choose terrace seats. Candlelight wall chandeliers and candles on the table add to the ambiance. (My oldest son liked the draped stage curtains, too.)

Dinner is served for almost two hours before the show begins. (If kids get antsy, wander outside on the cement pathways, near the fish pond.) Entrees include tri tip; breast of chicken stuffed with pancetta, bacon, and jack cheese; grilled salmon with shrimp mousse strudel; or a vegetarian taco salad. Meals come with vegetables and delicious hot rolls. The children's menu offers chicken strips with french fries. Full waiter service makes dining here a real treat. The dessert selection includes cheesecake, honey orange ice cream in an almond phyllo nest, and (my personal favorite), chocolate strawberry euphoria - brownies topped with ice cream, fresh strawberries, chocolate mousse, and chocolate. Note: The show and dinner are included in the admission price, but appetizers, beverages, and desserts are extra. Champagne brunches are served Saturdays, Sundays, and selected Thursdays. A performance is included with the brunch.

The seven, yearly musical productions are first rate, and most of them are suitable for children. Past shows have included *Secret Garden, Joseph and the Amazing Technicolor Dreamcoat, Ben Bollinger's Broadway, The Sound of Music*, and the annual *Wonderful World of Christmas*. Reservations are required for all shows. Appropriate attire is requested.

Ask about school group productions, when children can see a show and bring a sack lunch to eat at the picnic tables outside. Also inquire about their Children's Series.

**Hours:** Dinner seatings are Thurs. - Sat., 6pm; Sun., 5pm. Brunch seatings are Sat., Sun., and selected Thurs. at 11am. Shows begin at 8:15pm, 7:15pm, and 1:15pm, respectively.

**Admission:** $31 - $56 per person, depending on where you sit (terrace is the most expensive) and your entree selection. Children's rates for Fri. evenings and Sat. matinees are $19 in section A and the main floor, only. Children must be 12 years or under to order a children's entree. (If a child's entree is desired at another show time, you must call ahead of time.)

**Ages:** 6 years and up.

# BOB BAKER MARIONETTE THEATER

(213) 250-9995

*1345 West 1st Street, Los Angeles*

(Exit Hollywood Fwy [101] S. on Glendale, L. on 1st St., which is just before the bridge.)

The Bob Baker Marionette Theater has been around since 1963, proving its staying power in this ever-changing world. Interactive marionette performances are given while children sit on a horseshoe-shaped carpet around the stage, and parents sit in chairs behind them.

The musical revues feature marionettes, and some stuffed animals, that range in size from very small to the size of a two-year-old. They "sing" and "dance" their way right into your child's heart. The puppeteers, dressed in black, become invisible to the audience as the kids get swept away in the magic of the show. The performance is done within touching distance of the kids, and sometimes the marionettes even sit in their laps! This is a great way to keep short attention spans riveted. If the story line seems a little thin to you and your attention drifts, watch the puppeteers manipulate the strings - it's a good show in itself. If it's your child's birthday, for an additional $6, he/she will get special recognition with a crown, a song just for him/her, and a little present.

After the forty-five-minute show, chat with the puppeteers and enjoy a sack lunch (that you supply) at the picnic tables in the lobby. Reservations are required for all shows.

**Hours:** Performances are given Tues. - Fri. at 10:30am; Sat. - Sun. at 2:30pm. There are additional shows given during the month of December.

**Admission:** $10 for ages 2 years and up; $8 for seniors; children under 2 years (lap sitters) are free. Free parking next to the theater.

**Ages:** 2½ - 11 years.

## CARPENTER PERFORMING ARTS CENTER

(562) 985-7000  / www.csulb.edu/~cpac          $$$$
*6200 Atherton Street, on the campus of California State University of Long Beach, Long Beach*
(From San Diego Fwy [405], exit S. on Palo Verde Ave. Follow CSULB signs. R. on Atherton St. From San Gabriel River Fwy [605] exit W. on 7th Street R. on Bellflower Blvd., R. on Atherton Street. Enter the Carpenter Center parking lot on your left.)

Lovers of musical theater, dance, dramatic theater, and children's performances will enjoy shows given at this center. One-hour-plus family matinees are given on six Sundays during the season. Troupes have entertained youngsters with magic, comedy, circus-type acts, dance, storytelling, ballet, etc. Ask about their seasonal, wide-screen film festival. Come join the fun!

**Hours:** Family matinees are given on selected Sun. at 2pm. Call for other show dates and times.

**Admission:** Tickets for the family matinees are $8 - $11 per person, depending on your seat. Call for prices for other shows.

**Ages:** Some shows are for 5 years and up; some shows are recommended for older kids.

## CERRITOS CENTER FOR THE PERFORMING ARTS

(800) 300-4345 - show info; (562) 916-8530 - tour info.  /          $$$$$
www.cerritoscenter.com
*12700 Center Court Drive, Cerritos*
(Going W. on Artesia Fwy [91], exit W. on Artesia Blvd., L. on Bloomfield. Going E. on 91, exit S. on Bloomfield. From Bloomfield, L. on Town Center Dr., R. on Center Court Dr.)

Every season this Center features four or five performances just for kids,

such as puppetry or dance. Call for times and dates. Cerritos also features star-studded headliners such as Bill Cosby; Peter, Paul, and Mary; etc.
   **Admission:**   Show prices usually range from $16 - $21.
   **Ages:**   5 years and up.

## CHILDREN'S THEATRE NETWORK (Northridge)          ☼

(818) 706-9884 / www.thectnetwork.com                    $$$$
*18111 Nordhoff Street, at the California State University of Northridge,*
*Northridge*
(Exit San Diego Fwy |405| E. on Nordhoff. Or exit Simi Valley - San Fernando Valley Fwy
|118| W. on Reseda Blvd., L. on Nordhoff.)
   See CHILDREN'S THEATRE NETWORK (San Diego) for details.
Numerous other performances are also given at this theater.

## CHILDREN'S THEATRE NETWORK (Torrance)          ☼

(310) 376-1740 / www.thectnetwork.com                    $$$$
*3330 Civic Center Drive, James Armstrong Theatre at the Torrance*
*Cultural Arts Center, Torrance*
(Exit Harbor Fwy |110| W. on Carson St., R. on Madrona Ave., R. on Civic Center Dr. Or
exit San Diego Fwy |405| E. on Artesia, L. on Prairie Ave., turns into Madrona Ave., L.
on Civic Center Dr.)
   See CHILDREN'S THEATRE NETWORK (San Diego) for details. This
theater also offers numerous other family-oriented, as well as adult, productions.

## DEAF WEST THEATER          ☼

(213) 660-0877                                           $$$$
*660 North Heliotrope Drive, Los Angeles*
(Going N. on Hollywood Fwy |101|, exit N. on Vermont, L. on Melrose, L. on Heliotrope.
Going S. on 101, exit E. on Melrose, R. on Heliotrope.)
   A children's play is performed at this theater at least once a year. The hour-and-a-half show is performed in American Sign Language, while a spoken version can be heard through headsets. What a great opportunity for both hearing-impaired and hearing children to enjoy a show together!
   **Hours:**   Call for show times.
   **Admission:**   $15 for adults; $12 for seniors, students, and kids high-school
                    age and under.
   **Ages:**   6 years and up.

## ENCINO COMMUNITY CENTER          ☀

(818) 995-1690                                           $$
*4935 Balboa Avenue, Encino*                             ⛲
(Exit Ventura Fwy |101| S. on Balboa Ave.)
   The children's theater company, Imagination-in-Residency, presents innovative, interactive shows, so kids get opportunities to participate in pretending. Past shows have included *The Velveteen Rabbit* and *Three Tales by Hans Christian Anderson.*

**Hours:** Shows are usually on Sat. and Sun. at 1pm.
**Admission:** $7 per person.
**Ages:** ages

## GLENDALE CENTER THEATRE

(818) 244-8481
*324 North Orange Street, Glendale*
(Going E. on Ventura Fwy [134], exit S. on N. Central Ave., L. on Lexington Dr., R. on Orange St. Going W. on 134, exit S. on N. Brand Blvd., R. on Lexington Dr., L. on Orange St.)

This theater puts on terrific, one-and-a-half-hour, shows for children. Past productions have included *The Little Mermaid*, *Sleeping Beauty*, *Hansel and Gretel*, and *Jack and the Beanstalk*. The season begins in March and ends in November. Many block-buster musicals and comedies suitable for the family are also performed throughout the year.

**Hours:** Children's shows are usually performed Sat. at 11am. Call for other show times.
**Admission:** $14 for adults; $10 for children 12 years and under.
**Ages:** Depends on the show.

## GRIFFITH PLANETARIUM AND LASERIUM SHOWS

(213) 664-1191 - Planetarium; (818) 997-3624 - Laserium /
www.griffithobservatory.org; www.laserium.com
*On the slope of Mount Hollywood, in Griffith Park, Los Angeles*
(Exit Golden State Fwy [5] W. on Los Feliz Blvd., take Hillhurst Ave. N. past the Greek Theater to the Observatory.)

The Planetarium has a gigantic projector that fills the dome ceiling with realistic views of the nighttime sky, even though you're inside and it might be daytime. The hour-long show is an eye-opener for citified kids (and adults) who have not seen starry wonders. Children 4 years and under are admitted only to the 1:30pm show on Saturdays and Sundays, but do take them then as the show, *Voyage to the Planets* is geared for young kids. A friendly, green, animated space alien is the tour guide, "talking" with the real-life lecturer, and taking the intrigued audience on a trip to different planets.

The Laserium shows are laser-beam concerts with rock, classical, or other music, and incredible special effects. Your audio, visual, and kinesthetic child will love this illuminating production. A variety of different shows are offered each week. (See GRIFFITH OBSERVATORY AND PLANETARIUM, under the Museums section, for other things to do here.)

**Hours:** Planetarium shows are given in the summer Mon. - Fri., 1:30pm, 3pm, and 7:30pm; Sat. - Sun., 1:30pm, 3pm, 4:30pm, and 7:30pm. Shows are given the rest of the year are Tues. - Fri., 3pm, and 7:30pm; Sat. - Sun., 1:30pm, 3pm, 4:30pm, and 7:30pm. Laserium shows are presented Tues. - Thurs. and Sun. at 6pm and 8:45pm; Fri. - Sat. and various holidays at 6pm, 8:45pm, and 9:45pm.

**Admission:** The Planetarium show is $4 for adults; $3 for seniors; $2 for ages 5 - 12. Children 4 years and under are admitted free to the 1:30pm weekend show with a paying adult. The Laserium show is $7 for adults; $6 for senior citizens and ages 5 - 12; children 4 years and under are not admitted. (Certain discounts are available through AAA.)

**Ages:** 3 years and up for the Saturday planetarium show; 5 years and up for all other shows.

## HARRIET AND CHARLES LUCKMAN FINE ARTS COMPLEX

(323) 343-6610                                                          *$$$$*

*5151 State University Drive, on the Cal. State L.A. campus, Los Angeles*
(Exit San Bernardino Fwy [10] N. on Eastman Ave., R. on State University Drive.)

The Luckman fine arts theater presents modern dance, ballet, opera, and other musical performances. Many of them are suitable for families, such as the *Nutcracker Suite*.

**Hours:** Call for show dates and times.
**Admission:** Prices vary greatly depending on the show. Parking is $5.
**Ages:** Depends on the show.

## JEWEL BOX THEATRE

(818) 760-PLAY (7529) - fairy tales; (323) 254-9568 - Fundamentals       *$$$*
*10426 Magnolia Boulevard, North Hollywood*
(Exit Ventura Fwy [134] N. on Chuenga Ave., R. on Magnolia.)

This forty-five-seat theater offers a few different ways for kids to see and be a part of performances. One group presents youth actors, with an adult lead, in one-hour fairy tales that encourage audience participation. The second performance offered here is through the Fundamentals group, who present shows that are both entertaining and educational. Their one-hour *Fun and Discovery With Bubbles* interactive presentation combines high energy, music, and bubbles. Kids will learn how to create unique bubbles and where the different colors on bubbles come from, plus a few lucky ones are chosen to be put inside a bubble at the end of the show.

**Hours:** Call for hours on the fairy tales shows. The bubble show is usually given on Sat. at 11am.
**Admission:** Fairy tales shows are $8 per person. The bubble show is $6 per person.
**Ages:** 2 years and up.

## L. A. CONNECTION COMEDY THEATER

(818) 710-1320                                                          *$$$*
*13442 Ventura Boulevard, Sherman Oaks*
(Exit Ventura Fwy [101] S. on Woodman, L. on Ventura Blvd.)

Tickle your children's funnybones and bring them to the Comedy Theater for comedy improv performances by kids, for kids. The almost hour-long improvisational show is given in a small room with tiered, theater-type seating. The performers consist of one adult and usually six kids that are between 5 to 14 years old. The kids are members of the Kids Repertory Company and they are trained in the L.A. Connection's Improv Workshops.

Audience participation is mandatory as the actors ask for help in creating characters, or supplying ideas to use in a skit. Your children love to see their suggestions acted out. Remember, the performers are kids, so there is a lot of kid-type humor. As with any improv show, the success of a skit depends on the improvisationalists and the audience. The L.A. Connection really connected with my kids!

If your child thinks the whole world is a stage, then maybe he should be on it. Sign him up for comedy improv classes and the next performance you see could be his.

**Hours:** Performances are Sun. at 3:30pm.

**Admission:** $7 per person.

**Ages:** 5 years and up - younger ones won't get the humor.

## LOS ANGELES CENTRAL LIBRARY

(213) 228-7000 - Children's Literature Department; (213) 228-7040 - cultural and educational activities

*630 West Fifth Street, Los Angeles*

(Exit Harbor Fwy [110] E. on 6<sup>th</sup> St., L. on Grand, L. on 5<sup>th</sup>. It's at Hope and 5<sup>th</sup> St.)

This 125-year old library is a classic. From the unique architecture to the millions of books to the areas and exhibitions that focus on special interests, it is an oasis to researchers and readers of all ages who can easily spend hours here. The children's section is a haven for young book lovers with it comfy furniture and shelves of books that open their imagination to new worlds.

On the second floor, in the Children's Literacy Department, the KLOS Story Theater presents a free, one-hour show on Saturdays at 2pm. Various past shows have featured magic tricks, instructions on how to make a book (followed by actually making one), and storytelling with puppets. On Sundays at 2pm a free, one-hour children's video is shown. At least once a month, on the first floor of the library, at the Mark Taper Auditorium (which seats 225), a free, one-hour, usually culturally-themed performance, such as folk-dancing, is given. Call for specific themes and shows. One-hour school tours are given Mondays (for pre-K to second graders only), and Thursdays and Fridays (for third to fifth graders) at 10am and 11am. Tours consist of a half-hour tour of the library and a half hour of story time or making a craft. Call (213) 228-7055 to make a reservation.

**Hours:** The library is open Mon., Thurs. - Sat., 10am - 5:30pm; Tues. and Wed., noon - 8pm; Sun., 1pm - 5pm. Closed most major holidays.

**Admission:** Free. Enter the parking structure under the library on Flower St. - $1 for the first hour, $2.20 for the second hour - with validation.

**Ages:** 3 years and up.

## LOS ANGELES PHILHARMONIC TOYOTA SYMPHONIES FOR YOUTH SERIES

(323) 850-2000 / www.laphil.org   $$$$
*135 North Grand Avenue, Dorothy Chandler Pavilion in the Music Center, Los Angeles*
(Exit Harbor Fwy [110] E. on Temple, R. on Grand. Or, exit Santa Ana Fwy [101] S. on Grand.)

Five times a year the Los Angeles Philharmonic offers one-hour concerts under the collective title of Toyota Symphonies for Youth. They are designed to excite kids, particularly between the ages of 6 to 12, about the wonderful world of orchestral music. Meet in the lobby first for a variety of pre-concert activities. Different stations can include arts and crafts, storytellers, dance, and/or meeting with musicians who will demonstrate their instruments. All the activities help to introduce (and reinforce) the morning's concert theme. Move into the grand hall for the concert. Past concerts include *Magical Melodies*, *Fun with Bach*, and *Peter and the Wolf*.

**Hours:** Pre-concert activities begin at 10am. Concerts begin at 11am on selected Sat., usually in the months of November, January, February, April, and May.

**Admission:** $6 - $10 per person, depending on your seat. Parking is available in the Music Center Garage ($7); in the Mall Garage, across Grand Avenue ($6), and at the corner of Temple and Grand ($6).

**Ages:** 6 years and up.

## MAGICOPOLIS

(310) 305-0336 / www.magicopolis.com   $$$$$
*1418 4th Street, Santa Monica*
(Exit Santa Monica Fwy [10] N. on Lincoln Blvd., L. on Wilshire, L. on 4th St.)

Abracadabra - make a magical place appear. Poof! Magicopolis, meaning "City of Magic," was actually created by veteran magician, Steve Spill, to present magic in various forums for the public, as opposed to other venues that are private clubs. Penn and Teller have given their blessing to Magicopolis by having their hands and feet cast in cement out front. Street magicians entice pedestrians from the Promenade to come inside by performing tricks and illusions. Curiosity seekers on Fourth Street can peek in through a glass facade and see the "hallway into infinity," and a top-heavy sculpture of objects precariously balanced, looking ready to topple. While waiting for the shows to begin, watch what a resident magician has up his sleeve, and grab a bite to eat from the inside cafe that serves fresh baked goods, coffee, and juice.

There are two main rooms where magic is executed. The first, the Hocus Pocus Room, is an intimate setting (forty seats) where resident magicians perform twenty-minute shows incorporating sleight-of-hand and "mind-reading." Being close-up to the performers, however, does not insure that audience members will "get" the trick; at least it usually doesn't in my case. Kids sit here with mouths open and ask, "How did he do that?" In the main theater, which holds 150 people, get ready to be entertained and mystified by larger-scale illusions. The one-hour shows vary, depending on the featured magicians, so every time you come to Magicopolis you'll see something new. For those who want to try a little magic of their own, check out the retail shop. Note: Look for the nine, stained glass magician windows on display here. They portray Houdini escaping from chains, Aladdin releasing the genie, Kellar performing levitation, and more.

**Hours:**     Performances in the main room are scheduled for Wed. and Thurs., 8pm; Fri., 8pm and 10pm; Sun., 2pm and 7pm. Shows in the Hocus Pocus room run continuously, beginning the same hours as shows in the main theater.

**Admission:**  $10 per person per show in the Hocus Pocus room; $20 per person per show in the main room; Sun. matinees are $15.

**Ages:**      10 years and up.

## MORGAN-WIXSON THEATRE
(310) 828-7519
*2627 Pico Boulevard, Santa Monica*
(Exit Santa Monica Fwy [10] S. on Cloverfield, L. on Pico Blvd.)

*$$$*

Once a year, the youth production features young actors performing for young audiences. The show is usually an abbreviated version of a full-scale musical. There are other theater shows for the whole family, as well as comedies, musicals, etc. for older audiences.

**Hours:**     Call for shows hours.
**Admission:**  Prices range from $7 - $15, depending on the productions.
**Ages:**      Depends on the show.

## NORRIS THEATRE FOR PERFORMING ARTS
(310) 544-0403 / www.norristheatre.org
*27570 Crossfield Drive, Rolling Hills Estates*
(Exit Pacific Coast Highway S. on Hawthorne Blvd., L. on Silver Spur, R. on Crossfield)

*$$$$*

Eight productions specifically for children are performed every year. Past shows have included *Winnie the Pooh*, *The Ugly Ducking*, and *Pippi Longstocking*. Other productions are geared mainly for adults.

**Hours:**     Children's productions are on certain Sun. at 1pm and 4pm.
**Admission:**  $13 per person.
**Ages:**      2 - 12 years.

## PANTAGES THEATRE
(213) 468-1770
*6233 Hollywood Boulevard, Hollywood*
(Exit Hollywood Fwy [101] W. on Hollywood Bvld.)

*$$$$$*

Outstanding productions - musical, drama, comedy, etc. - are performed here regularly. Call for a current schedule. A few of our favorite past productions include *Peter Pan*, which starred Cathy Rigby, and *Phantom of the Opera*.

**Hours:**      Call for show dates and times.
**Admission:**  Varies, depending on the show.
**Ages:**       5 years and up.

## PASADENA SYMPHONY MUSICAL CIRCUS

(626) 793-7172
*300 E. Green Street, at the Pasadena Civic Auditorium, Pasadena*
(Exit Pasadena Fwy[110] N. on Fair Oaks Ave, R. on Green.)
Five, one-hour presentations of the Musical Circus are given throughout the year. The first half hour is spent in the lobby of the auditorium where children are invited to try out the various instruments and ask questions of the musicians. In the second half hour, a soloist or a small group of musicians give a mini concert. I bet this show will strike a chord with some of your children!
**Hours:**      Presentations are given one Sat. a month at 9am, usually in the months of October, November, February, March, and May.
**Admission:**  Free
**Ages:**       2 - 12 years.

## PEPPERDINE CENTER FOR ARTS

(310) 456-4522 / www.pepperdine.edu                                   *$$$$*
*24255 Pacific Coast Highway, Malibu*
(Exit Ventura Fwy [101] S. on Las Virgenes Rd., which turns into Malibu Cyn. Rd. Go to the end, R. on Pacific Coast Hwy.)
The Childrens Series consists of five different, one-hour shows performed throughout the season. Past titles include *Jungle Book*, *Treasure Island*, and *Ugly Duckling*. Pepperdine offers just a few other presentations geared for all ages, including magic shows and concerts.
**Hours:**      The Childrens Series is presented one Sat. a month at 11am and at 1pm, usually in the months of October, January, February, March, and April. Call for other show dates and times.
**Admission:**  $14 per person for the Childrens Series. Inquire about prices for other shows.
**Ages:**       3 years and up.

## PIERCE COLLEGE

(818) 719-6488 / www.lapc.cc.ca.us                                    *$$$*
*6201 Winnetka Avenue, Woodland Hills*
(Exit Ventura Fwy [101] N. on Winnetka Ave. It's in the Performing Arts Building.)
The college usually performs at least one children's show a year, such as *Willy Wonka and the Chocolate Factory* and *Wind in the Willows*.
**Hours:**      Call for a program schedule.
**Admission:**  $8 - $10 per person.
**Ages:**       6 years and up.

# PUPPET AND MAGIC CENTER

$$$

(310) 656-0483 / e-mail:smpuppets@aol.com

*1253 B Third Street, Santa Monica*

(Exit Santa Monica Fwy [10] N. on Lincoln Blvd., L. on Wilshire Blvd. to the Promenade entrance. The center's entrance is in the alley behind the Third Street Promenade.)

What do you get when you mix Harry Houdini with Edgar Bergen? Steve Meltzer! Steve puts on forty-five minute, musical, one-man puppet/ventriloquist/magic shows that intrigue youngsters, confound older kids, and entertain everyone. The intimate theater, tastefully decorated with pictures and posters of magic and puppeteer greats, seats up to fifty people in comfortable theater-style chairs. The first half of the show consists of puppets, marionettes, etc., that speak, sing, tell jokes, and even dance (with Steve's help, of course). This former elementary school teacher has a delightful range of voices and "personalities." I was surprised my children didn't clap more during the second part of his performance, the magic show, until I realized that they were amazed at the tricks and kept trying to figure out how he did them, usually to no avail. Audience interaction throughout the show is an added highlight. Tip: It's no illusion - this is a great place for a birthday party!

After the performance, you'll get the opportunity to see (with your eyes, not your hands) his hundreds of puppets. You may also peek into his puppet workshop where you might see one of his creations in process. Steve has a small Magic Shop here, too where he sells puppets and magic tricks. Anytime you are in the neighborhood, make sure you stop off at the Puppet and Magic Center - no strings attached.

**Hours:** Weekend shows are usually given at 1pm and 3pm. Please call first. Call, also, for Magic Shop hours and for special performance times.

**Admission:** $6 per person for the weekend show.

**Ages:** 1½ to 12 years.

# SANTA MONICA COLLEGE PLANETARIUM

$$

(310) 452-9396 or (310) 452-99223 /

www.smc.edu/events/weeklyevents.htm

*1900 Pico Boulevard, Santa Monica*

(Exit Santa Monica Fwy [10] S. on Cloverfield, R. on Pico Blvd. It's located on the 2nd floor of the Technology building.)

Do your kids have stars in their eyes? Bring them to the planetarium, then lean back, look up at the nighttime sky, and watch some of the mysteries of the heavens unfold. The lecture and shows, with titles like *Alien Skies*, focus on space exploration, astronomy, and the possibility of extra-terrestrials.

**Hours:** Shows are every Fri. night at 7pm and 8pm. (The latter time is the feature presentation.)

**Admission:** $4 for a single show; $7 for both shows; elementary-school-aged kids are half price.

**Ages:** 6 years and up.

## SANTA MONICA PLAYHOUSE

(310) 394-9779
$$$
*1211 4<sup>th</sup> Street, Santa Monica*
(Exit Santa Monica Fwy [10] N. on 4<sup>th</sup> St.)

This ninety-two seat Playhouse offers original, one-hour, family-style musicals every weekend. Most of the productions are based on well-known characters and have titles like *Alice's Wonderful Teapot* and *Captain Jack and the Beanstalk*. There is a cookies and punch intermission. Young and old will enjoy this theater experience. Ask about their special classes and workshops.

**Hours:** Every Sat. and Sun. at 1pm and 3pm.
**Admission:** $8 for ages 2 and up.
**Ages:** 3 years and up.

## SHUBERT THEATRE

(800) 233-1770 or (800) 233-3123
$$$$$
*2020 Avenue of the Stars, Los Angeles*
(Exit San Diego Fwy [405] E. on Santa Monica Blvd., R. on Avenue of the Stars.)

This theater presents the finest in Broadway musicals, hit plays, and hot comedies. Many of the productions are great for the entire family. This is one of our favorite places for "real" theater shows.

**Hours:** Call for show dates and times.
**Admission:** Varies, depending on the show.
**Ages:** 5 years and up.

## SOUTHERN CALIFORNIA CONSERVATORY OF MUSIC

(818) 767-6554
$$
*8711 Sunland Boulevard, Sun Valley*
(Exit Golden State Fwy [5] N. on Sunland Blvd.)

Four operas a year are performed fourteen times each in this small theater. The children's operas (i.e. every word is sung) are performed by children, ages 8 to 14 years. Most of the musicals have been designed and composed for this group. Past show titles include *Snow White and the Seven Dwarfs*, *Robin Hood*, and *Mother Goose*. Come to watch, or sign up your future star to be in the next production!

**Hours:** Call for a schedule.
**Admission:** $5 for adults; $2.50 for ages 4 - 11; children 3 years and under are free.
**Ages:** 3 - 13 years.

## STORYBOOK THEATRE AT THEATRE WEST

(818) 761-2203
$$$
*3333 Cahuenga Boulevard West, Los Angeles*
(Exit Hollywood Fwy [101] at Lankershim Blvd., S. on Cahuenga. If going N. on 101 Fwy, go back over Fwy on Lankershim, R. on Cahuenga.)

Every Saturday, Storybook Theatre presents a fun, musical, audience-participatory play geared for 3 to 9 year olds. Classics are re-done to appeal even more to children (with all the violence eliminated), like *Little Red Riding Hood* and *Jack In The Beanstalk*. There is an apple juice intermission in this hour-long show. Afterward, the cast stays around to talk with the kids. What a wonderful "first theater" experience! Call to find out what's playing.

**Hours:** Sat. at 1pm.
**Admission:** $8 per person.
**Ages:** 3 - 9 years.

## U.C.L.A. CENTER FOR PERFORMING ARTS

☼

$$$$$

(310) 825-2101 / www.performingarts.ucla.edu
*University of California in Los Angeles, Los Angeles*
(Exit San Diego Fwy [405] E. on Wilshire Blvd., L. on Westwood Blvd. to the information kiosk. Make sure you ask for a map.)

Name it, and it plays at U.C.L.A. There are several different concert and theater venues here that feature a wide variety of musicals, dance, theater, concerts, etc. One of our favorites was *Stomp,* a high-energy show where performers created rhythm and music using brooms, trash can lids, and other unusual "instruments."

**Hours:** Call for a schedule of current shows.
**Admission:** Prices vary depending on the show. Parking is $5.
**Ages:** It depends on the show.

## BALLET PACIFICA

☼

$$$

(949) 851-9930 / www.ocartsnet.org/ballet_pacifica
*650 Laguna Canyon Road, Festival of Arts Forum Theater, Laguna Beach*
(Exit San Diego Fwy [405] or Santa Ana Fwy [5] S. on Laguna Canyon Rd. [Hwy 133]. It's on the R., on the Festival of the Arts grounds.)

Ballet Pacifica has a Children's Series, consisting of four productions a year at the Forum Theater. The ballet productions are held in September or October, February, March, and April. Past performances include *The Emperor's New Clothes, Winnie-the-Pooh,* and *Puss in Boots.* Note: The *Nutcracker* is performed over fifteen times in December. Each show is a winner for the whole family, especially your blossoming ballerina. Check for time and location, as the company also performs at other locations such as the Irvine Barclay Theater.

**Hours:** Call for a schedule.
**Admission:** Tickets are usually $11 for adults; $8 for children 12 years and under.
**Ages:** 5 years and up.

## BROADWAY ON TOUR CHILDREN'S THEATER

☼

$$$

≣

(714) 282-8148
*2190 Canal Street, Orange*
(Exit Costa Mesa Fwy [55] W. on Lincoln/Nohl Rd., L. on Tustin, R. on Heim Ave., L. on Canal St.)

This theater encourages intimacy by filling only the first five rows of seats. Kids 10 to 18 years old put on presentations for younger children who delight in seeing just slightly older versions of themselves on stage. The one-hour musicals are usually based on classic fairytales, and they run for six weeks. Broadway on Tour's motto is, "Children bringing theater to children." Call for show information, and to find out how your child could become a performer.

**Hours:** Shows are performed on Fri. evening, and Sat. - Sun. at 2pm.
**Admission:** $6 per person.
**Ages:** 4 - 12 years.

## BROWN BAG PLAYERS ☼

(949) 581-5402 / members.aol.com/ctworkshop                    *$$*
*21801 Winding Way, Lake Forest*
(Exit San Diego Fwy [5], N.E. on Lake Forest Dr., L. on Serrano Rd., L. on Winding Way. It's held across the street from Heritage Park at Rancho Canada School.)

The Brown Bag Players are sponsored by the Children's Theatre Workshop. The Workshop teaches theater to children ages 7 to 16, who then put on a production. The Brown Bag Players are seasoned actors whose goal is to make theater accessible to children via interaction. Kids are invited to bring their own brown bag lunch (hence the name of the company) between 11:30am and noon to eat while watching the actors prepare for the performance. As the actors put on their make-up, children are invited to join in by putting on make-up (or face paint). During the show, kids are intermittently invited on stage to help tell the story. Afterward, the actors answer questions about scenes, scenery, costumes, technical equipment, or whatever other things kids wonder about. What a great way to encourage kids to be involved with theater! Past one-hour presentations have included *Tale of the Frog Prince* and *The Future of Maid Marion*.

**Hours:** Each of the 3 yearly productions are put on for 3 consecutive weekends. The doors for lunch are open at 11:30am; the play starts at 12:15pm.
**Admission:** $5 per person.
**Ages:** 2 - 12 years.

## CALIFORNIA STATE FULLERTON PERFORMING ☼ ARTS

(714) 278-3371                    *$$$*
*Nutwood and State College, Fullerton*
(Exit Orange Fwy [57] W. on Nutwood.)

The Kaleidoscope Players put on special presentations every February, just for kids.

**Hours:** Call for show date and time.
**Admission:** Call for prices.
**Ages:** 5 years and up.

# CURTIS THEATRE / CITY OF BREA GALLERY

(714) 990-7722 - theater; (714) 990-7730 - gallery / www.ci.brea.ca.us
*1 Civic Center Circle, Brea*
(Exit Orange Fwy [57] W. on Imperial, R. on Randolf, R. on Birch, R. on Civic Center Circle.)

Curtis Theatre boasts Brea's Youth Theatre and Kids Culture Club. The Youth Theatre is comprised of a talented cast of young actors and actresses (i.e. kids) who put on two musical extravaganzas a year. Past productions include *Peter Pan* and *Joseph and the Amazing Technicolor Dreamcoat*. Call for information about signing your kids up to be in a future production. The Culture Club is comprised of eight professional productions a year. Previous year's forty-five-minute headliners have included a music and laser show, a magic show, the *Nutcracker Suite*, and Jim Gamble's puppets. Call for a current schedule.

Across from the theater, the Civic Center also has a small gallery called City of Brea Gallery. We saw an exhibit on Japanese dolls, but exhibits do change periodically. The gallery also has a Children's Art Space where young visitors may create their own masterpiece that is related to the current exhibit. The Brea Gallery is usually open on performance nights and gives kids something to look at while waiting for the theater doors to open.

**Hours:**     Call for a schedule of shows. The gallery is open Wed. - Sun., noon - 5pm (open Thurs. and Fri. until 8pm). The Children's Art Space is open Wed. - Thurs., 3:30pm - 4:30pm; Sat. - Sun., 2:30pm - 3:30pm.

**Admission:**  Tickets for the Youth Theatre usually run $9.50 for adults; $7.50 for children 12 years and under. Tickets for the Culture Club and other family shows generally run between $5 - $10 per person. The gallery is $1 for adults; free to youth 17 years and under.

**Ages:**       5 years and up.

# EDWARDS IMAX 3D THEATER (Irvine)

(714) 832-IMAX (4629); or (949) 450-4900
*At the junction of the 405 and 5 Fwy., at the Irvine Spectrum Center, Irvine*
(Going S. on Santa Ana Fwy [5], exit W. on Alton Pky. At the end of the off ramp, go straight into the Spectrum. Going N. on 5, exit W. on Alton Pky. Going S. on San Diego Fwy [405], exit N. on Irvine Center Dr., R. on Pacifica.)

For your viewing pleasure, Edwards Theater has a twenty-one screen theater complex in the heart of the Irvine Spectrum entertainment center. The crown jewel of this Hollywood-looking building is a 3D IMAX theater. The giant screen is six stories high and ninety-feet wide. The lightweight headsets, which look like heavy duty sunglasses, help create three-dimensional images that look incredibly real. You become part of the forty-five-minute movie as you swim with fish, fly in an airplane, etc. You feel like you're really living the adventure! Watch your kids reach out to try to touch objects that seemingly jump right off the screen. The movies can be a terrific educational tool, too. If you make reservations to come on a class field trip, request a Teacher's Resource Guide for the group. Also see IRVINE SPECTRUM CENTER, under the Malls section, for information on the rest of the mall.

**Hours:** The first show starts daily at 10am.
**Admission:** The 3D IMAX is $8 for adults; $7 for seniors; $6 for ages 12 and under.
**Ages:** 4 years and up.

## ELIZABETH HOWARD'S CURTAIN CALL DINNER THEATER ☼

(714) 838-1540                                                    $$$$$
*690 El Camino Real, Tustin*                                        ⚏
(Going S.E. on Santa Ana Fwy [5], exit N.E. on Newport Ave., L. on El Camino Real. Going N. W. on 5, exit N.E. on Red Hill Ave., L. on El Camino Real.)

Prepare for an evening of fine dining and a terrific Broadway musical when you come to the Curtain Call Dinner Theater. The restaurant/theater holds up to 300 people, and tiered seating insures that every seat has a good view of the stage. Seating for your meal begins two hours prior to show time, although younger kids will get antsy if you actually arrive this early. Your three-course meal is waiter served. The main entree selections include baked chicken with herbs, ham, New York roast, or prime rib. A vegetarian lasagna, may be preordered. Soup, salad, and vegetables come with the meal, while desserts and beverages cost extra. Savor the food and enjoy the service! (It's just like the kind of meals we have at my house. Oh, never mind, that's Martha Stewart's house I'm thinking of.)

The ninety-minute musicals are enthralling, especially for children who appreciate the opportunity of seeing live theater. Most of the shows are suitable for the family, but call first and ask to see what is currently playing. Five different shows are performed each year. Past titles include *Camelot*, *Sound of Music*, and *The King and I.*

**Hours:** Meal seating begins Tues. - Sat. at 6:15pm; Sun. at 11:15am and at 5:15pm.
**Admission:** $25.95 - $36.95 per person, depending on the night you visit. (Tues. is the least expensive.)
**Ages:** 6 years and up.

## IRVINE BARCLAY THEATER ☼

(949) 854-4646 / www.ocartsnet.org/ibt                            $$$
*4242 Campus Drive, Irvine*                                        ⚏
(Exit San Diego Fwy [405] S. on Culver Dr., R. on Campus Dr. to Bridge Rd.)

This theater offers four to five family-oriented shows a year, plus several touring shows geared for kids. The various types of shows include circus acts, folk singers, Indian dancers, acrobats, and the *Nutcracker Suite*. Applause, applause - not a seat in the house is more than sixty feet away from the stage.

**Hours:** Call for show dates and times.
**Admission:** Tickets range from $5 - $50.

**Ages:**   5 years and up.

## THE LAGUNA PLAYHOUSE
(949) 497-9244  / www.lagunaplayhouse.com
*606 Laguna Canyon Road, Laguna Beach*

(Exit San Diego Fwy [405] or Santa Ana Fwy [5] S. on Laguna Canyon Rd. [Hwy 133]. It's on the R., in the Laguna Moulton Theater, on the Festival of the Arts grounds.)

"Orange County's Award-Winning Theater for Young People and the Young at Heart!" Four, great-for-the-kids plays are presented here each year. Past productions include *Wind in the Willows*, *How to Eat Like a Child*, and *The Best Christmas Pageant Ever*.

**Hours:**   Call for show dates and times.
**Admission:**   Tickets are usually between $8 - $11.
**Ages:**   5 years and up.

## LA MIRADA THEATRE FOR THE PERFORMING ARTS
(562) 944-9801
*14900 La Mirada Boulevard, La Mirada*

(Exit Artesia Fwy [91] or Santa Ana Fwy [5] N. on Valley View, R. on Rosecrans, R. on La Mirada.)

Golden State Children and Programs for Young Audiences are two production companies that present children's programs here three to five times a year.

**Hours:**   Call for show dates and times.
**Admission:**   Tickets are usually between $8 - $10.
**Ages:**   5 years and up.

## MEDIEVAL TIMES
(714) 521-4740  / www.medievaltimes.com
*7662 Beach Boulevard, Buena Park*

(Exit Artesia Fwy [91] S. on Beach Blvd. It's N. of KNOTT'S BERRY FARM.)

The sight of this eleventh-century-style castle sets the mood for a "knight" to remember. Before entering the arena, the Museum of Torture welcomes visitors for $2 for adults, $1 for kids 12 years and under. This unusual museum displays over thirty reproductions of instruments of torture and ridicule used during the Middle Ages, like the Rack, and the Stock and Pillories. Each instrument is explicitly labeled as to its use. Personally, I wouldn't go through the museum again.

Upon entering the castle, wear the crowns to given ye, good Lords and Ladies, as the color designates which of the knights you'll cheer for. The Lord of the Castle has invited you, and 1,100 of your closest friends, neighbors, and foes to a two-hour royal tournament. First, silky-maned horses prance and high-step, delighting horse fans young and old. These elegant displays of horsemanship are the highlight of the pre-show activities.

Then comes the main event - the tournament. Six knights on horseback joust and perform feats of real skill. After every game, the winning knight throws flowers out to his rooting section. The final battle looks real, with swords actually sparking as they strike each other. The knights fight on horseback, and then on foot, until there is just one knight left "alive" - the victor. (Reassure younger kids that this is just a show.)

Throughout the evening serfs and wenches serve a four-course feast, eaten without utensils, of course. The delicious meal consists of vegetable soup, whole roasted chicken, spare ribs, potatoes, pastries, and drink. We enjoyed the food and were riveted by the action. After the show, the gift shop selling medieval memorabilia is open, or dance at the in-house Knight Club.

One-hour, educational Castle Tours are offered for a minimum of twenty students. Kids are guided by a costumed Master of Ceremonies through the decorated halls. Life in the Middle Ages is explained as they look at authentic medieval artifacts, and learn about chivalry and knighthood. The highlights are meeting a "real" knight, and seeing demonstrations of horsemanship and actual medieval weapons. Tours are given Monday through Thursday, at 10:30am and noon. Call to make a reservation. The cost is $4 per person.

Student Matinees are offered January through August, on certain Tuesdays and Thursdays, from 11:30am to 1pm for grades kindergarten through twelfth. A medieval history lesson is given, by a Master of Ceremonies on horseback, instead of some of the pageantry of a nighttime show. Kids still see, though, the knights engaging in period games and sword fights. This educational "tour" includes a lunch of chicken, apples, cookies, drink, etc. The cost is $15.95 per person. The castle is also open during the day for those who want to simply come in and look at the horses and the arena.

**Hours:** Call for times for the knightly performances and for matinees on Sun.

**Admission:** The price, including dinner, show, and tax, is $34.95 for adults; $22.95 for ages 12 and under. Reservations are required. (Certain discounts available through AAA, but not on Sat.) Note: If three people pay in full, the fourth person, (i.e. the birthday person, who must show proof of his/her birthday) gets in for free on the date of his/her birthday.

**Ages:** 3 years and up.

# ORANGE COUNTY PERFORMING ARTS CENTER ☼
(714) 755-5799 - symphony; (714) 556-2787 - center /                $$$$
www.ocartsnet.org/ocpac
*600 Town Center Drive, Costa Mesa*
(Exit San Diego Fwy [405] N. on Bristol St., R. on Town Center.)

Six Saturdays a year, Pacific Symphony puts on Mervyn's Musical Mornings, which are concerts geared for families. The performances vary in content, but aim to be pieces that children are familiar with, such as music from *Nutcracker Suite* or even from cartoons. They are always fun for kids. See the

Tours section for information on taking a tour of this center.
> **Hours:** Select Sat. at 10am and at 11:30am.
> **Admission:** $12 for adults; $10 for children 12 years and under.
> **Ages:** 5 years and up.

## PLAZA GARIBALDI DINNER THEATER
(714) 758-9014                                                    *$$$$*
*1490 S. Anaheim Boulevard, Anaheim*
(Going S. on Santa Ana Fwy [5], exit E. on Ball Rd., R. on Anaheim Blvd. Going N. on 5, exit E. on Katella, R. on Anaheim Blvd.)

Experience the finest Mexican entertainment and cuisine this side of the border. Your two-hour, dinner/show features a variety of acts such as Mariachis, singers, folkloric dancers, cowboy ropers, tango dancers, etc. The fiesta atmosphere, authentic costumes, and colorful decor enhance your visit here. Adults can choose from numerous entrees, ranging from traditional Mexican fare to seafood. Kids can choose from hamburger with fries, carne asada, or chicken with rice. Beverages are extra. Sunday brunches, at 1pm and 3pm, are all-you-can-eat buffets that come with champagne. Ole!
> **Hours:** Shows begin Thurs., 8:30pm and 10:30pm, Fri. - Sat., 8:30pm, 10:30pm, and midnight; Sun., 1pm, 2:30pm, 7:30pm, 9:30pm, and 10:45pm.
> **Admission:** $16.95 for adults; $8.95 for children 10 years and under. The price includes dinner and the show.
> **Ages:** 4 years and up.

## RANCHO SANTIAGO COLLEGE PLANETARIUM
(714) 564-6220 or (714) 564-6600                                        *$*
*West 17ᵗʰ Street and North Bristol, Santa Ana*

West $17^{th}$ Street and North Bristol, Santa Ana
(Exit Santa Ana Fwy [5] W. on 17ᵗʰ St. at Bristol in Rancho Santiago College)

Twinkle, twinkle little star, how I wonder what you are? Your kids can begin to find the answers to this question in the 100-seat planetarium. The hour-long show, *Introduction to the Sky*, is a trip around the galaxy, as you see and learn about planets and constellations. The Christmas show is *Star of Bethlehem*. There is time after the shows for questions and answers.
> **Hours:** Shows are given mid-September through Mid-May, Mon. - Wed., and Fri. at 9:30am. A second show on Tues. is offered at 11am. Reservations are needed.
> **Admission:** $2 per person.
> **Ages:** 5 years and up.

## ROBERT B. MOORE THEATER
(714) 432-5880 / www.occ.cccd.edu                                       *$$$$*
*2701 Fairview Road, at Orange Coast College, Costa Mesa*
(Exit San Diego Fwy [405] S. on Fairview.)

This college puts on <u>fourteen</u> children's productions throughout the year, which is two or three favorites for each person in my family.

**Hours:** Call for show dates and times.
**Admission:** Tickets range from $8 - $15. Matinees are less expensive.
**Ages:** 5 years and up.

## SADDLEBACK CHILDREN'S FESTIVAL

(949) 364-ARTS (2787)
*2700 Marguerite Parkway, Mission Viejo*
(Exit San Diego Fwy [5], E. on Crown Valley Pky., L. on Marguerite Pky. First level of Mission Viejo Mall, the storefront theater next to Robinsons May.)

Saddleback College is the proud sponsor of a wonderful series of children's plays. One-hour plays are either musical or classic stories acted out. Past productions have included *A Tale of Peter Rabbit*, *A Little Princess*, and *Little Red Riding Hood and the Three Little Pigs*. The plays are thoroughly enjoyable and the theater location is great too, especially if you want to go shopping at the mall or grab an ice-cream cone after a performance. The productions run in July, August, and September, but I hope they'll expand their season soon! During the summer, plays are also sometimes performed at Saddleback College at the outdoor theater.

**Hours:** Performances are given Wed. and Thurs. at 5pm and 7pm; Sat. - Sun., at 11am and 1pm.
**Admission:** $6 per person; children under 2 years are free.
**Ages:** Plays are usually geared for children ages 4 -12.

## SAM'S SEAFOOD "POLYNESIAN SPECTACULAR"

(562) 592-1321 / www.letseatoc.com
*16278 Pacific Coast Highway, Huntington Beach*

See SAM'S SEAFOOD "POLYNESIAN SPECTACULAR", under the Edible Adventures section, for details.

## SOUTH COAST REPERTORY

(714) 708-5555 / www.ocartsnet.org/scr
*655 Town Center Drive, Costa Mesa*
(Exit San Diego Fwy [405] N. on Bristol St., R. on Town Center.)

A few times a year, this theater offers productions for families. At least once a year, a performance is given by young actors. Kids get excited about seeing their peers on stage!

**Hours:** Call for show dates and times.
**Admission:** Varies, depending on the show.
**Ages:** 5 years and up.

## TIBBIE'S MUSIC HALL

(949) 252-0834 / www.tibbiesmusichall.com
*4647 MacArthur Boulevard, Newport Beach*
(Exit San Diego Fwy [405] S. on MacArthur, just S. of the John Wayne Airport.)

More than just dinner, and more than just a show - Tibbie's is a two-hour, dinner, musical song and dance revue. Past shows titles have included *From Stage to Screen* (favorite Broadway show tunes and movie music), *Solid Gold* (songs from the 70's), and the fantastic, annual Christmas show, *Holiday Follies*. The eight waiters and waitresses are also the entertainers. They start the show by singing as they bring in the salad, and they entertain all the way through dessert. (Dinner selections include prime rib, salmon, a chicken entree, or chef's special for adults; hamburger or chicken strips for kids.) They perform on the stage, as well as all around you. Audience participation, a code-word game, and other surprises throughout the evening add to your family's enjoyment.

If your child is celebrating a birthday, graduation, or other special occasion, be sure you tell Tibbie's beforehand so they will mention it sometime during the show. And don't tell the kids, but dessert is mud pie served in a flower pot, with a silk flower! Enjoy this delightful night out on the town where the food is good and the entertainment is fun and clean. One to two week reservations are suggested. Five or six different shows are presented throughout the year, so call for particular show titles.

**Hours:**   Shows are Fri. at 7:30pm; Sat. at 7pm; and selected Sun. at 2pm.
**Admission:**   Tickets, which include the show, dinner, and dessert are $28.95 for adults; $15.95 for children 12 years and under.
**Ages:**   6 years and up.

## TINSELTOWN STUDIOS                                              ☼

(714) 937-9090 / www.tinseltownstudios.com                         *$$$$$*
*2200 E. Katella Avenue, Anaheim*
(Exit Santa Ana Fwy [5] E. on Katella Ave. It is adjacent to the Edison International Field.)

Have you ever wondered what it's like to be a famous television or movie star? Now is your chance to find out! In front of Tinseltown, the lit-up water tower and the swirling searchlights indicate that a special event is going on. As at any Hollywood gala, the television crews, autograph seekers, and paparazzi vie for the attention of the arriving stars. This time, however, the celebrities are you and your family. This evening of star treatment is an evening to participate in and celebrate the (make-believe) *Tinseltown Awards Show*.

Walk on the red carpet inside to an art deco-style theater lobby. Besides the large bar, the room is filled with Hollywood memorabilia, a movie set, and T.V. monitors showing film clips. Guests may peruse the adjacent retail store called The Prop Shop. A musical number will announce the opening of the main dining room doors where inside, over 700 "stars" can be seated. Decorated as a lavish television show set, the stage, along with two large screens, dominates one wall. A program at your seat gives you the story of the mythological founder of Tinseltown, as well as what is in store for the evening. The three-course dinner includes your choice of top sirloin, salmon filet, chicken breast, or vegetarian pasta. As you dine, watch to see if your interview on the front walk, the *Pre-Award Show* telecast, is shown on the side screens. (This could be a few minutes of your fifteen minutes of fame.) As dessert is being served, the hour-long *Tinseltown Awards Show* begins. The show consists of emcees, and seventeen singers and dancers performing major Hollywood production numbers and ballads. True to an awards-show format, in between numbers and emcee remarks, the Oggie statuette is given for several categories, including Best Actor and Best Actress. Some of the winners are actually members of the audience who will be inserted into real motion pictures via the ulti-mat (i.e. green screen) process. You always knew that you should be in pictures! Scheduled to open after this book goes to print, Tinseltown promises to be a dazzling Hollywood dining experience!

**Hours:**    The dinner/show is Tues. - Sun., beginning at 6pm and at 8:30pm.

**Admission:**    $39.50 for adults; $29.50 for children 11 years and under. Soft drinks and other beverages are an additional fee. A $5 per person additional charge covers gratuities.

**Ages:**    7 years and up.

## TRINITY CHRISTIAN CITY INTERNATIONAL

(714) 708-4805 / www.tbn.org
*3150 Bear Street, Costa Mesa*
(Exit San Diego Fwy [405] S. on Bristol St., R. on Paularino Ave., R. on Bear St.)

A lavish fountain surrounded by beautiful landscaping and white archways is the serene garden setting of this T.C.C.I. building. The lobby of this international headquarters building is opulently decorated in whites and golds, along with beveled mirrors on the walls and around the columns. (I kept wishing for my own bottle of Windex™, so my children's visit here wouldn't be *so* obvious, although they were never looked at disparagingly. I've rarely encountered friendlier staff.) A powerful-looking angel at the top of the ornate central staircase immediately draws your attention. He is made out of white marble, brandishes a real sword, and is stepping upon a representation of Satan. The ceiling of the rotunda, just over his head, depicts heavenly scenes painted in a Victorian style.

Take the stairs, or a glass-enclosed elevator, to the second floor where you'll see a non-traditional church and a broadcasting room. Check out all the equipment! You are invited to attend free broadcasts and tapings of the Trinity Broadcast Network programs that air from either room. Call for dates and times.

After my boys and I stopped gaping, we went back downstairs into a small theater room. Tip: Just before you enter, note the "mirror room" where you look through several sets of beveled mirrors, seemingly into infinity. A fifteen-minute preview, hosted by Paul Crouch, president and founder of T.B.N., presents the history and Christian heritage of Orange County, and T.B.N. Afterward, as the screen and curtain rise, you are invited to walk along an excellent re-creation of Via Dolorosa, the cobblestone street in the city of old Jerusalem where Jesus carried his cross to Calvary. The street ends at the entrance of another theater.

Three, one-hour-long movies are shown in this forty-nine seat Virtual

Reality Theatre. (Virtual Reality, or "surround" sound, means that you'll literally feel the rumblings of earthquakes and thunder, and that the loud noises and music are amplified.) These outstanding re-enactments vividly bring Biblical events to life. Each film, shot on location in Israel, is presented a few times throughout the day. Note that the films powerfully and realistically portray their subject, so certain scenes are graphic and thereby intense for younger children. *The Revolutionary* shows the life of Christ, from His birth to His resurrection. Graphic scenes include a demon being cast out and Christ being nailed on the cross. *The Revolutionary II* is about the miracles of Jesus' ministry. Graphic scenes include a demon being cast out and Christ being nailed to the cross. (I know that last part sounded familiar.) *The Emissary* depicts the Apostle Paul's life, his conversion, his subsequent new life of faith, and his struggles. Graphic scenes include the stoning of Stephen, beatings, and a shipwreck.

A beautiful, fully-stocked gift shop is also on the premises. See TRINITY BROADCAST NETWORK, under the Tours section, for an associated attraction. Tip: Pack a sack lunch because Shiffer Park is just across the street. The park has a few playgrounds, large grassy areas, shade trees, and picnic tables.

**Hours:** The building is open Mon. - Thurs., 10am - 6pm; Fri. - Sat., 10am - 9pm; Sun., 1pm - 6pm. Movies, beginning on the half hour, run Mon. - Thurs., 10:30am - 4:30pm; Fri. - Sat., 10:30am - 7:30pm; Sun., 1:30pm - 4:30pm. Call for a program schedule.

**Admission:** Free

**Ages:** 6 years and up.

## RIVERSIDE COMMUNITY COLLEGE PLANETARIUM ☼

$

(909) 222-8090 / www.rccd.resources4u.com/cs
*4800 Magnolia Avenue, Riverside*
(Exit Riverside Fwy [91] W. on 14th St., L. on Market St./Magnolia Ave.)

Come see a truly star-studded show at the college planetarium! The theater seats sixty people and each presentation has a live narrator. Different shows study various aspects of astronomy such as constellations, revolutions (the earth's, not a country's), galaxies and measuring distances between them, lunar eclipses, and what makes the sun shine.

School groups, or other groups, can schedule a time to see fifty-minute shows such as *Sun's Family*, or *Finding Your Way in the Sky*, or others. These shows are geared specifically for elementary-aged kids. There are several shows and programs geared for secondary grade levels, too. *Christmas Star* is offered only in the month of December.

**Hours:** Public shows are offered year round, usually on Fri. nights at 7pm. Groups can see shows Mon. - Thurs. at noon. Reservations are required.

**Admission:** Public shows are $3 for adults; $2.50 for students; $1.50 for children 11 years and under. Tour shows are $75 for up to sixty people.

**Ages:**   6 years and up.

## CHAFFEY COLLEGE PLANETARIUM

(909) 941-2758 / e-mail:mprovence@yahoo.com          *$$*
*5885 Haven Avenue, Rancho Cucamonga*
(Exit San Bernardino Fwy [10] N. on Haven.)

A forty-five minute introduction to celestial bodies is given most Friday nights here at the college. See and learn about our solar system and other galaxies as you gather under the indoor nighttime stars. School tours are given during the week with advanced registration. Some of the show titles to choose from include *Our Solar System*, *Finding Your Way in the Sky*, and *Eclipses.*

**Hours:**   Shows for the general public are given most Fri. nights at 7pm. Call to book a weekday school tour.

**Admission:**   $4 per person for the public shows. School groups are $60 for up to seventy-six people.

**Ages:**   5 years and up.

## EDWARDS IMAX 3D THEATER (Ontario)

(909) 476-1525 or (909) 941-4487          *$$$*
*4900 E. 4ᵗʰ Street, Ontario*
(Exit Ontario Fwy [15] to 4ᵗʰ St. It is just outside Ontario Mills Mall.)

Going to the movies is a lot more fun if you are part of the action, not just watching it happen. Besides the twenty regular movie screens, this Edwards allows you to "experience" a movie on the giant IMAX screen by using lightweight headsets that create three-dimensional images. Objects will jump out at you, float around you, and seemingly become a part of your immediate surroundings. (Watch your kids try to reach out and touch the objects.) Live whatever adventure you see on the screen, whether it's underwater with fish, in the sky with birds, etc. Use your visit as an educational tool if you come with a group of students, and request a Teacher's Resource Guide, which are very well put together. See ONTARIO MILLS MALL, under the Malls section, for other nearby attractions.

**Hours:**   The first show starts at 10am.

**Admission:**   Prices for 3D movies are $7 for adults; $6 for seniors; $5 for ages 2 - 12 years.

**Ages:**   4 years and up

## THEATRE AT THE GROVE

(909) 920-4343          *$$$$*
*276 E. 9ᵗʰ Street, Upland*
(Exit San Bernardino Fwy [10] N. on Euclid, R. on 9ᵗʰ.)

Fine, professional, dramatic live theater is performed at the grove, along with comedies, concerts, six musicals per season, and children's workshops. Past shows have included *Jesus Christ Superstar*, and *Barnum.*

**Hours:**   Call for show dates and times.

**Admission:**   Varies, depending on the show.
**Ages:**         Varies, depending on the show.

## CALIFORNIA BALLET COMPANY

(619) 560-5676
San Diego

$$$$$

This professional ballet company tours throughout San Diego. They perform three to four, ninety-minute ballets a year. Past family-oriented shows, usually put on in the spring, have included *Alice in Wonderland* and *Snow White*. The associated junior ballet company, with performers between the ages of 12 and 17 years, put on a yearly show, usually in January. The company also offers dance classes of ballet, jazz, and modern dance for children 3 years and up.

**Hours:**        Call for a schedule.
**Admission:**   Prices depend on the theater venue.
**Ages:**         6 years and up.

## CALIFORNIA CENTER FOR THE ARTS

(800) 98-TICKETS (988-4253) /
coyote.csusm.edu/community/hold.artcenter/ccae.home.html
*340 N. Escondido Boulevard, Escondido*

$$$

(Exit Escondido Fwy [15] E. on Valley Parkway; take the east bound lane which turns into Grand Ave., L. on Escondido Blvd.)

All the world's a stage and kids are invited to come watch the world, or at least a production or two. Several of the yearly performances given at the center are perfect for the entire family. Past productions have included *The Sound of Music*, *The Magic Schoolbus*, and *The Hobbit*, which was performed with large puppets.

**Hours:**        Call for the names and dates of productions.
**Admission:**   Tickets are usually about $10 for children's productions.
**Ages:**         5 years and up

## CHILDREN'S CLASSICS

(619) 268-4494
*1540 Camino del Mar at the L'Auberge del Mar Garden Amphitheater, Del Mar*

$$

(Exit San Diego Fwy [5] W. on Del Mar Heights Rd., R. on Camino Del Mar.)

An entertaining, thirty-five-minute presentation of classic children's literature is performed by the San Diego Actors Theater a few times each month. Past productions have included *The Giving Tree*, *Snow White and the Seven Dwarfs* (where kids came up on stage to help be the dwarfs), *Hansel and Gretel*, and *Goldilocks*. These theater presentations are great for the younger (and older) set! Sometimes acting workshops are offered after the shows. Workshops are geared for kids 4 to 9 years old and cost $10 per child.

**Hours:**        Performances are given the second and fourth Sat. of each month at 11am.

**Admission:**   $4 per person.
**Ages:**   3 years and up.

## CHILDREN'S THEATRE NETWORK (San Diego)

(619) 238-8280 / www.thectnetwork.com

*Performed at Lyceum Theater at Horton Plaza, Broadway Cir, & 4th Ave.,
San Diego; and the Center for Performing Arts, 15498 Espola Rd., Poway*
(San Diego: Going S. on San Diego Fwy [5], exit W. on Ash St., L. on 4th Ave. Going N.
on 5, exit S. on 6th Ave., R. on Broadway. Poway: Exit Escondido Fwy [15] E. on Rancho
Bernardo Rd., turns into Espola Rd.)

This terrific, everyone-gets-a-role, theater group is comprised of kids 4 years
old through college-age, as well as a few adult performers. What a great "first-
theater" exposure for kids who are acting, and those in the audience. Past
productions have included *Joseph and the Amazing Technicolor Dreamcoat*, *The
Wiz*, *Peter Pan*, *Aladdin*, and *Fiddler on the Roof*. If your child is a thespian
"wannabe", call about enrolling him/her for the next production. The twelve-
week Saturday course costs $160, which includes rehearsal workshops, training,
and productions. Participants also have the opportunity to go abroad once a year.
There are three other locations of the theater network: Northridge, Torrance, and
West Covina.

**Hours:**   Call for show locations, dates, and times.
**Admission:**   Tickets are usually $15 for adults; $12 for children 4 - 12 years.
**Ages:**   4 years on up to watch or participate.

## CHRISTIAN YOUTH THEATER

(800) 696-1929 or (619) 588-0206 / www.cctcyt.org/cyt
*San Diego*

Enjoy live, musical theater, performed by students 8 through 18 years, and
put on at six locations throughout San Diego County. Past productions have
included *Aladdin*, *Jungle Book*, *The Secret Garden*, *Tom Sawyer*, *Willy Wonka &
the Chocolate Factory*, and *Alice in Wonderland*. The theater presents
wholesome entertainment for the whole family!

**Hours:**   Call for show locations, dates, and times.
**Admission:**   Tickets usually cost about $7 for adults; $6 for children 12 years
and under.
**Ages:**   4 years and up.

## MARIE HITCHCOCK PUPPET THEATER

(619) 685-5045
*Balboa Park, San Diego*
(Going S. on Cabrillo Fwy [163], exit N. on Park Blvd. Going S. on San Diego Fwy [5],
exit at Ash St. / "A" St., L. on "A" St., L. on Park Blvd. Going N. on 5, exit W. on "B" St.,
R. on Park Blvd. Once on Park Blvd. turn L. on Presidents Way to get to the museums.)

This intimate theater, located behind the San Diego Automotive Museum,
presents kid-approved, half-hour, puppet shows. The type of puppets vary from
show to show, and can include hand puppets, marionettes, dummies (for

ventriloquists), and puppets made from anything and everything found around the house. The shows themselves are similar in that they never fail to capture a child's imagination. From *Cinderella* to *The Ugly Duckling* to *The Frog Prince*, stories are told as only puppets can tell them! Shows change weekly so watch out - bringing the kids here can become habit forming. (See BALBOA PARK [San Diego], under the Museums section, for a listing of all the museums and attractions within walking distance.)

**Hours:** Performances are usually given Wed., Thurs., and Fri. at 10am and 11:30am; Sat. - Sun. at 11am, 1pm, and 2:30pm.
**Admission:** $2 for adults; $1.50 for children 2-12 years.
**Ages:** 1½ - 10 years

## POWAY CENTER FOR THE PERFORMING ARTS

(619) 748-0505 / www.inetworld.net/eldend
$$$
*15498 Espola Road, Poway*
(Exit Escondido Fwy [15], E. on Rancho Bernardo Rd., which turns into Espola Rd., follow as it turns right.)

This Center offers a few outstanding children's programs a year. Last year's highlights included Jim Gamble puppets, and a troop that performed juggling, acrobatics, and comedy, combined with a laser light show.

**Hours:** Call for performance times.
**Admission:** Tickets usually run between $5 - $8.
**Ages:** 4 years and up.

## SAN DIEGO JUNIOR THEATRE

(619) 239-1311
$$$
*Performed in Balboa Park, Casa del Prado Theatre, San Diego*
(Going S. on Cabrillo Fwy [163], exit N. on Park Blvd. Going S. on San Diego Fwy [5], exit at Ash St. / "A" St., L. on "A" St., L. on Park Blvd. Going N. on 5, exit W. on "B" St., R. on Park Blvd. Once on Park Blvd. turn L. on Space Theater Way.)

The San Diego Junior Theatre is a comprehensive workshop program for student 4 to 18 years old, who present six family-oriented shows a year. Past performances of the for-kids-by-kids group have included *Annie, Master Prince and the Pauper*, and *The Adventures of a Bear Named Paddington*. Ask about special performances that are interpreted for the deaf.

**Hours:** Call for show dates and times.
**Admission:** Prices usually range from $7 - $9.
**Ages:** 4 years and up.

## WELK RESORT THEATER

(888) 802-7469 / www.welkresort.com
$$$$$
*8860 Lawrence Welk Drive, Escondido*
(Exit Interstate 15 L. on Gopher Canyon, R. on Champagne Blvd., L. onto Lawrence Welk Dr.)

This "wannaful" (i.e. that's the way Welk used to say "wonderful") dinner/theater offers buffet meals and five different, full production Broadway musicals a year. Audiences in the 330-seat theater have seen the likes of *My Fair Lady*, *The King and I*, *Seven Brides for Seven Brothers*, and its annual, *Welk Musical Christmas Show*. As you can tell by the titles, many of the musicals are family-oriented.

Buffet-style eating is great for picky eaters! The delicious array of food consists of ham, roast beef, chicken, fish, pastas, salads, breads, vegetables, fruit, dessert, etc. Lunch or dinner is served for a full two hours before each show, so there is plenty of time to enjoy your meal before the two-hour extravaganza. Tip: Come an hour into serving time if you think your child might get restless being here for the entire time.

**Hours:** Lunch buffets are served Tues. - Thurs., Sat. - Sun. (not Mon. or Fri.) from 11:15am - 1:15pm. The performance begins at 1:45pm. Dinner buffets are served Tues., Thurs. - Sat. from 5:30pm - 7:30pm. The performance begins at 8pm.

**Admission:** $32 - $37 for adults for a meal and a show; $28 - $32 for adults for just the show. $18 for children 3 -12 years for a meal and a show; $15 for children for just a show.

**Ages:** 6 years and up.

## MOORPARK PLAYHOUSE
(800) 597-1210 or (805) 529-1212 / www.moorparkplayhouse.com     $$
*45 E. High Street, Moorpark*
(Exit Simi Valley/San Fernando Valley Fwy [23] E. on New Los Angeles Ave. [23/118], N. on the Moorpark Ave. [23], R. on High St.)

This theater was built in 1928, and its antiqueness adds to its uniqueness. There are several different venues to enjoy great performances here. The Playhouse series offers vaudeville, melodrama, musical spoofs, comedy, and drama. The Celebrity series showcases concerts performed by touring groups. Rock 'n roll, country, etc. have all taken center stage. Magic shows have also been featured. The Children series presents puppets and children's fairy tales, and even classes where kids can learn to be performers.

**Hours:** Call for a schedule.

**Admission:** Prices vary, depending on the show. Ticket for the Children series are usually $5 per person.

**Ages:** It varies, depending on the show.

## PERFORMING ARTS CENTER
(805) 486-2424 / www.west.net/~oxnardcty/performingarts.html     $$$
*800 Hobson Way, at the Performing Arts Center, Oxnard*
(Exit Ventura Fwy [101] S. on Hwy 1 [or Oxnard Blvd.], R. on 9th St., R. on Hobson.)

Shows performed here for the general public include *Sesame Street*, *Nutcracker*, *Anne Frank*, etc. School groups often rent the theater for special performances put on by American Theatre for Youth, or other touring groups. Call for a schedule.

**Hours:** Call for show dates and times.

**Admission:**   Varies, depending on the show.
**Ages:**   3 years and up, depending on the show.

## THOUSAND OAKS CIVIC ARTS PLAZA

(805) 449-ARTS (2787)

*2100 E. Thousand Oaks Boulevard, Thousand Oaks*

(Coming W. on Ventura Fwy [101], exit on Hampshire Blvd., R. on Thousand Oaks, Blvd., L. on Civic Arts Plaza Dr. Coming E. on 101, exit L. on Rancho Rd., R. on Thousand Oaks Blvd.)

This arts plaza offers two theaters: the Forum, which seats 500 people, and the Kavli, which seats 1,800. Professional local and national touring production groups put on numerous, first-class shows ranging from ballet, to musicals, to dramas. A variety of family and children's concerts are offered, as well as several different children's series. Past programs include Jim Gamble's Marionettes, *Do Jump! Acrobatic Theater*, *Freedom Train*, *The Music Man*, *Oregon Trail*, and *Sesame Street Live*. Call for a complete schedule.

**Hours:**   Call for show dates and times.
**Admission:**   Prices vary, depending on the show.
**Ages:**   Varies, depending on the show.

# TOURS

Insight into ordinary and unique places is what this section is all about. Many tours are offered under Museums, and other sections, too. Tip: See the Ideas / Resources section toward the back of the book for general tour ideas regarding a particular profession or subject.

## CLAIM JUMPER                                              ☼

(800) 949-4538 / www.claimjumper.com                         *$$$*

While studying the Gold Rush, come jump a claim at this restaurant. A guided tour begins with a talk in the lobby about the discovery of gold at Sutter's Mill, the Gold Rush, and what a claim jumper really was. The class is then divided. One group learns about any furnishings here from this era. Then they learn about careers in the food service industry, which Claim Jumper has turned into their own gold mine. Meanwhile, the other group is seeing the behind-the-scenes part of the restaurant, the kitchen. They see the different work stations, visit the storeroom and walk-in refrigerator, grind some coffee, and see how dining room food orders are put together. After both groups have had a complete tour, strike it rich with lunch. Select either chicken tenders or mini-burgers, both of which come with french fries, a soft drink, and a piece of Claim Jumper Mud Pie. Groups must consist of a minimum of twelve people and a maximum of thirty-two; this number includes students and adult chaperones. Make sure to give the restaurant the names of all the students, as name badges are given out. Call for the Claim Jumper nearest you.

**Hours:** Tours are given Tues., Wed. and Thurs. at 9:30am. Lunch is served around 11am.

**Admission:** $5 per student, plus tax and gratuity. Adults may pay $5 for the same meal choice as the kids, or pay the regular price for something from the menu.

**Ages:** Geared for 4th graders.

## AIR FORCE FLIGHT TEST CENTER                              ☼

(805) 277-3510 or (805) 277-3512 / www.edwards.af.mil         *!*

*Edwards Air Force Base*

(Exit the Golden State Fwy [5] N. on the Antelope Valley Fwy [14], E. on Edwards/Rosamond and drive for a few miles.)

Your ninety-minute tour starts off with a half-hour film, called *First Flights,* on the history of flight testing. The movie has general public appeal, but it is geared for those who are aeronautically inclined. The hour-long, narrated bus tour takes visitors past the hangers and to the flight line, along the taxiway and to the edge of the dry lake beds that are fondly referred to by everyone on base as "the greatest natural landing fields." You ride the length of the flight line and, weather and operations permitting, can get out to take a closer look at the lake beds. Along the way, you'll see test planes taking off, several unmanned vehicles, and whatever else is on base that particular day. The tour is comprehensive and, when coupled with a visit to the AIR FORCE FLIGHT TEST CENTER MUSEUM (see the Museums section) and/or the NASA DRYDEN FLIGHT RESEARCH CENTER (see this section), you have a thorough overview on aeronautics and flight testing.

**Hours:** Tours are given on Fri. at 10am. Reservations are required.

**Admission:** Free

**Ages:** 8 years and up.

# NASA DRYDEN FLIGHT RESEARCH CENTER
(805) 258-3446 / www.dfrc.nasa.gov
*Lilly Avenue, Edwards Air Force Base*
(Exit the Golden State Fwy [5] N. on the Antelope Valley Fwy [14], E. on
Edwards/Rosamond., R. on Lilly Ave., almost to Hwy. 58)

A mural of twenty aircraft that reflect the aeronautical heritage of NASA
Dryden is in the lobby of the Visitors' Center. This is the primary research and
test center for flight research and the space shuttle program, as well as a backup
landing site. Your tour begins with a fifteen-minute, somewhat technical film
that gives insight to the importance and accomplishments of the space program.
During your ninety-minute guided walking tour you'll go into a large hanger to
see and learn about past research aircraft, particularly the "X" series of
experimental aircraft; some of the current planes being tested; the massive dry
lake bed used for a runway and NASA landing site; and, time permitting, the
control tower. Admittedly, my children also liked seeing the doors to the office
building because it was a shot frequently used in the TV show, *I Dream of
Jeannie*. We saw a lunar aircraft (LLRV), too, that helped train Apollo astronauts
how to land on the moon. Note: Neil Armstrong was a research pilot here before
joining the space program. Much of the information on the tour is technical, so I
was a little surprised how much my boys (as they range in ages) enjoyed it. Any
and all questions (and my kids had a lot) are fully answered, and the knowledge
that does sink in make this a memorable tour. Outside, next to the parking lot are
several more test planes to look at.

The large gift shop is also part mini-museum. An aircraft display features
phones in front of model planes so visitors can hear explanations on the history
and achievements of particular planes and pilots. In another section, panels light
up according to the planes being discussed by a recording. The last display has
mannequins modeling pressure suits used by test pilots - one was worn by Neil
Armstrong.

Combine your visit here with a trip down the street to the AIR FORCE
FLIGHT TEST CENTER MUSEUM (under the Museums section) and the AIR
FORCE FLIGHT TEST CENTER tour (under this section).

**Hours:** Tours of NASA are given Mon. - Fri. at 10:15am and 1:15pm.
**Admission:** Free
**Ages:** 8 years and up.

# A.D. EDMONSTON PUMPING PLANT
(805) 858-5509
*Edmonston Road*
(Exit Golden State Fwy [5] E. at the Grape Vine exit, past Denny's and continue on
Edmonston Road for about 6 miles. It's about a half hour south/east of Bakersfield.)

Edmonston pumping plant is located at the foot of the Tehachapi Mountains
and is the largest pumping facility of the State Water Project. A ninety-minute
tour, given for a minimum of twelve people and maximum of thirty-five, begins
with a twenty-minute video on water safety. Visitors start the walking tour at the

top floor, which contains the control room, then they go down into the depths of the plant, five stories underground. The fifth floor is the electrical gallery, where numerous power lines enter the building. Keep descending and on the fourth floor, you'll see the top of pump motors, where 80,000 (hp) electric motors turn the pumps. The enormous machinery is impressive, and a bit overwhelming. (Water pipes weigh 220 tons!) On the lower level, water enters the plant from the bottom of the fore bay.

Kids see plant machinery as they learn about water conservation, water safety, and how the pumping plant lifts water over the mountains. It gives you a lot to think about the next time you drink tap water or take a long, hot shower.

**Hours:** Tours are given by request.
**Admission:** Free
**Ages:** 8 years and up.

## A.E.S. REDONDO GENERATING STATION

(310) 318-7430
*1100 Harbor Drive, Redondo Beach*
(Exit San Diego Fwy [405] S. on Western, R. on 190th St., which turns into Anita St., then turns in to Herondo, L. on Harbor.)

Have you ever walked through a generating plant? Have you ever wanted to? Here's your opportunity for a ninety-minute, *electrifying* experience. Groups must consist of ten to twenty-five people. The first half hour is spent learning about the principles and components of electricity and of a steam plant, and the various ways electricity is generated (i.e. solar, wind, etc.), as well as a little history about Redondo Beach. During the next half hour visitors walk around the plants, including those built and used from the 1940's through today. (This part of the tour is not wheelchair accessible.) Kids will notice the differences in the architecture of the buildings and the technology in processing electricity. They'll visit turbine decks and control rooms, and be *shocked* at the equipment size and amount of power generated. The tour also includes, weather permitting, a look at and a brief history on the Whaley wall, painted by marine muralist, Wyland. Walk across the street for the last half hour of the tour, which is spent inside the marine lab. Marine education science center docents will explain the sea life exhibits and how the creatures arrived here. (Mostly through intake pipes.) A few tanks and aquariums hold horn sharks, sand sharks, bat rays, lobsters, and more. Outside are a few more aquariums, plus a tidepool tank and a touch tank with sea stars, sea slugs, etc. The marine biologists working here study the sea animals and then release them.

**Hours:** Tours are available Mon. - Thurs. between 9:30am - 2pm.
Reservations are needed.
**Admission:** Free
**Ages:** Second graders and up.

## CALIFORNIA INSTITUTE OF TECHNOLOGY - SEISMOLOGY TOUR

(626) 395-6811 / www.gps.caltech.edu/seismo/seismo.page.html                    !
*1201 East California Boulevard, Pasadena*
(Exit Foothill Fwy [210] S. on South Lake Ave., L. on California Blvd. It is on the Caltech campus in the Mudd Building, on the N.E. corner of Wilson Ave. and California Blvd.)

Too often in Southern California there is a whole lot of shakin' going on. What causes this? Find out by taking a seismology tour. Much of the information is technical, but older children can appreciate it. You'll start the one-hour tour in the lobby, which has a time line that shows how information comes into the lab. The lobby also has a computer that shows recent earthquake activity around the world and a computer with a touch screen that shows (with sound and animation) information on the Northridge quake and others. From here you go through the seismology lab to see giant drums where seismic data are recorded, and learn how to read the seismographs. The aim of the tour is to allow students to see and learn about a working lab. This is not a hands-on tour. You also go through the media center, where press conferences are held after a quake. There is plenty of time to ask earthquake-related questions. The tour is wheelchair accessible.

Tours are given for a group of at least ten people, maximum twenty five. If your group has less than ten people, you will be assimilated in with another group, if possible, to reach the minimum number. Students must be 12 years old or in the sixth grade. School tours must book the date at least one month in advance so the class will receive educational and instructional materials before coming. Non-school group tours must be scheduled two weeks in advance.

**Hours:**  Tour are offered on the first Tues. and first Thurs. of the month at 10am, 11am, 1:30pm, 2:30pm, and 3:30pm. They are not offered during the months of January, July, August, or September.

**Admission:** Free

**Ages:**  At least 12 years old or 6th grade and up.

## GOODWILL INDUSTRIES (Long Beach)                                 ☀

(562) 435-3411 / www.goodwill.org                                              !
*800 W. Pacific Coast Highway, Long Beach*
(Exit San Diego Fwy [405] S. on Long Beach Blvd., R. on Pacific Coast Hwy.)

See GOODWILL INDUSTRIES (Santa Ana), in this section, for details. This facility also has a cafeteria that visitors may use. The minimum number for the tour is ten people.

**Hours:**  Tours are offered Mon. - Fri. between 9am - 2pm.

**Admission:** Free

**Ages:**  At least 8 years old.

## GOODWILL INDUSTRIES (Los Angeles)                                ☀

(213) 223-1211 / www.lagoodwill.org                                            !
*342 San Fernando Road, Los Angeles*
(From the Golden State Fwy [5], exit E. on Broadway, R. on Ave 20, which turns into San Fernando. From the Pasadena Fwy [110], going N. exit W. on Figueroa, L. on San Fernando. Going S. on 101, exit N. on Ave 26, L. on Figueroa, L. on San Fernando.)

See GOODWILL INDUSTRIES (Santa Ana), in this section, for details.

This facility doesn't have a shrink wrap machine on the premises, but it does have a computer recycling center, which techno kids will love. Note that a cafeteria, open to the public, is here also. A minimum number for this tour is five people.

**Hours:** Tours are offered Mon. - Fri. between 9am - 3pm.
**Admission:** Free
**Ages:** Preferably 5th graders and up.

## GUIDE DOGS OF AMERICA

(818) 362-5834 / e-mail:gdaguidedogs@earthlink.net
*13445 Glenoaks Boulevard, Sylmar*
(Going N. on Golden State Fwy [5], exit N. on Roxford St., R. on Glenoaks Blvd. Going E. on Foothill Fwy [210], exit S. on Roxford St., L. on Glenoaks Blvd.)

Guide Dogs of America is a center that breeds, raises, and trains Labrador Retrievers, Golden Retrievers, and German Shepherds for the blind. It is also a school that teaches blind men and women how to use guide dogs. These services are offered free of charge. Free tours, which last about an hour and a half, are given of the facility. First you'll watch a twenty-minute video that shows puppies frolicking, students getting to know their dogs, and testimonies on their lives being changed by being mobile. The film tugs at your heart. You'll walk past the administrative offices and hallways lined with photos of graduates and tour the dormitories where students stay for a month while receiving training. Note: If students are in residence, this part of the tour is bypassed. The best part, according to kids, is seeing the kennels and whelping bays of future guide dogs. Tip: Call first to see if there is a puppy litter because seeing them makes the field trips extra special for children. Tours are offered for groups of ten or more people with an advance registration of thirty days. Walk-in tours, for individuals, are also available.

Have you ever thought about being a foster parent - for a dog? Guide puppies, or future guide dogs, need temporary homes for their first eighteen months of life. If you are willing to teach them basic obedience, love them, and encourage them to be well socialized (sort of like raising children), call for more information. The heartbreak of separation from your pup comes in the knowledge that your family enabled a blind person to be mobile and independent. You're invited to attend the graduation ceremony of your dog and the student you've helped.

**Hours:** Group tours are given Tues. and Wed. at 10am and 2pm, by reservation only.
**Admission:** Free
**Ages:** Geared for fourth graders and up, but younger children may come, also.

## JET PROPULSION LABORATORIES

(818) 354-9314 / www.jpl.nasa.gov/faq/tours
*4800 Oak Grove Drive, Pasadena*

(Going N.W. on Foothill Fwy [210], exit S.E. on Foothill Blvd., go to end and turn L. on
Oak Grove Dr. Going S.E. on 210, exit S. on Gould Ave., L. on Foothill Blvd., go to end
and turn L. on Oak Grove Dr.)

"Space, the final frontier." JPL is a leading research and development center
for NASA, with 160 buildings on 177 acres of land. Its mission is to observe
earth, explore new worlds (via unmanned spacecraft) and send back pictures, and
ultimately, find the answer to the question, "Are we alone?" The twenty-minute
film *Welcome to Outer Space* shows spectacular pictures of stars, moons, and
various planet surfaces. It made my family aware of the incomprehensible
vastness of our universe. My boys were awed by this realization - I just felt very
small and insignificant. (Did you know that one light year translates as six
trillion miles?) The theater room/auditorium contains vivid photographs of star
fields and pillars of gas; replica models of the Voyagers; and a Voyager gold
record made for other intelligent life forms to listen to and learn about planet
earth. Press the display button and listen to a sampling of the recording. The
actual recording contains greetings in fifty-nine languages as well as photographs
of our culture, and sounds of music, the rain forest, a heartbeat, and much more.

The adjacent museum has replicas of early and modern space craft including
the 1958 Explorer, the Mars Pathfinder, the 1989 Galileo, and the Cassini, which
is currently on its way to Saturn. Our tour guide talked extensively about the
models and their actual missions. Although some of it was a bit too technical for
my kids (and me - I guess I'm no rocket scientist), we learned a lot.

Trekking over to another building, we watched Mission Control in action.
The viewing room allows you to see the Operations Chief tracking and (maybe)
listen to him communicate with spacecraft - it depends on what's going on. The
last stop is the assembly area where, again, depending on what is in process, you
might see actual spacecraft being assembled. Maybe you'll see a piece of history
in the making!

JPL facilities can only be seen on a tour. Individuals, up to ten people, may
come for a tour on the first and last Monday of each month from 1pm to 3pm.
Tours are given Monday through Friday from 10am to noon for groups of fifteen
to forty people. Tours are two hours long and require a lot of walking, although
the center is also wheelchair accessible. You are welcome to take pictures.
Reservations are required. Bring your space cadets here and have a blast! Note:
See the May Calendar section for details about the JPL's annual Open House.

    **Hours:**   See above information for details.
  **Admission:**   Free
     **Ages:**   7 years and up.

# LONG BEACH AIRPORT TOUR

(562) 570-2611                                                                                  !
*4100 Donald Douglas Drive, Long Beach*
(Exit San Diego Fwy [405] N. on Lakewood Blvd., L. on Donald Douglas Dr.)

Invite your preschool-aged kids (and older) to come to the airport and take a
pretend trip. (No minimum group number is required.) A customized, forty-five
to seventy-five-minute tour answers all their questions about what goes on here.

They'll see lots of different things, depending on the busyness of the airport. Kids can talk to skycaps, go to the boarding lounges, and walk through the screening area where monitors show items going through the conveyor. Be prepared to answer questions like, "How does it take pictures of the insides of things?" and "Why?"

The Observation Deck is great for, well, observing planes landing and taking off. Your trip might include a visit to the baggage area (you just never know what your child might find interesting), and for smaller groups of older kids, the Control Tower, where air-traffic controllers are at work. Kids might even get to see an Airport Fire and Rescue truck with all of its heavy-duty equipment. Lastly, they'll board a mock wooden aircraft and watch a video that simulates a flight. Afterwards, the kids are given little souvenirs of their "trip." Flexibility is a key for this high-flying tour.

**Hours:** Tours are available at your convenience, but preferably given Mon. - Fri. Two week reservations are needed.
**Admission:** Free
**Ages:** 4 years old and up.

## LOS ANGELES MEMORIAL COLISEUM AND SPORTS ARENA

(213) 748-6136 / www.stadia.com/lacoliseum                                          $$
*3939 S. Figueroa Street, Los Angeles*
(Exit Harbor Freeway [110] on Martin Luther King Blvd. It's on the corner of Martin Luther King and Figueroa.)

Host of two Super Bowls, two Olympics, the World Series, and many other exciting games, the L.A. Coliseum seems like more than just a building. The forty-five-minute walking tour shows you the training facilities, team locker rooms, press box, and the site that held the Olympic flame. Visitors are allowed to roam the track and fields, and dream of crowds cheering them on. All this happens as a guide explains the history of the events and the people that made them famous. This excursion is fascinating for young (and older) sports enthusiasts. Tip: Knowledge of sports' past glories can be helpful. (See CALIFORNIA SCIENCE CENTER and NATURAL HISTORY MUSEUM OF LOS ANGELES COUNTY, under the Museums section, for other attractions in the immediate area.)

**Hours:** Tours are given Tues., Thurs., and Sat. at 10:30am, noon, and 1:30pm.
**Admission:** $4 for adults; $3 for seniors; $2 for students with ID; $1 for children 11 years and under. Parking is $5 per vehicle.
**Ages:** 5 years and up.

## LOS ANGELES TIMES

(213) 237-5757
*202 W. 1st Street, Los Angeles*

(Exit Harbor Fwy [110] E. on 4$^{th}$ St., L. on Main St., L. on 1$^{st}$ St. Or, exit Santa Ana Fwy [101] S. on Alameda, R. on 1$^{st}$ St.)

Children, who are at least 10 years old or in the fifth grade, with journalistic tendencies will enjoy seeing how a newspaper is put together. The forty-five-minute tour goes through the editorial offices, where news from all over the world is gathered, written, and edited; the composing room, where news stories and advertisements are put together in page format; the library; the photography department; and the test kitchen, where recipes are tested for the Times' Food Section.

If your group is between ten and thirty-five people, you may take the above tour and/or a one-hour tour through the Olympic plant, where you'll pass through a pressroom, which is twice the size of a football field; the newsprint storage area, where robot-like automated vehicles carry rolls of newsprint weighing 2,500 pounds; the plate-making area, where newspaper pages go from photographic negatives to aluminum printing plates; and the mail room, where an automated distribution system takes newspapers from presses to the delivery trucks.

Kids (and adults) rarely realize what it takes, on a daily basis, to put together the internationally acclaimed newspaper that gets read with a cup of coffee every morning. Groups need to make reservations thirty days in advance.

**Hours:**  Tours for individuals are available Mon. - Fri. at 11:15am. No reservations are needed. Tours for groups between ten and thirty-five people are offered Mon. - Fri. at 10am and 1:15pm. Reservations are required.

**Admission:**  Free. Park for free at the Times garage at 213 S. Spring St.

**Ages:**  Children must be at least 10 years or older.

# NBC STUDIO TOURS

(818) 840-4444

*3000 W. Alameda Avenue, Burbank*

(Going E. on Ventura Fwy [134], exit S. on Pass Ave., L. on Alameda. Going W. on 134, exit, at Hollywood Way, R. on Alameda.)

Start your seventy-minute walking tour of the NBC Studios by, fittingly enough, watching TV. A six-minute film depicts the history of NBC, including clips of classic shows. You'll then walk through huge warehouses filled with props from past and present shows. It helps to be a fan of either *Days of Our Lives* or *The Tonight Show* since the tour emphasizes these particular shows. You might see, depending on availability, *The Tonight Show* set, the wardrobe department, a video demonstration of make-up, an NBC Sports Presentation, set construction, production studios, and maybe even a star or two. It's all contingent on what is going on at the studio that day, but it's usually a wonderful opportunity to see behind the scenes of a working studio. In the last room, a few visitors are asked to stand against a blue background. Via screen magic, on the video monitor they look like they are flying. Note: Free tickets for *The Tonight Show*, for ages 18 years and older, are available at the studio, so you can combine a behind-the-scenes tour with watching a live show all in the same day.

Be forewarned that the tickets go fast.

Bring a sack lunch and go to the JOHNNY CARSON PARK (look under the Great Outdoors section), right across the street from the studio.

**Hours:** Tours are given Mon. - Fri. between 9am - 3pm, every hour on the hour. Tours are also given on Sat. between 10am - 2pm during the summer.

**Admission:** $7 for adults; $3.75 for ages 5 - 12; children 4 years and under are free.

**Ages:** 6 years and up.

## PACIFIC STOCK EXCHANGE

(213) 977-4700

*233 South Beaudry, Los Angeles*

(Exit Harbor Fwy [110] W. on 3<sup>rd</sup> St. It's at the corner of 3<sup>rd</sup> and Beaudry.)

Do you have older kids who are studying Wall Street's ups and downs? The twelfth floor offers a viewing gallery that will give them a first-hand look at the action that makes our financial world go 'round.

**Hours:** The best time for watching the trading is between 7am and 1pm.

**Admission:** Parking is available in the building - $1 for every twenty minutes, or behind the Stock Exchange - $3.25 for all day.

**Ages:** 10 years and up.

## PARAMOUNT PICTURES

(323) 956-4848

*860 N. Gower Street, Hollywood*

(Exit Hollywood Fwy [101] W. on Santa Monica Blvd., L. on Gower.)

Paramount Pictures offers a two-hour, guided walking tour of its studio for ages 10 and up. This tour includes a historical and informative behind-the-scenes look of a major motion picture and television facility during its day-to-day operations. This is great insight for actor/director/producer "wannabes"!

**Hours:** Tours leave every half hour Mon. - Fri. between 9am - 2pm.

**Admission:** $15 per person.

**Ages:** 10 years and up.

## RIO VISTA WATER TREATMENT PLANT

(805) 297-1600 / www.clwa.org

*27234 Bouquet Canyon Road, Santa Clarita*

(Exit Golden State Fwy [5] E. on Valencia Blvd., L. on Bouquet Canyon Rd.)

Aaah - nothing like a drink of cold water to refresh your body. But how does the water magically appear in our tap? Take a one-hour tour of this plant to learn about the need for water, Santa Clarita Valley water sources, and water conservation. You climb up stairs and walk around to see filters, huge generators, and containers of liquid oxygen and the chemical ozone. Outside in the small conservation garden, see and learn about water-conserving plants and drip irrigation. The tour is bested suited for older children, but the docents, who are educators, will tailor the talk for whatever age and interest group is represented, including youth service organizations trying to meet merit badge requirements. Between ten to thirty participants comprise a group. Note: School buses to and from the plant will be provided for students within the Santa Clarita Valley school district.

**Hours:** Public tours are conducted Thurs. at 1pm and the third Sat. at 1pm. Groups may take tours Mon. - Fri. Call to make a reservation.
**Admission:** Free
**Ages:** 3rd graders and up.

## SEBASTIAN INTERNATIONAL'S RAIN FOREST
(800) 829-7322 / www.sebastian-intl.com
*6109 DeSoto Avenue, Woodland Hills*
(Exit Ventura Fwy [101] N. on DeSoto Ave., L. on Erwin. It's on the corner.)
 Sebastian International is a beauty care company that really cares about the environment and in particular, stopping the depletion of the rain forest. The corporate headquarters is in an angular, artsy building and has a room with displays pertaining to the rain forest. The Wall of Life has holes with objects in it, such as fake plants or animals, to pull out, look at, and read their descriptions. Its purpose is to demonstrate how species depend upon each other. Other exhibits include a big globe that shows how much of the earth used to be covered by rain forests compared to now-a-days, and a wall-size aquatic terrarium containing live fish and plants. Walk through the exhibits on your own, or take a guided, forty-minute tour, that includes some hands-on reinforcements. Use Sebastian's as a supplemental aid in teaching your kids about the rain forest.

**Hours:** Open to the public daily 9am - 3:30pm. Open for group tours, between ten to twenty-five people, on Mon., Wed., and Fri. between 9am - 3pm. Call for an appointment.
**Admission:** Free
**Ages:** 7 years and up.

## VAN NUYS AIRPORT TOUR
(818) 785-8838
*16700 Roscoe Boulevard, Van Nuys*
(Exit the San Diego Fwy [405] Fwy W. on Roscoe Blvd. The actual address is on Sherman Way, but this is where visitors meet for a tour.)
 Here's a way to stay grounded while touring an airport - take the ninety-minute bus tour of the Van Nuys airport. If you have a group of at least fifteen people, the airport will provide a bus at the 9:30am tour. All 11am tours must provide their own buses. There are several stops along the way, depending on what's available on the day of your visit. You will cruise along the service road and runway, and look inside hangers. Stops could include seeing the fire station, the radar facilities, boarding a Highway Patrol helicopter, a commercial plane, and/or smaller aircraft. As the kids watch planes land and take off, they'll learn

the history of the airport and gain some high-flying knowledge. Bring a sack lunch and eat at the observation site while watching the planes in flight.

**Hours:**     Tours are offered for groups of fifteen or more people, Mon. - Fri. at 9:30am and 11am. Reservations are required.

**Admission:** Free

**Ages:**      6 years and up.

## WARNER BROS. STUDIOS VIP TOUR                                ☼

(818) 954-1744 / www.wbsf.com/cmp/reserve.htm                    *$$$$$*
*4000 W. Warner Boulevard, Burbank*
(Going E. on Ventura Fwy [134], exit S. on Pass Ave., L. on Olive/Warner. Going W. on 134, exit at Hollywood Way, L. on Alameda., L. on Hollywood Way to Warner.)

Kids must be at least 9 years old to participate in this two-hour, walking tour that gives an intimate and educational look at how a studio works. Start off your tour in the waiting room which has props from *Casablanca* and *Batman*. What you see, exactly, depends on what is happening that day at the studio. You'll see numerous exterior sets from classic to current movies and television shows, interior sets (*E.R.* is filmed here), and the wardrobe department (and the miles of costume racks). You also might see the building of a set, or even filming in a sound studio. No matter what, this tour affords visitors a great opportunity to see what actually goes go on behind the scenes. It will also either take some of the romance out of picture-making, or make your child want to be involved in the process! Reservations are required.

**Hours:**     Tours, for no more than 12 people at a time, leave every half hour and are given Mon. - Fri. between 9am - 3pm.

**Admission:** $30 per person.

**Ages:**      9 years and up.

## BODEGA FUDGE AND CHOCOLATES                                   ☼

(714) 489-0708 / www.drbodega.com                                 !
*34255 Pacific Coast Highway, #106, Dana Point*                   ♨
(Exit San Diego Fwy [5] N. on Pacific Coast Highway.)

My middle son has never met a chocolate he didn't like, so he loved Bodega. This family-owned and operated retail store has received numerous awards for their fudge truffle confectionary concoctions. Groups of ten or more preschoolers through elementary-school-aged children are invited, along with their parents, to take a half-hour tour of the Bodega "factory." (Tours are also offered for senior citizens.) Visitors will learn how the chocolates are made, what makes the products kosher, how the machines run, and how quality control is maintained by making small batches at a time. Best of all, samples are given out. (You know how vital it is to taste test.) Children may also draw their initials, with chocolate, in a candy bar that they can take home to eat. The store sells seven different flavors of truffle bars, including rocky road and butter vanilla, plus chocolate truffle sauce and traditional English toffee. How sweet it is!

**Hours:** The store is usually open Tues. - Sun., 9am - 6pm. Tours are
given by appointment.
**Admission:** Free.
**Ages:** 4 years old to 6th graders.

# CRYSTAL CATHEDRAL OF THE REFORMED     ☼
# CHURCH IN AMERICA
(714) 971-4013 / www.crystalcathedral.org                    !
*4201 Chapman Avenue, Garden Grove*
(Exit Santa Ana Fwy [5] E. on Chapman Ave.)
This spectacular sanctuary, enclosed by 10,000 mirrored windows, is an
impressive place to stop. The windows are panes of glass that overlay a massive
amount of steel trestled framework. Kids (and adults) look up and around in
amazement at this church. Tour on your own, or take a forty-minute guided tour
which goes through the church and around the other facilities. Your tour guide
will explain how and why the cathedral was built, as well as offer information
about the different ministries going on here. The grounds are beautiful, with a
fountain between the office buildings and a large gift/book shop. Look down at
the concrete floor panels to read various Bible verses. The tower of the Cathedral
contains a fifty-two bell carillon that rings every fifteen minutes. Look in the
Calendar section for details on the spectacular shows, *Glory of Christmas* in
December, and *Glory of Easter* in March.
**Hours:** Tours are given Mon. - Sat. between 9am - 3:30pm. (Church
functions affect tour times.) Closed major holidays.
**Admission:** Donations are accepted.
**Ages:** 6 years and up.

# FULLERTON MUNICIPAL AIRPORT     ☼
(714) 738-6323                                               !
*4011 W. Commonwealth, Fullerton*
(Exit Artesia Fwy [91] or Santa Ana Fwy [5] N. on Magnolia to end, L. on
Commonwealth, 1 block to the Tower.)
Help navigate your kindergartner or older child on this one-hour walking
tour. A docent, who is a member of the Fullerton's Pilot Association, will show
your group, of at least five people, around the airport.
Tours are modified to fit your particular children's interests and questions. A
highlight is sitting in a small Cessna plane and in a helicopter owned by the Fire
Department. Small groups of older kids may visit the Control Tower - depending
on how busy the air traffic is. They'll get a bird's eye view of planes landing and
taking off, and see how radar works. The tour ends on a high note as souvenirs,
like plastic wings for future pilots, are given out.
**Hours:** Hours and days are flexible, although Mon. - Fri. is preferred.
**Admission:** Free
**Ages:** 5 years and up.

## GOODWILL INDUSTRIES (Santa Ana)                    ☀

(714) 547-6308 / www.ocgoodwill.org                    !
*410 N. Fairview Street, Santa Ana*
(Going E. on Garden Grove Fwy [22], exit S. on Fairview St. Going W. on 22, exit S. on Haster St., L. on Garden Grove Blvd., R. on Fairview St. From the Santa Ana Fwy [5], exit W. on 1st St., R. on Fairview St.)

Learn how to spread goodwill as you accompany your kids on a half-hour tour of this facility. You'll get an overview of what Goodwill Industries does by watching people, including many disabled people, being trained to work in several different areas. Watching assembly lines are interesting, as things are put together and packages are shrink wrapped. Kids will also see recycling in action, as old stuffed animals and toys get fixed up for someone else to play with and love. Check out the receiving dock where the donations are piled. Idea: Clean out your closets and have your kids bring their old toys and clothes to Goodwill on your tour date. Tip: Next door to the facility is a thrift store and an "as is" store where kids can hunt for treasure amidst the junk. (I think we bought as much as we brought!) There is no minimum number of people required for a tour, but a week's notice is requested. Also see GOODWILL INDUSTRIES, under this section, located in Los Angeles and Long Beach.

**Hours:**  Tours are given Tues. and Thurs. between 10am - 2pm.
**Admission:**  Free
**Ages:**  At least 7 years old.

## GOURMET LOLLIPOP CO.                                ☀

(714) 841-2000                                         $
*7351 Heil Avenue, Sweet J, Huntington Beach*
(Exit San Diego Fwy [405] S. on Beach Blvd., R. on Heil Ave. [near Gothard])

Suckers are born every minute; lollipops, however, are made here daily. The Gourmet Lollipop Company is a small, family-owned retail store that offers a wide variety of tasty candies, most of them made on the premises. It also sells candy molds, flavors, toppings, and everything else needed to make sweet treats. What a fun family activity!

One of the attractions here, besides the obvious of purchasing (and eating) candy, is taking a twenty-minute tour of the back room kitchen where the concoctions are created. You'll see and learn how the lollipops are made (there are forty-eight different flavors), from stirring in the ingredients to pouring the mixture in the mold, putting in the sticks, trimming off the excess (no sampling, sorry), and putting on the wrappers. Up to 1,500 lollipops can be made in one day - imagine how happy this makes your dentist! We also saw hand-decorated chocolate products and a variety of special order candy. The tour is short, sweet, and to the point. Tip: Grab bags for your group can be purchased ahead of time.

Afternoon candy-making classes are also offered for groups of at least ten or more participants who are at least 5 years old. The cost is $5 per person, as you make it and take it home, and reservations are required.

**Hours:** The store is open Tues. - Fri., 9am - 6pm; Sat., 9am - 4pm.
Candy-watching tours are given Wed., Thurs., and Fri. at 10am,
11am, and noon, for groups of at least 20 people. Candy-making
tours are given Wed., Thurs., and Fri. at 4pm and 5pm.
**Admission:** The candy-watching tour is free. The candy-making tour is $5
per person. Lollipops start as low as 10¢.
**Ages:** Children must be at least 5 years old for all tours.

## JOHN WAYNE AIRPORT TOUR

(949) 252-5219                                                                 !
*3151 Airway Avenue, Costa Mesa*
(Exit San Diego Fwy [405] S. on Bristol, L. on Red Hill, R. on Baker, L. on Airway.)

This one-hour tour is tailored toward the participants' ages. It shows how
the airport is similar to a small city, with different people doing different jobs,
each one making a contribution to the community. Kids will see the places that
the public has access to while learning about the history of the airport and some
basic information on aviation. Most docents are involved in aviation in one form
or another. The tour goes to the departure and arrival levels to see the various
activities that happen at each one, including baggage claims areas, etc. There are
huge windows all along the field, and a V-shape one jutting into it that offers a
wonderful view of the planes landing and taking off, planes being serviced, and
baggage being loaded and unloaded. A fun remembrance, like an airplane
coloring book, is given out at the end of the tour. Happy landings! A minimum
of ten people are needed for a tour.

**Hours:** Tours are available Mon. - Sat. between 10:30am - 3:30pm.
Reservations are required.
**Admission:** Free
**Ages:** 6 years and up.

## ORANGE COUNTY PERFORMING ARTS CENTER
## (tour)

(714) 556-2787 / www.ocartsnet.org/ocpac                                       !
*600 Town Center Drive, Costa Mesa*
(Exit San Diego Fwy [405] N. on Bristol St., R. on Town Center.)

All the world's a stage! Get a behind-the-scenes look at the 3,000-seat
Segerstrom Hall, where major symphony concerts, operas, ballets, and Broadway
musicals are presented. Take a tour, beginning at the ticket box office, through
the theater, and finishing up backstage. Tour routes may vary due to rehearsal
and performance schedules.

**Hours:** Guided tours are offered Mon., Wed., and Sat. at 10:30am.
Reservations are required for a group of 10 or more people.
Closed on some holidays.
**Admission:** Free
**Ages:** 8 years and up.

## TRINITY BROADCASTING NETWORK

(714) 832-2950 / www.tbn.org
*14131 Chambers Road, Tustin*
(Exit Santa Ana Fwy [5] S. on Tustin Ranch Rd., L. on Walnut Ave., L. on Franklin Ave., L. on Michelle Dr., L. on Chambers. Trinity owns several buildings in this section, but the tour starts in the main lobby.)

This forty-minute walking tour starts in the plush lobby of T.B.N. where token visitor gifts are handed out. (We like any kind of gifts!) The docent will take you to the prayer room on the third floor, a room that has cushioned benches around the perimeters and ornately-painted Biblical scenes on the ceilings and walls. In another building across the street, you'll see another prayer room with more of the colorful scenes from the Old and New Testament. The tour guide explains the scenes as well as the work that T.B.N. does. Walk down a hallway lined with photos of Paul and Jan Crouch - hosts of the *Praise the Lord!* program and co-founders of T.B.N. - along with many of their celebrity guests. The studio, where the program is shot before a live audience, holds the opulent living room setting that includes a chandelier, fireplace, and three huge stained glass pictures as part of the backdrop. Impressive! The guests waiting to appear are seated on purple and gold cushioned chairs (that look like thrones). There is, of course, lighting equipment and numerous cameras in here, too. Walk through the adjacent room filled with rows of telephones and computers for handling the multitude of calls. The tour ends back across the street in the T.B.N. library. I could live in this room. Oak shelves are filled with books that the public is welcome to use, but not check out. Oak panels reach to the ceiling. Plush carpeting, subdued lighting, and a fireplace complete the ambiance. Just off the library is a chapel with oak pews and another beautiful stained glass picture.

Tip: See TRINITY CHRISTIAN CITY INTERNATIONAL, under the Shows and Theaters section, for their other location which features three of their production movies.

**Hours:**     Tours are given Mon. - Fri. at 11am and 3pm.
**Admission:**     Free
**Ages:**     6 years and up.

## WYCLIFFE BIBLE TRANSLATORS

(714) 969-4600 or (714) 969-4630 / www.wycliffe.org
*19891 Beach Boulevard, Huntington Beach*
(Going S. on San Diego Fwy [405], exit S. on Beach Blvd. Going N. on 405, exit S. on Harbor Blvd., R. on Adams Ave., R. on Beach Blvd.)

"Then Jesus came to them and said, 'All authority in heaven and on earth has been given to me. Therefore go and make disciples of all nations. . .'"
(Matthew 28: 18-19) In order to teach peoples around the world about Jesus and for them to have a New Testament, communication is necessary. For communication to happen, languages must be studied, learned, and translated into writing - hence, Cameron Townsend founded Wycliffe Bible Translators. Even with all the available technology, it takes, on the average, fifteen years for a two-person team to produce grammar, a dictionary, and a New Testament in a

new language. There are over 6170 languages in the world today and less than half have God's written word!

Now that you know the mission, come explore the headquarters that enable linguists, missionaries, and countless helpers to spread the Good News - it's like taking a trip around the world! The tour is an hour and a half. An eleven-minute movie in the uniquely decorated Visitors' Center Room shows the purpose and realities of Wycliffe. One of the second story windows is a huge "family" tree done in stained glass. Also in this immediate area is Martin Luther's impressive German Bible, printed in 1652. Other displays here include pictures of the founder in Guatemala and a bookshelf filled with New Testaments translated into various languages. The hallways are filled with fascinating exhibits such as primitive shields, dolls, bowls, clothing, drums, a necklace of monkey teeth, feather headdresses, spears, baskets, statues, and pictures of tribal people from all parts of the earth. The artifacts are riveting, and introduce kids (and adults) to little-known cultures and customs. Downstairs is a life-size diorama depicting a portion of a primitive village that incorporates 3D props of a hut, large tree, canoe, and drum. You are invited to attend chapel afterward where visiting missionaries speak. Interested in becoming a part of Wycliffe's vision? Kids can volunteer to do something as simple as stuffing envelopes, and/or adopt a missionary by becoming a pen-pal.

**Hours:** Wycliffe is open Mon. - Fri. from 8:30am - 4:30pm. Drop-in tours are given Mon., Wed., and Fri. at 10am - no minimum number needed. Group tours are given by appointment and are geared for that particular age group.
**Admission:** Free
**Ages:** 6 years and up. (Tours are long for young children, but interesting.)

# RIVERSIDE PRESS ENTERPRISE
(909) 320-7875 - tours; (909) 684-1200 - general / www.pe.net
*3512 14th Street, Riverside*
(Exit Riverside Fwy [91] E. on 14th St.)

Students can get a behind-the-scenes look at the different aspects of how a newspaper is put together on this one-hour tour of the Enterprise. The tour covers the composing room, the newsroom, and telemarketing for the classified section. Lots of interesting facts about newspapers are given and students will be surprised at how much paper is used for just one edition. Tours are open to schools that have classes participating in a newspaper and education program, and for kids involved in the girl and boy scouts. Groups over twenty students will be divided into smaller groups. If the above sentences do not apply to you, but you would like a tour, call for information.

**Hours:** Two tours are given every Fri. during the school year.
**Admission:** Free
**Ages:** Must be in 3rd grade or above.

## ONTARIO INTERNATIONAL AIRPORT            ☽

(909) 937-2883 or (909) 937-2700                              !

*Vineyard Avenue, Ontario*

(From the San Bernardino Fwy [10], exit S. on Vineyard Ave. From the Pomona Fwy [60], exit N. on Grove Ave., R. on Airport Dr., R. on Vineyard Ave.)

Your youngsters can pretend to fly the friendly skies on their hour-and-a-half, guided tour of the airport. They will see the hustle and bustle as passengers arrive and depart; walk through a metal detector; see the baggage claim area and, find out, maybe, where luggage actually goes; learn about the people who work at an airport; watch planes land and take off; and more. Tours are given for school groups.

Hours:     Tours are given Mon. - Fri. between 9am - noon during the
           school year. Reservations are needed.
Admission: Free
Ages:      Children must be of kindergarten age or older.

## RILEY'S FARM - Living History            ☼

(909) 797-7534 or (909) 797-5145  / www.rileysfarm.com        $$$$

*12261 S. Oak Glen Boulevard, Oak Glen*

(Exit San Bernardino Fwy [10] L. on the Yucaipa exit, L. onto Oak Glen Rd. In about 6 miles, you'll reach the "Welcome to Oak Glen" sign. This farm is at the end of the windy road.)

The year is 1775. The Revolutionary War is imminent. Students can learn first hand how it felt to be involved with this radical war by participating in a four-hour re-enactment. Upon arrival, students are broken into "townships" to experience life in this era. Some of the activities they participate in include visiting a blacksmith, witnessing Colonel Fenton's attempt to bribe Sam Adams, encountering British soldiers, going through a court trial, training with arms (using fake muskets), and marching across the farm in a re-creation of Lexington's famous battle road. While these scenes are being re-enacted, kids become a part of the history - living it and learning it. A typical fare of lunch is also served: bread, cheese, fruit, and beef jerky.

If kids are studying the Civil War, Riley's also has a re-enactment tour for this pivotal time period that is just as engrossing and just as authentic as the Revolutionary War. Riley's Farm, set in the hills of Oak Glen, has a naturally rural ambiance with running streams, apple orchards, and dirt trails. Two-hour field trips are also offered, as well as other living history programs, plus old-fashioned Tavern dinners, and more. If your group is too small to meet the minimum number for a war re-enactment tour (thirty-five participants), ask about joining up with another group.

Hours:     Tours are offered April through November by reservation.
Admission: $12 per student; one adult free with every fifteen students.
Ages:      Geared for 5th graders and up.

## EAGLE MINING COMPANY

(760) 765-0036

$$

*North end of "C" Street, Julian*

(From San Diego Fwy [5] or Escondido Fwy [15], take 78 Fwy E. to Julian. 78 is Washington St. in Julian. From the 8 Fwy, take 79 N. to Julian, at 78 Jct. turn left on Main St. Go N. on "C" St. from Main St., in the heart of Julian. Follow the signs.)

Eureka! There's gold in them thar hills! Original mining equipment and a few old buildings make it look like time has stood still here. One of the buildings is a small museum/store with rock specimens, mining tools, and a glass-cased display of memorabilia from the early 1900's.

Trek through time on your one-hour, guided, walking tour through two genuine gold mines that were founded in 1870: the Eagle Mine and the connecting, High Peak Mine. My kids have studied about the forty-niners, but to actually go through a gold mine, walk on ore-cart tracks, see stone tunnels hand carved by picks, and learn the hardships of mining, really made a lasting impact on them. We saw the vein that the miners worked and realized, along with hundreds of other people both past and present, that gold wasn't easily obtainable. It took one ton of rock to yield a sugar-cube-size amount of gold! We went up two of the eleven levels in the mines, saw the hoist room where ore buckets were used as olden-day elevators, and experienced darkness so black that we couldn't see our hands in front of our faces. I admire the fortitude of our early engineers. It's interesting to note the difference between the earlier smooth rock tunnels that were hand drilled and the later jagged edges left from blasting with charges. Don't forget to look up at the amazing shaft tunnels (and duck your head)!

Outside, we saw the milling equipment used to crush rocks, and learned the tedious process of extracting gold. Try your hand at panning for gold (it's harder than it looks) in a "stocked" water trough on the premises, but warn kids that they can't keep the gold. And just remember: All that glitters isn't gold.

Julian is a quaint town with unique shops along Main Street. Your kids will enjoy a stop-off at the Julian Drugstore for an ice cream at its old-fashioned soda counter. The drugstore is located on the corner of Main and Washington Sts. Also see the JULIAN PIONEER MUSEUM under the Museums section.

**Hours:**     Open daily from 9am - 3pm.
**Admission:** $7 for adults; $3 for ages 5 - 16; children 4 years and under are free.
**Ages:**      4 years and up.

## HOTEL DEL CORONADO

(619) 435-6611 / www.hoteldel.com

$$$$

*1500 Orange Avenue, Coronado*

(Exit San Diego Fwy [5] W. on 75 and cross over the Coronado Bridge, L. on Orange Ave. The toll is $1 to Coronado and the return trip is free. If you are car pooling, cross the bridge using the right lane, at no charge.)

I don't normally mention hotels as an outing to take your children, but the Hotel Del is an exception. Just the outside of this architectural marvel will elicit a few "wow's" from your family. Built in 1888, it is one of the most luxurious and celebrated buildings in the world, as well as one of the largest wooden structures in existence. The dark, wooden interior of the hotel is equally impressive and ornate. Tell your kids that this was the first hotel in the world to have electric lights. If that doesn't turn them on, be a name dropper and mention that none other than Thomas Edison supervised the installation of the lights.

You may walk around the elegant hotel on your own, or sign up for a one-hour, guided tour. Your family will learn about the hotel's intriguing history, including the story of the haunted room. Note: Your children *will* ask if they can stay at the hotel. It's worth it if you can afford it, as each of the 692 rooms are unique, especially the 400 historic rooms. Rates start at $190 a night. The food is outstanding, the surroundings are lush, the pool is crystal clear, the stretch of beach is incredibly beautiful, the tennis courts are great, etc. Also see CORONADO BEACH HISTORICAL MUSEUM and HOTEL DEL CORONADO - TEA TIME (under separate listings in the Alphabetical Index).

**Hours:** Guided tours are offered Wed. - Sun., at 10am and 11am. Come during the week if possible, as weekends are usually crowded.

**Admission:** Guided tours are $10 per person (ages 3 years and up) if you are a hotel guest; $15 per person if not. Parking in the hotel lot costs $2.50 per hour; street parking, which is hard to come by, is free.

**Ages:** 6 years and up.

# NAVY SHIP'S OPEN HOUSE

(619) 437-2765 - ship tours; (619) 556-7359 - naval base tour
*U.S. Navy Pier of Harbor Drive, near Broadway on the Embarcadero, San Diego*
(Going S. on San Diego Fwy [5], exit W. on Ash St., L. on 4$^{th}$, R. on Broadway, L. on Harbor. Going N. on 5, exit S. on 6$^{th}$ Ave., R. on Broadway, L. on Harbor.)

The Navy offers a unique opportunity for the public to tour a destroyer, frigate, amphibious cruiser, submarine, aircraft carrier, or other naval craft, as well as the Navy base. There are two types of ship tours offered: One is a forty-five-minute tour given for a minimum group of twenty, maximum of 100. Groups must sign up two weeks in advance. The other tour is given on weekends for the general public to come on board and explore - no reservations are needed. The type of ship you actually see on either tour depends on what is in the harbor on the day you plan to visit. A military tour guide will take you through the ship and answer any questions, and we all know that kids always have plenty of those. Note that neither tour is stroller/wheelchair accessible and that there are incline ladders to climb. (Don't wear dresses or skirts, ladies!) A favorite room is the combat information center, where radar equipment is on display. Please call first to make sure a ship is available, and to find out which kind it is. Aircraft carriers are on the north island and are often on deployment, so call for availability.

The Navy will provide a guide and van for a group of up to six people to take a thirty-minute "windshield" tour of the base. A group of more than six passenger must provide their own vehicle and the guide will ride with them.

**Hours:** Groups tours are given Tues. and Thurs. between 9am - 3pm. Public tours are given Sat. and Sun. from 1pm - 4pm. Tours of the base are given during the week with advanced notice.

**Admission:** Free

**Ages:** 5 years and up.

## SAN DIEGO UNION-TRIBUNE

(619) 221-7215 - tour; (619) 299-3131 - general

*350 Camino de la Reina, San Diego*

(Going W. on Mission Valley Fwy [8], exit E. on Hotel Cir. N., which turns into Camino de la Reina. Going E. on 8, exit E. on Hotel Cir. S., R. on Hotel Cir. N., which turns into Camino de la Reina.)

A one-hour tour to see how a newspaper is put together may be just the thing to spur your child's interest in journalism. Tours may include walking through the newsroom to see reporters and editors at work, seeing the production area where composing and paste-up work is done, and learning about circulation, advertising, and numerous other newspaper components. Tours are given to groups between twenty to thirty-five students and require advance registration. If you, as an individual, would like to take the tour, you may join in with a pre-registered group tour that is usually comprised of students. The facilities are wheelchair accessible.

**Hours:** Tours are given Tues., at 10:30am and 1:30pm; Wed. - Thurs., at 10:30am.

**Admission:** Free. A school group may be charged a minimal fee simply to cover the cost of materials which are sent to the school before the visit.

**Ages:** Children must be 9 years and up.

## ST. VINCENT DE PAUL VILLAGE

(619) 233-8500 / www.neighbor.org

*1501 Imperial Avenue, San Diego*

(Going S. on San Diego Fwy [5], exit W. on Imperial Ave. Going N. on 5, exit N. on Crosby St., L. on 25th St., L. on Imperial Ave. From Escondido Fwy [15], exit E. on Imperial Ave.)

". . . Give me your tired, your poor, your huddled masses yearning to be free. . ." (Part of a poem that is engraved on the pedestal of the Statue of Liberty.) St. Vincent's Village is a "network of residential centers providing a continuum of care to over 2,000 men, women, and children daily." This incredible, state-of-the-art, self-contained facility aids the poor and homeless in very practical ways. It offers them a new lease on life with homes, meals, life-skills programs, counseling, and medical programs.

A one-hour tour takes your group of ten people through most of the facility - the lobby, office, kitchen courtyard, residential buildings, food storage, and medical buildings. This is quite an operation, so a behind-the-scenes tour is eye opening. If you are seeking to instill compassion in your children and/or if they are looking for a venue to help those less fortunate, a visit to this village is a good starting point. Coming here will make an indelible mark upon hearts because the homeless are then no longer faceless or nameless, but real people with real needs.

**Hours:** Tours are offered Mon. - Fri. at 9am, 11am, 1pm and 3pm. Please call at least a week ahead of time to reserve a tour date and time.

**Admission:** Free

**Ages:** 8 years and up.

# TRANSPORTATION

Take a journey with your child by plane, train, automobile, ship, carriage, etc., for a truly "moving" experience together. Note: There are numerous boating companies up and down the coastline. I've mentioned only a few, giving just some pertinent facts. Anchors away!

## ALFREDO'S
(562) 434-6121

Alfredo's has seventeen concessions throughout Southern California, along the beach and in many parks. They rent kayaks - $5 an hour for single, $15 an hour for double; pedal boats - $15 a half hour; as well as bikes, skates, and boogie boards. The boat rentals are available usually daily in the summer, and on weekends only the rest of the year. Call for their locations.

## THE CALIFORNIAN                                                         ☼
(800) 432-2201 / www.californian.org                                    $$$$$

Set sail in this full-scale re-creation of the 1848 vintage *Revenue Cutter* tallship, once one of the fastest ships of its kind. It's magnificent to look at. The primary purpose of the *Californian* is to serve students and adults as a unique training vessel. On board the ship, participants will learn maritime history, the art of sailing tallships, and how shipmates must work together as a team.

The *Californian* offers three programs. In the Sea Chest program, for fourth through eighth graders, a container that looks like an old sea chest is sent to the classroom about a month before the sail date. The chest holds a workbook for each student, a teacher's guide (thank goodness!), a video tape of the ship's sailing adventures, an audio tape of sea chanteys, and line for students to practice knot-tying techniques. On the sail date, the student crew receives dockside orientation before their three-hour tour; that's right - their three-hour tour. Hoisting all the sails takes quite a bit of time. Once out at sea, students attend twenty-minute workshops at each of the three stations: One emphasizes what a sailor's life was like in the 1850's; a second teaches basic navigation skills and how to chart a ship's course; and the third allows attendees to participate in actually sailing the ship, by raising sails, steering, etc. Tip: Bring snacks on board and have lunch waiting for the kids afterwards! A minimum of thirty-five students and maximum forty-five students are required for this cruise. Smaller groups can be combined together to reach the necessary numbers.

The Cadet Cruise is a five-day experience for ages fifteen to nineteen years. Program topics include earth sciences, environmental awareness, California history, applied sciences, and, of course, learning how to sail a tallship. Besides receiving hands-on learning on these topics, the cadet crew members will learn teamwork and responsibility, and how to sleep next to someone who might snore. A group of sixteen students is required for this cruise.

The Tallship Day Sail program is a four-hour excursion where the public can just enjoy the ride, or participate in sailing the ship - hauling on lines to raise sails, taking a turn at the ship's helm to steer the ship, etc. Passengers will also learn the history of tallship vessels and all about the life of a sailor. Lunch is provided on board. The recommended age for this cruise is at least ten years old.

Note: About ten days a year the *Californian* docks at a harbor and is open to the public, for free, to board and simply look around. Guided tours are not given.

**Hours:** Call for program dates. The *Californian* docks at Oxnard, Marina del Rey, Long Beach, Dana Point, Oceanside, San Diego, and Chula Vista at various times throughout the year.

**Admission:** The Sea Chest program is $38 per person; the Cadet Cruise is $495 per person; and the Tallship Day Sail is $75 per person.

**Ages:** 10 years and up; certain programs have other age requirements.

## METROLINK

(800) 371-5465 / www.metrolinktrains.com                    *$$*
*Serves almost all of Southern California*

The metro commuter train links several counties in Southern California, from Ventura, to San Bernardino, to the Antelope Valley (and everything in between). Dial the above phone number for specific route information. It's a fun excursion and saves the hassle of driving in traffic.

**Hours:** The rail runs Mon. - Fri. from early morning until evening. Only the San Bernardino - Santa Clarita/Antelope Valley line runs on Sat.

**Admission:** Varies, depending on starting point and destination.

**Ages:** All

## VOYAGES OF REDISCOVERY

(800) 401-7835 / www.ladywashington.org;                    *$$/$$$*
www.hawaiianchieftain.com                                    *$$*

The *Lady Washington* is a faithful replica of the first American square rigged ship to round Cape Horn and come to the Pacific Northwest. The *Hawaiian Chieftain* is an authentic replica of a typical European merchant trade ship, similar to those used by Spanish explorers in the late eighteenth century. Both ships set sail from their base in northern California and travel together to our southern harbors for a few months in the winter. They will dock in Ventura, Marina Del Rey, Long Beach, and San Diego, periodically during the months of December, January, and February. Boarding the ship, kids can experience first hand the life of sailors, coastal explorers, traders, missionaries, and Native Americans. This is accomplished by a dockside tour or sailing expedition. In preparation for either tour, Voyages will send the class a packet of suggested pre-trip activities and a bibliography. Costumed, docent educators are the instructors on the tours, both of which are geared specifically for fourth and fifth graders.

At the one-hour dockside tour, students visit each of three learning stations. The first one teaches line handling and the life of a sailor; the second, navigation and the work of officers; and the third, the history of the many cultures along the coast over 200 years ago. The three-hour expedition incorporates the same kind of "classes" as in the dockside tour, as well as actually setting and trimming the sails, steering the ship, and using traditional navigation tools. Kids will be learning mathematics, cartography, astronomy, and other sciences, and most of all, how to work together as a team.

Programs run rain or shine, just like sailors of old, who sailed (almost) no matter what the weather conditions were like. Each tour must have a minimum of thirty participants (this number includes chaperones and teachers) for either ship, with a maximum of forty-five, or ninety, for both ships. Smaller groups may be able to share their tour with another group.

Individuals and families wishing to explore the ships may do so in two ways. One is by going sailing on a three-hour, battle re-enactment trip led by period-dressed crew members. The passengers are spectators as the two ships try to out maneuver each other by sailing furiously. A highlight is the firing of the cannons. (The cannons don't use real ammunition, just lots of noise and smoke.) The second opportunity to explore the ships is offered when they are docked. A formal tour is not given, but docents are on hand to answer questions. Whatever you choose to do, come sail the high seas of adventure!

**Hours:** All tours take place from the above mentioned ports during the months of December through February. Dockside tours for school groups are given Mon. - Fri. at 9am, 10am, and 11am. Sailing expeditions for groups are offered once a day, Mon. - Fri. from 12:30pm - 3:30pm. Battle re-enactments are conducted Sat. from 2pm - 5pm; Sun. from 10am - 1pm and 2pm - 5pm. Dockside exploration for individuals and families is available Mon. - Fri. between 3pm - 6pm; Sat. between 10am - 1pm.

**Admission:** Dockside tours for groups are $5 per participant. Sailing expeditions are $30 per participant. Battle re-enactments are $40 for adults; $25 for children 12 years and under. Dockside exploration for individuals is $7 for a family (i.e. immediate family members), or $3 for adults; $2 for seniors and students; $1 for children 12 years and under.

**Ages:** 4th and 5th graders for tours; 6 years and up for battle re-enactments; 3 years and up for dockside exploration for families.

# AMTRACK - ONE-DAY TRAIN RIDES
(800) 872-7245 / www.amtrak.com                      $$$$
*800 North Alameda Street, Union Passenger Station, Los Angeles*
(Exit Santa Ana Fwy [101] N. on Alameda.)

A train ride is a treat for any age child! The Union Station in Los Angeles is a wonderful starting place for this exciting journey. The station is grandly old, and with its high ceiling, arched doorways, marble floors, and wood and leather seats (and a little imagination), it is a nostalgic and romantic reminder of the era when train travel was the only way to go. By incorporating a train trip into your day's excursion, whether it's simply to a park, to a special restaurant, or to a major destination, you make your outing and time together more memorable. The train cars have bathrooms and most have snack cars, too. Note: Amtrack leaves from various other cities.

The prices quoted are for unreserved round trips; reserved seats are at least an additional $7 per rider. Reserved summer rates are slightly higher. Always ask for special promotions. The age definition for children is 2 through 15 years. Listed below are just six Amtrak routes, departing from L.A. and arriving at various cities. Call for destinations closer to you, and please always call for current departure times and prices:

L. A. -        Fullerton; a thirty-three-minute ride that ends five miles north of Knott's Berry Farm.
           Departs at 8:30, 10:30, etc. Adults are $13; children are $6.50.


L. A. -        Anaheim; a forty-two-minute ride, where you can walk across the street to Katella Street, and take a commuter rail to Disneyland, or the Disneyland Hotel.
           Departs at 8:45, 10:45, etc. Adults are $14; children are $7.


L. A. -        Santa Ana; a fifty-two-minute ride.
           Departs at 6:45, 8:45, 10:45, etc. Adults are $16; children are $8.


L. A. -        San Juan Capistrano; a one-hour and fifteen-minute ride. (It lets off two short blocks from Mission San Juan.)
           Departs at 6:45, 8:45, 10:45, etc. Adults are $20; children are $10.


L. A. -        San Clemente; a one-hour and twenty-six-minute ride.
           Departs at 8:45. Adults are $22; children are $12.


L. A. -        San Diego; a two-hour and forty-five-minute ride.
           Departs at 8:45, 10:45, etc. Adults are $40; children are $20.
    **Ages:**  All

# ANGELS FLIGHT RAILWAY
(800) 371-5465 or (213) 626-1901                                                      $
*Bunker Hill, Los Angeles*
(Exit Hollywood Fwy [101] S. on Alameda St., R. on 3$^{rd}$ St. It's between 3$^{rd}$ and 4$^{th}$ Sts., on Hill.)
    A ride on the world's shortest railway is one of those cool little excursions that kids enjoy. Starting at the restored station house, with Victorian carvings, the funicular (new word for the day) takes passengers up and down the steep hill. Go for the brief thrill of it, or go shopping at the bottom of the hill. Add this "trip" onto another local attraction.
    **Hours:**  Open daily from 6:30am to 10pm.
**Admission:**  One-way fare is 25¢.
    **Ages:**  All

# BELMONT PIER
(562) 434-6781                                                                    $$$
*29 39$^{th}$ Place, Long Beach*
(Exit Long Beach Fwy [710] E. on Broadway, R. on Redondo Ave., L. on Ocean Blvd., R. on 39$^{th}$ Pl.)

Take a whale-watching cruise, available January through March.

**Admission:**   During the week, fare is $15 for adults for a three-hour tour; $12 for children 12 years and under. Call for weekend prices.

## BEVERLY HILLS TROLLEY

(310) 285-2551                                                                                    *$$*

*Departs from the corner of Rodeo Drive and Dayton Way, Beverly Hills*

(Exit San Diego Fwy [405] E. on Santa Monica Blvd., R. on Rodeo Dr.)

This is the best bargain in Beverly Hills! If you are in the area and want to give your kids a taste of the posh lifestyle, at an affordable price to you, hop on board a trolley for your choice of mini-adventures. A forty-minute Sites and Scenes narrated tour shows riders some of the most famous sights in Beverly Hills, including a few celebrity homes, some of the high-priced boutiques, and the elegant hotels. The ninety-minute Art and Architecture tour points out some of the most significant art and architectural locations around town, including City Hall, galleries, Creative Artists Agency, Museum of Television and Radio, and more.

**Hours:**   The Sites tour usually runs July through Labor Day and the latter part of December, Tues. - Sat. every hour from noon - 5pm. It runs May through June, and September through November on Sat. only on the hour from noon - 4pm. The Art tour is offered July through New Year's on Sat. at 10:30am. All tours are canceled if it is raining.

**Admission:**   $5 for adults per tour; $1 for children 11 years and under. Tickets are available from the trolley driver on a first come, first serve basis.

**Ages:**   5 years and up.

## CALIFORNIA AQUATICS

(562) 431-6866 - office; (562) 434-0999 - beach #                                *$$$*

*Bayshore Avenue and 2nd Street, Long Beach*

(Take San Diego Fwy [405] or San Gabriel River Fwy [605] to 22 Fwy W. Exit S. on Studebaker Rd., R. on Westminster, turns into 2nd. Bayshore is just over second bridge.)

Kayak rentals are $5 to $7 an hour, and peddle boats are $15 an hour. California Aquatics also offers weekend water field trips for the family. Another option is to sign up to become a member of the Snorkeling By Kayak Club. The $35 membership fee is good for four years, entitling the card bearer and family members (best suited for junior high schoolers and up) to rent kayaks, peddle boats, wetsuits, and skindiving equipment for only $10 per day! There is another Aquatics location on Appian Way, by Mother's Beach.

**Hours:**   Open weekends only in the winter. Call for all hours.

**Ages:**   5 years and up.

## GONDOLA AMORE

(310) 376-6977                                                                                    *$$$$$*

*260 Portofino Way, at the Portofino Hotel and Yacht Club, Redondo Beach*
(Take Artesia Fwy [91] as it turns into Artesia Blvd., turn S. on Pacific Coast Highway, R.
on Beryl, which turns into Portofino Way. Your gondolier will meet you in the lobby.)
O solo mio! This one-hour gondola cruise is a unique way to see the
Redondo harbor and shoreline. During the day you'll also see Catalina Island (on
a clear day), sailboats, waterfowl, and maybe a few seals. Nighttime rides bring
about their own magic (and romance). The two gondolas, operated by the owner
and by lifeguards, seat up to four people, have canopies for privacy, and small
twinkling lights around the boat and canopies. Amore provides blankets, as the
ocean air can get chilly even on a summer night, cups for your drinks, fresh fruit,
and bread and cheese. Your list of things to bring includes jackets, a music
cassette, beverages, and your camera. Tips: Before or after your cruise, check out
the nearby Cheesecake Factory for scrumptious food and/or walk around the
pier. (Look up REDONDO BEACH PIER under the Piers and Seaports section.)
**Hours:** Open daily from noon - 9pm. Reservations are required. Note:
Holiday seasons book quickly.
**Admission:** $75 for two people; $10 for each additional person. Note: AAA
members receive a substantial discount.
**Ages:** 4 years and up.

## GONDOLA GETAWAY
(562) 433-9595 / www.clever.net/gondolas
*5437 E. Ocean Boulevard, Long Beach*
(Exit San Diego Fwy [405] S. on Cherry Ave., L. on Ocean Blvd.)
Long Beach, California is transformed into Venice, Italy when you take your
child on a gondola ride. I know this attraction is thought of as a romantic
excursion, and it is. It is also a wonderful treat for your child. Step into a
Venetian gondola and for one hour, gently slip in and out through the waterways
and canals of Naples. Your gondolier will serenade you with Italian music,
regale you with interesting tales, or quietly leave you alone. After our kids plied
my husband and I with questions about the possibility of sharks and whales, they
settled down to enjoy the ride and look at the incredible homes along the
waterfront. Christmas time is particularly spectacular, as many of the houses are
decked out with lights, animated figures, etc. Make reservations for this time
period far in advance.
Bread, cheese, salami, and a bucket of ice are provided, as is a blanket for
the colder nights. Bring your own liquid refreshment. Your child will now be
dreaming of visiting a tiny little town far away in a boot-shaped country. Ciao!
**Hours:** Open daily for cruises from 11am - 11pm. Suggested reservations
are two weeks in advance.
**Admission:** Gondolas carry two to six people - $55 for the first two
passengers; $10 for each additional person. The Carolina carries
eight to fourteen people - $17 per person. Fleet cruises carries
twenty to fifty-six people - $15 per person.
**Ages:** 4 years and up.

# HYDROSPHERE ☼

(310) 230-3334 / www.hydrosphere-expedition.com  *$$$$$*

*Long Beach*

Looking for adventure with a bite to it? Hydrosphere was founded by a former Cousteau Society diver and documentary film producer. On board the *Pacific Explorer,* you have the choice of going on several expeditions, the most unique one being the Shark Tagging and Research Expedition, off the coast of Catalina Island. Suited-up in a wetsuit and lowered into the ocean in a four-feet deep, open-top snorkel cage is the way you'll observe marine life while in a protected environment. The adventure takes a predatorial turn when blue, and sometimes mako sharks, nudge the cage, drawn by chum thrown out by Hydrosphere's operators. The sharks can't get to you, but that fact doesn't stop your heart from pounding wildly. Oftentimes, the sharks are brought on board for closer observation, an in-depth lesson, and/or tagging purposes. Other excursions, also educational in nature, include Sea Lion Observations, Catalina Island Adventure, and more.

**Hours:** Call for a schedule of dates and times.

**Admission:** Weekday prices for the Shark Expedition are $119 for adults; $99 for ages 8 - 18. The Sea Lion Observation is $79 for adults; $59 for college students and ages 8 - 17. All weekend prices are higher. Rent a mask and snorkel for $5; a child's wetsuit for $5. Adult wetsuits may be rented elsewhere. Reservations for any expedition is required.

**Ages:** 8 years and up.

# LONG BEACH MARINE INSTITUTE ◗

(714) 540-5751 / www.longbeachmarineinst.com  *$$$*

*5857 Appian Way, Long Beach*

(Take San Diego Fwy [405] or San Gabriel River Fwy [605] to 22 Fwy W. Exit S. on Studebaker, R. on Westminster, R. on Appian Way, near the bridge, first L. in the Marina lot parking, on the Sea Explorer Base.)

"The Long Beach Marine Institute, formerly the Newport Institute of Oceanography, is an association of researchers and educators dedicated to bringing marine field research into the classroom and the classroom into the field." (A quote from the institute's brochure.) L.B.M.I. offers a myriad of different programs to encourage hands-on learning about marine life and their habitats. Most programs are offered for groups of twenty-five or more. If your group number is smaller, the L.B.M.I. workers will hook you up with another group. Besides going on the guided kayak tours, snorkeling excursions, and guided tidepool tours, being on board the *Conqueror* is a main attraction. This ninety-foot, ship-shape vessel is the host and means of transportation for several field trips.

The three-hour Sea Creature Trawl is a popular expedition. After a slide presentation and boat orientation, set sail for adventure. Organisms from the sea floor are gathered (by use of a trawl) on board to be inspected and sorted through. Kids love being able to put their hands in this fascinating pile of gunk to find "treasures." They can also examine their findings under a microscope. Combine the Sea Creature Trawl with the Marine Mammal Safari (more than just a whale-watching cruise) for only a few dollars more. Another special outing combines a sleep-over on the boat with the Sea Creature Trawl, and a morning kayak trip in the back bay. Life doesn't get any better than this!

**Hours:** Call for times for various excursions.

**Admission:** Prices range from $7 per person for a tidepool tour to $14 for a Sea Creature Trawl to $69 for the sleep over, etc.

**Ages:** 4 years and up, depending on the activity.

## LONG BEACH SPORT FISHING

(562) 432-8993                                                                      *$$$$*

*555 Pico Avenue, Long Beach*

(Exit Long Beach Fwy [710] W. on Anaheim St., E. on Santa Fe Ave., L. on 9th St., which turns into Pico.)

Fishing and whale-watching cruises (January through March) are offered here.

**Admission:** $12 for adults for the two-and-a-half hour whale-watching cruise; $9 for children 12 years and under.

## LOS ANGELES HARBOR CRUISES

(310) 831-0996                                                                      *$$$*

*Ports O' Call Village, berth 78, San Pedro*

(Exit Harbor Fwy [110] S. on Harbor Blvd. and follow the signs.)

Enjoy a one-hour cruise of the inner and outer harbor, past supertankers, cruise ships, a Coast Guard station, Terminal Island, a Federal Prison, and Angels Gate Lighthouse. Two-hour coastline cruises along the Palos Verdes Peninsula, and whale-watching cruises are also available.

**Hours:** One-hour cruises depart from the Village Boat House on the hour, Mon. - Fri., noon - 4pm; Sat. - Sun. and holidays, noon - 5pm. Two-hour cruises depart on the weekends at 11:30am, 1:30pm, and 3:30pm. Closed Thanksgiving and Christmas.

**Admission:** One-hour cruises are $6 for adults; $3 for ages 6 - 12; children 5 years and under are free. Two-hour cruises are $10 for adults; $5 for ages 6 - 12.

## MARINA BOAT RENTALS

(310) 574-2822 / www.boats4rent.com                          *$$$$*

*13719 Fiji Way, Marina del Rey*

(Take Marina Fwy [90] to the end, L. on Mindanao, L. on Lincoln, R. on Fiji Way.)

Located in FISHERMAN'S VILLAGE (see the Piers and Seaports section), Marina Boat Rentals includes kayaks - $10 per hour for a single, $15 an hour for a double; sailboats - $25 an hour for a fourteen footer; motor boats - $30 an hour for a six-passenger boat that doesn't leave the harbor, and $55 an hour for a six-passenger boat that does; and electric boats - $45 an hour.

**Hours:** Open in the summer daily from 9am - 9pm. Open the rest of the year daily from 9am - 6pm or so, depending on the weather.

**Admission:** Prices listed above.

**Ages:** 4 years and up.

## METRO RAIL

(213) 626-4455 / www2.mta.net

*Los Angeles*

This rail mode of transportation is a work-in-progress, but the rail lines that are complete make going to a destination an adventure. The Blue Line runs north and south between Long Beach and downtown Los Angeles. Trains run every ten minutes. The Green Line runs east and west, connecting Norwalk, so far, to El Segundo. Trains run alongside, but separate from, the 105 freeway. The Red Line currently runs from Union Station in downtown Los Angeles to Wilshire/Alvarado. Eventually, it will go through Hollywood and out to the San Fernando Valley. The advantages of riding the rails are numerous, such as it's inexpensive, you don't have to fight traffic, you don't have to try to find a parking spot, and kids consider it a treat.

**Hours:** Trains usually run daily from 6am - 11pm.

**Admission:** $1.25 on up, depending on your route.

**Ages:** All

## SHORELINE VILLAGE CRUISES

(562) 495-5884

*401 East Shoreline Drive, Long Beach*

(Take Long Beach Fwy [710] to the end, E. on Shoreline Dr.)

Enjoy a forty-five-minute cruise through Queen's Way Bay, past the QUEEN MARY, SCORPION, and LONG BEACH AQUARIUM. Whale-watching cruises are also available the end of December through March.

**Hours:** Summertime departures are daily at 1pm, 2pm, 3pm, and 4pm. Wintertime departures are usually weekends only.

**Admission:** $6 for adults for the harbor cruise; $3 for children 12 years and under. $15 for adults for the two-and-a-half whale-watching cruise; $8 for children.

**Ages:** 4 years and up.

## SPIRIT CRUISES

(310) 548-8080

*Berth 77, Ports O' Call, San Pedro*

(Exit Harbor Fwy [110] S. on Harbor Blvd. and follow the signs.)

Cruise through the main channels and see the sights! Reservations are suggested.

**Hours:** Forty-five-minute cruises are offered on Sat. and Sun. One-and-a-half-hour cruises are offered daily May through October; weekends only the rest of the year.

**Admission:** $6 for adults for the shorter cruise; $3 for children 12 years and under.

**Ages:** 5 years and up.

## U.C.L.A. MARINA AQUATIC CENTER

(310) 823-0048 / www.saonet.ucla.edu/recreate                *$$$*

*14001 Fiji Way, Marina Del Rey*

(Take the Marina Fwy [90] to the end where it turns into the Mariana Exwy, L. on Mindanao Wy., L. onto Admiralty Wy., R. on Fiji Wy.)

Chart your own course to explore the marina! Go windsurfing, kayaking, sailing, rowing, canoeing, etc., via the aquatic center. You can either rent a particular boat for an hour or so, or sign up for a class. At various times throughout the year, an experienced naturalist offers a four-hour natural history cruise on board the sixty-foot research vessel, *Sea World U.C.L.A.* Learn about the animals, and plants, that live in the Santa Monica Bay, and what can be done to take better care of them. Year-round classes are offered, such as oceanography, scuba diving, etc. The summer youth programs make a big splash with kids.

**Hours:** Open Tues. - Fri., 6am - 9am, and 1pm - 7pm; Sat. - Sun., 6am - 7pm. Hours vary, depending on the season, so please call ahead of time.

**Admission:** Windsurfing, kayaking, and canoeing rentals are $10 an hour; sailboats are $12; rowboats are $8. Become a member for $45 a year, which allows you discounts on rentals and access to any of the classes.

**Ages:** Most classes are geared for older children. Although kayaks are single-seaters, kids can join in on canoes, sailboats, and rowboats.

## THE VELODROME

(310) 516-3907

*1000 E. Victoria Street, Carson*

(Exit Artesia Freeway [91] S. on Avalon Blvd. L. on Victoria St. The entrance is a right turn at Tamcliff Ave. At Cal. State University at Dominguez Hills.)

The 1984 Olympics brought many good things to Los Angeles, including the Velodrome. This bicycle racing track is still used for this purpose, for a wide variety of age groups. It is also a great place for skateboarding and my favorite sport, swap meeting. Call for a schedule of bicycle and skateboard classes, demonstrations, and competitions. (Classes and competitions are not available in the swap meet category, though. Oh well!)

**Hours:** Call for hours.

**Admission:** Depends on the event.

**Ages:**   Depends on the event.

# YOUNG EAGLES PROGRAM (Lancaster)   ☼

(805) 940-1709  / www.youngeagles.com                                    !
*4555 W. Avenue G, Fox Field, Lancaster*                                 ♨
(Exit Antelope Valley Fwy [14] W. on Ave. G and drive for about 3 miles.)
   See YOUNG EAGLES PROGRAM (Pacoima), under this section, for
details. Reservations are needed.
   **Hours:**   Usually offered on the second Sat. of the month, starting at 8am.
   **Admission:**   Free
   **Ages:**   8 - 18 years.

# YOUNG EAGLES PROGRAM (Pacoima)   ☼

(818) 725-4AIR (4247) - Pacoima; (800) 843-3612 - national number  /      !
www.youngeagles.com
*12653 Osborne Street, Whiteman Airport, Pacoima*                         ♨
(Exit the Golden State Fwy [5] E. on Osborne, past San Fernando Rd., turn L.)
   "They will soar on wings like eagles." (Isaiah 40:31) I think all kids (and
adults) dream of flying, and the Young Eagles Program helps those dreams
become a reality. Young Eagles is a national program sponsored by the E.A.A.
(Experimental Aircraft Association), who desire to introduce children to the joy
of aviation. There are several Young Eagle chapters throughout Southern
California who offer aviation camps, educational programs, etc., as well as an
opportunity to actually fly (for free!) in an airplane. Kids, between the ages of 8
and 18 years, are invited to participate, one time only, in this unique flying
experience. Please remember that everyone here is volunteering their time,
including pilots, so be patient with a process that can take up to two hours.
Although the following information is fairly standard, call the particular program
you're interested in for specific dates, times, and other details. Reservations are
highly suggested, and necessary at some of the airports. A signed consent form
for each child is required.
   At the airport, after your child registers, he/she will (in no particular order):
• Participate in a pre-flight inspection training, which means looking over an
airplane to make sure it's mechanically sound while learning some technical
aspects of how to fly a plane. • Fly! The flight is usually twenty minutes round
trip. What a thrill! If it becomes too thrilling for your child, airsick bags are
provided. The planes are either two-seaters or four-seaters. • Take a tour of the
control tower if available. Kids will need to keep their voices low so they don't
disturb the tower operators. Two more wonderful freebies are a certificate upon
completion of the flight, and a magazine called *Sport Aviation for Kids* that
comes later in the mail. Plan on bringing something to munch on as many
airports have picnic tables available. Kids who are grounded will enjoy watching
the planes take off and land. Blue skies and tail winds to you!
   At the Pacoima airport, kids will fly over Magic Mountain, which makes
their flight extra special.

**Hours:** One Sat. a month, starting at 10:30am. Call for specific dates.
**Admission:** Free
**Ages:** 8 - 18 years old.

## YOUNG EAGLES PROGRAM (Santa Monica)                    ☼

(310) 390-8000 - program; (310) 458-8591 - airport /                            !
www.youngeagles.com
*3200 Airport Drive, Santa Monica Airport, Santa Monica*                         ⛄
(Exit Santa Monica Fwy [10] S. on Bundy Dr., R. on Airport Ave.)

See YOUNG EAGLES PROGRAM (Pacoima), under this section, for
details. This airport features the program three or four times a year on selected
Saturdays. When kids have flown with the eagles, so to speak, they can get into
the nearby MUSEUM OF FLYING (look under the Museums section) for free!
Ask about this chapter's other Young Eagle events and educational programs.

**Hours:** Three or four selected Sat. throughout the year.
**Admission:** Free
**Ages:** 8 - 18 years.

## YOUNG EAGLES PROGRAM (South Bay)                    ☼

(310) 374-4812 / www.youngeagles.com                                            !
*Compton Airport, Long Beach Airport, and Torrance Airport*                      ⛄

See YOUNG EAGLES PROGRAM (Pacoima), under this section, for
details. Most pilots at this program try to let the kids have a turn at the controls,
for just a short period of time. They fly out of the above airports when they have
a group of thirty, or so, young pilot "wannabes."

**Hours:** Offered about seven times a year on selected Sat., starting at
1pm.
**Admission:** Free
**Ages:** 8 - 18 years.

## ADVENTURES AT SEA YACHT CHARTERS                    ☼

(800) 229-2412 / www.gondola.com                                          *$$$$$*
*3101 West Coast Highway, Suite 209, Newport Beach*
(Take Costa Mesa Fwy [55] S. to end where it turns into Newport Blvd. After about 2
miles take right lane which exits to Coast Hwy [1]. Don't go over the bridge, but turn L.
on W. Coast Hwy. Adventures at Sea is about 250 yards down on the right.)

These luxurious, electric gondolas are made out of mahogany, have leather
seats, a canopy, and are operated by gondoliers either dressed in a tuxedo
(depending on the occasion), or in the traditional, Venetian outfit. Take a
peaceful cruise along the waterways of Newport Beach Harbor and Newport isle
to view the boats and waterfront homes. The gondoliers will begin your cruise
from the harbor office, or pick you up at one of several harbor-side restaurants.
Adventures at Sea provides a chilled bottle of Martinellis and Godiva chocolates,
or it can provide a complete dinner served on china. This is definitely an upscale
adventure!

**Hours:** Open daily, call for reservations.
**Admission:** $125 for two people, $10 each additional person.
**Ages:** 5 years and up.

## AIR COMBAT USA, INC.                                             ☼

(800) 522-7590 / www.aircombat.com                              *$$$$$*
*230 N. Dale Place, Fullerton*
(Exit Artesia Fwy [91] or N. Santa Ana Fwy [5] N. on Magnolia, L. on Commonwealth, R. on Dale St., veer right for Dale Pl. Or, exit S. on the Santa Ana Fwy [5], E. on Artesia, R. on Dale Pl. (just after Dale St.). It's at Beach/Aviation, on the N. side of airport.)

If being a Top Gun is your top dream, here's the opportunity to make it a reality. You, perhaps being an unlicenced pilot and leading an otherwise normal life, will actually fly and fight air-to-air combat. "The SIAI Marchetti SF260 is a current production, Italian-built, fighter aircraft. It has 260 horsepower, can fly at 270 MPH, FAA certified to +6 to -3 G's and can perform unlimited aerobatics. It was originally designed to transition student pilots to jet fighters. It is maneuvered by the stick grip complete with gun trigger, identical to the F4 Phantom. The pilot and guest pilot sit side-by-side with dual controls." (Excerpted from Air Combat's brochure.) If all this has your adrenaline pumping, go for it!

You'll be prepped for your flight in a one-hour ground school, which covers the basics, with emphasis on tactical maneuvers. After being fitted with a flight suit, helmet, and parachute, you'll soar for one hour with the birds over Catalina waters. You're actually in control of the aircraft 90% of the time, while receiving constant instruction on how to get the "enemy." After practicing maneuvers, you'll engage in six "g-pulling" (i.e. gut wrenching) dogfights against a real opponent (e.g. friend, spouse, etc.) A direct hit registers through an electronic tracking system, complete with sound effects and smoke trailing from the other aircraft. This is as close to the real thing as you can possible get without being in the military. I will confess that after a few high/low yo-yos and roll overs, I used that special white bag and became part of the 10% that share in this ritual.

After you've landed, and come down from your high, you can view the videos, complete with sound, that were simultaneously recorded from each aircraft. Relive your flight and your "hits" again and again on the copy you receive to take home. This is an unforgettable experience!

**Hours:** Four classes/flights that accommodate two people each, are offered every day. Class times are 7am, 9:30am, noon, and 2:30pm.
**Admission:** $795 a flight. Ask about specials, such as discounts for two people, or ready/alert, which means you'll be called to come over A.S.A.P. if there is a cancellation.
**Ages:** 8 years old and up - large enough to wear a parachute and in good health.

## BALBOA BOAT RENTALS

(949) 673-7200                                                          *$$$*
*510 East Edgewater, Balboa*
(Take Costa Mesa Fwy [55] to the end, which turns into Newport Blvd., which turns into Balboa Blvd., L. on Island Ave, R. on Edgewater.)
   Kayaks and eight-seater electric boat rentals are offered here.
   **Admission:**   $10 an hour for a single kayak; $15 an hour for a double. Boats
                    that seat up to 8 passengers are $45 an hour; up to 12, $55 an
                    hour.

## DAVEY'S LOCKER

(949) 673-1434                                                          *$$$*
*400 Main Street, Balboa*
(Take Costa Mesa Fwy [55] to the end, which turns into Newport Blvd., which turns into Balboa Blvd., R. on Main St.)
   Skiff rentals, fishing, and whale-watching cruises (January through March) are offered here.
   **Admission:**   $38 for a half day for skiffs. $12 for adults for the two-and-a-half
                    whale-watching cruise; $8 for children 12 years and under.

## NEWPORT HARBOR CRUISE, BALBOA PAVILION

(949) 673-5245                                                          *$$*
*400 Main Street, Balboa*
(Take Costa Mesa Fwy [55] to the end, which turns into Newport Blvd., which turns into Balboa Blvd., R. on Main St.)
   Forty-five and ninety-minute cruises aboard the Pavilion Queen or Pavilion Paddy are available here. Depending on the length of your cruise, you'll see stars' homes such as George Burns and John Wayne; Pirate's Cove, where Gilligan's Island was filmed; and tour around six of the eight islands in the immediate area.
   **Hours:**   Daily departures are 11am - 5pm in the summer; 11am - 3pm the
                rest of the year. Closed Christmas.
   **Admission:**   $6 for adults for the forty-five-minute cruise; $4 for seniors; $1
                    for ages 5 - 12; children 4 years and under are free. $8 for adults
                    for the ninety-minute cruise; $4 for seniors; $1 for ages 5 - 12;
                    children 4 years and under are free. (Certain discounts available
                    through AAA.)
   **Ages:**   4 years and up.

## NEWPORT HARBOR SHOWBOAT CRUISE

(949) 673-0240                                                          *$$*
*700 E. Edgewater Avenue, Balboa*
(Take Costa Mesa Fwy [55] to the end, which turns into Newport Blvd., which turns into Balboa Blvd., L. on Island Ave, R. on Edgewater.)
   This forty-five-minute cruise is perfect for kids as they'll go around Balboa Island and, hopefully, see some sea lions. A ninety-minute cruise is also

available. Seeing several star's homes and hearing the history of Balboa Island and Peninsula are interesting parts of the cruise.

**Hours:** Daily departures for the forty-five-minute cruise are at 11am, 1pm, and 3pm. Daily departures for the ninety-minute cruise are on the hour between 11am - 6pm in the summer, 11am - 3pm the rest of the year.

**Admission:** $6 for adults for the forty-five-minute cruise; $2 for ages 5 - 11; children 4 years and under are free. $8 for adults for the ninety-minute cruise; $2 for ages 5 - 11; children 4 years and under are free. Closed December 24 - 25.

**Ages:** 4 years and up.

## NEWPORT LANDING SPORTFISHING

(949) 675-0550                    *$$$$*

*309 Palm, Suite F, Balboa*

(Take Costa Mesa Fwy [55] to the end, which turns into Newport Blvd., which turns into Balboa Blvd., L. on Palm.)

Whale-watching cruises from January through March are available here.

**Admission:** $15 for adults for the two-and-a-half hour cruise; $10 for children 12 years and under.

## PADDLEPOWER

(949) 675-1215                    *$$$*

*500 West Balboa Boulevard, Balboa*

(Take Costa Mesa Fwy [55] to the end, which turns into Newport Blvd., which turns into Balboa Blvd.)

Kayak rentals are available here.

**Admission:** Prices start at $9 an hour for a single, $12 an hour for a double.

## RESORT WATERSPORTS

(800) 585-0747 or (949) 729-1150                    *$$$*

*Newport Dunes Resort, Newport Beach*

(Take Newport Fwy [55] S.W. to end, which turns into Newport Blvd., L. on W. Coast Hwy., L. on Jamboree Rd., L. on Backbay Dr. Or, from Corona Del Mar Fwy [73], exit S.W. on Jamboree R., R. on Backbay Dr. before E. Coast Hwy.)

Located in NEWPORT DUNES RESORT (look under the Beaches section), this rental facility has everything you need to make your day at the beach more exciting. Going rates are: $15 an hour for pedal boats, $45 for electric-powered boats, $18 an hour for windsurfers, $17 an hour for sail boats, $13 an hour for single kayaks, and $16 an hour for double kayaks. Bike rentals, skate rentals, and California chariots (a cross between a skateboard and scooter) start at $6 an hour. They also offer guided kayak tours of an adjacent wildlife estuary reserve every Sunday at 10am, weather permitting. In the estuary, you can see crabs, blue herons, snowy egrets, and other birds and animals in their natural habitat. We took this tour and learned why this reserve is becoming endangered, as well as some of the clean up projects that we can get involved with. A two-hour tour is $20 per person; $15 for ages 12 years and under. What a work-out for those of us not physically fit! But it is also a fun and educational way to spend some family time together.

**Hours:** Open daily in the summer from 9am - 8pm. Open year round on the weekends, usually from 10am - 5pm. Call for other hours of operation.

**Admission:** Prices are stated above, plus a $6 per vehicle entrance fee.

## THE CARRIAGE HOUSE

(909) 781- 0780

*Mission Inn, Riverside*

$$$

Take a ride in a beautiful horse-drawn carriage through the historic Mission Inn district. The carriage holds four adults comfortably or two adults, three kids. With horses named Cinderella and Belle, children feel like they are living out a storybook fantasy, if only for a short ride.

Tea parties are a perfect occasion to incorporate a carriage ride. Or, rent the wagon, which seats up to sixteen people, for a cowboy party. At Christmas time, even though there isn't any snow to glisten, the carriage sleigh bells ring if you're listenin', plus Christmas lights are even more dazzling when seen from this old-fashioned vantage point. Note: Take a ride around the block with Santa Claus for only $3 per person at Christmas time, weather permitting.

**Hours:** Carriages can often be found along the Mission Inn district, but calling for a reservation is your best bet.

**Admission:** A twenty-minute ride is $35 for the entire carriage; an hour ride is $70.

**Ages:** All

## CARRIAGES BY MARGARET

(909) 370-8691 or (909) 370-8691

*Riverside*

$$$

What Cinderella or Prince Charming child hasn't dreamed of riding in a horse-drawn carriage, if only because of fairy tales? Take a ride in an immaculate white or black carriage pulled by a beautiful, silky horse that is gentle enough to pet. The carriages seat up to six people, four adults comfortably. If you have a party, reserve the horse-drawn trolley car that seats up to twelve people! Choose your own route for a ride or call for using the carriage for special events

**Hours:** Call for hours you'd like to book a ride.

**Admission:** Prices vary, depending on the length of the ride and the destination.

**Ages:** All

## ORANGE EMPIRE RAILWAY MUSEUM

(909) 657-2605 / www.oerm.mus.ca.us

*2201 South "A" Street, Perris*

!/$$$

(Exit Escondido Fwy [215] W. on 4th St. A more direct route than following the signs is to turn L. on "A" St., then go down a few miles until you reach the museum on the left.)

If you love trains, make tracks to the Orange Empire Railway Museum where you can really go full steam ahead! This huge, unique, outdoor museum is best described as a work-in-progress. Railcars from all over the country, in various states of disrepair, find their way here. Some are being restored while others are just stationed here. Walk around to see which railcars the volunteers are working on.

The museum is open daily, but weekends are the prime time to visit as this is the only time when train and trolley rides are available. Purchase an all-day ride ticket, which is good for rides on a locomotive, electric trolley, streetcar, freight car, and/or passenger car. (Three types of cars are usually running.) Each ride lasts about fifteen minutes and a conductor explains the history of the vehicles and the museum, and the impact of train transportation in Southern California. The train's whistle, the clickety-clack of its wheels, and the clanging of streetcar bells add excitement to your adventure.

Walk through the several car houses (i.e. buildings that house railcars) to see historic Yellow Cars (which my kids thought looked like school buses); a San Francisco cable car; electric railway streetcars and locomotives dating from 1900; steam engines; and wood passenger cars. The car houses are usually open on weekends. They are open during the week whenever volunteer staff is available.

Check out the Middleton Collection that includes old toy and scale model railroad cars, etc. There is an ongoing video that shows how tracks are laid. We got derailed at the gift shop, which offers videos, books, and all sorts of train paraphernalia. There are also a few picnic tables and grassy areas here.

**Hours:** The grounds are open daily from 9am - 5pm. Train and trolley rides are available only on weekends and major holidays from 11am - 5pm. Closed Thanksgiving and Christmas.

**Admission:** The museum is free. All-day ride passes are $7 for adults; $5 for ages 5 - 11; children 4 years and under ride free.

**Ages:** All

## YOUNG EAGLES PROGRAM (Riverside)

(909) 686-1318 / www.youngeagles.com
*4130 Mennes Street at Flabob Airport, Riverside*
(Exit Pomona Fwy [60] S. on Rubidoux (not the Valleyview/Rubidoux exit), go to the end, turn L. and a quick R. through the airport gates.)

See YOUNG EAGLES PROGRAM (Pacoima), in this section, for a complete description. This particular airport also features a twenty-five minute video on aviation starring Cliff Robertson, hot dogs and soft drinks for $1 each, t-shirts for $10 each, and perhaps a chance at the controls while in the air. If time permits, adults may get an opportunity to fly for a $15 donation. Call to make reservations.

**Hours:** The second Sat. of the month, except August and December, starting at 8am.

**Admission:**  Free
**Ages:**  8 - 18 years old.

## CALIFORNIA SPEEDWAY

(800) 944-RACE (7223)  / www.racingwest.com/tracks/california.shtml    *$$$$$*
*9300 North Cherry Avenue, Fontana*
(Exit San Bernardino Fwy [10] N. on Cherry Ave.)

    The best in NASCAR racing roars to life in Southern California! Located on over 525 acres, this state-of-the-art speedway features a two-mile, D-shaped oval super speedway with a 1.3 mile infield road course. The track can accommodate three to four cars side by side. (Racers clock average speeds of up to 180mph!) The three major race weekends occur in May, for the Winston Cup Series; July, for the NASCAR Truck and Busch Series; and October/November, for the CART Series. The stadium seats allow great views of the races. Gigantic screens and hundreds of smaller monitors show the action to spectators, too. Thirteen huge message boards, an incredible speaker system, a car-themed children's play area, sometimes live entertainment, and "real" food (including lobster), as well as standby's of hot dogs and hamburgers, all aid in making this a very fan-friendly speedway.

    **Hours:**  Major races occur in May, July, and October/November. Call for a race schedule.
**Admission:**  $30 general admission; $35 for reserved seats; $45 for a pit pass (only for those 18 years and older). AAA members are given certain discounts.
    **Ages:**  4 years and up.

## YOUNG EAGLES PROGRAM (Chino)

(714) 758-7035  / www.youngeagles.com                                        *!*
*Merrill Avenue, Chino Airport, Chino*
(Exit Riverside Fwy [91] N. on the 71, N. on Euclid [or the 83]. Exit Hwy 83 R. on Merrill Ave., R. on Airport Way. It is near hanger #3, by the Fighter Jets Museum part of the Air Museum.)

    See YOUNG EAGLES PROGRAM (Pacoima), under this section, for details. This program allows kids the opportunity to control the aircraft - for a short period of time! Each young pilot gets a Polaroid picture taken of himself/herself, too. The program gives boy scouts half of what they need for their aviation merit badge. Since you are here, check out the adjacent AIR MUSEUM "PLANES OF FAME" museum. (Look under the Museums section for details.)

    **Hours:**  Offered four times a year on selected Sat., starting at 10am.
**Admission:**  Free
    **Ages:**  8 - 18 years.

## YOUNG EAGLES PROGRAM (Redlands)

(909) 798-3933  / www.youngeagles.com                                        *!*

*1745 Sessums Drive, Mentone Airport, Redlands*                              ⛪
(Exit San Bernardino Fwy [10] E. on University Ave., R. on Colton Ave., L. on Wabash,
which dead ends into the airport.)
     See YOUNG EAGLES PROGRAM (Pacoima), under this section, for
details. Reservations are needed.
    **Hours:**  Offered four or five times a year on selected Sat., starting at 9am.
  **Admission:**  Free
     **Ages:**  8 - 18 years.

## YOUNG EAGLES PROGRAM (Upland)                                   ☼

(909) 982-8048 / www.youngeagles.com                                         !
*1749 W. 13th Street, Cable Airport, Upland*                                ⛪
(Exit San Bernardino Fwy [10] N. on Central, E. on Foothill, L. on Benson one block and
L. into the airport.)
     See YOUNG EAGLES PROGRAM (Pacoima), in this section, for details.
Reservations are required for this program.
    **Hours:**  Offered nine times a year on selected Sat.
  **Admission:**  Free
     **Ages:**  8 - 18 years.

## BIPLANE AND AIR COMBAT ADVENTURES                              ☼

(800) 759-5667 / www.barnstorming.com                                   $$$$$
*2198 Palomar Airport Road, McClellan Palomar Airport, Carlsbad*
(Exit San Diego Fwy [5] E. on Palomar Airport Rd.)
     Flying in a restored open-cockpit biplane, wearing helmet, goggles, and a
pilot scarf reminds me of another flying ace, Snoopy, and his adventures with the
Red Baron. (Yes, I do know that Snoopy isn't real.) You'll fly over the stunning
San Diego coastline for twenty minutes, side-by-side with another passenger
(your child!), while the pilot sits behind you. It's like riding a motorcycle in the
sky!
     Another adventure offered here is Air Combat. After a crash course, so to
speak, on general aviation and specifically, tactical maneuvers during combat,
you'll suit up and take off for the wild blue yonder. When you've gotten a feel
for the controls, get ready for combat with a real "enemy." You'll fly for over
thirty minutes, experiencing high low yo-yos (where the plane dips abruptly
downward and zooms upward and your stomach heads in the opposite direction),
and other maneuvers in a dogfight - let the fur fly! This exhilarating experience
is one that you'll remember and talk about for the rest of your life.
    **Hours:**  Call to schedule a flight.
  **Admission:**  Biplane Adventures start at $98 for one or two people, for twenty
                minutes of flight time. Air Combat starts at $199 per person and
                a $20 discount if you B.Y.O.E. (Bring Your Own Enemy). Ask
                about current specials.
     **Ages:**  6 years and up.

## CINDERELLA'S CARRIAGE                                                ☼

(619) 239-8080 / www.cinderella-carriage.com                           *$$$$$*

*In front of the Harbor House Restaurant at Seaport Village, or in front of* ▥
*Crowces Restaurant at 5ᵗʰ Avenue and "F" Street in the Gaslamp Quarter,*
*San Diego*

(Seaport Village: Going S. on San Diego Fwy [5], exit W. on Ash St., L. on 4ᵗʰ, R. on Broadway to end, L. on Harbor Dr. Going N. on 5, exit S. on 6ᵗʰ Ave., R. on Broadway to end, L. on Harbor Dr.

Gaslamp Quarter: Going S. on San Diego Fwy [5], exit W. on Ash St., L. on 6ᵗʰ Ave., R. on "F" St. Going N. on 5, exit S. on 6ᵗʰ Ave., R. on "F" St.)

The largest carriage company on the coast still makes every ride feel special and intimate. Enjoy the waterfront from a different vantage as you take a carriage around Seaport Village, or explore the historic and romantic Gaslamp Quarter. The one-horse powered carriages are pulled by a large draft horse (e.g. a Clydesdale or a Belgium horse). Kids (and adults) will get a thrill out of clip-clopping along the streets of downtown San Diego. And don't worry, your Cinderella's carriage won't turn into a pumpkin before your ride is over.

**Hours:** Carriages are available at Seaport Village daily from noon - 11pm, and at the Gaslamp District nightly from 6pm - 11pm. You may just show up, or make reservations.

**Admission:** Half-hour rides cost $45 for up to four people.

**Ages:** All

## H & M LANDING                                                       ◐

(619) 222-0427 / www.hmlanding.com                                     *$$$$*

*2803 Emerson, San Diego*

(Going S. on San Diego Fwy [5], exit S. on Rosecrans St., L. on Emerson. Going N. on 5, exit at Hawthorne St., go straight on Brant St., L. on Laurel, R. on N. Harbor Dr., L on Rosecrans St., L. on Emerson.)

San Diego's oldest whale-watching expedition company offers two, three, and even five-hour cruises during whale-watching season, which is January through mid-March. Three-hour cruises depart at 10am and 1:30pm and head to the coastal waters of Point Loma. Five-hour trips depart at 10am and travel to the Coronado Islands and Mexico's marine wildlife sanctuary. Be on the lookout for whales, sea lions, dolphins, and elephant seals.

**Hours:** Stated above.

**Admission:** The three-hour whale watching excursion is $17 for adults; $12 for children 17 years and under.

**Ages:** 6 years and up.

## OCOTILLO WELLS STATE VEHICULAR                                      ◐
## RECREATION AREA

(760) 767-5391                                                         *!*

(Take 78 E. out of Julian, beyond Ocotillo Wells.)

For a little off-roading fun, try Ocotillo Wells Recreation Area where you can go up hills, over sand dunes, and through dry washes! You must provide your own vehicles (and have them registered), but the entrance is free and so are primitive camping sites.

**Hours:** Open daily.
**Admission:** Free
**Ages:** 6 years and up.

## OLD TOWN TROLLEY TOURS

(619) 298-8687 / www.historictours.com          $$$$
*4040 Twigg Street, San Diego*
(Exit San Diego Fwy [5] E. on Old Town Ave., L. on San Diego Ave., R. on Twigg St. This is the main depot.)

Really get to know the city of San Diego by taking a narrated tour on board an old-fashioned looking trolley. The tour guide will tell you about the history of San Diego, plus lots of fun stories. One of the best features about this tour is that you can take a continuous two-hour tour, or jump off (so to speak) and rejoin the tour at any time throughout the day. There are nine locations covered on the loop, including Old Town, Seaport Village, Horton Plaza, Hotel Del Coronado, San Diego Zoo, and Balboa Park. Appropriately nicknamed "transportainment," we enjoyed the commentary, the freedom of stopping at attractions, staying for a bit, and getting back on board when we were ready. Hassle-free parking is another plus. Ask about their specialty tours, such as the three-hour, Navy tour, where you'll see various aspects of the military in San Diego. Also see SAN DIEGO TROLLEY, under this section, for another way to get around San Diego.

**Hours:** Trolleys run daily from 9am - 5pm. They do not run on Thanksgiving or Christmas. The Navy tour departs every Fri. at 9:15am.
**Admission:** The prices for all tours are $20 for adults; $8 for ages 4 - 12; children 3 years and under are free.
**Ages:** 5 years and up.

## POINT LOMA LANDING

(619) 223-2390          $$$$
*1403 Scott Street, San Diego*
(Going N. on San Diego Fwy [5], take the first exit after Cabrillo Fwy exchange, turn L. on 6th St. at end of off ramp, R. on Ash St. to end. R. on Harbor Dr. around bay, L. on Scott St. Going S. on 5, exit S. on Rosecrans St., L. on Harbor Dr., R. on Scott St.)

Three-hour, whale-watching cruises are offered twice daily during the whale-watching season.

**Hours:** Open daily, January through March. Call for times.
**Admission:** $17 for adults; $12 for children 12 years and under.
**Ages:** 6 years and up.

## SAN DIEGO HARBOR EXCURSION

(619) 234-4111 / www.sdhe.com          $$$
*1050 North Harbor Drive, Broadway Pier, San Diego*

(Going S. on San Diego Fwy [5], exit W. on Ash St., L. on 4<sup>th</sup>, R. on Broadway to end. Going N. on 5, exit S. on 6<sup>th</sup> Ave., R. on Broadway to end.)

Enjoy a one or two-hour narrated cruise along San Diego's coast in a nice excursion ship. A snack bar is on board. During a one-hour cruise, you'll see the Star of India, the Naval Air Station, and the San Diego shipyards that hold merchants' vessels, fishing boats, and more. During the two-hour cruise, you'll also travel by the Cabrillo National Monument. Whale-watching trips are given January through March. Tip: Bring a jacket or sweater on any journey by sea!

**Hours:** One-hour cruises depart daily, starting at 10am. Two-hour cruises depart Mon. - Fri. at 2pm; Sat. - Sun., 9:45am, 12:30pm, and 2pm. Call first as hours may change in the winter.

**Admission:** One-hour cruises cost $12 for adults; $10 for seniors and military; $6 for ages 4 -12; children 3 years and under are free. Two-hour cruises are $17 for adults; $15 for seniors and military; $8.50 for ages 4 - 12 years. Parking at the Broadway pier is $1 per hour; $3 maximum.

**Ages:** 3 years and up

# SAN DIEGO RAILROAD MUSEUM

(619) 595-3030 / www.sdrm.org                                          $$$

*Highway 94, Campo*

(Exit 8 Fwy [45 miles from downtown San Diego] S. on Buckman Springs Rd., travel 10.5 miles to junction Hwy 94., bear right [1.5 miles] to Old Stone Store, L. after railroad tracks and follow signs to the Museum.)

The sound of a train whistle blowing has always been a signal for adventure! Come aboooooard the San Diego Railroad Museum train for an hour-and-a-half ride your children will never forget. You'll ride in restored classic steam or diesel locomotives, depending on what is available. My boys loved the freedom of moving about while traveling. They walked in between the cars (parents are asked to accompany minors), watched the scenic mountains and meadows roll past, saw a few cows, and played cards. Tip: We brought a picnic lunch, as only snack food is available to purchase on the train. At the halfway point, kids can view (from the windows) the engine being switched around to pull you back the way you came. The conductors were friendly and shared a lot of information about railroads and the history of the area.

Free walking tours are offered one stop before the end of the excursion. You'll see numerous old and restored rail cars such as passenger, Pullman, and freight cars; learn about the historical significance of the railways; and walk through a caboose. The forty-five minute tour leads you back to the Campo Depot.

At the museum (depot) there are a few stationary pull carts to climb on, a Box Car Theater that shows continuously running videos about the railway system, a gift shop, and picnic tables. In addition to weekly rides, special trips are arranged to Tecate in Mexico, and Jacumba in California.

**Hours:**  The Museum hours are 9am - 5pm on weekends and holidays.
Trains depart at 11am and at 2:30pm on Sat., Sun., and most
holidays. Closed Thanksgiving and Christmas.
**Admission:**  To simply come and look at the trains is free. Train rides cost
$10 for adults; $8 for seniors and active military; $3 for ages 6 -
12; children 5 years and under are free.
**Ages:**  3 years and up.

## SAN DIEGO TROLLEY

(619) 685-4900 - 24-hour information express line; (619) 233-3004 -
office; (619) 234-5005 - for persons with hearing impairments. /
www.sandag.cog.ca.us/sdmts/trolleypage.htm
*San Diego*

The San Diego Trolley (and bus) line is a great way to get around San
Diego. The North-South line extends from Old Town all the way down to San
Ysidro. From this last stop at the border, you can either walk into Mexico, or
take a cab. Park for free at the Old Town Transit Center, or all day at the MTS
tower garage at 12th and Imperial for $6. The East line goes from Santee to
Seaport Village. There are several places to catch the trolley line along the
routes, with many of the stops being at major attractions. Part of the fun for a
child is just the ride. Also see OLD TOWN TROLLEY TOURS, under this
section, for another way to get around San Diego.
**Hours:**  It runs daily from 5am - 1am, with service every fifteen minutes
most of the day.
**Admission:**  One-way fares range from $1 - $2.25, depending on how far you
go. Children 4 years and under ride for free. Tickets are usually
dispensed from machines.
**Ages:**  All

## TORREY PINES GLIDER PORT

(619) 452-9858
*2800 Torrey Pines Scenic Drive, La Jolla*
(Exit San Diego Fwy [5] W. on Genesee Ave., L. on N. Torrey Pines Rd., R. on Torrey
Pines Scenic Dr., to the end onto the dirt parking lot.)

Man has had dreams and aspirations of flying since the beginning of time.
Hang gliding and paragliding are the closest things we'll get to it in this lifetime
(and they are much better than Icarus' attempt!) Kids may participate in this
uplifting sport, or come to just watch. We brought a picnic lunch, as there are
tables at the cliff tops, although a full-service snack bar is here, too. Besides the
exhilarating sight of gliders soaring and dipping along the coastline, there is a
breathtaking view of the ocean and beach. The small planes you see flying
overhead are really remote control planes that have a take-off/landing site right
next "door."

**Hours:** Flights are scheduled daily, although if you're coming to watch, you might want to call first to see if anyone is actually flying that day. Closed Christmas.

**Admission:** Free, unless you're flying! Tandem introductory lessons, starting at $125, usually take about an hour which includes ground school instruction and about 30 minutes of flight time. Solo lessons, starting at $125, can take all day with actual gliding practice done off "bunny slopes."

**Ages:** All to come and watch; 5 years and up for tandem; at least 100 pounds for solo flights.

## YOUNG EAGLES PROGRAM (San Diego)                ☼

(619) 390-7510 - program; (619) 661-6520 - airport  /                !
www.youngeagles.com
*1409 Continental Avenue, Brown Field, San Diego*                 ≞
(Exit San Diego Fwy [5] E. on Route 905 (only 1 ½ miles from the border) and drive about 3 miles. Look for airport and E.A.A. signs.)

See YOUNG EAGLES PROGRAM (Pacoima), under this section, for details. At this location, the flight is over the city of San Diego and over the ocean. Younger children who are grounded can ride in a simulator that has a radio, earphones, and all the instruments that are in a cockpit. The ride moves and turns as the wheel is turned. Ask about this chapter's other Young Eagle programs.

**Hours:** Usually offered the second Sat. of each month.

**Admission:** Free

**Ages:** 8 - 18 years.

## BAY QUEEN HARBOR CRUISE                ☼

(805) 642-7753                                           $$
*Spinnaker Drive, Ventura*
(Going S. on Ventura Fwy [101], exit S. on Harbor Blvd. Going W. on 101, exit S.W. on Seaward Ave., L. on Harbor Blvd. From Harbor, go R. on Spinnaker Dr.)

Enjoy a forty-minute cruise out of the harbor, past the boats and homes along the coastline. See VENTURA HARBOR and VILLAGE, under the Piers and Seaports section, for other things to do in this area.

**Hours:** Cruises depart daily between noon - 4pm, every hour on the hour.

**Admission:** $6 for adults; $3 for children 12 years and under.

**Ages:** All

## CHANNEL ISLAND'S LANDING                ☼

(805) 985-6059                                           $$$
*2950 S. Harbor Boulevard, Oxnard*
(Exit Ventura Fwy [101] S. on Victoria Ave., R. on Channel Islands Blvd., L. on Harbor Blvd.)

Set sail on sailboats that rent for $15 an hour, or on an electric boat that seats up to ten people and rents for $40 an hour. (Somehow it doesn't sound right to say, "Set sail on an electric boat" - oh well!)

**Hours:** Open Mon. - Fri., 8am - 5pm; Sat. - Sun., 8am - 5:30pm.
**Admission:** Prices listed above.
**Ages:** All

## FILLMORE & WESTERN RAILWAY

(800) 773-TRAIN (8724) or (805) 524-2546                          $$$$
*351 Santa Clara Avenue, Central Park Depot, Fillmore*
(To reach the Central Park Depot in Fillmore: Exit State Route 126 N. on Central Ave. and proceed 1 block. To reach the Santa Paula Depot: Exit State Route 126 N. on State Highway 150 [or 10th St.] and proceed 3 blocks.)

"More powerful than a locomotive"; *The Great Train Robbery*; *The Little Engine that Could* - what does this potpourri of things bring to mind? A train ride, of course! Riding on a train is a real adventure for children. The countryside is scenic along this route with citrus groves and beautiful landscapes. This railway line is also a favorite Hollywood location, so many of the trains you'll see and ride on have appeared in movies and television shows. Snacks are available on board.

There are several types of weekend excursions offered. Hop on board for a two-hour, round-trip steam or diesel ride between Fillmore and Santa Paula. You might have time to stop off at your destination city for a little while - check with the ticket agent about space availability for the return trip. Spirit of the West train rides include a stop at a private location for a barbecue dinner (which is provided), musical entertainment, and dancing to live music. Other specialty rides, such as murder/mystery rides (for adults), are offered throughout the year.

**Hours:** Trains usually depart from Fillmore on Sat. at 2pm; Sun., 11am, and 2pm. Spirit of the West rides depart at 6pm and return at 9:30pm.
**Admission:** Round-trip fare is $15 for adults; $12 for seniors; $8 for ages 3 - 12; children 2 years and under are free. Spirit of the West rides are $46.50 for adults; $40 for seniors; $38.50 for ages 8 - 12; $15 for children 7 years and under. Other specialty rides vary in price.
**Ages:** 3 years and up.

## JIM HALL RACING SCHOOL

(805) 654-1329 / www.jhrkartracing.com                           $$$$$
*675 Harbor Boulevard, Ventura*
(Exit Ventura Fwy [101] S. on Victoria, R. on Olivas Park Dr., L. on Harbor Blvd.)

What child doesn't like racing around? Now he/she can learn how to do it in karts! Besides the adult classes, this racing school offers cadet classes, for kids 8 to 12 years old. Classes range from half-day instruction to a week, or more. On a modified course, the cadet group will learn safety (yea!), how to drive, braking techniques (this could be especially valuable in just a few years), and they'll

even get timed. Watch out, Mario Andretti!
**Hours:** Call for class hours.
**Admission:** Varies, depending on the length of class. A half day for cadets, which is three hours of instruction and driving, starts at $95.
**Ages:** 8 years and up.

## SANTA PAULA AIRPORT / CP AVIATION, INC.    ☼
(805) 933-1155 or (805) 525-2138 / www.cpaviation.com        !/$$$$
*830 E. Santa Maria Street, Santa Paula*
(Exit the 126 Fwy N. on State Highway 150 [or 10ᵗʰ St.], L. on Harvard Blvd., L. on 8ᵗʰ St., L. on Santa Maria St.)

This small airport is kid-friendly; partly because of its size, and partly because it's always fun to watch planes land and take off. Instead of just watching, however, why not take the kids up for a spin, literally! At the instructor's discretion, if your child is at least 12 years old (and doesn't get motion sickness), he/she can take an exhilarating half-hour aerobatic ride with loops, rolls, and G's (better than a roller coaster!) for $87. For those who enjoy a calmer scenic ride, a Cessna 172, which seats three passengers, is only $42 (total) for a half-hour flight. Other aircraft are available for flights, too. Lunch at the airport restaurant will complete your lofty adventure.

One Sunday a month, take a free tour of the fifteen or so antique aircraft (and vintage automobiles) on display here. Depending on the docent, kids can look at and maybe touch these unique airplanes.
**Hours:** The airport is open daily. Call for hours for a flight. The antique aircraft and tour is only offered on the first Sun. of the month from 10am - 2pm.
**Admission:** Free, unless you are going to fly.
**Ages:** 4 years and up for a look around the airport and a scenic flight.

## ZOOS AND ANIMALS

Kids and animals seem to go hand-in-hoof - both are adorable and neither is easy. Animal lovers - this section is for you! Tip: Take a trip to a pet shop. See "Pets" in the Ideas and Resources section for some of our local favorites.

## EXOTIC FELINE BREEDING COMPOUND ☼

(805) 256-3793 / www.cathouse-fcc.org !

*Rhyolite Avenue, Rosamond*

(Exit Antelope Valley Fwy [14] W. on Rosamond Blvd. [to the E. is Edwards Air Force Base], R. on Mojave-Tropico Rd., L. on Rhyolite Ave.)

This place is the cat's meow! There are fifty exotic wild cats living here, representing over fifteen different species. Since it is a breeding compound, you're almost guaranteed to see a few kittens, too. Unlike traditional zoos, the safety fences keep you only a few feet (not yards) away from the caged animals. This allows for plenty of up-close viewing. Picture-taking, however, is not allowed unless you are an E.F.B.C. member.

Stroll along the cement pathways to see jaguars, panthers, pumas, lynxes, fluffy Amur leopards, regal-looking servals, weasel-like jaguarundi, and lots of Chinese leopards. Do take a tour to see the cats in the back, where you'll see more leopards, plus three huge Siberian tigers that play with toys such as truck tires and bowling balls. You'll learn about the animals - what they eat, how much they weigh, their life span, etc. - and about the importance of this breeding compound. Tip: Hold on to young children while on the "back lot" tour. Cats tend to see them as potential meals, and although they are in cages (the cats, not the kids), only ropes further separate kids from cats who can stick their paws between the bars.

The gift shop has a few displays showing some of the reasons these cats are facing extinction - one fur coat was made from fifteen bobcats, and another was made from over fifty leopards. Tip: Late afternoon and cooler months are the best times to visit the compound as this is when the felines are more active. Please call if you want to schedule a tour for ten or more people. Educational outreach programs are also available.

**Hours:**   Open Thurs. - Tues. from 10am - 4pm. Closed Christmas.
**Admission:**   Free. Membership is $15 for an individual; $25 for a family.
**Ages:**   4 years and up.

## ARABIAN HORSE SHOWS ☼

(909) 869-2224 / www.kelloggwest.org/arab.htm $

*Kellogg Drive, California State Polytechnic University, Pomona*

(Going E., exit San Bernardino Fwy [10] S. on Kellogg Dr. Going N., exit Orange Fwy [57] W. on Temple, R. on S. Campus Dr., L. on Kellogg Dr. Parking is on the R., in the campus parking lot. Cross the street to the university farm.)

The Kellogg Arabian Horse Center at Cal Poly houses over eighty-five purebred Arabian horses. Scenically set in the hills, the center's thirty-eight acres encompass a huge pasture, three barns, foaling stalls, a breeding area, a veterinary clinic, a farrier shop, an arena, and a covered grandstand.

Staff and students of horse husbandry and equine sciences present hour-long shows that put the horses through their various paces. You see demonstrations of English and western riding, with riders in appropriate costumes, as well as drill team/precision maneuvers, and horses going over small jumps. Riders in silver and gold flowing Arabian dress are a hit with the crowd as their horses, decorated in jewel-toned brocade and tassels, prance around the ring. Our favorite act was the horse that performed several tricks, including walking and rocking a baby carriage.

After the show, children can ride a horse around a path for $2; watch a thirty-minute video on the history of Kellogg's center (note that the small video room contains a horse skeleton); and walk around the stables. Tip: Bring carrots to feed the horses. Families can pet the beautiful horses, watch them being bathed and groomed, and simply enjoy the ambiance. Springtime is the best time to visit as there are newborn colts to see. Ask about rodeos presented at the college, as well as those sponsored by Cal Poly, but performed off campus.

**Hours:**   The shows are offered October through June on the first Sun. of each month at 2pm.

**Admission:**   $3 for adults; $2 for ages 6 - 17; children 5 years and under are free.

**Ages:**   3 years and up.

## CABRILLO MARINE AQUARIUM

(310) 548-7562 / www.cabrilloaq.org
*3720 Stephen M White Drive, San Pedro*
(Take Harbor Fwy [110] to the end, L. on Gaffey St., L. on 9th St., R. on Pacific Ave. almost to the end, L. on 36th St. which turns into Stephen M White.)

Explore the underwater treasures of Los Angeles Harbor without ever getting wet! Cabrillo Marine Aquarium specializes in the marine life of Southern California. It features quite a few tanks, mostly at kids' eye-level, filled with a wide variety of sea life.

The front courtyard has full-size killer whale, shark, and dolphin models, plus a full-grown gray whale outlined on the cement. Kids are welcome to touch the whale bones in the adjacent Whale Graveyard.

The exhibit halls have tanks filled with live jellies (usually referred to as jellyfish), crustaceans, octopuses, fish, leopard sharks, moray eels, and other sea animals. There are numerous displays of preserved animals, such as seals and sea lions; bones, skeletons, jaws, and teeth of sharks and whales; pictures; and other models of sea life. My boys liked pushing the button to hear the recording of a whale singing, although their renditions of it were more grating than musical. We also watched a shark blend into the sandy ocean floor; touched a sample of shark skin and compared it to a sample of sandpaper; and saw a slide presentation at the auditorium. Call to see what's currently showing.

As most kids have this inherent need to explore the world with their hands and not just their eyes, a definite favorite is the tidepool touch tank. Here kids can gently touch sea anemones, sea stars, etc.

The Cabrillo Aquarium offers seasonal events such as grunion hunting (March through July) and whale watching (January through April), plus various workshops. At low tide - call for particular times and seasons - tidepool tours are given at the beach in an area called Pt. Fermin Marine Refuge.

Don't forget to pack your swimsuits and beach towels as Cabrillo Beach is

right outside the aquarium. Wonderful sandy stretches and a play area await your
children. For more adventuresome kids (or whosoever's parents will let them),
there are rock jetties to explore. Enjoy your day playing by the ocean, and
learning more about it.

**Hours:** The Aquarium is open Tues. - Fri., noon - 5pm; Sat. - Sun., 10am
- 5pm. Closed Thanksgiving and Christmas. The touch tank
doors open for twenty minutes at a time Tues. - Fri. at 1:30pm,
2:30pm, and 3:30pm; Sat. - Sun. at 11:30am, 1:30pm, 2:30pm,
and 3:30pm. Slide shows are presented Tues. - Sun. at 11am and
2pm. The beach is open daily from 6am - 10pm.

**Admission:** The aquarium is free; donations are appreciated. Parking is $6.50
per car. If you get here early enough, you can park on the street
and just walk through the beach/aquarium entrance gate.

**Ages:** All

## ENDANGERED SPECIES ECOPARK

(562) 436-5844 / e-mail:ecopark@aol.com
*429-E Shoreline Village Drive, Long Beach*
(Exit Long Beach Fwy [710] E. on Shoreline Dr., R. on Shoreline Village Dr. It's located
in the red barn-like building, near Parker's Lighthouse Restaurant.)

At first glance this medium-sized room doesn't look like it would hold a
child's attention for any length of time. But come in, look around, and you and
your family will be drawn into observing and learning about the live exotic
animals on display. In this rainforest-like setting, with simulated vegetation
crawling up the walls and covering the ceiling, the captive-bred animals are
displayed in glass enclosures that imitate their natural environments. The
exceptions are the Scarlet Macaw and the Moluccan Cockatoo, who are perched
on stands in uncaged areas. The other inhabitants of EcoPark include prehistoric-
looking Cuban Rock Iguanas, boa constrictors, Indigo snakes, chinchillas, Giant
African Millipedes, whiptail scorpions, and the venomous and colorful South
American Poison Arrow Frogs. The animal exhibits are at a child's eye level.

The staff members are friendly and very knowledgeable, eager to explain
animal habitats, behavior, diet, their names (all-important information to a child),
etc. You might even get to gently stroke a scaly snake or furry chinchilla. A
small side room contains six computers with terrific educational programs such
as Create Play Safari, Guidebook, and a veterinary program. The well-supplied
arts and crafts table is ready for youngsters to create animals masks, jungle
jewelry, drawings, etc. A hands-on table allows visitors to touch feathers and
snake skins. Look closer at an object via a fiber optics microscope that projects
its findings on a monitor. Animal videos can be seen on a small screen in the
little theater area.

A seventy-five-minute school program is offered to groups of twenty-five to
seventy students. It includes a fifteen-minute presentation on the preservation of
rare, threatened, and endangered wildlife; teaching time, and touching time, at
the animal stations; and working on a craft project. Programs are tailored

according to age: preschoolers will learn the basics, while high schoolers can learn exactly how to set up and maintain habitats.

Enjoy the surrounding shops and eateries that comprise Shoreline Village. Use the Alphabetical Index to look up nearby attractions - LONG BEACH AQUARIUM OF THE PACIFIC, QUEEN MARY, and SCORPION.

**Hours:** Open daily from 10am - 6pm. Closed Thanksgiving and Christmas.

**Admission:** $4.95 for adults; $2.95 for seniors and ages 2 - 12; children under 2 years are free. School groups are about $3.50 per student; teachers are free. The first two hours of parking is free with validation and a minimum $3 purchase. Parking is $1 per half hour after that; $6 maximum.

**Ages:** 2 years and up.

## THE FARM

(818) 341-6805 - recording; (818) 885-6321 - The Farm on the weekends.

*8101 Tampa Avenue, Reseda*

(Exit Ventura Fwy [101] N. on Tampa)

This Farm reminds me of Old MacDonald's place in that song with all those vowels. There are over 100 animals to pet, and even a few to hold. The llamas, cows, chickens, bunnies, turkeys, sheep, ducks, pigs, peacocks, and goats are readily accessible to pet through the fence pens. If you come at the right time of year, you'll also see baby animals and have the opportunity to cuddle lambs and kids (i.e. baby goats). Animal feed is available for purchase for an additional 50¢. Old tractors, bales of hay, and the aroma of farm animals add to the barnyard atmosphere. Riding lessons, and/or pony rides around a track, are available, too. And yes, The Farm does birthday parties.

**Hours:** Open Sat. - Sun. and holidays from 10am - 5pm, weather permitting. Open in the summer one hour later.

**Admission:** $3 for ages 1 and up. Pony rides are an additional $2.50. Call for horse riding lessons.

**Ages:** All

## HOLLYWOOD PARK

(310) 419-1500 / www.hollywoodpark.com

*1050 South Prairie Avenue, Inglewood*

(Exit San Diego Fwy [405] E. on Century, L. on Prairie, or exit Century Fwy [105] N. on Prairie.)

Do your kids like horsing around? At Hollywood Park they can see thoroughbred horses, and enjoy a children's play area located at the north end of the park. The play area has a grassy lawn for picnicking as well as some playground equipment. Arcade games are also available here. The landscaping of the park, with its lagoons and tropical trees, is pleasing to the eye.

**Hours:** The season goes from mid-April through mid-July, and
November through mid-December. Call for racing information
and times.
**Admission:** $6 for adults (which includes parking and a program); children
17 years and under are free with a paid adult.
**Ages:** 4 years and up.

# INTERNATIONAL CENTER FOR GIBBON STUDIES ☀

(805) 296-2737 / www.izoo.org/icgs                                    *$$$*
*Esquerra Road, Santa Clarita*
(Exit Golden State Fwy [5] E. on Valencia Blvd., L. on Bouquet Canyon [about 5 ½
miles], R. on Esquerra Rd., which is a dirt road on the right-hand side that is easy to
miss - it is before you enter the Angeles National Forest. Go through the stream bed
(hard to cross if it's raining), a quick R. on Galton, another dirt road to a dirt driveway
outside the six-foot high chain-link fence.)

What's the difference between a monkey and an ape? If you answered,
"monkeys have tails," you are correct. Next question: Are gibbons monkeys or
apes? Hint - they have no tails. A one-hour guided tour of this outdoor facility
takes you past sixteen enclosures that hold over thirty-five gibbons in their
natural family groupings. The enclosures are sizable, chain-link cages, scattered
over the hard-packed dirt grounds and under shade trees. The tours are
informative, entertaining, and vary according to the interests and ages of each
tour group. Note: To ensure the safety of the gibbons, visitors must be in good
health, not have had any recent contact with a person or animal with an
infectious disease, and stay a minimum of five feet away from all enclosures.

Gibbons are arboreal apes - they swing from tree to tree - and are found in
the rainforests of Southeast Asia. This research facility, which has six out of the
eleven species, studies their behavior and helps to increase their endangered gene
pool, which means you could see babies on your visit here. Gibbons are the only
primates to walk upright and they have earned the name of loudest land mammal.
Every species has a different way of singing (that's the technical name - I call it
screaming) to each other, usually in the morning hours. They can project their
voices a distance of up to two miles. We heard them. I believe it. The kids loved
it. Siamangs have vocal sacs that inflate to the size of a large grapefruit when
they sing (reminiscent of a bullfrog). This is fascinating to listen to and watch.
Males and females in certain species are born one color and change colors as
they mature. (Is this the same thing as going gray?) We also learned about
gibbons' nutrition, why they are dying off, preventative medical care, and more.
My boys went ape over this center!
**Hours:** Open by appointment for groups of ten or more people.
**Admission:** $7 per person.
**Ages:** 4 years and up.

# LAKEWOOD PONY RIDES AND PETTING ZOO ☀

(562) 860-1108                                                           *$*
*11369 E. Carson Street, Lakewood*

(Exit San Gabriel River Fwy [605] W. on Carson. It's in the Lakewood Equestrian Center.)

If you're in the *neigh*borhood, saddle-up for a pony ride in this small, attractive, park-like, riding center. Choose from either a pony sweep, a parent-led walk around the track, or a trotting track (for ages 3 years and up). There is also a small petting zoo with a llama, a turkey, a pot belly pig, goats, rabbits, and sheep. Ponies and/or the petting zoo can be brought to your home, school, church, or fair for a party, too.

**Hours:**   Open Wed. - Sun. from 10am - 5pm.
**Admission:**   Pony rides are $2 each. The petting zoo is 50¢ per person.
**Ages:**   Children 1 year old and up to 100 pounds may enjoy the pony rides. All ages for the petting zoo.

# LONG BEACH AQUARIUM OF THE PACIFIC ☼
(562) 590-3100 / www.aquariumofpacific.org                    *$$$$*
*100 Aquarium Way, Long Beach*
(Exit San Diego Fwy [405] S. on the Long Beach Fwy [710] to the end of the Downtown exit, which will turn into Shoreline Dr., R. on Aquarium Way.)

Something fishy's going on at the fourth largest aquarium in the United States. The first stop in this multi-level aquarium is the spacious entryway, or Great Hall of the Pacific, where your attention is immediately riveted by a life-size, eighty-eight-foot blue whale (no way can a creature be so large!) hanging overhead with her calf "swimming" beside her. This hall also contains preview tanks of the main exhibit regions. Watch a short video about the aquarium in the theater, or one of several other sea-related films. Description cards, with the names and color photos of all the creatures, accompany each gallery. Information and breath-taking footage on the audio/video screens throughout the aquarium answer many of the questions visitors have about the animals here. Note that almost everything in the tanks, besides the fish, is man-made, although it is incredibly realistic looking. Note, too, that small Discovery Labs are located in each area and staffed with docents to answer questions, give demonstrations, and allow you to touch selected sea creatures. All exhibits are handicapped accessible. Now it's time to view the three main exhibit areas: California/Baja, Northern Pacific, and Tropical Pacific.

The natural flow of the aquarium leads visitors toward the back of the building, to the California/Baja area. Watch the enthralling moon jellies and other exotic drifters float gracefully around in their tanks. Peek at the Swell Shark egg cases where baby sharks are getting ready to be born. A kelp display shows those of us who aren't marine biologists that kelp is used as an ingredient in lipstick, Jell-O, toothpaste, and other household items. Catch an underwater look at the seals and sea lions splashing around. (Ask about feeding times, when divers often come in and play with the animals.) Walk up the stairs and outside to see these mammals sun themselves on the surface of the rocky "shoreline." Tiered cement seating allows good viewing for everyone. This outdoor plaza also features sea turtles, shore birds (who are unable to fly away), and a touch tank that holds stingrays and batrays. They feel like rubber. The Discovery Lab contains sea urchins, anemones, sea stars, and crabs to gently touch. Back inside, on the second floor of the gallery, you'll see aptly-named garden eels and a rocky reef that holds unusual looking fish, particularly the Lookdowns, a vertically flattened fish.

For a change in venue and temperature, enter the Northern Pacific gallery. The most popular attraction here are the playful sea otters in a tank with underwater and above-water viewing. Ample information is given about their fur (for which they've been voraciously hunted), their food, their habitats, and more. Other draws include the tank of anchovies (no pizza!), diving puffins (seabirds), monstrous-looking Giant Japanese Spider Crabs, and a Giant Pacific Octopus, which is not menacing, but so shy you might not even see him.

The Tropical Pacific is one of the most colorful sections here. It's set up so you'll "travel" through the reef and into deeper waters as you venture deeper into this gallery. The coral lagoon showcases brilliantly-colored fish - electric blue, canary yellow, jade green, vivid purple, etc. The largest tank, containing a tropical reef and its 1,000 inhabitants, offers various levels of viewing which is interesting because of the diversity of life shown in here. You'll see clown fish, zebra sharks, giant groupers, and more. At feeding time the divers are equipped with aquaphones to answer any questions. A partial water tunnel allows visitors to see sharks, and every parent knows that an aquarium visit is not complete without seeing sharks. Other outstanding exhibits in this gallery include deadly sea snakes; sea horses; the strange-looking leafy sea dragons and weedy sea dragons; upside-down jellies, who were created to live like this; orange-spined unicorn fish; sex reversal fish (mainly wrasses) who change from females to males as they mature or undergo stress - go figure; and beautiful, but venomous or poisonous fish, such as the lionfish.

The Kids' Cove, outside by the California/Baja gallery, is a semi-enclosed area with ocean-themed murals and several hands-on stations for kids. A canopied-covered theater, a sand play area, and a plexiglass whale that you can walk through to see its skeletal structure complete this cove.

Cafe Scuba has indoor tables, and outdoor tables that overlook the seal and sea lion exhibit and Rainbow Harbor. And yes, fish is on the menu.

Ask about the multitude of special events and programs offered to families and school groups including sleep overs, behind-the-scenes tours, studies of a particular animal or species, etc. Two classrooms in the educational wing are fully stocked with lab equipment, live systems (touch-tank animals), terrestrial aquariums, craft projects, etc. An educator's room, available for teachers, contains computers, books, arts and crafts resources, and more.

The aquarium is adjacent to Rainbow Harbor. In between the aquarium and harbor is an esplanade and a large green lawn. Feel free to bring a blanket and a picnic lunch. Head out on the esplanade (i.e. cement walkway) to the colorful-looking buildings of SHORELINE VILLAGE, a shopping and eating complex. Head the other way around the harbor toward a quasi park (i.e. an expanse of green lawn with a few picnic tables) where you can view the QUEEN MARY and SCORPION just across the waters. (Look under the Alphabetical Index for a listing of the places mentioned in capital letters.) Aquabuses (i.e. boats), which run from 8am to 8pm, will take you to and from those attractions for a minimal fee. Call (800) 429-4601 for more information.

**Hours:** Open daily 10am - 6pm.

**Admission:** $13.95 for adults; $11.95 for seniors; $6.95 for ages 3 - 11 years; children 2 years and under are free. Parking is $6. Catch a free ride to the aquarium on a bright red Long Beach Passport shuttle bus that cruises Pine Ave., Shoreline Dr., and Ocean Blvd. in the downtown area, and connects to the Metro Blue Line at the Transit Mall on First Street. Passports will also deliver you to the Queen Mary and Scorpion.

**Ages:** All

## LOS ANGELES ZOO                                                ☼

(323) 644-4200 / www.lazoo.org                                 *$$$*

*Griffith Park, Los Angeles*

(Going N. on Golden State Fwy [5] or W. Ventura Fwy [134], exit at Zoo Dr. and follow the signs. Going E. on 134, exit S. on Victory Blvd., L. on Zoo Dr. Going S. on 5, exit S. on Western, L. on Victory Blvd. to Zoo Dr.)

All the big-name animals star at the Los Angeles Zoo - elephants, tigers, mountain lions, giraffes, bears, kangaroos, polar bears, etc. Our favorites are the gorillas, apes, chimps, and other primates - they provide entertainment that tops television any day! An aquatic area features otters and seals. The darkened Koala House has koalas in their nighttime environment, since they are supposed to be more active at that time. Don't forget to ssssstop by the Reptile House! Tip: Zoo keys can be purchased for $3 and are good for a year. Insert a key in boxes at various animal enclosures to hear more information (and a jingle) about that particular species. If you get tired of walking around this huge and hilly zoo, purchase an all-day shuttle pass for $3 for adults, $1 for seniors and ages 2 to 12. The shuttle goes around the perimeter of the zoo, and will drop you off or pick you up at various stops along the way.

The entrance to Adventure Island is a cave. Inside it, kids can crawl through tunnels, look at exhibits on cave creature dwellers, and see a (pretend) stalactite and stalagmite. In this Adventure portion of the zoo, there are a few barnyard animals to pet through the fence pens, occasionally baby animals to observe through nursery windows, and some great interactive displays that teach about various zoo inhabitants and their habitats. The *Animals and You* live demonstration/show allows visitors to see, maybe touch, and definitely learn about an assortment of animals in an intimate setting.

At the prairie dog exhibit kids can pop their heads up from underneath the ground into a plexiglass dome while real prairie dogs are looking at them! This is a fun photo opportunity.

In the summer months, join in a Sundown Safari where your family can sleep in tents on the zoo grounds and enjoy special nighttime and behind-the-scenes tours. What a great experience! Ask about their numerous other special programs and events.

**Hours:**      Open daily from 10am - 5pm. Closed Christmas.
**Admission:**  $8.25 for adults; $5.25 for seniors; $3.25 for ages 2 - 12. (Certain discounts are available through AAA.) Sundown Safari costs $75 per adult; $50 per child.
**Ages:**       All

## MARINE MAMMAL CARE CENTER AT FORT MACARTHUR

(310) 548-5677 / www.mar3ine.org
*3601 South Gaffey Street, San Pedro*
(Exit the Harbor Fwy [110] S. on Gaffey St. Go almost to the end of Gaffey, turn R. through the gates on Leavenworth Dr., just past the FORT MACARTHUR MUSEUM.)

Injured or sick marine mammals, like sea lions and seals, are brought here, doctored, and taken care of until they can be released back into the wild. Rehabilitation can take one to three months, depending on the case. We saw one seal that was severely underweight and another that had numerous shark bites. This small facility usually houses five to twelve marine mammals outside in chain link fence pens. Your children have an opportunity to learn more about these animals as knowledgeable volunteers are on hand to answer any questions kids might ask. And they do ask! There are also classes offered through the Los Angeles school system that utilize the laboratory inside the adjacent building. (Look up FORT MACARTHUR MILITARY MUSEUM, under the Museums section, as it is located just across the street.)

**Hours:**      Open daily from 8am to 5pm.
**Admission:**  Free
**Ages:**       All - younger ones will just enjoy seeing the animals, while older ones can learn about them and appreciate what the Center does.

## MONTEBELLO BARNYARD ZOO / GRANT REA PARK

(323) 887-4595 - park; (323) 727-0269 - pony and horse rides
*600 Rea Drive (Grant Rea Park), Montebello*
(Exit San Gabriel River Fwy [605] E. on Beverly Blvd., R. on Rea Dr.)

A small Barnyard Zoo is at one corner of the Grant Rea Park. It has a small pond for ducks; an aviary with doves and peacocks; and pens holding goats, pigs, a cow, llamas, horses, and sheep that kids can pet through the fences. Visiting this "zoo" makes a stop at the park a little more special. Other activities include a short, truck-drawn hayride around part of the park for $1 per person; train rides around the same "track" for $1.50 per person; and pony rides, for younger children, twice around the walking track for $2.

The surrounding, nice-sized park is pretty. It has baseball diamonds, batting cages (open at certain times), picnic tables under shade trees, barbeques, a playground, and bike trails along the river bed.

**Hours:**      The park is open daily from 7am - dusk. The zoo is open daily 9:30am - 5pm. Specialty rides are usually available during zoo hours, except on Mondays, when the rides are closed. Call first.

**Admission:**  Free to the park and zoo. Prices for rides are given above.
**Ages:**  All

# MOUNT SAN ANTONIO COLLEGE FARM TOUR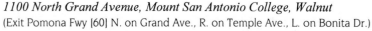
(909) 594-5611                                                                        *!*
*1100 North Grand Avenue, Mount San Antonio College, Walnut*
(Exit Pomona Fwy [60] N. on Grand Ave., R. on Temple Ave., L. on Bonita Dr.)

Take a forty-five minute guided tour of the farm animals on this college campus. You'll see cows, horses, goats, and sheep and, depending on your guide, learn about what the animals eat, how to take care of them, etc. The tour is geared for younger children and is simply a fun introduction to farm animals. Pack a sack lunch and enjoy a picnic area under nearby shade trees and the hilly, grassy field.

**Hours:**  Call for tour hours.
**Admission:**  Free, but donations are appreciated.
**Ages:**  3 - 10 years.

# ROUNDHOUSE AQUARIUM
(310) 379-8117 / www.commpages.com/roundhouse                                      *!/$*
*Manhattan Beach Boulevard, at the end of Manhattan Beach Pier,*
*Manhattan Beach*
(Exit San Diego Fwy [405] W. on Rosecrans Ave., L. on Pacific Coast Highway. Take the next R. on Valley Dr., R. on Manhattan Beach Blvd.)

Come see the stars of Manhattan, sea stars that is. The Roundhouse Aquarium is a very small marine learning center, but packed with information and exhibits. The various tanks contain leopard sharks and moray eels; two octopuses; a fifty-year-old, seventeen-pound spiny rock lobster (God definitely created some odd-looking creatures); and a touch tank containing mostly sea stars. A few other tanks with tropical fish and local invertebrates round out the collection at Roundhouse Aquarium. There are also whale bones and shark's teeth to examine.

Upstairs is a play and study center complete with sea animal puppets, books, and videos. Note: It gets crowded quickly inside the aquarium.

The aquarium offers marine science programs and field trips for students. For example, a one-hour class, for at least eight or more people of any age, includes learning about the marine environment and teaching time by the touch tanks. The cost is $4 per person. A three-hour class, given for kindergartners through twelfth graders, includes a lot of fascinating information, as well as hands-on fun such as touching sea stars and even petting a shark. The cost is $160 for forty students. Sleeping with the Sharks is an overnight field trip that includes a pizza party (i.e. similar to a shark feeding frenzy), touching sharks and shark teeth, dissecting parts of a shark, and more. The cost is $50 per person.

On your way out to the aquarium, which is located at the end of a concrete pier, check out all the beach activity - sand volleyball, surfing, swimming, and of course, sun bathing. You can also, ironically, fish from the pier. Sidewalk shops are just down the street.

**Hours:** Open Mon. - Fri., 3pm to sunset; Sat. - Sun., 10am - sunset. Call for tour and program times.

**Admission:** Free entrance to the aquarium; donations encouraged. Tour prices are given above. Metered parking is available on Manhattan Beach Blvd. by the stores, or wherever you can find it!

**Ages:** 2 years and up.

## SANTA ANITA PARK
(626) 574-7223 / www.santaanita.com
*285 W. Huntington Drive, Arcadia*
(Exit Foothill Fwy [210] S. on Baldwin Ave., L. into the parking lot for Gate 8. The park is located next to a shopping mall.)

Hold your horses! One of the most famous thoroughbred horse racing parks in the United States is surprisingly family-friendly. Watch the horses being put through their paces during their morning workouts from 7:30am to 9:30am. Grab a bite to eat at Clocker's Corner Cafe breakfast counter which offers inexpensive items that can be eaten at the outside patio area overlooking the track. On Saturdays and Sundays, weather permitting, between 8am and 9am take a free, fifteen-minute, behind-the-scenes, narrated tram ride. Catch the tram near Clocker's Corner Cafe in the parking lot near the west side of the grandstands. You'll ride along dirt "roads", through a hub of horse activity, and past rows of stables where walkers, trainers, and jockeys are exercising, bathing, and grooming horses. Tip: Call first as the tram ride is not offered on days of major races.

Walk in the beautifully landscaped Paddock Gardens, located just inside the admission gate, to look at the flowers, statues, and equine-themed topiary plants. In the gardens, twenty minutes prior to post time, there is a brief "show" as jockeys, in their colorful silks, walk and ride their mounts around the walking ring before going on to the race track. Note: The first race usually begins at 1pm. Weekends bring special events such as mariachi bands and dancers, costumed park mascots strolling about, etc.

Go through a paved tunnel from the gardens to the infield (i.e. interior of the racetrack) to reach a playground. Kids can horse around on the large play structure that has wavy slides, metal domed monkey bars, a merry-go-round, and a circular swing set. The infield also features large grassy areas for running around and picnicking, so pack a lunch. Note: You may stay in the infield during races.

From the time the starting gates (which are portable) and jockeys are in position, to the finish line, enthusiasm runs rampant through the crowd. The actual races, although over quickly, are thrilling, even for non-betters. (The numerous manned windows and wagering machines receive a lot of frantic activity.) My boys "scientifically" deduced who to root for - according to the horse's name and/or the color of the jockey's silks. Tip: Sitting in grandstand seats is the best way to see the action as the slanted cement standing area in front of the seats fills up quickly with people who are always taller than you. Note: It is almost a half an hour between races.

Lunchtime food can be purchased at snack bars, the cafeteria, the casual, but nice Turf Club, or the posh Club House, where appropriate dress is required. Prices vary according to venue.

I wager your kids will have a good time watching the "Sport of Kings."

**Hours:** The season runs the month of October to mid-November, and the end of December through April.

**Admission:** Free admission before 9:30am includes watching the daily horse workouts and, on weekends, going on the tram ride. If you arrive after 9:30am, admission is $4 for adults; free for kids 17 years and under when accompanied by an adult. Parking is $3 after 9:30am.

**Ages:** 4 years and up.

# STAR EXPLORATION STATION CHILDREN'S ☼ MUSEUM

(310) 445-1428 / e-mail:starincorp@earthlink.net            *$$*
*3909 Sepulveda Boulevard, Culver City*
(Exit San Diego Fwy [405] E. on Venice Blvd., R. on Sepulveda Blvd. It's on the right hand side of the street with metered parking out front.)

Step into a re-created rainforest, complete with (fake) rock walls, plants, murals, camouflage, and a front desk decorated as a thatched-roof hut. The museum's purpose is to teach kids the importance of preserving the environment and protecting wildlife. In fact, it is a designated wildlife sanctuary and works with the Department of Fish and Game. Illegal articles, seized from people trying to smuggle them into the country via airports, seaports, and over the border, are displayed here for show and tell.

Groups must squeeze into the several small rooms in this compact museum to see and touch the live animals, but the interaction and comprehensive information make it worth your while. The first room contains cockatoos. Visitors will hear what the birds eat, all about their behavior, and how they are treated cruelly (the majority die) while being imported for profit. Kids are encouraged to gently stroke a cockatoo's feathers and even hold the birds. The next room has terrariums and aquariums that contain newts, eels, colorful angelfish and blue tangs, coral that's been harvested, a unique pillow starfish, and other aquatic creatures taken from people attempting to bring them into the U.S. An adjoining room holds a Nile monitor, a Komodo dragon, and tortoises. The chameleons in here may be touched and held. Kids (and adults) are invited to wrap the pythons around themselves, or for the more squeamish, to merely stroke them (or not). The last room contains confiscated goods, that children may touch, such as boots made out of rattlesnakes; a purse made out of an alligator, including its head and paws; animals' skins such as tiger, zebra, and cheetah; an elephant foot stool; and more. Again in here, children will be educated about endangered species.

School or group tours generally run two hours, which can be a bit long for younger children. During public hours, visitors may roam around the museum. A staff person is stationed in each room to answer any questions and assist you in holding the animals.

**Hours:** Open to the public Sat. from 10am - 4pm. Open for school/group tours, minimum 35 students and maximum 80, Mon. - Fri. between 9am - 3pm.

**Admission:** $5 for adults; $4 ages 2 - 12 years; children under 2 years are free. For a school/group tour the cost is $3 per child; one adult is free for every ten children.

**Ages:** 2 years and up.

## SUNSET RANCH HOLLYWOOD STABLES

(323) 464-9612 / www.usrc.net/sunsetranch

*3400 N. Beachwood Drive, Los Angeles*

(Exit the Ventura Fwy [101] S. on Cahuenga Blvd., E. on Franklin Ave., N. on Beachwood Dr., all the way up to the top.)

Many places offer scenic horseback riding during the day, including this one, but this stable also offers guided, moonlit rides. You'll leave around 6pm and ride over the hills of Griffith Park. Parts of this trail are very secluded, and beautiful. At 8pm or so, you'll arrive at Vivas Mexicas restaurant. After dinner, head back to arrive at the stables around 11pm. It's a long night, but a special one, too.

**Hours:** Fri. nights from 5:30pm - 11pm.

**Admission:** $35 per person; dinner costs extra.

**Ages:** 12 years and up.

## TROUTDALE

(818) 889-9993

*2468 Troutdale Drive, Agoura*

(Exit Ventura Fwy [101] S. on Kanan Rd., L. on Troutdale Dr.)

"Fishy, fishy in a brook/ Daddy caught him with a hook./ Mammy fried him in a pan/ And baby ate him like a man." (Childcraft, Poems and Rhymes, 1966)

Troutdale is in a woodsy setting with two small ponds to fish from - perfect for beginners. There are logs to sit on around the perimeter of the ponds. The entrance price includes a bamboo fishing pole and bait. For an extra 50¢, you can get your fish cleaned. Munch at the snack bar or bring a picnic lunch to eat while you're catching dinner. Be sure to pick up a flyer that has recipe ideas.

**Hours:** Open Mon. - Fri., 10am - 4pm; Sat. - Sun., 9am - 5pm. Weekend hours are extended during the summer.

**Admission:** $3 per person, fishing or not. Fish prices vary depending on its length. For instance, a rainbow trout that is 10" - 11" long costs $4.25.

**Ages:** 3 years and up.

## U.C.L.A. OCEAN DISCOVERY CENTER

(310) 393-6149 / www.lifesci.ucla.edu/odc                     *$$*
*1600 Ocean Front Walk, Santa Monica*
(Exit Santa Monica Fwy [10] N. on 4<sup>th</sup> St., L. on Colorado Ave. It is at the foot of the
Santa Monica Pier.)

Discover what really lives in the Santa Monica Bay at the Ocean Discovery
Center, located under the Santa Monica Pier. This small, but fascinating center
has several tanks of live sea creatures to look at and touch. The changing exhibit
is the open ocean tank. We saw moon jellies that were mesmerizing to watch as
their milky white bodies floated gracefully around in their tank. Another large
aquarium holds crabs, sea stars, and various fish. Use the flashlight provided to
see tiny Swell Sharks developing inside their hanging egg cases. Mature Swell
Sharks, sand crabs, sand dollars, leopard sharks, and batrays are too fragile for
fingers, but they are easily seen in shallow tanks placed at a child's eye level.
Kids can, however, gently touch tidepool life such as sea stars, sea anemones,
and sea slugs. A touch table displays a shark's jaw and individual teeth. It also
has a microscope for closeup look at scales, shells, etc.

Another prime attraction in the center is the numerous Discovery boxes that
are filled with age-appropriate activities, games, and/or books. Choose from
Diving Deep, Knot Relay, Ocean Life Puzzles, Beach Bingo, and more. The
beautiful, marine-muraled classroom was designed for the instructional use of
the school programs that are offered here. These informative and interactive one-
hour-plus programs are offered year round.

Make a day of your visit to the Discovery Center by taking a walk on the
pier (see SANTA MONICA PIER under the Piers and Seaports section),
enjoying some rides at PACIFIC PARK (see this entry under the Amusement
Parks section), or just playing at the beach!

**Hours:**    Open Sat. - Sun., 11am - 5pm. It is open in the summer Tues. -
            Fri., 2pm - 6pm, as well as the normal weekend hours. Call for
            holiday hours.
**Admission:**  $3 for adults; children 2 years and under are free. School
            programs are $120 for up to sixty students.
**Ages:**    3 years and up.

## WILDLIFE WAYSTATION

(818) 899-5201 - info; (800) 540-2373 - reservations /          *$$$*
www.waystation.org
*14831 Little Tujunga Canyon Road, Angeles National Forest*
(From Golden State Fwy [5], go N.E. on San Fernando Fwy [118], E. on Foothill Fwy
[210], N.E. on Foothill Blvd., L. [or N.] on Osborn, up the winding road that turns into
Tujunga Canyon Rd. You'll see the signs.)

This donor-supported waystation is in existence to help wild animals with
the three "r's": rescue, rehabilitate, and refuge. Our tour guide told us that they
sometimes rehabilitate and release baby animals in the wild and, when
appropriate, they release adults in the wild, too. My 8-year-old heard this, and
with an incredulous look said, "They release adults in the wild?"

This can be a wonderful wildlife experience as long as you and your children follow the necessarily stringent rules. The shelters here provide homes to over 1,000 animals - lions, tigers, the rare ligers (a cross between a lion and a tiger), bears, wolves, bobcats, jaguars, leopards, primates, etc. We were in awe of seeing so many "zoo" animals up close, separated by almost nothing more than a chain link fence. This is where the rules come in. Since carnivores tend to look at children as dinner, and the unpaved trails are narrow, parents must keep a really close eye, and/or hand, on their kids.

We learned fascinating facts about the animals and their habitats on our forty-five-minute walking tour. Note: Not all of the paths, especially the ones with wooden steps, are stroller/wheelchair friendly. The tour guides are committed and knowledgeable volunteers, but they do vary greatly in their ability and desire to relate to kids.

Make sure to spend time at the Waystation either before or after your tour to watch the animal presentations. Every half hour, or so, individual animals are brought out on a small stage by a learned handler who provides excellent opportunities to learn more about particular species. We have seen and learned about rattlesnakes, birds of prey, wolves, lions and, even the unusual binturong (i.e. "bear/cat").

Feed the animals at the petting zoo for an additional 50¢, or just pet them for no additional cost. The zoo contains pigs, goats, llamas, emus, and donkeys. Snacks for humans are available for purchase, but bringing outside food is not allowed. If you are interested in supporting the Waystation, ask about being a financial donor and/or call before your visit to see what items on their wish list you can bring, such as shovels, toilet paper tubes, towels, etc.

**Hours:** Tours are offered every hour between 10am - 5pm on the first and third Sun. of each month, weather permitting. Group tours can be arranged on other days. Reservations are required for all tours.

**Admission:** $12 for adults; $6 for ages 3 - 11; children 2 years and under are free. (Your "donation" is tax deductible.)

**Ages:** 3 years and up.

## CASA DE TORTUGA

(714) 962- 0612         *!*

*10455 Circulo de Zapata, Fountain Valley*

(Going N. on San Diego Fwy [405], exit N. on Brookhurst, R. on Slater, L. on Ward, L. on Circulo de Zapata. Going S. on 405 , exit E. on Warner. R. on Ward, R. on Circulo de Zapata. Casa De Tortuga is in a residential section and is actually outside [and inside] a large house.)

Come out of your shell to see the wonderful variety of turtle and tortoise species - over 100 - at this "House of Turtles." A favorite is the large Galapagos Island tortoise. In this one-hour, outdoor tour children walk around the turtle pens, within touching distance of the turtles. Kids will hear what tortoises like to eat, which are endangered species, what "endangered species" means, and the difference between a turtle and a tortoise. Docents welcome questions, which makes your curious child very happy.

We also loved the "really neat" pond in the backyard filled with turtles. If your child is interested in adopting a turtle, he/she will be given information to help make the best choice. Note: Narrow pebbled walkways make strollers difficult to push.

Slow and steady might win the race, but tours here fill up almost a year in advance, so hurry and make your reservation. (No more than twenty-five people are allowed in any group.) Casa De Tortuga has a free, annual open house, usually held the third weekend in August - no reservations are needed (or accepted).

**Hours:**     Tours are given Mon. - Sat. at 10am.
**Admission:** Free
**Ages:**      3 years and up.

# CENTENNIAL FARM

(714) 708-1618
*88 Fair Drive, Costa Mesa*
(Exit Costa Mesa Fwy [55] S.W. on Newport Blvd., R. on Fair Dr., through Gate #1. It's in the Orange County Fair Grounds.)

This outdoor working farm has pigs, chickens, sheep, bunnies, ducks, Clydesdale horses, and a buffalo. During the springtime, in particular, be on the lookout for the many animal babies that are born here. The bee observatory is fascinating and with their nonstop motion, it's easy to see where the term "busy boys" oops, I mean "busy bees," came from.

Walk around the grounds to learn about other aspects of farming. Younger kids will probably be amazed to see vegetables such as carrots, zucchini, lettuce, and corn being grown, not already picked and packaged as in the grocery stores. (Please do not pick the vegetables or feed the animals.)

A ninety-minute free tour of the farm is available for grades kindergarten and up, for groups of ten or more students. The tour includes going into the main building and seeing chicks hatch in the incubator, planting a seed (and then taking it home), and learning about the food groups. Reservations are required.

A few picnic tables are here at the farm too, so pack a sack lunch. The huge parking lot is usually empty at this time, so bring skates or bikes.

**Hours:**     The farm is open to the public August through May, Mon. - Fri. from 1pm - 4pm; Sat. - Sun., 9am - 4pm. Tours are given October through May, Mon. - Fri. at 9am and 11am. The farm is closed to the public in June, and open in July only with paid admission to the Orange County Fair. (See the July Calendar section.)
**Admission:** Free
**Ages:**      2 years and up during public hours; kindergarten and up for the tours.

## FRIENDS OF THE SEA LION MARINE MAMMAL CENTER ☼

(949) 494-3050 / www.fslmmc.org !

*20612 Laguna Canyon Road, Laguna Beach*

(Exit San Diego Fwy [405] or Santa Ana Fwy [5] S. on Laguna Canyon Rd. [Hwy 133]. It's just S. of El Toro Rd.)

This Center is a small, safe harbor for sea lions and harbor seals that are abandoned, ailing, or in need of medical attention. The animals are kept outside in bathtub-like pens until they are ready to be released back into the wild. This is a good opportunity for kids to see these animals up-close, while learning more about them and the effect that we have on our oceans (i.e. their habitats). The volunteers are great at answering the numerous (and sometimes off-the-wall) questions they are asked.

Feeding time, usually around 3pm or 4pm, is lively as the sea lions go wild, barking in anticipation of a meal. (It sounds like mealtime at our house.) There are usually between five to twelve mammals here, but more arrive toward the end of pupping season, which is the end of March through July. (Also see LAGUNA KOI PONDS, in this section, located just north of the center.)

**Hours:** Open daily from 10am - 4pm.
**Admission:** Free; donations gladly accepted.
**Ages:** 3 years and up.

## JONES FAMILY MINI FARM / LOS RIOS DISTRICT ☼

(949) 831-6550 $

*31791 Los Rios Street, San Juan Capistrano*

(Exit the San Diego Fwy [5] W. on Ortega Hwy [74]., L. at Camino Capistrano, R. on Verdugo. It's behind the Amtrack Station in the Los Rios Historic Section.)

This working "mini-farm" will become a favorite stopping place whenever you visit San Juan Capistrano. Inside the barn is a small petting pen with goats, sheep, rabbits, and guinea pigs. The farm also has a few other animals to pet through the fence pens, such as donkeys, horses, and a pot-bellied pig. Feed is available to purchase for the animals - 50¢. Starting at 8 months old, kids up to eighty pounds can ride a pony around a track. For a birthday party with a real farm, or western flavor, rent the large outside picnic area for $100 for two hours.

Leave your car at MISSION SAN JUAN CAPISTRANO (see the Museums section), which is just down the street, or park by the Amtrack depot off Verdugo Street. Either way, enjoy a short walk to the farm and around this quaint, historic area. In front of the farm is the 100-year-old Olivares Home, and next door is the O'Neil Historic Museum, (949) 493-8444. Older kids might enjoy a walk through these Victorian homes to see antique furniture and clothing.

**Hours:** The Farm is open Wed. - Sun. from 11am - 4pm. O'Neil Historic Museum is open Tues. - Fri., 9am - noon and 1pm - 4pm; Sun., noon - 3pm.

**Admission:** Free to walk around outside of the farm. For 50¢ per person, you may go inside the petting farm. Pony rides are $2 per ride. O'Neil Museum is free; donations of $1 per person are appreciated.

**Ages:** All

## LAGUNA KOI PONDS

(949) 494-5107 / www.lagunakoi.com

*20452 Laguna Canyon Rd., Laguna Beach*

(Exit Santa Ana Fwy [5] S. on Laguna Canyon Rd. [Hwy 133]. It's just S. of El Toro Rd.)

This fun little stop off has several cement tanks filled with Koi fish, and a store carrying fish supplies. We enjoy just looking at these colorful fish with their beautiful patterns. Who knows, you may want to purchase a few to raise at home. You may also feed them - 25¢ for a handful of pellets. It's fun to watch their large mouths open quickly and bite at the food. Combine a trip here with a visit to the FRIENDS OF THE SEA LION MARINE MAMMAL CENTER (see this section), which is located just south of the ponds.

**Hours:** Open Mon. - Sat., 9am - 5pm; Sun., 11am - 5pm

**Admission:** Free

**Ages:** All

## LOS ALAMITOS RACE COURSE

(714) 995-1234 / www.losalamitos.com

*4961 E. Katella Avenue, Los Alamitos*

(Exit San Gabriel River Fwy [605] E. on Willow/Katella, or going N. W., exit San Diego Fwy [405] or Garden Grove Fwy [22] N. on Valley View, L. on Katella.)

Thoroughbreds, quarter horses, Arabian horses, and harness racing are the attractions here. Have your child cheer for his favorites! Call for schedule information.

**Hours:** Open year round - call for specific races and hours.

**Admission:** $3 for adults, or $5 for the clubhouse; kids 15 years and under are free. Free parking.

**Ages:** 4 years and up.

## MAGNOLIA BIRD FARM (Anaheim)

(714) 527-3387

*8990 Cerritos, Anaheim*

(Exit the Santa Ana Fwy [5] W. on Ball Rd., L. on Magnolia, R. on Cerritos. It's on the corner.)

Take your flock of kids to visit their fine feathered friends at the Magnolia Bird Farm pet shop. Birds here range from common doves and canaries to more exotic cockatoos and macaws. Upstairs is a small-bird aviary and a bird room with cement walls that echo their continuous squawking.

The Bird Farm has bird accessories, including a wide assortment of bird cages. Here's a craft idea: Buy a simple wooden cage for your kids to paint and decorate, then fill it with bird seed, and hang it up in your backyard. While you're here, have your kids take the bird challenge - see if they can get one of the talking birds to actually speak to them! (Also see MAGNOLIA BIRD FARM, La Sierra.)

**Hours:** Open Tues. - Sat. from 9am - 5pm.
**Admission:** Free
**Ages:** All

## ORANGE COUNTY ZOO

(714) 633-2022 / www.oc.ca.gov/pfrd/hbp/oczoo.htm
*1 Irvine Park Road, Orange*

(Exit Newport Fwy [55] E. on Chapman, N. on Jamboree, ends at Irvine Regional Park.)

Take a trip to the zoo while you're in the park! Tucked away in the massive IRVINE REGIONAL PARK (see the Great Outdoors section) is the eight-acre Orange County Zoo. The zoo has barnyard animals such as cows, sheep, goats, and pigs to pet through fence pens. Food dispensers are here, too. The main section of the zoo features animals native to the southwestern United States, such as mountain lions, bobcats, deer, coyotes, brown pelicans, a black bear, and a variety of birds.

**Hours:** Open daily from 10am - 3:30pm.
**Admission:** $1 for ages 6 and up; children 5 years and under are free. This admission is in addition to the vehicle entrance fee to the park.
**Ages:** All

## SANTA ANA ZOO

(714) 835-7484 / www.santaanazoo.org
*1801 E. Chestnut Avenue, Santa Ana*

(Going S. on Santa Ana Fwy [5], exit at 4ᵗʰ St. go straight on Mabury St., turns into Elk Ln., L. on Chestnut. Going N. on 5, exit W. on 1ˢᵗ St., L. on Elk Ln., L. on Chestnut. It's at Prentice Park.)

Lions and tigers and bears - not here! This small zoo, however, is perfect for young children. They can easily walk around it all, see all the animals, and still have of time to play on the playground, in just a few hours. The Santa Ana Zoo houses llamas; cavies; small mammals, such as porcupines; birds, including bald eagles; and a wide variety of monkeys - our personal favorites. Walk through the wonderful aviary where you can see beautiful and exotic birds close up. The Children's Zoo has pigs, goats, and sheep to pet through pens, plus reptiles and amphibians to look at. Kids can take a short elephant ride ($2.50 per person), between 11am to 3pm on most weekends October through May. The playground has a small climbing hut, slides, and turtle statues. The gift shop has a wonderful variety of animal-oriented merchandise. Purchase lunch at the snack bar, which is usually open, or enjoy a sack lunch right outside the zoo gates at the adjoining Prentice Park which offers picnic tables, grassy areas, and shade trees.

Breakfast with the Beasts is a once-a-month Saturday morning program offered for ages 3 and older. It includes a light breakfast, a guided tour, and a chance to feed some animals in the Children's Zoo. The fee is $15 for one parent and one child; $7.50 for each additional person. A variety of other educational and interactive programs for kids are also offered throughout the year.

Hours:    Open Mon. - Fri., 10am - 4pm; Sat. - Sun., 10am - 5pm. Closed New Year's Day and Christmas.

Admission:    $4 for adults; $2 for seniors and ages 3 - 12; children 2 years and under and the physically impaired are free. (AAA discounts available.)

Ages:    All

## MAGNOLIA BIRD FARM (La Sierra)

(909) 278-0878

*12200 Magnolia Avenue, La Sierra*

(Exit Riverside Fwy [91] S.W. on Magnolia Ave.)

See MAGNOLIA BIRD FARM, Anaheim, for a more complete description of the bird farm. The main difference between the two is size, with this location being almost three times larger. The aviary here includes parakeets, love birds, finches, and quail, as well as doves and pigeons.

As springtime brings the birth of new baby birds, kids can sometimes see them being hand fed through the glass walls. Tour groups, of at least ten or more people, will learn about seed, such as which kind is best for what species; see and study a (live) white dove; and more.

Hours:    Open Tues. - Sat. from 9am - 5pm. Reservations are needed for the free, half-hour tour.

Admission:    Free

Ages:    All

## AMERICAN WILDERNESS ZOO AND AQUARIUM

(909) 481-6604 / www.wildernessexp.com    $$$

*4557 One Mills Circle, in Ontario Mills Mall, Ontario*

(Exit San Bernardino Fwy [10] L. on Milliken Ave., R. on 4th Street or exit Ontario Fwy [15] W. on 4th St. It's next to the food court and AMC Theaters.)

Where can you see forest, mountains, desert, ocean, and a rainforest all in one day? At American Wilderness Zoo and Aquarium, which consists of five carefully recreated regions (or rooms) inside this building in the mall. The regions are complete with the sights, sounds, and live animals native to each habitat. Talk about going wild at the mall!

Start your visit with a six-minute Star Tours-style simulator ride that jolts you along with an on-screen, computer-animated journey through animal habitats as seen from the animal's point of view. Then, enter the Redwood Forest room where fake trees and lush foliage look real. One wall, made of faux rocks, houses banana slugs (ugh), and a variety of snakes and other reptiles behind glass enclosures. Walk through a huge, carved-out "redwood" to reach the High Sierras room. In here, behind glass, live bobcats and marmots are in separate enclosures only a few feet away from you. In the adjoining Mojave Desert room observe roadrunners, quail, jackrabbits, tortoises, kangaroo rats, a coatimundi, Gila monsters, and other lizards up close. The Pacific Shore room has a large aquarium containing colorful fish, sea stars, and sea cucumbers. Ethereal-looking moonjellies occupy a smaller aquarium. In a tank along one wall watch a few harbor seals frolic in the waters. A small tidal touch tank encourages visitors to gently touch sea stars, sea anemones, and sea urchins. In the adjacent Amazon Valley room, enclosures contain two-toed sloths, ocelots, marmosets (small monkeys), a toucanet, and Brazilian Agoutis, which look like large guinea pigs with long legs. The far wall has an aquarium tank with turtles, glow-in-the-dark fish, and prehistoric-looking lizards. The hallway just before you exit has glass cases containing tortoises, tarantulas, snakes, and unique-looking poisonous frogs. Each region, or "biome," has at least one knowledgeable "ranger" available to answer any questions. Experience Wilderness on your own, or take a guided tour to learn about the animals and climates you encounter.

Check out Wilderness' well-stocked retail store and the neighboring Wilderness Grill, which serves good food in a rustic, log cabin type of atmosphere. You will also want to spend some time in the gigantic ONTARIO MILLS MALL (look under the Malls section for more details), a tourist attraction in its own right. Other "shoppertainment" features at the mall include UltraScreen and 3D IMAX movies, a virtual reality arcade, a fancifully-decorated food court, and hundreds of outlet and specialty retail stores.

**Hours:** Open Sun. - Thurs., 10am - 9pm; Fri. - Sat., 10am - 10pm
**Admission:** $9.95 for adults; $8.95 for seniors; $7.95 for ages 3 - 11; children 2 years and under are free. Combined entrance to Wilderness and an UltraScreen movie is $14.95 for adults; $12.95 for seniors; $11 for ages 3 - 11; children 2 years and under are free.
**Ages:** All

# FLYING HOP RANCH

(760) 249-3795  / robertk@snowline.net
*4757 Hwy 138, West Cajon Valley*
(Exit Mojave Fwy [15] W. on Hwy. 138, the Palmdale/Silverwood Lake exit. Go 3.2 miles and look for ranch on the right.)

Come on over to "Down Under." This twenty-acre working ranch, dubbed Little Australia, is home to 100 emus (which are native only to Australia), over 600 bunnies (the ranch supplies pet stores), as well as chickens, llamas, goats, pigs, donkeys, sheep, ducks, foxes, and a few turtles. The forty-five-minute hands-on tours encompass petting some of the animals (feed is available to purchase), gathering an egg from the chicken coop, holding bunnies, and looking into the emu nursery. Note: Emus hatch from November through April. You'll learn about the animals, their care and breeding; Australia; life on a ranch; and lots more. An informational pamphlet, a child's activity booklet, a certificate (stating that you've learned how to care for bunnies), and an emu feather are given out to visitors. The hard-packed dirt "roads" make the ranch stroller/wheelchair accessible. There are picnic tables and shade trees, so pack a lunch. Don't forget to check out the Aussie-themed gift shop! The ranch also offers tent and RV camping. Each site has a picnic table and fire pit.

**Hours:** Open daily 9am - 5pm. School tours are given by appointment.
**Admission:** $4 for adults; $2.50 for seniors and ages 2 - 15; children under 2 are free. School tours are $2.50 per person. Camping is $18 a night.
**Ages:** All

## CHULA VISTA NATURE CENTER

(619) 422-2473 / sdcc12.ucsd.edu/~wa12/cvnature.html
*1000 Gunpowder Point Drive, Chula Vista*
(Exit San Diego Fwy [5] W. on "E" St. to park, or exit E. on "E" St, to park at the Visitor's Center and take the free trolley into the Nature Center.)

Putting their hands in a pool of hungry sharks is only one of the special things that kids (and adults) are invited to do at the Chula Vista Nature Center, located in the Sweetwater Marsh National Wildlife Refuge. You'll start your visit by taking an old-fashioned trolley (free of charge) into the refuge - cars are not allowed. The medium-sized center is full of interactive exhibits such as pulling apart tabs with suction cups attached to them to experience the grip of an octopus; using a bioscanner (i.e. a mounted camera with a zoom lens) to see anemones close up on a monitor; and poking your head up into a glassed-enclosed exhibit to watch mice run around. (Mice use the marsh as hunting grounds.) The touch table has pelican bones, bird skulls, whale vertebrae, and shells. There are several tanks with live sea creatures, such as seahorses, halibut, lobsters, and rainbow trout. Listen for the snapping sounds of the snapping shrimp as they try to frighten predators away. Like a good mystery? Then try to find the California scorpionfish, who are hiding in plain sight.

My boys proudly boast that they've touched a shark, and lived! The outside petting pool contains leopard and horn sharks as well as batrays, stingrays, and the odd-looking shovel-nose guitarfish. (These creatures actually come within petting distance.) Join in the feeding fun, which usually takes place around 4pm.

An outside overlook affords an opportunity to observe terns, killdeer, plovers, sandpipers, and more wetlands wildlife. A walk-through bird aviary features the clapper rail, as well as some interactive exhibits such as rubbing tables and an oversized clapper rail nest for kids to crawl inside. A hummingbird and a butterfly garden are also on the grounds. Stroller-friendly trails in front of the Center branch off in various directions and allow kids to get close to the bay to see geese, egrets, or smaller water inhabitants. Look for other wildlife along the trail such as bunnies, turtles, and lizards.

The Nature Center offers a variety of on-site special programs, such as Make It Take It craft workshops for ages five and up, given on Saturdays and Sundays from 1pm to 2pm for 50¢. Call to get a complete schedule, or to sign up for a guided group tour.

**Hours:** Open Tues. - Sun. from 10am - 5pm. Open in the summer the same hours, plus Mondays. Closed New Year's Day, Easter, Thanksgiving, and Christmas. Trolleys run approximately every 25 minutes.

**Admission:** $3.50 for adults; $2.50 for seniors; $1 for ages 6 - 17; children 5 years and under are free. Prices subject to change. The first Tues. of every month is free admission day.

**Ages:** 3 years and up.

## DEL MAR FAIRGROUNDS / RACETRACK

(619) 755-1141 / www.delmarfair.com

*Del Mar Fairgrounds, Del Mar*

(Exit San Diego Fwy [5] W. on Via de la Valle)

Horse racing season at the famous Del Mar Fairgrounds begins in July and runs through mid-September. Kids have good horse sense - they aren't here to bet, but to enjoy the races. Also inquire about horse shows, rodeos, and polo games.

**Hours:** Gates are open Mon., and Wed. - Fri. at noon; Sat. - Sun., 11:30am. Post time is usually 2pm, although it's at 4pm for the first five Fri.

**Admission:** General admission is $3 for adults; $6 for clubhouse; free for children 17 years and under.

**Ages:** 5 years and up.

## FREEFLIGHT

(619) 481-3148

*2132 Jimmy Durante Boulevard, Del Mar*

(Exit San Diego Fwy [5] S. on Via de la Valle [toward the ocean], L. on Jimmy Durante, follow around the fairgrounds.)

This boarding house for birds is also a breeding facility with baby birds available for sale. When you walk along the pathway in the yard you'll see over thirty perches, and between thirty to ninety birds. Over twenty of them may be handled and touched by visitors. Bring 25¢ to purchase peanuts to feed the birds. Freeflight offers half-hour tours that explain the different types of birds, their habitats, etc. Please note that children under 13 years must be accompanied by a parent. Tip: Bring a sweater because the beach weather is often cool.

**Hours:** Open daily from 10am - 4pm. Closed on rainy days.

**Admission:** $1 per person.

**Ages:** 3 years and up.

## LEELIN LLAMA TREKS

(800) LAMAPAK (526-2725) or (760)765-1890 / www.llamatreks.com   *$$$$$*

*1645 Whispering Pines Drive, Julian*

(Exit 78 Fwy E. on Whispering Pines Dr. It's just N. of the town of Julian)

Looking for an unusual outing? Sign up for a llama trek! Choose from a variety of destinations - to the lake, through the mountains, through the town of Julian, etc. - in the beautiful Julian countryside. Each member of the group leads his/her own llama that carries trekkers' lunches and other necessities. Most kids, and adults, aren't used to being around llamas, so the intrigue, as well as the scenery, makes the four-hour expeditions unique experiences. The animals are gentle, enjoy being pet, and by the end of the trek, your children will want to take theirs home. They can't. A deli sandwich, cold salad, cookie, and cold drink are included in your outing. Even young children will enjoy the shorter treks, while ages 8 and older are eligible to go on overnight trips to the Sierras. The latter excursion includes four or five nights of camping in the mountains, hiking, and delicious, home-cooked food!

LeeLin Wickiup is a bed and breakfast owned by LeeLin Llama Treks. Each room is decorated in different decor - Native American, Victorian, or rustic. The Wickiup is situated on a heavily-wooded, three-acre hillside, so kids can run around outside, as well as pet the llamas. Combine a day-long llama trek with staying here overnight.

**Hours:** Call for reservations. At least two people must sign up for any of the treks.

**Admission:** Prices range from $55 - $85 for the day trip, depending on destination, duration, and difficulty of hike. Children 11 years and under are half price. Prices are about $750 per person for the six-day excursions. Wickiup rates start at $105 per couple during the week.

**Ages:** 4 years and up.

## THE MONARCH PROGRAM

(760) 944-7113

*450 Oceanview Avenue, Encinitas*

(Exit San Diego Fwy [5] W. on Encinitas Blvd., R. on Vulcan, R. on Orpheus, R. on Union, R. on Oceanview.)

I'm not particularly fond of most insects, so I think butterflies should be in a classification by themselves, called beautiful winged creatures, or something. This research facility/butterfly house has two rooms devoted to our fluttery friends. The education room is classroom-size and contains maps that show the path of butterfly migrations, plus real caterpillars, chrysalides, and other stages of metamorphosis. A docent is on hand to answer any questions. A video, showing the life cycle of a butterfly, can be watched upon request.

The second room, or vivarium, is 1,200 square feet of plants, flowers, a few trees, a waterfall, and butterflies alighting on everything. Most of the butterflies in here are native to California, except the zebra butterfly. You'll see monarchs, red admirals, swallowtails, the California dogface (which doesn't look like its namesake), and more. Children can hold out a piece of fruit (provided by the Monarch Program), such as a watermelon, to attract the butterflies. But, please, don't try to catch them - it could hurt them. A small butterfly garden is just outside.

School/group tours are welcome during the week. A one-hour tour consists of a half-hour slide show and talk, and a hands-on activity. Students may pet the velvety soft caterpillars, draw butterfly body parts on paper, etc. The other half hour is spent in the vivarium. Note: Caterpillars are available for purchase.

Bring a sack lunch to enjoy at Orpheus park, which is just down the street. The park has picnic tables, grassy areas, shade trees, and a playground.

**Hours:** Open to the public Sat. - Sun., 11am - 2pm. Open for school tours Mon. - Fri. Call to make a reservation.

**Admission:** $4 for adults; children 12 years and under are free. Group tours are a flat fee of $70 for up to thirty people.

**Ages:** 2 years and up.

# SAN DIEGO WILD ANIMAL PARK

(619) 234-6541  / www.sandiegozoo.org                *$$$$*

*15500 San Pasqual Valley Road, Escondido*

(Going S. on San Diego Fwy [5] or Escondido Fwy [15], exit E. on Hwy 78, which turns into San Pasqual Valley Rd. Going N. on 15, exit E. on Via Rancho Pkwy., which turns into Bear Valley Rd., R. on San Pasqual Rd., which turns into Via Rancho Pkwy., go to end, R. on San Pasqual Valley Rd.)

Go on a safari and see the exotic animals that live in the African veldt and Asian plains, without ever leaving Southern California. The 2,000-acre San Diego Wild Animal Park has tigers, rhinos, elephants, giraffes, etc., in atypical zoo enclosures. The animals here roam the grasslands freely, in settings that resemble their natural habitats. The best way to see a majority of the animals is via the Wgasa Bush Line monorail, a five-mile, fifty-minute, narrated journey (tour). This ride is included in your admission price. I suggest going on the monorail first as the lines get longer later in the day.

The ride ends back at Nairobi Village, which is a great starting point for the rest of your wild animal adventure. From here you can walk through some of the thirty acres that comprise the Heart of Africa. This circuitous path is three-quarters-of-a-mile long and can take a few hours. The trail will take you into the forest where antelope and okapi roam; along a stream - look for warthogs and foxes; near waterfalls; and to a large watering hole where rhinos, waterbuck, etc., congregate. Cross over a bridge to the one small island (out of five islands total) that has a mock research station and see lab equipment, dart guns, etc. A live aardvark and hornbill dwell here, too. The plains are home to wildebeest, cheetahs, and even a station - open at designated times - where visitors can hand-feed giraffes.

There are numerous other attractions at the wild animal park. Watch the antics of the monkeys and gorillas. The Petting Kraal has small deer, goats, sheep, etc., to pet and feed. Check the time for the unusual animal shows performed here. Hand-feeding rainbow lorikeets, which look like small parrots, is thrill. Check for feeding times. I was enchanted by the Hidden Jungle. This "room" is filled with lush green plants and colorful butterflies fluttering all around. Mombasa Lagoon is a terrific, interactive way to experience animal behavior "firsthand": Put on a furry pair of bat ears and look silly, but hear acutely; sit in a large turtle shell (and maybe hatch an idea or two); explore the inside of the weaver bird dwelling; climb a giant spider web; hop from one huge lily pad to another; and more! Enjoy all your travels through the animal kingdom.

For summertime fun, walk along a seemingly prehistoric trail to Dino Mountain, where twenty, life-size, roaring, moving, and spitting dinosaurs are brought to "life" by robotics.

Want to make your day picture perfect? The Photo Caravan (ages 8 and up) offers two photo opportunities to go on an open, flat-bed truck into some of the animal enclosures. The cost ranges from $65 to $89, depending on the length of the adventure. Your kids can feed some of the animals, take pictures of them, and learn all about them. Call (760) 738-5049 for tour dates and more information. Roar and Snore overnight tent-camping safaris include nature hikes, a campfire and snacks, photo opportunities, and close-up encounters with wild beasts! The cost is $87.50 for adults; $67.50 for kids, who must be at least 8 years old. Call (760) 738-5022 for more information. These are just a few of the special programs offered - call for a complete schedule.

**Hours:**   Open daily in the summer 7:30am - 8pm. Open daily the rest of the year from 9am - 5pm.

**Admission:**   $21.95 for adults; $19.75 for seniors; $14.95 for ages 3 - 11; children 2 years and under are free. Parking is $3. A combination ticket with the SAN DIEGO ZOO (to be used within five days) is $35.15 for adults; $21.55 for ages 3 - 11. Admission to the Wild Animal Park is free one day in May in celebration of Founder's Day.

**Ages:**   All

# SAN DIEGO ZOO ☼

(619) 234-3153 / www.sandiegozoo.org                                      $$$$
*Park Boulevard in Balboa Park, San Diego*
(Exit San Diego Fwy [5] to Pershing Dr., take Balboa Park exit and follow the signs.)

The world famous San Diego Zoo is home to some of the rarest animals in captivity, and almost every animal imaginable, at least that's what it seems like. Put your walking shoes on because this zoo covers a lot of ground! In fact, you'd be hard pressed to try to see all 4,000 animals in one day, at least with young children in tow. The flamingos, just inside the entrance, are a colorful way to start your day. Tiger River, Elephant Mesa, the Horn and Hoof Mesa, Gorilla Tropics, and the Reptile House are just a few of the exhibit areas to visit. Be amazed at how enormous hippos really are and the size of polar bears in two underwater viewing exhibits - Hippo Beach and Polar Bear Plunge, respectively. Experience panda-monium and see the two giant pandas that are visiting from China - what unique-looking animals! Enjoy a walk through the bird aviary; watch the antics of the bears at Sun Bear Forest; see koalas in their trees; and take the opportunity to observe kangaroos, camels, primates, etc., in enclosures that simulate their natural habitat. If you want to find out more about particular animals and plants, and hear stories about the zoo, as well as test your zoo trivia, rent an audio guide for $4.

A thirty-five-minute, double-decker, narrated bus tour is not only fun and informative, but it's a great way to get a good overview of most of the animals here. A narrated Kangaroo Bus Tour also covers about seventy-five percent of the zoo, but you can hop on and hop off (hence the name), at eight locations, as often as you want throughout the day. The Skyfari Aerial Tram ride is another way to view a portion of the zoo at $1 per person, each way.

The *Sea Lion Show* and the *Wild Ones Show*, presented twice daily, are an entertaining and interesting way to see some favorite animals close up. The Children's Zoo is always a highlight as there are animals to pet; mole-rats and other unique animals to look at; and an animal baby nursery that shows off the newest zoo additions. Ask about the many special programs the zoo offers during the year, including zoo sleepovers and Close Encounters of the Zoo Kind.

**Hours:** Open daily in the summer 7:30am - 9pm. Open daily the rest of the year from 9am - 5pm.

**Admission:** $16 for adults; $7 for ages 3 - 11; children 2 and under area free. The bus tour is an additional $4 for adults; $3 for ages 3 - 11. The Kangaroo bus tour is $8 for adults; $5 for kids. A combination package with the SAN DIEGO WILD ANIMAL PARK (to be used within 5 days) is $35.15 for adults; $21.55 for children. Admission is free on the first Monday of October in celebration of Founder's Day.

**Ages:** All

## SEAL ROCK MARINE MAMMAL RESERVE

*Coast Boulevard, La Jolla*
(Exit San Diego Fwy [5] W. on La Jolla Village Dr., L. on Torrey Pines Rd., R. on Prospect Pl., R. on Coast Blvd.)

From a distance, we saw what looked like lumpy rocks on the beach. As we got closer, however, we could see that they were really numerous seals sprawling on the sand and on the nearby rocks. My boys and I were thrilled that we were almost close enough to touch the seals, although doing so and getting too close is forbidden. (Even seals are protected by harassment laws!) A normal family might be here for just a few minutes; we were here for an hour because we were enthralled. Warning: Seals are not sunbathing here constantly, so seeing them is a hit or miss deal.

**Hours:** Open daily.
**Admission:** Free
**Ages:** All

## SEA WORLD

(619) 226-3901 / www.seaworld.com
*Sea World Drive, San Diego*
(Exit San Diego Fwy [5] W. on Sea World Dr.)

Sea World entertains and educates people of all ages with its wide variety of sea animal exhibits. The dazzling dolphin and silly sea lion shows get top ratings. The killer-whale show, starring Shamu and friends, is a crowd-pleaser with its thrills - a trainer riding a whale gets catapulted - and chills - those sitting in the splash-zone bleachers get wet. Shamu Backstage allows visitors to wade into shallow water, reach over an acrylic panel, and touch the killer whales. Trainers also invite a few volunteers to help out and train the whales by holding targets, carrying food buckets, and rewarding the giant mammals for a behavior correctly performed. View the animals underwater at the viewing gallery.

Other unique attractions include: Shark Encounter, which culminates in a fifty-seven-foot-long enclosed people-mover tube that takes you through shark-infested waters(!); Rocky Point Preserve, where kids can actually touch and feed bottlenose dolphins (they feel rubbery); Forbidden Reef and the California Tide Pool, where you can touch bat rays and other marine animals if you stretch your arms far enough; the penguin exhibit, which also features the penguins' cousins, the funny-looking puffins who fly through the air and sea; the sea turtles; four other huge aquariums for kids to "oooh" and "aaah" at; and Wild Arctic, where a simulated helicopter ride lands you at a remote research station. Blasts of Arctic air greet you at the research station which is equipped with tools of the trade. (Actually, you're still at Sea World.) Here you'll see beluga whales, harbor seals, walruses, and polar bears.

Shamu's Happy Harbor is two acres of pure kid delight. This play area has tubes, slides, ropes, balls, a sandy beach, a moon bounce, an outdoor theater for kid-oriented entertainment, and a Funship for pretend pirates to climb aboard. For those who want (or are allowed) to get wet, there are a few water fountains to splash in, and water tubes to go through. Tip: Bring a towel or change of clothing.

For an additional $2 per person, each attraction, the Skytower, which offers a panoramic view, and the Bayside Skyride, which is a gondola ride over Mission Bay, are fun treats. Sea World also offers various outstanding educational tours, such as the ninety-minute, behind-the-scenes tour for an additional $7 for adults, $6 for seniors and ages 3 to 11. Sleep over with sharks or other animals. What fun! Ask about their dolphin interaction program. Call for information on the times, hours, and admission for these (and more) unique field trips. Note: Although no outside food is allowed inside, a picnic area is set up just outside the park. Spending a day (or night) here is a great way for the whole family to "sea" the world!

**Hours:** Open daily in the summer Mon. - Fri., 9am - 10pm; Sat. - Sun., 9am - 11pm. (Check for seasonality.) Open daily the rest of the year 10am - 6pm.

**Admission:** $35.95 for adults; $26.95 for ages 3 - 11; children 2 years and under are free. A two-day package, where you may visit Sea World twice within a 7 day period, is a great deal at $36.95 for adults; $27.95 for ages 3 - 11. Parking is $6 per day.

**Ages:** All

# STEPHEN BIRCH AQUARIUM-MUSEUM ☼
(619) 534-FISH (3474) / aqua.ucsd.edu $$$
*2300 Expedition Drive, San Diego*
(Exit San Diego Fwy [405] W. on La Jolla Village Dr. Stay to the R. as La Jolla Village Dr. turns into N. Torrey Pines. Take the next L. on La Jolla Shores Dr. and follow it to Scripps Institute of Oceanography. Stephen Birch is at the University of California, Scripps Institute of Oceanography.)

Statues of leaping, large gray whales are in the fountain outside the entrance of the Stephen Birch Aquarium - Museum. This outstanding, sizable, aquarium-museum has three main exhibit areas. The aquarium section contains over thirty-three large tanks filled with an incredible variety of creatures found in the Earth's oceans - from eels to sharks to flashlight fish that glow in the dark. Just some of our favorite sea animals showcased here include the almost mesmerizing moon jellies; chocolate chip starfish; garden eels that look like hoses "standing" upright in the sand; bizarre-looking, weedy sea dragons (related to the seahorse); the amazing giant octopus; and the beautiful, but venomous, striped lionfish. The largest tank has a huge kelp forest which makes it easy to view animals that are normally hidden on ocean floors. See divers feed the fish in the forest Tuesdays and Thursdays at 12:20pm and Sundays at 10:30am. (These times may change.)

Outside, the rocky Tidepool Plaza connects the aquarium and the museum. A wave machine gently creates natural water motion in a simulated tidepool. Kids will see up close (and can gently touch) sea stars, sea urchins, sea cucumbers, etc. Also, take in the magnificent panoramic view of the La Jolla coastline (and the world famous Scripps Institute).

The museum features Exploring the Blue Planet, a fantastic oceanographic exhibit with seven different, interactive display areas. Each area incorporates touch screens or an activity that shows and explains the integral part that oceans play in relation to how the Earth functions. Kids will learn about various aspects of ocean sciences from the displays on currents, tides, and waves; from earthquakes and plate tectonics; and as they experience a simulated, submersible ride to the ocean floor. My kids really enjoyed the Ocean Supermarket, where they used scanners on common household products to see which ingredients came from the ocean. (Did you know that ice cream uses carrageenan [i.e. red seaweed] to make it smooth and creamy?!)

The above is a sampling of what the Stephen Birch Aquarium- Museum has to offer - come "sea" it for yourself! There is also an Aquarium Bookshop, and outdoor picnic areas that are stroller and wheelchair accessible. Call about the many special activities and programs offered through the aquarium-museum including tidepools tours, whale-watching cruises, grunion running, etc.

**Hours:** Open daily from 9am - 5pm. Closed Thanksgiving and Christmas.
**Admission:** $7.50 for adults; $6.50 for seniors; $5 for students; $4 for ages 3 - 17; children 2 years and under are free. Parking is $3.
**Ages:** 3 years and up.

# AMERICA'S TEACHING ZOO

(805) 378-1441 / www.vcnet.com/gwhiz
*7075 Campus Road, Moorpark*

(Exit Simi Valley/San Fernando Valley Fwy [118] N. on Collins Dr. Continue all the way up Collins, behind the college, R. into the dirt parking area where you'll see signs for the zoo.)

Students attend this teaching zoo, that contains 130 exotic animals, to become zoo keepers, veterinarians, animal trainers, etc. If your child aspires to one of these professions, or is just intrigued with animals, come visit. As this is a teaching zoo and not just here for public enjoyment, many of the caged animals are in rows, making it difficult, or impossible, to see a lot of them. However, the animals that are readily viewed can be seen more up close than at a typical zoo. Note: Picnic tables are here for your lunching pleasure.

Demonstrations, featuring three to five animals per show, such as primates, hoofed animals, or reptiles, are given every hour on a small outdoor stage. The student trainers talk about the animal's habitats, nutrition, and training. Afterward, kids can come up, ask questions, and usually touch the animals. One of the reptiles we saw and touched was a boa. We were amazed at its strength and its under-belly softness. Trainer talks, where one animal is showcased and discussed, are given in the morning.

Don't miss the 4pm feeding of the carnivores! Actually, get there a little early and see animals being fed that aren't on the scheduled program. We saw a trainer go inside a cage to feed the tigers and to "show-off" the tigers' learned behavior. The trainers and students willingly answered all the questions they were asked. My kids and I learned so much here!

Watch out for a type of monkey called langurs. One growled and leapt at the bars toward my kids. We were told that this species considers eye contact to be a sign of aggression, and smiling children to be teeth-baring, aggressive adversaries. As parents, we often feel the same way.

**Hours:** The Zoo is open weekends only from 11am - 5pm. Trainer talks are given at 11:30am. The demonstrations are every hour on the hour from noon - 3pm, weather permitting. You can call to see what animals will be shown. Feeding of the carnivores is at 4pm.

**Admission:** $4 for adults; $3 for seniors; $2 for children 12 years and under.

**Ages:** All

# CASTLE EARTH CHILDREN'S MUSEUM

(805) 583-5243
*77 Tierra Rejada Road, Unit A, Simi Valley*

See CASTLE EARTH CHILDREN'S MUSEUM, in the Museums section, for details.

# FILLMORE FISH HATCHERY

(805) 524-0962
*612 E. Telegraph Road, Fillmore*

(Exit Hwy 23 R. on Hwy 126, look for signs)

Stop off and take a look around the fish hatchery to see hundreds of thousands of rainbow trout. The compartments of the concrete tanks are labeled with the various species names. Coin-operated fish food dispensers are here and the fish always seem to be hungry.

**Hours:** Open daily 7:30am - 3:30pm

**Admission:** Free

**Ages:** 2 years and up.

## PARTY ANIMALS

(805) 523-2957

*3370 Moorpark Road, Moorpark*

(Exit Ventura Fwy [101] N. on 23 Fwy, L. on Tierra Rejada Rd., L. on Moorpark Rd. It is located just behind Tierra Rejada Family Farm.)

The phrase "party animals" has several different connotations. Here, Party Animals refers to the farm animals that are available for birthday parties, as well as to simply look at and pet. Your family can wander the dirt grounds to see pens of chickens, sheep, ducks, rabbits, goats, and horses. Some of the animals come close enough to touch, especially if you purchase feed in the nearby food machines. (Bring quarters!) You are welcome to wander around on your own, making a trip here a pleasant, rural experience. You may also take a twenty-minute, guided, animal feeding tour, which includes information on and feed for the above-mentioned animals. The tour is by reservation only and your group must consist of at least ten people.

Other activities here include tractor-drawn hayrides, and pony rides, led around inside a very small enclosure by an attendant. The maximum rider weight is seventy pounds. On-site birthday parties include unlimited pony rides, the animal feeding tour, and use of the covered party shelter that has grills and a few picnic tables. Bring your own food. While at Party Animals, visit the adjacent TIERRA REJADA FAMILY FARMS. (See the Edible Adventures section).

**Hours:** Open June through October from 9am - 6pm, with pony rides usually available daily. Open November through May 10am - 5pm, with pony rides available on the weekends, weather permitting.

**Admission:** 50¢ per person. Guided animal feeding tours are $2 per child. Hayrides are $1.50 per person. Pony rides are $2.50 per ride. Rental of the party shelter is $100 for two hours for ten children; additional children are $10 each.

**Ages:** Birth to 12 years.

## BIG BEAR
## (and the surrounding area)

This four-season mountain resort is close enough to escape to for a day or a weekend, though it offers enough activities for at least a week's vacation. The pine trees and fresh air that beckon city-weary folks, plus all the things to do, make it an ideal family get-away. November through March (or so) the mountains become a winter wonderland with lot of opportunities for snow play and skiing. This section, however, covers a broader base of activities because Big Bear is great any time of year! For specific information on events held during the time you plan to visit, "call" www.BigBeartodaymag.com.

## ALPINE SLIDE at MAGIC MOUNTAIN

(909) 866-4626

*Big Bear Boulevard, Magic Mountain Recreation Area, Big Bear*
(Exit Big Bear Blvd. It's ¼ mile W. of Big Bear Lake Village.)

Alpine Slide lifts family fun to new heights! Take the chairlift up the mountain. Then, you and your child sit on a heavy-duty plastic toboggan and rip down the quarter-mile, cement, contoured slide that resembles a bobsled track. Control your speed by pushing or pulling on the lever. We were cautious only on our first ride. Your child can go down by himself if he's at least 7 years old.

If you don't succumb to motion sickness, take a whirl on the Orbitron. You'll be harnessed to the inside of this big sphere and spun around in all directions. Doesn't that sound like fun? The miniature golf course, Putt 'N Around, has just a few frills, but kids still enjoy puttin' around on it. Go karts are available here, too. Inside the main building are a few video games, of course, and a snack bar. That delicious food you smell is a burger or hot dog being barbecued right outside.

Summer play is enhanced by two zippy waterslides. You'll end with a splash in the three-and-a-half-feet deep pool, but it's not for swimming in. Winter allows you and the kids a chance to inner tube down the snow-covered hill, or cultivate the fine art of throwing snowballs. You'll have mountains of fun any season you come to Alpine Slide at Magic Mountain.

**Hours:** The Alpine Slide, Orbitron, miniature golf, and go karts are open mid-June through mid-September and November through Easter, daily 10am - 5pm (weather permitting). In the summer, these attractions are often open later on weekends. The rest of the year they are open same hours, but on weekends only. The waterslide is open mid-June to mid-September, daily from 10am - 6pm. The snow play area is open as long as there is snow, daily from 10am - 4pm.

**Admission:** Alpine ride - $3.50 for one ride; $15 for a five-ride book. Orbitron - $4 a ride. Miniature golf - $4 a round for adults; $3 for kids. Go karts - $3.50 a single car; $5.50 a double car. Waterslide - $1 for one ride; $7 for a ten-ride book; $12 for an unlimited day pass. Snow play - $12 for an unlimited day-pass with a tube; $8 for an unlimited day-pass using your own tube. Children 6 years and under are free on the Alpine slide, waterslide, and snow play area, as long as they are accompanied by a paying adult.

**Ages:** 3 years and up.

## ALPINE TROUT LAKE

(909) 866-4532

*Catalina Road, Big Bear*
(Exit Big Bear Blvd. S. on Catalina.)

This beautiful tree-lined lake is a restful place to fish. Chairs, picnic tables, and barbecue pits are around the perimeters of the stocked lake, so you can catch your meal and eat it, too.

**Hours:** Open Mon. - Fri., 10am - 5pm; Sat. - Sun., 9am - 6pm, weather permitting.

**Admission:** $5 for a family or group of up to 6 people. Rod rentals, reel, and bait are an additional $3.50 per person. Fish cost $4.89 per pound.

**Ages:** 3 years and up.

## BALDWIN LAKE STABLES                                            ☼

(909) 585-6482                                                    *$$$$*

*Baldwin Lake Road, Big Bear*

(Head E. on Big Bear Blvd., past the Hwy 38 turnoff, and follow it as it turns into Shay Rd., then Baldwin Lake Rd.)

Leave the city behind and horseback ride through the scenic national forest. The breathtaking mountain views, and sore bottoms for those unused to trotting along, are all included in your ride price. Enjoy a one to four hour ride along the Pacific Crest Trail, or see things in a different light by taking a sunset ride!

**Hours:** Open daily most of the year, weather permitting, from 9am - 5pm. Winter hours are daily 10am - 4pm. Call before you come.

**Admission:** $20 an hour per person. Sunset rides are $35 per person - no children allowed.

**Ages:** At least 6 years old.

## BEAR MOUNTAIN RIDING STABLES                                    ☼

(909) 878-4677                                                    *$$$$*

*At the top of Lassen Drive, Big Bear*

(Exit Big Bear Blvd. S.E. at Moonridge Rd. Go to the end of Moonridge and turn L. on Lassen Dr. It's at the foot of Bear Mountain Ski Resort.)

There is only so much you can see of Big Bear from the car! A horseback ride is an ideal way to experience the beauty of the mountains. Children 7 years and up can take a one or two-hour guided horseback ride through the pine trees and over mountain ridges. At the stables, younger children can take pony rides around the track.

**Hours:** Open daily 9am - 5pm, during good weather. Call first, just in case.

**Admission:** $20 per hour per person for horseback riding. $5 for three laps around the track on a pony.

**Ages:** 1 - 6 years for pony rides; 7 years and up for horseback rides.

## BEAR MOUNTAIN TRADING CO.                                       ☀

(909) 585-9676                                                    *!/$*

*42646 Moonridge Road, Big Bear*

(Exit Big Bear Blvd. S.E. at Moonridge Rd.)

This two-story trading company store is a fun little stop off. There is a wonderful selection of old-fashioned gifts, including wooden toys, lots of candy

favorites, and Indian accessories. Stop here on your way to or from
MOONRIDGE ANIMAL PARK, which is described later in this section.

**Hours:** Open daily from 10am - 5:30pm.
**Admission:** Free
**Ages:** 4 years and up.

## BEAR VALLEY BIKES
(909) 866-8000 $$$

*Big Bear Boulevard, Magic Mountain Recreation Area, Big Bear*
(It's ¼ mile W. of Big Bear Lake Village, on top of Red Ant Hill, across from the Alpine
Slide at Magic Mountain.)

Pedal your way around town or sign up for a guided tour. Bear Valley has
mountain bikes, tandems cycles, BMX bikes, trailers for children, toddler bikes,
and even helmets. An adjacent BMX track is open Wednesday evenings at
5:30pm to practice. Races are held on Sunday afternoons. Sign up and join in the
fun!

**Hours:** Open daily 10am - 5pm. Call for winter hours.
**Admission:** Mt. bikes are $6 an hour; tandems are $10 an hour; BMX bikes
are $5 an hour. $8 to race on the BMX tracks.
**Ages:** All

## BIG BEAR BIKES
(909) 866-2224 / www.publiconline.com/=bigbearbikes $$$
*41810 Big Bear Boulevard, Big Bear*
(On Big Bear Blvd., near Snow Summit Blvd.)

Need some wheels to get around town? Big Bear Bikes offers, fittingly
enough, mountain bikes and suggests trying out the beautiful North Shore bike
path. This bike shop also rents snowshoes and can suggest numerous destinations
for putting them to good use. (Note: This is a winter-time activity.) They also
host three-hour, guided moonlight snowshoe tromps for $20. The price includes
equipment rental, hiking for a few hours, and stopping off to warm yourselves
near a campfire. (Bring your own munchies.)

**Hours:** Open Mon. - Fri., 10am - 5pm, weather permitting. Open one
hour later on the weekends.
**Admission:** Bike rentals start at $6 per hour. Tandems are $10 an hour.
Snowshoe rentals begin at $10 a day.
**Ages:** All for bikes; 6 years and up for snowshoes.

## BIG BEAR DISCOVERY CENTER
(909) 866-3437 $$$$$
*Highway 38 (North Shore Drive), Big Bear*
(between Fawnskin and Stansfield Cutoff, at the Ranger Station)

This ranger station is the best place to call or visit for trail maps, camp sites,
and special program information. Some programs include weekend campfire
programs offered in the amphitheater behind the center, nature programs on

Thursday nights, canoe tours around the lake, and numerous other activities. The center has informational and pictorial panels regarding the forest and the lake and their inhabitants. Pick up an Adventure Pass here, too. An Adventure Pass is required for all vehicles parking on National Forest property for recreational purposes.

Pick up your free *Eagle Discovery Guide and Games* booklet at the center. The guide will help you find eagles on your own, plus it offers fun ways to learn about eagles and their habitats. Another option to "hunt" for eagles during their winter season in the mountains is to board the Eagle Discovery Tour bus for a three-hour journey through Big Bear. There are several stops along the way. A professional naturalist will aid you in identifying eagle habitats and the surrounding eco system, while informally teaching interesting facts about our national symbol. You'll receive the use of binoculars and a spotting scope. A light snack is included, too.

> **Hours:** Open daily from 8am - 5pm. Closed New Year's Day, Thanksgiving, and Christmas. Eagle tours are given in the winter on weekends and daily during holiday periods, from 9:30am - 1pm. Reservations are required.
>
> **Admission:** The Adventure pass is $5 per day or $30 for an annual pass. The Eagle Discovery Tour is $25 for adults; $20 for youth.
>
> **Ages:** All

## BIG BEAR HISTORICAL MUSEUM and CITY PARK ☼
(909) 585-8100 or (909) 866-5753                                                        $

*Greenway Drive, Big Bear*

(Exit Big Bear Blvd. E. on Greenway. The museum is in the N.E. portion of the Big Bear City Park, E. of the airport.)

The past is definitely present at the Eleanor Abbott Big Bear Valley Historical Museum. The buildings that comprise the museum are very old (and old looking). The small main building contains a good assortment of taxidermied animals such as a golden eagle, skunk, red fox, badger, etc., displayed mostly behind glass in "natural" settings. Other exhibits include birds' nests, eggs, arrowheads, rocks, fossils, unique leather carvings, old photographs of old Big Bear, and old-fashioned toys. Outside on the porch are turn-of-the-century post office boxes, plus mining equipment and mining artifacts. An old barn and lots of old, rusted agriculture equipment are also on the grounds.

An on-site, furnished, 1875 one-room log cabin offers a real look into the pioneer lifestyle. The docents in here are wonderful at explaining to kids how pioneer families lived, and the uses of some of the household items. My boys couldn't believe that chamber pots were really used as portable potties. It finally dawned on them that entire families lived together in this one room; sleeping, cooking, eating, and playing together. I hope they'll be more thankful about their own living arrangements!

The adjacent park has a few pieces of play equipment and some old tennis courts. The park is good mostly for just running around in its overgrown fields.

Shade is scarce, but there are a few picnic tables here.

**Hours:** Open May through October only, Sat. 10am - 4pm; Sun. and
holidays, 11am - 2pm.
**Admission:** $1 per person donation.
**Ages:** 3 years and up.

## BIG BEAR JEEP TOURS
(909) 878-5337 / www.bigbearjeeptours.com                    *$$$$$*
*Stationed in Big Bear Village - call for specifics.*

For rugged kids, who like bumpy adventures, jeep tours are the way to go.
There are so many historical, beautiful places to explore in these mountains and
some of them are only accessible via four-wheel drive. Take a one-hour trip to
the top of the ridgeline, or go for several hours to explore Holcomb Valley where
kids will learn about the Gold Rush, a ghost town, and gold mines. What a great
way to see and experience a bit of golden history!

**Hours:** Call for tour times.
**Admission:** Prices range from $37.95 per person for a one-and-a-half-hour
tour, to $64.95 per person for a four-hour tours.
**Ages:** 4 years and up.

## BIG BEAR MARINA
(909) 866-3218                                                   *$$$*
*Corner of Lakeview Drive and Paine Road, Big Bear Marina, Big Bear*
(Exit Big Bear Blvd. S. on Paine Rd.)

The Marina offers a boatload of fun for the family. Fishing boats are $12 an
hour and seat up to five people. Pedal boats are $10 an hour and seat up to four
people. Canoes are $10 an hour and seat up to three people (depending on
weight). Tiger Sharks (similar to wave runners) are $60 an hour and seat up to
three people. Take an hour-and-a-half, narrated tour around Big Bear Lake on
the Big Bear Queen. Tours are given daily, in season, always at 2pm, and
sometimes at noon and 4pm, if at least fifteen people are signed up. Prices are
$9.50 for adults; $8 for seniors; $5 for ages 3 to 12; children 2 years and under
are free. Rent a small pontoon, a flat-bottomed boat that is almost seasick proof,
for $35 an hour. It seats up to eight people. A large pontoon, which seats up to
twelve people, is $45 an hour.

Where can your family go for dinner that is a fun, kid-friendly treat (and I
don't mean McDonald's)? Somewhere that is exotic, yet cost efficient?
Different, but agreeable to all? The answer to all these questions is - on a
pontoon sunset dinner cruise! Cruise around Big Bear Lake on your own, in and
out of the coves. Let the kids steer the boat, but not too near the shore. Anytime
during your cruise, pig out on the delicious dinner supplied by Hall's Chicken,
which includes broasted chicken, potatoes, coleslaw, and rolls. Bring dessert and
drinks, and you are set to sail! The pontoon sunset cruise is $75 for eight people,
or $100 for twelve people. Dinner is included in this price.

Big Bear Queen also offers dinner cruises on Thursday nights from 6pm to

7:30pm for $14.95 per person, which includes a guided tour and dinner.

**Hours:** Open daily, seasonally, usually spring through November 1 from 7am - 7pm. Pontoon sunset cruises are 5pm - 8pm in the summer, 4pm - 7pm at other times. You must prepay by 2pm on the day of your cruise, and don't forget to pick up your dinner at Hall's, which is just down the road. Reservations are strongly suggested.

**Admission:** Prices are listed above.

**Ages:** 3 years and up.

## BIG BEAR PARASAIL

(909) 866-IFLY (4359)                              $$$$$

*At the north end of Pine Knott Boulevard, Big Bear*

(Exit Big Bear Blvd. S. on Pine Knott Blvd.)

Ever had dreams where you can fly? Parasailing is the next best thing. Start off on dry land, attached by a harness to the parasail and by a tow rope to the boat. As the boat pulls away, you are lifted into the air for ten minutes of flight. You can stay dry if you want, and if all goes well, or take a quick dip (more like a toe touch) in the lake before being airborne again. This is a thrill-seeking experience for kids and adults.

**Hours:** Seasonal only - late spring through early fall - Mon. - Fri., 9am - 5pm; Sat. - Sun., 8am - 6pm.

**Admission:** Single - $35 weekdays; $40 weekends. Tandem - $60 weekday; $70 weekends.

**Ages:** 90 pounds and up.

## BIG BEAR SOLAR OBSERVATORY

(909) 866-5791 / www.bbso.njit.edu                              $

*North Shore Lane, Big Bear*

(Exit North Shore Dr. on North Shore Ln. It's past Fawnskin.)

The small, thirty-foot dome solar observatory offers a unique way to study the often sunny skies in Big Bear. Three telescopes monitor and record images of the sun, which are then displayed on video monitors. Cameras can show sharper details than the unaided eye can see. Take a twenty-minute tour to get the hot facts about the sun.

**Hours:** Open July 4th through Labor Day, Saturdays only from 4pm - 6pm.

**Admission:** $1 donation per person.

**Ages:** 8 years and up.

## CHILDREN'S FOREST

(909) 337-5156                              $

*Off Highway 18, between Running Springs and Big Bear*

(Exit Highway 18 on Keller Peak Road for the information center, interpretive trail, and lookout tower.)

The Children's Forest is 3,400 acres within the San Bernardino National

Forest. Maintained primarily by youths, its purpose is to encourage children to develop a passion for the environment. Using a self-guided brochure, walk the only established trail, which is a three-quarter-mile paved trail. Or, choose any other place to wander around in the forest. Among the pine trees and along the mountain stream be on the lookout for wildlife such as birds, deer, squirrels, unusual insects, etc. Youth naturalists lead free walks along the interpretive trail during the summer, on weekends only, between 1pm to 3pm. With a minimum of twenty participants, you can schedule an appointment for special programs, such as Finding the Wild Things, Charting Your Course, and Rappers and Raptors. These programs are the same ones offered to school groups - see below for descriptions. Most programs are recommended for ages 6 and up, although younger children will especially enjoy the program, Preschool Small Worlds of Wonder. Don't forget to pack lunch, water, sunscreen, and binoculars.

The Keller Peak lookout tower is open to the public daily in the summer and during fire season from 9am to 5pm - what a view! On a clear day you can see all the way to the ocean. When the tower is open, you may drive out to it or hike to it. The trail to the tower is four miles from the highway.

School exploration programs are offered Monday through Friday, year round. Each program is four hours long. The majority of the time is spent in the forest, plus there are games and hands-on activities. Groups are limited to forty students and students must be at least in third grade. Note that smaller groups generally see and do more. A sampling of topical studies includes, Finding the Wild Things - learn how animals adapt to their environments, where they live, what they eat, and how to read the signs of their presence; Birds - Rappers and Raptors - learn to identify many species by their markings, habits, and songs; Get Green and Growing - learn to identify plants and their function in the ecosystem; and Charting Your Course - learn elementary map and compass reading techniques. Seasonal snowshoe field trips are available to aid in learning about winter ecology. Get a workout while following animal tracks!

Other programs include training youths between fifteen to eighteen years to become naturalists, and once-a-month Investigation Days, where conservation topics such as survival skills, birding, art/music, etc., are taught. With all that it offers and set in such beautiful surroundings, I'm glad the Children's Forest is open to adults, too!

**Hours:** The paved trail and the forest is open daily sunrise to sunset. Program times vary - call for a schedule or to make an appointment.

**Admission:** $5 per vehicle per day to stop anywhere in the forest. Public and school programs cost $150 for minimum twenty participants; $300 for twenty-one to forty participants.

**Ages:** All for the paved trail and walking around; other age requirements depend on the program.

# HIKING

(909) 866-3437

There are many, *many* places to go hiking in the Big Bear area. See BIG BEAR DISCOVERY CENTER, in this section, for information on the ranger station. Note: Anywhere you park in the national forest for recreational reasons, you must pay for an Adventure Pass. Just two of the places my family has enjoyed trekking include:

CASTLE ROCK:

(From Highway 18, the trailhead is about one mile east past the dam.)

The trail is only eight-tenths of a mile, but it is an uphill walk over some rocky terrain. The destination is Castle Rock, a large rock that kids love to climb on. Its name gives lead to a lot of imaginative play time here. All of my kids wanted to be king - what a surprise! If everyone still has the energy, keep hiking back to the waterfalls, and/ or to Devil's woodpile. The scenery along the way is spectacular.

WOODLAND TRAIL

(On Highway 38, parking is almost directly across the street from M.D. Boat Ramp, just west of the Stanfield Cutoff Road.)

This one-and-a-half-mile loop is an easy walk, as the dirt trail follows more along the side of the mountain, rather than into the mountain. Although you can hear the traffic from certain sections of the trail, the changing landscape, from pine trees to coastal shrub to cactus, still offers the sense of being immersed in nature. An interpretative trail guide is available through the Ranger Station. Make it an educational field trip as well as a nice walk!

**Hours:** Open daily.

**Admission:** $5 a day for an Adventure Pass.

**Ages:** 4 years and up.

# THE HOT SHOT MINIATURE GOLF COURSE

*Corner of Catalina and Big Bear Boulevard, Big Bear*
(On Big Bear Blvd., just N. of Moonridge.)

Putt around under shady pine trees at this basic, but fun miniature golf course. Encourage your kids to be hot shots here!

**Hours:** Open daily seasonally, weather permitting, from 10am - 6pm. Closed during the winter.

**Admission:** $4 for adults; $3 for kids 12 years and under. Replays are $1 per person.

**Ages:** 3 years and up.

# ICEOPLEX ICE CASTLE

(909) 336-2111 / www.iceoplex.com

*27307 Highway 189, Blue Jay*

(Take Riverside Fwy [91] N.E. until it turns into the San Bernardino Fwy [215]. Stay to the right and take the 259/30 fwys. Stay on the 30 then exit N. on Waterman Ave. Waterman turns into Highway 18. Go past Rim Forest, turn L. on Daily Canyon which turns into Hwy. 189.)

Enjoy this open-air ice-skating rink all year round! It has a roof overhead and is enclosed on three sides (one side has a lobby), leaving the fourth side open to a great view of the surrounding pine trees. The Castle offers open skating sessions, skating classes, and youth hockey. For the more adventuresome, try broom ball. This sport is played using brooms as hockey sticks, and wearing tennis shoes instead of ice skates. Yes, it's painful to fall on the ice, but this is a fun, exhilarating game!

**Hours:** Open skating sessions held Mon. - Fri., 8:30am - 11:15, and 12:45 - 5:15; Wed. an additional session is held 7:30pm - 9pm; Sat. - Sun., sessions are 1pm - 4pm. Additional sessions are held Fri. - Sat., 8pm - 10pm.

**Admission:** $6 for adults; $5 for children 12 years and under. Skate rentals are $2 a session. A family pass on Sun. is $17 for two adults and two children.

**Ages:** 3 years and up.

## LAKE ARROWHEAD CHILDREN'S MUSEUM

(909) 336-1332 - recorded information; (909) 336-3093 - front desk / www.mountaininfo.com/kids

*Highway 18, in the Village Shopping Center, Lake Arrowhead*

(Exit San Bernardino Fwy [10] N. on the 215, E. on the 30. Take the Waterman Ave. [Hwy 18] exit 'up the hill' to Lake Arrowhead. The museum is located in the lower level of the Village, at the end of the peninsula, just past the G.R. Toy Shop and Rocky Mt. Chocolate Factory.)

In the Lake Arrowhead Village shopping center, kids now have a place of their own to "shop" for fun. This museum is comprised of a large room, decorated with beautiful nature murals, divided into interactive exhibit areas. Some of the permanent exhibits include the Ant Wall - where children are the ants, climbing up and down carpeted ramps and tunnels; Inventor's Workshop - where recyclable "trash" is crafted into take-home treasure; a Bubble Area - where bubbles can be kid-size; a Theater - with face paint and great costumes for dressing up and acting out; a Toddlers' Room - with several toys, and Peter Pan's ship to climb aboard and sail off to Never Land; Science Stations - where kids can throw a ball and clock its speed, speak through tubes to each other, and experiment with magnets, hand batteries, etc.; Space - which has glow in the dark chalk and a chalkboard, black lighting, and control panels of a space ship; and Village Merchants - with playhouse-size "stores" like a fire station, a post office, a photo shop with a photosensitive shadow room, and a Vet's office with lots of stuffed animals. Technologically-minded children enjoy playing educational games on the computers. Check out the imaginative temporary exhibits here, too. There is always something fun to do at this children's museum! Note: RIM OF THE WORLD HISTORICAL MUSEUM, described later in this section, is adjacent to the children's museum.

**Hours:** Open in the summer daily from 10am - 6pm. Open the rest of the year Wed. - Mon. from 10am - 5pm. Closed Thanksgiving and Christmas.

**Admission:**  $4 for ages 2 years and up; $3 for seniors.
**Ages:**  2 - 10 years.

## MCDILL SWIM BEACH / MEADOW PARK

(909) 866-0130
*Park Avenue, Big Bear*
(Exit Big Bear Blvd. N. on Knight St. to the end.)

This waveless lagoon, with a lifeguard on duty, offers a refreshing respite during the hot summer months. Kids can play in the water, or build castles on the sandy beach. Swimmers enjoy going beyond the roped area, out to the floating dock that they can lay out on or dive off. A small playground, a volleyball court, and a snack bar round out the facilities at this beach. And the view of the mountains is spectacular! Children 10 years and under must be supervised by an adult.

Meadow Park is just outside the Swim Beach gates. This large, grassy park has a small playground, nice tennis courts, volleyball courts, baseball diamonds, and horseshoe pits. Bring a picnic dinner to cook at the barbecue pits, and enjoy the sunset.

**Hours:**  The swim beach is open seasonally on weekends from noon - 5pm, and daily in the summer from noon - 5pm. The park is open sunrise to sunset.
**Admission:**  $2.50 for adults; $2 for ages 5 - 10; children 4 years and under are free. The park is free.
**Ages:**  All

## MOONRIDGE ANIMAL PARK

(909) 866-0183 / www.bigbear.net/moonridgezoo
*18012 Goldmine Drive, Big Bear*

(Exit Big Bear Blvd. S.E. on Moonridge Rd. The Animal Park is toward the end of the road, on Goldmine Dr.)

Get a little wild up in the mountains! Animals from the surrounding mountains that need extra care, whether they are orphaned or hurt, find sanctuary in this small animal park. A grizzly bear, a snow leopard, black bears, wolves, coyotes, bobcats, raccoons, deer, eagles, and other animals and birds now consider the animal park their home. It's just the right size for kids, and since the enclosures are not too large, it's easy to see the animals up close here. Special daily events include animal presentations at noon, where an animal is brought out and talked about, and a feeding tour at 3pm (except on Wednesdays). We've always found the docents and trainers willing, even eager, to answer our kids' questions, so it makes our visit here more memorable. A small education center has a few prepared specimens, such as a snowy owl, and some hands-on exhibits. The Animal Park also offers special programs, such as flashlight tours and the tasty ice cream safaris.

| **Hours:** | Open daily Memorial Day through October, 10am - 5pm, weather permitting. Open the rest of the year on the weekends, 10am - 4pm, weather permitting. After a snowfall, come take a guided "snow tour" through the Animal Park from 11:30am - 1:30pm. Always call first! |
|---|---|
| **Admission:** | $2.50 for adults; $1.50 for ages 3 - 10; children 2 years and under are free. |
| **Ages:** | All |

## RIM OF THE WORLD HISTORICAL MUSEUM

(909) 336-5884 / www.mountaininfo.com                                        *$*

*Highway 18, in the Village Shopping Center, Lake Arrowhead*

(Exit San Bernardino Fwy [10] N. on the 215, E. on the 30. Take the Waterman Ave. [Hwy 18] exit 'up the hill' to Lake Arrowhead. The museum is located in the lower level of the Village, at the end of the peninsula, adjacent to the Lake Arrowhead Children's Museum.)

This small museum is adjacent to LAKE ARROWHEAD CHILDREN'S MUSEUM, which is listed in this section. Displays represent this area's past, as well as its present. Exhibits include dioramas of the old village, arrowheads found locally, pictures and explanations on the making of the lake, the Lollipop lady's dress (from Santa's Village), old skis, pictorial collages, and more. The museum is a special place to visit for those who have lived and grown up in this area. Tip: While adults are reminiscing and learning history, kids can enjoy a look around and then go play in the children's museum.

| **Hours:** | Open daily in the summer from 10am - 6pm. Open daily the rest of the year from 10am - 5pm. |
|---|---|
| **Admission:** | $1 per person. Admission is free for those who have paid to come into the children's museum. |
| **Ages:** | 6 years and up. |

## SCENIC SKY CHAIR

(909) 866-5766 / www.snowsummit.com                                      *$$$*

*At Snow Summit ski area, Big Bear*

(Exit Big Bear Blvd., S. on Summit Blvd.)

Do your kids appreciate the awesome scenery of mountains, trees, and Big Bear Lake, plus breathing clean air? If not, they'll still enjoy the mile-long, thirteen-minute (each way) chair ride up the mountaintop. At the top, there is a picnic and barbecue area, so bring your own food, or purchase a burger, chicken sandwich, etc., from the snack bar. As there are over forty miles of trails through the forest and wilderness areas, hikers and biking enthusiasts are in their element up here. The terrain varies, meaning that trails range from easy, wide, forest service roads to arduous, single-track, dirt trails. What better way to spend a day than up here in a place readily described as "God's country."

Bike rentals are available at the base of Snow Summit at Team Big Bear Mountain Bikes, (909) 866-4565 / www.teambigbear.com. Mountain bikes are the recommended cycle, and helmets are required for all riders. The store has maps for all the Big Bear trails.

**Hours:** The sky chair operates May through mid-June and mid-September through October (or the beginning of ski season) on weekends only, 9am - 4pm. It's open daily, mid-June through mid-September, Mon. - Fri., 9am - 4pm; Sat., 8am - 5pm; Sun., 8am - 4pm, weather permitting.

**Admission:** One-way ride (no bike) - $5 for adults; $2 for ages 7 - 12; children 6 years and under are free when accompanied by a paying adult. One-way ride with bike or round trip no bike - $7 for adults; $3 for ages 7 - 12. An all-day pass with bike - $19 for adults; $8 for kids. Ask about half-day prices.

**Ages:** 3 years and up.

## SPORTLAND ARCADE

*672 S. Pine Knot Avenue, Big Bear*                                          $

(Exit Big Bear Blvd. S. on Pine Knot Ave.)

This arcade features skee ball, air hockey, pool tables, a few kiddie rides, and arcade games. It also has sports cards for sale.

**Hours:** Open daily.

**Admission:** Technically, free

**Ages:** 4 years and up.

## SUGARLOAF CORDWOOD CO.

(909) 866-2220                                                              !/$

*42193 Big Bear Boulevard, Big Bear*

(At the corner of Big Bear Blvd. and Stanfield Cut-off)

The gigantic, wooden, chain-saw carvings of bears, Indians, etc., will attract your attention as you drive along Big Bear Boulevard. This unique store is worth a stop. Take a walk through the lot and inside the rooms to see smaller carvings and other unusual, artistic, gift items.

**Hours:** Usually open Mon. - Fri., 10am - 5pm; Sat. - Sun., 9am - 6pm.

**Admission:** Free

**Ages:** 3 years and up.

## SUGARLOAF PARK

*Baldwin Lane, Big Bear*                                                     !

(Exit Big Bear Blvd. [38] S. on Maple Ln., L. on Baldwin.)

It is a beautiful drive to this park, but where up here isn't the scenery beautiful? Sugarloaf Park has a softball field, a few tennis courts, a sand volleyball court, and older metal playground equipment, plus picnic shelters and barbecue pits. It also has a mini-forest, which is a small grouping of short trees that feels like the real thing to younger kids (only they won't get lost!).

**Hours:** Open daily from sunrise to sunset.

**Admission:** Free

**Ages:** All

## SUPER BEAR ARCADE
(909) 866-8620                                                                    *$*
*Big Bear Boulevard, Big Bear*
(Located in the Big Bear Village.)

    For those who need their video and arcade game fix, this arcade center has a wide variety of games to choose from, plus a few kiddy rides. It is conveniently located in Big Bear Village.

| | |
|---|---|
| **Hours:** | Open Mon. - Thurs., 11am - 9pm; Fri., 11am - 10pm; Sat. - Sun., 10am -10pm. |
| **Admission:** | Token money. |
| **Ages:** | 2½ years and up. |

## VICTORIA PARK CARRIAGES, LTD
(909) 584-2277  / www.buggies.com                                         *$$$$*
*Big Bear*

    There is no more elegant, storybook way to explore Big Bear than by horse and carriage. A carriage can usually be found in the heart of the Village, across from Chad's, on the weekends. Take a fifteen or twenty-minute ride through the Village, and down to the lake. The carriages seat between four to seven people. Ask about taking a hayride, too.

| | |
|---|---|
| **Hours:** | Call to make a reservation. |
| **Admission:** | $25 a couple during the day; $30 a couple at nighttime; no charge for small children. Additional adults are half-price. |
| **Ages:** | 2 years and up. |

## WILD WINGS UNLIMITED
(909) 584-4295                                                                   *!/$*
*42656 Moonridge Road, Big Bear*
(Exit Big Bear Blvd. S.E. on Moonridge Rd.)

    Tweet, tweet, chirp, chirp - these are the recorded sounds you'll hear upon entering this store for birding enthusiasts. Bird houses, bird feathers, birdseed, bird baths, and binoculars are just a few of the practical items for sale. More decorative merchandise includes bird figurines, paintings, carvings, etc. Bird lovers of all age flock to this store!

| | |
|---|---|
| **Hours:** | Open Mon. - Tues., Thurs. - Sat., 10am - 5pm; Sun., 10am - 4pm. Closed Wed. |
| **Admission:** | Free |
| **Ages:** | 3 years and up. |

## PALM SPRINGS
### (and the surrounding area)

A collage of words and images used to come to mind when I thought about Palm Springs - desert; hot; resort; homes of the rich and famous; golf; shopping mecca; etc. Now that my family has thoroughly explored it, I can add to this list - kid-friendly; fun; beautiful; great hiking opportunities; and educational treasures. This area is one oasis that is no mirage!

Note: Although this section is titled Palm Springs, it also includes attractions in the surrounding desert cities.

## BIG MORONGO CANYON PRESERVE ☼

(760) 363-7190 / www.ca.blm.gov/palmsprings/morongomap.html    !
*East Drive, Morongo Valley*
(Exit Interstate 10 N. on Route 62, E. on East Dr.)

The quietness of this peaceful preserve was broken only by shouts from my kids whenever they spotted a lizard, bunny, roadrunner, or other animals. The trails are relatively easy to walk, and many of them go in and through the canyon and the fire-blackened trees. There are several short looping trails, as well as a longer hike of five-and-a-half miles along the Canyon Trail, which extends the length of the canyon. Fresh water marshes and a variety of trees and plants add to the otherwise more traditional desert landscape. Wildlife here includes Bighorn sheep, raccoons, coyotes, and so many species of birds that people come just to observe them. Bring binoculars!

**Hours:** Open daily from 7:30am - sunset.
**Admission:** Free
**Ages:** 3 years and up.

## CAMELOT PARK FAMILY ENTERTAINMENT ☼
## CENTER

(760) 321-9893                                                          *$$$*
*67-700 E. Palm Canyon Drive [111], Cathedral City*                     ♨
(Exit Interstate 10 S. on Gene Autry Tr., L. on E. Palm Canyon Dr. [Hwy 111].)

In short, there's simply not a more congenial spot for happy ever aftering than here in Camelot! This huge family fun center (the first castle off Highway 111), offers a variety of entertainment for everyone. Choose from three themed **miniature golf** courses - $6 per round for ages 6 years and up, $4.25 for seniors, children 5 years and under are free; **go carts** - $4.75 a ride; **bumper boats** (avoid the shooting fountain waters or get refreshed) - $4 a ride; **laser tag** (a five-minute game of going through mazes in the dark, and zapping the other team with laser guns to score points) - $4; a **simulator** ride - $4; a castle **fun jump** (inflated bounce) - $1 for ages 12 and under; **batting cages;** and over 200 video and sport games, plus a prize redemption center.

**Hours:** Open Mon. - Thurs., 11am - 10pm; Fri., 11am - midnight; Sat., 10am - midnight, Sun., 10am - 10pm.
**Admission:** Attractions are individually priced above, or purchase one of the super saver packages.
**Ages:** 4 years and up.

## CHILDREN'S DISCOVERY MUSEUM OF THE DESERT ☼

(760) 321-0602                                                          *$$*
*71-701 Gerald Ford Drive, Rancho Mirage*                               ♨
(Exit Interstate 10 W. on Ramon, L. on Bob Hope Dr., R. on Gerald Ford Dr.)

The desert, well known for golf and retirement living, boasts of a terrific museum for children. The building is deceptive. Its architectural style befits an art museum, and its high ceilings are complemented by numerous windows and tall, pastel, modular room dividers. Upon entering the lobby, my 11-year old whispered, "Are you sure this is a hands-on place for kids?" Most definitely!

The exhibits flow easily from one to another. Some of the scientific exhibits in the front include a music machine of sorts, where a touch on a metal sculpture produces a jazz or percussion musical sound, and a stroboscope, which is a display where kids can draw their own design, attach it to the fan, and watch it "dance" in the strobe light. Follow any one of three colored ropes through a kid-size, spider-web-looking rope maze. A reading corner has several books, tables and chairs, and colorful wooden pattern pieces. Indigenous rock and flora displays add local color to one section. Put together a life-size skeleton in another area. Get properly suited up with a safari hat, goggles, and gloves and use the tools provided to find faux artifacts in a simulated dig. Climb a (fake) rock wall, complete with hand and foot holds. The relatively large Make-It-Take-It work area is a real treat for kids who like to take apart radios, computer components, and other household gadgets. They can even use the screwdrivers, glue, pieces of wood, and recycled materials to make a new creation to take home. Painting a car is not normally allowed, but the VW Beetle here is a much-decorated canvas on wheels. Smocks, paints, and brushes are supplied. The Art Corner has paper, markers, a computer with art programs, and even a giant loom for young weavers. Toward the back of the museum is a well-stocked grocery store with mini-carts and a checkout counter. Pizza, every child's favorite food, can be made to order just next door. This pizzeria has all the ingredients (made from cloth) to make pizzas, as well as aprons, hats, and a pretend brick oven, plus tables and chairs for customers. An enclosed toddlers' play area and a real CHP motorcycle are also located in this wing.

Walk up the snake-like, winding ramp to the second story Attic Room. This area is decorated with old trunks, hat boxes, fishing poles, pictures, and adding machines and telephones. One of the best features is the quality costumes in which to play dress up. They range from princess dresses with sequins to military uniforms to suits and everything in between. Lots of hats, an assortment of shoes and boots, plus boas and ties are some of the accessories.

The above merely lists the highlights of the museum! Parental supervision is required at all times but, as each activity was so much fun, I was delighted to comply. Both the adjacent Dinah Shore theater and the outdoor amphitheater put on a variety of performances year round. Ask about numerous special programs and classes offered for children, such as art classes, ballet lessons, and the Writers' Club for third to fifth graders where local writers will share their talents and excitement about writing.

**Hours:** Open Tues. - Sat., 10am - 5pm; Sun., noon - 5pm. School field trips here are offered Tues. - Fri. from 9:30am - 11:30am and 12:30pm - 2pm.

**Admission:** $5 per person; children 2 years and under are free. Yearly membership is a great deal at $15 per person. School groups, consisting of a minimum of ten students, are $3 per student; teachers and chaperones are free.

**Ages:** 1 year and up.

# COACHELLA VALLEY MUSEUM & CULTURAL CENTER

(760) 342-6651   *$*

*82-616 Miles Avenue, Indio*

(Exit Interstate 10 S. on Monroe, L. on Miles Ave.)

Each city desires to preserve its history and make it available for future generations. The Coachella Valley Museum has displays inside the small 1928 adobe home that reflect Indian and pioneer heritage. Some of the permanent displays include Indian pottery and arrowheads; dioramas of date picking, and an interesting thirteen-minute video about growing dates; old-fashioned clothing; original kitchen appliances; and a large panel displaying various fire alarms.

Outside, on the beautiful grounds, are lots of old agricultural tools and machinery. Peek inside the blacksmith shop to see forges, anvils, tongs, etc. Take a guided tour to learn background information on the items here or, although nothing is hands-on, look around by yourself to get a rich, visual sampling of history.

 **Hours:** Open October through May, Wed. - Sat., 10am - 4pm; Sun., 1pm - 4pm. Open weekends only in June and September. Closed July and August.

 **Admission:** $2 for adults; $1 for seniors and ages 5 -1 4; children 4 years and under are free.

 **Ages:** 5 years and up.

# COACHELLA VALLEY PRESERVE

(760) 343-1234   *!*

*Thousand Palms Canyon Road, Coachella*

(Exit Interstate 10 N. on Ramon Rd., L. on Thousand Palms Canyon Rd.)

This 18,000-acre preserve is not only immense, but it is diverse in topography and wildlife. The preserve straddles Indio Hills and the infamous San Andreas Fault. Thousand Palms Oasis (yes, it contains at least this many palm trees) is at the heart of the Coachella Valley Preserve. The oasis is supported by water constantly seeping along the fault line.

Kids begin to appreciate the many faces of the desert as they hike through here. It is sandy, dry, and rocky, and these elements create sand dunes, bluffs, and mesas. It is also mountainous and interspersed with dense palm trees, cacti, and various other vegetation. Some of the trails are as short as one-quarter mile, while others are longer at one-and-a-half miles, and more.

Start at the rustic Visitors Center that has natural history exhibits behind glass. The displays include arrowheads, mounted insects, birds' nests, and eggs. Bring a water bottle and/or a picnic lunch and have a delightful time exploring desert wilderness at its finest.

 **Hours:** Open daily from sunset to sunrise.

 **Admission:** Free

**Ages:**    4 years and up.

## COVERED WAGON TOURS

(760) 347-2161                                                                              *$$$$$*

*Ramon Road outside Thousand Palms*

(From Palm Springs, go E. on Ramon Rd., or go N. on Washington from La Quinta. It's on the E. side of Ramon Rd.)

Travel in a mule-drawn, covered wagon for a two-hour, narrated tour of the Coachella Valley Preserve. You'll go along the San Andreas fault, occasionally getting out along the way, and see three oases, and lots of wildlife. The wagons are not the primitive ones your pioneer ancestors used, as these have padded seats, springs, tires, etc., although part of the fun is the bumpiness of the ride. Take just the tour, or add on a chuck wagon cookout dinner and sing-a-long for the full western experience.

**Hours:**    Call for tour times.

**Admission:**    The tours are $30 for adults; $15 for ages 7 - 16; children 6 years and under are free. Tour and dinner costs $55 for adults; $27.50 for ages 7 - 16; children 6 years and under are free.

**Ages:**    5 years and up.

## DESERT ADVENTURES

(760) 864-6530 / www.redjeep.com                                                            *$$$$$*

*67555 E. Palm Canyon Drive, suite A104, Cathedral City*

(Exit Interstate 10 S. on Gene Autry Tr., L. on E. Palm Canyon Dr. [Hwy. 111])

Choose from three different tours to take your two-hour or four-hour jeep trip, and explore the wonders of the desert. The Indian Canyon tour takes you through archaeology sites, two lush oases, and to a waterfall, all the while learning about the history of Palm Springs. The Santa Rosa Mountains tour is a great combination of an off-road adventure, and a naturalist tour. The Mystery Canyon Adventure tour goes through the Coachella Valley, across the San Andreas, and involves hiking around the area. Bighorn sheep, coyotes, and other wildlife are abundant along the back roads, so keep your eyes open. The jeeps seat up to seven people.

**Hours:**    Two-hour tours usually leave at 8am, 10am, 1pm, and 3pm. Four-hour tours leave at 8am and 1pm. Ask about their sunset tours. Call to make a reservation.

**Admission:**    Two-hour tours cost $69 for adults; $64 for ages 6 - 12 years. Four-hour tours cost $99 for adults; $94 for kids.

**Ages:**    6 years and up.

## DINOSAURS / SKYLINE AVIATION HELICOPTER RIDES / WHEEL INN RESTAURANT

(909) 849-8309 - dinos; (909) 699-3048 - helicopter rides; (909) 849-    *!/$*
7012 - restaurant.

*Off Interstate 10, Cabazon*

(Going E., exit Interstate 10 N. on Main St. It's E. of Hadleys; and about 20 minutes N.W. of Palm Springs.)

While cruising down the desert highway, looking out the window, your kids see the usual things, such as big trucks, cactus, and dinosaurs. Screech go the brakes! The gigantic (150-feet long) Apatosaurus, with fiery eyes, is almost triple the size of the actual dinosaur that roamed the earth long ago. The same goes for the Tyrannosaurus behind him. Enter the steel and concrete Apatosaurus through its tail. Along the cave-like stairway are a few fossils and rocks behind glass displays, plus information and explanations regarding these two huge time travelers. Up in the Apatosaurus' belly is a gift shop, specializing in everything dinosaur. The fun for a child is just being inside here. The T-Rex, however, can only be looked at, but do look up at his mouth to see the remains of the last ~~victim~~ visitor.

Located behind the dinosaurs, Skyline Aviation helicopter rides take you to the skies on the weekends and holidays. Take a three or four-minute flight to see the great creatures from the sky, or go on a longer trip to see Whitewater Windmills, Palm Springs, etc.

Wheel Inn Restaurant is a folksy truck-stop cafe with merchandise for sale, like gift items, sculptures, etc., displayed throughout. Retail pictures on the walls range from Disney to the Southwest. (Note: There are pictures of scantily-clad women toward the back.) Note: A Denny's restaurant and Burger King are also at this stop.

All in all, it's a *dino*-mite little stop!

| | |
|---|---|
| **Hours:** | The dinosaur gift shop is usually open daily from 9am - 8pm. The restaurant is open twenty-four hours. The helicopter rides are offered on weekends and holidays only. |
| **Admission:** | It's free to look and walk around the dinosaurs. The helicopter rides start at $12.50 for two passengers for a three to four-minute flight; $100 for two passengers for a twenty-minute flight, etc. |
| **Ages:** | All |

# GENERAL PATTON MEMORIAL MUSEUM          ☼
(760) 227-3483                                                                $
*Chiriaco, Chiriaco Summit*
(Exit Interstate 10 at Chiriaco. The museum is right off the freeway, 30 miles east of Indio.)

Any study of World War II includes at least one lesson on war hero, General George Patton. Even if kids don't know who he is yet, they will like all the "war stuff" at the museum. Outside the memorial building are over a dozen tanks. Kids can't climb on them, but they can run around and play army!

Inside, the front room is dominated by a five-ton relief map depicting the Colorado River Aqueduct route and surrounding area. The large back room is filled with General Patton's personal effects, and WWII memorabilia such as uniforms, weapons, flags, and artillery. Our favorite exhibits include a jeep, a lifelike statue of General Patton (who looks amazingly like George C. Scott), and rounds of machine gun bullets. Special displays showcase Nazi items taken from fallen Nazi soldiers; a small, but powerful pictorial Holocaust display; and items found on the battlefield of Gettysburg.

Over one million servicemen and women were trained at this huge Desert Training Center site during WWII. If your child is especially interested in this period of military history, take him to the remnants of the training camps, accessible by four-wheel vehicles. Call the museum for directions and more details.

**Hours:** Open daily from 9:30am - 4:30pm.

**Admission:** $4 for adults; $3.50 for seniors; children 11 years and under are free.

**Ages:** 3 years and up.

# HARD CLAY CAFE

(760) 341-3755

*Sage Street, Palm Desert*

(From Hwy 111, heading toward Indian Wells, go past Monterey, R. on Sage St.)

An artist is defined as "a person who uses deliberate skill in making things of beauty." I can, in all honesty, say that my children and I try to be artists; we are deliberate in our attempts. Actually, I'm often pleasantly surprised at how wonderful their creations turn out at paint-your-own ceramic stores. Hard Clay Cafe offers a wide range of items to paint, including plates, picture frames, tiles, mugs, etc. This is a great activity to share in together, and kids come home thrilled with their creations. Note: This is a great place to make gifts for hard-to-shop-for relatives!

**Hours:** Open in the summer Wed. - Sat., 10am - 5pm. Open the rest of the year daily 10am - 5pm.

**Admission:** The price of your item, ranging from $2.50 - $40, plus $6 an hour per painter which includes paints, brushes, glazing, and firing.

**Ages:** 4 years and up.

# HEARTLAND (The California Museum of the Heart)

(760) 32-HEART (324-3278)

*39-600 Bob Hope Drive, Rancho Mirage*

(Exit Interstate 10 W. on Ramon, L. on Bob Hope Dr. N. of Country Club Dr. It's in the Heart Institute.)

You'll receive a "hearty" welcome at this small, Smithsonian-quality museum that is in the Heart Institute. Listen - do you hear a heartbeat? The sound grows louder as you enter the museum through the pink plastic and white rubbery strands of a model heart valve. Stand in a pinkish tube, which is actually a replica of an artery, and touch the bumpy rubber walls. Look up to see a video describing the process of how plaque attacks and constricts the function of this vessel. The next display looks and feels like rubbery red doughnuts, but they're "actually" blood platelets. A video explains blood cells' relationship to the heart.

A ten-foot model of a real heart isn't as cute looking as the typical renderings of a heart shape. Different buttons either make the model light up, tracing the circulatory system, or make this heart seemingly come alive: moving, beating, pulsating. Another interactive display that got my kids really pumped is called Sound of the Heart, where you can place a stethoscope over your child's heart, record the heartbeat, and then play back the magnified version. Have your child jog in place, then play the recording again for a comparison. Listen to series of recorded heartbeats that have irregularities, such as mitrostenosis.

No "butts" about it, the large, literally smoking cigarettes certainly drew my boys' attention. I hope that the cartoon about not smoking extinguished any desire to puff their lives away.

The 104-seat Happy Heart Theater shows any one of three films upon request. One is a fifteen-minute cartoon for young kids. Another is for school-aged kids called *I Am Joe's Heart*. After this twenty-eight-minute film is shown, catch the three-minute "music video" - open heart surgery accompanied by jazz music. Reactions range from "cool" to "gross." The third film, *How to Beat a Heart Attack,* is geared for general viewing. Look for this theater to incorporate 3D and sensurround special effects in the near future.

Although the information in many of the exhibits is too technical for younger kids to fully digest, the hands-on features and outstanding visuals make an impact on the hearts and minds of all ages.

>    **Hours:**     Operating hours are usually Mon. - Fri., 7:30am - 6pm, although
>                   summer hours may be shorter. It is also open September - May
>                   on Sat. from 7am - noon. Call to check on hours before you visit.
> **Admission:**    Suggested donations are $2 for adults; $1 for kids or students 6 -
>                   17 years; children 5 years and under are free.
>     **Ages:**     4 years and up.

## HI-DESERT NATURE MUSEUM

(760) 369-7212
*57-116 Twentynine Palms Highway, Yucca Valley*
(Exit Twentynine Palms Highway [62] N. on Dumosa, just E. of Sage Ave.)

I *hi*ghly recommend the Hi-Desert Nature Museum. It offers lots of activity, and has fascinating exhibits on wildlife, geology, culture, and science.

The rotating exhibits in the front room have included Wild on Wildflowers; Shake, Rattle & Roll, Living With Earthquakes; Holiday Traditions (from around the world); etc. We saw Black Widow. Arachniphobia aside, the fantastic photographs, video, and information combined with live and dead specimens made learning about this feared insect interesting. The far wall in this room contains encased displays of Indian baskets, arrowheads, pottery, and Kachina dolls.

Another room has taxidermied waterfowl plus animals that are unique to the desert such as mule deer, quail, roadrunners, jack rabbits, and coyotes. A hands-on area in here has skulls and soft fur to match with the stuffed animals.

Fossils, shells, and a wonderful rock and mineral collection comprise the earth science room. The petrified logs are unusual, as are the sphere balls. Rocks like amethyst and malachite are shown in their rough, natural state, and also in a polished version. Original minerals are shown next to their commercial counterpart such as fluorspar next to toothpaste, and talc next to baby powder; this helps kids to make connections and understand that man-made products were first God-created resources.

A mini-zoo has live squirrels, lizards, snakes, and a tarantula. A docent is often on hand to assist your child in holding one of the animals. I'm proud to write that after recovering from my cold sweat, I held the (large!) tarantula.

The Kids' Corner is action packed. There is a small sand pit (I mean archaeological dig); animal puppets; a butterfly and insect collection; stone mortar and pestles with corn kernels to grind; discovery boxes to reach in and guess what you're touching; animal tracks to match with animals; a touch table with whale bones, rocks, and shells; books; and containers of construction toys. The Hi-Desert Nature Museum also offers themed traveling classroom programs on recycling, insects, wildflowers, a particular animal, etc.

The community center/park just behind the museum is equally fine. It has four basketball courts, a baseball field, a skateboard park with cement ramps, a sand volleyball court, a covered picnic area, grassy areas, and three playgrounds complete with slides, climbing apparatus, and swings. All this and a few shade trees are against the backdrop of Joshua trees and the desert mountains.

Opening an oyster and finding the pearl that's been created by a grain of sand, is like opening the doors to this museum and finding a part of the sandy desert that has been transformed to a treasure of great worth.

**Hours:**   Open Tues. - Sun. from 10am - 5pm. Closed major holidays.
**Admission:**   Free
**Ages:**   1 years and up.

# INDIAN CANYONS

(760) 325-5673
*S. Palm Canyon Drive, Palm Springs*
(Exit Interstate 10 S. on Indian Canyon Dr., which turns into Palm Canyon Dr. Keep going S. for a few miles.)

Vast, spectacular, and awesome are three words that come to mind when exploring Indian Canyons. Long ago, ancestors of the Agua Caliente Cahuilla Indians made their homes in these canyons and the surrounding area. Today, a large number of Indians still reside on the reservation here. The Tribal Council has opened three out of four canyons for the public to explore.

A mile or so past the entrance gate is the trading post. Kids enjoy looking at the trinkets, jewelry, and Indian art work. Beyond the store are picnic grounds, and hiking and horse trails.

Palm Canyon is fifteen miles long and abundant with palm trees; a stark contrast to the surrounding rocky hills. The moderately-graded, paved walkway into this valley leads you along a stream, and to a picnic oasis. The scenery almost makes you forget that you're hiking! Andreas Canyon is unexpectedly lush with fan palms and more than 150 species of plants, all within a half-mile radius. Hike along a stream and see unusual rock formations. Challenge your kids to look for shapes or people in the rocks. There are also Indian caves back in the canyon and old grinding stones. You can hike to Murray Canyon from Andreas Canyon. Murray is smaller and less accessible, but no less beautiful. There are caves here also, which always sparks a child's imagination. Hiking in Indian Canyons is a wonderful opportunity to explore the desert wilderness surrounded by the stunning backdrop of the rocky mountains.

**Hours:** Open daily from 8am - 5pm. Summer schedule may vary.
**Admission:** $5 for adults; $2.50 for seniors; $3 for students; $1 for ages 6 - 12. Children 5 years and under are free.
**Ages:** All, but older kids for real hiking.

## JOSHUA TREE AND SOUTHERN RAILROAD MUSEUM

(760) 366-8503 - museum; (760) 363-6446 - tours                                    *$*
*Willow Lane, Joshua Tree*
(Exit Highway 62 S. on Park Blvd., turns into Quail Springs Rd., S. on Willow Lane.)

Both the Live Steam Club and the railroad museum are located here. Model railroad enthusiasts can not only work on their hobby, but some have engineered it so that they live here, too. The trains range from two-and-a-half-inch scale models to full-size rail cars. If it's running, you're invited to ride on Uncle Bert's gasoline-powered model train, which covers about a mile of track. Take a tour of the full-size cars including a diner, with its old-fashioned stove and icebox; a mail car, with small pigeonholes that are labeled with city names; a Pullman sleeping car, which always makes sleeping on a train seem romantic; and the grand finale - a caboose.

Inside the museum are model steam engines and lots of railroad memorabilia from Francis Moseley's collection. Ask to watch the video which shows how a model train operates. This site is great for those who are loco about trains!

**Hours:** Open to the public on the second and third Sat. - Sun. of the month from 10am - 4pm.
**Admission:** $1 donation.
**Ages:** 3 years and up.

## JOSHUA TREE NATIONAL PARK

(760) 367-5500  / www.nps.gov/jotr                                                 *$*
*Joshua Tree*
(The south entrance: Exit Interstate 10 N. on Cottonwood Springs, 25 miles east of Indio. The north entrance: Exit Twentynine Palms Highway |62| between the town of Joshua Tree and Twentynine Palms. The west entrance: Exit Twentynine Palms Highway |62| at the town of Joshua Tree. This is the best way to reach Keys View and Hidden Valley.)

This 800,000-acre park gets its name from the unique Joshua trees that Mormon visitors likened to the biblical Joshua reaching up to God. Explore the riches of this national treasure by car, by foot, and/or by camping.

Entire books are written on Joshua Tree National Park, so consider the following information a very condensed version. Just a few phrases attributed to this enormous park are "wind-sculpted boulders"; "massive granite monoliths"; "five fan palm oases dotting the park"; "wildflowers and wildlife"; "mountainous"; and "rugged." Start your visit at the main headquarters/Visitors Center in Oasis of Mara, located off the north entrance. You can get a map here, look at the botanical displays, and watch a slide show that gives a good overview of the park.

If you are automobile adventurers, which is a good way to get a lay of the land, there are many roads to travel. Keys View is the most popular destination because of its breathtaking view of the valley, mountains, and deserts. (Bring a panoramic camera.) If you don't mind a few bumps along the way, and kids usually don't, there are many dirt roads accessible only by four-wheel drive. Particularly outstanding is the eighteen-mile Geology Tour Road, which showcases some of the most incredible landscape the park offers.

Hiking runs the gamut from easy, one-tenth-of-a-mile trails, to strenuous, over thirteen-mile long trails. Three of the trails that offer fascinating terrain also lead to special destinations. The first one is Hidden Valley, with trails winding through massive boulders. It leads to and through legendary cattle rustlers' hideouts. The second is Barker Dam, which was built almost 100 years ago, and is now a reservoir that many desert animals frequent. Approach it in whispers, if possible, so as not to scare away any critters. Encourage your children to look for some of the "hidden" wildlife in the water. The third is Lost Horse Mine, which is a rugged one-and-a-half-mile hike. This mine was used for prospecting and gold mining. Maybe there still is gold in them thar hills! **Bring water** no matter which trail you take because it is not supplied in the park.

Rock climbing is a popular sport here. Even if your kids are too young to participate, they'll get a vicarious thrill at watching more experienced climbers. Boulder hopping is also fun, and that can be done by kids of all ages.

Camping is primitive at most of the 500 sites in Joshua Tree. Many campsites are located in the shelter of rocks, while others, at higher elevations, offer spots of shade. It is hot during the day, much cooler at night (even cold), and at times quite windy, but kids revel in it all. Water is only provided at Cottonwood and Black Rock Canyon campgrounds, so other sites are really back to basics.

National parks are sometimes called "universities of the outdoors." Joshua Tree National Park is an outstanding university to attend. Everyone will go home with a special memory, and a different reason for wanting to come back.

**Hours:** Open daily sunrise to sunset.

**Admission:** $5 per vehicle, which is good for a week's admittance. The Visitors Center is open daily from 8am - 5pm. Camping starts at $10 a night.

**Ages:** All

# KID OASIS

(760) 360-6192 / e-mail:kidoasis1@aol.com

$$$

*42-215 Washington Street, Palm Desert*                              ♨

(Exit Interstate 10 S. on Washington Street. It is located in a shopping center that also features a Lucky's food store, an ice cream shop, and a few restaurants.)

It is obvious, just by entering this clean, bright, well-designed oasis for kids, that the owners are also conscientious parents. One entrance/exit door, and a wristband, with matching numbers for parents and their children, are just a few of the safety measures. The food counter - there is no kitchen - is located right by the entrance. You may order sandwiches ($3.75), tossed salads ($2.75), corn dogs or bagel dogs ($1.75 each), pizza delivered by Little Caesar's ($10 for a medium), snack food, and beverages. The adjacent Adult Oasis room, with its big window, is almost soundproof so it blocks the noise, but not the view. It's comfortably outfitted with couches, tables and chairs, and lots of magazines.

The main room contains a large, two-level play structure that has ball pits; a bounce room; a soft play obstacle room; an area with huge, clear plastic balls to roll around on; kid-size plastic tubes and tunnels to crawl through; rope bridges; rope stairs; a mini-zip line; a long, curvy slide; a punching/kicking bag; and, for visual entertainment, a see-through tube which continuously filters colorful balls. Just a few yards away is a separate, enclosed, carpeted toddler area. It has a few small slides, a ball pit, a short tunnel, and a large plastic train car. The eating area, or relaxing area for parents too pooped to play, is also in this room, directly in front of the toddler playland.

Another attraction is a Synth-A-Beam. $1 buys a player five rhythmic minutes to make his/her own kind of music. Eight multi-colored track lights shine on the floor, but when the beam is disrupted by a hand stuck between the light and floor, the floor sensor makes a percussion or drums sound.

Children are kept busy at Kid Oasis - playing, jumping, and squealing with delight. Note that socks are required to play here and that there are no video games (yea!). And yes, themed party rooms are available!

**Hours:**       Open Sun. - Thurs., 10am - 8pm; Fri. - Sat., 10am - 9pm.

**Admission:**   $6 per child; $3 for adults who want to play in the main play structure; free for non-paying adults and children under one year, as long as there is one paid admission.

**Ages:**        3 months - 10 years old.

# LAKE CAHUILLA                                                      ☼

(760) 564-4712 - lake; (800) 234-PARK (7275) - camping reservations   $

*58-075 Jefferson, La Quinta*                                         ♨

(Exit Interstate 10 S. on Monroe St., R. on Avenue 58.)

Escape from the heat at Lake Cahuilla recreation park. The gigantic, stocked lake is a prime spot for fisherboys and girls to reel in the catch of the day. Kids over 16 years need a state fishing license. Night fishing is open Friday and Saturday during the summer. Although swimming in the lake is prohibited, there is a pool open for your aquatic pleasure. A wooden playground is located behind the pool - youngsters always have energy to play, no matter what temperature it is!

The park is not abundantly blessed with shade trees, but there are large grassy areas and palm trees to enhance its beauty. Hiking trails traverse the park, so make sure you've got plenty of sunscreen and water. Over 150 campsites are available here, complete with barbecues and other amenities. Come escape the city life, if just for a day or night!

**Hours:** The park is open mid-October through April daily from sunrise to sunset, and May 1 through mid-October, Fri. - Mon., sunrise to sunset. The pool is open weekends only April through May, and September through October, 11am - 5:45pm. It is open during the summer Fri. - Mon. from 11am - 5:45pm.

**Admission:** $2 for adults; $1 for children 10 years and under. The swimming pool is an extra $1 per person. Primitive camping (space and a table - no shade trees) is $12 a site; an upgraded site is $16 a night. Fishing is $5 for ages 16 and up; $4 for ages 5 - 15; children 4 years and up are free.

**Ages:** All

# LIVING DESERT WILDLIFE AND BOTANICAL GARDEN PARK ☼

(760) 346-5694 / www.livingdesert.org                                *$$$*
*47-900 Portola Avenue, Palm Desert*
(Exit Interstate 10 S. on Monterey Ave., L. on Palm Canyon, [Hwy 111], R. on Portola.)

Kids can experience a lot of living in the 1,200-acre Living Desert! Choose one of three areas of interest - botanical gardens, wildlife, or hiking - or partake in some of each.

The nocturnal (this can be your child's new word for the day) animals exhibit is to your immediate left through the entrance gate. Bats are always a highlight in here. Behind this exhibit is the good-sized Discovery Room. Children can get a real "feel" for desert life as they touch live snakes, turtles, and a big hairy tarantula, plus feathers, bones, rocks, and fur. They can also put on animal puppet shows at the box theater, put together puzzles, or make crayon rubbings of desert animals.

The northern section of this "like a zoo, only better" park is mostly botanical. The pathways weave in and out amongst an incredible variety of desert floral including saguaros, yuccas, and towering palm trees. Caged bird life is abundant along the walkways, too. We took the time to really watch our feathered friends' activities and learned quite a bit.

Eagle Canyon houses twenty desert animal species living in their natural element. Powerful mountain lions, Mexican wolves, and the small fennec foxes dwell in their own craggy retreats that are easily viewed through glass. Don't miss the tree-climbing coyote!

A trail system lies to the east, traversing through some of the 1,000-acre wilderness section of the park. Three loops offer something for every level hiker: An easy three-quarter mile hike; a moderate one-and-a-half-mile hike; and a strenuous five-mile, round-trip hike to the base of Eisenhower Mountain. Don't get me wrong, however, the walk around the park is a hike in itself. If you get tired, take the fifty-minute guided tram tour that goes all around the park.

Animals in the Living Desert dwell in outdoor enclosures that resemble their natural habitat. A rocky mountain is home to the Bighorn sheep. Look for them leaping among the boulders. Other exotic animals include Arabian oryx, aardwolves, zebras, cheetahs, small African mammals, and birds. We saw several other animals in the wild, too, such as a snake slithering across our path and the ever-speedy roadrunner darting out of the bushes. Seeing them authenticated the unique setting of this park. Want to see more animals, more up close? See Wildlife Wonders, a live animal presentation at the outdoor theater, featuring your favorite desert critters.

Visit here during the spring when the desert flowers and trees explode in a profusion of colors, or come in the winter to see Wildlights (see the December Calendar section for more information). Anytime you choose to visit the Living Desert will be a time of wonder, relaxation, and education.

**Hours:**      Open October 1 through June 15 daily from 9am - 5pm. Open June 16 through July 31, and September daily from 8am - noon. Closed the month of August and on Christmas Day. The Children's Discovery Room is open daily 10am - 4pm, but closed the first Tues. of the month. Times for weekend Wildlife Wonders show vary.

**Admission:**  $7.50 for adults; $6.50 for seniors; $3.50 for ages 3 - 12; children 2 years and under are free. The tram tour is $5 a person. School groups, with reservations, are free, however, spaces fill up fast so make your reservation soon.

**Ages:**       All

## MCCALLUM THEATRE

(760) 340-2787 / www.mccallum-theatre.org                    *$$$$*
*73000 Fred Waring Drive, Palm Desert*
(Exit San Bernardino Fwy [10] W. on Ramon Rd., L. on Bob Hope Dr., R. on Fred Waring Dr. It's in the Bob Hope Cultural Center.)

This beautiful theater seats over a thousand people and has three levels of seating, including box seats. Several one-hour, just-for-kids plays and musicals are put on throughout the year. Past titles include *Romana Quimby*, *Pippi Longstocking*, and *Pinocchio*. There are also several productions that are enjoyable for the entire family.

**Hours:**      Call for a program schedule.
**Admission:**  Tickets for the kids' shows range between $5 - $15 per person, depending on the seat.
**Ages:**       4 years and up.

## MOORTEN BOTANICAL GARDEN

(760) 327-6555                                                   *$*
*1701 S. Palm Canyon Drive, Palm Springs*
(Exit Interstate 10 S. on Indian Canyon, turns into Palm Canyon Dr.)

This place has plenty of prickly plants along pleasurable pathways. In other words, this compact botanical garden, specializing in cacti, is a delightful stroll and an interesting way to study desert plant life. There are over 3,000 varieties of cacti, trees, succulents, and flowers, plus lots of even birds! You'll see giant saguaros, ocotillos, and grizzly bear cactus, plus you can walk through a greenhouse (or cactarium). Toward the entrance are petrified logs, and a few, small desert animals in cages. Enjoy this spot of greenery in the midst of the sandy, brown desert.

**Hours:** Open Mon. - Sat., 9am - 4:30pm; Sun., 10am - 4pm.

**Admission:** $2 for adults; 75¢ for ages 5 - 15; children 4 years and under are free.

**Ages:** All

# OASIS WATERPARK

(760) 325 - SURF (7873) /
www.palmsprings.com/hotels/oasis/waterpark.html
*1500 Gene Autry Trail, Palm Springs*
(Exit Interstate 10 S. on Gene Autry Trail. S. of Ramon Rd., N. of Palm Canyon [Hwy 111].)

This twenty-two-acre waterpark is truly an oasis in the desert. Built in and on top of a rocky hill, with an adjoining resort health club, the surroundings are luxurious. Eight waterslides for big kids range from mild, uncovered slides, to an enclosed forty-m.p.h. Rattlers slide, to a seventy-foot free fall slide. Catch a wave, dude, in the wave pool where kids can body or board surf. Get carried away in the gentle, three-foot-deep, circular Lazy River inner tube ride. Younger children can take the plunge in their own small water play area. Tots have a place to call their own with a wading area, kiddie slides, inflatable toys, and even a bounce. Oasis Waterpark also offers locker rentals, private cabana rentals, full-service snack bars, and an indoor restaurant for all your creature comforts. Note: You cannot bring your own food inside the park. And yes, there is a video arcade here, too.

Tip: For a rocky mountain high in the desert, try your hand (and foot) at the UPRISING ROCK CLIMBING CENTER (described later in this section), which is located right next door.

**Hours:** Open daily, mid-March through Labor Day, plus weekends through October, from 11am - 5:30pm.

**Admission:** $10.95 for local residents (bring proof of residency). For non-residents - $18.95 for adults; $9.95 for seniors; $11.95 for kids 36" - 60" tall; kids under 36" are free. After 3pm, admission is $12.50 for two residents; $18.95 for two non-residents. Body boards rentals are $5. Parking is $3, or $5 for preferred (i.e. closer) parking.

**Ages:** All

## OFFROAD RENTALS

(760) 325-0376                                                              *$$$$$*
*59511 Highway 111, Palm Springs*

(Exit Interstate 10 S. on White Water, go one mile S. on Hwy. 111. It's 4 miles N. of the Palm Springs Aerial Tramway. The office is in a white train caboose.)

Come ride the sand dunes in Palm Springs! After watching a ten-minute video on safety, put on the helmet and goggles (provided by Offroad), hop on your single-seater, four-wheel ATV, and go for an exhilarating ride. An expansive, flat area immediately in front of the rental facility is great for beginners, and it is the only place children may ride. The "course" has circle eight figures, too. More experienced riders (i.e. older) can venture on the large sand hills beyond this area. Machines are suited to the age and size of the rider, and speed limits are built into the vehicles. (Yea!) For instance, children 6 to 10 years, or so, are assigned vehicles that can't exceed four mph. A beverage is included in your admission price, but bring your own sun block.

    **Hours:** Open daily from 10am - sunset. Hours might vary during the summer.

    **Admission:** Forty-five-minute rides start at $30 per person.

    **Ages:** 6 years and up to drive their own vehicle.

## THE OLD SCHOOLHOUSE MUSEUM

(760) 367-2366                                                              *!*
*6760 National Park Drive, Twentynine Palms*

(Take Highway 10 east to 29 Palms Hwy. [62]. Take [62] approximately 42 miles to the town of Twentynine Palms. Once in town, look for National Park Drive - one block east of Adobe Road (1st stop light) - and turn right.)

Originally built in 1927, the old schoolhouse now houses historical exhibits of the early settlers, mostly via pictures and written information. The books on display are on Native Americans, gold miners, cowboys, and homesteaders. A re-created schoolroom, complete with wood desks, a flag, and a blackboard, is now a small research library. The gift shop carries pamphlets on the history of this area as well as cards and gift items. Call if you would like information on a school field trip.

    **Hours:** Open most of the year Tues. - Sun., 1pm - 4pm. Open in the summer weekends only from 1pm - 4pm.

    **Admission:** Free

    **Ages:** 7 years and up.

## PALM SPRINGS AERIAL TRAMWAY

(760) 325-1391 / www.pstramway.com                                         *$$$$*
*Valley Station is located on the north edge of Palm Springs*

(Exit Interstate 10 S. on Palm Canyon [Hwy.111], R. on Tramway Rd., 3½ miles up the hill.)

In fourteen minutes an eighty-passenger, enclosed car, carries you seemingly straight up the side of Mount San Jacinto. The scenery change in this short amount of time is almost unbelievable - from cactus and desert sand below, to the evergreen trees and cool air up above. (Call ahead to see if there is snow.) The altitude up at Mount San Jacinto State Park is 8,516 feet!

The Mountain Station at the top has an Alpine Restaurant, which opens at 11am, a snack bar, a game room, a gift shop, and observation areas where you can see the entire valley, including the Salton Sea which is forty-five miles away. The bottom floor of the Station has a few taxidermied animals and an interesting twenty-two-minute film on the history of the tramway.

Behind and down the Mountain Station building is Mount San Jacinto Wilderness State Park, with fifty-four miles of great hiking trails, campgrounds, and a ranger station. Though we just walked along the easier trails, the mountain scenery anywhere up here is unbeatable! Just remember that the trail you go down, you must also come back up to catch the tram. Horse rentals are available for a guided tour. Snow equipment rentals are available in the winter, November 15 through April 15, conditions permitting. There are plenty of areas to go sledding and cross country skiing.

Catch the package deal called Ride 'n' Dine, which includes tram fare and dinner. The meal is your choice of chicken, ribs, or vegetable lasagna, with a salad bar, bread, and dessert served from 4pm to 9pm at the Alpine Restaurant. Tickets may be purchased after 2:30pm; no advanced reservations are accepted. Otherwise, the cost of a buffet dinner, served 4pm to 10pm, is $11.95 for adults; $8.95 for children. The lunch menu, served daily from 11am to 3:30pm, is a la carte. Tip: Bring jackets for everyone and wear closed-toed shoes - it **really** does get cold up here!

    **Hours:**    Cars go up every half hour Mon. - Fri., starting at 10am; Sat. - Sun., starting at 8am. The last car goes up at 8pm, and the last car comes down at 9:45pm.

**Admission:**    $17.65 for adults; $14.95 for seniors; $11.65 for ages 5 - 12; children 4 years and old are free. Ride 'n' Dine costs $21.95 for adults; $14.65 for ages 5 to 12; children 4 years and under can eat off your plate, or you can purchase a meal for them. (Discount fare is offered to AAA members.)

      **Ages:**    3 years and up.

# PALM SPRINGS AIR MUSEUM     ☼

(760) 778-6262 / www.air-museum.org     *$$$*
*745 Gene Autry Trail, Palm Springs*
(Exit Interstate 10 S. on Gene Autry Trail.)

Enjoy happy landings at this classy air museum, conveniently located next to the Palm Springs Airport. Two hangers house between fifteen to thirty vintage WWII aircraft that are being restored or are in flight-ready condition. The collection includes Hellcats, Tomcats, B-17's, a P-40 Warhawk, and more. The planes are not cordoned off, making it easier to look at them close up, although touching is not allowed. Walk under and look up into the belly of an A-26 Invader attack bomber. My kids were thrilled to see the places where it actually held real bombs! The planes are fascinating for the part they've played in history, and visually exciting for kids because most have decorative emblems painted on their sides. Bunkers and displays around the perimeter of the airy hangers honor different eras of flight by featuring various uniforms, flight jackets, photographs, patches, combat cameras, etc. Other exhibits include gleaming antique cars, maps of missions, and touch screens. Tour the inside of a B-17 for a donation of $3 per person, or just admire it from the outside. Starting at 10am, the Wings Theater continuously shows war movies, combat videos, or interviews with war heroes. Kids always enjoy watching small planes land and take off at the adjacent runway. For more entertainment with an altitude, come see fly-overs on Memorial Day, Veterans Day, Armed Forces Day, Pearl Harbor Day, etc. Call for a schedule and for more details.

**Hours:** Open daily 10am - 5pm.

**Admission:** $7.50 for adults; $6 for seniors and military with I.D.; $3.50 for ages 6 - 12 years; children 5 years and under are free.

**Ages:** 4 years and up.

# PALM SPRINGS DESERT MUSEUM ☼

(760) 325-7186 / www.psmusuem.org                                         $$$
*101 Museum Drive, Palm Springs*
(Exit Interstate 10 S. on Indian Canyon Dr., R. on Tahquitz Canyon Way, R. on Museum Dr.)

There are many facets of this museum jewel. The lobby displays an impressive giant ground sloth. The Natural Science Wing has wall murals and life-size dioramas featuring taxidermied desert animals. Pick up a phone to hear about their habits and habitats. A rock "wall" with windows allows visitors to see live animals such as a variety of snakes (e.g. sidewinders and kings), gila monsters, scorpions, and kangaroo rats. An adjacent room has rotating science exhibits that often include hands-on experiments.

The left wing is a fine arts gallery with changing exhibits of paintings, sculptures, and other forms of art. As the gallery is not overwhelmingly large, exploring the art world is a feasible journey for youngsters. My middle son has an artistic temperament, so I'm hoping art exposure will develop the talents, too!

Further back on the main floor are a few rooms devoted to Western and Native American art. One room consists mainly of paintings, blankets, and numerous baskets. Another, called the George Montgomery Collection, features the western star's movie posters, furniture, paintings, and bronze sculptures of cowboys and Indians. The William Holden Collection offers some of Holden's prized art pieces. Also in this area is a Miniature Room, which displays miniature dioramas in the perimeter of the walls.

The upper level room and mezzanine level have rotating exhibits of twentieth century art, which means expect the unexpected. I love seeing what's new up here.

The downstairs theater presents shows mostly for adult audiences, such as plays, ballets, and concerts. Even if you don't eat here, take a stroll through the Gallery Cafe to check out its colorful mobiles and funky decor. Outside, all-age visitors will enjoy the small, twentieth-century sculpture garden. Ask about the variety of classes offered in the on-site classrooms.

The classy Palm Springs Desert Museum is an interesting way to learn about natural history and different art styles, plus it's a respite from the heat!

**Hours:** Open Tues. - Sat., 10am - 5pm; Sun., noon - 5pm. Closed major holidays. Docent guided tours are conducted each day at 2pm.

**Admission:** $7.50 for adults; $6.50 for seniors; $3.50 for ages 6 - 17; children 5 years and under are free. The first Fri. of each month is free admission day.

**Ages:** 3 years and up.

## PALM SPRINGS VILLAGEFEST

(760) 325-1577                                                                    !/$

*Palm Canyon Drive, Palm Springs*

(Exit Interstate 10 S. on Palm Canyon Dr. It's between Barristo Rd. and Amado Rd.)

It's Thursday night and you're in Palm Springs with the kids, wondering what to do. You pick up this terrific book called *Fun and Educational Places to go With Kids* and read about VillageFest - problem solved! The VillageFest, or international old-time street fair, is held along several blocks on Palm Canyon Drive in the heart of Palm Springs. There is food, arts and crafts vendors, boutiques, cafes, and entertainment such as live music. For kids, various attractions could include pony rides, magic shows, a party bouncer, a gyroscope, school band competitions, and a stage for children's productions.

**Hours:** Thurs. nights from 6pm - 10pm. The fair is usually not held during July and August.

**Admission:** Free entrance, but attractions cost $.

**Ages:** 4 years and up.

## SUNRISE PARK / SWIM CENTER

(760) 323-8278                                                                    !/$

*On Sunrise Way and Ramon Road, Palm Springs*

(Exit Interstate 10 S. on Indian Canyon Dr., L. on Ramon Rd., L. on Sunrise Way.)

This park has activities that will keep your family busy and refreshed from sunrise to sunset. Besides the wonderful grassy areas and big playground with bridges, slides, and swings, the most important feature here is the Olympic-size swimming pool. (It has a shallow end for younger kids to cool off.) The deck has lawn chairs and a picnic area.

After spending a day at the park, take your kids out to the ball game next door. The baseball stadium has night lights.

**Hours:** The park is open daily from sunrise to sunset. The pool is open year-round, Mon., Wed., and Fri., 11am - 5pm; Tues., Thurs., Sat. - Sun., 11am - 3pm. Night swimming is available in the summer.

**Admission:** The park is free. Swim sessions are $3.25 for adults; $2.25 for ages 4 - 12; children 3 years and under are free with a paid adult. Such a deal - pay a $20 one-time fee for membership and then pay an additional $20 for a card worth twenty-five swims!

**Ages:** All

## TOMMY JACOB'S BEL AIR MINIATURE GOLF GREENS

(760) 322-6062                                                                                        $$
*1001 South El Cielo Road, Palm Springs*
(Exit Interstate 10 S. on Gene Autry Tr., R. on Ramon, L. on El Cielo Rd.)

This deluxe miniature golf course might not have the bells and whistles, or castles and windmills, that others have, but it is a beautiful course. Located next to the real golf course, it has shade trees and stone walls surrounding the "greens." The course itself is just difficult enough to make it fun, and it's lighted at night.

**Hours:** Open daily from 7am - 7pm.
**Admission:** $5 per round for adults; $3 for ages 17 and under.
**Ages:** 4 years and up.

## UPRISING ROCK CLIMBING CENTER

(760) 320-6630 / www.uprising.com                                                       $$$
*1500 S. Gene Autry Trail, Palm Springs*
(Exit Interstate 10 S. on Gene Autry Trail. S. of Ramon Rd., N. of Palm Canyon [Hwy 111]. It's in the same complex as OASIS WATERPARK.)

Do your kids have you climbing the walls? Then you'll feel right at home at Uprising Rock Climbing Center. The three, outdoor climbing structures have micro mists systems and are covered with an awning to block out direct sunlight. Kids can test their rock climbing skills here and train to reach new heights. The tallest wall is forty feet high while another, connected structure, has a thirty foot repelling tower. There are forty top ropes in all. All climbers are belayed and wear harnesses, although lead climbing for advanced climbers is available. The twenty-foot "teaching" wall might not look that high, but it seemed tall to me when I was at the top! It's a great spot for beginners to get a grip on this sport. A small bouldering area (i.e. no ropes needed) is also here.

Rental gear is available, or you can bring your own. Climb a few times during your visit, or make it an all-day workout. Ask about climbing excursions to Joshua Tree, Idyllwild, and out-of-state sites.

**Hours:** Usually open Mon. - Fri., noon - 8pm; Sat. - Sun., 10am - 6pm.
**Admission:** Prices vary greatly, depending on your skill level, if you bring any people with you, etc. For instance, an "opener" class includes one hour of climbing, equipment rental, and a belayer for $35. Harness, shoes, helmet, and chalk bag are available to rent.
**Ages:** At least 6 years, and up.

## WHITEWATER TROUT CO. / RAINBOW RANCHO TROUT FISHING

(760) 325-5570

$$

*Whitewater Canyon Road, Whitewater*

(Exit Interstate 10 N. on Whitewater Canyon Rd, along the Whitewater Cut Off. Across from the Whitewater Rock Supply Company, L. (N.) on Whitewater Canyon Rd. It's located 5 miles back.)

Grilled, baked, and fried are just a few savory suggestions as to how you can fix the trout lunch or dinner that you're almost sure to catch. In fact, you can rent the BBQ area, fix your fish, and eat 'em right there. Two stone-lined ponds with benches around them, shade trees, a picnic area (bring your own food just in case), and a grassy expanse offer a visual and physical respite from the desert surroundings. Bring your fishing poles or rent them here. Tip: Bring your own cooler for your fish.

Come early for a half hour tour of the adjacent fish hatchery, which has been here since 1939. Learn about its history and how to raise trout; see the various size fish; and feed them.

Note: Before you turn north on Whitewater Canyon Road and just past the Rock Supply Company, there is a seasonal stream bordered by big rocks. While it's not usually deep enough to swim in, it is a great place to at least get your feet wet. Wear a bathing suit and bring a towel.

**Hours:** Open Wed. - Sun. from 10am - 5pm. The fish hatchery tour is given Wed. - Sun. at 9am with advanced reservations.

**Admission:** 50¢ a person entrance fee; $2.50 per person fishing fee which include a pole, bait, and tackle. It's the same price if you bring your own pole. A state license is not required. Fish cost $2.72 per pound and 25¢ (per fish) for cleaning. The fish hatchery tour is free to day fishermen. Rental of the BBQ area is $10 for up to four people, $2.50 for each person thereafter, and each adult must catch (and pay for) a minimum of one fish. Use of the adjoining picnic area is free for day fishermen.

**Ages:** 3 years and up.

## WIND FARM TOUR

(760) 251-1997 / windtours@aol.com.

$$$$

*Indian Road (frontage), Palm Springs*

(Exit Interstate 10 N. on Indian Rd., L. on the frontage road of 20th Ave. 1 ¼ mile to the trailer buildings.)

If you like learning about alternative energy sources and are fascinated by the power that wind can generate, you'll be (literally) blown away by this tour put on by EV (Electric Vehicle) Adventures. To state the obvious, it is usually very windy out here. Why? Because cool coastal air comes inland and pushes the hot air through the narrow mountainous San Gorgonio Pass.

The ninety-minute tour, of one of the six wind farms in the world, takes place via a golf-cart-style electric vehicle, powered by the on-site giant turbines. You'll be driven around on the grounds and hear the thumping noise created by the huge pinwheels in motion. At selected stops you'll hear about the history and future of the wind machines, and you'll have the opportunity to inspect components (e.g. blades and nacelle [battery covers]) up close. Blades, by the way, can span more than half the length of a football field. You'll see the older style wind turbines, with lattice towers (reminiscent of the Eiffel Tower), and the newer, sleeker, more efficient ones with hollow steel towers. And, yes, you'll finally find out if these wind mills are simply tax shelters or actually producing usable, affordable energy! A lot of information is given and although much of it is technical, even I understand a bit more now about electricity, sources of clean energy, and what comprises a kilowatt hour. Although the tour got a little long winded for my boys, they particularly liked hearing about the wind smiths, those brave people who climb up the 150-foot tower ladders to do maintenance work.

Bring sunscreen, sunglasses, and water bottles. A visitors' center sells wind farm paraphernalia as well as solar-powered products. In the works are plans for electric vehicles to be on exhibit for viewing and possibly for test riding.

**Hours:** Tours are usually offered daily at 9am, 11am, 1pm, and 3pm, except during the summer when it's just too hot. Reservations are suggested, but not required. Call first as during gale winds or incredibly hot days, tours are canceled.

**Admission:** $20 for adults; $14 for kids 8 - 16 years; $7 for children 7 years and under. Call for group tour prices.

**Ages:** 9 years and up.

# CALENDAR
(A listing of annual events)

Many places listed in the main section of this book offer special events throughout the year. Below is a calendar listing of other annual stand outs. If you are looking for more local events, like fairs, etc., call the Recreation Department of your City Hall; call your Chamber of Commerce; or check the front pages of your local phone book. The prices given here are from 1998 and are quoted to give you a general idea of the cost. **Please call an event a month in advance as dates sometimes fluctuate.**

## JANUARY:

FESTIVAL OF THE WHALES, Dana Point. (714) 496-2274 / www.ocmi.org, 24200 Dana Point Harbor Dr., Orange County Marine Institute. This twenty-three-day festival, that usually spreads out over a few months, celebrates the California gray whales' migration south. The whole family can enjoy a variety of events offered throughout Dana Point, such as parades, art shows, kite flying, sand castle workshops, tidepool explorations, street fairs, kid's coloring contests, film festivals, and whale-watching excursions. Prices vary according to the event. Have a whale of a time!

TOURNAMENT OF ROSES PARADE, Pasadena. (626) 449-7673 - recording; (626) 449-4100 - real person / www.tournamentofroses.com, Pasadena City Hall. This two-hour, world-famous parade of fancifully, elegantly, decorated floral floats, plus bands and equestrian units, is held on New Year's Day. Camp out on the streets to guarantee a viewing spot, (626) 744-4501 - police (ask about camping regulations on parade route); try your luck in arriving in the early morning hours on the actual day; or call Sharp Seating Company, (626) 795-4171, for grandstand seating. Prices for seats range from $27 - $60. Please make reservations at least two months in advance. The parade starts at 8am.

TOURNAMENT OF ROSES VIEWING OF FLOATS, Pasadena. (626) 449-4100 / www.tournamentofroses.com, along Sierra Madre Blvd., between Paloma St. and Sierra Madre Villa Ave. The famous floats can be viewed up close for a few days after the parade. Let your kids "oooh" and "aaah" at the intricate workmanship, and bring your camera! Admission is $2 per person; children 2 years and under are free.

WHALE WATCHING. See the Transportation section in the main portion of the book for places to call to take a whale-watching cruise. The season goes from the end of December through March. Cruises are usually two and a half hours of looking for (and finding!) gray whales as they migrate to Baja. Also, be on the lookout for dolphins, pilot whales, and sea lions. Dress warmly.

WINTER WONDERLAND, Beverly Hills. (310) 550-4765, 471 S. Roxbury Dr., Roxbury Park. Over a hundred tons of snow turns the park into a winter wonderland for a day. Go down sled runs, build a snowman, and enjoy a horse-drawn carriage sleigh ride, a petting zoo, game booths, and children's craft center. Pre-registration is required for either of the two, two-and-a-half-hour sessions. Admission is $3 for adults; $6 for ages 3 - 18.

## FEBRUARY:

CAMELLIA FESTIVAL, Temple City. (626) 287-9150, corner of Las Tunas Dr. and Golden West Ave., Temple City Park. The festival, held the last weekend in February, is complete with carnival rides, and an art show on Sunday. The highlight, the festival parade, is held on Saturday. Camellia-covered floats (which must be finished with parts of camellias - no other materials are allowed), are designed and made by youth groups. Prizes, including a Sweepstakes Trophy, are given out. Over twenty marching bands and drill teams, plus other organizations that promote the welfare of children, like Brownies and Cub Scouts, participate. Carnival rides are open Fri. night. The parade begins Sat. at 10pm and festivities go on to 6pm. The festival runs on Sun. from noon - 8pm. Admission is free. Certain activities cost.

CHINESE NEW YEAR CELEBRATION, Los Angeles. (213) 617-0396, Chinatown. This month long celebration starts off with the elaborate Golden Dragon Parade that has floats, bands, and dragon dancers (in wonderful costumes), plus the Little King and Queen contest and the Children's Lantern Procession. Other goings-on include arts, crafts, and music. Admission is free, although certain activities cost. "Gung Hay Fat Choy." (Happy New Year.)

COIN & COLLECTIBLES EXPO, Long Beach. (562) 436-3661 or (562) 436-3636, 100 S. Pine Ave., Long Beach Convention Center. A penny for your thoughts! Over 400 vendors buy and sell rare coins, paper money, foreign currency, collectible postcards, autographs, historical documents, jewelry, and stamps. A free coin and stamp are usually given out to younger children at the Young Numismatists and Young Stampers table, respectively. Open Thurs. - Sun., 10am - 7pm. Admission is $4 per person for all four days.

NATIONAL DATE FESTIVAL, Indio. (760) 863-8247 / www.datefest.org, 46350 Arabia St. at the Desert Expo Center. This ten-day event usually begins the Friday before President's Day. There are hundreds of exhibits and activities! Some with particular kid-appeal include the gem and mineral show, carnival-type rides, a model railroad, a livestock show, a petting zoo, elephant rides, camel rides, pony rides, virtual reality rides, a Mexican village, and a Renaissance Village. The camel and ostrich races are some of the festival highlights. These races take place twice a day, and you just never know what is going to happen with two such stubborn species of animals. On President's Day

Monday there is a colorful Arabian Nights parade and pageant - don't miss this! The festival is open daily from 10am - 10pm. Admission is $6 for adults; $5 for seniors; $4 for ages 5 - 12; children 4 years and under are free. Rides and some attractions have additional fees. Parking on the fairgrounds is $3.

PRESIDENT'S DAY, Yorba Linda and Simi Valley. (714) 993-3393 / www.nixonfoundation.org, 18001 Yorba Linda Blvd., Richard Nixon Presidential Library and Birthplace and/or (805) 522-8444 / www.lbjlib.utexas.edu/reagan, 40 Presidential Dr., Ronald Reagan Presidential Library and Museum. These museums usually hold special presidential tributes near President's Day. In the past, these celebrations have included game booths, food booths, presidential look-a-likes, and sometimes free admission to the museum! Call for details.

SCOTTISH FESTIVAL, Long Beach. (562) 435-3511 / www.queenmary.com, adjacent to the Queen Mary. Wear a kilt and bring your bagpipes for this two-day event. Over fifty Scottish clans will be on hand to entertain visitors with a parade, traditional and contemporary music, Highland dances, storytelling, a parade of British automobiles, food, and much more. Open Sat. - Sun., 10am - 6pm. Admission is $12 for adults; $10 for seniors and military personnel; $7 for ages 4 - 11; children 3 years and under are free. Parking is $6.

VISIT WITH LINCOLN AND WASHINGTON, Hollywood Hills. (800) 204-3131 or (818) 241-4151, 6300 Forest Lawn Dr., Forest Lawn Memorial Park. Meet George Washington and Abraham Lincoln (educators dressed in costume) who talk about "their" lives and "their" accomplishments for about thirty minutes each, near the Court of Liberty. Walk the grounds to see statues of these men, and see the fifteen-minute film called *Birth of Liberty*. This living history program is presented on two weekdays for up to 350 people, every half hour from 9:30am - 11:30am. Reservations are necessary. Admission is free. See the Forest Lawn entry in the main part of the book for more details about the park.

WHALE WATCHING. See the January entry for details.

## MARCH:

BLESSING OF THE ANIMALS, Los Angeles. (213) 628-1274, El Pueblo de Los Angeles State Historic Park. This event is held on the Saturday before Easter. Children can dress up their pets - all domestic animals welcome - and bring them to the Plaza Church to be blessed by priests. This is done to honor the animal's contributions to the world. It gets wild with all different kinds of animals "held" in children's arms! Admission is free.

COWBOY POETRY AND MUSIC FESTIVAL, Santa Clarita. (805) 255-4910, Arch St. and 12th St. at Melody Ranch Motion Picture Studio. Howdy-doo! Over

12,000 people attend this four-day event that acknowledges that cowboys are still heroes. Browse in shops at Melody Ranch (which resembles a western town), grab some grub, and listen to some of the finest poetry, stories, and music that the west has to offer. Several specifically family-oriented programs are offered, including western farces, trick ropers, and old Western flicks on Friday night, plus off-site events, such as gold panning at Placerita Canyon Nature Center. The festival just gets bigger and better every year! Tip: Dress up in western duds and don't forget to wear your Stetson. The festival runs Thurs., 8pm - 9:30pm; Fri., 7pm - 10pm; Sat., 10am - 11:30pm; Sun., 10am - 6pm. (Trail rides into the ranch begin at 8am on the weekends and cost $60.) Admission is $7 per person per day, which includes a shuttle ride to the ranch. Parking is $2. Note that while a majority of the shows are included in the admission price, certain shows are ticketed events and cost extra.

EASTER BUNNY CARNIVAL AND EGG HUNT, Mission Viejo. (949) 589-4272, Antonio Parkway and Las Flores at Trabuco Mesa Park. Usually held the Saturday before Easter, this event (with over 2,000 participants last year and 17,000 plastic eggs!) is really *egg*citing. Start your morning off at 7am with a pancake breakfast - $3 for adults; $2.50 for ages 7 to 12. Then join in the Easter egg hunt for children 2 to 10 years. (Each age group is given a different starting time.) Don't forget your Easter basket! Visit the costumed characters of Mr. and Mrs. Bunny, the petting zoo, and the bounce house, plus make and decorate a child-size kite - all for free! There are also arts and crafts booths. At the Baby Goods Swapmeet you can buy good quality, used baby and children's clothes and toys. Hours for the *egg*stra special carnival and hunt are 9am - noon.

EASTER EGG HUNTS. Many parks and schools put on free Easter egg hunts and/or Easter craft activities the weekend or Saturday before Easter. Call the Recreation Department at your local City Hall for more information.

FIESTA DE LAS GOLONDRINAS (Festival of the Swallows), San Juan Capistrano. (714) 493-1976. This week-long festival celebrating the return of the swallows from their annual migration to Argentina takes place in different areas throughout San Juan Capistrano, including the Mission. The swallows actually return every year on March 19th, so all of the festivities happen around this date. Some of the festivities include parades (like a children's pet parade), pageants, petting zoo, pony rides, carnival rides, carnival games, a kid's hat contest, arts and crafts, music, and more! Free admission and parking. Certain activities and attractions cost. Call the Mission, (714) 248-2048, to find out what special activities they have planned.

FLOWER FIELDS, Carlsbad. (760) 431-0352, 5802 Paseo del Norte, off Palomar Airport Rd. During March and April, walk through fifty acres of rows of blooming ranunculus. The colors are amazing, and the trails lead to bluffs overlooking the shoreline. Call first to make sure the flowers are in full bloom.

Open daily 9:30am - dusk. Admission is $4 for adults; $3 for ages 4 - 12; children 3 years and under are free.

GEM SHOW, Costa Mesa. (760) 931-1410 / www.ocfair.com, 88 Fair Dr., at the Orange County Fairgrounds. This three-day show for rock hounds brings over fifty vendors that buy, sell, and trade a wonderful variety of rocks, minerals, beads, and jewelry. Open Fri., noon - 7pm; Sat., 10am - 7pm; Sun., 10am - 5pm. Admission is $4 for adults; $3 for seniors; children 12 years and under are free.

GLORY OF EASTER, Garden Grove. (714) 54-GLORY (544-5679) / www.crystalcathedral.org,12141 Lewis St., Crystal Cathedral. This hour-long, spectacular production with live animals and actors, celebrates the resurrection of Jesus Christ in a powerful way. The last days of his life; the events leading up to his death, including the crucifixion; and his resurrection are presented in a dramatic and realistic re-enactment. The show runs for about twelve nights, with the curtain rising at 6:30pm and at 8:30pm most nights (there are no shows on Mon.), and an additional show at 4:30pm on selected weekend days. Tickets are $20, $25, or $30 for adults; $2 less for seniors and children 12 years and under. Ask about family days discounts, when tickets are $15 per person.

GREAT AMERICAN TRAIN SHOW, Long Beach. (562) 436-3661, 100 S. Pine St., at the Long Beach Convention Center. Chug over to the weekend show that features operating train models as well as several hundred tables selling train paraphernalia. Free workshops are offered so you can learn modeling tips and more. Open 11am - 5pm. Admission is $5 for adults; children 12 years and under are free. Parking is $7.

GREEN MEADOWS FARM, Orange. (800) 393-3276 / www.greenmeadows.com, 1 Irvine Rd., in Irvine Regional Park. From mid-March through mid-April take a guided, two-hour, walk around this unique, completely hands-on, petting farm. There are over 500 animals to see, touch, snuggle, and sometimes feed, such as rabbits, chicks, ducks, cows, pigs, sheep, goats, turkeys, and a buffalo. Spring is in the air, so kids are almost assured of seeing animal babies. Your admission price also includes milking a cow and taking a pony ride and a tractor-driven hayride. This is a wonderful, informative, and memorable field trip for kids and adults. A nice gift shop is here, too. Open Mon. - Fri., 9:30am - noon (last tour); Sat., 10am - 2pm (last tour). General admission is $9 for ages 2 and up. Admission for groups of twenty or more is $7 per person. Reservations for groups are required. Also see the May and September Green Meadows Farm entries.

GRUNION RUNS, up and down the coast. Call beaches, the Cabrillo Marine Aquarium, the Orange County Marine Institute, or Stephen Birch Aquarium Museum for more details, dates, and times. Look in the main section of the book for more info on the above-mentioned places. Grunions are small, silvery fish that venture out of the waters from March to August to lay their eggs on sandy beaches. They are very particular about when they do this - after every full and new moon, and usually around midnight. No nets or gloves are allowed; only bare hands. (Did I mention that the fish are slippery?) Eat what you catch, and enjoy a unique night of grunion hunting. Minimal cost.

LIFE OF CHRIST MOSAIC PROGRAM, Covina Hills. (800) 204-3131, at 21300 Via Verde at Forest Lawn Memorial Park. A costumed educator, representing Christ, talks for about a half hour about "his" life and purpose. The talk is given in the forecourt of the Heritage Mausoleum. This living history program is given on one weekday at 9:30am, 10:30am, and 11:30am. Reservations are necessary. Admission is free.

OCEAN BEACH KITE FESTIVAL, Ocean Beach. (619) 531-1527, between Santa Monica and Newport Sts. at Ocean Beach Elementary School and across the street at Ocean Beach Recreation Center. The first Saturday of the month offers a colorful, high-flying festival celebrating the joy of kiting. You are invited to build, decorate, and fly kites. There are contests for all ages, a parade, and a crafts fair. There is no charge for admission or for materials for kite making.

POPPY RESERVE, Lancaster. (805) 942-0662 - state park; (805) 724-1180 - recorded info from the poppy reserve / www.calparksmojave.com, 15101 W. Lancaster Rd., located 13 miles west of the Antelope Valley Fwy (14), off W. Avenue I. At this time of year I hear echos of the wicked witch's voice in *The Wizard of Oz* cackling, "poppies, poppies." During the months of March and April our bright orange California state flower blooms in this 800-acre reserve, as do several other types of wildflowers. (You'll also notice wonderful patches of flowers along the roadside, too.) Call first to see how rains have affected the bloom schedule. Hike along the seven miles of hilly trails that run through the reserve, including a paved section for stroller/wheelchair access. Don't forget your camera!! Although poppies only bloom seasonally, the reserve is open year round. The Visitors' Center is open seasonally, however. It provides orientation to the reserve and educational information. Parking during poppy season is $5 a vehicle; $3 off season.

POW WOW, Indio. (760) 342-2593, 84245 Indio Springs Dr. at Fantasy Springs Casino. This Powwow brings together Native Americans and non-Indians in a celebration of music, dance, food and arts, and crafts. Don't miss the "grand entrance" where all the Indians, in full costume, dance as the come in. The powwow is usually held Fri., 5pm - midnight (grand entrance at 7pm); Sat., 11am - midnight (grand entrance at 1pm and 7pm); Sun., 11am - 6pm (grand entrance at 1pm). Admission is $4 for adults; $2 for ages 6 - 12; children 5 years and under are free.

SPRING DINGER, Santa Fe Springs. (562) 946-6476, 12100 Mora Dr.,
Heritage Park. This day of old-fashioned fun is held around Easter. Kids can ride
on a fire engine; pet animals in the petting zoo; pump water from a well; dress-
up in old-fashioned clothing; hunt for Easter eggs; listen to story-tellers; try
square dancing; churn butter; crank a wheel to make ice-cream; and play turn-of-
the-century games - all for free!! The hours are noon - 4pm. Admission is free.

VISIT WITH MICHELANGELO and LEONARDO DA VINCI , Glendale.
(800) 204-3131 or (213) 254-3131, 1712 S. Glendale Ave., at Forest Lawn
Memorial Park. A costumed Michelangelo and Da Vinci talk to an audience of
up to 350 people for about a half hour about "their" lives and achievements -
history comes alive! A short guided tour around some of "their" art on the
premises follows. (Note: The art does contain some nudity.) This two-day,
weekday, program is presented at 9:30am, 10:30am, and 11:30am. Reservations
are necessary. This event repeats in October. Admission is free. See Forest Lawn
in the main section of the book for details about the park.

WHALE WATCHING. See the January entry for details.

# APRIL:

CIRCUS VARGAS, San Diego. (619) 235-1100 / www.balboapark.com, the
lower level off Park Blvd., Balboa Park. For one week Circus Vargas, one of the
largest circuses under the big top, presents everything a child dreams about in a
circus. Animal acts, daring acrobatics, and talented clowns are all part of this
extravaganza. Tickets are usually $8 for adults; $6 for children.

EARTH DAY, San Diego. (619) 239-0512, Balboa Park. Celebrate the
preservation of the environment in this one-day event. Several hundred
organizations host booths and exhibits on organic materials; alternatives to
lighting, power, and energy; and more. Kids (and parents) who attend Earth Day
will hopefully become more planet smart. Activities begin at 10am and end at
6pm. Admission is free.

GLORY OF EASTER, Garden Grove. See the March entry for details.

GREEN MEADOWS, Irvine. See the March entry for details.

IMAGINATION CELEBRATION, Orange County. (714) 833-8500. The
Orange County Performing Arts Center hosts this fifteen-day event that's held
during the latter part of April, and spills into May. At least fifty of Orange
County's artistic and educational organizations bring performances, workshops,
and exhibitions to over seventy locations. This festival of arts for families takes
place at malls, museums, parks, schools, etc. Some of the activities include
puppet making, family art days, folk tales, band and theater performances, and

dancing. Almost every event is free in this county wide celebration of imagination! Call for a schedule of events.

KALEIDOSCOPE, Long Beach. (562) 985-2288, Bellflower and Atherton Sts. at California State Long Beach campus. This open house, sponsored by the various departments of the college, is a wonderful, one-day community event. There is face painting, carnival rides, cultural dances, an African marketplace, a Powwow, a solar car (from the Engineering Dept.), a Renaissance faire, and more. The hours are from 11am - 5pm. Admission is free.

LOS ANGELES TIMES FESTIVAL OF BOOKS, Los Angeles. (800) LATIMES (528-4637), ext. 7BOOK (2665), U.C.L.A. campus. This weekend festival has a very festive atmosphere and it's the place for book lovers of all ages. Hundreds of publishers have booths in which to sell their books. Well-known authors and celebrity authors sign their books and do book readings. Special programs on-going at the children's stages include storytellers, clowns, musicians, and more. Festival hours are Sat., 10am - 6pm; Sun., 10am - 5pm. Admission is $5 per vehicle.

PET EXPO, Pomona. (800) 999-7295, 1101 W. McKinley Ave., Fairplex at the L.A. County Fairgrounds. Bark, meow, oink, baaa, sssss, neigh - this is the three-day weekend for animals lovers. Over 1,000 animals - dogs, cats, reptiles, goats, mini horses, llamas, rabbits, pigs, fish, etc. - are at the expo. See bird shows, cat shows, a petting zoo, Frisbee dogs, celebrity animals, pet products, stage shows, and educational demonstrations. Check out the pet adoption services. (Animals are not for sale here.) Open Fri., 10am - 6pm; Sat., 9am - 7pm; Sun., 9am - 6pm. Admission per day is $7 for adults; $5 for seniors; $2 for ages 6 - 12; children 5 years and under are free.

POINT MUGU'S NAVAL AIR WEAPONS STATION'S AIR SHOW, Point Mugu. (805) 989-8095, Las Posas exit off Ventura Fwy 101. At this weekend show, the air is filled with flight demonstrations of solo routines and formation flying, including the Air Force Thunderbirds, and acrobatic stunts. The ground displays are equally exciting with aircraft on exhibit, a flight simulator, children's rides, a home show, food booths, etc. Gates open at 8am; demonstrations begin at 9:30am. Open-air, unreserved seating and parking are free; reserved seats are between $4 - $35. Bring suntan lotion!

POPPY FESTIVAL, Lancaster. (805) 723-6077, Lancaster City Park. The poppy festival, located fifteen miles east of the poppy reserve, is held for one weekend in April. The festival offers carnival rides, a twenty-minute helicopter ride over the reserve ($30 for adults, $25 for children), craft workshops, environmental displays, etc. Open Sat., 10am - 6pm; Sun., 10am - 5pm. Admission is $4 for adults; $2 for ages 6 - 12; children 5 years and under are free. Parking is $2.

POPPY RESERVE, Lancaster. See the March entry for details.

RAMONA PAGEANT, Hemet. (800) 645-4465, 27400 Ramona Bowl Road. A cast of over 350 people use an entire mountainside as a stage, plus quite a few horses, to tell the romantic story of Spanish Ramona and her Indian hero, Alessandro. The tale, which also reflects our early California heritage, is incredibly well told. Going into its 75th year, this epic is performed for three weekends. All performances begin at 3:30pm. Tickets range from $10 (for children 11 years and under sitting in the upper section) to $25 (for adults sitting in the lower section). Bring a blanket and picnic dinner.

RENAISSANCE PLEASURE FAIRE, San Bernardino. (800) 523-FAIR (2473); (626) 795-3397 - Presenters of the Past / www.renfair.com, 2555 Glen Helen Parkway, Glen Helen Regional Park. Heare ye, heare ye, this annual faire runs for nine weekends from April to June, bringing the renaissance time to life. Eat, drink, and be merry as you cheer on knights; play challenging games from times of yor; be entertained by juggling, dancing, and singing; and enjoy the delicious food and faire! Educational field trips, put on by Presenters of the Past, are offered Tues., Wed., and Thurs. from 9:15am - 2:30pm for $16 per student. (Adults chaperones are free.) Geared for 4th graders through high schoolers, students, who must be dressed in period costume, will watch and/or partake in jousting demonstrations, chainmail knitting, Elizabethan country dance, basketry, and more. Students learn about this time period as they see it being relived before their eyes! (They also receive a free pass to come to the faire.) The faire is open to the public Sat. - Sun. from 10am - 6pm. Admission is $17.50 for adults; $15 for seniors and students; $7.50 for ages 5 - 11; children 4 years and under are free. Parking is $6.

SCANDINAVIAN FESTIVAL, Thousand Oaks. (805) 493-3151 / www.clunet.edu, 60 W. Olsen Rd. at California Lutheran University. Valkommen! This two-day festival usually takes place on the third weekend of April. Enjoy a presentation/program of a 16th century Swedish royal court, plus folk dancing, arts and crafts booths, and a replica of Tivoli Gardens, though it's not quite as large as the one in Denmark. Kids will particularly enjoy the jugglers, magicians, clowns, and moon bounces. A smorgasbord is served here, too. The festival is open Sat., 10am - 6pm; Sun., noon - 5pm. Admission is $5 for adults; $2 for ages 6 - 13; children 5 years and under are free. Certain activities cost extra.

SPEEDWAY, Costa Mesa. (714) 708-3247 or (949) 492-9933 / www.wient.com/speedway, 88 Fairview Drive at the Orange County Fairgrounds. The Speedway roars to life every Saturday night (although some years it's Friday nights) from April through September. This spectator sport of motorcycle racing can include sidecars, go karts, Quads, a kids' class (ages 6 to 12), and more. After the two-hour show, which can get long for younger ones, take the kids into the pits to get racer's autographs, or, when the bikes cool down, to sit on a cycle or two. Wear jeans and t-shirt (and bring a sweatshirt) as dirt tracks aren't noted for cleanliness. Gates open at 6:30pm; races start at 7:30pm. Admission is $9 for adults; $5 for seniors and ages 13 - 17; $2 for ages 6 - 12; children 5 years and under are free. Parking is free.

SUNKIST ORANGE BLOSSOM FESTIVAL, Riverside. (800) 382-8202, historic downtown Riverside. "Orange" you glad you came to this weekend festival? Traditionally held the third weekend in April, it celebrates life in Riverside as it was over 100 years ago with a parade featuring floats, marching bands, and equestrian units; tasty orange treats; cooking demonstrations; live entertainment; magic shows; circus acts; carnival rides; a recreated "living history" town; a children's grove with crafts, petting zoo, and elephant rides; steam train engine rides; a fireworks display on Saturday night; and arts and crafts booths. The hours are Sat., 10am - 8:30pm; Sun., 10am - 6pm. Admission is free, although certain activities cost.

TEMECULA BALLOON AND WINE FESTIVAL, Temecula. (909) 676-4713, Temecula Valley. Rise and shine for this colorful weekend festival. The balloons are filled with hot air starting at 6am, an event that is fascinating to watch. Lift-off is around 7am, with numerous balloons filling the sky in a kaleidoscope of color. Other, less lofty, activities include live entertainment, arts and craft, and a kid's fair with kiddie rides, pony rides, a petting zoo, etc. General admission is $15 for adults; $5 for ages 7 - 12; children 6 years and under are free. Certain activities cost extra.

TOYOTA GRAND PRIX RACE, Long Beach. (800) 752-9524 or (562) 981-2600 / www.longbeachgp.com, E. Shoreline Dr. and Seaside Way, downtown Long Beach. This three-day event includes practice and qualifying runs on Friday; celebrity racing, final qualifying runs on Saturday; and final cart car races on Sunday. General admission is $26 for Friday and Saturday for adults, and $34 on Sunday for adults; kids 12 years and under are free when accompanied by a paying adult. Reserved grandstand seats are $48 - $58 for adults on Sunday; $33 for kids. See you at the races!

WEEK OF THE YOUNG CHILD. Various parks in the Southland and San Diego participate in celebrating kids by hosting different events. Some of the activities include arts and crafts, hands-on science fun, blowing bubbles, family entertainment, and sometimes a petting zoo. Preschools, Y.M.C.A.s, Scout troops, etc., are on hand to provide a resource for parents to get information about education and services for kids. Check your local newspaper for a listing of events or call your local city hall. In San Diego, call (619) 239-0512 for information on this event held at Balboa Park.

YOUTH EXPO, Orange County. (714) 708-3247 / www.ocfair.com, 88 Fairview

Dr., Orange County Fairgrounds. This huge, three-day expo highlights the talents of Orange County kids from elementary through high school age. Their artistic endeavors are showcased in different buildings according to age groups and categories, such as fine arts, photography, woodworking, and ceramics. 4-H Club members also have wonderful exhibits. The Science Fair is a highlight which draws people from all over the United States who offer money and/or scholarships to students whose experimentally-based research designs are outstanding. The Expo is great for admiring other kids' works, and for sparking the creative genius in your child. Hours are Fri., 9am - 3pm (this day can get crowded with school tours); Sat. - Sun., 9am - 5pm. Admission is free.

## MAY:

CALIFORNIA STRAWBERRY FESTIVAL, Oxnard. (805) 385-7578 or (888) 288-9242 / e-mail:berryland@juno.com, 3250 S. Rose Ave. and Channel Island Blvd., at College Park. This big, juicy festival, held on the third weekend of May, offers unique strawberry culinary delights, and a strawberry shortcake contest. Kids enjoy Strawberryland, in particular, because it has a petting zoo, puppet shows, arts and crafts, and carnival rides. Have a berry good time here! Open Sat. - Sun., 10am - 6:30pm. Admission is $7 for adults; $4 for seniors and ages 2 - 12. Certain activities cost extra.

CHERRY FESTIVAL and CHERRY PICKING, Beaumont. See the June entry for details.

CHILDREN'S DAY, Los Angeles. (213) 628-2725, Little Tokyo. This two-day traditional Japanese celebration is for families, and particularly children ages 4 - 12. They are invited to participate in a running race, as well as making arts and crafts. Other attractions include magic shows, dancing, fine arts exhibits, etc. Admission is free, although certain activities cost.

CINCO DE MAYO CELEBRATION - The fifth of May, Mexican Independence Day, is celebrated throughout Southern California. In Los Angeles, for instance, call (213) 628-1274, at El Pueblo de Los Angeles State Historic Park in downtown. The festival celebrates this Mexican holiday with several days of Mexican folk dancing, mariachi music, parades, puppet shows, booths, piñatas, and fun! Also call Bazaar del Mundo in Old Town San Diego, (619) 296-3161 / www.bazaardelmundo.com; or Borrego Springs, (800) 559-5524 / www.borregosprings.com; or Oceanside, (760) 471-6549.

FRONTIER RENDEZVOUS, Oak Glen. (909) 797-1005, 39610 Oak Glen Rd. at Los Rios Rancho. A long Memorial Day weekend (Wed. to Sun.) is celebrated in the mountains with Mountain Man events. Authentic encampments from the 1500's through Civil War era encompass men and women in period dress, pioneer cooking, tomahawk throwing contests, setting bear traps, making clothing, craft booths, and musicians playing everything from mandolins to pump organs. Camp is open daily from sunup to sundown. Admission is free, but bring money for bartering.

GEM SHOW, Costa Mesa. See the March entry for details.

GREEN MEADOWS FARM, Los Angeles. (800) 393-3276 / www.greenmeadows.com, 4235 Monterey Rd., Ernest Debs Regional Park. The Farm is open May - June. See the March entry for details.

INSECT FAIR, Los Angeles. (213) 763-3466 / www.nhm.org, 900 Exposition Blvd., Natural History Museum of Los Angeles. See the museum entry in the main section of the book for a description of the museum. Kids go buggy at this weekend event where every kind of insect product is available to look at and/or purchase. Items include jewelry, t-shirts, toys, silkworms, live critters, a butterfly house, chocolate-covered crickets (poor Jimminy!), mounted insects, and lots more. The fair includes educational presentations and hands-on activities. Creep, crawl, or fly here on the second weekend of May between 10am - 5pm. Admission to the fair includes admission to the museum: $8 for adults; $5.50 for seniors and students; $2 for ages 5 - 12; children 4 years and under are free.

INTERNATIONAL MUSEUM DAY. Here is a little known fact - May 18 is International Museum Day. Many museums offer free admission, while others sponsor a family day of art and craft activities, storytelling, entertainment, celebrity appearances, or other special programs. Call your local (or favorite) museum and see what they have to offer.

MIRAMAR ARMED FORCES DAY FESTIVAL, Miramar. (619) 537-6289 / www.mwrmiramar.com, Miramar Naval Air Station. This one-day event has a little of something for everyone including a car show, craft fair, kiddie rides, Native American Pow Wow, and military static displays such as planes, jets, helicopters, tanks, etc. The Festival usually runs from 10am - 6pm. Admission is free.

OPEN HOUSE AT JET PROPULSION LABORATORY, Pasadena. (818) 354-4321 or (818) 354-7006 / www.jpl.nasa.gov, 4800 Oak Grove Dr. This annual open house is out of this world. The space research center offers a glimpse into outer space with over 30 exhibits ranging from planetary imaging to spacecraft tracking; presentations; commercial technology booths that display state-of-the-art instruments and products; robotic demonstrations; thinking games for kids; and much more. Open Sat. - Sun., 9am - 5pm. Admission is free.

RAMONA PAGEANT, Hemet. See the April entry for details.

RAMONA RODEO, Ramona. (760) 789-1311 / www.ramonamall.com, 5th St.

and Aqua Ln. Kick up your heels 'cause the rodeo's in town! Although activities start Friday night, the weekend brings rodeo shows, a parade, and a carnival-like atmosphere. This all takes place the second weekend in May. Rodeo admission is usually $8 for adults; $5 for kids 12 years and under. Reserved seating is $2 more, but worth it since shows can sell out.

RANCHO SANTA MARGARITA FIESTA RODEO, Rancho Santa Margarita. (949) 589-4272, corner of Santa Margarita Prkwy. and Los Flores St., next to Target. Yipee-aye-ay! This five-day fiesta begins on Thursday night with family activities. Friday starts with a cattle drive from Casper Wilderness Park ending at the rodeo grounds. Friday night is team-roping competition. Professional rodeos are held on the weekend. The two-hour shows (which seat 5,000) include bull riding, calf roping, women's barrel racing, kids' rodeos, bronco riding, bareback riding, and rodeo clowns. There are also carnival rides for kids, game booths, pony rides, and lots of arts and crafts booths. The nights bring country western dancing and more fun. The rodeo grounds are open Fri., 3pm - 11pm; Sat., 10am - midnight; Sun., 10am - 6pm. Admission to the grounds is $2 for adults; $1 for kids. Tickets for the rodeo are $12 for adults in advance ($2 more at the gate); $10 for kids 3 - 12 years ($2 more at the gate). Parking is $3.

RENAISSANCE PLEASURE FAIRE, San Bernardino. See the April entry for details.

SAN BERNARDINO COUNTY FAIR, Victorville. (760) 951-2200 / www.sbcfair.com, 7th St. For nine days, the desert really heats up with excitement when the county fair comes to town. 86 acres of rides, attractions, farm animals, Destruction Derby, a rodeo, entertainment, and more fun. Open Mon. - Fri., 4pm - 11pm; Sat. - Sun., noon - 11pm. General admission is $5 for adults; $3 for seniors; $2 for ages 6 - 12; children 5 years and under are free. Activities cost extra.

SAN DIEGO WILD ANIMAL PARK, Escondido. (619) 234-6541 / www.sandiegozoo.org, 15500 San Pasqual Valley Rd. Get a little wild in the beginning of May as the Wild Animal Park celebrates founder's day and admission is free! Call for the exact date.

SCOTTISH FESTIVAL AND HIGHLAND GATHERING, Costa Mesa. (714) 708-3247 / www.ocfair.com, 88 Fair Drive, Orange County Fairgrounds. This Memorial weekend festival features everything Scottish - tossing the caber, hammer throws, shot put, sheepdog herding, good food, and a lot of tartan. Bagpipes and highland and country dancing also entertain you and the kids throughout the day. Admission is $13 for adults; $3 for ages 5 - 12; children 4 years and under are free.

SPEEDWAY, Costa Mesa. See the April entry for details.

STRAWBERRY FESTIVAL, Garden Grove. (714) 638-7950 or (714) 638-0981, 12862 Euclid Ave. This four-day event, usually held over Memorial Day weekend, features carnival rides, games, parades, arts and crafts booths, a pie eating contest, the annual redhead round-up, and lots and lots of strawberries! Free admission, although certain activities cost.

U.C.L.A. POW WOW, Los Angeles. (310) 825-7513, U.C.L.A. campus. Representatives from many Native American tribes gather for a weekend of dance, music, crafts, games, and food. Bring your own tribe! (i.e. family) Open Sat. 10am - 8pm; Sun., 10am - 5pm. Admission is $5 per vehicle.

VISIT WITH MONTEZUMA, Hollywood Hills. (800) 204-3131 or (818) 241-4151, 6300 Forest Lawn Dr. at Forest Lawn Memorial Park. A costumed Montezuma talks at the Plaza of Mexican Heritage to an audience of up to 350 people for about thirty minutes about "his" life and achievements - history comes alive! A short, guided explanation of some of the artifacts from the Mexican museum follows the talk. This one or two-day program takes place during the week at 9:30am, 10:30am, and 11:30am. Reservations are necessary. This event repeats in October. Admission is free.

## JUNE:

ADVENTURE PLAYGROUND, Huntington Beach. (714) 842-7442 - playground; (714) 536-5486 - surrounding park, 7111 Talbot, Huntington Beach Central Park. Open mid-June through mid-August, young Huck Finns can use a raft (push poles are provided) in the shallow waters of a man-made lake. Kids will also love the slide (i.e. tarp-covered hill) which ends in a little mud pool; a rope bridge leading to a tire swing and mini zip line; sand box; and a kid-built "city" of shacks and clubhouses (only for ages 7 years and up). Lumbers, hammers, and nails are provided. Open Mon. - Sat., 10am - 5pm. Admission is $1 for kids who are Huntington Beach residents; $2 for non-residents; free for adults.

CHERRY FESTIVAL and CHERRY PICKING, Beaumont and Cherry Valley. (909) 845-9541 - Beaumont Chamber of Commerce; (909) 845-3628 - Cherry Growers Association. I tell you no lie - June is a ripe month for cherry picking, but the season could start in mid-May, depending on the weather. Call first. The three-week, or so, season starts with a festival ($1 admission) that includes a parade, carnival-type rides, and a lot of family fun and entertainment. One of our favorite places to pick cherries, and the place with the largest acreage, is Wohlgemuth's Orchard, (909) 845-1548, 1106 E. 11th St. in Beaumont. Admission to the orchards at Wohlgemuth's is $2 per person (or you may purchase pre-picked cherries). Use the provided cans with ropes and hang them around your neck so cherries can be picked (and sampled) with both hands, working from the ground. Ladders aren't allowed or necessary. The per pound cost of cherries varies according to market value. There are also picnic tables under shade trees here, too, and a bakery. Look for roadside signs announcing other U-Pics. Dowling Orchard, (909) 845-1217, is not a U-Pic, but it does offer just-picked cherries and a year-round produce market.

COIN & COLLECTIBLES EXPO, Long Beach. See the February entry for details.

COLORADO LAGOON MODEL BOAT SHOP, Long Beach. (562) 570-1719, at Colorado Lagoon. Beginning in mid-June, the shop is open through the summer. Kids 7 years and up can learn how to build model boats and sail them in the lagoon. Help your kids chart their course to a great summer pastime. Store hours are Mon. - Fri. from 10am - 4pm. Materials are available to purchase starting at $15.

DEL MAR FAIR, Del Mar. (619) 793-5555 - recording; (619) 755-1161 - fairgrounds / www.delmarfair.com, Del Mar Fairgrounds. The major, three-week event features everything wonderful in a county fair - carnival rides, flower and garden shows, gem and minerals exhibits, farm animals, livestock judging, food, craft booths, and a festive atmosphere. Call for a schedule of events. General admission is $7 for adults; $3 for ages 6 - 12 years; children 5 years and under are free. Parking is $4. Certain activities cost extra.

FORD FAMILY FUN SUMMER NIGHTS, Hollywood. (323) 461-3673 / www.lacountyarts.org, 2580 Cahuenga Blvd. E., at the John Anson Ford Amphitheater (just N. of the Hollywood Bowl). This outdoor amphitheater presents wonderful, one-hour family performances almost every Saturday in July and August, along with a few Sunday afternoon shows. Bring a picnic lunch and enjoy an intimate setting with shows that feature top-name entertainment in magic, puppetry, storytelling, music, dance, or plays designed for children to enjoy. Saturday shows starts at 10am; Sundays shows at 4:30pm. Seats cost $7 per person, though discounts are offered of five admissions for $25. Ask about Family Day admission. Parking on site costs $5. Shuttle services from 1718 Cherokee in Hollywood are 25¢.

HUCK FINN'S JUBILEE, Victorville. (909) 780-8810 / www.huckfinn.com, Mojave Narrows Regional Park, just south of Victorville. The huge, three-day jubilee always falls on Father's Day weekend. It kicks off with a fishing derby at 8am on Fri., followed by a weekend of river raft building contests, egg-tossing contests, a big-top circus, arm wrestling championships, a mountain man encampment, arts and crafts, a Becky Thatcher and Tom Sawyer look-alike contest, country music, and lots more down home fun. Put on a straw hat and join the throngs of people. Open Fri. - Sat., 8am - 10:30pm; Sun., 7:30am - 7pm. Admission $9 per day for adults; $5 for ages 6 - 11; children 5 years and under are free.

INDIAN FAIR, San Diego. (619) 239-2001 / www.museumofman.org, Museum of Man, Balboa Park. This weekend fair provides one of the largest forums for Native American artistry in the West Coast. It features costumed tribal dancers, traditional storytellers, and a market with arts, crafts, and authentic cuisine. Admission is $5 per person.

IRISH FAIR AND MUSIC FESTIVAL, Arcadia. (626) 574-7223 / www.irishfair.org / www.santaanita.com, 285 W. Huntington Dr., at the Santa Anita Race Track infield. Top o' the mornin' to ye. This weekend Irish fair features top-name entertainment, such as Clancy, and Hal Roach; parades; traditional contests, such as fiddle playing and dancing; sheep-herding demonstrations; a dog show featuring Irish breeds; bagpipe music; vendors of Irish wares; and Leprechaun Kingdom for kids. The kingdom features storytelling, jugglers, pony rides, carnival rides, etc. Another favorite at the festival is a recreation of a medieval Irish village, Tara, where sword-yielding performers recount the Island's legends and history. The festival runs Sat. - Sun., 10am - 6pm. Admission is $12.50 for adults; $9.50 for students and seniors; children 12 years and under are free. Certain activities cost extra.

OPEN HOUSE AT THE HOLLYWOOD BOWL, Hollywood. (323) 850-2000 / www.hollywoodbowl.org, 2301 N. Highland. For six, musically hot weeks, forty-five-minute, multi-cultural performances are given at the Bowl that could incorporate dance, music, storytelling, etc. A craft workshop for kids, ages 3 - 12, that pertains to the theme follows each performance. Each week brings a different show which is performed twice daily. Shows are Mon. - Fri. at 10am and 11:15am and the workshops are at 11am and 12:15pm. Open House visitors are invited to watch orchestra rehearsals inside the Bowl for no additional charge. On most days, rehearsals take place from 9:30am - 12:30pm. Tickets for Open House are $3 per person, plus $1 workshop materials fee for each participating child. Parking is free.

OUTDOOR FAMILY FILM FESTIVALS. Call your local park or Chamber of Commerce to ask for information about the many parks that offer free, nighttime, out-door family entertainment such as concerts and G, or PG, movies. Bring a blanket, picnic dinner, and enjoy a show together!

PEARSON PARK AMPHITHEATER, Anaheim. (714) 765-5274, Lemon and Sycamore Sts. The terrific programs put on here throughout the summer are geared for kids in the K - 6th grades. They vary in length from one to three hours. Past programs have included Make-a-Circus, magic shows, and audience participation shows with songs or a storyteller. The shows are on Friday night and usually start at 7:30pm. Tickets usually cost $3 for adults; children 10 years and under are free. Call for specific show information.

RENAISSANCE PLEASURE FAIRE, San Bernardino. See the April entry for details.

SAN DIEGO SCOTTISH HIGHLAND GAMES AND GATHERING OF
CLANS, San Diego. (619) 645-8080 / e-mail:smwsrp@aol.com, Brengle Terrace
Park, Vista. The last weekend in June is the one for Scottish merrymaking, which
includes highland dancing, Celtic harping, bagpipe competitions, sheep dog
herding trials, athletic competitions (such as caber tossing), and lots of good
food. In past years, admission has been $9 for adults (per day); $7 for seniors, $3
for ages 3 - 12. Ask about two-day passes. Parking is $2.

SPEEDWAY, Costa Mesa. See the April entry for details.

THRESHING BEE AND ANTIQUE ENGINE SHOW, Vista. (760) 941-1791 /
www.ziggyworks.com/~museum, 2040 N. Santa Fe Ave., at  the Antique Gas &
Steam Engine Museum. (See this museum listing in the Museums section of the
book.) This show is held on two consecutive weekends in June, and again in
October. There are demonstrations of American crafts, farming, log sawing, and
blacksmithing, plus many of the restored tractors are put in a parade, making it
an unusual-looking parade! Join in some of the activities and try some good,
home-cooked food. Admission is $6 for adults; $3 for ages 6 - 12; children 5
years and under are free.

## JULY:

ADVENTURE PLAYGROUND, Huntington Beach. See the June entry for
details.

ANIFEST, Los Angeles area. (818) 842-8330 / home.earthlink.com/~asifa. The
International Animated Film Association brings together professional animators,
collectors, and fans for this animated event. Exhibits include cels, movies,
figurines, and other memorabilia. Activities throughout the day include cartoon
voice shows, seminars, etc. What a fun family outing! Call for current location
and admission prices. Tickets for past shows have been between $5 - $10.

COLORADO LAGOON MODEL BOAT SHOP, Long Beach. See the June
entry for details.

CORN FESTIVAL, Norwalk. (562) 863-4567, 11951 Imperial Hwy., Paddison
Farm. Corny though it might be, this one-day festival, usually held the last
weekend in July, includes hayrides ($1), pony rides ($2), a petting farm,
mountain clogging, country-western dance demonstrations, antique farm
equipment displays, carnival booths, and old-fashioned contests like corn-
shucking, hog-calling, frog-jumping, and turtle racing. Admission is $8 for
adults; $6 for children 12 years and under.

CYPRESS COMMUNITY FESTIVAL, Cypress. (714) 827-2430, Brethren
Christian High School. This one-day event gets bigger and better every year.
There are kiddie rides, a moon bounce, carnival-like games, crafts to make, and
family entertainment throughout the day. In addition, there are lots of food
booths, craft booths, and a business expo. Put on the sunscreen and enjoy the
day. Free admission. Various activities have a minimal cost.

FESTIVAL OF ARTS AND PAGEANT OF THE MASTERS, Laguna Beach.
(949) 494-1145 / www.foapom.com, 650 Laguna Canyon Rd. at Irvine Bowl
Park. This annual event, which runs from July through August, draws thousands
of visitors. More than 150 artisans and craftsmen display their work here -
jewelry, wood crafts, paintings, etc. - and at the nearby Sawdust Festival. Kids
will be particularly drawn to the ongoing demonstrations such as glass blowing,
print making, water color, Japanese pottery making, etc. Young aspiring artists
should visit the Art Workshop, open daily from 11am - 5pm. It supplies free
materials for paintings, paper hat making, etc. The Jr. Art Gallery is juried art
work of over 150 school children from Orange County. Kids love looking at
other kids' work. Bands play continuously. Call for a schedule of special events.
Pageant of the Masters is people in full makeup and/or costumes who pose and
recreate live "pictures" of well-known art works, both classical and
contemporary. Each ninety-second picture is accompanied by a narration and full
orchestral music. Note that some of the live art works contain nudity (i.e. real,
semi-naked bodies). This one-and-a-half-hour production (with over 250
participants) is staged nightly at 8:30pm. The cost ranges between $10 - $50 per
person. Festival admission is included in the pageant tickets. The festival is open
daily from 10am - 11:30pm. Admission to the festival is $5 for adults, for an
unlimited number of visits during the run of the festival; $3 for seniors and
children 12 years and under. Metered parking is available on the streets, or take a
shuttle for $1 from Lot 5. Certain activities cost extra.

FIREWORKS and 4TH OF JULY SHOWS - Call your local parks or City Hall
for information. Note: The Hollywood Bowl, (213) 850-2000 /
www.hollywoodbowl.org, features a fireworks spectacular, along with
outstanding lively music.

FORD FAMILY FUN SUMMER NIGHTS, Hollywood. See the June entry for
details.

HOLY SPIRIT FESTIVAL, Artesia. (562) 865-4693, 11903 Ashworth Ave., in
the Artesia DES. Held the last Sunday and Monday in July, this two-day event
celebrates several elements of the Portugese culture. On Sunday, a grand
religious procession is followed by marching bands, food booths (including a
free lunch or dinner for every visitor), and entertainment. Monday night is the
three-hour culmination of the festival with bloodless bullfights, put on with
professional matadors. The festival hours are Sun., 10am - midnight; Mon., 6pm

- 9pm. Admission is free.

OLD FORT MACARTHUR DAYS, San Pedro. (310) 548-7705 /
www.ftmac.org, 3601 S. Gaffey St., Fort MacArthur. Military encampments, set
up chronologically, and re-enactments, representing the time periods from 1776
through present day, are at the Fort on the weekend following the 4th of July.
Observers can mingle with the soldiers and ask questions about their lives. Re-
enactments of historic military skirmishes can include the Indian wars, the
Calvary, both World Wars, and/or the Korean War. There are also marching
drills, rifle-loading drills, and firing demonstrations, plus military vehicles are on
the grounds. On Sunday, some of the cannons are shot, too. Bring a sack lunch
or purchase food from the vendors. Booths sell military paraphernalia. Open 9am
- 5pm, with shows usually at 11am, 1pm, and 3pm. Admission per day is $5 for
adults; $3 for ages 5 - 11; children 4 years and under are free.

OPEN HOUSE, Hollywood. See June entry for details.

ORANGE COUNTY FAIR, Costa Mesa. (714) 751-3247 / www.ocfair.com, 88
Fair Dr., Orange County Fairgrounds. This huge ten-day event is great fun for
the whole family. There are lots of carnival rides and games; rodeos (that last a
few hours); speedway racing; farm animals, featured in shows and races, and to
pet; craft booths; acrobats; exhibits; demonstrations, such as a firefighter combat
challenge, etc.; great food; and top-name entertainment. Each day brings new
attractions and events. There is so much to see and do that one day might just not
be enough! Call for discount days and the calendar of special events. General
admission is $6 for adults; $5 for ages 13 - 17; $2 for ages 6 - 12; children 5
years and under are free.

PEARSON PARK AMPHITHEATER, Anaheim. See the June entry for details.

RINGLING BROS. & BARNUM AND BAILEY CIRCUS, Anaheim, Long
Beach, and Los Angeles. Call Arrowhead Pond for the Anaheim location - (714)
704-2500 / arrowheadpond.com; Long Beach convention center - (562) 436-
3661 or (562) 436-3636; and Los Angeles convention center - (213) 741-1151 or
the sports arena - (213) 748-6136. This is a traditional month for "The Greatest
Show on Earth" to come to town. Catch some of the most amazing animal and
acrobatic acts ever performed!! Tickets range from $11.50 - $32.50, depending
on performance date and time, and your seat location.

SAWDUST FESTIVAL, Laguna Beach. (949) 494-3030 /
e-mail:sawdust@dettanet.com, 935 Laguna Canyon Rd. This three-acre, outdoor
arts and crafts festival, with over 200 artisans, goes from the end of July through
August (almost simultaneous with the Festival of Arts). There are on-going
demonstrations of ceramics such as throwing pots (so to speak), etching, glass
blowing, etc. The Children's Art booth is for kids to create art projects - for free!

Family-oriented daytime entertainment includes storytelling and juggling. Nighttime entertainment includes listening and dancing to bands. Tram service is available for a nominal fee. Hours are daily from 10am - 10pm. Admission is $6 for adults for an unlimited number of visits during the run of the festival; $1 for ages 6 - 12; children 5 years and under are free.

SPEEDWAY, Costa Mesa. See the April entry for details.

SOUTHERN CALIFORNIA INDIAN CENTER'S ANNUAL POWWOW, Costa Mesa. (714) 751-3247 / www.ocfair.com, 88 Fair Dr., Orange County Fairgrounds. Come see spectacular traditional Native American dancing. (The hoop dance is our favorite.) Also enjoy handcrafted arts and crafts, and food. Call for hour and admission fees.

U.S. OPEN SANDCASTLE COMPETITION, Imperial Beach. (619) 424-6663 / www.ci.imperial-beach.ca.us/sand_hm.htm, Imperial Beach Pier. This three-day sandcastle competition and parade is fun to either sign up as a competitor, as there are various age categories, or just to watch other creative people at work. We are amazed at the fantastic designs the sand sculpturers dream up. Free admission to watch.

## AUGUST:

ADVENTURE PLAYGROUND, Huntington Beach. See the June entry for details.

CASA DE TORTUGA, Fountain Valley. (714) 962-0612, 10455 Circulo de Zapata. One weekend a year, this "House of Turtles" hosts an open-house. You'll see and learn about over 800 turtles and tortoises. The pens are staffed by knowledgeable docents. Casa is normally booked a year in advance for their tours, so this is a great opportunity to bring your 3-year-old (and up) child! No strollers permitted. Free admission.

COLORADO LAGOON MODEL BOAT SHOP, Long Beach. See the June entry for details.

FESTIVAL OF ARTS AND PAGEANT OF THE MASTERS, Laguna Beach. See the July entry for details.

FORD FAMILY FUN SUMMER NIGHTS, Hollywood. See the June entry for details.

LONG BEACH SEA FESTIVAL, Long Beach. (562) 570-3100. This month-long festival occurs on a weekend at various locations throughout Long Beach. Join the fun with boat races, swimming contests, a fishing contest, and a sand sculpture contest for professionals and amateurs. Free admission to watch.

NISEI WEEK JAPANESE FESTIVAL, Los Angeles. (213) 687-7193 / members.aol.com/niseiweek/niseiweek.htm, Little Tokyo. This week-long festival, the biggest Japanese festival of the year, takes place at several locations throughout Little Tokyo. A sampling of events include martial arts demonstrations, traditional Japanese dancing, games, arts and crafts, Yabusame archery on horseback, taiko drumming (on huge drums), tofu tasting, and a grand parade with floats. Most of the activities and programs occur on the weekends, Sat.,10am - 6pm; Sun., 10am - 4pm. Call for a schedule of events. Admission is free, although various activities cost.

MIRAMAR AIR SHOW, Miramar. (619) 527-6289 or (619) 537-4119 / www.mwrmiramar.com, Miramar Naval Air Station. This two-day air show features the Blue Angels, civilian pilots, etc., performing thrilling aviation stunts and maneuvers. On the ground are over 200 displays of airplanes, helicopters, and military equipment. Admission and parking are free.

MUD MANIA, Long Beach. (562) 570-1755, 4600 Virginia Rd. at Rancho Los Cerritos. Get down and dirty at this one-day event. Stomp around in an adobe mud pit, make real adobe bricks, play Tug O' War over a mud pit, and help whitewash the adobe oven. Bring a change of clothing. Cleaner activities include making bars of soap, and crafting an adobe model out of cardstock. Refreshments and live musical entertainment round out the day. Open Sun., 12:30pm - 4:30pm. Admission is $3 per person; children 3 years and under are free.

OLD MINERS DAYS, Big Bear. (909) 866-4607 / www.bigbearchamber.com, on Big Bear Blvd. This three-weekend event features a logger's jubilee with tree cutting and log rolling contests; arts and crafts booths; a doo dah parade; and a grand finale parade. Parade entries range from elegant equestrian units, to floats, to old wagons (old flatbed wagons and the red Radio Flyer types, too), and clowns. Admission is free.

OPEN HOUSE AT THE HOLLYWOOD BOWL, Hollywood. See the July entry for details.

PEARSON PARK AMPHITHEATER, Anaheim. See the June entry for details.

RENAISSANCE ART FESTIVAL, Long Beach. (562) 438-9903 at Rainbow Lagoon. Heralding all Lords and Ladies who wish to participate in two days of festivities that harken back to days of old! Renaissance period events include jugglers, magicians, children's games, hands-on exhibits, fencing instructions, and musical entertainment. Admission is $10 for adults; $4 for ages 5 - 12; children 4 years and under are free. Tickets bought in advance are less expensive.

RINGLING BROS. & BARNUM AND BAILEY CIRCUS, Anaheim, Long Beach, and Los Angeles. See the July entry for details.

SAWDUST FESTIVAL, Laguna Beach. See July entry for details.

SPEEDWAY, Costa Mesa. See the April entry for details.

VENTURA COUNTY FAIR, Ventura. (805) 648-3376 / www.seasidepark.org, at Seaside Park. This major event is a week and a half long. The fair offers lots of carnival rides, plus rodeos, pig races, a petting zoo, pony rides, on-going entertainment, and several buildings that have arts and crafts for sale as well as vendor demonstrations. Whew! The fair is open daily from 10am - midnight. A fireworks show is put on nightly at 9pm. Admission is $6 for adults; $3 ages 6 - 12; children 5 years and under are free. Certain activities cost extra. Parking is $5.

WORLD BODYSURFING CHAMPIONSHIP, Oceanside. (760) 966-4535, Oceanside Beach, near the pier. This three-day event is coming up on its 23rd year. Over 300 contestants participate, several from foreign countries. They are judged on length of ride and style, such as barrel rolls and somersaults. You must be at least 12 years old to enter. It is held Fri., 7am - noon; Sat., 7am - 1pm; Sun., 7am - 3pm. The semi-finals and finals are held on Sun. Admission to watch is free; $15 to participate.

# SEPTEMBER:

CALIFORNIA AMERICAN INDIAN DAYS CELEBRATION, San Diego. (619) 281-5964, Balboa Park. Usually held on the third weekend of the month, the celebration showcases American Indian singers and fantastic dancers, as well as tribal arts and crafts to purchase or try making yourself. Open from 9am - dusk. Admission is free.

COIN & COLLECTIBLES EXPO, Long Beach. See the February entry for details.

CORNELIUS JENSEN BIRTHDAY CELEBRATION, Riverside. (909) 369-6055, 4307 Briggs St. The Jensen-Alvarado Ranch Historic Park celebrates Cornelius's birthday on the last Saturday in September with a lot of hoopla. Watch and/or join in the gold panning, soap making, sheep shearing, branding, and spinning and weaving demonstrations. Kick up your heels and dance with the country music. The party goes from 10am - 4pm. Admission is $3 for adults; $1.50 for kids 12 years and under.

FREE FISHING DAY, all over. The last weekend in September usually includes a free fishing day, meaning that no license is required. Call a park or your favorite fishing hole to see if they are participating in this "reel" deal.

GREEN MEADOWS FARM, Los Angeles. (800) 393-3276 / www.greenmeadows.com, 4235 Monterey Rd., Ernest Debs Regional Park. The Farm is here from the end of September through October. See the March entry for details.

"HART" OF THE WEST, Santa Clarita. (805) 259-0855 or (805) 222-7657, 24151 San Fernando Rd. at the William S. Hart Park and Museum. This celebration of "California is a nation" that encompasses many facets of the Old West, usually takes place the fourth weekend of the month. A pow wow is held on the large picnic area. It kicks off around noon with the all tribes and nations procession, followed by the Blessing, and on-going dancing (with narration and interpretation) from each of the Indian nations. Native American wares are for sale at booths. Mountain men, set up in encampments next to the pow wow, show how people lived in the mid 1800's, by using period tools, campfire cooking, and display booths. Civil War re-enactments and skirmishes take place near the adjacent train depot. Shows, which may include cannons firing, take place at 11am, 1pm, and 3pm. Sometimes President Lincoln shows up and recites the Gettysburg Address. A street fair is located just across the street. Parking is tight. The celebration hours are Sat., 9am - 6pm; Sun., 9am - 5pm. Admission is free to most of the events, although admission to the re-enactments is $1 per person.

INDIAN CULTURAL DAYS, San Diego. (619) 239-0512, Balboa Park. This weekend cultural event includes incredible Native American dancing, singing, tapestry displays, bead work, and crafts for kids to watch and/or make. Admission is free.

LOMBARDI'S RANCH, Saugus. See the October entry for details.

LONDON BRASS RUBBING CENTER, Long Beach. (562) 436-4047, 525 E. 7th Street at St. Luke's Episcopal Church. Cheerio! Your child will thoroughly enjoy making a medieval brass rubbing, offered from the end of September through November. (This has become one of our favorite fall activities.) On black background paper, use a wax rubbing crayon of gold, silver, or bronze to capture the intricate designs. The facsimiles of over sixty tombstones from England vary in size, and depict knights, ladies in fancy dress, griffons, Shakespeare, etc. Groups, of at least ten people, can incorporate a half-hour talk, given by a docent in period dress, to learn more the medieval time and the stories of some of the engravings. A complete English tea can be added on to your time here, too, with advanced reservations and a group of at least ten people. The center is open to the public Thurs. - Sun., 10am - 4pm. It is open to groups during this time, too, as well as Tues. and Wed., 10am - 4pm. Teas are served upon request. The price to rub cost between $3 - $12, depending on the size of the brass plate. Groups between ten to twenty pay $4.50 for a piece worth up to $7.50. Groups with twenty-one people or over pay $3.75. Teas are $15 for adults; $8.50 for children 17 years and under. This price includes a rubbing and a half-hour lesson/talk, too.

LOS ANGELES COUNTY FAIR, Pomona. (909) 623-3111 / www.fairplex.com, off the 10 Fwy. at Fairplex. Billed as the world's largest county fair, this three-week event is wonderful (and exhausting). It has lots of carnival rides and games, workshops, country contests, livestock shows, horse-racing, flower and garden shows, music, dancing, booths, and several long buildings filled with exhibits, and truly unique items and products for sale. An interactive space exhibit was a big hit in the '98 (only in an L.A. county fair!) Come early and plan to spend the whole day - there is a lot to see and do (and buy!). Fair hours are Mon. - Thurs., 11am - 10pm; Fri., 11am - 11pm; Sat., 9am - 11pm; Sun., 9am - 10pm. General admission is $9 for adults; $7 for seniors; $5 for ages 6 to 12; children 5 years and under are free. Call to find out about discount admission days. Certain activities cost extra. Parking is $5.

POWAY DAYS COMMUNITY CELEBRATION AND RODEO, Poway. (619) 748-0016 or (619) 748-0022 or (760) 736-0594 / www.powayrodeo.com, on Tierra Bonita Rd. at the PRCA Arena. This is definitely a reason to come to Poway! The multi-day event kicks off with a parade that will have your kids hootin and hollerin'. PRCA rodeos (i.e. Professional Rodeo Cowboys Association) are one of the best in the nation with cowboys competing in several categories. See a show and stay for the entertainment, food, and booths. Tickets range from $10 - $14.

SEAFEST, Corona del Mar. (714) 729-4400 / newportbeach.com. This two-weekend fest has two major events; a sand castle and sand sculpting contest, and Taste of Newport - a sampling of the many restaurants in the area. Call about participating in the sandy events or just come to "sea" the most imaginative things created with sand.

SPEEDWAY, Costa Mesa. See the April entry for details.

TALLSHIPS FESTIVAL, Dana Point. (949) 496-2274 / www.artseek.com/tallships, 24200 Dana Point Harbor Dr. at the Orange County Marine Institute. The two-day festival, usually held the first weekend after Labor Day, begins as the majestic tall ships sail into port. Tour the ships and enjoy demonstrations of the sailing arts. Pirates and sailors are everywhere. Music, crafts, and food make this festival worth *sea*ing. Free admission.

VISIT WITH MONTEZUMA, Los Angeles. See the May entry for details.

# OCTOBER:

ARBORFEST, Fullerton. (714) 278-3579 / arboretum.fullerton.edu, 1900
Associated Rd. at Fullerton Arboretum. Pumpkins and bales of hay add to the
atmosphere of celebrating harvest time for two days here in early October.
There's an apple press to make cider, opportunities to make butter, "wash"
clothes the old-fashioned way, and watch lace being made. The Heritage House
is also open. The fest runs Sat. - Sun., 10am - 4pm. Admission is $5 for adults;
children 17 years and under are free.

CALABASAS PUMPKIN FESTIVAL, Agoura. (818) 222-5680 /
www.pumpkin-festival.com, Cornell Rd. at Paramount Ranch. Kick up your
heels for a weekend of autumn country fun in a Wild West setting. On-going live
entertainment includes country bands, kids dancing troupes, cloggers, and more.
Join in a contest of pumpkin pie eating, pumpkin seed spitting, pumpkin carving,
etc. Visit the Native American Indian Village and watch authentic dancers. Shop
at the numerous arts and crafts vendor booths. And don't forget to pick up a
pumpkin or two. Open Sat., 9am - 5pm; Sun., 9am - 4pm. Admission is $8 for
adults; $6 for seniors; $4 for ages 4 - 12; children 3 years and under are free.
Parking is $4.

EDWARDS AIR FORCE BASE AIR SHOW, Kern County. (805) 277-3510 or
(805) 277-3510 / www.edwards.af.mil., Edwards Air Force Base. Come see an
outstanding, one-day air show, complete with acrobatic teams, biplanes, wing-
walking, military air-ground task force demonstrations, and much more. (Be
prepared for crowds!) Bring folding chairs, water bottles, sunscreen, and hearing
protection because some of the planes are loud! Gates are open at 7am; the show
begins at 10am; events end at 3:30pm. Admission is free.

FALL HALLOWEEN FAIR AND CELEBRATION, Fullerton. (714) 738-6595,
1201 W. Malvern Ave. at the Muckenthaler Cultural Center Foundation. This
one-day affair offers face-painting, pumpkin decorating, games, and yummy
cookies, followed by two concert performances. In the past, the Irvine Youth
Orchestra has performed *Phantom of the Opera*, with an intermission of a
costume parade on stage, followed by *Carnival of the Animals*, a reading
accompanied by music. A fun, cultural way to celebrate fall. Call for hours.
Admission is $3 per person.

FAULKNER FARM, Santa Paula. (805) 525-3975, 14292 W. Telegraph Rd., off
Briggs Rd. This seven-acre pumpkin farm, part of a larger working farm, offers a
month of family fun in the country. One of the farm's major attractions is
pumpkins ranging in size from mini up to 200 pounds. Afternoon weekday
hayrides are $1. Weekends also offer a petting zoo (50¢ admission), pumpkin
painting, face painting, western dancing, craft booths, live country and bluegrass
entertainment, special farm demonstrations (i.e. milking cows, shearing sheep,

etc.), and a variety of fresh foods to purchase, such as jams and squash. Bring your own little punkins here, and have a picnic, too! Call to reserve special school-group "tours," which include educational information about pumpkins, a hayride, a pumpkin, and other goodies for $2.50 per person. The farm is open from the first Saturday in October through October 30 daily from 10am - 5:30pm. Admission is free.

GEM-O-RAMA, Trona. (760) 372-5356, 3 ½ hours north of L.A. in the small city of Trona, near Ridgecrest. This two-day event, which occurs the second weekend in the month, is worth the trek! A gem and mineral show and a bus trip around the chemical plant are the clean activities. Messy highlights include mineral collecting in the gooey black mud for hanksite and borax crystals; trudging in the salt lake for halite; and an opportunity to collect flourescent rocks. Bring a short-wave black light for the latter "tour." Also bring sacrificial clothes, water (to use to wash off), gloves, a heavy hammer, a crowbar (for prying out the specimens), and large boxes lined with trash bags to bring home your treasures. What a unique opportunity to rock collect! Activities begin at 8am on both days. Admission is $5 per vehicle - such a deal!

GEM SHOW, Costa Mesa. See the March entry for details.

GREEN MEADOWS, Los Angeles. See the September entry for details.

HALLOWEEN ALTERNATIVES - For alternatives to door-to-door trick or treating, check your local park or church as many of them offer carnival-type of fun, a safer atmosphere, and still plenty of candy!

HARVEST FESTIVAL, Anaheim. (714) 999-8900 / www.harvestfestival.com, 800 W. Katella Ave., Anaheim Convention Center. This three-day event is the place to go for all your shopping needs and desires. Life in the nineteenth-century is the theme here, so an old-fashioned ambiance is prevalent through the Harvest Festival. Over 1,400 craftsman and artisans sell unique items, from hand-carved train whistles to elegant jewelry, and everything in between. There is on-going entertainment of craft demonstrations (which keeps kids intrigued) and live bands. Good food is on the premises, too. Admission is $7.50 for adults; $6.50 for seniors; $4 for ages 6 - 12; children 5 years and under are free. Admission is $1 off if you bring a can of food. Parking is $7.

HARVEST FESTIVAL, San Diego. (619) 236-6500, San Diego Concourse. See above Harvest Festival entry for a description.

INTERNATIONAL FESTIVAL OF MASKS, Los Angeles. (213) 937-4230, at the corner of Wilshire and Curson Sts., at Hancock Park. Folkloric dance from all over the world, ethnic music, theater, storytelling, mask makers, and mask vendors contribute to this unusual weekend festival. Sunday's mask parade is an absolute hit with kids. The festival runs from 11am - dusk on both days. Admission is free.

LEGO CONSTRUCTION ZONE, San Diego. (619) 239-8180, Horton Plaza on the Sportsdeck. Everyone likes Legos™! Each participant is given the same number of Legos™ and the assignment to make a unique design within a certain time limit. The competition is fun and creative, and who knows - your child might be an engineering genius! Free admission to watch. The price to participate is $17 per person. You can keep your creation and might win a great prize.

LIVE OAK CANYON CHRISTMAS TREE FARM, Redlands. (909) 795-TREE (8733), 32335 Live Oak Canyon Rd. See this entry in the main section of the book for a full description. Now is the farm's season for a pumpkin patch and so much more!

LOMBARDI'S RANCH, Saugus. (805) 296-8697, 29527 Bouquet Canyon Rd. This family-owned and operated working farm opens its gates at the end of September and during the month of October. It offers forty-five-minute school tours during the week that include seeing and learning how pumpkins are grown, harvested, etc., and walking around the farm to see farm animals. Tours are free, need a minimum of twelve people, and are for ages 4 years and up. Attractions here include a few vehicles to climb in (a paddy wagon and a real firetruck), a giant fiberglass pumpkin slide, a walk through scarecrow alley (with over eighty scarecrows), bales of hay to sit on while munching on a hot dog (sold at the snack bar here), and hundreds of pumpkins (up to 150 lb.), squash, gourds, and Indian corn to purchase. Weekend activities include a petting zoo, with goats, sheep, llama, etc. ($1 per person), wagon rides ($3), pony rides ($2), and face painting ($1 to $3). Ask about entering the scarecrow contest as it offers hundreds of dollars in cash prizes! Open daily from 9am - 6pm. The farm is also open June through September, and in November until Thanksgiving to sell fresh fruits and vegetables. Admission is free.

LONDON BRASS RUBBING CENTER, Long Beach. See September entry for details. Ask about the Medieval Feast put on this month. Enjoy a theater presentation and great, traditional food - English bangers, Cornish game hens, ale, pumpkin bread, etc. The cost is $35 per person.

MCGRATH STREET PUMPKIN PATCH, Ventura. (805) 647-0365, corner of Knoll Dr. and McGrath St. During the month of October, walk the eight-acre field and choose a vine-cut pumpkin from the patch. Multi-colored Indian corn, squash (heirloom variety), and gourds (the hard-shell kind used by artists and musicians), are for sale here year round. Free, tractor-drawn hayrides are given on the weekends. One weekend, a local school puts on a fair geared for younger children. Groups of ten or more can take a field trip during the week to learn all about pumpkins, Indians, etc. Call to make a reservation. Open daily 9am - dusk. Admission is free.

MOUNTAIN MAN DAYS (RENDEZVOUS), Banning. (909) 922-9200, 16th and Wilson at Gilman Historic Ranch and Wagon Museum. From Wed. - Sun., "meet" the trappers, mountain men, and cowboys of the Old West. Visit an 1700 - 1800's-era living history encampment and see clothing, tools, and equipment from this time period. Bring your gold dust ($) to use at the trading posts. Food and drink is available. School tours are by reservation during the week and admission is $2 per person for ages 3 years and up. General public admission on the weekends is $2 for adults; $1 for children 3 - 12 years. Public parking is $4.

NATIONAL FIRE PREVENTION WEEK, all over. Call your local fire station to see if they are doing something special this week. Many offer tours of the fire engines and station houses, and sometimes kids can even dress up like a fireman. The safety tips are lifesavers.

ONCE UPON A STORY, San Juan Capistrano. (714) 768-1916, at various locations in San Juan. Enjoy a weekend of tall tales and some great storytelling from some of the best storytellers in the country. Learn fundamentals of storytelling from masters, or come to just be entertained. Your kids might even get their fill of stories, for a day or two at least. Hours are Sat., 8:30am - 10:30pm; Sun., 2pm - 10pm. Individually priced story sessions range from $3 to $10 per person. Ask for package deal pricing.

PUMPKIN CITY'S PUMPKIN FARM, Laguna Hills. (949) 768-1103 - pumpkin city; (949) 586-8282 - mall, 24203 Avenue De La Carlota, Laguna Hills Mall. This one-acre, fenced-in farm takes over part of the mall parking lot for the month of October. The ground is covered with hay, while tractors, cornstalks and bales of hay all around help enhance the autumn mood. There are Indian tepees to go in, and kids can take a ride on a pony ($3.50), a scale train ($1.25), an elephant (weekends only), or a few kiddie rides. There is also entertainment by costumed characters and country bands. Group reservations are offered that include special rates on pumpkins and pony rides. And oh yes, there are thousands of pumpkins here of all shapes and sizes - mini pumpkins to ones that weigh up to 200 pounds! The farm is open daily from 9:30am - 9pm. Free admission.

PUMPKIN PATCH, Pomona. (909) 869-2224, Kellogg Dr., Cal State Poly University. Call to see which weekends the pumpkin patch is offered. Kids can walk the acres of fields, purchase a vine-cut pumpkin, play games at the booths, and enjoy some refreshments. Admission is free, and the pumpkins are relatively inexpensive.

SAN DIEGO ZOO, San Diego. (619) 234-3153 / www.sandiegozoo.org, Park

Blvd. in Balboa Park. The world-famous zoo is free for all ages on the first Monday of October in celebration of Founder's Day. Kids, ages 11 years and under, are free for the entire month! What a way to celebrate!

THRESHING BEE AND ANTIQUE ENGINE SHOW, Vista. See the June entry for details.

VISIT WITH MICHELANGELO AND LEONARDO DA VINCI, Glendale. See the March entry for details.

## NOVEMBER:

CIVIL WAR RE-ENACTMENT AND ENCAMPMENT, Oak Glen. (909) 797-5145, 12261 S. Oak Glen Blvd., Riley's Farm / www.rileysfarm.com The third weekend in November brings 250 re-enactors to Riley's Farm to show what life was like during the Civil War time period. Visit soldiers at their encampment, see battle skirmishes, and be immersed in this pivotal time, if only for a day or two. Farm Stays are offered for people who *really* want to live history - they may stay on the farm for two nights, share in five meals, and be a participant (as part of the civilian attachment) in the re-enactments. Overnight farm stays are $250 for adults; $185 for children 3 - 12 years. Watch the re-enactment Sat. - Sun., 10am - 4pm. Admission is $5 for adults; $3 for ages 3 - 12.

DISNEYANA DREAMERS, San Diego. (760) 747-2990, 1895 Camino del Rio at the Scottish Rite Center. Old and new Disney collectables are available to look at and purchase, such as animation cels, drawings, books, buttons, ornaments, cast member items, and more. Prices range from inexpensive to practically buying a piece of the Matterhorn. Call for dates and hours. Admission is $4 for adults; kids 12 years and under are free.

DOO DAH PARADE, Pasadena. (626) 449-2447 or (626) 795-3355, near the heart of Old Town in downtown Pasadena. This spoof of parades is held the Sunday before Thanksgiving. There are no actual rules regarding the parade or the participants, but the wackier the groups or presentation, the better. Kids laugh it up as they see some of the funkiest outfits and most unique dance routines ever performed. Everyone may act up and act out! The parade goes from 11am - 1pm. Admission is free.

FRONTIER RENDEZVOUS, Oak Glen. See May entry for details. This particular event happens over Thanksgiving weekend.

GLORY OF CHRISTMAS, Garden Grove. See the December entry for details.

HOLLYWOOD CHRISTMAS PARADE, Hollywood. (323) 769-5990 or (213) 469-2337, starting at Gower St. and Sunset Blvd. All the stars come out at night -

I mean the stars of Hollywood - for this celebrity-packed parade that is put on the Sunday after Thanksgiving. There are fantastic floats, live bands, equestrian units, and of course, Santa Claus. The two-hour parade goes along a three-mile course through the streets of Hollywood. Reserved grandstand seating is $30 - $40 per person. Standing room is free, but it does get crowded, so get here early. The parade goes from 6pm to 8pm. All-day parking in nearby lots runs from $5 - $15.

LIVE OAK CHRISTMAS TREE FARM, Redlands. (909) 795-TREE (8733), 32335 Live Oak Canyon Rd. See this entry in the main section of the book for a full description.

LOGANS CANDY, Ontario. (909) 984-5410, 125 W. "B" St. This small retail candy store makes candy canes starting in November. A limited number of tours are offered to visitors to watch the striped candy become a sweet reality. During the twenty-minute tour, first the process is described, then kids see the candy canes being made, followed by a time for questions. Tours are given Mon. - Fri. at 5:30pm, 7pm, and 8:30pm. The cost is $2.25 per person and includes a small bag of candy.

LONDON BRASS RUBBING CENTER, Long Beach. See the September entry for details.

MOTHER GOOSE PARADE, El Cajon. (619) 444-8712. Chambers and Main Sts. This two-hour parade has been going strong and gaining momentum since 1946. It features over 5,000 participants - bands, equestrian units, clown acts, and the best part of all - lots of floats depicting Mother Goose rhymes and fairy tales. The parade takes place the Sun. before Thanksgiving beginning at about 12:30pm. Admission is free.

PILGRIM PLACE FESTIVAL, Claremont. (909) 621-9581, 660 Avery Road. This timely festival takes place on the second Friday and Saturday in November. Thanksgiving is a time to be thankful (and to eat), but do your kids know how this holiday began? Find out by watching the educational highlight here, an hour-long, live re-enactment called, *The Pilgrim Story*. It accurately and biblically retells an important story of our heritage. This play is performed at the outside theater at 1pm each day by the retired church professionals who live at this center. Call for special school performances. Other activities (50¢ each) include riding the Mayflower-on-Wheels, taking a mini-train ride, and visiting the Wampanoag Indian Village for story time, games, etc. A favorite activity at the festival is called the Glue In. Tables full of recycled items are available for kids to glue onto a piece of cardboard to create a masterpiece (50¢). The festival runs from 10am - 4pm. Free admission and free, but hard-to-find, parking.

POWWOW, Indio. See the March entry for details.

SAWDUST WINTER FANTASY, Laguna Beach. (714) 494-3030 /
e-mail:sawdust@deltanet.com, 935 Laguna Canyon Rd. Three acres of fun in the
snow and other cool activities are offered for nine days. Real snow is brought in
daily so you can teach your little angels how to make snow angels. Family
entertainment includes jugglers and carolers. Children's art activities, like mask
making, are different each day and are free! Over 150 artists have booths here,
with on-going crafting demonstration. Get your holiday shopping done and keep
the kids happy - all at the same time! To complete the fantasy, Santa Claus
makes his rounds. Open from 11am - 7pm. Admission is $4 for adults for
unlimited entrance during the run of the festival; $1 for ages 6 - 12; children 5
years and under are free. Parking fees vary depending on which lot you choose.

## DECEMBER:

BELMONT SHORE CHRISTMAS PARADE, Belmont Shore. (562) 434-3066,
on 2nd St. between Bayshore and Quincy. This two-hour street parade starts at
5pm on a Sat. and has over 100 entries, including bands, homemade floats, and
Santa Claus. Call for exact date. Admission is free.

CHRISTMAS BOAT PARADE OF LIGHTS, Newport Beach. (714) 729-4400,
Newport Beach Harbor. The largest and oldest boat parade, with more than 200
participants, usually sets sail nightly, December 17 through December 23.
Consider taking the kids on a cruise for a closer look at the beautiful boats. The
ideal location for viewing is Balboa Island, but you should arrive before 5:30pm
as parking is limited. If you are going to have dinner in this area, be sure to make
reservations. The parade hours are from 6:30pm - 8:45pm.

CHRISTMAS BOAT PARADE OF LIGHTS, Oceanside. (760) 722-5751. Call
to find out when and where, specifically, the boat parade will be held this year.
The parade is a highlight of the season for my kids.

CHRISTMAS OPEN HOUSE AND PARADE, San Diego. (619) 437-8788,
Ferry Landing Marketplace on Coronado. Start off your holiday season with a
bang as this one-day event, usually held on the first Friday in December,
concludes with a fireworks display. During the day, kids will enjoy a parade
along Orange Avenue, entertainment, and Santa's arrival by ferry (the reindeer
are taking a rest). Admission is free.

CRUISE OF LIGHTS, Huntington Beach. (714) 840-7542, Peter's Landing. The
Huntington Harbor Philharmonic Committee sponsors this event, raising money
to donate to the youth music programs in Orange County. From December 13
through December 21 or so, forty-five-minute boat tours are given around the
decorated homes of the harbor area. These homes have entered a competition, so
you will see the creme de la creme, like the Sweepstakes winner, the Most
Beautiful, the Most Traditional, etc. You'll also hear interesting commentary.

Some boats along the way are also decked out in their Christmas best. Tours are offered every hour on the half hour from 5:30pm - 8:30pm. Tickets Mon. - Thurs. are $8.50 for adults, $5 for ages 2 to 12; Fri. - Sun., $10 for adults, $5 for ages 2 to 12. Book early!

DISNEY'S WORLD ON ICE. (714) 704-2400 - Arrowhead Pond in Anaheim; (213) 748--6136 - L.A. Sports Arena, (562) 436-3636 - Long Beach arena / www.ticketmaster.com. This ninety-minute, beautiful (and sometimes comical) show on ice usually features characters from Disney's newest film release. Very well done. Tickets range from $11.50 - $18.50. Opening night tickets are only $10!

FIRST NIGHT, Fullerton. (714) 738-6575 or (714) 738-5332 / www.ci.fullerton.ca.us, bordered by Lemon, Malden, Chapman, and Commonwealth Sts. Bring in the New Year all night long! Activities include entrance to the Fullerton Museum Center, music and dancing in the streets, and a fun zone for kids that includes kid's karaoke, face painting, a petting zoo, and rides. Fireworks light up your life at midnight! First Night fun happens between 7pm - midnight. Tickets are $12 for adults; $8 for kids 11 years and under.

FLOATING PARADE OF 1,000 LIGHTS, Long Beach Harbor. (562) 435-4093. Come enjoy the boats on parade that are adorned with Christmas lights and decorations. Prizes are awarded in several categories. The best views are from Shoreline Village, particularly Parkers Lighthouse, although parking is at a premium.

GARDEN GROVE WINTERFEST CARNIVAL, Garden Grove. (714) 741-5200, 9301 Westminster at Garden Grove Park. A lot of holiday fun is packed into the first Saturday of this month! There is a snow play area, pictures with Santa, games, and a crafts area where kids can make a variety of projects such as ornaments, wrapping paper, Christmas cards, etc. The carnival runs from 10am - 3pm on a selected Sat. General admission is free. Each activity takes one to two tickets, and tickets are only 25¢ each!

GLORY OF CHRISTMAS, Garden Grove. (714) 54-GLORY (544-5679) / www.crystalcathedral.org, 12141 Lewis St. at the Crystal Cathedral. Come see this one-hour, absolutely spectacular, musical production that is a re-enactment of the miraculous birth of Jesus Christ. It's complete with live animals and angels soaring overhead. (Arrive a little early and see the animals in a farm enclosure towards the back of the parking lot.) Although show times vary they are usually at 6:30pm and 8:30pm nightly (no shows on Mon.), with additional shows at 4:30pm on selected Sat. and Sun. Tickets are $20, $25 or $30 for adults; $2 less for seniors and children 12 years and under. Ask about family discount days, when tickets are $15 per person.

HOLIDAY BOWL PARADE, San Diego. (619) 283-5808, Harbor Drive. Although football is the focal point of this one-day event, the colorful parade is also a highlight. Floats, inflatable balloons, numerous bands, and other entertainment await sports fans of all ages. The two-hour parade begins at 10am. Admission is free.

LIGHTED STREETS. Is there a street or two in your neighborhood that the owners have gone all out to decorate every year? One of our family traditions is to choose one special night during the Christmas season, go out to a restaurant, and walk up and down the festive streets to enjoy the lights and displays.

LIVE OAK CHRISTMAS TREE FARM, Redlands. (909) 795-TREE (8733), 32335 Live Oak Canyon Rd. See this entry in the main section of the book for details. Now is the season for Christmas trees!

LONG BEACH CHRISTMAS WATER PARADE, Long Beach. (562) 436-3645, Naples Canals. Boat-owners cover their boats with Christmas lights, and parade past decorated homes along Naples canals. If you miss the boat parade, just seeing the homes along here is a special treat.

LOS ANGELES HARBOR CHRISTMAS BOAT PARADE, San Pedro. (310) 832-7272, Ports O' Call. Owners go all out to decorate their boats and compete for the best in a wonderful parade that is put on the second Sat. of December.

LOS POSADAS, Los Angeles. (213) 628-7833, Olvera Street. Guests join in a candlelight procession led by actors portraying Mary and Joseph as the couple searches for shelter. The Christmas pageant ends with a more modern celebration of breaking open a pinata. The procession starts at about 7pm. Admission is free.

MARINA DEL REY CHRISTMAS BOAT PARADE, Marina del Rey. (310) 821-7614. On the second Saturday of December over eighty boats, decorated to the hilt with Christmas lights and decorations, sail around the marina's main channel. The parade is exciting with winners chosen for Best Theme, Best Humor, Best Music, etc. The best views are from Burton Chase Park or Fisherman's Village.

MUSEUMS, all over. Many of your favorite museums get all decked out for the holidays, particularly the historical homes. Many also offer holiday programs with special family activities.

PARADE OF LIGHTS, Ventura. (805) 642-7753, at the Ventura Village. This festive boat parade is usually held the first or second weekend in December. Call for specific dates. Take the Bay Queen for an hour-and-a-half cruise, as it goes around the harbor to see homes that are decorated for the holidays. Also, call for the dates when a white Christmas is celebrated at the Village with snow brought in specially for kids.

ROSE BOWL FAMILY FESTIVAL, Pasadena. (626) 440-ROSE (7073), 1001 Rose Bowl Dr. Several days before the big parade and football game, visitors can watch final touches being applied to the floats, see marching bands and equestrian units practice, shop at souvenir booths, and more. General admission is free, but there are charges for some events.

ROSE PARADE DECORATING. (626) 440-ROSE (7073) - call to ask where your assistance might be used in helping to decorate the Rose Parade floats. AAA Club members who are least 13 years old, can help decorate the AAA float. Call (714) 424-8190 for more information.

ROSE PARADE FLOAT VIEWING, Pasadena. (626) 440-ROSE (7073), Rosemont Pavilion - 700 Seco St. (Exit Foothill Freeway [210] at Seco St. and Rose Palace - 835 S. Raymond Ave. Come see the famous floats as they are being made, from December 28 through December 31. Workers spend weeks meticulously decorating them using plants, seeds, tree bark, flowers, and single petals. Viewing times are from 9am - 9pm. Minimal fee.

STAR OF BETHLEHEM, Santa Ana. (714) 564-6600, W. 17th St. and North Bristol at Rancho Santiago College Planetarium. For the first three Thursday nights in December, the planetarium sky is reset to the time of Jesus' birth. This is a scientific look at the configurations and causal effect of this miraculous star. The show starts at 7:30pm and costs $2 per person.

VICTORIAN CHRISTMAS, El Toro. (714) 855-2028, 25151 Serrano Rd., Heritage Hill Historical Park. On the first Saturday in December, experience Christmas as it was during the turn-of-the century. Walk through these four historic buildings, which are festooned with old-fashioned decorations. Over fifty exhibits display and demonstrate homemade handicrafts like wooden carvings and lace making. A popular display is on antique engines that includes a milking machine, a corn husker, and a corn grinder. A free children's crafts area is available for kids to make their own special creations. Genteel entertainment is provided, and Saint Nicholas also pays a visit. Open from 10am - 4pm. Admission is $3 for adults; $2 for kids.

WILDLIGHTS, Palm Desert. (760) 346-5694 / www.livingdesert.org, 47900 Portola Ave., at the Living Desert Wildlife and Botanical Park. A special display, up for only six-weeks, features nearly a dozen, larger-than-life animal and other sculptures illuminated in lights. This can include a gigantic teddy bear, a thirty-foot snowman, assorted desert critters, and a golfing Santa. Live entertainment, good food, and a visit from Santa Claus (bring your own camera) add to the holiday festivities. The park reopens at 6pm and stays open until 9pm for these wild nights. (The animals are put to bed - it's a people-only party.) Admission is

$4 for adults; $2.50 for children 11 years and under.

WINTER WONDERLAND, Corona del Mar. (714) 644-3151, Grant Howald Park, between Iris and 5th Ave. If you don't feel like driving a few hours to the snow, just drive to Corona del Mar for this one-day event. Bring your mittens and have a great time building a snowman or ~~starting~~ having a snow ball fight with your kids. Food and beverages are available for purchase. The hours are 10am - 1pm. Admission is free.

# IDEAS / RESOURCES

(General ideas of where else to go and what to do, plus where to find specific resource information.)

**AIRPLANE or HELICOPTER RIDES -**
Look in the phone book, call small, local airports for flight information, and check the Transportation section for specific flying venues.

**ANIMALS -**
AA Laboratories, (714) 893-5675 or www.egglab.com, located in Westminster, sells fertilized eggs - $12.50 for a dozen chick eggs. They also have duck and quail eggs. Incubators rent for $10 a week - home births without the labor pains! Be forewarned, however, that very little instruction comes with your eggs and incubator. Tip #1: Go tu the library to research the process by checking out picture books of developing chicks and ducks, etc.; # 2: Pick up an information sheet, and feed, at Blacksmith's Corner, (562) 531-0386 in Bellflower, or at a similar pet store near you. And yes, if you do not want to raise the birds, AA Labs will (usually) take them back and donate them to farms, zoos, etc.
*Insect Lore*, (800) LIVE BUG (548-3284) or www.insectlore.com. This catalog offers living science kits, giving families the opportunity to observe insects growing and transforming. Our favorite kits are the butterfly, earthworms and compost, praying mantis, silkworm, ladybird beetles (i.e. ladybugs, to lay people), and frog hatchery. Each kit comes with instructions, information, and eggs or embryos. The catalog also offers owl pellets, plus other science experiments, books, and visual aids.

**ARTS AND CRAFTS -**
Many places offer free or minimal fee classes/workshops for kids. Check out your local craft stores, such as Michaels (ask about Kids Club Saturdays); Ben Franklin Crafts; Home Depot (many offer free Sat. workshops), and Lakeshore Learning Materials store. Also, look under the Arts and Crafts section in the main part of the book.

**AUDIO TAPES -**
The following are just a few of our favorite, non-musical, tapes:
Adventures in Odyssey, (800) A-FAMILY (232-6459) or www.family.org - 6 tapes for about $25. Focus on the Family puts out this tape series consisting of 12 half-hour-long, Biblically-based, radio dramas. The stories are centered around a fictional soda shop/Bible room/imagination station/kid's hang-out called Whit's End, and the people that live in the small (made-up) town of Odyssey. Each episode involves kids, families, dilemmas, solutions, morals, wit, and wisdom. I can't recommend these adventures highly enough!

Boomerang, (800) 333-7858 - $7.95 per tape; $43.95 for 12 tapes. This audio magazine is filled with 70 minutes of stories of famous people, jokes, mysteries to solve, current events, and fun and factual information about the 50 states. Each issue is presented by kids, for kids, and is designed for ages 6 and up.

Classical Kids Series - about $10.98 per tape. The tapes can be found in most larger retail record stores or ordered through catalogs such as Rainbow Re-Source Center, (800) 705-8809. Each tape in this wonderful series tells the story, told in play format, of a famous composer while the composer's music plays in the background. Titles include *Beethoven Lives Upstairs*, *Mozart's Magical Fantasy*, etc.

Greathall Productions, (800) 477-6234 or e-mail:greathall@greathall.com - about $9.95 per tape. Be enthralled by award-winning storyteller, Jim Weiss. Kids (and adults) of all ages will enjoy the masterful retelling of (mostly) classic stories. Tape titles include *Arabian Nights*, *Sherlock Holmes for Children*, *Three Musketeers*, *Giants!*, *Greek Myths*, *Shakespeare for Children*, *Animal Tales*, etc.

## BASEBALL -

Call for a game schedule and ask about special days, such as fan appreciation day, etc.

Angels, at Edison International Field in Anaheim, (714) 663-9000 or (714) 634-2000 or www.angelsbaseball.com

Dodgers, at Dodger Stadium, (213) 224-1400 or www.dodgers.com

Padres, at Jack Murphy Stadium, (619) 283-4494 or www.padres.com

Minor league games can be major league fun. Check out teams such as Bakersfield Blaze, (805) 322-1363 or www.bakersfieldblaze.com; High Desert Mavericks, (619) 246-6287; Lake Elsinore Storm, (909) 245-4487; Lancaster Jethawks, (805) 726-5400; Mission Viejo Vigilantes, (714) 699-1616 or www.vigilantes.com; Rancho Cucamonga Quakes, (909) 481-5000, www.fanlink.com/na/cal/quakes; and San Bernardino Stampede, (909) 888-9922.

High school and college games are exciting, too.

## BASKETBALL -

Clippers, at L.A. Memorial Coliseum and Sports Arena, (213) 748-6136 or www.clippers.com

Lakers, at Great Western Forum, (310) 419-3100 or www.lakers.com

Sparks, (a women's pro team), (310) 419-3100 or www.wnba.com

Also check out high school and college games.

## BATTING CAGES -

"Hey batter batter." Cages are great for hitting practice, in season or out.

## BILLIARDS -

Many billiard parlors have a family-friendly atmosphere.

## BOOKS -

Numerous book stores offer story times and/or craft times. Some of the bigger book stores, such as Barnes and Noble, Borders, etc., have a huge children's selection, as well as a children's reading area. Many smaller bookstores cater specifically to kids and are delightful to browse through. Also see Educational Toys, Books, and Games in this section.

Used book stores are a terrific bargain. To name just a few, try:

Acres of Books, in Long Beach, (562) 437-6980 or
e-mail:acresofb@aol.com

Book Baron, in Anaheim, (714) 527-7022 (vintage books and used books)

Book City, in Hollywood, (213) 466-2525 or www.hollywoodbookcity.com or in Burbank, (818) 848-4417 ( new and used books).

Brindles, in Tustin, (714) 731-5773 (new and used books).

Thrift stores and garage sales are another great resource for used books.

## BOWLING -

Many alleys offer bumper bowling for kids, where the gutters are covered so kids almost always knock down a pin or two. (This sounds like something right up my alley, too.)

## CAMPING -

Campgrounds mentioned in this book are usually listed under the or Great Outdoors sections. Call Parknet, at (800) 444-7275, to make camping reservations at any California State Park. Check your library or local book store for books written just on camping.

## CELEBRITIES -

Call the Walk of Fame at Hollywood Chamber of Commerce, (213) 469-8311 or chamber.hollywood.com, to find out when the next celebrity will be honored with a ceremony dedicating his/her star along this famous "walk." Ceremonies occur almost monthly.

## CIRCUS -

Check sports arenas, newspapers, or try the following numbers to see when the circus will be in town:

Carson & Barnes - (405) 326-3173. It features five rings of continual action, with hundreds of animals, international performers, and lots of razzle dazzle.

Circus Flora - (314) 531-6273. Named for its African elephant, this circus specializes in new circus-style ensemble acts. An intimate show performed in a 1,500-seat Big Top.

Circus Vargas - (619) 793-0748. This one-ring circus, with that small-town feel.

Cirque Du Solei - (800) 392-1999 or (800) 678-2119. These artsy and eccentric productions change their theme often and focus on "impossible" body movements. Very unique! Note: No animals are used in this circus

Make A Circus - (415) 242-1414. A circus troupe from No. Cal. presents two-hour workshops to large groups, for free, at parks throughout So. Cal. Kids first see a short show; then learn how to tumble, juggle, act like a circus animal, etc.; and then put on a show for the audience.

New Pickle Circus - (408) 429-1324. American and Russian circus acts are presented along with Chinese acrobats, dance, and original music.

Ringling Bros. & Barnum and Bailey Circus - (703) 448-4000. Billed as "the greatest show on earth," this mult-ring circus is one of the best known in the Western world. It involves daring animal acts, clowns, and feats of skill presented with theatrical flare and state-of-the-art lighting.

## CONSTRUCTION SITES -

If you're toolin' around, these sites can give your youngster constructive ideas to build on.

## CONVENTION CENTERS -

They host a multitude of activities, many of them geared for children, such as Kid's Stuff Expos, toy shows, circuses, etc. Call them intermittently to see what's going on:

Anaheim, (714) 999-8925 ext. 9888 - recorded info, (714) 999-8999 - real person info, or www.anaheimoc.org

Long Beach, (562) 436-3661 or (562) 436-3636.

Los Angeles, (213) 741-1151 or www.lacclink.com

Ontario, (909) 937-3000 or www.ontariocva.org

San Diego, (619) 525-5000 or www.sdccc.org

## COUNTY FAIR GROUNDS -

Numerous events are held here throughout the year, such as gem shows, reptiles expos, the fair, cat shows, circuses, Scottish games, horse shows, etc. Call for schedule.

Los Angeles, (909) 623-3111 or www.fairplex.com.

Orange, (714) 708-FAIR (3247) or www.ocfair.com.

Riverside, (760) 863-8247 or www.datefest.org

San Bernardino (760) 951-2200 or www.sbcfair.com.

San Diego, (619) 755-1161 or www.delmarfair.com.

Ventura, (805) 648-3376 or www.seasidepark.org.

## COUPONS -

Call the Visitors Center (or Chamber of Commerce) of the city you are planning to visit as they often offer discount coupons good towards attractions. For instance, "The Family Values Coupon Book" for Orange County, features savings at over 50 area attractions, hotels, restaurants, and shops. Call (714) 999-8999 or www.anaheim.org for information. The San Diego Visitors Center, (619) 236-1212 or www.sandiego.org, offers a free "value coupon" booklet that saves on main attractions, harbor cruises, restaurants, and more.

## CPR CLASSES -
Call your local Red Cross or hospital for class information. (This is a great idea for babysitters, too!)

## EDUCATIONAL TOYS, BOOKS, and GAMES -
There are numerous stores and catalogs that offer good quality, educational products. Some of our favorite stores include Bright Ideas for Learning (in Camarillo), F.A.O. Schwartz, Imaginarium, Lakeshore Learning, Learning Express, Parent Teacher Aids (in Simi Valley) and Zany Brainy (an immediate favorite). Look in your telephone directory for these listings, and for two other great resources - teacher supply stores and children's bookstores. Many museum gift shops offer a terrific line of educational (and fun) supplies. Also check out the following companies that offer catalogs and/or home workshops for their products:

    Discovery Toys, (800) 426-4777 or www.discoverytoysinc.com - carries a fantastic line of toys, books, games, and computer software.
    Dorling Kindersley Books, (888) 225-3535 (Ellen Knowles, independent consultant) - offers outstanding books.
    Usborne Books, (800) 442-2812 or www.usborne-usa.com - top notch books.

## EQUESTRIAN SHOWS -
English and Western riding, jumping, prancing, etc., are all part of seeing a horse show. Call your local equestrian center for dates and times.

## FARMER'S MARKETS -
See Edible Adventures in the main section of the book for details.

## FILMING -
Interested in seeing actual filming? The L.A. Film Office, at (323) 957-1000 or www.eidc.com, provides a free "shoot sheet" that lists expected location shots for any given day. The Hollywood Visitor Information Center, (213) 689-8822, can help with directions.

## FOOTBALL -
Chargers, at Jack Murphy Stadium, (619) 280-2121 or www.chargers.com High school and college games are fun, too.

## GYM CLASSES FOR KIDS -

Some suggestions are:

Gymboree - Check your local phone book for listings. Classes are offered for parents and their children - newborns through 4 years old - that include easy exercise, songs, bubbles, and visits from Gymbo, the clown.

My Gym - Classes in tumbling, songs, games, and gymnastics are offered for the younger set. The franchises are everywhere in Southern California. For examples, in Newport Beach, call (714) 261-5252.

Y.M.C.A. - They offer fun fitness programs for kids.

## HOBBIES AND MODELS -

Kids like to collect - anything! For example - bottlecaps, dolls, miniatures (dollhouses), postcards, rocks, sports cards, stamps, etc. Other hobby ideas include model-making (i.e. cars, planes, rockets, and trains), creating jewelry, sewing, etc.

## HOCKEY -

Ice Dogs, at Long Beach Arena in Long Beach, (562) 423-3647 or www.icedogshockey.com

Kings, at Great Western Forum in Inglewood, (310) 419-3100 or www.lakings.com

Mighty Ducks, at Arrowhead Pond in Anaheim, (714) 704-2400 or www.mightyducks.com

San Diego Gulls, at the Sports Arena in San Diego, (619) 225-9813 or www.sandiegoarena.com

## HORSEBACK RIDING -

*Neigh* doubt about it, this is a terrific family outing!

## HOT AIR BALLOON RIDES -

Up, up and away! Hot air balloon rides are recommended for ages 10 and over, as younger children might get scared of the flames shooting out (i.e. the "hot air"); they might get bored; and they can't see very well over the basket. All ages, however, are enthralled by watching the balloon being inflated, either in the morning or at sunset! Inquire about Hot Air Balloon Festivals for a real colorful outing. Most of the companies listed fly over Del Mar, Palm Springs, and/or Temecula. Flights are about an hour and include a champagne breakfast. Prices are per person. Here are just a few names and numbers to get you started:

Fantasy Balloon Flights, (800) GO ABOVE (462-2683) or www.gtesupersite.com/balloonride - about $135.

Skysurfer Balloon Company, (619) 481-6800 - about $135.

Sunrise Balloons, (800) 548-9912 - between $125 - $140.

## ICE SKATING -

Go figure! Call, for instance, the arenas listed below:

Glacial Garden Skating Arena, in Lakewood, (562) 429-1805, has three
rinks - two for the ice, and one for in-line skating. They also offer
broomball which is *fun*tastic!

Disney Ice, in Anaheim, (714) 535-7465, offers public sessions, plus
figure skating and hockey classes and it's the rink where the Mighty
Ducks practice!

## JUNKYARDS -

One man's trash is another man's treasure. For kids who like to take things
apart and make new creations, junkyards are inspiring places to investigate.

## KITE FLYING -

Go fly a kite!

## LIBRARIES -

Your local library has a lot to offer. Besides book, video, and cassette
lending, many offer free storytelling on a regular basis and/or finger
plays, puppet shows, and crafts. Some libraries also encourage your
bookworms by offering summer reading programs. Get a group together
and ask for a tour. *A Treasure Hunt in My Library*, by Candace Jackson,
is an outstanding book, with curriculum, that takes kids on a tour of the
library and teaches them how to use it. Order it through a bookstore or by
calling (888) 707-4289 or www.museummania.com. Check out her
website to do some on-line treasure hunts. She has also written several
great books for kids on specific museums in Southern California.

## MAGAZINES -

If you only receive one magazine, make it *Family Fun*. Put out by Disney,
each edition is packed with do-able crafts, snacks, party ideas, games,
activities, and family-friendly places to travel. Pick it up at the newsstand or
call (800) 289-4849 or www.familyfun.com for subscription information.
(Currently, $14.95 for 10 issues.)

## MALLS -

Going to the mall can be a fun excursion with kids (honest!), especially if the
mall has "extra" features, such as a merry-go-round or fountains, or, if it's
spectacular in design, has unique shops and restaurants, etc. See the Malls
section in the main part of the book for some of our top picks.

## MONEY -

Collect money from foreign countries without the expense of traveling there.
Call (800) CURRENCY (287-7362) to find the nearest Thomas Cook
Foreign Exchange Currency. You may exchange any sum of money for
currency from an unlimited number of countries, for only one transaction fee.
The fee is a $4.95 service fee or 1% of the U.S. amount, whichever amount is
greater.

**MOVIE THEATERS -**
An obvious choice, but movies, and especially matinees, can be a
relatively inexpensive and fun treat. For instance:
> Super Saver Cinema, in Seal Beach, (562) 594-9411 - each show costs
> $2.
> Super Saver, in Norwalk, (562) 868-9694 - showings on certain days of
> the week are only $1.
> AMC Theaters, in Long Beach, (562) 435-4262 - sometimes offer a book
> of 10 movies for $7.50 during the summer.

**MUSEUMS -**
You can $ee L.A., or ¢.E.E. L.A. The Cultural Entertainment Events card
(C.E.E.) offers entrance to 19 top museums for only $40 a year for the
family!! These museums include Autry Museum, George C. Page, Kidseum,
Natural History, Petersen, and Richard Nixon. Call (818) 957-9400 for more
information. The card will also save you money on sporting and theater
events.
Note: International Museum Day is May 18, so many museums offer free
admission and/or arts and crafts for your family to do.

**PARKS -**
Almost every local park offers classes or programs for free, or at a
minimal cost. Ask about kid's cooking classes, sidewalk chalk art day,
etc.

**PET STORES -**
This is a fun, mini-outing. Ask about tours. Cuddly puppies and adorable
rabbits are great, but so are unusual and exotic animals found at some of
the stores listed below:
> Blacksmith's Corner in Bellflower, (562) 531-0386 - It's like visiting a
> mini farm, with its chickens, ducks, pheasants, etc.
> Last Straw Feed Store in Fallbrook, (760) 728-6482 - The animals are
> mostly outdoors. See a llama, camel, goats, turkeys, chickens, a
> gigantic Burmese python, etc.
> Prehistoric Pets in Fountain Valley, (714) 964-3525 or
> www.prehistoric.com - Incredible! See exotic snakes (some 20 ft.
> long) and monitor lizards from all over the world, plus a small fish
> pond in the middle of the store, and more.
> Petco - A chain store, so look in your local phone book. They have fish,
> snakes, bunnies, iguanas, turtles, and birds.

**PHOTO ALBUMS -**
Tapped dry on how to put together a creative and memorable photo
album? Call the magazines and the multi-level company listed below for
innovative ideas and acid-free products:
> *Creative Keepsakes* magazine, (888) 247-5282 or

www.creatingkeepsakes.com - Browse through and implement the
many ideas given here. Current subscription price is $19.95 for 6
issues.

Creative Memories (company), (800) 468-9335 or
www.creative-memories.com - Call for information on purchasing
craft scissors, and acid-free pages, stickers, cut outs, etc. Or, learn
artistic techniques to organize and crop your photos by hosting or
attending a workshop for you and your friends.

*Memory Maker* magazine, (303) 452-0048 or
www.memorymakersmagazine.com - Pick up a copy of this
beautifully laid out and inspirational magazine. Current subscription
price is $24.95 for 6 issues.

## PLAYGROUPS -

Check local parks, newspapers, and "Parenting" for information on
hooking up magazine to hook up with a playgroup. This is a great way to
share the joys and trials of raising children. Other resources include:

MOMS, e-mail:momsclub@aol.com, is an international, non-profit
support group specifically for stay-at-home moms. Weekly meetings
consist of talking and eating together, listening to a speaker, and going
on various outings. All age children are welcome at all meetings and
activities. For information on a club near you, write to: MOMS Club,
25371 Rye Canyon, Valencia, CA 91355.

MOPS (Mothers Of Preschooler), (303) 733-5353 or www.mops.org, is
an international, Christian-based organization that has local meetings
in almost every city. Moms usually meet at a church and talk, eat,
listen to a speaker, and make a craft while their preschoolers are being
cared for by a Moppet helper. Great organization! Call the
headquarters to find a MOPS near you.

Tot Lot is a playgroup designed for preschoolers (and their parents) to
meet and play together at parks on a regular basis during the week,
building those all-important socialization skills. Registration fees go
towards crafts, snacks, and even field trips. Call, for example,
Lakewood Recreation and Community Services, (562) 866-9771 for
information on Tot Lot at Biscailuz, Bolivar, Boyar, Del Valle, and
Mayfair parks.

## RESTAURANTS -

See the Edible Adventures section in the main part of the book. Try
eating at some unusual locations, such as at airports, on boats (such as the
Queen Mary), etc. Take your kids out for ethnic foods, too.

## ROLLER HOCKEY -

Bullfrogs, at Arrowhead Pond in Anaheim, (714) 704-2400.

**ROLLER SKATING -**
   Roll on the sidewalks, around parks, etc., and at rinks, such as:
      Fountain Valley Skating Center, in Fountain Valley, (714) 847-6300.
         This rink also offers stroller skating, which is skating around a rink
         while pushing your baby in a stroller, on Thurs. from 1pm - 3pm for
         $4 per mother/child pair.
      Surf City Skatezone, in Huntington Beach, (714) 842-9143. Skatezone
         offers roller skating and ice skating under one roof!

**SAN DIEGO THEATRE -**
   The San Diego Performing Arts League puts out a bimonthly booklet called
   *What's Playing*? It has a complete listing of the music, dance, theater groups,
   specific show, dates, prices, etc., in the San Diego area. $10 for a year's
   subscription. Call (619) 238-0700 or www.sandiego-online.com/sdpal for
   more information.

**SCIENCE PROGRAMS -**
   Check science museums for on-site programs and workshops, as well as
   traveling programs. Science-2-U, (562) 630-6987 or e-mail:jjjill@aol.com, is
   one example of a program that comes to you. A minimum group of 8 students
   have a fantastic array of hands-on, one-hour classes to choose from, such as
   Slimy Critters, Kids' Chemistry, and Marine Life. The cost is generally $10
   per student, per session.

**SPORTS ARENAS -**
   Many special events are held at sports arenas including sporting events,
   concerts, Walt Disney's World on Ice, circuses, etc:
      Anaheim, at Arrowhead Pond, (714) 704-2400.
      Inglewood, at Great Western Forum, (310) 419-3100.
      Long Beach, at Long Beach Arena, (562) 436-3636.
      Los Angeles, at L.A. Memorial Coliseum and Sports Arena, (213) 748-
         6136 or www.stadia.com/lacoliseum.
      San Diego, at Sports Arena, (619) 225-9813 or www.sandiegoarena.com

**SPORTING EVENTS -**
   Check out high school and college events. These local games are a fun,
   inexpensive introduction to sports.

**SWAP MEETS -**
   Give your kids a dollar or two to call their own, as there are a lot of
   inexpensive toys or jewelry items for them to choose from at swap meets.
   Everyone goes home happy with their treasures! Here's a list of just a few
   good swap meets:
      Alpine Village (indoor/outdoor) in Torrance, (213) 770-1961. Open Tues.
         - Sun., 8am - 2pm. Admission is free on Thurs.; 50¢ per person other
         days.

Anaheim Marketplace (indoor) in Anaheim, (714) 999-0888. Over 250 variety shops and a food court. They also have adjacent batting cages and arcade games. Open Wed. - Mon. from 10am - 7pm. Free admission.

Kobey's Swap Meet (outdoor) at the sports arena parking lot in San Diego, (619) 226-0650. Taking up the equivalent of 12 footballs fields, this swap meet offers bargains on everything under the sun. Open Thurs. - Sun., 7am - 3pm. Admission is 50¢ on Thurs. and Fri.; $1 on Sat. and Sun. No charge for children 11 years and under.

Orange County Marketplace (outdoor) in Costa Mesa, (714) 723-6616. One of the best, with over 1,200 vendors, plus a food court. Open on weekends from 8am - 3pm. Admission is $1 for adults; children 11 years and under are free.

Roadium (outdoor) in Torrance, (213) 321-3902. 500 merchants sell new items, collectibles, bargains, and food daily from 7am - 4pm. Admission on Mon., Tues., Thurs., and Fri., is 50¢ per person; Wed., $1.25 for adults; 75¢ for seniors and children; Sat. and Sun., $1.50 per car, plus 50¢ per person.

Rosebowl Flea Mart (outdoor) in Pasadena, (626) 577-3100. Held the second Sun. of each month. Admission is $15 from 6am - 7:30am; $10 from 7:30am - 9am; $5 from 9am until it closes. Parking is $2.

Saugus Speedway Swapmeet (outdoor) in Saugus, (805) 259-3886. With over 700 vendors, this huge swap meet is held every Tues. and Sun. from 8am - 3pm. Swapmeets are held on Fri. only in the summer. Admission on Tues. is free; Sun., $1 for adults; children 11 years and under are free.

Tip: Also check out 99¢ Stores, which are along the same lines as swap meets.

## SWIMMING and WADING POOLS -

Community pools are open seasonally. Call your local park or city hall for information.

## THRIFT STORES -

Teach your children the gift of thrift! Give them a few dollars to buy a "new" article of clothing, a toy, or a book. Tip: Main Street, in the city of Ventura, has at least 10 thrift stores in a row.

## TICKETS -

Audiences Unlimited, (818) 506-0067 or www.tvtickets.com, offers free tickets to watch the filming of almost all of the network television shows and many of their specials. For some shows, the minimum age for kids is 12 years old; for most, it's 18 years old.

Times Tix, (213) 688-2787, located in W. Hollywood allows cash-only, day-of-show tickets to be purchased Thurs. - Sun., noon to 6pm for 50% off.

Call (310) 659-3678 for a list of today's shows and availability.
Times Arts Tix, (619) 497-5000, located in San Diego next to Horton Plaza,
has half-price, day-of-performance, theater tickets available on a first-
come, first-served, cash-only basis. Call for a listing of the day's half-
price shows.

## TOURS -

See Tours in the main section of the book. The following are general ideas of
where you can go for group tours:
Animal Shelter
Airport
Bakery
Bank
Chiropractor
College/University
Dairy
Dentist
Factory
Fire Station
Florist
Grocery Store
Hospital
Hotel
Newspaper Office
Nurseries (plant)
Pet Store
Police Station
Post Office
Printer
Restaurant

## TOYS -

Look in this part of the book under Educational Toys, Books, and Games.
Two other listings worth mentioning are:
U.S. Toy Constructive Playthings, in Garden Grove, (714) 636-7831 -
Call for a catalog or visit their store. They offer top-of-the-line toys,
books, games, puzzles, etc., as well as lower priced, carnival-type
"prizes."
Oriental Trading Company, (800) 228-2269 or www.oriental.com - This
catalog company offers bulk and individual novelty items, usually
priced at the lower end of the scale.

## VOLUNTEERING -

Volunteering is a terrific way to spend time with your children while
teaching them the real values of life - giving and serving. Check with
local churches and temples, as many have regular times when they go to

help feed the homeless. Here are a few other volunteer agencies:

Fullerton Arboretum, (714) 278-3404. They encourage family participation in nursery projects, such as propagation, transplanting, weeding, etc.

Green Networking for Orange County, (949) 548-2393. If you're concerned about the environment and don't know how to help or where to find information, this group provides you with names and numbers of more than 200 environmental groups, businesses, and agencies in Orange County.

Habitat For Humanity, (714) 895-4331 or www.habitatoc.org. A non-profit organization committed to providing low-income, owner-occupied housing by utilizing volunteer labor and donated materials. (Former President Jimmy Carter is one of the more prominent members.) Volunteers are needed to build homes and serve on committees such as finance, construction, and public relations. Kids must be at least 16 years old to work on construction sites, but younger children can help with off-site activities such as registration, making lunches, etc.

St. Vincent de Paul - (619) 233-8500. Look up Tours in the main section of the book for details.

Volunteer Center of Greater Orange County, (714) 953-5757. A clearinghouse for a huge variety of age-appropriate opportunities, from feeding the homeless, to visiting the elderly, to planting trees, cleaning up parks, and removing graffiti. They even have a guide book on family volunteer activities.

# WILDFLOWER HOTLINES -

Anza Borrego Desert State Park, (760) 767-4684.

Joshua Tree National Park, (760) 367-5500 or www.nps.gov/jotr

Mojave Desert Information Center, (760) 733-4040 or www.calparksmojave.com

Poppy Reserve, (805) 724-1180 or (805) 942-0662 or www.calparksmojave.com

Southern California Hotline, Theodore Payne Foundations, (818) 768-3533

# ALPHABETICAL INDEX

## - H -

# INDEX BY CITY

**BIPLANE AND AIR COMBAT
ADVENTURES, 456
CARLSBAD CHILDREN'S MUSEUM,
310
LEGOLAND CALIFORNIA, 14
PLAZA CAMINO REAL MALL - KIDS'
CLUB, 212
**Carson**
GO KART WORLD, 74
INTERNATIONAL PRINTING
MUSEUM, 243
SOUTHBAY PAVILION - LI'L
SHOPPERS CLUB, 206
THE VELODROME, 447
**Castaic**
CASTAIC LAKE RECREATION
AREA, 118
**Catalina**
CATALINA ISLAND, 360
**Cathedral City**
CAMELOT PARK FAMILY
ENTERTAINMENT CENTER, 512
**Century City**
DIVE!, 44
**Cerritos**
CERRITOS CENTER FOR THE
PERFORMING ARTS, 388
HERITAGE PARK (Cerritos), 130
LIBERTY PARK, 132
**Chatsworth**
CHATSWORTH PARK, 119
STONEY POINT, 146
**Chino**
THE AIR MUSEUM "PLANES OF
FAME", 298
PRADO REGIONAL PARK, 180
Q-ZAR (Chino), 96
YOUNG EAGLES PROGRAM (Chino),
455
**Chiriaco Summit**
GENERAL PATTON MEMORIAL
MUSEUM, 516
**Chula Vista**
ARCO OLYMPIC TRAINING
CENTER, 377
CHULA VISTA NATURE CENTER,
487
FUN-4-ALL, 102
WHITE WATER CANYON, 16
**City of Industry**
THE HOMESTEAD MUSEUM, 241
MALIBU SPEEDZONE, 79

**Clairemont**
SOUTH CLAIREMONT RECREATION
CENTER / POOL, 193
**Claremont**
BEN BOLLINGER'S CANDLELIGHT
PAVILION, 386
KENNETH G. FISKE MUSICAL
INSTRUMENT MUSEUM, 245
RANCHO SANTA ANA BOTANIC
GARDEN, 141
RAYMOND M. ALF MUSEUM, 264
**Coachella**
COACHELLA VALLEY PRESERVE,
514
**Colton**
FIESTA VILLAGE, 95
**Corona**
S.C. VILLAGE PAINTBALL GAMES,
94
TOM'S FARMS, 60
**Corona Del Mar**
CORONA DEL MAR STATE BEACH
and TIDEPOOL TOURS, 32
CRYSTAL COVE STATE PARK &
BEACH, 158
IT'S YOU, 25
**Coronado**
CORONADO BEACH, 36
CORONADO BEACH HISTORICAL
MUSEUM, 311
HOTEL DEL CORONADO, 433
HOTEL DEL CORONADO - TEA
TIME, 65
SAN DIEGO BAY FERRY / OLD
FERRY LANDING, 380
SILVER STRAND STATE BEACH, 36
**Costa Mesa**
CENTENNIAL FARM, 481
JOHN WAYNE AIRPORT TOUR, 429
LAUNCH PAD, 282
ORANGE COUNTY PERFORMING
ARTS CENTER, 403
ORANGE COUNTY PERFORMING
ARTS CENTER (tour), 429
RAINFOREST CAFE (Costa Mesa), 55
ROBERT B. MOORE THEATER, 404
ROCKREATION (Costa Mesa), 92
SOUTH COAST REPERTORY, 405
SOUTH COAST STORYTELLERS
GUILD, 373
TEWINKLE PARK, 169
TRINITY CHRISTIAN CITY

# INDEX BY PRICE

**Free Occasionally** - The following attractions have special days when no admission is charged:

**Los Angeles County**
Arboretum of Los Angeles County - third Tues. of each month, pg. 116
Fowler Museum - every Thurs. (located under Mathias Botanical Garden), however parking is still $5, pg. 134
George C. Page Museum - first Tues. of each month, pg. 228
Huntington Library, Art Collections and Botanical Gardens - first Thurs. of each month, pg. 242
Kidspace - last Mon. of each month (except Oct.) from 5pm - 8pm, pg. 245
Los Angeles County Museum of Art - second Tues. of each month, pg. 248
Museum of Contemporary Art / Geffen - each Thurs. from 5pm - 8pm, pg. 252
Museum of Neon Art - second Thurs. of each month from 5pm - 8pm, pg. 254
Natural History Museum of L. A. County - first Tues. of each month., pg. 258
Raymond M. Alf Museum - every Wed., pg. 264
South Coast Botanical Garden - third Tues. of each month, pg. 146

**Riverside County**
California Museum of Photography - every Wed., and the first Sun. from Oct. through June, pg. 291
KidZone - first Sun. from Oct. through June, pg. 294

**San Diego County**
Balboa Park Museums - see BALBOA PARK (San Diego), as the museums vary in their "free day," pg. 306
Chula Vista Nature Center - first Tues. of each month, pg. 487
Firehouse Museum - first Thurs. of each month, pg. 312
Museum of Contemporary Art (both locations) - first Sun. and first Tues. of each month, pg. 322
San Diego Wild Animal Park - one day in early May, call for date, pg. 490
San Diego Zoo - first Mon. in Oct., pg. 491

**Ventura County**
Carnegie Art Museum - Every Fri. from 3pm - 6pm, pg. 338

**Palm Springs**
Palm Springs Desert Museum - first Fri. of each month, pg. 528

### - Free (!) -

**various counties - !**
SIERRA CLUB, 114
**KERN - !**
AIR FORCE FLIGHT TEST CENTER, 416
AIR FORCE FLIGHT TEST CENTER MUSEUM, 214
EXOTIC FELINE BREEDING COMPOUND, 466
NASA DRYDEN FLIGHT RESEARCH CENTER, 417
TWENTY MULE TEAM MUSEUM, 215
**LOS ANGELES - !**
A.D. EDMONSTON PUMPING PLANT, 417
A.E.S. REDONDO GENERATING STATION, 418
AFRICAN AMERICAN FIREFIGHTER MUSEUM, 217
APOLLO PARK, 116

on

SANTA ROSA PLATEAU
　ECOLOGICAL RESERVE, 176
**SAN BERNARDINO - $**
A SPECIAL PLACE, 299
GLEN HELEN REGIONAL PARK, 178
JURUPA HILLS REGIONAL PARK,
　178
MARTIN TUDOR, 178
RAINS HOUSE - CASA DE RANCHO
　CUCAMONGA, 302
**SAN DIEGO - $**
AGUA CALIENTE SPRINGS COUNTY
　PARK, 182
ANZA BORREGO STATE PARK, 182
CABRILLO NATIONAL MONUMENT,
　377
CHULA VISTA NATURE CENTER,
　487
CLYDE E. REXRODE WILDERNESS
　AREA, 187
CUYAMACA RANCHO STATE PARK,
　184
DEL MAR FAIRGROUNDS /
　RACETRACK, 488
EDEN CREEK ORCHARD, 64
FIREHOUSE MUSEUM, 312
FREEFLIGHT, 488
GASKILL STONE STORE MUSEUM,
　312
GUY B. WOODWARD MUSEUM OF
　HISTORY, 313
HERITAGE OF THE AMERICAS
　MUSEUM, 314
JULIAN PIONEER MUSEUM, 315
JUNIPERO SERRA MUSEUM, 316
LA JOLLA SHORES BEACH, 35
LAKE CUYAMACA, 184
LAKE POWAY RECREATION AREA,
　187
MARIE HITCHCOCK PUPPET
　THEATER, 411
MISSION BASILICA SAN DIEGO DE
　ALCALA, 319
MISSION SAN ANTONIO DE PALA,
　320
MISSION SAN LUIS REY DE
　FRANCA, 321
THE MONARCH PROGRAM, 489
MOTOR TRANSPORT MUSEUM, 321
MUSEUM OF CONTEMPORARY ART
　(La Jolla), 322

MUSEUM OF CONTEMPORARY ART
　(San Diego), 322
MUSEUM OF PHOTOGRAPHIC
　ARTS, 324
PALOMAR MOUNTAIN STATE
　PARK, 189
QUAIL BOTANICAL GARDENS, 190
RANCHO BUENA VISTA ADOBE, 328
SAN DIEGO HALL OF CHAMPIONS -
　SPORTS MUSEUM, 332
SAN DIEGO MODEL RAILROAD
　MUSEUM, 332
SAN DIEGO TROLLEY, 460
SANTEE LAKES REGIONAL PARK
　AND CAMPGROUND, 192
TORREY PINES STATE RESERVE,
　195
WILLIAM HEISE COUNTY PARK, 195
**VENTURA - $**
CARNEGIE ART MUSEUM, 338
CHUMASH INTERPRETIVE CENTER,
　341
MISSION SAN BUENAVENTURA, 344
OJAI VALLEY HISTORICAL
　SOCIETY AND MUSEUM, 344
PARTY ANIMALS, 496
RONALD REAGAN PRESIDENTIAL
　LIBRARY AND MUSEUM, 345
SPACEPLAY, 110
STAGECOACH INN MUSEUM, 347
STRATHERN HISTORICAL PARK
　AND MUSEUM, 348
TIERRA REJADA FAMILY FARMS, 67
VENTURA COUNTY MARITIME
　MUSEUM, 348
VENTURA COUNTY MUSEUM OF
　HISTORY AND ART, 349
**BIG BEAR - $**
BIG BEAR HISTORICAL MUSEUM
　and CITY PARK, 501
BIG BEAR SOLAR OBSERVATORY,
　503
CHILDREN'S FOREST, 503
HIKING, 505
MCDILL SWIM BEACH / MEADOW
　PARK, 507
MOONRIDGE ANIMAL PARK, 507
RIM OF THE WORLD HISTORICAL
　MUSEUM, 508
SPORTLAND ARCADE, 509
SUPER BEAR ARCADE, 510

**PALM SPRINGS - $**
  COACHELLA VALLEY MUSEUM &
    CULTURAL CENTER, 514
  GENERAL PATTON MEMORIAL
    MUSEUM, 516
  HEARTLAND (The California Museum
    of the Heart), 517
  JOSHUA TREE AND SOUTHERN
    RAILROAD MUSEUM, 520
  JOSHUA TREE NATIONAL PARK, 520
  LAKE CAHUILLA, 522
  MOORTEN BOTANICAL GARDEN,
    524
  WHITEWATER TROUT CO., 531
    **- $5.01 to $10 ($$) -**
**various counties - $$**
  DISCOVERY ZONE, 70
  METROLINK, 439
  VOYAGES OF REDISCOVERY, 439
**LOS ANGELES - $$**
  ABALONE COVE, 115
  AMERICAN HERITAGE PARK /
    MILITARY MUSEUM, 218
  ANGELS ATTIC, 218
  ARBORETUM OF LOS ANGELES
    COUNTY, 116
  BEVERLY HILLS TROLLEY, 442
  BRIGHT CHILD, 70
  CABRILLO BEACH, 30
  CABRILLO MARINE AQUARIUM,
    467
  CASTAIC LAKE RECREATION
    AREA, 118
  DESCANSO GARDENS, 121
  DISCOVERY ZONE (Lakewood), 72
  ENCINO COMMUNITY CENTER, 389
  ENDANGERED SPECIES ECOPARK,
    468
  THE FARM, 469
  FIGHTER TOWN ENTERTAINMENT
    (Pasadena), 73
  FRANK G. BONELLI REGIONAL
    COUNTY PARK, 126
  GOLFLAND ARCADE, 74
  GRAND CENTRAL MARKET, 47
  GRIER MUSSER MUSEUM, 232
  GRIFFITH PLANETARIUM, 390
  HERITAGE SQUARE MUSEUM, 237
  HOLLYWOOD PARK, 469
  HUNTINGTON LIBRARY, ART
    COLLECTIONS AND BOTANICAL

  GARDENS, 242
  INTERNATIONAL PRINTING
    MUSEUM, 243
  JAPANESE AMERICAN NATIONAL
    MUSEUM, 244
  KIDSPACE, 245
  LASER STORM (Torrance), 77
  LASERTREK, 77
  LEO CARRILLO STATE BEACH, 30
  LOS ANGELES MEMORIAL
    COLISEUM AND SPORTS
    ARENA, 422
  MISSION SAN FERNANDO REY DE
    ESPAÑA, 251
  MUSEUM OF FLYING, 253
  THE MUSEUM OF TELEVISION AND
    RADIO, 254
  MY JEWISH DISCOVERY PLACE, 256
  NATIONAL HOT ROD ASSOCIATION
    MOTORSPORTS MUSEUM, 257
  NATURALIZATION CEREMONY, 367
  NBC STUDIO TOURS, 423
  PACIFIC PARK, 2
  PEPE'S KARTLAND, 81
  PUDDINGSTONE LAKE, 126
  PYRAMID LAKE, 140
  RACE CITY, 82
  SANTA FE DAM RECREATIONAL
    AREA, 145
  SANTA MONICA COLLEGE
    PLANETARIUM, 396
  SANTA MONICA PIER, 353
  SEASIDE LAGOON, 31
  SHERMAN OAKS CASTLE PARK, 83
  SHORELINE PARK, 115
  SHORELINE VILLAGE CRUISES, 446
  SKIRBALL CULTURAL CENTER, 267
  SOUTH COAST BOTANICAL
    GARDENS, 146
  SOUTHERN CALIFORNIA
    CONSERVATORY OF MUSIC, 397
  SOUTHWEST MUSEUM, 268
  SPIRIT CRUISES, 446
  STAR EXPLORATION STATION
    CHILDREN'S MUSEUM, 477
  TEMESCAL GATEWAY PARK, 146
  TREEHOUSE CLUB, 83
  U.C.L.A. OCEAN DISCOVERY
    CENTER, 479
  UNDER THE SEA, 85
  UNIVERSAL CITYWALK, 369

## ABOUT THE AUTHOR:

Fun and education are key words in our home. I enjoy home schooling my children; speaking to various groups; writing a weekly column for the Los Angeles Times; and whatever else God brings my family's way!

I would appreciate your ideas about this book. Do you have a wonderful place to go with kids that wasn't included in this edition? Please let me know and I'll share it in the next one. You can write to me at:

FUN PLACES TO GO WITH KIDS
P.O. Box 376
Lakewood, CA  90714 - 0376
(562) 867-5223
email: susan@funplaces.com

# Fün Places to go With Kids
### and educational

## $16.95 plus tax and shipping

Please send copy(s) of this wonderful, innovative, well-written, absolutely fantastic, fun book to . . .

NAME _____

ADDRESS _____ CITY _____

STATE _____ ZIP _____ PHONE _____

ENCLOSED IS MY CHECK FOR $ _____ ($18.95 per book, includes tax and $2.00 for shipping.)

Make check payable to: **Fun Places**. Send to: **Fun Places Publishing, P.O. Box 376, Lakewood, CA  90714-0376**

- - - - - ✂ - - - - - - - - - - - - - - - - - - - - - - - - - - - - - - - - - - - - - - - - - - - -

# Fün Places to go With Kids
### and educational

## $16.95 plus tax and shipping

Please send copy(s) of this wonderful, innovative, well-written, absolutely fantastic, fun book to . . .

NAME _____

ADDRESS _____ CITY _____

STATE _____ ZIP _____ PHONE _____

ENCLOSED IS MY CHECK FOR $ _____ ($18.95 per book, includes tax and $2.00 for shipping.)

Make check payable to: **Fun Places**. Send to: **Fun Places Publishing, P.O. Box 376, Lakewood, CA  90714-0376**

# Fün Places to go With Kids
### *and educational*

**$16.95 plus tax and shipping**

Please send copy(s) of this wonderful, innovative, well-written, absolutely fantastic, fun book to . . .

NAME _____

ADDRESS _____ CITY _____

STATE _____ ZIP _____ PHONE _____

ENCLOSED IS MY CHECK FOR $ _____ ($18.95 per book, includes tax and $2.00 for shipping.)

Make check payable to: **Fun Places**. Send to: **Fun Places Publishing, P.O. Box 376, Lakewood, CA 90714-0376**

- - - - - ✂ - - - - - - - - - - - - - - - - - - - - - - - - - - - - - - - - - - - - - - - - - - -

# Fün Places to go With Kids
### *and educational*

**$16.95 plus tax and shipping**

Please send copy(s) of this wonderful, innovative, well-written, absolutely fantastic, fun book to . . .

NAME _____

ADDRESS _____ CITY _____

STATE _____ ZIP _____ PHONE _____

ENCLOSED IS MY CHECK FOR $ _____ ($18.95 per book, which includes tax and $2.00 for shipping.)

Make check payable to: **Fun Places**. Send to: **Fun Places Publishing, P.O. Box 376, Lakewood, CA 90714-0376**

Notes: